Date Due

3/26/99		
APR 2 1 2005		

WHAT IS NSSM 200?

NSSM 200 is White House shorthand for National Security Study Memorandum. NSSM 200 was the definitive interagency study of world population growth and its implications for United States and global security, requested by President Nixon in 1974. The study was undertaken by the National Security Council, the CIA, the Defense, Agriculture and State Departments, and the Agency for International Development. **Among its conclusions: "World population growth is widely recognized within the Government as a current danger of the highest magnitude calling for urgent measures....There is a major risk of severe damage [from continued rapid population growth] to world economic, political, and ecological systems and, as these systems begin to fail, to our humanitarian values."**

THE LIFE AND DEATH OF NSSM 200

THE LIFE AND DEATH OF NSSM 200

How the Destruction of Political Will Doomed a U.S. Population Policy

STEPHEN D. MUMFORD

Center for Research on Population and Security
Research Triangle Park, North Carolina   1996

Library of Congress Catalog 96-70965

ISBN 0-937307-04-1 Hardcover
ISBN 0-937307-05-X Paperback

COMMENTS BY READERS OF THE
ADVANCE COPY

"*The Life and Death of NSSM 200* is a tour de force. It explains
incisively, with extraordinary documentation, how the Vatican
works, time after time, to torpedo its opposition in the realm of
population policy. Dr. Mumford focuses almost surgically on
the Catholic hierarchy's strategies and motives in the sinking of
the NSSM 200 study recommendations, and those of the
Rockefeller Commission on Population Growth and the
American Future on which I served from 1970 to 1972. Much
the same strategies and motives were put in play by the
Vatican, behind the scenes, at the 1992 UN Conference on the
Environment, in Rio. There is a direct relationship, of course,
between population growth and environmental degradation,
especially deforestation and desertification. Yet in the 1000 page
report on the Rio meeting there is no mention of this
relationship, and what must be done about it. —Why? The UN
requires consensus for full approval of policy statements. I was
a member of the U.S. delegation to the Rio Conference, and I
watched Argentina and The Philippines serve as surrogates for
the Vatican as they blocked all efforts to include any mention of
the population/environment relationship. The outcome of the
environmental conference was, in this respect, a disgrace.
Mumford's book vividly illuminates why the Vatican behaved as
it did in Rio, as well as in its total annihilation earlier of NSSM 200.
The book is the scholarly equivalent of investigative journalism at
its best, and performs an invaluable service for us all."

■ JAMES H. SCHEUER
U.S. Congressman, 1965-1994
New York

"The Life and Death of NSSM 200 does a major service in calling attention to the strong link between world overpopulation and U.S. national security. The point needs to be hammered home. Americans have perhaps begun to see the connection in the cases of Somalia, El Salvador, and Haiti, but the media unfortunately continues to concentrate on proximate and superficial political events. Population policy should be central to foreign policy."

■ **EDWARD O. WILSON**
Pellegrino University Professor, Harvard University
Museum of Comparative Zoology
The Agassiz Museum
Cambridge, MA

"The greatest danger to humanity is, without doubt, the tremendous increase in human population together with depletion of resources to fulfill human needs and desires. President Nixon was aware of this more than 25 years ago when he appointed the Commission on Population growth and the American Future, and again in 1974 when he directed a study of the implications of worldwide population growth on U.S. security. Dr. Mumford makes a telling argument as to the reasons these two reports were never implemented. The book is extremely interesting and a most important document. It is well worth reading."

■ **EDGAR WAYBURN, M.D.**
Former President, Sierra Club
Albert Schweitzer Award Laureate
San Francisco

"In his new work, *The Life and Death of NSSM 200,* Stephen
Mumford points out that you can't have a foreign policy
without a population policy. An engrossing book."

■ **RICHARD D. LAMM**
Former Governor of Colorado,
Executive Director, Center for Public Policy and Contemporary
Issues, University of Denver

"With courage and scholarship, Stephen Mumford has during
20 years stood as a rock against the media code-of-silence tide
which has fostered the incessant anti-democratic and
anti-American machinations of the Vatican and Catholic
Bishops — glaringly revealed in the 1975 'Bishops' Pastoral Plan
for Prolife Activities.'

"To rescue its tyrannical religious empire from encroaching
scientific enlightenment, the Roman Catholic Church asserts the
dogma of papal infallibility and thereby seeks to establish
Vatican control of reproductive rights and democratic
processes. The extent to which they succeeded during the 1970s
and 80s in suppressing highest-level U.S. determinations of
actions needed to protect the security of the U.S. and the world
from explosive population increase — derailing the
world-leading U.S. population/family planning assistance
program — makes for dismal but essential reading for every
true patriot concerned about our democratic future and the
global environment."

■ **REIMERT T. RAVENHOLT, M.D.**
President
Population Health Imperatives
Seattle, WA
Former Director, 1966-79,
Office of Population, USAID
Department of State

"The Life and Death of NSSM 200 is essential reading for every serious scholar and activist in world population matters—and all others interested in this subject, central to the survival of our environment and ourselves. It is the best source of the actual documents of the early and developmental period of United States and world-wide policies and programs. It belongs in every library with a serious collection on this subject.

"This book presents NSSM 200 itself, which consolidated the policies and programs of the Johnson, Nixon and Ford administrations. Although after its approval by President Ford in November 1975, internal and external religious and ideological forces of opposition were able to prevent its publication, they were in fact frustrated because it was available to all members of the United States government involved in administering population policies and programs. It was and has remained the basis for U.S. and world policies and action, absorbed and expanded in the Recommendations of the International Population Conference at Mexico City in 1984 and the Program of Action of the International Conference on Population and Development at Cairo in 1994.

"Those who have not read it will not know the history of the great work they are involved in."

■ **PHILANDER P. CLAXTON, JR.**
World Population Society
First Special Assistant to the Secretary of State
for Population Matters

"Steve Mumford's illuminating disclosure of Vatican pressure on U.S. international population policy is a powerful message, not only for the American public but for the United Nations as well. The Holy See delegation has accelerated its efforts at recent U.N. conferences to block universal access to modern contraceptives. Mumford's book provides chilling insight into why the Vatican's permanent observer status at the U.N. — whereby it uses its influence at the world's most important secular forum to spread religious dogma — should be reconsidered. *The Life and Death of NSSM 200* is must reading for all students of public policy."

■ **WERNER FORNOS, President**
The Population Institute
Washington, DC

"The Roman Catholic Church has been steadfastly opposed to all mechanical or chemical means of birth control. Stephen Mumford brings to bear overwhelming evidence that, from its beginning, the doctrine of Papal infallibility committed the Church to rejecting the reality of a world population crisis and led, indeed, to highly successful efforts to block timely U.S. interventions and responses (including strict immigration control). This is a dramatic exposé of the undermining of democratic institutions and political will, in the service of interests *antithetical* to U.S. population stabilization and the long-term survival of the nation."

■ **DR. VIRGINIA ABERNETHY**
Editor, Population and Environment
Professor of Psychiatry (Anthropology)
Vanderbilt University Medical Center
Nashville, TN

"This book gives extremely helpful background information about the hidden coordination of Vatican and American policy with regard to population growth and birth control. It is high time that certain problematic maneuvers of the Vatican are discussed in public."

■ **DR. HANS KÜNG, Catholic theologian**
Professor of Ecumenical Theology and
Director of the Institute for Ecumenical Research
University of Tübingen, Germany

"This sobering book raises a grave question: will it be possible to assure the reproductive rights of women and men, internationally recognized for the first time by the landmark 1994 Cairo International Conference on Population and Development? In a well-documented account, Mumford tells how in December 1974 the U.S. government adopted a policy on world population crucial for peace and development; how the policy was concealed in a restricted document (NSSM 200) for 14 years because of political influence by the Catholic Church; and how the Vatican and the Catholic Church have undermined and thwarted implementation of population policy vital for the security of the United States and other nations. Every American should be concerned about this alarming cover-up and subversion of democratic decision-making."

■ **RUTH ROEMER, J.D.**
Adjunct Professor Emerita
UCLA School of Public Health
Past President
American Public Health Association

"In *The Life and Death of NSSM 200*, Dr. Mumford gives us a uniquely clear account of how the Vatican manipulated the American government, causing it to distance itself from the compassionate control of population. Tragically, the relevance of this keen analysis grows with every new population-fueled horror."

■ **GARRETT HARDIN**
University of California
Santa Barbara, CA

"In the long run the security of the United States cannot be divorced from the security of all nations. Nor can our security be measured solely in military terms...The information in this book will be of enormous value to those in the U.S. and elsewhere who wish to encourage elected officials to recognize the need to develop policies and programs that address the problems resulting from the world's rapid population growth."

■ **GENE R. LA ROCQUE**
Rear Admiral, USN (Ret.)
President, Center for Defense Information
Washington, DC

"A fascinating and disturbing insight into a population policy that could have changed the world but for the machinations of the Vatican."

■ **TIM BLACK**
Chief Executive
Marie Stopes International
London

"In his new book, Stephen Mumford details with meticulous care the demise of a sensible population policy for the U.S., as commissioned by President Nixon and later buried by one political faction after another, since it was opposed by the Vatican and other religious right-wing leaders — of whom politicians seem to be ever afraid. Dr. Mumford has spoken out on overpopulation as a danger to national security for years, and we are now seeing the chaotic anarchy that continued rapid population growth brings.

"Political instability is the result of population pressures. So is environmental destruction. For over 20 years Mumford has been a lead scientist in the evaluation of all kinds of medical fertility control, including the quinacrine pellet nonsurgical method of sterilization. The book also shows that in the battle to save the papacy, the Vatican has no qualms about infiltrating U.S. politics, and has done so to purposely erode our democracy. If our political will had not been destroyed by the Catholic hierarchy, and the recommendations of NSSM 200 had been implemented in 1975, the world would be a safer place today."

■ **ELAINE STANSFIELD**
Director
Save Our Earth
Former Director, Zero Population Growth
of Los Angeles

"Stephen Mumford's book, The *Life and Death of NSSM 200* is a consummate and engrossing study of how the Vatican has worked ceaselessly to negate U.S. population policy. The alliance of Fundamentalist and Catholic conservatives has heightened this attack. With the increasing power of the right-wing in Congress, family planning and abortion rights are in severe danger. Mumford has been a pioneer in analyzing this onslaught on the right of women to control their fertility. His writing and campaign deserve to be brought to the widest possible audience.

■ **LARRY LADER**
President
Abortion Rights Mobilization
Founding Chair,
National Abortion & Reproductive Rights Action League
Recipient,
"Feminist of the Year Award," Feminist Majority Foundation

"For the Global Women's Rights Movement nothing is more important than control over our bodies and reproduction. This fundamental human right that forms the basis of all democratic institutions and equality is under attack as never before by the Vatican and the organized Catholic Church. Joined by the Christian Right in this unholy alliance, their push for absolute power takes place on the battlefield of population control, using women's fertility and lives as pawns. The high stakes and ruthless political power campaigns involved are clearly set out and lucidly explained in the new book by Stephen D. Mumford. This is essential reading."

■ **FRAN P. HOSKEN**
Editor and publisher WIN NEWS
(Women's International Network)
Lexington, MA

"The Vatican City's population policy is for 'No Growth.' It's birth rate is zero (presumably) and it has a zero net immigration policy: it admits for residence only replacements for those who exit by death, transfer or defection. The message to the rest of the world is: 'Do as I say' not 'Do as I do.'

"Let Steve Mumford tell you the story of the Vatican's effort to get others to live by rules that the Vatican itself won't abide. I say: 'If you don't play the game, you can't make the rules.'"

■ **JOHN H. TANTON, M.D.**
Founder, The Federation for American Immigration Reform (FAIR)
Editor and Publisher, *The Social Contract*

"Those who are new at efforts to promote population stabilization are often amazed to discover the prescience embodied in the 1972 report of the Commission on Population Growth and the American Future — and dismayed by the lack of implementation which followed it. Dr. Mumford's new book sheds light on the maneuvers which prevented development of an effective population policy stemming from these recommendations and those of the subsequent study requested by President Nixon and known in the White House as 'NSSM 200.' In California we suffer on a daily basis the diminished quality of life effected by years of our third world population-growth rates, a result of our national failure to develop a population policy."

■ **RIC OBERLINK, J.D.**
Executive Director,
Californians For Population Stabilization

"To understand the demise of NSSM 200 is to begin to understand why U.S. policymakers still will not act to solve the problem of population growth. Dr. Mumford's book represents decades of intensive scholarship and is an important contribution to this controversial and complex subject. We are grateful that this book is being published."

■ MONIQUE A. MILLER
Executive Director
Carrying Capacity Network
Washington, DC

"Even if last year's UN Conference on Population and Development in Cairo had accomplished little else, the behavior of the Vatican contingent vividly demonstrated the essence of what Steve Mumford has been saying all along: Namely that the pope and the Catholic hierarchy are "the enemy" of family planning and world population stabilization, and should be labeled and dealt with as such.

"Mumford is a forerunner. A few people like him are needed, it seems to me, in the dynamics of most effective social movements. The family planning movement has had its share of forerunners. These are men and women willing to make a fuss, often quite tiresome to their colleagues, to send up flares, in order to alert us all — to some crisis unfaced, some major human need unmet — and to energize a constructive response. I hope publication of Dr. Mumford's new book — *The Life and Death of NSSM 200* — will cause the forces of influence in the population field to turn toward him, rather than against him. Then his work can be seriously discussed on its merits."

■ DONALD A. COLLINS
Pioneer Population Activist

"Since President Nixon ordered the NSSM 200 study, world population has increased by 50 percent. Thanks in large part to that report's suppression, the world is much closer to the global disaster that will inevitably follow failure to bring population and resource use into line with our planet's carrying capacity. Steve Mumford is to be commended for bringing this important document to light and for exposing those who are making it unnecessarily difficult to solve the population/ecology problem."

■ **EDD DOERR**
Executive Director
Americans for Religious Liberty
Silver Spring, MD
President, American Humanist Association

"What may be perceived as 'Catholic-bashing' in Stephen Mumford's *The Life and Death of NSSM 200* should not be allowed to detract from this book's important argument: Roman Catholic theology and moral teaching in the area of population growth are a danger to humanity.

"More people means more intense problems for the planet, for nations, and for the United States — problems of security, as more and more people contend for the same amount of real estate and for other resources. Dr. Mumford performs a great service in bringing back into focus the bold initiatives of Richard Nixon and the Rockefeller Commission, and in bringing to light the resulting National Security Study Memorandum 200 and its fate."

■ **ROBERT KYSER,**
Retired Presbyterian (USA) minister, and
Managing Editor of *The Social Contract*

"In *The Life and Death of NSSM 200*, Stephen Mumford exposes the depressing story of America's retrenchment from the opportunity and commitment to lead the world in population control. The book is reminiscent of what Arnold Toynbee would call 'The Great Refusal.' Like Moses, the U.S. could only view the promised land and then back away. . . . The religious right and the Catholic hierarchy unquestionably now possess the clout with government, media and industry to frustrate the commitment, and to stifle the will, of the one nation that has the resources, and once had the vision and energy, to lead the world in salvation from uncontrolled human fertility."

■ **THE REV. W. W. FINLATOR**
Former Senior Pastor
Pullen Memorial Baptist Church
Pastor, Community Church
Raleigh, NC

"One must read this book to comprehend an ominous threat to each of us: the explosive growth of the anti-population control movement and its initiative to enact a Constitutional Amendment prohibiting abortion."

■ **WILLIAM C. PADDOCK**
Agricultural Scientist
West Palm Beach, FL

"I have read every word and am profoundly impressed by the book's scholarship and the author's passion. Having struggled in the field all my adult life, I am in a position to say that *NSSM 200* is a brightly shining light where light is most needed."

■ **MRS. ELIZABETH POOL**
Dublin, NH

"Stephen Mumford's latest book makes extremely disturbing
reading. In our daily life here in India, we see the impact of the
campaign by the Vatican — the misery of life in the urban slums
and the starvation of the rural poor. All of this cries out at the
injustices of religious politics, and is a far cry from what Jesus
preached! We fully agree that it is the politics of religion that
have derailed population control programs here in this country.
The Vatican, either directly or through its proxies, has seen to it
that population programs do not get ahead. China and
Indonesia have done far better in curbing population growth,
because there is minimal influence of the Vatican except
through the WHO. India has a Catholic population with
influence far in excess of its population percentage. Their
greatest influence comes from the wonderful charity work done
by the good nuns and padres. However, such profoundly
humanitarian service obscures the ways the Vatican has
crippled our population programs. The nuns and priests are
not at fault — they are merely innocent pawns of the Vatican. I
will be making *The Life and Death of NSSM 200* available to
policy makers throughout our population programs."

■ **PRAVIN KINI, MD**
Obstetrician and Gynecologist
Chief Investigator for South India
International Federation for Family Health
Bangalore

"In his new book, *The Life and Death of NSSM 200*, Dr. Mumford takes full advantage of the hitherto hidden—and most intriguing—archival material. It reveals with great clarity how the Catholic hierarchy subverted the efforts of our government, including two Presidents, to carry out the recommendations of perhaps the most comprehensive studies ever undertaken aimed at finding humane and effective ways to stop the world's disastrous population growth. Thus, the Vatican usurped control of US population policy, and left us with no policy at all."

■ **MARY S. MORAIN**
Fellow
World Academy of Art and Science
Carmel, CA

"To the large army of Americans who have so successfully introduced effective control of fertility to the American citizen, but who have failed so miserably as world leaders toward population control, here is the reason.

"A large cadre of America's brightest and best have given us, for the first time in human history, safe and absolute control of fertility (effective contraception backstopped by abortion). Everyone involved in this mission recognizes the dangers of overpopulation. Yet major efforts to control world population growth have fallen flat. Why? Here is your answer.

"The Roman Catholic Hierarchy has taken an immoral position on population control, inimical to the entire world, in an effort to protect its own power. This is what Steve Mumford's penetrating new book is all about."

■ **GEORGE C. DENNISTON, M.D.**
Seattle, WA

"The Life and Death of NSSM 200 fairly and accurately describes overpopulation and its disastrous consequences for humanity, and the implacable opposition by the Vatican to the effective control of population growth. It is far and away the best and most courageous book I have seen on these subjects."

■ **ALBERT D. WARSHAUER, M.D.**
Population Scholar
Wrightsville Beach, NC

"Very few have Dr. Mumford's insight or have done sufficient research on the role of the Vatican in population to appreciate, understand or believe what this book, *The Life and Death of NSSM 200,* contains. . . . Mumford's factual account of the harm that the Vatican has done and is doing regarding population and related vital areas of human welfare and global survival will alarm any thinking person regardless of their religious persuasion. . . . His book has the potential of being a best-seller and of major impact."

■ **CHARLES R. AUSHERMAN**
Executive Director
Institute for Development Training,
Ordained minister, Reformed Church in America

"The Life and Death of NSSM 200 is an eye-opener. We have often questioned how the United States can advise other nations to stabilize their populations without having a plan to stabilize our own. Now we understand what happened to the plan. To establish a realistic U.S. Population Policy, we must first expose and neutralize the foreign machinations of the Vatican."

■ **DR. VIVIAN HIATT-BOCK**
RAY BOCK
Poulsbo, WA

"All other efforts on behalf of social and environmental problems are useless unless population is stabilized. This must be faced forthrightly . . . . In his latest book, *The Life and Death of NSSM 200,* Dr. Stephen Mumford goes to great lengths to document the tragic behind-the-scenes record of how traditional U.S. separation of church and state has been cynically subverted. . . . Yet environmental and other groups shy away from the population issue. It's this fear of controversy, of stepping on sensitive toes. It's the old conflict between showing integrity by facing up to a problem, and thereby risking possible loss of influence or members, or of sticking to a relatively safe agenda. We must buck up our courage and get on with the job we all know must be done — stabilize world population."

■ **RICHARD VAN ALSTYNE**
Family farmer and environmentalist

"Stephen D. Mumford's *The Life and Death of NSSM 200* should be required reading for every member of the religious community who professes a genuine concern about population growth and the health and fate of humanity."

■ **THE REV. LAWRENCE D. RUPP**
Ordained Episcopal priest,
Vice-Chair, New Hampshire Citizens for a Sustainable Population

"I am delighted to see Stephen Mumford continuing the campaign for a rational approach to population with his *The Life and Death of NSSM 200*, which I have read with great interest. Rome is even more sinister than I thought!

"Tragically, the Church bears part of the responsibility for the recent catastrophe in intensely Catholic Rwanda. Were it not so opposed to contraception, Rwanda's population might not have increased in quite the way it has done, its carrying capacity might not have been exceeded in the way it has been, its population pressure would not be as intense as it is now, and the genocide that is endemic in the region might not have escalated in the way it has done."

■ **MAURICE KING, M.D.**
Honorary Research Fellow
The University of Leeds
England

"Reading Dr. Mumford's book brings to mind those saddest of words: "What might have been." The U.S. government's National Security Study Memorandum 200, carried out in 1974, analyzed the population problem and recognized the urgency of addressing it immediately. However, due to a massive, Vatican-led effort, the government's political will was dissipated and the public was confused with disinformation. The result was inaction on the population issue, and we are all paying the price as we see the grim predictions of NSSM 200 come true.

"Analyzing the population-denial movement without mentioning the Vatican is like analyzing the Holocaust without mentioning Germany. Yet the Vatican even now receives kid glove treatment from the media, its efforts at the suppression of information and the spread of disinformation are rarely exposed. Dr. Mumford has taken off the gloves and exposed the Vatican's ruthless agenda. One can only hope that this book is widely read, for disinformation that downplays the population problem is still rampant, and propagated by many news sources, including those of the highest reputation."

■ **MADELINE WELD, Ph.D.**
President, Global Population Concerns — Ottawa

TABLE OF CONTENTS

Reader Comments   i

A Postscript, Before   3

1994 Presidential Decision Directive   6

Foreword   15

Introduction   19

1   President Nixon's
    "Special Message" on Population   27

Marks the moment in 1969 when the President proposed
creation of the Commission on Population Growth and the
American Future.

2   The "Rockefeller Commission"
    on Population Growth   43

President Nixon's remarks upon signing the bill creating the
Commission in 1970, and the Commission's
recommendations submitted in 1972 on nearly 50 areas of
policy and action, including sex education, equal rights for
women, contraception and minors, voluntary sterilization,
abortion, and population stabilization.

3   The NSSM 200 Directive and the Study Requested   59

The 1974 Directive signed by Henry Kissinger on behalf of
President Nixon, and the text of the study report,
"Implications of Worldwide Population Growth for U.S.
Security and Overseas Interests."

**4   President Ford's Move
      toward a U.S. Population Policy   87**

The full text of National Security Decision Memo 314, signed
in 1975 by Brent Scowcroft on behalf of President Ford,
approving almost all of the NSSM 200 recommendations.

5   What Happened to the Momentum?   93

Traces the decline from its peak in 1975 of U.S. political will
to deal with the overpopulation problem.

6   Why Did Our Political Will Fade Away?   105

Describes the increasing involvement of the Roman Catholic
Church in scuttling any positive action toward
implementation of the NSSM 200 recommendations.

7   What Was the Role of the Vatican?   129

How the Reagan Administration altered its foreign aid
program to comply with Vatican insistence on an outright
ban on use of foreign aid funds for the performance or
promotion of abortions.

8   The Bishops' "Pastoral Plan"   135

The master blueprint for the infiltration and manipulation of
the American democratic process at all levels of government.
Includes the complete "unsanitized" text of the U.S. Bishops'
Pastoral Plan for Pro-Life Activities.

9   Implications of the Pastoral Plan   153

Analysis of the Plan and its implementation, including the
roles of the Catholic Press Association, Catholic physicians
guilds, Catholic lawyers associations, hospital associations,
lay organizations—and the paralyzing influence of
"ecumenical activity."

10   The Human Life Amendment—and Beyond   169

Evidence of the bishops' great success in killing American
political will through implementation of the Pastoral Plan
but without yet achieving passage of the Human Life
Amendment.

11   The Cross of Papal Infallibility   185

The history and dynamics of the dogma of papal infallibility.
Because of it, the Vatican has been forced to undermine the
political will of governments that are striving to deal with
overpopulation.

12   Postponing Self-Destruction of the Church   213

Strategies by which the Vatican and U.S. Catholic bishops
have been able to extend their institution's life.

13   Defection of the Faithful   227

Why American Catholics are not conforming to papal
teachings—with many leaving the Church and becoming
Protestants.

14   Vatican Rejection of Freedom of the Press   251

Examines 150 years of uninterrupted papal hostility toward
freedom of the press. Discusses techniques used to "bridle"
the press and the conclusion of George Seldes,
acknowledged dean of investigative reporters, that on
"Catholic issues" there is no free press.

15 The Catholic League and Suppression of The Press Today   277

The principles governing League behavior, the methods leading to its success, and a collection of specific acts designed to halt public criticism of the Church.

16 "Things Are Seldom What They Seem"   303

The "dis-uniting" of America. Explores the broad consequences of the Pastoral Plan, including the erosion of public confidence in our political system.

17 Conclusions   359

How the Vatican has no qualms about destroying American democratic institutions in its battle to save the Papacy.

References   373

Appendices
   1. The World Population Plan of Action   387
   2. NSSM 200 Study Report Text   433
   3. Vatican Control of World Health Organization Population Policy: An Interview   559

Index   569

GERALD R. FORD

March 26, 1993

Dear Mr. Schmidt:

Your letter of March 10, 1993, again requesting
that I author the suggested Foreword for the first
publication of NSSM200.

As you noted, I endorsed "the 227 - page NSSM
report and its recommendations on November 26,
1975, in National Security Decision Memorandum
314." My views are the same today.

I now write to reiterate my decision to not author
the suggested Foreword. This is a firm decision
which I hope you will respect.

Mrs. Ford and I have consistently supported the
Pro Choice point of view and will not change. I
was very disappointed with the 1992 GOP Platform
on this issue.

Best regards,

Gerald R. Ford

Mr. Adolph W. Schmidt
R D 4
Ligonier, Pennsylvania   15658

A POSTSCRIPT, BEFORE

No reader should feel that the findings presented in this book are outdated and irrelevant today. Quite the contrary — the information set forth here is as relevant now as when first written by the many authorities whose works are referenced herein.

The Rockefeller Commission and the NSSM 200 reports, contained in this volume, were undertaken in the 1970s. They were broad, intensive examinations, by our highest government officials, of the gravity of the population problem. Both reports offered appropriate responses to the issue.

Just how much do the recommended responses of President Nixon's time, over two decades ago, fit the facts and needs of today? The June 1, 1994 draft of President Clinton's Presidential Decision Directive (PDD), which outlined the problem and was prepared for the President's signature by the National Security Council (NSC), but since then has simply disappeared, emphatically answers this question.

A senior government official who had read an advance copy of this book was also an official reviewer of the PDD. This official recognized that I would have a keen interest in such a document and was kind enough to send me a copy. The advance draft of this Directive was to be finalized on June 3, 1994. This five page PDD, as well as a cover letter dated June 1 from Jane Bradley of the NSC, are presented below. As can be seen from the cover letter, the U.S. Departments of State, Health and Human Services, Treasury, the Agency for International Development, and the Environmental Protection Agency were officially involved in the preparation of this document. According to senior government officials who worked on the document, the PDD was never issued.

Thus, the same cycle has now been repeated, in almost the same way. The first cycle began in the 1970s, with the development of a rational U.S. population policy at the highest level, and ended with destruction of the policy before it could be implemented — destruction by the Vatican and its allies. The second cycle ended in the 1990s with burial of Mr. Clinton's Presidential Decision Directive.

The PDD was killed — suppressed — just as the Rockefeller Commission Report and the NSSM 200 reports were before it. Nothing came of this 1990s' attempt to address the issue of global overcrowding — despite the gravity of the threat to U.S. security posed by overpopulation and described in the draft PDD.

As Yogi Berra is said to have said, "It's déjá vu all over again!"

Nearly two years after the burial of the PDD, however, Secretary of State Warren Christopher courageously decided to pursue the proposed policies alone. He announced a new State Department policy which was consistent with the never-issued PDD in a speech at Stanford University in California. An April 18, 1996 *Washington Post* article by reporter Thomas W. Lippman, was headlined, "Christopher Puts Environment High on Diplomatic Agenda: Abuse of Natural Resources Imperils U.S. Interests Secretary of State Says", and summarized Christopher's speech. According to Lippman, the Stanford address had been planned and refined by Christopher and his aides for months.

The article begins, "Secretary of State Warren Christopher has seen the future and finds it alarming.

"He sees parched fields, poisoned air, toxic waters, rampant disease and societies driven to armed conflict by competition for dwindling resources — all potentially threatening to Americans.

"In that vision, those calamities resulted not from nuclear war but from worldwide abuse of the environment and overpopulation.

"It was those threats that impelled Christopher last week to proclaim a new definition of national security and a worldwide shift in the objectives of U.S. diplomacy. Christopher set environmentalism as a top priority, in addition to traditional goals such as preserving peace and promoting prosperity, in a speech outlining what senior aides said he hopes will be the legacy of his four years of directing the nation's foreign policy. . . .

"'Environmental forces transcend borders and oceans to threaten directly the health, prosperity and jobs of American citizens,' Christopher said . . . 'Addressing natural resource issues is frequently critical to achieving political and economic stability and to pursuing our strategic goals around the world. . . . A foreign policy that failed to address such problems would be ignoring the fundamental needs of the American people.'

"While continuing to grapple with 'traditional' security issues, Christopher said, 'we must also contend with the vast new danger posed to our national interests by damage to the environment and resulting global and regional instability.'"

Lippman goes on to describe the details of Christopher's policy. He also reports, "These decisions were not made overnight. The Stanford speech followed a spirited struggle within the State Department, which traditionally has emphasized political analysis and balance-of-power diplomacy, not pesticides or greenhouse gases."

Opposition to Christopher's policy, both within the State Department and without, was immediate. Lippman reports: "The approach has been criticized by some national security analysts, members of Congress and even State Department veterans as soft-headed and an inappropriate or ineffective use of diplomatic resources. . . . Many professional diplomats and foreign policy analysts . . . have expressed doubts about Christopher's approach, questioning the seriousness of the problems or diplomacy's usefulness in addressing them."

Unfortunately, given the success of the opposition to population growth control witnessed for more than two decades, we cannot be optimistic that Secretary Christopher's initiatives will succeed no matter how admirable his intentions. The new consensus necessary for success is nonexistent in the State Department and elsewhere in the government. Later in this book the opposition to Secretary Christopher's position and its institution will be described in detail.

Like the realities described by the authors of the Rockefeller Commission and NSSM 200 Reports, the opposition remains unchanged today.

The following PDD and its cover letter have been reformatted to fit the book page.

FOR OFFICIAL USE ONLY

BY FAX

June 1, 1994

To: Ellen Marshall, State   663-3068   663-3094
       Nils Daulaire, AID   647-8415   647-8595
       Sarah Kovner, HHS   690-6347   690-7098
       David Ogden, Treasury   622-0764   622-1228
       Bob Ward, EPA   260-2785   260-3828

FROM: Jane Bradley, OEP/NSC

SUBJECT: Revisions to Draft PDD on Global Population
Issues

Thanks again for your help today in reviewing and
recasting revisions to the draft Presidential Decision
Directive on population.   Attached is the revised
version resulting from our meeting. Please let me know
by c.o.b. Friday if your agency has any problems with
the revisions. If I don't hear from you, I'll assume
clearance.

Attachment

D RAFT

SUBJECT: Policy on Global Population Issues

Rapid global population growth is an urgent and substantial threat to international stability and sustainable development. This Presidential Decision Directive articulates objectives for, and guides the implementation of, United States policy on global population growth. The policy demonstrates our recognition of the linkages between population growth and long-term security, between population growth ~~in de-veloping countries~~ and high rates of consumption ~~in developed countries~~ as they impact on the environment, and between US leadership in addressing the population issue and the global effort to promote sustainable development. In addition, the policy is deeply-rooted in such fundamental national values as human rights, gender equality, and the rights of individuals and couples to determine the number and spacing of their children.

The United Nations estimates that the world's population in 2050 is likely to be between 7.8 and 12.5 billion people, compared with today's 5.5 billion, with ninety percent of this growth occurring in developing nations. High rates of growth in these nations are expected to exacerbate existing dilemmas of unemployment, stagnant economic development, depressed wages, declining per capita availability of cropland, food scarcity, rapid urbanization, depleted natural resource base and environmental degradation. The UN Food and Agriculture Organization estimates that by the year 2000, 31 low-income countries will be unable to feed their projected populations using their own land, and many will find it difficult to purchase food to meet shortfalls.~~, resulting~~ This may result in: disruptive migration flows ~~within and~~ between ~~developing countries, as well as significantly increased pressure to immigrate to the US and other developed countries~~; an increasing burden on the local ecosystems and the global environment; and threats to local and regional political stability.

The goal of US policy on global population growth is to marshall an immediate, concerted and comprehensive international response to population growth trends, based on three mutually reinforcing objectives: ~~promoting~~ respecting the rights and capabilities of individuals and couples to freely and responsibly determine the number and spacing of their children; improving individual reproductive health, with special attention to the reproductive health needs of women and adolescents, and the general health needs of infants and children; and reducing the rate of population growth as rapidly as possible to levels consistent with sustainable development.

The strategy for achieving this goal includes the following areas: fostering an international consensus for action; promoting targeted assistance to developing countries through both bilateral and multilateral channels; and demonstrating leadership by example in the United States. In each strategic area, US policy shall comprehensively target the determinants of fertility by addressing the unmet demand and need for family planning and reproductive health services, the desire for large families, and the impacts of current population growth momentum. Female education, gender equality — legal, economic and political — and efforts to reduce maternal and infant mortality can have a significant impact on population trends and sustainable development. Particular attention shall be paid to promoting the rights and roles ~~and responsibilities~~ of women.

The Department of State shall continue to coordinate overall interagency policy development and information clearinghouse functions for global population issues. In order to promote the Administration's policy on global population growth, the Department of State, in coordination with other appropriate agencies, shall develop and make available a public statement which articulates the policy set forth in this PDD and expresses the positive linkages to other Administration policies relating to global population issues.

1. FOSTERING AN INTERNATIONAL CONSENSUS FOR ACTION

A collective will toward action is fundamental to addressing global population growth. Therefore, at the International Conference on Population and Development (ICPD) scheduled for September 1994 in Cairo (and at the forthcoming World Summit for Social Development, the International Conference on Women, and in other relevant international fora) the US shall seek a consensus that provides a strong foundation for future

international cooperation on population, consistent
with US policy. Specifically, while avoiding quantitative near-term fertility reduction targets, the US
shall seek an international consensus on long-term
programmatic approaches to ~~goals for~~ reducing population growth on both global and regional bases. The US
shall also seek to reinforce ~~strengthen~~ the recommendations of previous conferences ~~in areas such as
reproductive rights, including the obligations of
governments to enable people to exercise these rights.~~
to ensure that individuals and couples have the right
to freely and responsibly decide the number and spacing
of their children, and that governments respect this
right. In addition, the US shall ensure that policy
statements on global population growth reference mutually strengthening commitments on closely related
issues, such as reproductive health, child survival,
environmental protection, development cooperation,
women's rights and migration. In preparation for the
ICPD, the Department of State, in consultation with
other appropriate agencies, shall develop for interagency review by [ONE MONTH AFTER SIGNATURE] a work
program to finalize a strategy for achieving US
objectives for the conference. The work program shall
ensure that adequate time is allocated for consultation
and cooperation with non-governmental organizations and
other governments in finalizing the strategy. In
addition, the strategy for achieving US objectives
should include a role for non-governmental organizations at the Conference.

2. PROMOTING TARGETED ASSISTANCE

The US currently provides assistance through both
bilateral and multilateral channels aimed at mitigating
population growth in developing countries. The level
of US budgetary commitment to overseas family planning
programs should continue to reflect their high priority
within the overall development assistance effort.
Therefore, their importance in the functional development assistance budget shall be maintained.

The US will continue its leadership role in supporting population assistance programs, implemented primarily through the Agency for International Development. Consistent with the overall restructuring of US foreign assistance, the determination of which recipient countries should have priority for future bilateral assistance in the area of population shall be based on the following criteria: a) global impact, as reflected in such indicators as overall contribution to population increases, levels of unmet need for contraception, lack of access to reproductive health services, maternal and child mortality, and population-related degradation of the global environment; and b) local and regional impacts, where population growth and reproductive conditions are key impediments to sustainable development. However, the US shall avoid attaching population conditions to efforts in other areas. Because population assistance should also be viewed as humanitarian, the US shall to the greatest possible extent avoid denying population assistance to countries due to concerns in other areas and shall seek to amend existing laws requiring such denial.

The emphasis for US bilateral assistance programs shall be based on a comprehensive approach to reproductive health that: a) incorporates multiple models of service delivery aimed at both men and women (including adolescents and young adults); b) links contraceptive information and services closely with other reproductive and primary health care intervention as appropriate; and c) addresses a broad range of reproductive health objectives (including screening and prevention of sexually transmitted diseases and reproductive tract infections). US assistance programs shall strengthen their current emphasis on quality of care and informed choice, while increasing the role of women in all phases of program design and implementation. In addition, attention shall also be paid to the need for additional investments in primary health care, HIV/AIDS prevention and services, maternal and child health, the role of women in development and female education.

Appropriate utilization of multilateral channels for
population assistance is also of critical importance
to a concerted international response to global population growth. As a result, the Administration shall
endeavor to ensure that adequate resources are directed
to such multilateral programs as the United Nations
Population Fund, the World Health Organization Human
Reproductive Research Program, as well as appropriate
private voluntary and non-governmental organizations.
In addition, the Department of State, the Agency for
International Development and the Department of Treasury, in cooperation with other relevant agencies, shall
undertake a review of the profile of assistance by other
bilateral donors and multilateral organizations in
population and human resource sectors in order to
develop a strategy for coordinating these modes of
assistance, avoiding duplication, and increasing participation.

3.   DEMONSTRATING LEADERSHIP BY EXAMPLE

Efforts toward international leadership by the US on
goals addressing health, security and sustainable
development concerns resulting from population growth
must be supported by a commitment to strive for these
goals ourselves. The Domestic Policy Council and the
Department of Health and Human Services, in consultation
with other appropriate agencies, shall develop a
statement describing US policies and programs that
address the broad range of population issues.

At the same time, the US and other developed countries
must maintain an awareness of their disproportionate
impacts on the global environment of their consumption
and production patterns. through consumption patterns
that are at several times the level of developing
countries. To effectively achieve the goal of marshalling an international response to population growth
trends, the US must also demonstrate leadership by
example in addressing the implications of these consumption patterns, with an aim toward reducing their
negative global environmental impacts. of consumption
of goods and services in the United States. The

DRAFT

Environmental Protection Agency, in coordination with
the Departments of Energy, ~~and~~ Transportation, Treasury, and other appropriate agencies, shall develop a
statement articulating US strategies for reducing such
negative impacts.

Finally, the State Department, ~~and~~ Agency for International Development, ~~and~~ the Department of Health and
Human Services ^and EPA, in consultation with other
appropriate agencies, shall review and report on the
potential for the US to demonstrate leadership with new
initiatives in the following areas: research and
development of new methods of fertility regulation,
particularly those methods that are especially designed
to respond to unmet needs in developing countries, to
give women greater control and also to protect against
sexually transmitted diseases; reproductive health
information and services for adolescents; access to
safe abortion and related services and counselling;
coordination of services and prevention of HIV/AIDS and
other sexually transmitted diseases with family planning and other reproductive health programs; reproductive health needs of the Former Soviet Union and Central
and Eastern Europe; and policy and program-relevant
research, especially on population/environment interrelationships, migration and urbanization, the popula-
tion/food situation, and interrelationships among
population growth, development, and sexual and reproductive behavior. A report on the potential for new
initiatives in the above areas should be presented to
the National Security Council by ~~July 1, 1994~~ [ONE MONTH
AFTER SIGNATURE], in order to maximize their utility
for ~~the ICPD process~~ implementing the ICPD action
program.

FOREWORD

President Ford's letter on page one was written shortly after a conversation between Adolph Schmidt and Mr. Ford's secretary. The conversation concerned an invitation to Mr. Ford to write a foreword to this book. His secretary conveyed the message that since Mr. Ford was now nearly eighty, he did not wish to take on any new projects.

Mr. Schmidt served as U.S. Ambassador to Canada during the Nixon administration; he knew President Nixon well, and has known President Ford for many years. So he is keenly aware that President Ford played a vital and positive role in one of the most important population projects ever undertaken by any government. This was a definitive study, initiated by President Nixon before Mr. Ford succeeded to the Oval Office, of the grave national and global security threat posed by world overpopulation. The study and its findings were successfully suppressed for eighteen years by the only institution categorically opposed to the project—a foreign-controlled institution whose security interests are quite different from those of the United States—the Vatican.

In this year 1996, world population will exceed an astonishing 5.9 billion persons. In 1975, world population had just reached the 4.0 billion mark. I choose 1975 for comparison here because that was the year President Ford, as his letter notes, endorsed the population policy recommendations contained in National Security Study Memorandum 200 (NSSM 200), the authoritative interagency study President Nixon had requested. Ford's endorsement was given in National Security Decision Memorandum 314 (NSDM

314). The complete texts of both memoranda are presented verbatim in this book.

NSSM 200 was the outgrowth of a gradually increasing concern over almost two decades about the world's rampant and totally unprecedented population growth. In effect, NSSM 200 verified and underscored a conclusion expressed earlier by a panel of the United Nations Association: namely, that sustained high rates of population growth "impair individual rights, jeopardize national goals, and threaten international stability."

The same grim tapestry of demographic facts that led the U.N. Association to this conclusion had also led President Richard Nixon, in July 1969, to deliver his Special Message to the Congress on Problems on Population Growth. That message set forth a far-reaching American commitment to helping limit the further unchecked increase of human numbers. It set in motion a broad range of government activities, both domestic and international. It called for creation of the Commission on Population Growth and the American Future, which collected and analyzed data that would make possible the formulation of a comprehensive, realistic U.S. population policy.

Other governmental activities called for in the message included: (1) increased research on birth control methods of all kinds and on the sociology of population growth; (2) expanded programs for training more people to work in the population and family planning fields, in this country and abroad; (3) expanded research into the effects of population growth on the environment and on world food supply; and (4) increased domestic family planning services aimed at extending such services to all those who want but cannot afford them.

The complete message as approved by Congress appears in Chapter One. President Nixon understood that the greatest threat ever faced by our species is its current unprecedented population growth. Here is part of President Nixon's concluding comments: "One of the most serious challenges to human destiny in the last third of this century will be the growth of the population. Whether man's response to that challenge will be a cause for pride or for despair in the year 2000 will depend very much on what we do today. If we now begin our work in an appropriate manner, and if we continue to devote a considerable amount of attention and energy to this problem, then mankind will be able to surmount this challenge as it has surmounted so many during the long march of civilization."

We made great strides toward fulfilling this commitment from 1969 through 1975. But as the record shows, the U.S. response began to unravel in 1976 and has been deteriorating ever since. As expressed in his March 26, 1993 letter to Ambassador Schmidt, President Ford's view of the implications of overpopulation remains today the same as it was in 1975 when he issued NSDM 314. The intervening years have shown this view, shared by so many knowledgeable people, to be remarkably sound.

I was among those who predicted dire consequences if our response to mounting population pressures was inadequate—if not enough were done to curb world population growth. Yet it surely gives me no satisfaction that so many of these consequences are now descending on us. My predictions were made in my first book on this subject—*Population Growth Control: The Next Move is America's* published by Philosophical Library (New York) in 1977. With the resurrection of NSSM 200, I am sensitized once again to the grave threat to international peace, to the domestic stability of all nations including our own, and to the global environment, posed by this inadequate response.

In setting the NSSM 200 project in motion, President Nixon specifically ordered a study of the "implications of worldwide population growth for U.S. security and overseas interests." The study examines in detail the ways in which uncontrolled population growth undermines national and global security. This study is as timely today as it was in 1974. Many predictions made in the report already have been realized. None of the predictions made over two decades ago has proved to be inaccurate. From our vantage point in 1996, it is clear that many of the anticipated consequences of our inadequate response to world population growth are now all but inevitable. While the NSSM 200 study may be one of the most important ever written on population policy, only a handful of people have seen it because it remained classified for fourteen years and has not been covered in the press.

This book contains NSSM 200 and its study report just as they were submitted to President Ford. I urge everyone concerned with human conflict, both domestic and global, with the social and economic welfare of the world's families, and with the global environment, to read this book. I urge you to ponder why our political will to deal with the population problem has so strangely and tragically withered since 1976. And I urge you to help us revive it.

STEPHEN D. MUMFORD
Research Triangle Park, NC
September, 1996

INTRODUCTION

The 1960s saw a surge in American public awareness of the world population problem. The invention of the contraceptive pill in 1960 stimulated broad public debate on birth control and the need for it. When Pope John XXIII created the papal Commission on Population and Birth in 1963, he gave the world hope that the Church was about to change its position on birth control. After all, why would the Vatican study the issue if the Church was not in a position to change its teaching on birth control? In 1968, Paul Ehrlich published his book, *The Population Bomb*, the most successful book of its kind, ever.[1] That same year, the journal *Science* published one of its most controversial articles ever, an essay by Garrett Hardin titled, "The Tragedy of the Commons,"[2] which sparked much discussion of the overpopulation threat.

Among mainstream protestant denominations, the Presbyterians were one of the first to call for a forthright response to the problem. In 1965, the General Assembly of the Presbyterian Church (U.S.A.) urged "— the government of the United States to be ready to assist countries who request help in the development of programs of voluntary planned parenthood as a practical and humane means of controlling fertility and population growth." In 1971, it recognized that reliance on private, voluntary decisions "— will not be sufficient to provide the necessary limitation of population growth unless there is a radical and rapid change in the attitudes and desires. The church must commit itself to effecting this change. The assumption that couples have the freedom to have as many children as they can support should be challenged. We can no longer justify bringing into existence as many children as we desire.

Our corporate responsibility to each other prohibits this. Given the
population crisis we must recognize and teach, beginning with
ourselves, that man has an obligation to limit the size of his family."And in 1972, the Presbyterians called on governments "to take
such actions as will stabilize population size...We who are motivated by the urgency of over-population rather than the prospect
of decimation would preserve the species by responding in faith:
Do not multiply—the earth is filled!"[3]

This kind of increasing outcry for action made it safe—almost
compelling—for American political leadership to identify with the
concept of population growth control and to call for new programs
to deal with the problem.

It was in this climate of rising concern that President Nixon sent
to Congress his "Special Message on Problems of Population
Growth." Special messages to the Congress are exceedingly rare
and this was the first such message on population. This action
punctuated the beginning of the peak of American political will to
deal with the mounting population crisis. The message, for the first
time, committed the United States to confronting the population
problem. Also rare, this special message was approved by the
Congress. Its passage was bipartisan, indicating broad political
support for American political action to combat this problem. The
message was a watershed development, yet few recall it. The
complete document appears as Chapter 1.

The most important element of the Special Message was its
creation of the *Commission on Population Growth and the American
Future.* During the signing of the bill establishing the Commission,
President Nixon commented on the broad political and public
support: "I believe this is an historic occasion. It has been made
historic not simply by the act of the President in signing this
measure, but by the fact that it has had bipartisan support and also
such broad support in the Nation." (See Chapter 2 for his complete
remarks.)

The 24-member Commission was chaired by John D. Rockefeller 3rd. It ordered more than 100 research projects which collected
and analyzed data that would make possible the formulation of a
comprehensive U.S. population policy. After two years of intense
effort, the Commission completed a 186-page report titled, *Population and the American Future* which offered more than 70 recommendations. The recommendations were a bold but sane response to

the challenges we faced in 1973. For example, they called for: passage of a Population Education Act to help school systems establish well-planned population education programs; sex education to be widely available, especially through the schools; passage of the Equal Rights Amendment (ERA); contraception to be available for all, including minors, at government expense if need be; abortion for all who want it, at government expense if necessary; vastly expanded research in many areas related to population growth control; and the elimination of all employment of illegal aliens.

The complete list of recommendations appears in Chapter 2. They represented the conclusions of some of the nation's most capable people. The scientists who completed the Commission's 100 research projects were among the best in their fields. These recommendations are included in this book because it is important for the reader to know what the U.S. response to the population problem could have been and should have been.

On May 5, 1972, at a ceremony held for the purpose of formally submitting the Commission's findings and conclusions, President Nixon publicly renounced the report.[4] This was six months before the President faced re-election and he was feeling intense political heat from one particularly powerful, foreign-controlled special interest group—the hierarchy of the Roman Catholic Church. Nothing happened toward implementation of any of the more than three score recommendations that collectively would have created a comprehensive U.S. population policy. Not one recommendation was ever adopted. To this day, the U.S. has no population policy, one of the few major countries with this distinction.

Had these 70 carefully reasoned recommendations been adopted as U.S. population policy in 1973—or if even a dozen or so of the most important ones had been adopted—America would be very different today. We would be more secure, subjected to less crime, better educated now with even greater educational opportunities ahead, living with less stress in a healthier environment, with more secure employment and greater employment opportunities, with better medical care, all in a physically less crowded America.

We would have set an example for the world, and we have good reason to believe that much of the world would have followed. Ironically, the American people were better prepared to accept these recommendations in 1973 than in 1996, even though world population during this brief period has mushroomed a horrendous 47 percent. For the past 20 years, all of us have been subjected to an intense disinformation program staged by the opposition to raise doubts in each of us regarding the seriousness of the population problem.

Despite the intense opposition President Nixon encountered in the wake of the Rockefeller Commission Report, his assessment of the gravity of the overpopulation problem and his desire to deal with it evidently remained unchanged. On April 24, 1974, nearly 18 months after his re-election, in the single most significant act of his presidency regarding the population crisis, Mr. Nixon directed, in NSSM 200, that a comprehensive new study be undertaken to determine the "Implications of World Population Growth for U.S. Security and Overseas Interests." The report of this study would become one of the most important documents on world population growth ever written. In NSSM 200, National Security Advisor Henry Kissinger, acting for the President, directed the Secretaries of Defense and Agriculture, the Director of the Central Intelligence Agency, the Deputy Secretary of State, and the Administrator of the Agency for International Development (AID), to undertake the population study jointly. The report on this study was completed on December 10, 1974 and circulated to the designated Secretaries and Agency heads for their review and comments.

On August 9, 1974, Gerald Ford succeeded to the Presidency. Revisions of the study continued until July, 1975. On November 26, 1975, the 227-page report and its recommendations were endorsed by President Ford in NSDM 314: "The President has reviewed the interagency response to NSSM 200...," wrote the new National Security Advisor, Brent Scowcroft. "He believes that United States leadership is essential to combat population growth, to implement the World Population Plan of Action* and to advance United States security and overseas interests. The President endorses the policy recommendations contained in the Executive Summary of the NSSM 200 response..."

President Ford, recognizing the gravity of the situation, directed NSDM 314 beyond the Departments and Agencies cited above. He

---

* The World Population Plan of Action was adopted at the UN World Population Conference at Bucharest in August, 1974. It is summarized and discussed in Chapter VI of NSSM 200. It is one of the most important population documents ever written and appears in its entirety in Appendix 1.

also directed it to the Secretaries of Health, Education and Welfare and Treasury, the Director of Management and Budget, the Chairmen of the Joint Chiefs of Staff, the Council of Economic Advisers, and the Council on Environmental Quality. He made it clear to *all* of the relevant Departments and Agencies of the United States Government that he intended this to become the foundation of population policy for our government.

Mr. Ford assigned responsibility for further action to the National Security Council (NSC): "The President, therefore, assigns to the Chairman, NSC Undersecretaries Committee, the responsibility to define and develop policy in the population field and to coordinate its implementation beyond the NSSM 200 response." To this day, the policy set forth in NSDM 314 has not been officially rescinded. In Chapter 4, NSDM 314 appears just as President Ford approved it.

NSSM 200 itself is a 2-page document and appears in Chapter 3. The report requested in NSSM 200 bears the title, *NSSM 200: Implications of Worldwide Population Growth for U.S. Security and Overseas Interests*. It consists of a 29-page Executive Summary and a two-part report 198 typescript pages in length. The report was never printed or published. It was typewritten, double-spaced. The Executive Summary appears in Chapter 3, while the main body of the report is in Appendix 2. Both appear just as President Ford read them, though we have typeset it for publication here, renumbering the pages correspondingly.

The potential importance of this document to U.S. security and the security of all nations was and remains immense. Both the findings and the recommendations have become increasingly relevant and urgent over the years. For this reason I have included the complete document in this book.

The NSSM 200 study details how and why continued rapid world population growth gravely threatens U.S. and global security. It also provides a blueprint for the U.S. response to this burgeoning problem, reflecting the deep concern of those who produced the report. Their strategy is complex, raising difficult questions. Some suggested policies are necessarily bold and the report's authors urged that it be classified for five years to prepare the American public for full acceptance of the goals proposed. However, it remained classified for 14 years for reasons that are unclear.

The intense concern of the authors is clearly evident. NSSM 200 reports: "There is a major risk of severe damage [from continued rapid population growth] to world economic, political, and ecological systems and, as these systems begin to fail, to our humanitarian values."[5] "World population growth is widely recognized within the Government as a current danger of the highest magnitude calling for urgent measures."[6] "It is of the utmost urgency that governments now recognize the facts and implications of population growth, determine the ultimate population sizes that make sense for their countries and start vigorous programs at once to achieve their desired goals."[7]

NSSM 200 made the following recommendations, to mention a few:

- The U.S. would provide world leadership in population growth control.[8]
- The U.S. would seek to attain its own population stability by the year 2000.[9] This would have required a one-child family policy for the U.S., thanks to the phenomenon of demographic momentum, a requirement the authors well understood (the Chinese did not adopt their one-child family policy until 1977).
- Have as goals for the U.S.: making family planning information, education and means available to all people of the developing world by 1980,[10] and achieving a 2-child family in the developing countries by 2000.[11]
- The U.S. would provide substantial funds to help achieve these goals.[12]

But, as with the Rockefeller Commission Report, the implementation of recommendations made in NSSM 200—approved by President Ford, with his approval communicated to all relevant Departments and Agencies in our government—was halted mainly through the influence of the same opposition that had precluded adoption of the Rockefeller Commission recommendations.

Had the recommendations of NSSM 200 been implemented in 1975, the world would be very different today. The prospects would have improved for every nation and people to be significantly more secure. There would be less civil and regional warfare, less starvation and hunger, a cleaner environment and less disease, greater educational opportunities, expanded civil rights, especially for women, and a political climate more conducive to the expansion of democracy.

Chapter 5 discusses the fate of the Rockefeller Commission and NSSM 200 initiatives. Chapter 6 examines the reasons for its demise. Chapter 7 identifies those responsible for the destruction of the initiatives and Chapters 8 and 9 describe how this was accomplished. The ultimate goal of the Vatican's anti-population efforts in the U.S. is passage of the Human Life Amendment, discussed in Chapter 10. The underlying cause of the world population problem is the dogma of Papal infallibility (1870), the foundation of the Catholic Church. Chapter 11 is the rationale of the Church in destroying these two initiatives: a ploy to insure its own institutional survival. The Catholic principle of infallibility, as it is challenged by the reality of overpopulation, is causing the Church to hurtle toward self-destruction as had been predicted by thoughtful bishops in 1870.

Chapter 12 discusses how self-destruction is being postponed. Most American Catholics reject the Church teachings on reproductive and population matters. The resulting steep decline in the American Church is discussed in Chapter 13. Given that we Americans are awash in information, it is inconceivable that all of this could have occurred without our knowledge. But it has. How? Chapters 14 and 15 are devoted to answering this vitally important question. The desperate attempt to protect Vatican security-survival interests, including its takeover of the Republican Party, is seriously undermining our democratic system of government. Many results of this campaign are described in Chapter 16. The last chapter focuses on an appropriate response to the only significant opponent of population growth control—the Vatican.

The documents presented in this book are fundamental to an understanding of the world population problem, the gravity of which is beyond dispute. This is also true of the issues presented in Chapters 5 to 17. Until these issues are effectively confronted, it will not be possible to deal with the world population problem successfully.

PRESIDENT NIXON'S SPECIAL MESSAGE ON POPULATION

1

This chapter consists of the President's "Special Message to the Congress on Problems of Population Growth," presented on July 18, 1969. It is reprinted here exactly as it was released by the White House.

1

T O THE CONGRESS of the United States:

In 1830 there were one billion people on the planet earth. By 1930 there were two billion, and by 1960 there were three billion. Today the world population is three and one-half billion persons.

These statistics illustrate the dramatically increasing rate of population growth. It took many thousands of years to produce the first billion people; the next billion took a century; the third came after thirty years; the fourth will be produced in just fifteen.

If this rate of population growth continues, it is likely that the earth will contain over seven billion human beings by the end of this century. Over the next thirty years, in other words, the world's population could double. And at the end of that time, each new addition of one billion persons would not come over the millennia nor over a century nor even over a decade. If present trends were to continue until the year 2000, the eighth billion would be added in only five years and each additional billion in an even shorter period.

While there are a variety of opinions as to precisely how fast population will grow in the coming decades, most informed observers have a similar response to all such projections. They agree that population growth is among the most important issues we face. They agree that it can be met only if there is a great deal of advance planning. And they agree that the time for such planning is growing very short. It is for all these reasons that I address myself to the population problem in this message, first to its international dimensions and then to its domestic implications.

IN THE DEVELOPING NATIONS

It is in the developing nations of the world that population is growing most rapidly today. In these areas we often find rates of natural increase higher than any which have been experienced in all of human history. With their birth rates remaining high and with death rates dropping sharply, many countries of Latin America, Asia, and Africa now grow ten times as fast as they did a century ago. At present rates, many will double and some may even triple their present populations before the year 2000. This fact is in large measure a consequence of rising health standards and economic progress throughout the world, improvements which allow more people to live longer and more of their children to survive to maturity.

As a result, many already impoverished nations are struggling under a handicap of intense population increase which the industrialized nations never had to bear. Even though most of these countries have made rapid progress in total economic growth—faster in percentage terms than many of the more industrialized nations—their far greater rates of population growth have made development in per capita terms very slow. Their standards of living are not rising quickly, and the gap between life in the rich nations and life in the poor nations is not closing.

There are some respects, in fact, in which economic development threatens to fall behind population growth, so that the quality of life actually worsens. For example, despite considerable improvements in agricultural technology and some dramatic increases in grain production, it is still difficult to feed these added people at adequate levels of nutrition. Protein malnutrition is widespread. It is estimated that every day some 10,000 people—most of them children—are dying from diseases of which malnutrition has been at least a partial cause. Moreover, the physical and mental potential of millions of youngsters is not realized because of a lack of proper food. The promise for increased production and better distribution of food is great, but not great enough to counter these bleak realities.

The burden of population growth is also felt in the field of social progress. In many countries, despite increases in the number of schools and teachers, there are more and more children for whom there is no schooling. Despite construction of new homes, more and more families are without adequate shelter. Unemployment and underemployment are increasing and the situation could be aggravated as more young people grow up and seek to enter the work force.

Nor has development yet reached the stage where it brings with it diminished family size. Many parents in developing countries are still victimized by forces such as poverty and ignorance which make it difficult for them to exercise control over the size of their families. In sum, population growth is a world problem which no country can ignore, whether it is moved by the narrowest perception of national self-interest or the widest vision of a common humanity.

INTERNATIONAL COOPERATION

It is our belief that the United Nations, its specialized agencies, and other international bodies should take the leadership in responding to world population growth. The United States will cooperate fully with their programs. I would note in this connection that I am most impressed by the scope and the thrust of the recent report of the Panel of the United Nations Association, chaired by John D. Rockefeller 3rd.[*] The report stresses the need for expanded action and greater coordination, concerns which should be high on the agenda of the United Nations.

In addition to working with international organizations, the United States can help by supporting efforts which are initiated by other governments. Already we are doing a great deal in this field. For example, we provide assistance to countries which seek our help in reducing high birthrates—provided always that the services we help to make available can be freely accepted or rejected by the individuals who receive them. Through our aid programs, we have worked to improve agricultural production and bolster economic growth in developing nations.

As I pointed out in my recent message on Foreign Aid, we are making important efforts to improve these programs. In fact, I have asked the Secretary of State and the Administrator of the Agency

The 57-page report, dated May 1969, is entitled "World Population, A Challenge to the United Nations and Its System of Agencies." The report was issued by the National Policy Panel established by the United Nations Association of the U.S.A. —Ed.

for International Development to give population and family planning high priority for attention, personnel, research, and funding among our several aid programs. Similarly, I am asking the Secretaries of Commerce and Health, Education, and Welfare and the Directors of the Peace Corps and the United States Information Agency to give close attention to population matters as they plan their overseas operations. I also call on the Department of Agriculture and the Agency for International Development to investigate ways of adapting and extending our agricultural experience and capabilities to improve food production and distribution in developing countries. In all of these international efforts, our programs should give further recognition to the important resources of private organizations and university research centers. As we increase our population and family planning efforts abroad, we also call upon other nations to enlarge their programs in this area.

Prompt action in all these areas is essential. For high rates of population growth, as the report of the Panel of the United Nations puts it, "impair individual rights, jeopardize national goals, and threaten international stability."

IN THE UNITED STATES

For some time population growth has been seen as a problem for developing countries. Only recently has it come to be seen that pressing problems are also posed for advanced industrial countries when their populations increase at the rate that the United States, for example, must now anticipate. Food supplies may be ample in such nations, but social supplies—the capacity to educate youth, to provide privacy and living space, to maintain the processes of open, democratic government—may be grievously strained.

In the United States our rate of population growth is not as great as that of developing nations. In this country, in fact, the growth rate has generally declined since the eighteenth century. The present growth rate of about one percent per year is still significant, however. Moreover, current statistics indicate that the fertility rate may be approaching the end of its recent decline.

Several factors contribute to the yearly increase, including the large number of couples of childbearing age, the typical size of American families, and our increased longevity. We are rapidly reaching the point in this country where a family reunion, which has typically brought together children, parents, and grandparents, will instead gather family members from *four* generations. This is a development for which we are grateful and of which we can be proud. But we must also recognize that it will mean a far larger population if the number of children born to each set of parents remains the same.

In 1917 the total number of Americans passed 100 million, after three full centuries of steady growth. In 1967—just half a century later—the 200 million mark was passed. If the present rate of growth continues, the third hundred million persons will be added in roughly a thirty-year period. This means that by the year 2000, or shortly thereafter, there will be more than 300 million Americans.

This growth will produce serious challenges for our society. I believe that many of our present social problems may be related to the fact that we have had only fifty years in which to accommodate the second hundred million Americans. In fact, since 1945 alone some 90 million babies have been born in this country. We have thus had to accomplish in a very few decades an adjustment to population growth which was once spread over centuries. And it now appears that we will have to provide for a third hundred million Americans in a period of just 30 years.

The great majority of the next hundred million Americans will be born to families which looked forward to their birth and are prepared to love them and care for them as they grow up. The critical issue is whether social institutions will also plan for their arrival and be able to accommodate them in a humane and intelligent way. We can be sure that society will *not* be ready for this growth unless it begins its planning immediately. And adequate planning, in turn, requires that we ask ourselves a number of important questions.

Where, for example, will the next hundred million Americans live? If the patterns of the last few decades hold for the rest of the century, then at least three quarters of the next hundred million persons will locate in highly urbanized areas. Are our cities prepared for such an influx? The chaotic history of urban growth suggests that they are not and that many of their existing problems will be severely aggravated by a dramatic increase in numbers. Are there ways, then, of readying our cities? Alternatively, can the trend toward greater concentrations of population be reversed? Is it a desirable thing, for example, that half of all the counties in the

United States actually lost population in the 1950's, despite the growing number of inhabitants in the country as a whole? Are there ways of fostering a better distribution of the growing population?

Some have suggested that systems of satellite cities or completely new towns can accomplish this goal. The National Commission on Urban Growth has recently produced a stimulating report[*] on this matter, one which recommends the creation of 100 new communities averaging 100,000 people each, and ten new communities averaging at least one million persons. But the total number of people who would be accommodated if even this bold plan were implemented is only twenty million—a mere one-fifth of the expected thirty-year increase. If we were to accommodate the full 100 million persons in new communities, we would have to build a new city of 250,000 persons each month from now until the end of the century. That means constructing a city the size of Tulsa, Dayton, or Jersey City every thirty days for over thirty years. Clearly, the problem is enormous, and we must examine the alternative solutions very carefully.

Other questions also confront us. How, for example, will we house the next hundred million Americans? Already economical and attractive housing is in very short supply. New architectural forms, construction techniques, and financing strategies must be aggressively pioneered if we are to provide the needed dwellings.

What of our natural resources and the quality of our environment? Pure air and water are fundamental to life itself. Parks, recreational facilities, and an attractive countryside are essential to our emotional well-being. Plant and animal and mineral resources are also vital. A growing population will increase the demand for such resources. But in many cases their supply will not be increased and may even be endangered. The ecological system upon which we now depend may seriously deteriorate if our efforts to conserve and enhance the environment do not match the growth of the population.

How will we educate and employ such a large number of people? Will our transportation systems move them about as quickly and economically as necessary? How will we provide adequate health care when our population reaches 300 million?

---

[*]   The report issued by the National Commission on Urban Growth Policy, an ad hoc group of Urban America, Inc., is included in the book, "The New City," published by Praeger and edited by Donald Canty. —Ed.

Will our political structures have to be reordered, too, when our society grows to such proportions? Many of our institutions are already under tremendous strain as they try to respond to the demands of 1969. Will they be swamped by a growing flood of people in the next thirty years? How easily can they be replaced or altered?

Finally we must ask: how can we better assist American families so that they will have no more children than they wish to have? In my first message to Congress on domestic affairs, I called for a national commitment to provide a healthful and stimulating environment for all children during their first five years of life. One of the ways in which we can promote that goal is to provide assistance for more parents in effectively planning their families. We know that involuntary childbearing often results in poor physical and emotional health for all members of the family. It is one of the factors which contribute to our distressingly high infant mortality rate, the unacceptable level of malnutrition, and the disappointing performance of some children in our schools. Unwanted or untimely childbearing is one of several forces which are driving many families into poverty or keeping them in that condition. Its threat helps to produce the dangerous incidence of illegal abortion. And finally, or course, it needlessly adds to the burdens placed on all our resources by increasing population.

None of the questions I have raised here is new. But all of these questions must now be asked and answered with a new sense of urgency. The answers cannot be given by government alone, nor can government alone turn the answers into programs and policies. I believe, however, that the Federal Government does have a special responsibility for defining these problems and for stimulating thoughtful responses.

Perhaps the most dangerous element in the present situation is the fact that so few people are examining these questions from the viewpoint of the whole society. Perceptive businessmen project the demand for their products many years into the future by studying population trends. Other private institutions develop sophisticated planning mechanisms which allow them to account for rapidly changing conditions. In the governmental sphere, however, there is virtually no machinery through which we can develop a detailed understanding of demographic changes and bring that understanding to bear on public policy. The federal government makes only a minimal effort in this area. The efforts of state and local governments are also inadequate. Most importantly, the planning which does take place at some levels is poorly understood at others and is often based on unexamined assumptions.

In short, the questions I have posed in this message too often go unasked, and when they are asked, they seldom are adequately answered.

COMMISSION ON POPULATION GROWTH AND THE AMERICAN FUTURE

It is for all these reasons that I today propose the creation by Congress of a Commission on Population Growth and the American Future.

The Congress should give the Commission responsibility for inquiry and recommendations in three specific areas.

First, *the probable course of population growth, internal migration and related demographic developments between now and the year 2000.*

As much as possible, these projections should be made by regions, states, and metropolitan areas. Because there is an element of uncertainty in such projections, various alternative possibilities should be plotted.

It is of special importance to note that, beginning in August of 1970, population data by county will become available from the decennial census, which will have been taken in April of that year. By April 1971, computer summaries of first-count data will be available by census tract and an important range of information on income, occupations, education, household composition, and other vital considerations will also be in hand. The Federal government can make better use of such demographic information than it has done in the past, and state governments and other political subdivisions can also use such data to better advantage. The Commission on Population Growth and the American Future will be an appropriate instrument for this important initiative.

Second, *the resources in the public sector of the economy that will be required to deal with the anticipated growth in population.*

The single greatest failure of foresight—at all levels of government—over the past generation has been in areas connected with expanding population. Government and legislatures have frequently failed to appreciate the demands which continued population growth would impose on the public sector. These demands are myriad: they will range from preschool classrooms to post-doctoral fellowships; from public works which carry water over thousands of miles to highways which carry people and products from region to region; from vest pocket parks in crowded cities to forest preserves and quiet lakes in the countryside. Perhaps especially, such demands will assert themselves in forms that affect the quality of life. The time is at hand for a serious assessment of such needs.

Third, *ways in which population growth may affect the activities of Federal, state and local government.*

In some respects, population growth affects everything that American government does. Yet only occasionally do our governmental units pay sufficient attention to population growth in their own planning. Only occasionally do they consider the serious implications of demographic trends for their present and future activities.

Yet some of the necessary information is at hand and can be made available to all levels of government. Much of the rest will be obtained by the Commission. For such information to be of greatest use, however, it should also be interpreted and analyzed and its implications should be made more evident. It is particularly in this connection that the work of the Commission on Population Growth and the American Future will be as much educational as investigative. The American public and its governing units are not as alert as they should be to these growing challenges. A responsible but insistent voice of reason and foresight is needed. The Commission can provide that voice in the years immediately before us.

The membership of the commission should include two members from each house of the Congress, together with knowledgeable men and women who are broadly representative of our society. The majority should be citizens who have demonstrated a capacity to deal with important questions of public policy. The membership should also include specialists in the biological, social, and environmental sciences, in theology and law, in the arts and in engineering. The Commission should be empowered to create advisory panels to consider subdivisions of its broad subject and to invite experts and leaders from all parts of the world to join these panels in their deliberations.

The Commission should be provided with an adequate staff and budget, under the supervision of an executive director of exceptional experience and understanding.

In order that the Commission will have time to utilize the initial data which results from the 1970 census, I ask that it be established for a period of two years. An interim report to the President and Congress should be required at the end of the first year.

OTHER GOVERNMENT ACTIVITIES

I would take this opportunity to mention a number of additional government activities dealing with population growth which need not await the report of the Commission.

First, increased research is essential. It is clear, for example, that we need additional research on birth control methods of all types and the sociology of population growth. Utilizing its Center for Population Research, the Department of Health, Education, and Welfare should take the lead in developing, with other federal agencies, an expanded research effort, one which is carefully related to those of private organizations, university research centers, international organizations, and other countries.

Second, we need more trained people to work in population and family planning programs, both in this country and abroad. I am therefore asking the Secretaries of State, Labor, Health, Education, and Welfare, and Interior along with the Administrator of the Agency for International Development and the Director of the Office of Economic Opportunity to participate in a comprehensive survey of our efforts to attract people to such programs and to train them properly. The same group—in consultation with appropriate state, local, and private officials—should develop recommendations for improvements in this area. I am asking the Assistant to the President for Urban Affairs to coordinate this project.

Third, the effects of population growth on our environment and on the world's food supply call for careful attention and immediate action. I am therefore asking the Environmental Quality Council to give careful attention to these matters in its deliberations. I am also asking the Secretaries of Interior, Agriculture, and Health, Education, and Welfare to give the highest priority to research into new techniques and to other proposals that can help safeguard the environment and increase the world's supply of food.

Fourth, it is clear that the domestic family planning services supported by the Federal Government should be expanded and better integrated. Both the Department of Health, Education and Welfare and the Office of Economic Opportunity are now involved in this important work, yet their combined efforts are not adequate to provide information and services to all who want them. In particular, most of an estimated five million low income women of childbearing age in this country do not now have adequate access to family planning assistance, even though their wishes concerning family size are usually the same as those of parents of higher income groups.

It is my view that no American woman should be denied access to family planning assistance because of her economic condition. I believe, therefore, that we should establish as a national goal the provision of adequate family planning services within the next five years to all those who want them but cannot afford them. This we have the capacity to do.

Clearly, in no circumstances will the activities associated with our pursuit of this goal be allowed to infringe upon the religious convictions or personal wishes and freedom of any individual, nor will they be allowed to impair the absolute right of all individuals to have such matters of conscience respected by public authorities.

In order to achieve this national goal, we will have to increase the amount we are spending on population and family planning. But success in this endeavor will not result from higher expenditures alone. Because the life circumstances and family planning wishes of those who receive services vary considerably, an effective program must be more flexible in its design than are many present efforts. In addition, programs should be better coordinated and more effectively administered. Under current legislation, a comprehensive State or local project must assemble a patchwork of funds from many different sources—a time-consuming and confusing process. Moreover, under existing legislation, requests for funds for family planning services must often compete with requests for other deserving health endeavors.

But these problems can be overcome. The Secretary of Health, Education and Welfare—whose Department is responsible for the largest part of our domestic family planning services—has developed plans to reorganize the major family planning service activities of his agency. A separate unit for these services will be established within the Health Services and Mental Health Administration. The Secretary will send to Congress in the near future legislation which will help the Department implement this important program by providing broader and more precise legislative authority and a clearer source of financial support.

The Office of Economic Opportunity can also contribute to progress in this area by strengthening its innovative programs and pilot projects in the delivery of family planning services to the needy. The existing network of O.E.O. supported community groups should also be used more extensively to provide family planning assistance and information. I am asking the Director of the Office of Economic Opportunity to determine the ways in which his Agency can best structure and extend its programs in order to help achieve our national goal in the coming years.

As they develop their own plans, the Secretary of Health, Education and Welfare and the Director of the Office of Economic Opportunity should also determine the most effective means of coordinating all our domestic family planning programs and should include in their deliberations representatives of the other agencies that share in this important work. It is my intention that such planning should also involve state and local governments and private agencies, for it is clear that the increased activity of the Federal government in this area must be matched by a sizeable increase in effort at other levels. It would be unrealistic for the Federal government alone to shoulder the entire burden, but this Administration does accept a clear responsibility to provide essential leadership.

FOR THE FUTURE

One of the most serious challenges to human destiny in the last third of this century will be the growth of the population. Whether man's response to that challenge will be a cause for pride or for despair in the year 2000 will depend very much on what we do today. If we now begin our work in an appropriate manner, and if we continue to devote a considerable amount of attention and energy to this problem, then mankind will be able to surmount this challenge as it has surmounted so many during the long march of civilization.

When future generations evaluate the record of our time, one of the most important factors in their judgment will be the way in which we responded to population growth. Let us act in such a way that those who come after us—even as they lift their eyes beyond earth's bounds—can do so with pride in the planet on which they live, with gratitude to those who lived on it in the past, and with continuing confidence in its future.

RICHARD NIXON
The White House

THE ROCKEFELLER COMMISSION ON POPULATION GROWTH

2

PART 1 of this chapter is the verbatim text of President Nixon's remarks when he signed the bill in 1970 creating the commission, and announced that John D. Rockefeller 3rd had accepted the commission's chairmanship.

PART 2 is the complete text of the commission's recommendations, submitted to the President in 1972.

2

P ART 1

March 16, 1970. Remarks of President Nixon on Signing Bill Establishing the Commission on Population Growth and the American Future.

Ladies and gentlemen:

We have asked you into this room because the Cabinet Room is presently being redecorated. The purpose is to sign the population message. I shall sign the message and then make a brief statement with regard to it.

First, this message is bipartisan in character as is indicated by the Senators and Congressmen who are standing here today. This is the first message on population ever submitted to the Congress and passed by the Congress. It is time for such a message to be submitted and also the time to set up a Population Commission such as this does.

Let me indicate very briefly some of the principles behind this population message.

First, it will study both the situation with regard to population growth in the United States and worldwide.

Second, it does not approach the problem from the standpoint of making an arbitrary decision that population will be a certain number and will stop there. It approaches the problem in terms of trying to find out what we can expect in the way of population growth, where that population will move, and then how we can properly deal with it.

It also, of course, deals with the problem of excessive population in areas, both in nations and in parts of nations, where there simply are not the resources to sustain an adequate life.

I would also add that the Congress, particularly the House of Representatives, I think, contributed very much to this message by adding amendments indicating that the Population Commission should study the problems of the environment as they are affected by population, and also that the Population Commission should take into account the ethical considerations that we all know are involved in a question as sensitive as this.

I believe this is an historic occasion. It has been made historic not simply by the act of the President in signing this measure, but by the fact that it has had bipartisan support and also such broad support in the nation.

An indication of that broad support is that John D. Rockefeller has agreed to serve as Chairman of the Commission. The other members of the Commission will be announced at a later time. Of all the people in this nation, I think I could say of all the people in the world, there is perhaps no man who has been more closely identified and longer identified with this problem than John Rockefeller. We are very fortunate to have his chairmanship of the Commission; and we know that the report that he will give, the recommendations that he will make, will be tremendously significant as we deal with this highly explosive problem, explosive in every way, as we enter the last third of the 20th century.

And I again congratulate the Members of the House and Senate for their bipartisan support. I wish the members of the Commission well.

And as usual we have pens for all the Members of Congress who participated in making this bill possible and for the members of the staff who are present here.

NOTE: The President spoke at 10:16 a.m. in the Roosevelt Room at the White House.

A White House release of March 16, 1970, announcing the signing of the bill and the appointment of John D. Rockefeller 3rd is printed in the Weekly Compilation of Presidential Documents (vol. 6, p. 734).

As enacted, the bill (S. 2701) is Public Law 91-213 (84 Stat. 67).

PART 2
Compilation of Recommendations of The Commission on Population Growth and the American Future

POPULATION EDUCATION

In view of the important role that education can play in developing an understanding of the causes and consequences of population growth and distribution, the Commission recommends enactment of a Population Education Act to assist school systems in establishing well-planned population education programs so that present and future generations will be better prepared to meet the challenges arising from population change.

To implement such a program, the Commission recommends that federal funds be appropriated for teacher training, for curriculum development and materials preparation, for research and evaluation, for the support of model programs, and for assisting state departments of education to develop competence and leadership in population education.

SEX EDUCATION

Recognizing the importance of human sexuality, the Commission recommends that sex education be available to all, and that it be presented in a responsible manner through community organizations, the media, and especially the schools.

CHILD CARE

The Commission recommends that both public and private forces join together to assure that adequate child-care services, including health, nutritional, and educational components, are available to families who wish to make use of them.

Because child-care programs represent a major innovation in child-rearing in this country, we recommend that continuing research and evaluation be undertaken to determine the benefits and costs to children, parents, and the public of alternative child-care arrangements.

CHILDREN BORN OUT OF WEDLOCK

The Commission recommends that all children, regardless of the circumstances of their birth, be accorded fair and equal status socially, morally, and legally.

The Commission urges research and study by the American Bar Association, the American Law Institute, and other interested groups leading to revision of those laws and practices which result in discrimination against out-of-wedlock children. Our end objective should be to accord fair and equal treatment to all children.

ADOPTION

The Commission recommends changes in attitudes and practices to encourage adoption thereby benefiting children, prospective parents, and society. To implement this goal, the Commission recommends:

Further subsidization of families qualified to adopt, but unable to assume the full financial cost of a child's care.

A review of current laws, practices, procedures, and regulations which govern the adoptive process.

EQUAL RIGHTS FOR WOMEN

The Commission recommends that the Congress and the states approve the proposed Equal Rights Amendment and that federal, state, and local governments undertake positive programs to ensure freedom from discrimination based on sex.

CONTRACEPTION AND THE LAW

The Commission recommends that: (1) states eliminate existing legal inhibitions and restrictions on access to contraceptive information, procedures, and supplies; and (2) states develop statutes affirming the desirability that all persons have ready and practicable access to contraceptive information, procedures, and supplies.

CONTRACEPTION AND MINORS

The Commission recommends that states adopt affirmative legislation which will permit minors to receive contraceptive and prophylactic information and services in appropriate settings sensitive to their needs and concerns.

To implement this policy, the commission urges that organizations, such as the Council on State governments, the American Law Institute, and the American Bar Association, formulate appropriate model statutes.

VOLUNTARY STERILIZATION

In order to permit freedom of choice, the Commission recommends that all administration restrictions on access to voluntary contraceptive sterilization be eliminated so that the decision be made solely by physician and patient.

To implement this policy, we recommend that national hospital and medical associations, and their state chapters, promote the removal of existing restrictions.

ABORTION

With the admonition that abortion not be considered a primary means of fertility control, the Commission recommends that present state laws restricting abortion be liberalized along the lines of the New York statute, such abortion to be performed on request by duly licensed physicians under conditions of medical safety. In carrying out this policy, the Commission recommends:

That federal, state, and local governments make funds available to support abortion services in states with liberalized statutes.

That abortion be specifically included in comprehensive health insurance benefits, both public and private.

METHODS OF FERTILITY CONTROL

The Commission recommends that this nation give the highest priority to research on reproductive biology and to the search for improved methods by which individuals can control their own fertility.

In order to carry out this research, the Commission recommends that the full $93 million authorized for this purpose in fiscal year 1973 be appropriated and allocated; that federal expenditures for these purposes rise to a minimum of $150 million by 1975; and that private organizations continue and expand their work in this field.

FERTILITY-RELATED HEALTH SERVICES

The Commission recommends a national policy and voluntary program to reduce unwanted fertility, to improve the outcome of pregnancy, and to improve the health of children.

In order to carry out such a program, public and private health financing mechanisms should begin paying the full cost of all health services related to fertility, including contraceptive, prenatal, delivery, and postpartum services; pediatric care for the first year of life; voluntary sterilization; safe termination of unwanted pregnancy; and medical treatment of infertility.

PERSONNEL TRAINING AND DELIVERY OF SERVICES

We recommend creation of programs to (1) train doctors, nurses, and paraprofessionals, including indigenous personnel, in the provision of all fertility-related health services; (2) develop new patterns for the utilization of professional and paraprofessional personnel; and (3) evaluate improved methods of organizing the delivery of these services.

FAMILY PLANNING SERVICES

The Commission recommends: (1) new legislation extending the current family planning project grant program for five years beyond fiscal year 1973 and providing additional authorizations to reach a federal funding level of $225 million in fiscal year 1973, $275 million in fiscal year 1974, $325 million in fiscal year 1975, and $400 million thereafter; (2) extension of the family planning project grant authority of Title V of the Social Security Act beyond 1972, and maintenance of the level of funding at approximately $30 million annually; and (3) maintenance of the Title II OEO program at current levels of authorization.

SERVICES FOR TEENAGERS

Toward the goal of reducing unwanted pregnancies and child-bearing among the young, the Commission recommends that birth control information and services be made available to teenagers in appropriate facilities sensitive to their needs and concerns.

The Commission recommends the development and implementation of an adequately financed program to develop appropriate family planning materials, to conduct training courses for teachers and school administrators, and to assist states and local communities in integrating information about family planning into school courses such as hygiene and sex education.

POPULATION STABILIZATION

Recognizing that our population cannot grow indefinitely, and appreciating the advantages of moving now toward the stabilization of population, the Commission recommends that the nation welcome and plan for a stabilized population.

ILLEGAL ALIENS

The Commission recommends that Congress immediately consider the serious situation of illegal immigration and pass legislation which will impose civil and criminal sanctions on employers of illegal border-crossers or aliens in an immigration status in which employment is not authorized.

To implement this policy, the Commission recommends provision of increased and strengthened resources consistent with an effective enforcement program in appropriate agencies.

IMMIGRATION

The Commission recommends that immigration levels not be increased and that immigration policy be reviewed periodically to reflect demographic conditions and considerations.

To implement this policy, that Congress require the Bureau of the Census, in coordination with the Immigration and Naturalization Service, to report biennially to the Congress on the impact of immigration on the nation's demographic situation.

NATIONAL DISTRIBUTION AND MIGRATION POLICIES

The Commission recommends that:

The federal government develop a set of national population distribution guidelines to serve as a framework for regional, state, and local plans and development.

Regional, state, and metropolitan-wide governmental authorities take the initiative, in cooperation with local governments, to conduct needed comprehensive planning and action programs to achieve a higher quality of urban development.

The process of population movement be eased and guided in order to improve access of opportunities now restricted by physical remoteness, immobility, and inadequate skills, information and experience.

Action be taken to increase freedom in choice of residential location through the elimination of current patterns of racial and economic segregation and their attendant injustices.

GUIDING URBAN EXPANSION

To anticipate and guide future urban growth, the Commission recommends comprehensive land-use and public-facility planning on an overall metropolitan and regional scale, and that governments exercise greater control over land-use planning and development.

RACIAL MINORITIES AND THE POOR

To help dissolve the territorial basis of racial polarization, the Commission recommends vigorous and concerted steps to promote free choice of housing within metropolitan areas.

To remove the occupational sources of racial polarization, the Commission recommends the development of more extensive human capital programs to equip black and other deprived minorities for fuller participation in economic life.

To reduce restrictions on the entry of low- and moderate-income people to the suburbs, that federal and state governments ensure provision of more suburban housing for low- and moderate-income families.

To promote a more racially and economically integrated society, that actions be taken to reduce the dependence of local jurisdictions on locally collected property taxes.

DEPRESSED RURAL AREAS

To improve the quality and mobility potential of individuals, that future programs for declining and chronically depressed rural areas emphasize human resource development.

To enhance the effectiveness of migration, the Commission recommends that programs be developed to provide worker-relocation counseling and assistance to enable an individual to relocate with a minimum of risk and disruption.

To promote the expansion of job opportunities in urban places located within or near declining areas and having a demonstrated potential for future growth, the Commission recommends the development of a growth center strategy.

INSTITUTIONAL RESPONSES

The Commission recommends the establishment of state or regional development corporations which would have the responsibility and the necessary powers to implement comprehensive development plans either as a developer itself or as a catalyst for private development.

POPULATION STATISTICS AND RESEARCH

The Commission recommends that the federal government move promptly and boldly to strengthen the basic statistics and research upon which all sound demographic, social, and economic policy must ultimately depend, by implementing the following specific improvements in these programs.

VITAL STATISTICS DATA

The Commission recommends that the National Center for Health Statistics improve the timeliness and the quality of data collected with respect to birth, death, marriage, and divorce.

ENUMERATION OF SPECIAL GROUPS

The Commission recommends that the federal government support, even more strongly, the Census Bureau's efforts to improve the completeness of our census enumeration, especially of minority groups, ghetto populations, and all unattached adults, especially males, who are the least well counted.

INTERNATIONAL MIGRATION

The Commission recommends that a task force be designated under the leadership of the Office of Management and Budget to devise a program for the development of comprehensive immigration and emigration statistics, and to recommend ways in which the records of the periodic alien registrations should be processed to provide information on the distribution and characteristics of aliens in the United States.

THE CURRENT POPULATION SURVEY

The Committee recommends that the government provide substantial additional support to the Current Population Survey to improve the area identification of those interviewed and to permit special studies, utilizing enlarged samples, of demographic trends in special groups of the population.

STATISTICAL REPORTING OF FAMILY PLANNING SERVICES

The Commission recommends the rapid development of comprehensive statistics on family planning services.

NATIONAL SURVEY OF FAMILY GROWTH

The Commission recommends program support and continued adequate financial support for the Family Growth Survey as almost the first condition for evaluating the effectiveness of national population policies and programs.

DISTRIBUTION OF GOVERNMENT DATA

The Commission recommends that the various statistical agencies seek to maximize the public usefulness of the basic data by making identity-free tapes available to responsible research agencies.

MID-DECADE CENSUS

The Commission recommends that the decennial census be supplemented by a mid-decade census of the population.

STATISTICAL USE OF ADMINISTRATIVE RECORDS

The Commission recommends that the government give high priority to studying the ways in which federal administrative records, notably those of the Internal Revenue Service and Social Security Administration, could be made more useful for developing statistical estimates of local population and internal migration.

INTERCENSAL POPULATION ESTIMATES

The Commission recommends that the government provide increased funding, higher priority, and accelerated development for all phases of the Census Bureau's program for developing improved intercensal population estimates for states and local areas.

SOCIAL AND BEHAVIORAL RESEARCH

The Commission recommends that substantial increases in federal funds be made available for social and behavioral research related to population growth and distribution, and for the support of nongovernmental population research centers.

RESEARCH PROGRAM IN POPULATION DISTRIBUTION

The Commission recommends that a research program in population distribution be established, preferably within the proposed Department of Community Development, funded by a small percentage assessment on funds appropriated for relevant federal programs.

FEDERAL GOVERNMENT POPULATION RESEARCH

The Commission recommends that the federal government foster the "in-house" research capabilities of its own agencies to provide a coherent institutional structure for improving population research.

SUPPORT FOR PROFESSIONAL TRAINING

The Commission recommends that support for training in the social and behavioral aspects of population be exempted from the general freeze on training funds, permitting government agencies to support programs to train scientists specializing in this field.

ORGANIZATIONAL CHANGES

The Commission recommends that organizational changes be undertaken to improve the federal government's capacity to develop and implement population-related programs; and to evaluate the interaction between public policies, programs, and population trends.

OFFICE OF POPULATION AFFAIRS, DEPARTMENT OF HEALTH, EDUCATION AND WELFARE

The Commission recommends that the capacity of the Department of Health, Education and Welfare in the population field be substantially increased by strengthening the Office of Population Affairs and expanding its staff in order to augment its role of leadership within the Department.

NATIONAL INSTITUTE OF POPULATION SCIENCES

The Commission recommends the establishment, within the National Institutes of Health, of a National Institute of Population Sciences to provide an adequate institutional frame work for implementing a greatly expanded program of population research.

DEPARTMENT OF COMMUNITY DEVELOPMENT

The Commission recommends that Congress adopt legislation to establish a Department of Community Development and that this Department undertake a program of research on the interactions of population growth and distribution and the programs it administers.

OFFICE OF POPULATION GROWTH AND DISTRIBUTION

The Commission recommends the creation of an Office of Population Growth and Distribution within the Executive Office of the President.

The Commission recommends the immediate addition of personnel with demographic expertise to the staffs of the Council of Economic Advisers, the Domestic Council, the Council on Environmental Quality, and the Office of Science and Technology.

COUNCIL OF SOCIAL ADVISERS

The Commission recommends that Congress approve pending legislation establishing a Council of Social Advisers and that this Council have as one of its main functions the monitoring of demographic variables.

JOINT COMMITTEE ON POPULATION

In order to provide legislative oversight of population issues, the Commission recommends that Congress assign to a joint committee responsibility for specific review of this area.

STATE POPULATION AGENCIES AND COMMISSIONS

The Commission recommends that state governments, either through existing planning agencies or through new agencies devoted to this purpose, give greater attention to the problems of population growth and distribution.

PRIVATE EFFORTS AND POPULATION POLICY

The Commission recommends that a substantially greater effort focusing on policy-oriented research and analysis of population in the United States be carried forward through appropriate private resources and agencies.

THE NSSM 200
DIRECTIVE
AND THE STUDY
REQUESTED

3

This chapter begins with the National Security Study Memorandum (NSSM) directive itself, signed in April, 1974, by Henry Kissinger on behalf of President Nixon. Then follows the Executive Summary of the report of the study conducted in response to the directive. The copiously detailed main body of the report consists of two parts, and can be found in Appendix 2, beginning on page 433

The complete report was presented to President Ford the following December. Following the Executive Summary, in this chapter several important points from the report are listed which do not appear in the Summary. These points are discussed elsewhere in the book.

3

NATIONAL SECURITY COUNCIL
WASHINGTON, D.C. 20506

April 24, 1974

National Security Study Memorandum 200

TO: The Secretary of Defense
             The Secretary of Agriculture
             The Director of Central Intelligence
             The Deputy Secretary of State
             Administrator, Agency for International Development

SUBJECT: Implications of Worldwide Population Growth for U.S.
           Security and Overseas Interests

The President has directed a study of the impact of world population growth on U.S. security and overseas interests. The study
should look forward at least until the year 2000, and use several
alternative reasonable projections of population growth.

In terms of each projection, the study should assess:

— the corresponding pace of development, especially in poorer
  countries;

— the demand for US exports, especially of food, and the trade
  problems the US may face arising from competition for resources; and

— the likelihood that population growth or imbalances will
  produce disruptive foreign policies and international instability.

The study should focus on the international political and economic
implications of population growth rather than its ecological, sociological or other aspects.

The study would then offer possible courses of action for the United States in dealing with population matters abroad, particularly in developing countries, with special attention to these questions:

— What, if any, new initiatives by the United States are needed to focus international attention on the population problem?

— Can technological innovations or development reduce growth or ameliorate its effects?

— Could the United States improve its assistance in the population field and if so, in what form and through which agencies — bilateral, multilateral, private?

The study should take into account the President's concern that population policy is a human concern intimately related to the dignity of the individual and the objective of the United States is to work closely with others, rather than seek to impose our views on others.

The President has directed that the study be accomplished by the NSC Under Secretaries Committee. The Chairman, Under Secretaries Committee, is requested to forward the study together with the Committee's action recommendations no later than May 29, 1974 for consideration by the President.

HENRY A. KISSINGER

cc: Chairman, Joint Chiefs of Staff

NSSM 200:

IMPLICATIONS OF WORLDWIDE POPULATION GROWTH
FOR U.S. SECURITY AND OVERSEAS INTERESTS

December 10, 1974

CLASSIFIED BY Harry C. Blaney, III
SUBJECT TO GENERAL DECLASSIFICATION SCHEDULE OF
EXECUTIVE ORDER 11652 AUTOMATICALLY DOWN-
GRADED AT TWO YEAR INTERVALS AND DECLASSIFIED
ON DECEMBER 31, 1980.

This document can only be declassified by the White House.

Declassified/Released on ___7/3/89___
under provisions of E.O. 12356
by F. Graboske, National Security Council

TABLE OF CONTENTS

Executive Summary   65 - 82
(*Reader:* For Parts One and Two, see Appendix 2)
Part One—Analytical Section   437 - 498
Chapter I World Demographic Trends
Chapter II Population and World Food Supplies
Chapter III Minerals and Fuel
Chapter IV Economic Development and
            Population Growth
Chapter V Implications of Population Pressures for
           National Security
Chapter VI World Population Conference

Part Two—Policy Recommendations   499 - 558
Section I A U.S. Global Population Strategy
Section II Action to Create Conditions for Fertility De-
            cline: Population and a Development Assis-
            tance Strategy
A. General Strategy and Resource for A.I.D. Assistance
B. Functional Assistance Programs to Create Condi
    tions for Fertility Decline
C.   Food for Peace Program and Population
Section III International Organizations and other Mul-
             tilateral Population Programs
A.   UN Organization and Specialized Agencies
B.   Encouraging Private Organizations
Section IV   Provision and Development of Family
             Planning Services, Information and Tech
             nology
A. Research to Improve Fertility Control Technology
B. Development of Low-Cost Delivery Systems
C. Utilization of Mass Media and Satellite Communi
    cations System for Family Planning
Section V Action to Develop Worldwide Political and
           Popular Commitment to Population Stability

EXECUTIVE SUMMARY

WORLD DEMOGRAPHIC TRENDS

1. World Population growth since World War II is quantitatively and qualitatively different from any previous epoch in human history. The rapid reduction in death rates, unmatched by corresponding birth rate reductions, has brought total growth rates close to 2 percent a year, compared with about 1 percent before World War II, under 0.5 percent in 1750-1900, and far lower rates before 1750. The effect is to double the world's population in 35 years instead of 100 years. Almost 80 million are now being added each year, compared with 10 million in 1900.

2. The second new feature of population trends is the sharp differentiation between rich and poor countries. Since 1950, population in the former group has been growing at 0 to 1.5 percent per year, and in the latter at 2.0 to 3.5 percent (doubling in 20 to 35 years). Some of the highest rates of increase are in areas already densely populated and with a weak resource base.

3. Because of the momentum of population dynamics, reductions in birth rates affect total numbers only slowly. High birth rates in the recent past have resulted in a high proportion in the youngest age groups, so that there will continue to be substantial population increases over many years even if a two-child family should become the norm in the future. Policies to reduce fertility will have their main effects on total numbers only after several decades. However, if future numbers are to be kept within reasonable bounds, it is urgent that measures to reduce fertility be started and made effective in the 1970's and 1980's. Moreover, programs started now to reduce birth rates will have short run advantages for developing countries in lowered demands on food, health and educational and other services and in enlarged capacity to contribute to productive investments, thus accelerating development.

4. U.N. estimates use the 3.6 billion population of 1970 as a base (there are nearly 4 billion now) and project from about 6 billion to 8 billion people for the year 2000 with the U.S. medium estimate at 6.4 billion. The U.S. medium projections show a world population

of 12 billion by 2075 which implies a five-fold increase in south and southeast Asia and in Latin American and a seven-fold increase in Africa, compared with a doubling in east Asia and a 40% increase in the presently developed countries (see Table I). Most demographers, including the U.N. and the U.S. Population Council, regard the range of 10 to 13 billion as the most likely level for world population stability, even with intensive efforts at fertility control. (These figures assume, that sufficient food could be produced and distributed to avoid limitation through famines.)

ADEQUACY OF WORLD FOOD SUPPLIES

5. Growing populations will have a serious impact on the need for food especially in the poorest, fastest growing LDCs. While under normal weather conditions and assuming food production growth in line with recent trends, total world agricultural production could expand faster than population, there will nevertheless be serious problems in food distribution and financing, making shortages, even at today's poor nutrition levels, probable in many of the larger more populous LDC regions. Even today 10 to 20 million people die each year due, directly or indirectly, to malnutrition. Even more serious is the consequence of major crop failures which are likely to occur from time to time.

6. The most serious consequence for the short and middle term is the possibility of massive famines in certain parts of the world, especially the poorest regions. World needs for food rise by 2-1/2 percent or more per year (making a modest allowance for improved diets and nutrition) at a time when readily available fertilizer and well-watered land is already largely being utilized. Therefore, additions to food production must come mainly from higher yields. Countries with large population growth cannot afford constantly growing imports, but for them to raise food output steadily by 2 to 4 percent over the next generation or two is a formidable challenge. Capital and foreign exchange requirements for intensive agriculture are heavy, and are aggravated by energy cost increases and fertilizer scarcities and price rises. The institutional, technical, and economic problems of transforming traditional agriculture are also very difficult to overcome.

7. In addition, in some overpopulated regions, rapid population growth presses on a fragile environment in ways that threaten longer-term food production: through cultivation of marginal lands, overgrazing, desertification, deforestation, and soil erosion, with consequent destruction of land and pollution of water, rapid siltation of reservoirs, and impairment of inland and coastal fisheries.

MINERALS AND FUEL

8. Rapid population growth is not in itself a major factor in pressure on depletable resources (fossil fuels and other minerals), since demand for them depends more on levels of industrial output than on numbers of people. On the other hand, the world is increasingly dependent on mineral supplies from developing countries, and if rapid population frustrates their prospects for economic development and social progress, the resulting instability may undermine the conditions for expanded output and sustained flows of such resources.

9. There will be serious problems for some of the poorest LDCs with rapid population growth. They will increasingly find it difficult to pay for needed raw materials and energy. Fertilizer, vital for their own agricultural production, will be difficult to obtain for the next few years. Imports for fuel and other materials will cause grave problems which could impinge on the U.S., both through the need to supply greater financial support and in LDC efforts to obtain better terms of trade through higher prices for exports.

ECONOMIC DEVELOPMENT AND POPULATION GROWTH

10. Rapid population growth creates a severe drag on rates of economic development otherwise attainable, sometimes to the point of preventing any increase in per capita incomes. In addition to the overall impact on per capita incomes, rapid population growth seriously affects a vast range of other aspects of the quality of life important to social and economic progress in the LDCs.

11. Adverse economic factors which generally result from rapid population growth include:
 – reduced family savings and domestic investment;

- increased need for large amounts of foreign exchange for food imports;
- intensification of severe unemployment and underemployment;
- the need for large expenditures for services such as dependency support, education, and health which would be used for more productive investment;
- the concentration of developmental resources on increasing food production to ensure survival for a larger population, rather than on improving living conditions for smaller total numbers.

12. While GNP increased per annum at an average rate of 5 percent in LDCs over the last decade, the population increase of 2.5 percent reduced the average annual per capita growth rate to only 2.5 percent. In many heavily populated areas this rate was 2 percent or less. In the LDCs hardest hit by the oil crisis, with an aggregate population of 800 million, GNP increases may be reduced to less than 1 percent per capita per year for the remainder of the 1970's. For the poorest half of the populations of these countries, with average incomes of less than $100, the prospect is for no growth or retrogression for this period.

13. If significant progress can be made in slowing population growth, the positive impact on growth of GNP and per capita income will be significant. Moreover, economic and social progress will probably contribute further to the decline in fertility rates.

14. High birth rates appear to stem primarily from:
a.   inadequate information about and availability of means of fertility control;
b.   inadequate motivation for reduced numbers of children combined with motivation for many children resulting from still high infant and child mortality and need for support in old age; and
c.   the slowness of change in family preferences in response to changes in environment.

15. The universal objective of increasing the world's standard of living dictates that economic growth outpace population growth.

In many high population growth areas of the world, the largest proportion of GNP is consumed, with only a small amount saved. Thus, a small proportion of GNP is available for investment—the "engine" of economic growth. Most experts agree that, with fairly constant costs per acceptor, expenditures on effective family planning services are generally one of the most cost effective investments for an LDC country seeking to improve overall welfare and per capita economic growth. We cannot wait for overall modernization and development to produce lower fertility rates naturally since this will undoubtedly take many decades in most developing countries, during which time rapid population growth will tend to slow development and widen even more the gap between rich and poor.

16. The interrelationships between development and population growth are complex and not wholly understood. Certain aspects of economic development and modernization appear to be more directly related to lower birth rates than others. Thus certain development programs may bring a faster demographic transition to lower fertility rates than other aspects of development. The World Population Plan of Action adopted at the World Population Conference recommends that countries working to affect fertility levels should give priority to development programs and health and education strategies which have a decisive effect on fertility. International cooperation should give priority to assisting such national efforts. These programs include: (a) improved health care and nutrition to reduce child mortality, (b) education and improved social status for women; (c) increased female employment; (d) improved old-age security; and (e) assistance for the rural poor, who generally have the highest fertility, with actions to redistribute income and resources including providing privately owned farms. However, one cannot proceed simply from identification of relationships to specific large-scale operational programs. For example, we do not yet know of cost-effective ways to encourage increased female employment, particularly if we are concerned about not adding to male unemployment. We do not yet know what specific packages of programs will be most cost effective in many situations.

17. There is need for more information on cost effectiveness of different approaches on both the "supply" and the "demand" side of the picture. On the supply side, *intense efforts are required to assure full availability by 1980 of birth control information and means to all fertile individuals, especially in rural areas* [emphasis added]. Improvement is also needed in methods of birth control most acceptable and useable by the rural poor. On the demand side, further experimentation and implementation action projects and programs are needed. In particular, more research is needed on the motivation of the poorest who often have the highest fertility rates. Assistance programs must be more precisely targeted to this group than in the past.

18. It may well be that desired family size will not decline to near replacement levels until the lot of the LDC rural poor improves to the extent that the benefits of reducing family size appear to them to outweigh the costs. For urban people, a rapidly growing element in the LDCs, the liabilities of having too many children are already becoming apparent. Aid recipients and donors must also emphasize development and improvements in the quality of life of the poor, if significant progress is to be made in controlling population growth. Although it was adopted primarily for other reasons, the new emphasis of AID's legislation on problems of the poor (which is echoed in comparable changes in policy emphasis by other donors and by an increasing number of LDC's) is directly relevant to the conditions required for fertility reduction.

POLITICAL EFFECTS OF POPULATION FACTORS

19. The political consequences of current population factors in the LDCs—rapid growth, internal migration, high percentages of young people, slow improvement in living standards, urban concentrations, and pressures for foreign migration—are damaging to the internal stability and international relations of countries in whose advancement the U.S. is interested, thus creating political or even national security problems for the U.S. In a broader sense, *there is a major risk of severe damage to world economic, political, and ecological systems and, as these systems begin to fail, to our humanitarian values* [emphasis added].

20. The pace of internal migration from countryside to over-swollen cities is greatly intensified by rapid population growth. Enormous burdens are placed on LDC governments for public administration, sanitation, education, police, and other services, and urban slum dwellers (though apparently not recent migrants) may serve as a volatile, violent force which threatens political stability.

21. Adverse socio-economic conditions generated by these and related factors may contribute to high and increasing levels of child abandonment, juvenile delinquency, chronic and growing under-employment and unemployment, petty thievery, organized brigan-dry, food riots, separatist movements, communal massacres, revolutionary actions and counter-revolutionary coups. Such con-ditions also detract from the environment needed to attract the foreign capital vital to increasing levels of economic growth in these areas. If these conditions result in expropriation of foreign interests, such action, from an economic viewpoint, is not in the best interests of either the investing country or the host government.

22. In international relations, population factors are crucial in, and often determinants of, violent conflicts in developing areas. Conflicts that are regarded in primarily political terms often have demographic roots. Recognition of these relationships appears crucial to any understanding or prevention of such hostilities.

GENERAL GOALS AND REQUIREMENTS FOR DEALING WITH RAPID POPULATION GROWTH

23. The central question for world population policy in the year 1974, is whether mankind is to remain on a track toward an ultimate population of 12 to 15 billion—implying a five to seven-fold in-crease in almost all the underdeveloped world outside of China—or whether (despite the momentum of population growth) it can be switched over to the course of earliest feasible population stabil-ity—implying ultimate totals of 8 to 9 billions and not more than a three or four-fold increase in any major region.

24. What are the stakes? We do not know whether technological developments will make it possible to feed over 8 much less 12

billion people in the 21st century. We cannot be entirely certain that climatic changes in the coming decade will not create great difficulties in feeding a growing population, especially people in the LDCs who live under increasingly marginal and more vulnerable conditions. There exists at least the possibility that present developments point toward Malthusian conditions for many regions of the world.

25. But even if survival for these much larger numbers is possible, it will in all likelihood be bare survival, with all efforts going in the good years to provide minimum nutrition and utter dependence in the bad years on emergency rescue efforts from the less populated and richer countries of the world. In the shorter run—between now and the year 2000—the difference between the two courses can be some perceptible material gain in the crowded poor regions, and some improvement in the relative distribution of intra-country per capita income between rich and poor, as against permanent poverty and the widening of income gaps. A much more vigorous effort to slow population growth can also mean a very great difference between enormous tragedies of malnutrition and starvation as against only serious chronic conditions.

POLICY RECOMMENDATIONS

26. There is no single approach which will "solve" the population problem. The complex social and economic factors involved call for a comprehensive strategy with both bilateral and multilateral elements. At the same time actions and programs must be tailored to specific countries and groups. Above all, LDCs themselves must play the most important role to achieve success.

27. Coordination among the bilateral donors and multilateral organizations is vital to any effort to moderate population growth. Each kind of effort will be needed for worldwide results.

28. World policy and programs in the population field should incorporate two major objectives:
  (a) actions to accommodate continued population growth up to 6 billions by the mid-21st century without massive starvation or total frustration of developmental hopes; and

(b) actions to keep the ultimate level as close as possible to 8 billions rather than permitting it to reach 10 billions, 13 billions, or more.

29. *While specific goals in this area are difficult to state, our aim should be for the world to achieve a replacement level of fertility, (a two-child family on the average), by about the year 2000* [emphasis added]. This will require the present 2 percent growth rate to decline to 1.7 percent within a decade and to 1.1 percent by 2000. Compared to the U.N medium projection, this goal would result in 500 million fewer people in 2000 and about 3 billion fewer in 2050. *Attainment of this goal will require greatly intensified population programs* [emphasis added]. A basis for developing national population growth control targets to achieve this world target is contained in the World Population Plan of Action.

30. The World Population Plan of Action is not self-enforcing and will require vigorous efforts by interested countries, U.N. agencies and other international bodies to make it effective. *U.S. leadership is essential* [emphasis added]. The strategy must include the following elements and actions:

(a) <u>Concentration on key countries.</u>

Assistance for population moderation should give primary emphasis to the largest and fastest growing developing countries where there is special U.S. political and strategic interest. Those countries are: India, Bangladesh, Pakistan, Nigeria, Mexico, Indonesia, Brazil, the Philippines, Thailand, Egypt, Turkey, Ethiopia and Colombia. Together, they account for 47 percent of the world's current population increase. (It should be recognized that at present AID bilateral assistance to some of these countries may not be acceptable.) Bilateral assistance, to the extent that funds are available, will be given to other countries, considering such factors as population growth, need for external assistance, long-term U.S. interests and willingness to engage in self-help. Multilateral programs must necessarily have a wider coverage and the bilateral programs of other national donors will be shaped to their particular interests. At the same time, the U.S. will look to the multilateral agencies—especially the U.N. Fund for Population Activities which already has projects in over 80 countries—to increase population assistance on a broader basis with increased U.S. contributions. This is desirable in terms of U.S. interests and necessary in political terms in the United Nations. But progress nevertheless, must be made in the key 13 and our limited resources should give major emphasis to them.

(b) Integration of population factors and population programs into country development planning. As called for by the world Population Plan of Action, developing countries and those aiding them should specifically take population factors into account in national planning and include population programs in such plans.

(c) Increased assistance for family planning services, information and technology. This is a vital aspect of any world population program. (1) Family planning information and materials based on present technology should be made fully available as rapidly as possible to the 85% of the populations in key LDCs not now reached, essentially rural poor who have the highest fertility. (2) Fundamental and developmental research should be expanded, aimed at simple, low-cost, effective, safe, long-lasting and acceptable methods of fertility control. Support by all federal agencies for biomedical research in this field should be increased by $60 million annually.

(d) Creating conditions conducive to fertility decline. For its own merits and consistent with the recommendations of the World Population Plan of Action, priority should be given in the general aid program to selective development policies in sectors offering the greatest promise of increased motivation for smaller family size. In many cases pilot programs and experimental research will be needed as guidance for later efforts on a larger scale. The preferential sectors include:

- Providing minimal levels of education, especially for women;
- Reducing infant mortality, including through simple low-cost health care networks;
- Expanding wage employment, especially for women;
- Developing alternatives to children as a source of old age security;
- Increasing income of the poorest, especially in rural areas, including providing privately owned farms;

  – Education of new generations on the desirability of smaller
    families.

While AID has information on the relative importance of the
new major socio-economic factors that lead to lower birth rates,
much more research and experimentation need to be done to determine what cost effective programs and policy will lead to lower
birth rates.

(e) <u>Food and agricultural assistance is vital for any population
sensitive development strategy</u>. The provision of adequate food
stocks for a growing population in times of shortage is crucial.
Without such a program for the LDCs there is considerable chance
that such shortage will lead to conflict and adversely affect population goals and developmental efforts. Specific recommendations
are included in Section IV(c) of this study.

(f) <u>Development of a worldwide political and popular commitment to population stabilization is fundamental to any effective
strategy</u>. This requires the support and commitment of key LDC
leaders. This will only take place if they clearly see the negative
impact of unrestricted population growth and believe it is possible
to deal with this question through governmental action. The U.S.
should encourage LDC leaders to take the lead in advancing family
planning and population stabilization both within multilateral organizations and through bilateral contacts with other LDCs. This
will require that the President and the Secretary of State treat the
subject of population growth control as a matter of paramount
importance and address it specifically in their regular contacts with
leaders of other governments, particularly LDCs.

31. *The World Population Plan of Action and the resolutions
adopted by consensus by 137 nations at the August 1974 U.N. World
Population Conference, though not ideal, provide an excellent
framework for developing a worldwide system of population/fam-
ily planning programs* [emphasis added]. (The Plan of Action
appears in Appendix 1, page 387.) We should use them to generate
U.N. agency and national leadership for an all-out effort to lower
growth rates. Constructive action by the U.S. will further our
objectives. To this end we should:

  (a) Strongly support the World Population Plan of Action and
      the adoption of its appropriate provisions in national and
      other programs.

(b) Urge the adoption by national programs of specific population goals including replacement levels of fertility for DCs
and LDCs by 2000.

(c) *After suitable preparation in the U.S., announce a U.S. goal
to maintain our present national average fertility no higher
than replacement level and attain near stability by 2000*
[emphasis added].

(d) Initiate an international cooperative strategy of national
research programs on human reproduction and fertility
control covering biomedical and socio-economic factors, as
proposed by the U.S. Delegation at Bucharest.

(e) Act on our offer at Bucharest to collaborate with other
interested donors and U.N. agencies to aid selected countries to develop low cost preventive health and family planning services.

(f) Work directly with donor countries and through the U.N.
Fund for Population Activities and the OECD/DAC to increase bilateral and multilateral assistance for population
programs.

32. As measures to increase understanding of population factors by LDC leaders and to strengthen population planning in
national development plans, we should carry out the recommendations in Part II, Section VI, including:

(a) Consideration of population factors and population policies
in all Country Assistance Strategy Papers (CASP) and Development Assistance Program (DAP) multi-year strategy
papers.

(b) Prepare projections of population growth individualized
for countries with analyses of development of each country
and discuss them with national leaders.

(c) Provide for greatly increased training programs for senior
officials of LDCs in the elements of demographic economics.

(d) Arrange for familiarization programs at U.N. Headquarters
in New York for ministers of governments, senior policy
level officials and comparably influential leaders from private life.

(e) Assure assistance to LDC leaders in integrating population
factors in national plans, particularly as they relate to health
services, education, agricultural resources and develop-

ment, employment, equitable distribution of income and social stability.

(f) Also assure assistance to LDC leaders in relating population policies and family planning programs to major sectors of development: health, nutrition, agriculture, education, social services, organized labor, women's activities, and community development.

(g) Undertake initiatives to implement the Percy Amendment regarding improvement in the status of women.

(h) Give emphasis in assistance to programs on development of rural areas.

Beyond these activities which are essentially directed at national interests, we must assure that a broader educational concept is developed to convey an acute understanding to national leaders of the interrelation of national interests and world population growth.

33. We must take care that our activities should not give the appearance to the LDCs of an industrialized country policy directed against the LDCs. Caution must be taken that in any approaches in this field we support in the LDCs are ones we can support within this country. "Third World" leaders should be in the forefront and obtain the credit for successful programs. In this context it is important to demonstrate to LDC leaders that such family planning programs have worked and can work within a reasonable period of time.

34. To help assure others of our intentions we should indicate our emphasis on the right of individuals and couples to determine freely and responsibly the number and spacing of their children and to have information, education and means to do so, and our continued interest in improving the overall general welfare. We should use the authority provided by the World Population Plan of Action to advance the principles that 1) responsibility in parenthood includes responsibility to the children and the community and 2) that nations in exercising their sovereignty to set population policies should take into account the welfare of their neighbors and the world. To strengthen the worldwide approach, family planning programs should be supported by multilateral organizations wherever they can provide the most efficient means.

35. To support such family planning and related development assistance efforts there is need to increase public and leadership information in this field. We recommend increased emphasis on mass media, newer communications technology and other population education and motivation programs by the UN and USIA. Higher priority should be given to these information programs in this field worldwide.

36. In order to provide the necessary resources and leadership, support by the U.S. public and Congress will be necessary. A significant amount of funds will be required for a number of years. High level personal contact by the Secretary of State and other officials on the subject at an early date with Congressional counterparts is needed. A program for this purpose should be developed by OES with H and AID.

37. There is an <u>alternate view</u> which holds that a growing number of experts believe that the population situation is already more serious and less amenable to solution through voluntary measures than is generally accepted. It holds that, to prevent even more widespread food shortage and other demographic catastrophes than are generally anticipated, even stronger measures are required and some fundamental, very difficult moral issues need to be addressed. These include, for example, our own consumption patterns, mandatory programs, tight control of our food resources. In view of the seriousness of these issues, explicit consideration of them should begin in the Executive Branch, the Congress and the U.N. soon. (See the end of Section I for this viewpoint.)

38. Implementing the actions discussed above (in paragraphs 1-36), will require a significant expansion in AID funds for population/family planning. A number of major actions in the area of creating conditions for fertility decline can be funded from resources available to the sectors in question (e.g., education, agriculture). Other actions, including family planning services, research and experimental activities on factors affecting fertility, come under population funds. *We recommend increases in AID budget requests to the Congress on the order of $35-50 million annually through FY 1980 (above the $137.5 million requested for FY 1975)* [emphasis added]. This funding would cover both bilateral programs and

contributions to multilateral organizations. *However, the level of funds needed in the future could change significantly, depending on such factors as major breakthroughs in fertility control technologies and LDC receptivities to population assistance* [emphasis added]. To help develop, monitor, and evaluate the expanded actions discussed above, AID is likely to need additional direct hire personnel in the population/family planning area. As a corollary to expanded AID funding levels for population, efforts must be made to encourage increased contributions by other donors and recipient countries to help reduce rapid population growth.

POLICY FOLLOW-UP AND COORDINATION

39. This world wide population strategy involves very complex and difficult questions. Its implementation will require very careful coordination and specific application in individual circumstances. Further work is greatly needed in examining the mix of our assistance strategy and its most efficient application. A number of agencies are interested and involved. Given this, there appears to be a need for a better and higher level mechanism to refine and develop policy in this field and to coordinate its implementation beyond this NSSM. The following options are suggested for consideration:

(a) That the NSC Under Secretaries Committee be given responsibility for policy and executive review of this subject:

Pros:
- Because of the major foreign policy implications of the recommended population strategy a high level focus on policy is required for the success of such a major effort.
- With the very wide agency interests in this topic there is need for an accepted and normal interagency process for effective analysis and disinterested policy development and implementation within the N.S.C. system.
- Staffing support for implementation of the NSSM-200 follow-on exists within the USC framework including utilization of the Office of Population of the Department of State as well as other.
- USC has provided coordination and follow-up in major foreign policy areas involving a number of agencies as is the case in this study.

Cons:

– The USC would not be within the normal policy-making framework for development policy as would be in the case with the DCC.
– The USC is further removed from the process of budget development and review of the AID Population Assistance program.

(b) <u>That when its establishment is authorized by the President, the Development Coordination Committee, headed by the AID Administrator be given overall responsibility:</u>[1]

Pros: (Provided by AID)

– It is precisely for coordination of this type of development issue involving a variety of U.S. policies toward LDCs that the Congress directed the establishment of the DCC.
– The DCC is also the body best able to relate population issues to other development issues, with which they are intimately related.
– The DCC has the advantage of stressing technical and financial aspects of U.S. population policies, thereby minimizing political complications frequently inherent in population programs.
– It is, in AID's view, the coordinating body best located to take an overview of all the population activities now taking place under bilateral and multilateral auspices.

Cons:

– While the DCC will doubtless have substantial technical competence, the entire range of political and other factors bearing on our global population strategy might be more effectively considered by a group having a broader focus than the DCC.
– The DCC is not within the N.S.C. system which provides a more direct access to both the President and the principal foreign policy decision-making mechanism.

1   NOTE: AID expects the DCC will have the following composition: The Administrator of AID as Chairman; the Under Secretary of State for Economic Affairs; the Under Secretary of Treasury for Monetary Affairs; the Under Secretaries of Commerce, Agriculture and Labor; an Associate Director of OMB; the Executive Director of CIEP, STR; a representative of the NSC; the Presidents of the EX-IM Bank and OPIC; and any other agency when items of interest to them are under discussion.)

–   The DCC might overly emphasize purely developmental aspects of population and under emphasize other important elements.

(c) That the NSC/CIEP be asked to lead an Interdepartmental Group for this subject to insure follow-up interagency coordination, and further policy development. (No participating Agency supports this option, therefore it is only included to present a full range of possibilities).

Option (a) is supported by State, Treasury,
Defense (ISA and JCS), Agriculture, HEW,
Commerce NSC and CIA.[1]
Option (b) is supported by AID.

Under any of the above options, there should be an annual review of our population policy to examine progress, insure our programs are in keeping with the latest information in this field, identify possible deficiencies, and recommend additional action at the appropriate level.[2]

---

1   Department of Commerce supports the option of placing the population policy formulation mechanism under the auspices of the USC but believes that any detailed economic questions resulting from proposed population policies be explored through existing domestic and international economic policy channels.

2   AID believes these reviews undertaken only periodically might look at selected areas or at the entire range of population policy depending on problems and needs which arise.

Table 1.   POPULATION GROWTH, BY MAJOR REGION: 1970-2075
(Absolute numbers in billions)

	1970 Actual	U.N. Medium Variant Projections for:				U.S. Proposed Goal for World Population Plan of Action Projections for:			
		2000		2075		2000		2075	
		Numbers	Multiple of 1970	Numbers	Multiple of 1970	Numbers	Multiple of 1970	Numbers	Multiple of 1970
WORLD TOTAL	3.6	6.4	x 1.8	12.0	x 3.3	5.9	x 1.6	8.4	x 2.3
More Developed Regions	1.1	1.4	x 1.3	1.6	x 1.45	1.4	x 1.2	1.6	x 1.4
Less Developed Regions	2.5	5.0	x 2.0	10.5	x 4.1	4.5	x 1.8	6.7	x 2.65
Africa	0.4	0.8	x 2.4	2.3	x 6.65	0.6	x 1.8	0.9	x 2.7
East Asia	0.8	1.2*	x 1.5	1.6*	x 2.0	1.4*	x 1.6	1.9*	x 2.3
South & South East Asia	1.1	2.4	x 2.1	5.3	x 4.7	2.1	x 1.9	3.2	x 2.85
Latin America	0.2	0.6	x 2.3	1.2	x 5.0	0.5	x 2.0	0.7	x 3.0

More Developed Regions: Europe, North America, Japan, Australia, New Zealand and Temperate South America.

Less Developed Regions: All other regions

* The seeming inconsistency in growth trends between the UN medium and the US-proposed projection variants for East Asia is due to a lack of reliable information on China's total population, its age structure, and the achievements of the country's birth control program.

SOME KEY POINTS FROM THE MAIN BODY
OF THE REPORT

All readers are urged to read the detailed main body of the report which is presented in full in Appendix Two. This will give the reader a better appreciation of the gravity of this new threat to U.S. and global security and the actions the many departments of our government felt were necessary in order to address this grave new threat—a threat greater than nuclear war. These 20 important points will be discussed in the remaining chapters of this book.

On the magnitude and urgency of the problem:

1. "...World population growth is widely recognized within the Government as a current danger of the highest magnitude calling for urgent measures." [Page 194]

2. "...it is of the utmost urgency that governments now recognize the facts and implications of population growth, determine the ultimate population sizes that make sense for their countries and start vigorous programs at once to achieve their desired goals." [Page 15]

3. "...population factors are indeed critical in, and often determinants of, violent conflict in developing areas. Segmental (religious, social, racial) differences, migration, rapid population growth, differential levels of knowledge and skills, rural/urban differences, population pressure and the spatial location of population in relation to resources — in this rough order of importance — all appear to be important contributions to conflict and violence...Clearly, conflicts which are regarded in primarily political terms often have demographic roots. Recognition of these relationships appears crucial to any understanding or prevention of such hostilities." [Page 66]

4. "Where population size is greater than available resources, or is expanding more rapidly than the available resources, there is a tendency toward internal disorders and violence and, sometimes, disruptive international policies or violence." [Page 69]

5. "In developing countries, the burden of population factors, added to others, will weaken unstable governments, often only marginally effective in good times, and open the way to extremist regimes." [Page 84]

6. The report gives three examples of population wars: the El Salvador-Honduras "Soccer War" [Page 71]; the Nigerian Civil War

[Page 71]; and, the Pakistan-India-Bangladesh War, 1970-71. [Page 72]

7. "...population growth over the years will seriously negate reasonable prospects for the sound social and economic development of the peoples involved." [Page 98]

8. "Past experience gives little assistance to predicting the course of these developments because the speed of today's population growth, migrations, and urbanization far exceeds anything the world has ever seen before. Moreover, the consequences of such population factors can no longer be evaded by moving to new hunting or grazing lands, by conquering new territory, by discovering or colonizing new continents, or by emigration in large numbers.

The world has ample warning that we all must make more rapid efforts at social and economic development to avoid or mitigate these gloomy prospects. We should be warned also that we all must move as rapidly as possible toward stabilizing national and world population growth." [Page 85]

Leadership is vital:

9. "Successful family planning requires strong local dedication and commitment that cannot over the long run be enforced from the outside." [Page 106]

10. "...it is vital that leaders of major LDCs themselves take the lead in advancing family planning and population stabilization, not only within the UN and other international organizations but also through bilateral contacts with leaders of other LDCs." [Page 112]

11. "These programs will have only modest success until there is much stronger and wider acceptance of their real importance by leadership groups. Such acceptance and support will be essential to assure that the population information, education and service programs have vital moral backing, administrative capacity, technical skills and government financing." [Page 195]

What must be done:

12. "Control of population growth and migration must be a part of any program for improvement of lasting value." [Page 81]

13. "...the Conference adopted by acclamation (only the Holy See stating a general reservation) a complete World Population Plan of Action" [Page 87]

14. "Our objective should be to assure that developing countries make family planning information, education and means available to all their peoples by 1980." [Page 130]

15. "Only nominal attention is [currently] given to population education or sex education in schools..." [Page 158] "Recommendation: That US agencies stress the importance of education of the next generation of parents, starting in elementary schools, toward a two-child family ideal. That AID stimulate specific efforts to develop means of educating children of elementary school age to the ideal of the two-child family..." [Page 159]

16. "...there is general agreement that up to the point when cost per acceptor rises rapidly, family planning expenditures are generally considered the best investment a country can make in its own future," [Page 53]

Contradiction of the Holy See's answer to the population problem:

17. "Clearly development per se is a powerful determinant of fertility. However, since it is unlikely that most LDCs will develop sufficiently during the next 25-30 years, it is crucial to identify those sectors that most directly and powerfully affect fertility." [Page 99]

18. "There is also even less cause for optimism on the rapidity of socio-economic progress that would generate rapid fertility reduction in the poor LDCs, than on the feasibility of extending family planning services to those in their populations who may wish to take advantage of them." [Page 99]

19. "But we can be certain of the desirable direction of change and can state as a plausible objective the target of achieving replacement fertility rates by the year 2000." [Page 99]

Abortion is vital to the solution:

20. "While the agencies participating in this study have no specific recommendations to propose on abortion, the following issues are believed important and should be considered in the context of a global population strategy...Certain facts about abortion need to be appreciated:

"— No country has reduced its population growth without resorting to abortion". [Page 182]

"— Indeed, abortion, legal and illegal, now has become the most widespread fertility control method in use in the world today." [Page 183]

"— It would be unwise to restrict abortion research for the following reasons: 1) The persistent and ubiquitous nature of abortion. 2) Widespread lack of safe abortion techniques..." [Page 185]

PRESIDENT FORD'S MOVE TOWARD A U.S. POPULATION POLICY

4

National Security Decision Memorandum 314 (NSDM 314) was signed in 1975 by National Security Adviser Brent Scowcroft on behalf of President Gerald R. Ford. The new President's forthright approval of virtually all of the NSSM 200 recommendations appeared to set the U.S. on a direct course toward development and implementation of a sophisticated national population policy.

4

NATIONAL SECURITY COUNCIL
WASHINGTON, D.C. 20506

CONFIDENTIAL (GDS)   November 26, 1975

National Security Decision Memorandum 314

TO: The Secretary of State
           The Secretary of the Treasury
           The Secretary of Defense
           The Secretary of Agriculture
           The Secretary of Health, Education and Welfare
           The Administrator, Agency for
           International Development

SUBJECT: Implications of Worldwide Population Growth for
           United States Security and Overseas Interests

The President has reviewed the interagency response to NSSM 200 and the covering memorandum from the Chairman of the NSC Under Secretaries Committee. He believes that United States leadership is essential to combat population growth, to implement the World Population Plan of Action and to advance United States security and overseas interests. The President endorses the policy recommendations contained in the Executive Summary of the NSSM 200 response, with the following observations and exceptions:

AID Programs

Care must be taken that our AID program efforts are not so diffuse as to have little impact upon those countries contributing the largest growth in population, and where reductions in fertility are most needed for economic and social progress.

Research and Evaluation

An examination should be undertaken of the effectiveness of population control programs in countries at all levels of development, but with emphasis on the LDC's. The examination should include an evaluation of AID program efforts as well as other efforts by national or international groups. The study would attempt to determine the separate effect of the population program, taking account of other economic or social factors which may have also influenced fertility.

Research on broader issues should be undertaken examining the factors affecting change (or lack of change) in the birth rate in different countries.

Funding for Population Programs:

The President desires that a review be undertaken quickly to examine specific recommendations for funding in the population assistance and family planning field for the period after FY 1976. The President wishes a detailed analysis of the recommended funding levels in the NSSM 200 study bearing in mind his desire to advance population goals. This analysis should include performance criteria to assure that any additional funds are utilized in the most effective manner. The appropriate level of funding of multilateral programs which effectively support this objective should be included in this review. The Chairman of the USC is responsible for preparing this analysis which is due 60 days from the date of this NSDM.

The Role of Other Countries:

Emphasis should be given to fostering international cooperation in reducing population growth in pursuing the recommendations of the World Population Plan of Action. It is important to enlist additional contributions from other developed and newly rich countries for bilateral and multilateral programs.

Basic Approach to Developing Countries' Population Programs:
Leaders of key developing countries should be encouraged to support national and multilateral population assistance programs.

The objective of the United States in this field is to work closely with others rather than to seek to impose our views on others. Our efforts should stress the linkage between reduced population growth and the resultant economic and social gains for the poorest nations. In all these efforts, we should recognize the basic dignity of the individual and his or her right to choose freely family goals and family planning alternatives.

National and World Population Goals:

The President believes that the recommendation contained in paragraph 31(c) of the Executive Summary dealing with the announcement of a United States national goal is outside the scope of NSSM 200. Of course, domestic efforts in this field must continue in order to achieve worldwide recognition that the United States has been successfully practicing the basic recommendations of the World Plan of Action and that the nation's birthrate is below the replacement level of fertility. In order to obtain the support of the United States citizens for our involvement in international population programs, it is important that they recognize that excessive world population growth can affect domestic problems including economic expansion as well as world instability.

Concerning the consideration of World Population Goals in paragraph 31(b), it should be understood that the general goal of achieving global replacement levels of fertility by the year 2000 does not imply interference in the national policies of other countries.

The Under Secretaries Committee, in conjunction with all appropriate agencies of the Executive Branch, may wish to make further recommendations to the President on these subjects.

Coordination of United States Global Population Policy:

Implementation of a United States worldwide population strategy will involve careful coordination. The response to NSSM 200 is a good beginning, but as noted above, there is need for further examination of the mix of United States assistance strategy and its most efficient application.

The President, therefore, assigns to the Chairman, NSC Under Secretaries Committee, the responsibility to define and develop policy in the population field and to coordinate its implementation beyond the NSSM 200 response.

The Chairman is instructed to submit an initial report within six months from this date on the implementation of this policy, with recommendations for any modifications in our strategy, funding programs, and particularly, the identification of possible deficiencies. Thereafter the Chairman is instructed to submit reports to the President annually.

The Chairman is authorized to request other appropriate bodies and agencies to assist him in this task as required. For the purpose of implementing this NSDM, the Under Secretaries Committee should include, in addition to the addressee members, ex officio representatives of the following agencies:

Council on Environmental Quality
Office of Management and Budget
The President's Science Adviser

                                        BRENT SCOWCROFT

cc: The Chairman, NSC Under Secretaries Committee
           The Director, Office of Management and Budget
           The Chairman, Council of Economic Advisers
           The Chairman, Joint Chiefs of Staff
           The Director of Central Intelligence
           The Chairman, Council of Environmental Quality

WHAT HAPPENED TO
THE MOMENTUM?

5

5

NOVEMBER 26, 1975 marked the end of the peak of American political will to deal with the overpopulation problem. This was the day that President Ford approved NSDM 314, committing the U.S. to a bold policy of population growth control. The peak lasted less than six years and then the momentum plummeted and our commitment has since diminished every year. In this Chapter, I will provide the details of what happened to the momentum. In the next Chapter, I will discuss why this happened and in Chapters 7 and 8, some additional details of how this was accomplished are provided.

As noted in the Introduction, when Mr. Nixon received the report, *Population and the American Future*, from Mr. Rockefeller in May 1972, the President publicly rejected it—just six months before he faced reelection. In his book, *Catholic Bishops in American Politics*, Timothy A. Byrnes, assistant professor of political science at the City College of New York, states, "Hoping to attract Catholics to his reelection campaign, Nixon publicly disavowed the prochoice findings of his own presidential commission on population in 1972. He communicated that disavowal in an equally public letter to Cardinal Terence Cooke [of New York], a leading spokesman for the bishops' opposition to abortion...The Catholic vote was especially important to Nixon and his publicists in 1972. They referred to Catholic support of the Republican ticket in order to refute the notion that Nixon had formed his new coalition by cynically appealing to the baser motives of Southern whites. They relied on Catholic participation in the new majority, in other words, as proof that the 'social issue' was much more than repackaged racial prejudice. As one of these publicists, Patrick Buchanan, put it: 'Though his critics were crying "Southern Strategy," the President's politics and policy decisions were not going unnoticed in the Catholic and ethnic communities of the North, East, and Midwest.'" [13]

Nixon was convinced that if he were to win in 1972, he must carry Southern whites and northern Catholics. He looked to the Catholic bishops for their support. Byrnes goes on to say, "Regardless of what it is based on, however, a perception that the bishops can influence votes has been enough to make candidates sensitive to the bishops..." And as the saying goes, in politics perceptions often create their own realities. He continues, "The bishops have more than just access to Catholic voters, of course. They also have virtually unparalleled institutional resources at their disposal. 'If you are a bishop,' Walter Mondale's 1984 campaign manager said to me, 'you've got some pretty substantial organizational capabilities....You've got a lot of people, you've got money, places to meet....You've got a lot of things that any good politician would like to have at his disposal.' You also have the ability, if you are the Catholic hierarchy collectively, to create or fortify movements in support of your preferred policy positions." [14]

Byrnes argues that: the bishops are able to bring virtually unrivaled resources to any cause or effort they decide to support; the bishops committed those resources to the fight against abortion in the 1970s; in the process they played a key role in the creation and maintenance of a large social movement. This movement was the so-called Religious New Right movement. This movement was still in its infancy at the time of Nixon's reelection bid in 1972 but the bishops were highly organized, single minded and prepared to deal. In his letter to Cardinal Cooke, Nixon made it clear that he too was prepared to deal. Nixon was reelected with the bishops' support.

During the year that followed the presentation of the Rockefeller Commission Report, it became clear that there would be no further response to the Commission's recommendations. In May 1973 a group of pioneer population activists acknowledged this inaction and asked Ambassador Adolph Schmidt to speak with his friend, Commission Chairman John D. Rockefeller 3rd. They met in June 1973 at the Century Club in New York City. Schmidt noted his own disappointment and that of his colleagues because no program had been mounted as a result of the Commission's recommendations. What had gone wrong? Rockefeller responded: "The greatest difficulty has been the very active opposition by the Roman Catholic Church through its various agencies in the United States." [15]

In 1992, one Rockefeller Commission member, Congressman James Scheuer (D.-NY), spoke out publicly for the first time on what had happened: "Our exuberance was short-lived. Then-President Richard Nixon promptly ignored our final report. The reasons were obvious—the fear of attacks from the far right and from the Roman Catholic Church because of our positions on family planning and abortion. With the benefit of hindsight, it is now clear that this obstruction was but the first of many similar actions to come from high places." [16]

None of the Commission's more than three score and ten recommendations was ever implemented. It is most disturbing that the American people were kept in the dark about this undemocratic and un-American intervention by the Vatican. It was not considered newsworthy simply because the press chose not to make it so. Why? Chapters 15 and 16 address this vitally important question. I believe both Catholic and non-Catholic Americans would have strongly rejected such interference in the American democratic process had they been aware of it. The quality of life for all Americans has been diminished by this unconstitutional manipulation of American policy, undertaken for the purposes of protecting papal interests.

NIXON AGAIN MOVES BOLDLY

Yet, as I noted earlier, President Nixon's assessment of the gravity of the overpopulation problem and his desire to deal with it were evidently unaltered by the intense Catholic hierarchy opposition he encountered in the wake of the Rockefeller Commission Report. On April 24, 1974, Mr. Nixon ordered that the NSSM 200 study be undertaken.

I can only speculate, but one may assume that President Nixon knew he would encounter the same implacable Vatican opposition to this report as to the one by the Rockefeller Commission. However, with his re-election safely behind him, perhaps he felt that if a definitive study of the national and global security implications of overpopulation showed that the very security of the United States were seriously threatened, it would generate public demand for action to curb U.S. and world population growth. This might serve to overcome the continued opposition mounted by the Vatican. Why else would he have asked for this study, given his painful experience with the Catholic Church after the Rockefeller Commission?

No doubt the Vatican was appalled to learn about NSSM 200. Only seven years before, the Vatican had created the National Conference of Catholic Bishops (NCCB), in part to counteract federal level threats to papal security interests. According to Byrnes, the primary activity of the Conference, to this day, has been its antiabortion effort.[17] (These issues will be discussed in other chapters.) The bishops correctly understood that NSSM 200 meant federally promoted and federally funded abortion for the U.S. and the world.

NIXON RESIGNS FROM THE PRESIDENCY

What role the bishops played in the removal of President Nixon from office, if any, has not been examined. Nixon was not aware of the Watergate break-in before it occurred. He was removed from office because of his role in the cover-up—and he lied to the American people about this role. Apparently he was willing to do anything to be President of the United States—including colluding with the bishops to undermine U.S. and global security by killing the Rockefeller Commission Report.

On August 9, 1974, Gerald Ford succeeded to the presidency. The report on NSSM 200 was completed on December 10, 1974 and circulated to the designated Secretaries and Agency heads for review and comment. Revisions of the study continued until July 1975. On November 26, 1975, NSSM 200 was made public policy in his NSDM 314.

NSSM 200 PROMPTLY DERAILED

NSSM 200 forthrightly opposes the Vatican on population strategy, family planning and abortion. It specifically notes that the only institutional opposition to population growth control is the Vatican and the Roman Catholic Church.[18] NSSM 200 acknowledged that only in countries where family planning and abortion are widely used had population growth rates fallen significantly.[19] The implications of NSSM 200 are obvious: its implementation would have meant extensive family planning and abortion efforts worldwide. The Vatican moved swiftly to block implementation of NSSM 200 policies already approved by President Ford. The result was that the new and concerted government activities needed to implement NSSM 200 never materialized. In the next chapter, I will explain why the Vatican felt it had to block implementation of the study's recommendations.

Byrnes discusses at some length the presidential election of 1976 and the remarkable role the Catholic bishops played in that election. The pivotal role that the candidates *perceived* the bishops would play made it possible for the bishops to kill the NSSM 200 initiative. According to Byrnes, "Catholics were seen as swing voters, and they were actively courted by both candidates. As a part of that courting process, each of the candidates also sought to establish a positive and, if possible, supportive relationship with the Catholic bishops. Jimmy Carter was concerned that the cultural gap between a 'born again' Southern Baptist candidate and northern ethnic voters would create a 'Catholic problem' for his campaign. In the hope of ameliorating such a problem, Carter went out of his way to assure Catholics at every opportunity that he was personally sensitive to their particular concerns. He also worked diligently throughout the campaign to establish a positive relationship with the Catholic hierarchy....Carter 'needed desperately to win the northern blue collar vote,' recalled one of his top aides. 'The bishops could affect that vote at the margin, and it is at the margin, after all, that elections are won and lost.'

"Ford had even more compelling reasons for seeking a friendly relationship with the Catholic hierarchy. Resigned to losing the South to his Georgian opponent, Ford's only chance for victory was to carry the heavily Catholic states of the Northeast and upper Midwest....The fact that Ford and Carter both *believed* that the bishops influenced the Catholic vote meant that the candidates were sensitive to the bishops' views and attentive to the bishops' statements and actions. The candidates' shared perception drew the bishops into the center of a closely fought national election campaign and granted the bishops an opportunity to advance their moral agenda in the public arena of presidential politics." [20] (As will be seen in Chapters 6 and 7, the term "moral agenda" is improperly used here.)

Carter and Ford and their campaigns had extensive interactions with the Catholic bishops as both the candidates and the bishops bargained for political advantage and concessions. According to Byrnes, "The key figure in these backchannel communications between the Catholic Conference and Carter's campaign was Bishop James Rausch. Rausch was, in effect, chief of staff of the entire NCCB/United States Catholic Conference bureaucracy."[21] Rausch took the initiative. One of Rausch's Democratic Party contacts was Thomas Farmer, a Washington lawyer. Farmer arranged a meeting between Bishop Rausch and Andrew Young, then a close aide to Carter.[21]

Byrnes continues, "According to Farmer, Rausch's initial meeting with Young was followed by a personal phone call from Carter in which the candidate expressed his desire to resolve his differences with the Catholic hierarchy....Discussions concerning Carter's relationship with the bishops proceeded on several different levels over the next few weeks. Farmer, for example, traveled to Atlanta for a meeting with Carter's top advisors; Rausch sent an aide from the Catholic Conference to observe one of Carter's strategy sessions in Plains, Georgia; and Rausch personally met with the Democratic vice-presidential candidate Walter Mondale (another old friend) to discuss their mutual interests in defusing further criticism of Carter's views by the NCCB leadership. In the end, Rausch, Farmer, and their interlocutors in Carter's campaign decided...to arrange a personal meeting between Carter and the leaders of the bishops' conference. At such a meeting, they decided, a whole range of issues could be discussed..."[22]

The meeting between Carter and the NCCB's executive committee, headed by Archbishop Joseph L. Bernardin,[23] took place on August 31, 1976 at the Mayflower Hotel in Washington, D.C. Many issues were discussed and deals struck. One of those deals has been described by Dr. R.T. Ravenholt, who directed the global population program of the U.S. Agency for International Development in the Department of State from 1966 to 1979. On March 4, 1991, he addressed the Washington State Chapter of Zero Population Growth (ZPG) on *Pronatalist Zealotry and Population Pressure Conflicts: How Catholics Seized Control of U.S. Family Planning Programs,*[24] and described one of the outcomes of this meeting.*

Ravenholt told the ZPG group, "Following a meeting of Presidential candidate Jimmy Carter and his campaign staff with fifteen

Catholic leaders...on which occasion they pressed to deemphasize federal support for family planning in exchange for a modicum of Catholic support for his Presidential race, President-elect Carter proceeded to put the two federal agencies with family planning programs under Catholic control.

"Joseph Califano became Secretary of Health, Education and Welfare, and the first one to whom President-elect Carter offered the U.S. AID Administrator position was Father Theodore Hesburgh, President of Notre Dame University. When Father Hesburgh declined the role of AID administrator, the appointment was given to John J. Gilligan, a Notre Dame graduate and a former governor of Ohio.

"Also, a long-time Catholic adversary of AID's family planning program, John H. Sullivan, moved from Congressman Clement Zablocki's office into AID during the Presidential transition and was given a key role in selecting Carter's political appointees. During previous years, Congressman Zablocki and Jack Sullivan had persistently worked to curb AID's high powered family planning program. In 1973, Jack Sullivan and allied zealots helped Senator Jesse Helms develop the Helms amendment to the Foreign Assistance Act. Since then, this amendment has prevented AID from providing assistance for the termination of unwanted pregnancies.

"Among the Carter political appointees selected by Jack Sullivan was Sander Levin, newly defeated Democratic candidate for Governor of Michigan. Not a Catholic but an opportunistic lawyer without previous family planning experience, Levin immediately upon entry to AID proceeded to maul and discombobulate AID's population program, as desired by his political superiors. He became the Assistant Administrator with direct responsibility for disorganizing and dispersing Office of Population personnel and for the removal of GS-18 Ravenholt. This was accomplished after several years.... Since then, AID's dismembered and otherwise crippled family planning program has been sustained to the extent possible by dedicated staff and likewise dedicated Members of Congress and other supporters. It has continued many operations,

---

* Copies of the Ravenholt Report are available from the Center for Research on Population and Security, P.O. Box 13067, Research Triangle Park, N.C. 27709, (919) 933-7491, for $3 each.

though certainly not all, despite continued harassment from the...anti-birth control zealots.

"...with the help of Jimmy Carter and his political appointees, religious zealots finally managed to degrade AID's population program."

Even during 1976, after NSDM 314 had been signed by President Ford and before the election, Catholic activists worked diligently to undermine population growth control efforts within the administration, according to Ravenholt. He offers examples in his Report.

During this period, Ford, as noted earlier, was intent on winning the support of the Catholic Bishops. According to Byrnes, "Ford to be sure was no right-to-lifer....However, once Ford had acquiesced in an abortion plank written by the right wing of his party, he was able to sharply distinguish himself from his opponent....At a Catholic Eucharistic Congress in Philadelphia, for example, Ford drew a standing ovation from a predominantly Catholic right-to-life crowd by declaring his concern over an increasing 'irreverence for life' in American society. More to the point for our purposes, the prolife Republican platform also allowed Ford to associate himself with the anti-abortion-centered agenda that had been firmly identified with Joseph Bernardin and the National Conference of Catholic Bishops. Acting on this opportunity, Ford invited Bernardin and the other members of the executive committee to meet with him at the White House....Ford, like Carter, assured the bishops that he shared their moral opposition to abortion. However, unlike Carter, Ford also expressed support for the so-called local option amendment that would reverse Roe v. Wade and return responsibility for abortion to the individual state legislatures." [25]

Despite the intensive efforts by both candidates, the bishops did not explicitly endorse either candidate for president in 1976. Clearly, the bishops were there to take credit when Carter won, as described by Ravenholt. Had Ford won, no doubt they would have taken credit too, as the stage was set for them to do so. After his forthright endorsement of the NSSM 200 recommendations, Ford showed no great enthusiasm for their bold and rapid implementation. Certainly, boldness and speed were called for in view of the threat overpopulation posed to U.S. and global security—as described so vividly in the NSSM 200 study. Like Presidents Nixon and Carter, Ford gave a higher immediate priority to being elected president than to protecting the security of the United States.

As in the case of the Rockefeller Commission Report, none of the recommendations of NSSM 200 was ever implemented. A grave threat to U.S. and global security had been identified in a definitive study by the most powerful departments in our government—departments that represent virtually all of our intelligence gathering capability. President Ford's approval of the policy recommendations of NSSM 200 in his Decision Memorandum 314 represented the high point of American political will to deal with the population problem. Then it plummeted.

Every year since 1975 has witnessed a diminishing commitment of the United States to both domestic and world population growth control. The Vatican and the Catholic bishops can take full credit for the destruction of American political will to deal with this threat. Why have they behaved in this manner? Is it really a question of morality?

WHY DID OUR POLITICAL WILL FADE AWAY?

6

6

THE ROCKEFELLER commission report and NSSM 200 are arguably two of the most important works on overpopulation ever written. Our country and the world would be different today if the recommendations contained in these two documents had been implemented. Many of the dire predictions made in these studies are coming true.

For example, had illegal immigration been controlled and legal immigration adjusted to meet the needs of Americans in 1971, as called for in the Rockefeller Commission Report, the U.S. population would peak at 243 million in 2035.[26] Instead, in 1995 our population increased to 259 million. According to Peter Brimelow, in the *Los Angeles Times*, "The Census Bureau projects that current immigration policy will drive the U.S. population up to 390 million by 2050, of whom 130 million will be post-1970 immigrants and their descendants. And that's moderate; the 'high series' estimate is 500 million."[26a] The quality of life of all Americans will be significantly diminished as we attempt to accommodate this additional 130-248 million people, and we will all be less secure. And this number can mushroom if we do not deal with excessive immigration soon.

In 1974, the NSSM 200 study predicted that growing scarcities of resources would lead to ever increasing dislocations and conflicts all over the globe which would diminish security for everyone everywhere. The February 1993 issue of *Scientific American* contains an article by Thomas F. Homer-Dixon, Jeffrey H. Boutwell and George W. Rathjens titled, *Environmental Change and Violent Conflict*.

This article reports on a study which documents that the predictions of NSSM 200 are already occurring around the world.

The authors state, "Within the next 50 years, the human population is likely to exceed nine billion, and global economic output may quintuple. Largely as a result of these trends, scarcities of renewable resources may increase sharply. The total area of highly productive agricultural land will drop, as will the extent of forests and the number of species they sustain. Future generations will also experience the ongoing depletion and degradation of aquifers, rivers and other bodies of water, the decline of fisheries, further stratospheric ozone loss and, perhaps, significant climatic change. As such environmental problems become more severe, they may precipitate civil or international strife."

To examine whether these problems are currently causing civil or international strife, the authors assembled a team of 30 researchers to review a set of specific cases. Their findings were then summarized: "The evidence that they gathered points to a disturbing conclusion: scarcities of renewable resources are already contributing to violent conflicts in many parts of the developing world. These conflicts may foreshadow a surge of similar violence in coming decades..."

The article examines case-studies of violent conflicts that are attributed to overpopulation by researchers from four continents: the migration of millions from Bangladesh to India which led to brutal ethnic conflicts; the persistent conflict in the Philippines driven by the desperate poverty caused by overpopulation; severe shortages of ground water in the Jordan River basin which are leading to conflict between Israelis and Palestinians; destruction of ecologically sensitive territories in South Africa which is forcing a migration to violent urban squatter settlements; expanding population in Senegal and Mauritania which spurred a violent conflict in the Senegal River Basin; similar factors which have stimulated the growth of the Maoist Shining Path rebels in Peru; the irreversible clear-cutting of forests and loss of soil which has led to violent social strife in Haiti, and which in turn has caused the exodus of boat people. There are many other examples.

NSSM 200 predicted that the U.S. would find itself in wars like the recent Iraq-U.S. war, as regional powers invade their neighbors to secure resources needed to provide for their ever expanding populations—just as Iraq invaded Kuwait. It also emphasized that the expense of U.S. involvement in such wars would far exceed the costs of worldwide population growth control.

In 1996, 22 years after NSSM 200 was completed and 23 years after the Rockefeller Commission Report was delivered to President Nixon, it is painfully clear that these two studies were right on target. They were based on the best intelligence available and their analysis undertaken by the most competent of U.S. researchers. Time is bearing out their soundness and accuracy of prediction.

The United States and all other countries are undeniably less secure than they were 20 years ago.

We can say with certainty that American political will to address the population problem did not begin to disappear on November 26, 1975 because this grave national and global security threat had been overestimated or was diminishing on its own. Something happened to cause its disappearance.

To identify what caused this disappearance, it is reasonable to first examine the institutional opposition to overcoming the population problem. I noted earlier that NSSM 200 had identified the Vatican as the only major institution opposed to population growth control. Sophisticated observers of governments recognize that political will is vital to mounting a successful response to a problem of this magnitude. If the opponent of a government action can kill the political will, the opponent need not worry about effective government action. The Vatican is a most sophisticated observer of governments.

It is logical to determine whether the Vatican played a role in this disappearance of political will. After all, this would be nothing new in America. In his history of Catholic bishops in American politics, Byrnes provides overwhelming documentation that the "bishops had participated in the political process to defend the parochial interests of their church and the viability of its institutions" from 1790 to the present.

What motive did the Vatican have for intervening to block implementation of the recommendations of the Rockefeller Commission and NSSM 200 reports? This is the subject of the rest of this Chapter.

VATICAN COUNCIL II SETS THE STAGE

Vatican Council II, which ended in 1966, set the stage for this intervention by the bishops. Recognizing that political changes were underway in the United States regarding family planning, abortion and population growth control, in significant part because of the discovery of the birth control pill and the rapidly growing awareness of the population problem, the Vatican prepared to respond. One of the outcomes, a product of Vatican II, was the *Pastoral Constitution on the Church in the Modern World.*

Part 2 of the Constitution was titled, "Some Problems of Special Urgency." Byrnes observes, "This list of problems to which the church was to turn its attention reads like a blueprint of the American hierarchy's political agenda of the 1970s and 1980s." [27] The first of these problems was abortion:

> God, the Lord of life, has conferred on men the surpassing ministry of safeguarding life—a ministry which must be fulfilled in a manner which is worthy of man. Therefore, from the moment of conception life must be guarded with the greatest of care, while abortion and infanticide are unspeakable crimes. [27]

The *Decree on the Bishops' Pastoral Office in the Church*, another Vatican Council II document, created the NCCB which was instituted according to universal church law. It was created to serve as a political instrument of the Vatican.[28] During a meeting of the American hierarchy in November 1966, the bishops formally established the NCCB as their official collective body and instituted the United States Catholic Conference (USCC) as their administrative arm and secretariat. [29] The Jesuit weekly *America*, editorialized that the national conference had been "converted from a confraternity into a government." [30] The Catholic lay *Commonweal* called the new organization, "a viable instrument with power adequate to national problems." [31]

The Vatican had determined that legalization of abortion was about to become such a national problem. From the very beginning until now, there has been a common and correct perception that the Catholic hierarchy was primarily an antiabortion political lobby. Byrnes summarizes his study of the history of Catholic bishops in American politics by saying, "Before I end, I want to address one final matter, namely the unique position that abortion occupies on the Catholic hierarchy's public policy agenda. Abortion is not simply one issue among many for the bishops. It is rather the bedrock, non-negotiable starting point from which the rest of their agenda has developed. The bishops' positions on other issues have led to political action and political controversy but abortion, throughout the period I have examined, has been a consistently central feature of the Catholic hierarchy's participation in American politics." [32]

VATICAN REJECTS CONCEPT OF AMERICAN DEMOCRACY

In 1974, the year the NSSM 200 study was ordered by President Nixon, the Vatican issued a document titled, *Vatican Declaration on Abortion*, which stated:

A Christian can never conform to a law which is in itself immoral, and such is the case of a law which would admit in principle the licitness of abortion. Nor can a Christian take part in a propaganda campaign in favor of such a law, or vote for it. Moreover, he may not collaborate in its application. [33]

This statement is an unequivocal rejection of the legitimacy of our democratically elected government to pass laws legalizing abortion. Obviously, no American Catholic who chose to follow this Vatican declaration could pay taxes to a government that would use tax money to perform abortions, counsel on abortion, educate on abortion, or to undertake any of the other numerous abortion-related activities that the government would be involved in if the recommendations of the Rockefeller Commission and NSSM 200 were implemented. Nor could American Catholics participate in any other way in any of the abortion-related activities that these recommendations would necessarily involve.

The Vatican had placed papal authority on the line. It had pitted papal authority against the authority of our government. If the Vatican was to avoid the destruction of papal authority, it must block implementation of those recommendations by our government.

This overt Vatican rejection of the principles of American Democracy is by no means new. The Papacy is implacably opposed to separation of church and state, the freedoms of speech, press, worship and assembly, and legislative authority vested solely with democratically elected representatives of the people. Today all Catholic priests must take a solemn oath to uphold and promote these views.

From the Catholic almanac:

> The Catholic citizen is in conscience bound to respect and obey the duly constituted authority provided faith and morals are thereby not endangered. Under no circumstances may the Church be subjugated by the State. Whatever their form may be, states are not conceded the right to force the observance of immoral or irreligious laws upon a people.[33a]

The 1974 *Vatican Declaration on Abortion* follows the instructions set forth by Pope Leo XIII in his encyclical on the "Chief Duties of Christian Citizens":

> If the laws of the state are manifestly at variance with the divine law, containing enactments hurtful to the Church or conveying injunctions adverse to the duty imposed by religion, or if they violate in the person of the Supreme Pontiff the authority of Jesus Christ, then truly, to resist becomes a positive duty, to obey, a crime."[33b]

The condemnation of current errors set forth in Pope Pius IX's encyclical *Quata Cura* and the list of 80 errors accompanying the encyclical were a direct assault on the American form of government. This is evident from even a partial listing:

#11 The Church has a right to occupy herself with philosophy, to refuse to tolerate its errors, and to assume the care of correcting them.

#12 It is false that the decrees of the Apostolic See and of the Roman Congregation impede the free progress of society.

#15 No man is free to embrace and profess that religion which he believes to be true, guided by the light of reason.

#19 The Church is [a] true, perfect, and entirely free association; she enjoys peculiar and perpetual rights conferred upon her by her Divine founder, and it neither belongs to the civil power to define what are these rights of the Church, nor the limits within which she may exercise them.

#20 The ecclesiastical power has a right to exercise its authority independent of the toleration or assent of the civil government.

#21 The Church has the power to define dogmatically the religion of the Catholic Church to be the only true religion.

#22 The obligation which securely binds Catholic teachers and writers is not limited to those things which are proposed by the infallible judgment of the Church as dogmas of faith for belief by all.

#23 The Roman Pontiffs and ecumenical councils have never exceeded the limits to their power, or usurped the rights of princes, much less committed errors in defining matters of faith and morals.

#24 The Church has the power of employing force and (of exercising) direct and indirect temporal power.

#27 The ministers of the Holy Church and the Roman Pontiff should be allowed the free exercise of the charge and dominion which the Church claims over temporal interests.

#30 Neither the immunities of the Church nor ecclesiastical persons have their origin in civil law.

#40 The doctrine of the Catholic Church is agreeable to the well-being and interests of society.

#42 In legal conflicts between both powers (civil and ecclesiastical) the ecclesiastical law prevails.

#44 No civil authority can interfere in matters relative to religion, morality, and spiritual government.

#53 Laws which protect religious establishments or secure their rights and duties may not be abrogated by civil government.

#54 Kings and princes are not only not exempt from the jurisdiction of the Church but are subordinate to the Church in litigated questions of jurisdiction.

#57 Philosophical principles, moral science, and civil laws may and must be made to bend (declinari) to divine and ecclesiastical authority.

#64 The violation of a solemn oath, as well as any vicious and flagitious action repugnant to the eternal law, is not only blamable, but is wholly unlawful, and deserving of the highest censure even when done from a love of country.

These are not medieval dicta, but indeed are current Church doctrine which the Vatican expects all Catholics to espouse, especially its priests. Every week these teachings are reinforced in the conservative Catholic press in America. For example, the August 1996 issue of Catholic Family News carries a front page article, "Religious Liberty and the Secular State," by Michael Davies.[33b1] This multi-page article reads: "The teaching of the Popes on this question has been consistent and unequivocal—that the Church and State should be united and should co-operate in promoting what will assist man in achieving his ultimate purpose and in repressing what will frustrate it. Pope Pius X condemned the principle of separation of Church and State as "an absolutely false and pernicious thesis."

Davies quotes Msgr. John A. Ryan in his book *Catholic Principles of Politics* (New York 1940): "If there is only one true religion, and if its possession is the most important good in life for States as well as individuals, then the public profession, protection, and promotion of this religion and the legal prohibition of all direct assaults upon it, becomes one of the most obvious and fundamental duties of the State. For it is the business of the State to safeguard and promote human welfare in all departments of life."

The Church's teachings unequivocally state that the pope rules in America whether non-Catholics like it or not. Davies contends that we are discussing a fundamental teaching of the Catholic Church: "His rule extends not merely to members of the Church, as most Catholics would imagine today, but to all men both as individuals and grouped together in a corporate body as a state. No state can claim to be exempt from the Kingship of Christ simply by declaring itself to be secular, and in a secular state the Church should use the religious liberty which it quite rightly claims for itself to campaign vigorously, militantly, for the laws of the state to conform to the norms required by the Kingship of Christ."

He continues: "If asked where those who govern their country derive their authority almost every English-speaking Catholic would reply: 'From the people.' They believe that, as legislators are elected by the people, they govern in the name of the people and as delegates of the people. Nothing could be more false. This is the fundamental error of the masonically inspired French Revolution...The Church is not opposed to democracy in the sense that legislators are elected by a ballot based on universal suffrage. What it cannot accept is that, once elected, legislators govern as delegates of the people and have a mandate to legislate only in accordance with the will of the majority. This evil concept destroys the basis of any objective standards of morality."

Davies presents the relevant Catholic teachings and then summarizes them in simple terms: "As I have already made clear, no one, Catholic or non-Catholic, can lay claim justly to anything that is contrary to the eternal or natural law of God, and this applies not simply to individuals but to states. No government can possibly have the right to legalize such moral abominations as abortion....The Catholic position is, then, perfectly simple. A true right, that is moral liberty, can exist to choose only that which is good and true. No human being can ever have a genuine right to choose what is evil or false, and legislators, who must govern as legates of God, can have no genuine right to promulgate legislation favoring what is evil or false."

Here we have in an August 1996 Catholic publication in America the current teachings of the Church which legitimize the undermining of the implementation of the Rockefeller Commission and NSSM 200 Report recommendations, as well as all other efforts by our government to control population growth initiated over the past two decades. How many American Catholics are receptive to these teachings?

In her book, *Being Right: Conservative Catholics in America*, (33b2) Mary Jo Weaver, estimates that the number of right-wing Catholics may reach as high as 10 million. Weaver has been for 21 years an Indiana University professor of religious studies. She has written five other books on Catholicism and this one is based on several years of research. According to her, right-wing Catholics can be defined by three dominant characteristics: (1) They express outrage at priests and laity who speak out in opposition of the pope. They point out that the Catholic Church is not a democracy and that error has no rights; (2) While they support the concept of the Second Vatican Council, they feel betrayed by its aftermath, believing most churches liberalized far beyond its intentions; (3) They feel extremely isolated because they believe there are so few true Catholics like themselves. They are filled with counterculture anxiety and anger.

In an interview with Cheryl Heckler-Feltz for the *National Catholic Reporter*,[33b3] Weaver offered the following findings: The right wing "avoids dialogue with outsiders in order to protect itself from contamination. It prefers the safe world of a shared outlook to the possibility of finding another point of view compelling. And it cannot afford to accept differences. Right- and left-wing Catholics live in parallel universes that will never meet. Being Catholic in the 1950s meant being right about God and belonging to a Church whose leaders did not make mistakes. But after 1968, the divide was ominous: American Catholics were increasingly described in bipolar terms as liberal or conservative. [The split between the two groups] is probably inexorable because liberals thrive in a climate of dissent, whereas conservatives, who stress obedience, cannot allow it to be part of any legitimate expression of Catholicism."

Weaver has done a great service to this country by methodically examining the stark differences between conservative and liberal Catholics in the United States. Among the laity there are really two very different Catholic Churches in America. The liberal Church, accounting for 50 million or more individuals, is mainly concerned with personal, family, community and country security-survival interests, and is largely powerless. The conservative Church, where almost all of the power of the Church (ecological, remunerative, coercive, social, legal, traditional, expert and charismatic, as described by Jean-Guy Vaillancourt (35)) is vested, controls the wealth, decision-making, administrative and political power of the Church. It is obedient to and owes its allegiance to Rome and is mostly concerned with defending the security-survival interests of the papacy. These two groups are incapable of communicating with each other and this schism is probably permanent. The far more powerful group is very much in the minority but it is completely obedient to Rome. These Catholics live in America, but just as Pope John Paul II called for in his encyclical in 1995 (and popes before him), they are not of America. Recognition of this split and understanding its basis and implications explains much of the behavior of American Catholics regarding population matters described in this book.

It is largely conservative Catholics who have obstructed implementation of the recommendations of the Rockefeller Commission and NSSM 200. Conservative clerics and laity alike are directed to use extensive covert means to undermine every United States family planning and population growth control effort, including the implementation of the NSSM 200 recommendations. In this they are enthusiastically assisted by their opportunistic nonCatholic collaborators.

In no nation does the Church honor the principle of separation of church and state, because the hierarchy is convinced of its "divine right" to direct nations in matters of faith and morals (and "morals" in some way touches on all human activities).

Thus, Pope John Paul II's 1995 encyclical *Evangelium Vitae* (Gospel of Life) came as no great surprise. It is largely a restatement of the teachings of earlier popes in his own words. *Evangelium Vitae* is a strident frontal assault on American Democracy in which he asks American Catholics to do whatever is necessary to impose papal teachings on all Americans even if it means sacrificing their lives. In her National Catholic Reporter article, "Defending life even unto death," Professor Janine Langan, of the University of Toronto, assesses *Evangelium Vitae*: "John Paul leaves no room for ghetto Catholicism. Excusing our silence about matters of truth because 'we should not push on other people our Christian God,' as one of my students put it last year, is not acceptable."[33c]

The October 8, 1995 *New York Times* headline reads "The Pope vs. the Culture of Death." According to *The New York Times*, in his *Evangelium Vitae*, the pope envisions a deepening war of the powerful against the weak [#12].[33d] In this war, the pope and his loyalists (a small minority of American Catholics) are on one side and American Democracy and Americans who support this government are on the other.

The Episcopalian publication, *The Churchman's Human Quest*, in its January-February 1996 article "Czech Philosopher Accuses Vatican of Undermining Democracy," cites the contemporary Czech philosopher, Vaclav Belohradsky's reaction to *Evangelium Vitae*:" [it is an] 'attack on the principles of liberal democracy.' The document, he said, questioned the legitimacy of national parliaments by casting doubt on the principle of majority rule."[33e]

This encyclical is so important to the security/survival of Americans and their democracy that all of us should familiarize ourselves with it. With insight will come recognition of the widespread subversion of our form of government and its processes by Catholics responding to this teaching, as well as nonCatholics collaborating with them to advance their own self-interests.

Included in the pontiff's 194-page *Evangelium Vitae* are:

"I declare that direct abortion, that is, abortion willed as an end or a means, always constitutes a grave moral disorder, since it is the deliberate killing of an innocent human being. This doctrine is based upon the natural law and upon the written Word of God, is transmitted by the church's tradition and taught by the ordinary and universal Magisterium [#62]."

"We are in fact faced by an objective 'conspiracy against life' involving even international institutions, engaged in encouraging and carrying out actual campaigns to make contraception, sterilization and abortion widely available. Nor can it be denied that the mass media are often implicated in this conspiracy, by lending credit to that culture which presents recourse to contraception, sterilization, abortion and even euthanasia as a mark of progress and a victory for freedom, while depicting as enemies of freedom and progress those positions which are unreservedly pro-life [#17]."

"To claim the right to abortion, infanticide and euthanasia, and to recognize that right in law, means to attribute to human freedom a perverse and evil significance: that of an absolute power over others and against others. This is the death of true freedom [#20]."

"Laws which legitimize the direct killing of innocent human beings through abortion or euthanasia are in complete opposition to the inviolable right to life proper to every individual...Laws which authorize and promote abortion and euthanasia are therefore radically opposed not only to the good of the individual but also to the common good; as such they are completely lacking in authentic juridical validity [#72]."

"Abortion and euthanasia are thus crimes which no human law can claim to legitimize. There is no obligation in conscience to obey such laws; instead there is a grave and clear obligation to oppose them by conscientious objection [#73]."

"It is precisely from obedience to God—to whom alone is due that fear which is acknowledgment of his absolute sovereignty—that the strength and the courage to resist unjust human laws are born. It is the strength and the courage of those prepared even to be imprisoned or put to the sword, in the certainty that this is what makes for the endurance and faith of the saints [#73]."

"In the case of an intrinsically unjust law, such as a law permitting abortion or euthanasia, it is therefore never licit to obey it, or to take part in a propaganda campaign in favor of such a law or to vote for it [#73]."

"The consequences of this gospel [the gospel of life]...can be summed up as follows: Human life, as a gift of God, is sacred and inviolable. For this reason procured abortion and euthanasia are absolutely unacceptable [#81]."

"No circumstance, no purpose, no law whatsoever can ever make licit an act which is intrinsically illicit, since it is contrary to the law of God which is written in every human heart, knowable by reason itself, and proclaimed by the church [#62]."

"Christians...are called upon under grave obligation of conscience not to cooperate formally in practices which, even if permitted by civil legislation, are contrary to God's law. Indeed, from the moral standpoint, it is never licit to cooperate formally in evil...This cooperation can never be justified either by invoking respect for the freedom of others or by appealing to the fact that civil law permits it or requires it [#74]."

"To refuse to take part in committing an injustice is not only a moral duty; it is also a basic human right [#74]."

"Democracy cannot be idolized to the point of making it a substitute for morality or a panacea for immorality. Fundamentally, democracy is a 'system' and as such is a means and not an end. Its 'moral' value is not automatic but depends on conformity to the moral law [#70]."

"Today...the powerful of the earth...are haunted by the current demographic growth and fear that the most prolific and poorest peoples represent a threat for the well-being and peace of their own countries [#16]."

"...it is possible to speak in a certain sense of a war of the powerful against the weak.... A person who..., just by existing, compromises the well-being or life style of those who are more favored tends to be looked upon as an enemy to be resisted or eliminated. In this way a kind of 'conspiracy against life' is unleashed. This conspiracy involves not only individuals in their personal, family or group relationships, but goes far beyond, to the point of damaging and distorting at the international level, relations between peoples and states [#12]."

"By virtue of our sharing in Christ's royal mission, our support and promotion of human life must be accomplished through...political commitment [#87]."

"[On]...the issue of population growth...It is...morally unacceptable to encourage, let alone impose, the use of methods such as contraception, sterilization and abortion in order to regulate births [#91]."

"Service of the Gospel of life is...a valuable and fruitful area for positive cooperation with our brothers and sisters of other Churches and ecclesial communities... [#91]."

"In the proclamation of this gospel, we must not fear hostility or unpopularity, and we must refuse any compromise or ambiguity which might conform us to the world's way of thinking. We must be in the world but not of the world [82]."

The Vatican is, in effect, reminding its faithful: We must be in America but not of America. We must be in America, but we must reject American democracy and the laws by which its citizens are governed.

Cardinal Alfonso Lopez Trujillo, president of the Pontifical Council for the Family, who spoke on October 3, 1995 on "Culture of Life, Culture of Death in the Encyclical *Evangelium Vitae*," makes it clear that the Church is at war with democratic America with its civil laws: "The Pope invites us with courage to the boycott of unjust laws which suppress the imperative of natural law carved into consciences by the Creator. And legislators, politicians, physicians, and scientists have the duty of conscience to be the defenders of life in the war against this culture of death."[33f]

According to Cardinal Joseph Ratzinger, head of the Congregation for the Doctrine of the Faith, the possibility of invoking "papal infallibility," was discussed but had been rejected as unnecessary because, as it is, the Pope's language on abortion invokes the full power of church doctrine, even if the word "infallible" is not there.[33g] This is true of all of the pope's pronouncements, and for this reason, for the believer, all of the pope's pronouncements are de facto accepted as infallible—just as Hasler reasons in Chapter 11.

In her National Catholic Reporter article to which we have referred,[33c] Professor Langan does not acknowledge that this encyclical is extremist in nature but she describes it forthrightly, referring to item #73: "In a situation as grave as the present one, Christians are bound to come into conflict with their co-citizens. They must have that courage....*Evangelium Vitae* is thus a challenge to defend life even at the cost of martyrdom. But it's also a promise that, with God, everything is possible. Finally, this encyclical does not merely state that being 'prochoice' is not an option, but that every one of us is also morally bound to oppose, at any cost, any public attack on any human person's right to life [#104]." Langan quotes the pope, "life finds its center, its meaning and its fulfillment when it is given up." [#51] In her view, and the pope's, martyrdom is admirable: "Martyrdom is the one witness to the truth about man which everyone can hear. No society, however dark, can stifle it."

This chilling view of martyrdom held by the pope and Professor Langan is not shared by most Americans when fanatical Moslem extremists resort to it. Martyrdom is almost universally condemned as religious extremism. Why should it be admirable behavior when exercised by Catholics?

In Italy, Evangelium Vitae was strongly criticized in the press, according to the National Catholic Register. The Italian press takes the Vatican much less seriously than does its American counterpart. In its article by Jeffrey Donovan, "At Home the Pope's Encyclical Takes Beating," the negative reactions were widespread and strongly worded.[33h] For example, the Rome daily *II Manifesto* termed the encyclical "fundamentalist and desperate" and offers: "The Pope multiples his condemnations, repeats his classic arguments and searches for new ones, too, but fails to consider the realities of modern life, which contradict everything he says." According to the Register, "Many commentators accused the Pope and the Church of interfering with the political process."

On the other hand, in the United States there was not one critical report of *Evangelium Vitae*. Not one American journalist or publisher declared that this encyclical calls for anarchy in this country in the attempt to destroy the principles of our government that so threaten the Papacy. This is perhaps the most serious attack on American democracy since Pope Pius IX's Syllabus of Errors.

Associate editor of the liberal Catholic Commonweal magazine, Paul Baumann, in his October 8, 1995 New York Times OP-ED article, "The Pope vs. the Culture of Death," writes "Americans are a notoriously pragmatic lot, and being lectured to about the theoretical foundations of democracy by those with little practical experience of democracy arouses an instinctive skepticism." This is a reasonable assumption.[33d]

However, amazingly, not a single American journalist published a report critical of this encyclical. *The New York Times* devoted nearly two full pages of text to it. None of the journalists involved offered any criticism whatever. Collectively, the articles simply spread the word on behalf of the Vatican, never questioning its implications for our cherished institutions.[33g,33i,33j]

In his contribution, Catholic *New York Times* writer, Peter Steinfels quoted only the responses of four other Catholics—Rev. Richard A. McCormick, Pamela J. Maraldo, Francis Kissling, and Richard Doerflinger—and their quoted criticisms were remarkably mild. No reactions of Protestants, Jews or secularists were cited in any of the *New York Times* articles.[33i]

Pope John Paul II has obviously dismissed the idea that American Protestants, Jews and secularists, who are in the majority among our democratic law makers, are capable of determining what is moral. Only he and other popes, as God's representative on earth, can make this determination. When the pope ruled that peace and the well-being of the peoples of the world are insufficient justification for the use of contraception, sterilization and abortion in this encyclical, it appears that he was referring to the NSSM 200 report.

VATICAN CLAIMS RIGHT TO PROTECT ITSELF AGAINST HARMFUL LAWS

At the same time, we must remember that the Vatican claims the right to protect itself against what it determines to be harmful laws—even when democratically legislated! The central difficulty here, of course, is that what the Vatican considers "harmful" to itself and its authority, is just what nonCatholic and lay Catholic men and women consider beneficial to themselves and their families (see Chapter 13). In a letter sent to all American bishops by the Sacred Congregation for the Doctrine of the Faith, the most powerful Vatican office, Cardinal Joseph Ratzinger reminded the bishops that "the Church has the responsibility to protect herself from the application of harmful laws." This letter was keep secret from 55 million American Catholics until a brief notice written by Peter Steinfels for *The New York Times* appeared July 10, 1992. The actual text remained hidden from the public until it was leaked to the press on July 15, 1992. [34]

Obviously, if an institution has the "responsibility," it also claims the "right." The Vatican exercised its "right" to protect itself from the application of harmful laws, in the autocratic way it defines "harmful," when it blocked U.S. adoption of the Rockefeller Commission recommendations and implementation of the NSSM 200 policies approved by President Ford. "To protect herself," in Ratzinger's words, the Church moved quickly and efficiently to kill the two most important initiatives in American history to help control world population growth.

HOW POPULATION GROWTH CONTROL THREATENS THE PAPACY

Why is the Vatican obliged to halt legalized abortion and contraception despite the strong wishes of Americans? When our government legalized contraception and abortion, it pitted civil authority against papal authority. The Vatican demands supremacy over civil governments in matters of faith and morals, but our government has rejected this concept. Thus, while the Church is saying that family planning and abortion are evil and grave sins, our government is saying they may be good and should be used. Obviously, most American Catholics are accepting morality as defined by the government and rejecting morality as defined by the pope. As a result, Papal authority is undermined.

There are a number of Catholic countries in Latin America with abortion rates two to four times as high as the U.S. rate. But the bishops ignore abortions there. Why? Because they are illegal abortions, not legal ones. They do not threaten Papal authority! Only legal abortions do, because their legalization establishes their morality. Thus, the bishops take no significant actions to halt abortions in Latin America.

In *Papal Power: A Study of Vatican Control Over Lay Catholic Elites,*[35] published by The University of California Press in 1980, Jean-Guy Vaillancourt, Associate Professor of Sociology at the University of Montreal, closely examines the sources of papal power and how it evolved. He found that papal authority is vital to the maintenance of papal power. This power is derived in significant part from papal authority. If the Pope's authority is diminished, papal power is diminished. However, some authority is derived from papal power and if papal power is diminished, then authority is undermined. The relationship is circular. Less authority means less power which means even less authority. With diminishing power, survival of the institution of the Roman Catholic Church in its present hierarchical form is gravely threatened. Thus, the very survival of the Vatican is threatened by programs of population growth control.

In his book, "Persistent Prejudice: Anti-Catholicism in America," published by *Our Sunday Visitor* in 1984, Michael Schwartz summarized the position of Catholic conservatives on the abortion issue: "The abortion issue is the great crisis of Catholicism in the United States, of far greater import than the election of a Catholic president or the winning of tax support for Catholic education. In the unlikely event that the Church's resistance to abortion collapses and the Catholic community decides to seek an accommodation with the institutionalized killing of innocent human beings, that would signal the utter failure of Catholicism in America. It would mean that U.S. Catholicism will have been defeated and denatured by the anti-Catholic host culture."[36]

In April 1992, in a rare public admission of this threat, Cardinal John O'Connor of New York, delivering a major address to the Franciscan University of Steubenville, Ohio, acknowledged, "The fact is that attacks on the Catholic Church's stance on abortion—unless they are rebutted—effectively erode Church authority on all matters, indeed on the authority of God himself."[37]

This threat to Papal authority was recognized decades ago by the Papal Commission on Population and Birth Control. The two tiered commission consisted of a group of 15 cardinals and bishops and a group of 64 lay experts representing a variety of disciplines. The commission met from 1964 until 1966. According to commission member Thomas Burch, Pope Paul VI himself assigned them the task of finding a way to change the Church's position on birth control without destroying papal authority.[38]

After two years of studying the dilemma, the laymen voted 60 to four and the clerics nine to six to change the Church's teaching on birth control even though it would mean a loss of papal authority *because it was the right thing to do*. The minority also submitted a report to the Pope.[39] Coauthor of the minority report was the young Archbishop of Cracow, Karol Wojtyla, now Pope John Paul II.

In 1967, two newspapers published without authorization the full texts of the Papal commission's report. Thus the world knew that a substantial majority of the double commission had recommended liberalization on birth control.[39] The commission, of course, failed to find an acceptable way to accomplish this, and the result was the publication in 1968 of the encyclical, *Humanae Vitae*, which banned the use of abortion and artificial means of contraception, such as birth control pills. It is true that Pope Paul VI is credited with authorship of *Humanae Vitae*; not until 1995 was Karol Wojtyla revealed as a major contributor. A Polish theologian who worked with him declares that "about sixty percent [of materials for the Encyclical of our draft] is contained in the encyclical."[39a]

It was not until 1985 that Thomas Burch, a professor at Georgetown University in the 1960s and more recently chairman of Western Ontario's Sociology Department, revealed to the world the real assignment of the commission. When Pope Paul issued *Humanae Vitae*, he admitted to the world that the Church cannot change its position on birth control without undermining papal authority—an unacceptable sacrifice. However, it was not until 1979, when August Bernhard Hasler published his book, *How the Pope Became Infallible*, that the world was given the text of the minority report which persuaded Pope Paul VI to reject the majority position.[40] Hasler was a Catholic theologian and historian who served for five years in the Vatican secretariat for Christian unity. During this period, he was given access to the Vatican Archives where he discovered numerous documents, never studied before, that revealed the story of Vatican Council I. Dr. Hasler died suddenly at age 43, four days after writing a critical open letter to Pope John Paul II and six months after completing the second edition of this book.[41]

The declaration of papal infallibility was a product of Vatican Council I, which preceded Vatican Council II more than a century ago, and was considered vital to the continuation of papal power. According to Vaillancourt, "During the Middle Ages and under feudalism, when the Catholic Church was a dominant institution in society, papal power grew in importance, relying often on force to attain its ends, which were political as much as they were religious. The Crusades and, later on, the Inquisition, stand as the two most notorious of these violent papal ventures. But with the decline of the Portuguese and Spanish empires, with the advent of the Reformation and of the intellectual, democratic, and industrial revolutions, the Catholic hierarchy lost much of its influence and power. Unable to continue using physical coercion, the Papacy was led to strengthen its organizational structure and to perfect a wide range of normative means of control. The declaration of papal infallibility by the first Vatican Council (Vatican I), in 1870, was an important milestone in that direction. The stress on the absolute authority of the pope in questions of faith and morals helped turn the Church into a unified and powerful bureaucratic organization, and paved the way for the establishment of the Papacy-laity relationship as we know it today." [42]

Pope Paul VI was faced with the prospect of personally destroying the concept of papal infallibility, a concept vital to the continuation of papal power. Hasler notes, "But for Paul VI there already were infallible declarations of the ordinary magisterium on the books concerning contraception. And so, unlike the majority of his commission of experts, the pope felt bound to these declarations by his predecessors." Thus the pope was forced to agree with the minority report of the commission.

ORIGIN OF TODAY'S ANTI-FAMILY PLANNING CRUSADE

Hasler quotes from that minority report — a paragraph that defined today's anti-family planning crusade:

"If it should be declared that contraception is not evil in itself, then we should have to concede frankly that the Holy Spirit had been on the side of the Protestant churches in 1930 (when the encyclical Casti connubii was promulgated), in 1951 (Pius XII's address to the midwives), and in 1958 (the address delivered before the Society of Hematologists in the year the pope died). It should likewise have to be admitted that for a half a century the Spirit failed to protect Pius XI, Pius XII, and a large part of the Catholic hierarchy from a very serious error. This would mean that the leaders of the Church, acting with extreme imprudence, had condemned thousands of innocent human acts, forbidding, under pain of eternal damnation, a practice which would now be sanctioned. The fact can neither be denied nor ignored that these same acts would now be declared licit on the grounds of principles cited by the Protestants, which popes and bishops have either condemned or at least not approved." [43]

Hasler concludes, "Thus, it became only too clear that the core of the problem was not the pill but the authority, continuity, and infallibility of the Church's magisterium."

This is at the very core of the world population problem. The Papacy simply cannot survive the solutions—i.e., contraception, abortion, sex education, etc. The Vatican believes, probably correctly, that if the solutions to the population problem are applied, the dominance of Vatican power will soon wither. Grasping the implications of the principal of infallibility are crucial to understanding the underlying basis of the world population problem. Chapter 11 is devoted to this topic.

It is most important to understand that the Vatican leadership can visualize a world where it no longer exists. It was this chilling vision that drove the conservative members of the Vatican leadership and Pope Paul VI to reject the majority report and accept the minority report of the Papal Commission on Population and Birth Control in 1968. This vision has driven Vatican behavior on family planning ever since. Thus, the security-survival of the Papacy is now pitted directly against the security-survival of the United States. The Vatican simply cannot accommodate the security interests of the United States.

This is not the first time our security interests have been in conflict. There are many examples of the American Catholic hierarchy supporting papal security interests at the expense of U.S. security interests. One example is the Spanish Civil War between the democratic constitutional government and the Vatican supported fascist Franco. Byrnes states, "The bishops also broke with Roosevelt over the issue of the Spanish Civil War....The bishops instinctively supported Franco in the war....Caught between mainstream views on foreign policy and the interests of their church, the bishops...opted for defense of the international church."[44]

It is institutional survival that governs the behavior of the Catholic hierarchy in all matters. The claim that "morality" governs its behavior in the matters of family planning and abortion is fraudulent. The hierarchy has a long history of determining which position is in the best interest of the Papacy—including the survival of the Papacy—and then framing that position as the moral position. Father Arthur McCormack was for 23 years the Vatican consultant to the UN on development and population, leaving that post in 1979. In 1982, he went public with his conclusion that the Vatican position on family planning and population growth control is immoral. A summary of his reasoning is offered in Chapter 13.

American political will to deal with the overpopulation problem fell victim to the Vatican's inexorable position. In the next chapter we will discuss how the Vatican achieved this vital objective, as it set about protecting its security interests.

WHAT WAS THE ROLE OF THE VATICAN?

7

7

BOTH the Rockefeller Commission and NSSM 200 studies were sophisticated undertakings. Complex activities generated the political will that led to them. The key people in our government examined the data and the logic that led to an inescapable conclusion: further rapid world population growth is a grave threat to American and global security. They agreed on this and they acted.

To reverse this process and to reverse it so quietly that only a few took notice, also required great sophistication. Only an exceeding well led, well financed, well connected, highly committed, autocratic organization could have succeeded. A politically sophisticated institution was necessarily involved.

The authors of NSSM 200 noted that the only institutional opposition to the World Population Plan of Action—adopted by consensus of 137 nations at the August 1974 United Nations World Population Conference—was the Vatican. The Vatican was intensely motivated to act against the Rockefeller Commission and NSSM 200 recommendations because the Catholic hierarchy was convinced that the survival of the institution of the Papacy was on the line.

Furthermore, as noted in the last chapter, the Vatican, with specific threats to papal interests in mind, had equipped the American hierarchy to intervene just a few years before. Did the American hierarchy act to destroy our political will to overcome the population problem?

In Byrnes's study of the history of Catholic bishops in American politics, he found that from 1790-1960, papal security interests were decided by local and state governments and not at the national level.[45] For this reason, bishops concentrated their political intervention efforts at the local and state levels. In the 1960s, a large package of federal legislation greatly increased the federal government's "authority and obligations for the health, safety, and morals of the community. It involved national agencies and officials in areas of family life that had been left, theretofore, either to the discretion of individuals and their families or to the regulation of state and local governments."[46] Furthermore, in the same period, the Supreme Court also expanded its role at the expense of state and local governments with Roe v. Wade and other decisions. The combined effect of these two trends was a shift of the political activity of greatest concern to the bishops from the local and state level to the federal level.[47]

The Vatican determined that if it were to survive intact it must become much more active in U.S. politics at the national level. Vatican control of politics in large Catholic cities is well known and undisputed. Only by being highly organized and active politically on *all* levels of government could the Vatican overcome the rapid increase in political will and momentum in demand for population growth control that had recently developed.

The Vatican, with its masterful political acumen, recognized the trends and quickly prepared to counteract them. Through Vatican Council II, U.S. bishops were given the necessary tools.

Did the Vatican succeed in changing U.S. policy on family planning, abortion and population growth control? *TIME* magazine concluded that it most certainly did. The headline on the cover of the February 24, 1992 issue of *TIME* magazine was: "*HOLY ALLIANCE: How Reagan and the Pope conspired to assist Poland's Solidarity movement and hasten the demise of Communism.*"[48] The cover article was written by Pulitzer prize-winning journalist Carl Bernstein. Bernstein listed Reagan's "Catholic Team," noting that "The key administration players were all devout Roman Catholics—CIA chief William Casey, [Richard] Allen [Reagan's first National Security Advisor], [William] Clark [Reagan's second National Security Advisor], [Alexander] Haig [Secretary of State], [Vernon] Walters [Ambassador at Large] and William Wilson, Reagan's first ambassador to the Vatican. They regarded the U.S.-Vatican relationship as a holy alliance: the moral force of the Pope and the teachings of their church combined with...their notion of American Democracy."

THE POPE CALLED THE TUNE

In a section of his *TIME* article headed "The U.S. and the Vatican on Birth Control," Bernstein included three revealing paragraphs:

"In response to concerns of the Vatican, the Reagan Administration agreed to alter its foreign aid program to comply with the church's teachings on birth control. According to William Wilson, the President's first ambassador to the Vatican, the State Department reluctantly agreed to an outright ban on the use of any U.S. aid funds by either countries or international health organizations for the promotion of...abortions. As a result of this position, announced at the World Conference on Population in Mexico City in 1984, the U.S. withdrew funding from, among others, two of the world's largest family planning organizations: the International Planned Parenthood Federation and the United Nations Fund for Population Activities.

"'American policy was changed as a result of the Vatican's not agreeing with our policy,' Wilson explains. 'American aid programs around the world did not meet the criteria the Vatican had for family planning. AID [the Agency for International Development] sent various people from [the Department of] State to Rome, and I'd accompany them to meet the president of the Pontifical Council for the Family, and in long discussions they finally got the message. But it was a struggle. They finally selected different programs and abandoned others as a result of this intervention.'

"'I might have touched on that in some of my discussions with [CIA director William] Casey,' acknowledges Pio Cardinal Laghi, the former apostolic delegate to Washington. 'Certainly Casey already knew about our positions about that.'"

Thus, Bernstein makes clear what the cadre of devout Catholics in the Reagan Administration did to protect the Papacy from the recommendations of NSSM 200. Simply put, these strategically-placed Catholic laymen, and the U.S. bishops with direct papal support and intervention, succeeded in destroying the American political will to deal with the population problem.

How they accomplished this goal so vital to the robust survival of the Papacy is the subject of the next three chapters.

THE BISHOPS'
PASTORAL PLAN

8

8

O N NOVEMBER 20, 1975, the American Catholic bishops issued their *Pastoral Plan for Pro-Life Activities*. This was just 6 days before President Ford endorsed the NSSM 200 study recommendations as public policy.

This Plan is a superbly detailed blueprint of the bishops' strategy for infiltrating and manipulating the American democratic process at the national, state and local levels. It creates a national political machine controlled by the bishops.

The Plan has been called by Timothy Byrnes the most "focused and aggressive political leadership" ever exerted by the American Catholic hierarchy.[49] So much for respect for the American constitutional principle of separation of church and state.

In 1973, when the Supreme court decided Roe v. Wade, James McHugh was a monsignor and the staff director of the National Catholic Family Life Bureau. He is now a bishop. In a March 4, 1987 interview by Byrnes,[50] McHugh observed that "within twenty-four hours" of the court's action, the bishops knew they would need to mount a political campaign in favor of a constitutional amendment prohibiting abortion. "Indeed," Byrnes observed, "by November 1973 the bishops had explicitly declared that they wished 'to make it clear beyond a doubt to our fellow citizens that we consider the passage of a prolife constitutional amendment a priority of the highest order.'" [51]

The Plan states: "It is absolutely necessary to encourage the development in each congressional district of an identifiable, tightly knit and well organized prolife unit. This unit can be described as a public interest group or a citizen's lobby." According to McHugh, some conference members asked, could the bishops credibly claim that these groups were not expressly subordinate to the NCCB? Byrnes states: "McHugh, who actually drafted the plan, told me that the NCCB's [50 member] administrative board (which first passed the plan and authorized its presentation to a plenary session for adoption by the conference as a whole) debated this section of the document for 'several hours,' searching for a way to formally distance these politically charged advocacy groups from the tax-exempt church." [52]

Byrnes continues, "As finally adopted, the Pastoral Plan defined a 'congressional district pro-life group' as 'an agency of citizens operated, controlled, and financed by these same citizens' and added that 'it is not an agency of the church, nor is it operated, controlled or financed by the church.' Some observers nevertheless pointed out that the actual—as opposed to the formal—independence of the lobby groups was belied by the highly detailed list of objectives and guidelines that directly followed this disclaimer."[53] In other words, the bishops themselves recognized that the disclaimer was ridiculous.

In many ways, the draft of the Plan that was approved earlier by the administrative board is more revealing as to the true intentions of the bishops to create a political machine they controlled than the sanitized version that was distributed to the bishops after the full body gave its approval in November. For this reason, I chose to include, in its entirety, the unsanitized plan as it was approved by the administrative board.

The Plan, as it appears here, is verbatim. However, it has been typeset for this book. Certain passages that appear in the sanitized final version which do not appear in the Bishops' Administrative Board approved version are also very revealing. For this reason, I quote these passages in a subsequent section.

["UNSANITIZED" PLAN]

**NCCB/USCC
DOCUMENTATION
November, 1975**

ACTION ITEM: #3

SUBJECT: <u>Pastoral Plan for Pro-Life Activities</u>

              <u>Ad Hoc</u> Committee for Pro-Life Activities

Action Required: Written or voice vote on approval of
                      Pastoral Plan

Vote Required: Majority of those present and voting

PASTORAL PLAN FOR PRO-LIFE ACTIVITIES

Introduction

The value of human life has been seriously endangered by the U.S. Supreme Court abortion decisions of January 22, 1973, and by decisions of other state and federal courts during the past three years. Although these decisions deal primarily with abortion laws, implicitly they also touch on euthanasia.

These decisions also contradict the commonly held belief that the right to life is a fundamental human right, guaranteed protection by the Constitution of the United States.

Many Americans of different faiths and convictions are convinced that abortion is morally wrong and that a policy of permissive abortion is contrary to American constitutional principles. As a religious community within this larger society, the Catholic Church teaches that abortion is morally wrong. We do not seek to impose our moral teaching on American society, but as citizens of this nation we find it entirely appropriate to ask that the government and the law be faithful to its own principle — that the right to life is an inalienable right given to everyone by the Creator. Furthermore, exercising our rights as citizens, and the freedom assured us by the First Amendment, we commit ourselves to the establishment of a system of law that will provide legal protection of human life from conception to natural death. The implications of this commitment are wide-ranging and demanding, but we feel morally impelled to pursue whatever course of action is required.

At present, this commitment leads us to put forth every effort to reverse the holdings of the U.S. Supreme Court in Roe and Doe, and to establish a constitutional base for laws that will protect unborn human life. For practical purposes this involves amending the Constitution of the United States to give a clear, unequivocal, and deliberate affirmation of the value of unborn human life, and to guarantee to unborn human beings the plethora of human and civil rights assured to all other persons.

Plan of Action for Constitutional Amendment
National Program

I. Mobilization of Leadership at National Level

a) Priests and Religious
b) Catholic Physicians Guilds
c) Catholic Lawyers Associations
d) USCC Advisory Council
e) National Conference of Catholic Charities
f) Catholic Hospital Association
g) Knights of Columbus, Catholic Daughters of America, National Order of Foresters, Ancient Order of Hibernians
h) Catholic Press Association
i) National Holy Name Society
j) NCCW - NCCL
k) National Catholic Education Association
l) Catholic Theological Society of America
m) Canon Law Society of America
n) Catholic Philosophical Society
o) Nurses
p) Social Workers
q) Catholic Universities
r) Ladies of Charity
s) Daughters of Isabella
t) Knights of St. George

Objectives

1. Inform leadership of each group of the deliberations at the Regional Working Sessions, and the points of consensus reached by the Bishops. Provide an explanation of current status of the proposed amendments, particularly in light of the Senate Subcommittee action. Enclose a copy of Respect Life — 1975, placing the abortion question in a broader context. Propose a meeting with leaders.
2. Explain political strategy and discuss how each group may participate. Show the National Organizations how to inventory their internal political capabilities systematically by

means of their own government relations audit which enables each organization to build its own support system.

3. Establish a communications structure from Washington to
the National Office of each organization to activate support
for the political program and to achieve readiness for necessary response action on our part.

4. Emphasize inherent link between abortion and euthanasia,
and necessity of preparedness for euthanasia struggle.

II. Ecumenical Activity

Objectives

1. Initiate contacts with or respond to Churches that wish to
discuss questions related to abortion or euthanasia.
2. Follow up with additional meetings or structured consultations with the Churches that we have already met with.
3. Engage in scholarly meetings with non-Catholic theologians and other scholars on pro-life issues.
4. In all ecumenical activity, the BCEIA should be appropriately informed and involved.

III. General Public Information Effort

NB. Although political activity to pass an amendment is directed primarily toward Congress, it is also important to generate understanding and support from other groups or
individuals who can be persuasive with Congress and with
those who inform or influence public opinion. Thus some activity should be directed toward:

– All leadership types (business, government, professions,
academic, labor) to inform them of our position and determination to carry through in a long range effort.

– State legislators and state and local party leaders (in all
parties) to inform them of our position and ask their support.

- Communications leaders (press, TV, radio) to generate understanding of our position even if they do not agree with it, and to emphasize the need for a fair hearing of that position. It is important to realize that although major networks may not be very cooperative, local stations are generally willing to provide opportunities to discuss issues.

IV. Judicial Activity

Although the U.S. Supreme Court is firmly committed to Roe and Doe, efforts should be made to reverse the decision, to restrain lower courts from interpreting and applying Roe and Doe more aggressively and more absolutely than the Supreme Court. The following efforts should be pursued:

1. Urge appointment of judges who are fairminded and objective on abortion, and on Roe and Doe.

2. Urge law professors and lawyers to write articles for law journals attacking the philosophical basis of Roe and Doe, and presenting the strictest and most guarded interpretations of Roe and Doe.

3. Set up a hot-line in each state so that injunctions, court challenges or prosecutions directed toward Catholic hospitals can be immediately and effectively met. This effort should include monitoring all cases in state and federal district courts challenging any hospital's policies in regard to sterilization or abortion.

V. Pro-Life Groups

The many pro-life groups operate at varying levels of competence and effectiveness, but their presence is important and valuable to the pro-life movement. Their objectives are certain to vary in type and degree. Uniformity of objective and method is by no means essential. The momentum, activity and support which they create are more helpful to the overall program. It is important to encourage them, to cooperate with them as closely as possible, and to assist their fundraising efforts at the diocesan or state level. The NCHLA and the Bishops' Pro Life Committee will take every opportunity to continue cooperation at the national level, without assuming financial responsibility for these independent groups.

VI. The Catholic Press

1. The National Committee for a Human Life Amendment might provide every diocese with a voter information profile on all of the incumbent members of Congress for inclusion in the diocesan papers prior to next year's general election. This would help to inform our people of where their elected officials stand.

2. The Catholic Press has a special role to play in the Church by providing people with information that enables them to vote on issues in a way that reflects their moral principles.

VII. Specific Educational Efforts

The Church as a Learning Community

1. Develop a comprehensive and systematic effort to conduct the annual Respect Life Program in every parish, school and church-sponsored agency. The Respect Life Program provides the occasion to show the wide spectrum of pro-life commitments of the Church, and it provides the opportunity to motivate Catholics to take an active role in support of human life.

2. Assure quick development and speedy dissemination of a "life and abortion-education" program for use with the rapidly increasing adult education programs throughout the country and in the senior year of Catholic high school "Problems of Democracy" classes as well as in senior C.C.D. programs. This program is especially important since a large portion of the electorate at the time of ratification is this year in senior high school.

3. To coordinate the teaching opportunities of other Church related organizations, initiate and develop liaison between the Pro-Life Committee and the diocesan coordinating agency for:

1. Priests and Religious
2. Hospitals
3. Health Care Workers
4. Catholic Social Services
5. Education and Catechetics
6. Lay Apostolate Organizations

Each of these groups could assume a large portion of the education responsibility among their individual and unique constituencies. They should, however, be presented with a specific project which they would agree to assume.

Proposed Diocesan Plan

I. Establish in Each Diocese a Pro-Life Committee

General Purpose — The purpose of the Committee is to coordinate groups and activities within the diocese with respect to federal legislative structures, particularly efforts to effect passage of a constitutional amendment to protect the unborn child. In its coordinating role, the Committee will rely on information and direction from the Bishops' Pro-Life Office and the NCHLA. The committee will act through the diocesan Pro-Life Director, who is appointed by the Bishop to direct pro-life efforts in the diocese.

Membership — Diocesan Pro-Life Director
　　　　　　　(Bishop's Representative)
　　　　　— Respect Life Coordinator
　　　　　— Liaison with State Catholic Conference
　　　　　— Public Affairs Advisor[2]
　　　　　— Congressional District Representative(s)
　　　　　— Representatives of Diocesan Agencies
　　　　　　　(Priests, Religious, Lay Organization)
　　　　　— Information Specialists

— Legal Advisor — Representative of
Pro-Life Groups

Objectives:

1. Coordinate parish and Congressional district activity.

2. Oversee the development of "Grass-roots" organizations,
    and direct their activity and involvement.

3. Maintain communications with NCHLA in regard to fed-
    eral activity, so as to be ready for necessary action in regard
    to local Senators and Representatives.

4. Maintain a local public information effort directed to press
    and media. Include vigilance in re public media, seek
    "equal time," etc.

5. Develop Core Groups with close relationships to each Sena-
    tor or Representative.

II. Organization of Grass Roots Effort in Every Congressional
    District

    Directed to: Parishes
                        DCCW/DCCM
                        Knights of Columbus
                        Catholic Daughters of America
                        Holy Name Societies/Other Groups

Objectives:

1. Make every Senator and Congressman aware of continuing
    effort to obtain a constitutional amendment. Both the na-
    tional office and the state/diocesan office must have access
    to each congressional district for all future political activity.
    A chairperson should be designated in each district who will
    coordinate the efforts of parish pro-life groups, K of C
    groups, and non-sectarian pro-life groups, including right-
    to-life organizations. In each district, the parishes will be

one basic resource, and the clergy will have to be activated to lead and/or collaborate in the overall effort. Each Congressional District Chairperson will need some basic resources, ie structure, small budget, endorsement and support of clergy.

2. The Congressional District Chairperson should be a member of the Diocesan Coordinating Committee. In a diocese with many congressional districts, one or two Congressional District Chairpersons may represent their many colleagues.

3. Prudently convince others — Catholics and non-Catholics — of necessity of constitutional amendment to provide base for legal protection for unborn.

4. Carry out the public information effort — create a presence at public functions; conduct symposia; be available to press and media.

5. Coordinate efforts with existing pro-life and Right to Life groups.

III. Local Plan for Congressional Effort

Directed to:

1. All States/Dioceses should increase contacts with Senators and Representatives urging positive support for a human life amendment. Senators should be made aware that we are not satisfied with the Senate Subcommittee's failure to report some amendment and we intend to continue our efforts to pass an amendment.

2. In States/Dioceses where Congressman who is a member of House Judiciary Committee comes from, we urge extended hearings.

3. In States/Dioceses where Congressman is in favor of constitutional amendment and may be willing to co-sponsor an amendment, do not invite cosponsorship, but do not inhibit

it if Congressman wishes to support any of the House amendments.

4. In States/Dioceses where Senators or Congressmen have endorsed states' rights amendments, establish communications, explore possibility of support for human life amendment.

Fall — 1975 — House Activity

1. Begin activity on House of Representatives, requesting Judiciary Sub-Committee to conduct <u>extended</u> hearings. Emphasize need to give people a chance to be heard. Since the House is larger, we should expect a long-range effort to build the two-thirds majority.

2. Contact members of House Judiciary Subcommittee, and get a commitment from each member. The same applies to the members of the full House Judiciary Committee. This renewal of commitment is pressing in light of the Senate Subcommittee action.

3. Establish contacts with friendly Congresspersons, urging general support in the House. Explore those who favor a States' Rights approach, and see if they will support a human life amendment.

4. As the House Sub-Committee progresses, there will be a need to step up contacts with the Subcommittee members to commit them to a positive vote.

5. N.B. The House Recess Schedule makes the task of visiting the representative in his/her own district both imperative and achievable.

STATE COORDINATING COMMITTEE

1. It is assumed that overall coordination in each state will be the responsibility of the State Catholic Conference or its equivalent. Where a State Catholic Conference is in process of formation or does not exist, Bishop's representatives from each diocese might be appointed as the core members of the State Coordinating Committee.

2. The State Coordinating Committee will be comprised of the Director of the State Catholic Conference, and the diocesan Pro-Life coordinators. At this level it would be valuable to have one or more persons who are knowledgeable about state politics and experienced in legislative activity. This may be the Public Affairs Specialist referred to in the Proposed Diocesan Plan, or it may be a retired legislator or lobbyist. In any case, it should be someone who understands and practices the new style of politics.

3. The primary purposes of the State Coordinating Committee are:

- to monitor the political trends in the State, and their implication regarding the abortion effort;

- to coordinate the efforts of the various dioceses; and to evaluate the progress in the diocese and the congressional districts

- to provide counsel regarding the specific political relationships within the various parties at the state level.

"Sanitized" Plan Excerpts

There are a number of revealing passages in the sanitized version of the *Pastoral Plan* that do not appear in the unsanitized version. These passages further highlight how the bishops have developed an extensive and nimble political machine in the U.S., in order to advance papal interests. What follows here are direct quotes from the sanitized final version of the plan approved by the bishops' conference. This final version calls for a full mobilization of the Church's pastoral resources focused in three major efforts including public policy. The three-fold public policy action would be "directed toward the legislative, judicial and administrative areas so as to ensure effective legal protection for the right to life." Here are excerpts from this section of the plan:

- "This Pastoral Plan is addressed to and calls upon all Church-sponsored or identifiably Catholic national, regional, diocesan and parochial organizations and agencies to pursue the three-fold effort. This includes ongoing dialogue and cooperation between the NCCB/USCC on the one hand, and priests, religious and lay persons, individually and collectively, on the other hand. In a special way we invite the continued cooperation of the national Catholic organizations.
- "At the same time, we urge Catholics in various professional fields to discuss these issues with their colleagues and to carry the dialogue into their own professional organizations. In similar fashion, we urge those in research and academic life to present the Church's position on a wide range of topics that visibly express her commitment to respect for life at every stage and in every condition.
- "Dialogue is most important—and has already proven highly fruitful—among Churches and religious groups. Efforts should continue at ecumenical consultation and dialogue....Dialogue among scholars in the field of ethics is a most important part of this interfaith effort.
- "Legislative/Public Policy Effort...The abortion decisions of the United States Supreme Court (January 22, 1973) violate the moral order, and have disrupted the legal process....A comprehensive pro-life legislative program must therefore include the following elements:

"a) Passage of a constitutional amendment providing protection for the unborn child to the maximum degree possible.

"b) Passage of federal and state laws and adoption of administrative policies that will restrict the practice of abortion as much as possible.

"Accomplishment of this aspect of this Pastoral Plan will undoubtedly require well planned and coordinated political action by citizens at the national, state and local levels. This activity is not simply the responsibility of Catholics, nor should it be limited to Catholic groups or agencies. It calls for widespread cooperation and collaboration...."

Program Implementation

The blueprint provided by the bishops was designed to encourage the development of "grassroots" political action organizations. A key element of the plan was "the Pro-Life Effort in the Congressional District."

The plan continues, "Passage of a constitutional amendment depends ultimately on persuading members of Congress to vote in favor of such a proposal.* This effort at persuasion is part of the democratic process, and is carried on most effectively in the congressional district or state from which the representative is elected.

"Essentially, this effort demands ongoing public information activity and careful and detailed organization. Thus it is absolutely necessary to encourage the development in each congressional district of an identifiable, tightly-knit and well organized pro-life unit. This unit can be described as a public interest group or a citizens' lobby. No matter what it is called, its task is essentially political, that is, to organize people to help persuade the elected representatives...

"As such, the congressional district pro-life group differs from the diocesan, regional or parish pro-life coordinator or committee, whose task is pedagogic and motivational, not simply political, and whose range of action includes a variety of efforts calculated to reverse the present atmosphere of permissiveness with respect to abortion. Moreover, it is an agency of the citizens, operated, controlled and financed by these same citizens. It is not an agency of

---

* An amendment to the U.S. Constitution, of course, also requires ratification by three-fourths of the states. —Ed.

the Church, nor is it operated, controlled, or financed by the Church....It is complementary to denominational efforts, to professional groups, to pregnancy counselling and assistance groups.

"Each congressional district should have a chairperson who may serve as liaison with the Diocesan Coordinating Committee. In a diocese with many congressional districts, this may be arranged through a regional representation structure."

District Pro-Life Group Objectives

The bishops' solid infrastructure at the Congressional district level is then to be applied to the achievement of specific objectives, as listed in the plan:

- "To convince all elected officials and potential candidates that "the abortion issue" will not go away and that their position on it will be subject to continuing public scrutiny.
- "To elect members of their own group or active sympathizers to specific posts in all local party organizations.
- "To maintain an informational file on the pro-life position of every elected official and potential candidate.
- "To work for qualified candidates who will vote for a constitutional amendment, and other pro-life issues.
- "To maintain liaison with all denominational leaders (pastors) and all other pro-life groups in the district.

"This type of activity can be generated and coordinated by a small, dedicated and politically alert group. It will need some financial support, but its greatest need is the commitment of other groups who realize the importance of its purposes...and the absolute necessity of working with the group to attain the desired goals."

A copy of the complete sanitized version can be obtained from the Center. The bishops apparently never had any second thoughts about their Pastoral Plan, and its implementation began immediately. After 10 years of experience—and success—with the implementation, the bishops formally reendorsed the Plan at their November 1985 annual meeting.

IMPLICATIONS OF THE PASTORAL PLAN

9

9

// ...LAW can override consensus and reshape it...history isn't made by majorities, but by minorities with the stamina and smarts to persevere against the establishment while co-opting its institutions."

Stephen Settle
Veteran contributor
National Catholic Register
February 21, 1993

In Chapter 6, I wrote that the Vatican recognized that if the new threat to papal security-survival posed by the population movement in the U.S. were to be neutralized, American political will would have to be undermined. The purpose of the Pastoral Plan was to accomplish this goal.

Jesuit priest Virgil Blum, founder and first President of the Catholic League for Religious and Civil Rights, proposed this strategy in a 1971 *America* magazine article titled, "Public Policy Making: Why the Churches Strike Out."[54] "If a group is to be politically effective, issues rather than institutions must be at stake," Blum acknowledged. Abortion was simply the issue chosen to galvanize the movement created to achieve this effectiveness.

Blum's article set the stage for the creation of the Pastoral Plan, offering the bishops a set of well thought out guidelines which capitalized on centuries of experience of Jesuit manipulation of governments. Blum's own words make clear the true motivations of the bishops and their plan. An analysis of Blum's article was published earlier.[55] Additional comments from it appear later in this Chapter and in the next. Analysis of the Pastoral Plan makes the intentions of the bishops evident.

ANALYSIS OF THE PLAN

As noted earlier, the draft of the plan approved by the NCCB Administrative Board is, in many ways, more revealing than the sanitized final product. I will analyze the earlier version first and then examine revealing statements that appear only in the final product.

In the Introduction, the bishops claim, "We do not seek to impose our moral teaching on American society..." Then they define their goal, "the establishment of a system of law that will provide legal protection of human life from conception..." (defining life according to papal security-survival needs) and launch into their plan for a political mobilization designed to achieve this end no matter what the majority of Americans believe. It is immediately apparent that their claim is ridiculous. The bishops had the good sense to remove this claim from the sanitized draft.

The first section, "Plan of Action for Constitutional Amendment," describes a mustering of literally millions of people into a political machine completely controlled by the bishops for the purpose of protecting papal security interests—at the expense of U.S. security interests. This mobilization includes virtually all Catholic institutions and agencies in the United States. From their list in the draft, I will discuss only a few:

1. Catholic Press Association.

The Catholic Press Association has played a crucial role in the implementation of the Pastoral Plan. The suppression of information about the Pastoral Plan and its implications for American women, about the plan's relationship to our constitutional democratic government, and about the differences between papal security-survival and U.S. security as defined by NSSM 200, has been a great success of Catholic journalists in the secular print and broadcast media and the Catholic Press Association. Largely through one kind of intimidation or another, or simply by blocking publication of this kind of information, Catholic journalists—including reporters, editors, publishers and producers—have successfully sought to "protect the faith" as directed by their clerical leadership. Less than

0.01 percent of Americans have ever heard of the Pastoral Plan much less seen an analysis of it implications. The same is true of NSSM 200 which was made available briefly in 1976 before being reclassified and then not declassified until 1989.

The bishops determined the rules of the abortion engagement and defined the terms of the debate. This was in response to another of Blum's guidelines: "Crucial to influencing public opinion is getting the people to define the issue your way. Since language not only defines the situation but also shapes attitudes, a group's cause has an almost insurmountable handicap if it permits opposing forces to define the terms of the discussion. 'He who defines the terms of the controversy has the controversy half won,' said a wise politician." [56]

Enforcing these rules set forth by the bishops required the unwavering support of Catholic journalists in both the print and broadcast media. We never see forced pregnancy of 10-year children discussed in terms of the extreme form of child abuse it really is. We are never exposed to a discussion of the powerful relationship between being an unwanted child and being a criminal, a drug abuser or alcoholic. Costs to all of us because of the bishops' success in forcing unwanted children upon American women, so that the bishops can protect papal security interests, are enormous, but these costs are never discussed as part of the abortion debate. We are only exposed to dimensions of the abortion debate that the bishops can either win or can argue to a draw. The Catholic journalists organized by the bishops as a part of their Pastoral Plan insure that all tow the line. Without this cadre, the bishops' plan would have failed miserably.

The pope has a keen awareness of the importance of the media to his agenda. In a letter to the world's Catholic journalists appearing in the February 27, 1992 issue of *The Wanderer*, titled "Mass Media Need Catholic Presence," the pope states: "It is in this connection that on World Communications Day I recall the activities of Catholics, individually and in a myriad of institutions, in this field. In particular I mention the three great Catholic media organizations: the International Catholic Office for Film and Cinema(OCIC), The International Catholic Press Union (UCIP), and the International Catholic Association for Radio and Television (Unda). It is to them in particular and to the vast resources of professional knowledge, skill, and zeal among their extensive international membership that the Church turns hopefully and confidently....The great body of Catholic media professionals, lay men and women for the most part, must be reminded on this special day of the awesome responsibility which rests upon them...to foster the Church's presence in the media and to work for greater coordination among the Catholic agencies involved."

2. Catholic Physicians Guilds.

In 1975, 80 percent of all American obstetrician-gynecologists performed abortions. In 1994, this figure is below 20 percent. Much of the bishops' success in restricting the availability of abortion to Catholic and nonCatholic American women can be attributed to the bishops' mobilization of Catholic physicians. Behind the scenes manipulation in medical societies and on hospital boards, etc., career advancement of anti-abortion physicians at the expense of pro-choice physicians and outright intimidation were some of the tools used by the members of the guilds to achieve this remarkable success.

3. Catholic Lawyers Associations.

The bishops recognized that these associations, if properly led, could secretly facilitate the placement of anti-abortion individuals, both lawyers and nonlawyers, in positions of power in elected and nonelected positions and in public and private life. Also, various organizations were created to defend anti-abortion activists and advance the bishops' agenda in other ways.

4. Catholic Hospital Association.

The bishops called upon this association to defend the Catholic hospitals against any effort to induce or require Catholic hospitals to offer abortion related medical services to women who want them. The association also was asked to begin a propaganda campaign against the evil of abortion directed at Catholic hospital patients. There were many other ways in which this association has advanced the bishops' agenda, including stripping hospital privileges from physicians, Catholic and nonCatholic, if they performed abortions anywhere or even referred for or counseled patients on abortion. Individuals, including physicians, advanced or failed to advance in their careers, depending on their position on abortion and many conformed most unethically—to the benefit of the bishops.

5. Lay organizations.

The lay organizations the reader sees listed by the bishops in their plan collectively have a membership nearly 10 million strong. Members have been asked through their organizations to take whatever steps they can against prochoice individuals and institutions and to promote the advancement of anti-abortionists into positions of power, in their careers, and socially and politically as well. Advancement of individuals based on merit has been corrupted in order to advance the interests of the Papacy. Reading the publications of these organizations over the past 15 years, I have been impressed with the creativity by which the American way of life has been corrupted by these desperate bishops through their lay organizations in order to achieve the goals of their Pastoral Plan. Every American has suffered serious consequences from this activity. Individuals are usually unaware that they are victims of this plan and its behind-the-scenes manipulations, and mistakenly attribute their misfortunes to other causes.

The Pastoral Plan specifically states that the bishops will assist each Catholic organization and agency in marshalling political power, and power to manipulate professional groups, in order to advance the objectives of the Vatican.

ECUMENICAL ACTIVITY

The importance of ecumenism to the bishops' Pastoral Plan is made evident by the position it occupies in the description of the plan, second only to the section on the mobilization of the troops.

In another of his guidelines, Blum concluded that if the Catholic leadership is to succeed, it must make their efforts look non-Catholic.[57] Blum also concluded that to accomplish this goal, the bishops must create a strong ecumenical movement.

Before the Vatican's need of ecumenism came along, the small fledgling ecumenical movement of the 1960s was going nowhere. Blum's article was published in 1971. Then, suddenly, ecumenical activity exploded. Most of the Catholic activity in the Christian ecumenical movement has taken place since that time. A leading motivation for the involvement of Catholic leadership in ecumenism has been the Catholic Church's need for wide-scale public participation by Protestant churches in the anti-abortion movement. Blum recognized early on that "ecumenism" would be an essential weapon to counter the criticism certain to come with the blatant involvement of the bishops in making public policy. He saw that constant defense of the Catholic bishops by Protestant leaders, in the name of "ecumenism," was critical. In hindsight, he was obviously correct. Protestant leaders have served as tools of the Catholic bishops to blunt criticism, by branding such criticism as anti-Catholic or anti-freedom of religion and thus un-American. Protestants with good intentions were used like pawns to advance papal security interests at the expense of our country's. (More on the Vatican's ecumenism success in Chapter 14.)

PUBLIC INFORMATION EFFORT

The thinly veiled objective of this effort is to intimidate all leaders—business, government, professional, academic, labor, including state legislative and state and local party leaders, and leaders of the press and broadcast media. This effort has been highly effective. These leaders virtually never confront the Catholic Church regarding the appropriateness of this religious intervention in the making of public policy—behavior I was taught from grade school onward is an unacceptable abridgment of the first amendment of the U.S. Constitution.

As a result of this intimidation, the bishops' unAmerican activities unleashed by this plan, go undiscussed in academia, the professions, business, labor, national, state and local governments, and most especially in the press.

JUDICIAL ACTIVITY

Although the bishops have not yet succeeded in reversing the Roe v. Wade decision, one of their stated objectives, they have had considerable success through the courts in restricting access to abortion of millions of American women, especially poor women. However, their objective to "restrain lower courts from interpreting and applying *Roe* and *Doe* more aggressively and more absolutely than the Supreme Court" has been completely successful. There is not a single example of this occurring anywhere.

The bishops' call to appoint only anti-abortion judges met with overwhelming success during the Reagan and Bush years. They succeeded in influencing judicial appointments during these administrations. Not one single pro-choice federal judge was named to the bench. Over 70 percent of our federal judges are now basically anti-abortion, as are all five Supreme Court Justices appointed during those years.

Much of the success of the bishops in their manipulation of the U.S. judicial selection process is owed to the Catholic controlled Free Congress Foundation (FCF), founded by Catholic activist Paul Weyrich in 1978 in response to the Pastoral Plan's call for the creation of "grassroots" organizations. FCF's Judicial Selection Monitoring Project was created specifically to accomplish the bishops' goals as set forth in this section of the Pastoral Plan.

The bishops' call for members of Catholic Lawyers Associations to write articles for law journals attacking the philosophical basis of *Roe* and *Doe*, and presenting the strictest and most guarded interpretations of *Roe* and *Doe*, has resulted in a plethora of such material appearing not only in law journals but in publications meant for wider readership.

PROPOSED DIOCESAN PLAN

A reading of the diocesan plan makes clear the sophistication and intensity of the bishops' effort. It is obvious that this organization has vast institutional resources and is committed to using them. It is also evident that they are providing the leadership—bishops under direct command of the Vatican.

Virgil Blum offered two guidelines to the bishops relevant to the leadership of this effort. "Most of the laity," he wrote, "will not, on their own initiative, become involved in any civic organization that concerns itself with educational, religious and moral values...Catholic laymen on the whole simply do not get involved in...politics, even for their own financial benefit, unless the pastors give their approval and strong encouragement. And most pastors will not do so unless the bishop pushes them into it."[58]

Blum seems to be suggesting that the laity is a mindless herd who must be pushed into involvement in politics. However, that there is not greater lay involvement can best be accounted for, obviously, by the fact that most Catholics disagree with the bishops on abortion. Some of the key reasons for this disagreement are discussed in Chapter 13.

In a second guideline on this topic, Blum states, "...religious leaders [must] begin to take seriously their role as leaders and moral persuaders...They must provide the leadership in the organization of issue-oriented interest groups that will be actively involved in the making of public policy." [59] Blum makes clear that the intent is the making of public policy—as determined by the bishops. He also says they must provide the leadership of what have become known as the New Right organizations. The bishops obviously accepted Blum's many guidelines, including these two.

Objective 2 of the Diocesan Plan states: "Oversee the development of 'grass-roots' organizations, and direct their activity and involvement." Is it legitimate to label a Vatican-created and bishop-controlled lobbying effort, "grass-roots"? In the section of the Diocesan Plan titled, "Organization of Grass Roots Effort in Every Congressional District," Objective 1 states, "In each district, the parishes will be one basic resource, and the clergy will have to be activated to lead and/or collaborate in the overall effort." The leadership down to the lowest possible level is clerical just as Blum had said would be necessary for success.

It is evident that the Diocesan Plan called for pressure directed at and intimidation of the secular press and electronic media. Furthermore, the plan went on to say, "Develop Core Groups with close relationships to each Senator or Representative," obviously referring to development of pressure groups (see Objective 1). Every Senator and Representative is to be contacted repeatedly by a multitude of pressure groups controlled by the bishops, to advance the Papal agenda. Intimidation to discourage opposition to the Papal agenda is implied, "—create a presence at public functions; conduct symposia; be available to press and media." And the bishops have achieved the desired result.

The sections titled, "House Activity" and "State Coordinating Committee" both further reflect the considerable experience of this foreign-controlled lobbying effort. In the sections on both the creation of function of the pro-life groups and the diocesan plan, the bishops state that they will insure that this lobbying effort will be funded.

THE SANITIZED VERSION OF THE PLAN

This final version of the Plan which was approved by the majority of the membership of the NCCB is more sensitive to public reaction. However, it is still clear that the Plan places the full force of the Church's resources behind an effort to set public policy. "The Pastoral Plan is addressed to and calls upon all Church-sponsored or identifiably Catholic national, regional, diocesan and parochial organizations and agencies to pursue the three-fold effort."

The plan boldly states: "A comprehensive pro-life legislative program must therefore include the following elements:

a) Passage of a constitutional amendment providing protection for the unborn child to the maximum degree possible.

b) Passage of federal and state laws and adoption of administrative policies that will restrict the practice of abortion as much as possible.

Accomplishment of this aspect of this Pastoral Plan will undoubtedly require well planned and coordinated political action at the national, state and local levels."

It further states: "Thus this Pastoral Plan seeks to activate the...resources of the Church in three major efforts:

3. a public policy effort directed toward the legislative, judicial and administrative areas so as to insure effective legal protection for the right to life."

Then the Vatican turned their "faithful" loose on America to achieve these objectives using any means they could muster. There is a mountain of evidence showing that the bishops and other faithful have resorted to all tools at their disposal to achieve these objectives.[60-62] The Vatican, at this point, had already determined that its very survival was on the line.

As noted, this version details a 3-pronged attack, one devoted to each of the three branches of our federal government: legislative, judicial and administrative. The success of the bishops in their "public policy effort directed toward the administrative area" was truly stunning. Within a year after the Pastoral Plan was initiated in November 1975, during the President-elect Carter transition team era, the bishops had already seized considerable control.

The bishops succeeded in their efforts to elect Presidents Reagan and Bush, the two most Catholic Presidents in American history. As the *TIME* article shows, with the election of anti-abortion Ronald

Reagan and anti-abortion George Bush in 1980, the Vatican seized control of the administrative branch of our government in the area of population and family planning.[63] The comments of U.S. Ambassador to the Vatican William Wilson and of Cardinal Pio Laghi, Vatican Ambassador to the U.S., say all that needs to be said. In these two administrations, U.S. policy was made to reflect Vatican policy.

These two Presidents took whatever administrative actions they could take to impose Vatican family planning, abortion and population policy on all Americans. They made numerous appointments from the ranks of the Religious Right. These executive appointees waged a campaign of bureaucratic harassment and obstruction against the family planning establishment.[63a] Those whom G. Gordon Liddy, imprisoned for his role in the Watergate scandal, refers to as "agents of influence"[63b] were surreptitiously placed in key posts. The list of actions taken is long and goes far beyond the better known ones, such as the Mexico City policy, the ban on abortions in overseas military facilities and the ban on fetal tissue research.

Through these two Presidents, the Vatican succeeded in crippling our government's population and family planning efforts. However, it has not succeeded in passage of its all-important "Human Life Amendment" to our Constitution. This amendment would, for obvious reasons, be very destructive of U.S. security interests but is vital to Papal security interests.

During the Carter-Reagan-Bush years, the bishops directed an infiltration of every U.S. government office and agency that has anything to do with family planning, abortion, immigration and population growth control, including those that produce information that would point to a need for national or international population growth control. The Vatican seeks to undermine the effectiveness of the population and family planning related missions assigned to the various government and government funded agencies as directed by Congress.

The Vatican used faithful Catholics like Jack Sullivan, as described by Ravenholt in Chapter 5, to implement their agenda. It directed this infiltration by a group of Catholics who owe their allegiance to the Papacy rather than America, opportunistic non-Catholics like Sander Levin [64] and Catholics who simply owe their jobs to the bishops and are also very disinclined to bring attention to the bishops' corrupting influences.   Evidence of the success of the bishops in this regard abounds.[65-67]

With the administrative area of our government under such strong Vatican influence, it was easy to impose its wishes in the judicial area. As noted earlier, Presidents Reagan and Bush appointed five Supreme Court Justices and 70 percent of all sitting judges in the federal court system. All were anti-abortion, another stated goal of their Plan.

The third branch of the government, the legislative branch, was also specifically targeted by the Pastoral Plan. This branch has been more difficult for the bishops, though they did achieve influence in Congress sufficient to the point where pro-choice Congressmen could not override a presidential veto. So long as the bishops controlled the White House, this was sufficient for their purposes.

However, in 1994 the bishops scored a stunning success. The Republicans seized control of both the House and the Senate. Every single freshman Republican elected to both houses was anti-abortion, a remarkable achievement for the bishops and their Pastoral Plan for Pro-Life Activities.

A PLAN TO INTIMIDATE LAWMAKERS

There are other stated objectives of the Plan that are clearly designed to intimidate American politicians and all others who stand in the Vatican's way:

- "Encourage the development of 'grassroots' political action organizations."
- "Convince all elected officials and potential candidates that 'the abortion issue' will not go away and their position on it will be subject to continuing public scrutiny."
- "Elect members of their own group or active sympathizers to specific posts in all local party organizations."
- "Maintain an informational file on the pro-life position of every elected official and potential candidate."
- "Work for qualified candidates who will vote for a constitutional amendment, and other pro-life issues."

The actions that have resulted from these objectives have meant the termination of the political careers of hundreds if not thousands of Americans who placed U.S. interests above Papal interests. We have all witnessed the seizure of local, state and national control of the Republican party by religious fanatics as a result of these objectives. But the Democratic party and many individual Democrats have been victimized as well.

THE PLAN CREATED THE 'NEW RIGHT'

The Pastoral Plan specifically directed the creation of "grassroots" organizations for the purposes of advancing the papal agenda. During the period 1976-1980, nearly all of the organizations that became known as the "New Right Movement" or the "Religious New Right" were organized. Examples are: The Moral Majority, the Heritage Foundation, the Free Congress Foundation, the Eagle Forum, American Life Lobby, Committee for the Survival of a Free Congress, Life Amendment Political Action Committee, the National Committee for a Human Life Amendment, the National Conservative Political Action Committee, National Right to Life Committee, Religious Roundtable, Right to Life Party, and the Right to Life Political Action Committee. There are many others. Catholics were key players in the creation of all of these organizations and in their leadership. This assessment of the creation of this movement and its control by the bishops is well documented.[68-70]

The creation of these "grassroots" organizations by the bishops had far reaching consequences for the governing of America. Many of these consequences are widely known. Others are not.

For example, the 1980 election cost $127.3 million. Trade and corporate PACs spent $61.6 million. New Right PACs raised a combined $19 million. Conservative challengers were given disproportionately far more by corporate and right-wing sources. In her book, *The Right to Lifers: Who They Are, How They Operate, How They Get Their Money,* Connie Paige states,"The most perplexing aspect of all this was the change in nature of corporate giving—the phenomenon that threw the Democratic candidates off balance even more than did the astonishingly large amounts. Never before had oil companies, savings-and loan associations, defense contractors, the real-estate and insurance industries, builders, truckers, auto manufacturers and dealers, and the utility, chemical and dairy industries directed their resources in such vast quantities toward so many political unknowns of the same ideological stripe."[71]

This dramatic change in corporate giving was a direct result of the bishops' Pastoral Plan and its call for the creation of this plethora of Catholic controlled "grassroots" organizations and its call to Catholic laymen in these secular institutions to do whatever possible in the political arena to advance the goals of the plan. This included lay Catholic manipulation of corporate giving to political campaigns in such a way as to advance the papal agenda.

THE COURAGE OF JUDGE DOOLING

One of the early great successes of the Pastoral Plan was the passage of the Hyde Amendment in 1976, the year after the Plan was implemented. This amendment to an appropriation bill, offered by Congressman and Catholic activist Henry Hyde of Illinois, restricted the use of Medicaid money for abortion, limiting access to abortion for poor women. Planned Parenthood asked Federal Judge John F. Dooling of the U.S. District Court, Eastern District of New York, to determine whether the law was constitutional.

According to the account of a lawyer who clerked for him, Dooling was responsible, thorough, and highly intelligent.[72] He was also a practicing Catholic.[73] He took thirteen months to hear the evidence, which ultimately amounted to dozens of witnesses and thousands of pages of testimony.[74]

On February 4, 1980, E. Willis, writing for *The Village Voice*, summarized the outcome: "[In] Judge John F. Dooling's 328-page decision [on January 15, 1980], striking down the Hyde Amendment...he demonstrates that the purpose of the Hyde Amendment was never to save the taxpayers' money, keep the government neutral on a delicate moral issue, or distinguish between 'necessary' and so-called 'convenience' abortions.

"The amendment," says Dooling bluntly, "was a ploy by anti-abortion congressmen frustrated in their attempt to pass a Constitutional amendment that would override the Supreme Court's 1973 pro-abortion decision; its purpose was quite simply to circumvent the Court's ruling and prevent as many abortions as possible." Dooling makes short work of the anti-abortionists' pretensions to being a spontaneous grassroots movement that owes political victories to sheer moral appeal. He confirms that right-to-life's main source of energy, organization, and direction has been the Catholic Church, and describes in detail how the movement uses one-issue voting to put pressure on legislators, candidates, and the party organizations that nominate them—a tactic that gains its influence far out of proportion to its numbers.

"After quoting various Christian and Jewish theologians' differing opinions on abortion and the question of fetal personhood, Dooling argues that the antiabortionist view is not based on any moral or religious consensus but reflects a sectarian position that 'is not genuinely argued; it is adamantly asserted'...The Hyde Amendment, he concludes, is religiously motivated legislation that imposes a particular theological viewpoint, violating dissenters' First Amendment rights."

Dooling carefully examined the bishop's Pastoral Plan as he prepared his decision. He documented that the Hyde Amendment became U.S. law only because of the considerable success enjoyed by the bishops in the implementation of their Pastoral Plan.

One might ask how the Catholic Church could have retained its tax exemption under these circumstances. The answer is simple. By this time, the bishops had mobilized their "faithful" with their Plan. In the critical government departments and agencies, the bishops held sufficient influence to block any challenges. Several attempts were made. All failed. The Pastoral Plan's mobilization of responsive lay Catholic judges and other government officials, including IRS decision-makers, ruled out any hope that American law would be enforced against the bishops and their obedient followers.

Judge Dooling clearly understood the grave implications for America of the Pastoral Plan. However, he was no match for the awesome power of his bishops: this decision was quickly overturned by an Appeals Court and the Hyde Amendment became law.

Had the Catholic Church been stripped of its tax exemption status when the bishops approved its Pastoral Plan, which was obviously in order, the Vatican would not have succeeded in killing American political will to confront the population problem. Without the tax exemption, the Vatican would not have succeeded in covertly "co-opting its [the U.S. government's] institutions," as Stephen Settle suggested. Every dollar of the Catholic Church's income and expenditures would have been publicly accounted for. Settle's "minority" would not be able to manipulate government policy to advance the security interests of the Papacy at the expense of U.S. security interests.

THE HUMAN LIFE AMENDMENT — AND BEYOND

10

10

THERE IS a mountain of evidence that the bishops enjoyed great success in killing American political will through implementation of their Pastoral Plan. Millions of abortions have been denied poor women because of the Hyde amendment. The U.S. domestic family planning program has shrunk by two-thirds since implementation of the Plan while the number of women of reproductive age has grown by several million. Population education and sex education have been severely crippled. Our international population program has been straitjacketed. None of the recommendations of the Rockefeller Commission and NSSM 200 has been implemented. However, the bishops have not yet been able to achieve their primary objective—passage of the Human Life Amendment (HLA). The HLA asserts that human life begins at conception and that the conceptus has all the rights afforded human beings.

The HLA is overwhelmingly the most important concern now faced by the Vatican. Nothing threatens the survival of the Papacy more than the continuing challenges to papal authority which are certain to come from our American democracy so long as our Constitution does not contain this amendment.

For this reason, American democracy is the greatest single threat faced by the Papacy. As long as our democracy continues to pass laws like legalizing abortion or supporting family planning, papal authority will be gravely at risk. Governments of other countries witness the U.S. successfully challenging the Papacy as our democracy determines what is moral behavior. These governments may then choose to follow the lead of the U.S. in rejecting papal authority and the pope's "morality." But with the passage of the HLA, abortion and most modern methods of contraception will cease to be legal. Papal authority will then be protected. U.S. Government civil authority in these matters will cease to take precedence over papal authority.

These other achievements of the bishops and their Plan are quite remarkable and have had devastating effects on individual, family, national and global security. However, if the HLA is not added to our Constitution, all of these successes will be in jeopardy. The bishops understand this stark reality as they witness the gradual implosion of papal authority around the world. Papal authority is under siege and a siege which will continue until passage of the HLA.

THE DRIVE FOR HLA INTENSIFIES

Recognizing its failure with the HLA, the Vatican recently decided it must step up its campaign for the passage of the HLA. In September 1991, Catholic activist William Bennett, former Secretary of Education, and other Catholic "conservatives" announced the formation of Catholic Campaign for America. [75] Creation of this organization even 20 years ago would have been unthinkable. For nearly 200 years, Protestants have warned that the Vatican plans to create such organizations in the U.S. and that American democracy was threatened. One need only listen to what these Catholics are saying now to understand that the strategy Stephen Settle described in the *National Catholic Register* is being implemented—and to recognize that this minority, with its "stamina, smarts and perseverance" intends to impose papal law using any means necessary and to "co-opt" our democratic institutions.

This escalation comes as no great surprise in 1996. The Papacy is in a desperate situation which is widely recognized by the Church leadership, both clerical and lay. The Vatican also recognizes that its behavior is highly risky—and they apparently accept this risk for all American Catholics.

The Catholic Campaign for America (CCA), according to the *National Catholic Register*, was initiated to "bring a politically powerful and distinctively Catholic voice to the U.S. political scene." The group will work to "increase Catholic influence on public policy issues." [76] According to a CCA document, the mission of

CCA is to activate Catholics to increase Catholic influence in formulating public policy. [77]

The leadership of the Catholic Campaign includes many of the
leading "conservative" Catholic activists. Syndicated columnist and
failed Presidential candidate Patrick Buchanan is typical of the leadership group. In an August 28, 1992 *Our Sunday Visitor* interview,
Buchanan was asked, "What kind of Catholic are you?" Buchanan
responded, "A believing Catholic, a practicing Catholic *and a papist*
[italics mine]. I think John Paul II is a singular leader of our time. He's
immensely attractive and charismatic, but more than that, he speaks
out with a sense of authority and moral courage. I think he's a
genuinely great man, really a gift of God to the Church. And in
virtually all the quarrels in which he's engaged I'm on his side." [78] In
1996, *Newsweek* reported: "In 1977 Buchanan, who says that his
childhood heroes were Joseph McCarthy and Generalissimo Francisco Franco, wrote that 'though Hitler was indeed racist and anti-
Semitic to the core...he was also an individual of great courage, a
soldier's soldier in the Great War, a political organizer of the first
rank...'"[78a] Few Catholic Americans hold these three Roman Catholics in such high esteem. The May 1996 issue of the Conservative
Catholic Family News, describes Buchanan and the source of his
agenda: "As a faithful son of Holy Mother Church, Pat Buchanan
has drawn extensively from these immortal papal encyclicals [the
social encyclicals of the past 100 years]. They form the very bedrock
for his political agenda."[78b]

Buchanan leaves absolutely no doubt in the reader's mind to
whom he owes his allegiance. It is clearly not to his country. The
security-survival interests of the Papacy are undeniably pitted
against the security-survival interests of the United States. Buchanan need say no more. Given the mission of the Catholic Campaign
and statements of its leaders offered below, all members must
necessarily be equally devoted to the Papacy.

The Catholic Campaign leadership also includes the following
individuals: New York Cardinal John J. O'Connor (CCA's "National Ecclesiastical Advisor"); Mary Ellen Bork, a former nun and
wife of failed Supreme Court nominee Robert Bork; former Vatican
ambassadors William A. Wilson and Frank Shakespeare; former
Reagan National Security Advisor Richard V. Allen; former governor of New York Hugh Carey; Congressman Robert K. Dornan;
Phyllis Schlafly of Eagle Forum; Russel Shaw of the Knights of

Columbus; Domino's Pizza magnate Thomas Monaghan; Bishop Rene Gracida of Corpus Christi; Wall Street executive Frank Lynch; Philadelphia business executive Rocco L. Martino; former Pat Robertson presidential campaign coordinator Marlene Elwell; Pat Robertson's American Center for Law and Justice head Keith Fournier; secretive Opus Dei staff members Joseph J. Astarita and Patrick M. Hanretty; Steven Schmieder of the Society for Tradition, Family and Property; director of the Institute of Religion and Public Life Richard J. Neuhaus, and Legatus's Tom Wykes. [79]

The words of these leaders leave little to the imagination regarding the intentions of the organization. Executive Director Wykes recently told the National Catholic Reporter, "It's not a Catholic campaign to take over America. It's a Catholic campaign *for* America. We believe that Catholic values are a generative base for the values that all Americans share." [80] In their spring 1994 issue of *UPDATE* Wykes makes clear one of their goals: "Imagine thousands of Catholic political leaders, business leaders, and sports and entertainment personalities bolstered by an emerging Catholic constituency who are no longer afraid to integrate their faith into public life. Leaders who see their faith as the foundational element of everything they do."

In their 1992 issue of *Update*, Martino demanded the enactment of tax subsidies for Catholic schools and wrote, "Separation of church and state is a false premise that must finally be cast aside and replaced by the true meaning of our Constitution." [81]

In a "challenge to Catholic Americans" published by the Campaign in the fall of 1992, board member Hugh Carey said, "We must move from the beginning to the end from a defensive to an activist position; are we not after all seeking to be members of the church militant?...We are a giant religious country. We have the power. We have the people. Let's organize and win this fight for the benefit of all Americans." [82] Carey is saying let's accomplish our goals regardless of the wishes of democratic America. Let's benefit Americans with the leadership of the pope, whether or not Americans want this "benefit."

The Catholic Campaign quietly goes about its work. Despite its remarkable activities, it has not been mentioned in the national secular press, no doubt benefiting from the silence achieved by the bishops on activities like these, a result of the mobilization of Catholic journalists.

There are other groups which have been mobilized to take part in the Vatican's intensification of the effort to achieve passage of the HLA. An event billed as "the Catholic event of the year" by the Catholic press, was a conference held in October 1993 in New Jersey. The keynote speaker at this Christi Fideles sponsored conference was Patrick Buchanan. According to an advance advertisement in *The Wanderer*, the conference was designed to "rally the Catholic troops in opposition to the hellish agenda of the 'Clintonistas'. [It] will give you a battle plan for the recapture of America—by Catholics as Catholics. Each speaker will focus on a different aspect of *the only possible solution to the crisis now confronting our nation: Catholic action—social, political and moral* [italics mine]." The ad further states, "America was discovered by a Catholic, who claimed her for Christ the king. If America is to be rediscovered and reclaimed for our king...it is Catholics who must act and act now." [83]

A group of traditionalist Catholic university professors recently formed The Society of Catholic Social Scientists. New York's Cardinal O'Connor is a member. The group will be advised by a board of bishops. According to the National Catholic Register, the society was formed to "analyze political, social and economic issues, focusing Church social teaching and the natural law on the challenges of modern culture." Notre Dame law professor Charles Rice, addressing the first meeting in March 1993, made the position of the new society clear: "The solution to problems of contemporary society, such as abortion, has to be found in an explicit reliance on the teachings of the Catholic Church."[84] The Society has formed a "rapid response" team to provide comment to the news media on breaking issues of the day, to further advance the influence of the Vatican on American journalism.

Patrick Buchanan's organization, American Cause, held its first conference in May of 1993. Its theme, Winning the Culture War, was first described by Buchanan in his speech to the 1992 Republican convention. He is in conflict with all Americans who do not share his traditionalist Catholic beliefs.[85]

It appears that the Vatican recognized by the time of the 1992 Republican convention that their efforts must be intensified if the HLA is to be added to our Constitution. Only Rome could direct the creation of so many Catholic organizations in the span of a few months, each with a similar mission. Nothing has appeared in the secular press regarding the creation of this array of organizations. They diligently go about their work.

The Republican Party retained the HLA in its 1996 platform, in significant part due to the efforts of presidential candidate Patrick Buchanan and his followers, including the Christian Coalition. In a February 1996 fundraising letter, Buchanan's primary motivation is made evident: "I want to talk to you today simply and directly, from my heart, about what I believe is the most important issue facing America today. That issue is the sacredness of human life, and the moral imperative facing us to fight to protect it from the moment of conception to the moment of natural death. A principal reason I'm running for president is to turn back the pro-abortion forces and keep the Republican Party firmly in the pro-life camp. And then I want to use the Presidency as a vital and powerful force to change what Pope John Paul II has so correctly called "the culture of death" that has arisen in America since 1973.

"On November 8, 1994, we made a tremendous start—electing 5 new pro-life Senators and 44 new pro-life Representatives. Now for the first time in 40 years, both houses of Congress are controlled by the Republican Party—a party solemnly sworn, in its platform, to a 100 percent pro-life position. If we elect a pro-life President in 1996, we can finally move forward to ending abortion in the United States."[86a] The stage will be set to achieve the Vatican's goal of a HLA in the U.S. Constitution. Buchanan suggests that the Republican Party has become the papal party.

Recall Bishop James McHugh's 1987 comment to Byrnes: "within twenty-four hours" of the court's action on Roe v. Wade in 1973, the bishops knew they would need to mount a political campaign in favor of a constitutional amendment prohibiting abortion. The Vatican has already seized control of the Republican Party. More on this later.

PAT ROBERTSON AND HIS CHRISTIAN COALITION

Vital to the success of the Pastoral Plan has been the creation of, first, the Moral Majority, followed by the Christian Coalition. The secular press has long maintained a remarkable silence regarding the overwhelming Catholic influence within both of these organizations. This silence can be explained only by the widespread influence of the Church on journalists and their superiors, Catholic and non-Catholic (see Chapters 14 and 15). The evidence shows that both of these organizations, for all practical purposes, were created by the bishops because of the Plan, and these organizations have derived their energy, organization and direction from the Catholic Church. [86-90]

Perhaps the most convincing link between Pat Robertson's Christian Coalition and the activists who are implementing the Pastoral Plan is Robertson's link with Paul Weyrich. Weyrich recruited Jerry Falwell to become the nominal leader of the Moral Majority. [91] The Pastoral Plan calls for such an arrangement in the section on "Ecumenical Activity." Weyrich also claims to have suggested the Moral Majority name. He further claims that Falwell did not even know how to spell abortion when he recruited him. [92] When Falwell dropped out of politics in the late '80s, Weyrich sought out another Protestant to take his place in order to continue the ecumenical activity called for in the Pastoral Plan: Pat Robertson.

Weyrich is deeply involved in the Christian Coalition and planned to serve as a faculty member at 70 Christian Coalition "leadership schools" in 1994. [93] Weyrich's Free Congress Foundation is one of the most strident Catholic organizations in the U.S. Weyrich also supports a Center for Catholic Policy and he formed the Siena Group, a coalition of 40 Roman Catholic public policy organizations in 1988. That's right—40.

Catholic leadership of Robertson's so-called Protestant network is clearly established. In an April 1993 article in *Church & State* magazine, Joseph L. Conn reveals the close connections between Weyrich and other Catholic activists and Robertson. Marlene Elwell, co-founder of the Catholic Campaign, has long been a close ally of Robertson. In 1985, she went to work for Robertson's first political unit, the Freedom Council. In 1988, she was active in Robertson's presidential campaign. In 1989, she was hired by Domino Pizza magnate and Catholic activist Tom Monaghan to manage Legatus, a Catholic businessmen's group. (Membership is limited to Catholics who head corporations with at least $4 million in annual revenues.) [94]

Thomas Patrick Monaghan (no relation to the pizza magnate) is senior counsel of Robertson's American Center for Law and Justice (ACLJ). Monaghan, based in New Hope, Kentucky, is a staffer of Free Speech Advocates, a legal firm sponsored by Catholics United for Life. Free Speech Advocates is a lay division of the Dominicans.

As noted earlier, Catholic activist Keith Fournier heads Robertson's American Center for Law and Justice and also serves on the Catholic Campaign's national committee. [95]

In the same article, Conn discusses another Weyrich enterprise: National Empowerment Television (NET), initiated in 1991 and now a 24-hour-a-day, 7-day-a-week "conservative news and entertainment television network" which is more accurately described as a Papal propaganda machine. Says Conn, "[NET] allows leaders of the conservative movement to talk directly with grassroots activists via satellite-hookup television and stir them to action. Allies across the country meet at a chosen site, and a nearby satellite dish beams Washington figures into the room for a 'live' conversation." According to Weyrich, NET has already resulted in some political victories. Joining Weyrich on the NET board is fellow Catholic extremist William Bennett and Robertson honcho Ralph Reed.

According to Conn, "Roman Catholics are playing a crucial part in providing Robertson's forces with political respectability and expertise, legal assistance and high-tech communications support....Simply put, the emerging alliance between these Protestant and Roman Catholic conservatives links Pat Robertson's grassroots army—estimated at 350,000—with the Catholic right's wealth, political expertise and high-tech capabilities." [96] It also gives that very desirable Protestant look to the movement as sought by the bishops' Pastoral Plan.

CHRISTIAN COALITION

In seven years, the Christian Coalition has matured into a major political player. According to Adelle M. Banks of the Catholic News Service, the 33 year-old Reed built the organization from the grassroots network left over from Robertson's failed 1988 presidential campaign. Beginning with a staff comprised of himself, his wife and a part-time secretary, by late 1990, the coalition had 125 local chapters and 57,000 members. In 1994, it claimed a membership of 1.5 million in 1,500 local chapters that distributed 33 million election guides on candidates' positions in November 1994.[96a] It is fantasy to think that Reed accomplished this considerable feat in 6 years single handedly. He obviously had enormous help from numerous

people with exceptional organizational skills and infinite resources—like those found in the Catholic Church.

Time magazine discussed plans for Coalition with Ralph Reed:
"Though [Reed] says he dislikes the word control, dominance of the
G.O.P. remains the movement's ultimate objective."

"He speaks about forming a cadre of at least 10 workers in each
of the country's roughly 175,000 political precincts, raising his
budget to between $50 million and $100 million and gaining access
to 100,000 churches, compared with his current reach of 60,000
churches."[96b]

How large is the Christian Coalition? According to *Time* magazine it has a $25 million annual budget[96b] and claims 1.8 million
members. But a recent investigation by the Americans United for
Separation of Church and State found that the Coalition's "magazine had a paid circulation of 310,296 in September 1995, down from
a reported 353,703 in September 1994. The magazine is mailed to all
with a $15 per year membership. Americans United executive
director Barry Lynn rejects the 1.8 million claim: "If you're not
willing to support them with $15 or more a year, you're not much
of a member or supporter."[96c]

It probably makes little difference. If it has 300,000 or 400,000
members, the number is sufficient to achieve its goals. The important question is what proportion of these 300,000+ members is
Catholic? Later we will discuss a claim by Maureen Roselli that the
Coalition has 250,000 Catholic members. Are they in the majority?
Are they the most dedicated workers and, if so, what proportion of
them are full-time paid staff in Catholic institutions? It is likely that
much of the work of the Coalition, even in targeting Protestants, is
accomplished by thousands of paid employees of the Catholic
Church.

The evidence continues to mount that the Christian Coalition is
fundamentally Catholic—not Protestant. For example, Catholic
Georgetown University political science professor Mary Bendyna
told the Religious News Service that she was surprised to find, even
before the creation of the Catholic Alliance, that all five staffers in
the Christian Coalition's Washington, D.C. Office are Catholic.

According to the National Catholic Register newspaper, the
October 1995 Christian Coalition "Road to Victory" conference
"had a distinctly Catholic flavor. As in the past, former Pennsylvania Gov. Robert Casey and former Education Secretary William

Bennett gave keynote addresses. Father Jerry Pokorsky, a leader in the fight against inclusive language in religious texts, and two other priests offered invocations at different times. Catholic presidential candidates Alan Keyes and Patrick Buchanan were crowd favorites."[96d]

Robertson has always had a close relationship with the Catholic Church. Prof. Charles Rice of Notre Dame University once recommended that the pope be given the power to approve all aspects of "natural law" that is binding on people and government. In October 1981, Robertson called for a new constitutional amendment to guarantee "religious liberty." The following year, his first political group, the Freedom Council, announced that it was working with Rice on the wording for the new amendment.[96e]

Church & State Managing Editor Joseph L. Conn recently observed: "John Paul's political views also find some overlap with Robertson's...John Paul urged his listeners to defend the right of churches to play a role in politics and resist those who would 'establish secularism as America's official religion.' American political life, he insisted, must include 'biblical wisdom.' ...Robertson...insists that government must enforce 'God's law.'"[96f]

Had Prof. Bendyna known the true history of the creation of the Christian Coalition, she surely would not have been surprised at the composition of the Coalition's Washington office. The exercise of Coalition power is largely reserved for Catholics who are in the organization's hierarchy.

THE CHRISTIAN COALITION'S CATHOLIC ALLIANCE

Since its creation, the press has given Americans the mistaken impression that the Coalition is a Protestant organization. This has never been true. As of September 1995, the Coalition claimed 1.7 million members including 250,000 Catholics. With the help of the news media, it had distanced itself from the Catholic Church just as was called for in the Bishop's Pastoral Plan for Pro-life Activities. By October 1995, it was deemed safe for this "Protestant" organization to more openly identify with Catholics but only as individuals. Reed was very careful to make this distinction: "It is a way for Catholics who hold to these values to have a place that they can call home politically," Reed told the Associated Press. "So I want to make it clear that, although we expect to make the bishops aware of what we're doing, we're not really asking them to bless it or anoint it."[96f]

The time had come to openly identify with the Catholic Church. Indeed, it had become dangerous to continue to conduct business as a "Protestant" organization with all of these Catholics running around. The credibility of the organization was threatened if it continued to represent itself as "Protestant," but it will always be remembered as such. It remains a matter of vital importance to the bishops' goal of giving the right-to-life political movement a "Protestant" appearance.

On October 7, 1995, Pope John Paul II presided at a mass in New York's Central Park attended by an estimated 125,000 people. As a part of the service an ecumenical procession trooped to the papal altar. Pat Robertson had a place at the head of the line. After the mass—and a more intimate meeting with the pope at Cardinal O'Connor's residence, Robertson announced: "Protestants and Catholics are drawing together against a tide of secularism that threatens to engulf our world, and we must join hands together to resist it. We may disagree on particulars, but on the essence of things, we agree." Four days later the Coalition's Catholic Alliance was launched, apparently with the blessing of the pope himself.[96f]

Writing for the *Wanderer*, Paul Likoudis offers an explanation of the origins of the Catholic Alliance: "Doing preparatory work for the new Catholic Alliance is an unpaid coalition volunteer, Catholic layman Gerry Giblin, a 1955 graduate of Holy Cross who spent 30 years in IBM's marketing department. After retiring from IBM last year, he told *The Wanderer*, he approached Ralph Reed...to ask if there was something he could do to help expand the coalition's Catholic base...'My two interests have always been the Church and politics,' Giblin continued. Giblin says he talked Reed into the idea of the Catholic Alliance and then helped him create it."[96g] According to Giblin, the alliance will concentrate on grassroots training and voter identification and membership.[96f]

The alliance is headed by Maureen Roselli, a former National Conference of Catholic Bishops National Right-to-Life Committee staffer and erstwhile campaign director for Congressman Chris Smith (R-N.J.),[96f] a Roman Catholic extremist.

A 1996 membership drive letter signed by Roselli reads: "My name is Maureen Roselli. I am a committed Catholic. And I am the Executive Director of the Catholic Alliance—which is the largest affiliate of the Christian Coalition.... Of Christian Coalition's 1.7 million members, about 250,000 are Catholic—making Catholics the largest Christian denomination represented on Christian Coalition's membership rolls....Our effort to distribute scorecards to 40,000,000 Catholics over the next 12 months is the centerpiece of our National Catholic Alliance Voter Mobilization Campaign....Your participation will help us: (1) send a powerful reminder to Congress and candidates for President that they cannot afford to ignore your concerns—or the concerns of hundreds of thousands of Catholic voters who join with us; (2) identify those Catholic Americans who would like to join with us to help produce a record-breaking turnout of informed Christian and pro-family voters in the 1996 elections."

In her appeal for contributions, the strategy of the Catholic Alliance is laid bare:

* "Achieve our goal of distributing Congressional Scorecards to 40 million Catholics in 1996."

* "Cover our cost to poll millions of Catholics on issues of vital importance to our families and our nation..."

* "...distribute the results to all 535 members of Congress, candidates for Congress, the Presidential candidates and their top advisors, as well as the news media."

* "Mobilize millions of Catholics nationwide to get involved in the political process..."[96h]

The strategy is simple. Unmistakably identify the candidates who share the Alliance's political agenda. Communicate its findings in a clear and concise manner to all Catholics who may vote. Poll millions of Catholics preselected in various ways to maximize returns on its investment. Determine who will vote for the Alliance's candidates by massive polling. Intimidate elected officials with the distribution of the findings of its polls. Through a highly organized and extensive network, contact, perhaps repeatedly, all voters identified through polling who will vote for its candidates and insure that they vote on election day.

This is a proven strategy to win elections. It was precisely how the Christian Coalition acted in 1994 when Republicans who share its agenda swept Congressional elections. This is compelling evidence that a dedicated minority can control elections. Despite efforts to make the Christian Coalition look Protestant, it was created by Catholics to promote Catholic interests and its creators certainly have not relinquished control.

The strategy of the imposition of minority (Catholic) law on the majority through "stamina, smarts and perseverance," while co-opting institutions, is a proven strategy. One cannot help but be impressed by the successes of the Religious Right because it remains a small minority. An October 8, 1995 *New York Times*/CBS poll found that only 13 percent of Catholics and 12 percent of non-Catholics said that they considered themselves a part of the New Right.[96i] The odds that they can succeed in passing their HLA to our Constitution still remain low. However, they are obliged to try if Papal authority is to continue into the 21st century. As this minority of Catholic activists becomes more strident and takes more risks, it will succeed in making more law that will advance papal security interests at the expense of our American security interests. They will no doubt further co-opt our institutions as they make their best effort.

The costs to all Americans of this desperate attempt to save the Papacy already have been great and they are certain to escalate. They are the subject of Chapter 16.

THE CROSS OF PAPAL
INFALLIBILITY

11

11

// THE ONLY way to solve the problem of contraception is to solve the problem of infallibility." [97]

> Hans Küng
> Catholic theologian
> 1979

For me, no other single statement better summarizes the world population problem. To protect the dogma of infallibility, the Vatican has been forced to undermine the political will of governments which have been striving to deal with overpopulation. It has been largely successful in killing the political will to deal with this problem in all countries (where it exists) except in China. And, political will is vital to halting rapid population growth. Thus the dogma of infallibility lies at the very heart of the overpopulation dilemma.

There is wide agreement that the world population problem cannot be successfully dealt with unless we solve the contraception problem. However, there is a nearly total lack of awareness that the problem of contraception is related to the problem of papal infallibility, as noted by Hans Küng above.

There is a time warp involved here—a decisive action, or event, that occurred more than a century ago. It had a direct bearing on the mushrooming of population that didn't really get up to speed until the 1930s. The event was the action of Pope Pius IX and Vatican Council I in 1870. Understanding the principle of infallibility and how it came to pass is essential to understanding the world population problem. This Chapter is devoted to how and why this principle was created and its implications.

For decades, Americans have been subjected to pseudodiscussion of the population problem as American writers and speakers have gone about deflecting attention from the only population issue that really matters—that the Papacy is threatened with annihilation as civil authorities make contraception and abortion legally available to their constituents. We are all deeply indebted to both Hans Küng, arguably the world's leading Catholic theologian, and certainly the best known, and to August Bernhard Hasler, for his book, *How the Pope Became Infallible*.[98] In this Chapter, the wisdom of Dr. Küng's statement will become evident.

THREAT TO THE PAPACY

In Chapter 6, I cite a paragraph from the minority report of Pope Paul VI's Commission on Population and Birth authored in 1966 by the man who latter became Pope John Paul II. This paragraph shows with great clarity the real motivation of the Papacy: institutional survival. It is so important, I repeat it here:

> "If it should be declared that contraception is not evil in itself, then we should have to concede frankly that the Holy Spirit had been on the side of the Protestant churches in 1930 (when the encyclical Casti connubii was promulgated), in 1951 (Pius XII's address to the midwives), and in 1958 (the address delivered before the Society of Hematologists in the year the pope died). It should likewise have to be admitted that for a half a century the Spirit failed to protect Pius XI, Pius XII, and a large part of the Catholic hierarchy from a very serious error. This would mean that the leaders of the Church, acting with extreme imprudence, had condemned thousands of innocent human acts, forbidding, under pain of eternal damnation, a practice which would now be sanctioned. The fact can neither be denied nor ignored that these same acts would now be declared licit on the grounds of principles cited by the Protestants, which popes and bishops have either condemned or at least not approved."[43]

The pope's claim that "morality" demands that the Church maintain its current position on contraception is merely deception.

This will become evident as we discuss the doctrine of papal infallibility and the doctrine of primacy of the pope, and why they are vital to the survival of the institution of the Papacy itself.

HISTORY OF THE POPE'S INFALLIBILITY

Two dogmas were proclaimed at Vatican Council I on July 18, 1870 and they are linked. The dogma of the primacy of papal jurisdiction means that the pope has universal jurisdiction. He has "direct sovereignty over the entire church": [99] "The pope can intervene authoritatively at any time in any situation in any diocese, and in every instance where the pope intervenes the bishops are obliged to obey and submit to his decisions." [100] The bishops were at that moment, according to Küng, reduced to mere lackeys of Rome, [101] and this arrangement continues to this day.

The second dogma proclaimed that day, the dogma of papal infallibility, means that the pope is incapable of error when he makes *ex cathedra* decisions on matters of faith and morals. However, virtually all matters, including political, social and economic, can be framed in terms of faith and morals. Hasler describes this dogma as elastic, meaning that it expands and contracts. Whenever it seems opportune, infallibility, thanks to its vagueness, can be stretched far beyond the limits of *ex cathedra* decisions. The ordinary papal teaching now becomes infallible too. In a sense, such "infallible" decisions are much more important to the Vatican and the Church's bureaucratic machine than the rare *ex cathedra* declarations. The aura of infallibility counts more than its actual use. [102] Papal infallibility means that the pope has an interpretive monopoly. He no longer needs the Church's approval. His decisions are beyond appeal.

Infallibility was first attributed to the pope in 1279 by a Franciscan priest. [103] In 1324 Pope John XXII condemned this idea as the work of the devil [104] (which may explain why Pope John XXIII chose this name, the first in 550 years, and then set about ignoring the dogma of infallibility). Later on, in their struggle against Protestantism, popes once more considered infallibility a practical weapon. [105] In 1800, papal infallibility was still generally rejected except in Italy and Spain. [106] Pope Gregory XVI (1831-46) was the first pope to claim that popes were infallible. His encyclical, *Mirari*, also viewed freedom of conscience as "a false and absurd concept," indeed a mad delusion. According to him, freedom of the press could never be sufficiently abhorred. [107]

Pope Pius IX (1846-78), was absolutely committed to making papal infallibility a dogma. Indeed, it is unlikely that it would have ever become a dogma had it not been for this man. In his first encyclical letter (1846), he laid implicit claim to infallibility. [108] In 1854 Pius IX, on his own authority, elevated the doctrine of Mary's Immaculate Conception—the belief that the mother of Jesus was born without any stain of original sin—to the status of dogma. [109] With this act, he had de facto demonstrated his own infallibility.

PAPACY FACED EXTINCTION IN 1870

The times set the stage for Pius IX to act. The Papacy seemed to be facing extinction. [110] The Church was under siege from many different forces: secularization, liberalism, rationalism and naturalism. The French Revolution had changed the Catholic world permanently.

Pius IX was responding to several events of the times. It is believed that he wished to extend his spiritual jurisdiction as compensation for his loss of secular power because of the loss of the Papal States. [111] He believed that the principle of authority would counteract the principles of the French Revolution. He desperately needed to contain the forces of unbridled journalism which were wreaking havoc. [112] There was a hope that this principle of authority would bring about the return of lands already lost by the Papacy. The French Revolution destroyed centuries old patterns of Church government, [113] threatening the very existence of the Church.

The Church no longer had at its disposal the option of physical coercion that ranged from detention to annihilation, which was not infrequently used by the pope. For example, in "1868 Pius IX ordered the Italian revolutionaries, Monti and Tognetti beheaded in the Piazza del Popolo for attempting to blow up a papal barracks. And just two weeks before Rome was taken by storm, a certain Paolo Muzi was hanged in Frosinone, the last citizen of the Papal States to be executed." [114] This hanging took place just 6 weeks after papal infallibility became a dogma. With great disappointment, the pope knew the power he derived from the threat of annihilation was rapidly coming to an end.

Professor Vaillancourt, cited in Chapter 6, states, "...it has become increasingly difficult to enforce unpopular decisions through coercion and exclusion. Consequently, the Vatican must now try to exercise its control over Catholics through normative and manipulative means (e.g., through socialization and co-optation) rather than through coercive and repressive power....The declaration of papal infallibility...was an important milestone in that direction. The stress on the absolute authority of the pope in questions of faith and morals helped turn the Church into a unified and powerful bureaucratic organization, and paved the way for the establishment of the Papacy-laity relationship as we know it today." [115]

In his encyclical Quanta Cura (1864), Pius IX had listed eighty contemporary errors and condemned them. This is referred to as the Syllabus of Errors. In it he condemned many of the freedoms Americans hold dearest: freedoms of conscience, speech, the press, and religion. He rightfully recognized that American style democracy gravely threatened the Papacy. (If Americans are permitted to exercise these rights, American democracy may yet bring about the extinction of the Papacy.) The Syllabus was the definitive challenge to the modern state. [116]

With the Syllabus and numerous actions, the pope set the stage for his counterattack against the modern world and all that was threatening the Church. Now he needed the authority to carry out his wide ranging plan.

Pius IX felt that he must acquire absolute authority over the entire Church if the Papacy was to survive. Even in the early days of his Papacy, he was untrusting of his bishops to hold the line against these threats, so he forbade the formation of national bishops' conferences and directed that there be as little contact as possible between bishops. They were to communicate with Rome. For this reason, Pius IX introduced the obligation of regular visits to the Holy See, a practice that still continues. Control was the objective. All bishops had to administer their diocese in strict subordination to the pope under the threat of coercion. [117]

PIUS IX, THE MAN

To understand what really brought about proclamation of the dogmas of papal primacy and infallibility, we must take a close look at the man himself. Hans Küng describes Pius IX as follows: "Pius

IX had a sense of divine mission which he carried to extremes; he engaged in double-dealing; he was mentally disturbed; and he misused his office." [118]

Hasler describes Pius IX in detail. In 1850, Pius IX branded freedom of the press and freedom of association as intrinsically evil. He determined that liberalism (out of which American democracy grew) was the mortal enemy of the Papacy and the Church. His rule was reactionary and dictatorial. His followers' practices bordered on papolatry. The most eminent bishops of the time viewed him as a great disaster for the Catholic Church. [119] He struck "many people as dangerous above all because he wished to dogmatize a teaching which, from a historical standpoint, was worse than dubious and which overturned the Church's basic organization." [120] In their eyes, these dogmas "would deprive the Catholic Church of the last shred of credibility." [121] In the end, it looks as if this assessment of these bishops is proving to be correct. (More on credibility later.)

According to Hasler, Pius IX had surrounded himself with mediocre, unbalanced, sometimes even psychologically disturbed people. [122] His fury in private audiences would become so violent that older prelates might suffer heart attacks. He was described as having a heart of stone and at times normal feelings of affection, gratitude, and appreciation would be totally absent—heartless indifference. [123]

Hasler describes a series of bizarre incidents: "In all these episodes Pius IX showed quite clearly how out of touch he was with reality. [124] Many bishops had the impression that the pope was insincere, that he was striving to get infallibility approved by the use of trickery and cunning. In the presence of many witnesses, one bishop called him false and a liar. [125]

The historian Ferdinand Gregorovius noted in his diary, "The pope recently got the urge to try out his infallibility....While out on a walk he called to a paralytic: 'Get up and walk.' The poor devil gave it a try and collapsed, which put God's vicegerent very much out of sorts. The anecdote has already been mentioned in the newspapers. I really believe that he's insane." [126]

Hasler states, "Some, even bishops, thought he was mad or talked about pathological symptoms. The Catholic Church historian Franz Xavar Kraus noted in his diary: 'Apropos of Pius IX, Du Camp agrees with my view that ever since 1848 the pope has been both mentally ill and malicious.'" [127]

The most distinguished bishops viewed Pius IX as "the greatest danger facing the Church...." They felt powerless struggling with a pope who was possessed by his monomania and not accessible to rational arguments. "'Oh, this unfortunate pope,' wrote Felix Dupanloup in his diary. 'How much evil he has done!...I mean, he has delivered the Church into the hands of these three or four Jesuit professors who now want to inflict their lessons on him!...This is one of the greatest dangers the Church has ever known.'" [128]

Hasler asked the question: Was the pope mentally competent during Vatican Council I? "Many of his personality traits suggest that this was not the case. The unhealthy mysticism, the childish tantrums, the shallow sensibility, the intermittent mental absences, the strangely inappropriate language...and the senile obstinacy all indicate the loss of a solid grip on reality. These features suggest paranoia." [129]

THE LEGACY OF PIUS IX

The leadership entrusted the future of the Church to this man. But as we continue to permit papal influence in public policy-making to spread worldwide, we are allowing Pius IX's legacy—the legacy of an unbalanced man—to determine the future of our planet even as we approach the end of the 20th century. In significant ways, our behavior today is being determined by the actions of Pius IX of 125 years ago.

Furthermore, the dogmas of infallibility and papal primacy ended any semblance of democracy in the church, and no self correction can be expected, no matter how insane the Church policy on overpopulation has become.

THE DOGMAS' IMPORTANCE TO SOME CATHOLICS

Infallibility made Roman Catholicism even more attractive to many. People often seek religion because of their fear of uncertainty and the unknown in their lives and in death. It provides emotional relief. According to Hans Küng, "Infallibility performed the function of a metadogma, shielding and insuring all the other dogmas (and the innumerable doctrines and practices bound up in them). With infallibility—and the infallible aura of the 'ordinary,' day-to-day magisterium is often more important than the relatively rare infallible definitions—the faithful seemed to have been given a superhuman protection and security, which made them forget all fear of human uncertainty...In this sense the dogma of infallibility has undoubtedly integrated the lives of believers and unburdened their minds..." [130] So now the Church offers a final, unsurpassable guarantee of security to believers. This is a powerful attraction to all who fear insecurity—which includes most of us. Infallibility provided many believers with a great sense of religious security all through life, imparting stability and freedom from anxiety, relieving emotional pressure and softening the cruel blows of reality. [131]

On the other hand, the dogma of infallibility is binding on the conscience of the entire Catholic world. According to Hasler, "For the Roman Catholic Church, the dogmas defined by the Council are strictly obligatory. Anyone who doesn't accept them is threatened with excommunication, that is, with exclusion from the Catholic community." [132]

INFALLIBILITY'S IMPORTANCE TO THE POPE

The dogma of Papal infallibility was important to the pope and the Vatican in many ways. States Küng, "[It] most effectively furthered the unity, uniformity, and power of Roman Catholicism." [133] Enhancement of the power of the Church was an important motivating factor. Indeed all three of these outcomes were vital if the Papacy was to avoid extinction. He says, "What could be better for legitimizing, stabilizing, and immunizing this system against criticism than the dogma of the infallibility of its highest representative(s)?" [134]

The Church still derives enormous power from the claim of infallibility. "Paul VI laid aside his tiara" writes Hasler. "Both his successors, John Paul I and John Paul II, dispensed with the throne and crown. But the pope's claim to infallibility has remained, and hence so has their position of power. For power was the issue in 1870..." [135] But, if the essential foundation of the Church laid by the dogma of infallibility is destroyed, faith collapses and the whole Church will crumble. [136] For this reason, it is imperative to the Vatican that this dogma be protected.

Hasler describes in two paragraphs [137] why infallibility was important to both the leadership and their followers. "...in the Middle Ages there was a conspicuous trend to look for an infallible authority, whether it be pope or council, to buttress the great edifice of the Catholic system. Its original religious power had been lost, and yet the entire social structure still rested on religion as much as ever. Behind the perfectly intact facade doubts and uncertainty began to spread. Signs of disintegration became apparent in philosophy and theology. The old spontaneity and unquestioning naturalness of the faith were largely gone. The quest for infallibility looks like a desperate attempt to recover a lost sense of security.

"The endeavor to shore up doctrinal structures was unusually momentous because religion still played such a unique part in most people's lives. Their personal happiness depended on it, first of all in this world, and still more in the next. The great majority of the population had neither the skill nor the desire to judge questions of faith: They wanted to rely on authorized teachers. This only heightened the power and influence of the religious elite, which held the fate of so many in its hand. This arrangement thoroughly suited the mutual interest of both groups. Only those who could offer certainty in matters of salvation would be of any use to the people of that time. And so it didn't sound like blasphemy when men of the Church appeared, claiming they had been given all power in heaven as well as on earth (Boniface VIII)."

The promoters of the infallibility dogma believed that by raising the pope's authority to its upward limit they could gradually break society of its liberal and democratic tendencies.[138] A bishop of that day describes the advocates' position, "The great evil of our day is that the principle of authority lies prostrate. Let us strengthen it in the Church and we shall save society." Stated one supportive newspaper of the day: "The infallible pope must counteract and cure the prevailing abuses of unbridled freedom of the press, thanks to which journalists daily spread lies and calumny." [139]

THE POWERLESS PRESS

According to Hasler, "The plan was to enhance the pope's authority as much as possible, not only in hopes of strengthening the old hierarchical order within the Church but, above all, in society at large." [140] This objective was largely achieved, especially in the United States, as bishops and lay Catholics marched in lock-step until 1968 when the encyclical *Humanae Vitae* was issued.

During the period 1870 to 1968, the American press was almost completely tamed.

The Knights of Columbus, the largest organization of Catholic laity in the world, was founded soon after the dogma of infallibility was adopted (1882) by a priest in New Haven, Connecticut. The mission: protect the faith. By 1914, the Knights had evolved into a national organization with considerable capability to intimidate those who spoke out against the Church regardless of whether the criticisms were justified. They created the Commission on Religious Prejudices, chaired by Patrick Henry Callahan, to shut down the press criticism of the Church. According to their 1915 report, the Commission sponsored an education campaign by "informing and correcting editors and journalists who allowed religious prejudices to surface in their newspapers." Callahan pointed out that between August 1914 and January 1917, the number of publications which published material critical of the Church dropped nationwide from 60 to two or three.[141]

Until this time, the American press was free to be critical of the pope, the Vatican and the bishops, who are undeniably agents of a foreign-controlled power. But since the days of Callahan's Commission, the American press has not been free to report on the considerable political activities, and, most important, the motivations behind those activities. As a result, few Americans are aware of just how much their access to information is restricted by the Church. For example, recently, New York's *Newsday*, following an investigation, reported that at least 83 percent of the income of the New York City Archdiocese comes from local, state and federal taxes.[142] Separation of Church and State? How did this come to pass? We will never know. But the pope's authority in both New York and Washington was vital. There was never any follow-up. And this article never appeared in any other newspaper in the country or in the news on television or radio. Is this a state church or a church state? It seems like one or the other. Eighty-three percent of the budget surely makes this so. The American press is not free to discuss these matters.

Mainstream media never identify arson and bomb attacks against abortion clinics as domestic terrorism. Doing so would be greatly to the disadvantage of the bishops. Since 1982, according to the Bureau of Alcohol, Tobacco and Firearms, there have been 169 such attacks in 33 states on women's health centers where abortions were performed. On April 20, 1995, the *New York Times*, reporting on the Oklahoma City Federal Office Building bombing, ran a list headlined "Other Bombings in America," which spanned four decades and included some attacks that claimed no injuries or lives. But none of the 40 officially documented bombings that have targeted women's clinics in that period were mentioned. Why?

For the year before the Oklahoma City bombing, Planned Parenthood's Fred Clarkson had communicated their research findings on anti-abortion militants and extremist militias. Just after the bombing, when it became evident that this was an act of a domestic terrorist, Clarkson was invited by a major cable network to appear in their broadcast. Just fours hours before his scheduled appearance, the invitation was rescinded by the news producer. Clarkson told *EXTRA!*: "He said they couldn't have someone from Planned Parenthood on about militias, because they'd have angry pro-life viewers calling in and they didn't want to take that heat."[142a]

Another example is Oliver North's religious affiliation. The press has gone to great lengths to give the impression that Oliver North is a Protestant fundamentalist. Everyone I have ever asked "knew" that he is a Protestant. Most of his political support in Virginia is coming from southern Protestants and if he is elected to the Senate this year, it will be because of that support. But North is a devout Catholic. This fact was reported by both the Wall Street Journal [143] and The Christian Science Monitor [144] in 1986. Other newspapers and the electronic media have avoided this fact. North would lose many votes and support if this fact becomes widely known and many voters do want to know. But the press is not free to ask Mr. North how his conservative Catholic views might affect his voting behavior in the Senate, and this Fall's voters won't know. Infallibility did dramatically strengthen the pope's authority in the United States. The American press is very reluctant to resist his authority. Chapters 13 and 14 are devoted to the documentation of this reality.

The free presses of Europe and North America were gravely undermining papal authority. The proponents of the doctrine of papal infallibility were convinced that this doctrine would lead to control of the world press on matters vital to papal authority. The control of individuals in the press, as well as individuals who could be used to manipulate the press in various ways, including intimidation, in order to protect papal authority, was a key argument for adoption. The proponents were correct on this account as we shall see in Chapters 13 and 14.

The dogma of infallibility is important because it shields the entire doctrinal structure of the Catholic Church from criticism. According to Hasler, "This claim extends not to one doctrinal statement but to all of them; it covers every single one. Papal infallibility—the formal principle, as it were, of Catholicism—becomes the crowning conclusion of the system. The insurance policy is flawless: There can be no appeal from the pope to any other authority....Presupposing the fundamental principle of infallibility, the Church's entire operation can run smoothly."[145]

Absolute control of the entire Church structure by a despotic pope was made much easier by this dogma. The majority rule on questions of dogma that had existed for nearly 2000 years ended the day infallibility officially became dogma.[146]

A NEW IMAGE FOR THE POPE

Papal infallibility and universal jurisdiction resulted in a new image for the pope—which was quite intentional. He became God's representative on earth. Pius IX also became an idol and papolatry came so much into vogue that even many of his supporters were embarrassed.[147] He was now referred to as "exalted king," "most beloved of kings," "supreme ruler of the world," king of kings," and "vice-God of humanity."[148] This of course was the desired outcome. One journal wrote, "When the pope meditates, it is God who thinks in him." St. John Bosco referred to the pope as "God on earth" and asserted: "Jesus has put the pope on the same level as God." [149]

The school of thought that worked so diligently to achieve a favorable vote of the bishops at Vatican Council I was referred to as the Infallibilists. It was their view that "the Church, as a community incapable of erring in matters of faith, had to have an infallible leader and judge. Otherwise it would not be safe from error, it would lack both unity and order, and it would be vulnerable to fragmentation, as could be seen so clearly in Protestantism." [150] And they had a second line of thinking similarly based on papal primacy. "Since the pope had a universal jurisdiction and therefore the supreme teaching authority, he had to be infallible. Otherwise he might lead all the faithful into error, carrying the entire Church with him into the abyss, since all Catholics were obliged to obey him on questions of faith."[151]

The Jesuits were the chief manipulators in the campaign for papal infallibility.[152-155] Apparently, the Jesuits felt that their never ending political agenda would be best served if the pope became an infallible despot. The Jesuits were chosen to write the official history of Vatican Council I some 20 years later.[156-157]

More than anything else, even the manipulation of the bishops by the Jesuits, it was the fear of schism, that was considered a worse misfortune than infallibility, that kept the bishops in line.[158] A schism did occur but unfortunately for America and the rest of humanity it was small, resulting in the creation of what is known today as the Old Catholic Church.[159]

THE DISSENTERS' PREDICTIONS COME TRUE

Negative reactions to the two new dogmas was extensive—and most telling. The impact of these two dogmas in 1994 on virtually everyone on this planet, Catholic and non-Catholic, is enormous and will be discussed later. These reactions at the time are important to us today and should be examined. The apocalyptic predictions of the dissenters are now coming true.

Hasler notes that even at the Vatican Council some individuals perceived this claim of infallibility—this claim to total truth—would ultimately be self-destructive: "The Papacy, they thought, had gone down a blind alley from whence there could be no escape without a critical loss of authority. 'The results of the Vatican decree of 1870 are only now beginning to come to light,' the Catholic Church historian Franz Xaver Kraus noted in his diary on February 9, 1900. 'Rome has locked the door leading to its only way out. There seems to be nothing left but for the whole papal system to break down.'" [160]

The Swiss theologian Hans Urs von Baltha called the Vatican dogma a "gigantic disaster." [161] One bishop described the pope as "an authority subject to no other control than his own whims and preferences. The new dogma, he felt, must lead to despotism." [162] Wrote Henri Icard, a priest, "This is truly a difficult situation for the Church. The most absolute power—in the hands of a man who will only listen to the people who think—or, rather, speak—the way he does." [163] The French bishops, in a minority petition, wrote, "The new dogma, which must lead to such grave consequences, is de-manded of a Council which is both deeply divided and not free." [164] Different bishops referred to the new dogmas in the following way: "the Vatican farce," "the pope is devouring us," "we have to eat what we have vomited up," "a crime against the Church and humanity." [165] Says Hasler, "For them [the Council minority], the credibility of the Church was on the line." [166] Professor Friedrich Michelis described Pius IX as a "heretic and devastator of the Church." Neither his cardinal nor his bishop contradicted him. [167]

An English bishop wrote, "The bishop of St. Gall was so violent in his speech against infallibility that through the very force of his enunciation he lost a false tooth. He had to pick it up from the ground and put it back into place before he could go on." [168] One archbishop "viewed the fetishist adoration of the Church's hierar-chy (and especially of the pope) as the chief error of Catholicism....It had, he said, transformed the office of the supreme shepherd into a despotic sultanate of Mohammed and Christ's sheepfold into a herd of slaves." [169]

In German-speaking countries alone, twenty professors of the-ology and clerical teachers of philosophy were excommunicated within a short time after the Council. Two-thirds of all Catholic historians teaching at German universities left the Church." [170]

But there is no turning back. Says Icard, "To affirm that the Council lacked the freedom necessary to validate its ordinances is impossible....Under no circumstances would God abandon his Church in such a way that we should one day be justified in going back and questioning what the great majority of the bishops, to-gether with the pope, decided on matters of faith!...Can we run the risk of such a scandal? And what would then become of the Holy Church?" [171]

Objections to the adoption of the dogmas of papal primacy and infallibility were extensive, thoughtful and loud but to no avail. We can be certain that the Church, as an institution, will become extinct before these two dogmas are terminated.

CONSEQUENCES FOR CATHOLICISM AND HUMANITY

These two dogmas produced vast consequences for both the institution and for virtually all of us who now inhabit this planet. Had these two dogmas not been proclaimed, life on this earth would be both far less threatened and less threatening. There is much evidence that rational responses to these threats would have begun occurring decades ago.

In a couple of paragraphs, Hasler provides an overview of these consequences: "The Church not only missed its chance for a rapprochement with scientific scholarship...[it became] an obstacle to cultural evolution and an enemy of the unprejudiced search for truth. It is hard to deny the justice of such complaints—the way the dogma came to be defined would be proof enough....The dogma of infallibility was not just one more doctrine among many others. It took a comprehensive position on the issue of truth. It involved a very broad claim, namely, that the pope could pronounce on questions of faith and morals with guaranteed certainty. The truth was no longer to be brought to light by laborious research and investigation but by the determination of an infallible authority."[172]

"The Church does indeed gain, at first, in unity and uniformity, but it blocks off its own free access to the real world and ultimately stands in danger of losing touch with reality completely....On the one hand, Catholicism gains in...political muscle; on the other, its conflict with science grows more intense. Its dogmatic commitments make it harder for the Church to adapt to circumstances; they lessen its flexibility and the chances for reform. The Church loses it credibility with many people and draws in on itself. This increases the danger of its stiffening into a sect and forfeiting its potential for social renewal. The machine may still remain intact, and the power structure may continue to stand firm, but the life has gone out of it."[173] Hasler has described the Church as we find it in 1996.

The Church did gain in unity and uniformity. At least this applies to all those people who really matter: those who blindly support the pope, either because of faith or opportunity, including all cardinals and bishops, most priests and a relatively small fraction of the laymen. The Papacy has acquired enormous political muscle as a result of these two dogmas. The political muscle that was needed to halt NSSM 200 in its tracks and bury it for almost two decades is truly impressive. In the April 25, 1993 issue of The Independent On Sunday published in London, Mark Hertsgaard states, "The Vatican has managed to derail every international effort to curb the population explosion," despite the fact that we are overwhelmed with evidence that the population explosion gravely threatens almost every thing we value. This accomplishment has required enormous political muscle.

Indeed, the machine remains intact and the power structure continues to stand firm in significant part because of the influence through Catholics within the U.S. government and its ability to use the U.S. government as an instrument to impose papal policy on the UN system and other international organizations and on many national governments either through rewards, punishment or threat of force. The fact that the Church has been permitted to accumulate enormous wealth has also been vital to keeping its machine and power structure intact. In the 1980s, the Chicago Sun newspaper, following an investigation, estimated the net worth of the Church in the U.S. at more than $200 billion. Its worth world-wide has been estimated at $2 trillion.

Science and the Vatican are enemies. The Church ignores the findings of science when their acknowledgment threatens to under-mine papal authority. The best examples are the innumerable findings of science which show that overpopulation is causing often permanent degradation of our planet and reducing the number of people Earth can support on a sustainable basis. The Church sets about deliberately undermining the credibility of science in its desperate attempt at institutional survival. As a result of the Vati-can's efforts to survive the onslaught of these findings, we are all continuously bombarded with disinformation which seeks to throw these findings into question. But science continues, on nearly a daily basis, to produce alarming evidence that the Church's position on family planning and contraception is indefensible.

Each day the physical potential for human life support is dimin-ished by abuse of our planet, and much of this loss is probably permanent. As a result, every day the number of people that Earth ultimately will be able to support on a sustainable basis grows smaller. This fact alone makes the bishops' claims of "concern for human life" and defense of "right-to-life" absurd. Their policies are destroying the earth's physical ability to provide for human needs.

The charge by Hasler that these dogmas have stifled intellectual development by Roman Catholics is supported by two prominent Catholics in the United States. On November 11, 1988, Jesuit theo-logian Father Avery Dulles spoke to the Washington Chapter of the Catholic League for Religious and Civil Rights. Says Dulles (son of John Foster Dulles), himself widely regarded as a leading light in

U.S. Catholic intellectual life for more than three decades, "In spite of our many Catholic schools, colleges and universities we have as yet very few eminent Catholic intellectuals on the national scene....Catholics, whether clerical or lay, are not prominent in science, literature, the fine arts, or even, I think, in the performing arts and communications." [174]

Dulles reopened a theme first argued in depth in the mid-1950s by Church historian Msgr. John Tracy Ellis: "That U.S. Catholics have failed to achieve a leadership stature in U.S. intellectual and public life commensurate with their numbers, wealth and organizational strength." Ellis said he "would basically agree" with Dulles's analysis of the current situation and that the influence of Catholic leaders has increased substantially in the business and political worlds since the 1950s. But in the field of culture and intellectual life, "I fail to find for the last 35-40 years any widespread love of learning for learning's sake in Catholic circles. I say this with great regret." He went on to say "there is a decided emphasis in Catholic circles on money...[with the result that]...the United States is now teeming with Catholic millionaires." [175]

It is reasonable to assume that the Catholic educational system is devoted to the advancement of the papal agenda in America through the growth of influence in the political system. Advancement in science (which frequently threatens Catholicism) and encouragement of the "love of learning for learning sake" (which also threatens it) are not part of the papal agenda in America. Given the observations of Father Dulles and Msgr. Ellis, it is apparent that the priorities of Catholic schools reflect the papal agenda.

Hasler observed, "...the life has gone out of it."[176] By this he means that the Church no longer has a conscience. Referring to the Church's teaching on contraception, *Humanae Vitae*, Küng states, "This teaching...has laid a heavy burden on the conscience of innumerable people, even in industrially developed countries with declining birthrates. But for the people in many underdeveloped countries, especially in Latin America, it constitutes a source of incalculable harm, a crime in which the Church has implicated itself." [177] The widespread premature death and suffering that the Church has wreaked upon developing world women because of their position on birth control has been a clear indication to millions that the Vatican does not really give a damn about "the little people." Institutional survival, political muscle, and authority dominate the attention of the Church leadership—not "the little people" they claim to protect, many of whom reached this conclusion on their own. For them, the hypocrisy has been too much to stomach and they have left the Church by the tens of millions. The Church's position cannot be reasonably defended.

The evidence supporting Hasler's assessment that these dogmas are resulting in a loss of credibility is overwhelming. The number of young men entering American seminaries has dropped 35 percent since 1977. [177] In 1966, there were 42,767 seminarians. Today, while the Catholic population has increased by more than 50 percent, they number only slightly more than 6,000 in the U.S.[177a] During the 1993-1994 school year there were 6,244 candidates for the priesthood; this year there are 6,030, a drop of 3.4%. For those closest to Ordination, the number of candidates for the priesthood fell over the past year from 2,915 to 2,817.[177b] No end is in sight. Only three percent of American nuns are under age 40 and 37 percent are over age 70.[178] The average age of priests here is 65 years. There are now 20,000 ex-priests—one-half of all U.S. priests quit the priesthood before reaching retirement age,[179] and they represent the best and brightest. Membership in Catholic orders has fallen 40 percent since 1962, while the nation's Catholic population grew by 36 percent.[180] The Vatican now regards North America as a missionary region. Younger priests from Eastern Europe, Africa, Asia and Latin America are being brought in to protect papal interests because American men are shunning the priesthood.[181]

The number of Catholic grade and high schools is down by 30 percent since 1960. [182] This does not bode well for the future of the Church because Catholic schools provide over 90 percent of bishops, 90 percent of sisters and over 85 percent of priests.[183] The number of Catholic general hospitals is down 22 percent in the same period.[184] Only 28 percent of Catholics attend mass on a typical Sunday while 30 years ago mass attendance was more than 70 percent.[185] Catholics contribute only 1.1 percent of their income to the Church while Protestants contribute 2.2 percent; 20 years ago they gave about the same.

In Latin America, Protestant churches are growing swiftly, with as many as 20 percent of Catholics abandoning their church to become members. Latin America represents 48 percent of all Catholics in the world, but it provides only one percent of the missionaries. [186] While Bolivia has been occupied by the Catholic Church for

500 years, yet only five percent of its priests are natives. In Europe, the credibility of the Catholic Church is plummeting. Italy has the lowest birth rate in Europe. Less than 25 percent of the vote is now controlled by the Vatican, compared to a substantial majority in the decades after World War II, and state funded abortions are available to all who want them. In France, only one percent of the population attends mass regularly. In the summer of 1995, a petition calling for drastic changes in the Church collected half a million signatures in Austria, about half of their Catholic churchgoers.[186a] In November 1995, millions of Catholics across Europe—in Germany, Poland and Ireland—sent powerful messages to the Vatican demonstrating that they were prepared not merely to ignore the Church's teachings, but to defy them openly. Poland elected an ex-Communist whom Church leaders called a "neo-pagan." Ireland legalized divorce. In Germany 1.5 million out of five million practicing Catholics signed a petition modeled after the Austrian one.[186b]

Just as predicted in 1870 by the dissenting bishops, the credibility of the Church has been greatly diminished. These statistics are compelling evidence. Likewise, the predicted loss of touch with reality has also come true.

LOSING TOUCH WITH REALITY

Perhaps the most important outcome described by Hasler, the most dangerous outcome, is that the Church has lost touch with reality. There is much evidence of this but none more convincing than Pope Pius XII's proclamation on November 1, 1950 of the new dogma that Mary was assumed into heaven body and soul. In this dogma, the pope declared that "the immaculate Mother of God and ever Virgin Mary was at the end of her life assumed into heaven body and soul." This dogma is based entirely on mythology. The myth was never mentioned in the first five centuries of the Church's existence.

The myth of Mary first appeared in the sixth century in a text. The myth was loaded with grotesque accounts of miracles. According to Hasler, the story goes something like this: "Mary lives in Bethlehem. The archangel Gabriel makes known to her that her end is nigh. At her request all the apostles are brought from all the different countries of the world on a wondrous journey through the clouds to Bethlehem. Numerous miraculous cures take place at

Mary's sickbed. Since danger threatens from the Jews, the Holy Spirit carries Mary and the apostles off on a cloud to Jerusalem..." [187] The story goes on and on.

There were no other historical sources for Mary's Assumption. There was no serious opposition to this infallible proclamation by Pope Pius XII. The story is quite simply preposterous. It is frightening to think that such a thing could happen in 1950. Consider the fact that the entire leadership of the Church in 1950 went along with such nonsense. It is more frightening to recognize that these men, the leadership of the Church in 1996, are making critical decisions that affect all of humanity. It is shocking to be faced with the fact that this leadership was permitted to impose a policy which undermined U.S. political will to deal with the mounting overpopulation threat to U.S. and global security.

After reading the complete 6th century myth which was accepted by the entire leadership of the Church as truth (in my lifetime), I better understand how the Church can continue to ignore the growing mountain of evidence that the planet and humanity are gravely threatened by overpopulation. Bishops in 1870 saw this coming and voiced their concerns. In the last section I quoted Hasler, "...but [the Church] blocks off its own free access to the real world and ultimately stands in danger of losing touch with reality completely."[188] Indeed, it has.

DESPOTIC AUTHORITY

Just as predicted in 1870, these two new dogmas created a system of concentrated despotic authority. The implications for scientific findings and scientific advancement became evident almost immediately. In his 1903 book, *The Church and the Future*, leading English theologian George Tyrell explored the relationship between science and the Church's magisterium or teaching authority. Do science and its representatives enjoy autonomy even within the Church or must they remain forever subordinate to the magisterium? What should be done in case of conflict? Who and what decides when science has come up with unequivocal results which contradict the doctrine or decisions of the Church? [189] These are vital concerns for everyone who seeks a humane solution to the overpopulation problem. Science does have unequivocal results on this question. Who decides? The pope does and he has. He possesses despotic authority and today he is permitted to exercise it.

Catholic insiders are well aware of the despotism of the Papacy, and that the practice of it brings rewards. In 1954, Pius XII canonized Pius X, who had authorized an elaborate system of spies and informers "to ward off modernist errors."[190] His covert methods, including espionage, were discussed at his canonization proceedings. According to Hasler, the prevailing attitude was: "Since the faith of the Church was threatened, all such means seemed justified."[191]

Americans are frequently reminded that the pope's authority is despotic. Wrote Ignaz von Dollinger on March 1, 1887, to the archbishop of Munich, "The new dogmas have come into being thanks to force and coercion. They will also have to be maintained by the constant use of force and coercion."[192] Since the encyclical *Humanae Vitae*, the press with regularity has exposed Americans to acts of repression by the Vatican as it has silenced all of its dissenters, the mark of a successful despot.

INFALLIBILITY COLLIDES WITH CONTRACEPTION

Apparently until the reign of Pope John XXIII, the dogma of infallibility went unchallenged. It appears that John XXIII had plans for this dogma. As noted earlier, even the selection of his name John was suggestive in that Pope John XXII, who had ruled in the early Fourteenth Century, had condemned the concept of infallibility as the work of the Devil. When John XXIII created his Commission on Population and Birth, it was a signal to the world that the Church *could* change its position on birth control. But this would have to be at the expense of the principle of infallibility.

To review the sequence of events discussed in Chapter 6. Pope Paul VI inherited the Commission from Pope John. The Commission consisted of 2 parts—64 laymen in one group and 15 cardinals and bishops in the other. The laymen voted 60 to four and the clerics 9 to 6 to change the Church's position on birth control even though they recognized that this change would diminish papal authority. This vote was leaked to the press, so the whole world knew the outcome of the vote. However, Paul VI rejected the majority position, and accepted the minority view which insisted that to make this change regarding contraception would destroy the fundamental principle of infallibility and with it, the Church itself. Paul VI then issued his encyclical, *Humanae Vitae* (1968), in which the pope condemned practically every form of birth control as morally reprehensible. According to Hasler, "After the promulgation of the encyclical...the Church conducted a massive purge of its key personnel wherever it could."[193]

Thus, contraception represents the first serious threat to the principle of infallibility to emerge. It also represents a great crisis of authority. Though the Vatican would like to think this issue has already been decided, the vast majority of Catholics (and non-Catholics) reject the teaching of *Humanae Vitae*. In 1968 Dutch Bishop Franceos Simons had argued that faith in infallibility was theologically dubious, raising the issue for the first time in decades. Soon after, papal infallibility was questioned by Küng in *Infallible? An Inquiry*.[194] As a result, Küng fell victim to papal repression and was silenced as a Catholic theologian.

Contraception is bringing about an implosion in papal authority. Contraception has resulted in the greatest crisis in the Church since the loss of the Papal States during the time of Vatican Council I in 1870. Very few people are aware of the real motivation for *Humanae Vitae*. But they do recognize that the behavior demanded by this encyclical is not in their best interests—behavior that in the long run will be suicidal for humanity. Contraception has initiated a collapse of the institution from within.

CHANGING THE AMERICAN VIEW OF THE BISHOPS

But more important to us as Americans, this despotic authority exercised by the pope has serious implications for the way in which we should view bishops who serve in America. As mentioned earlier, Küng acknowledged that the dogma of infallibility reduced all bishops to mere lackeys of the pope. Since American security-survival interests, as explored in NSSM 200, and the security-survival interests of the Papacy, as defined by Pope Paul VI and Pope John Paul II, are squarely in conflict, the American bishops cannot possibly represent the interests of both. It is evident they have chosen, without exception, to protect the security interests of the Papacy at the expense of the security interests of the United States. This is not a satisfactory exercise of American citizenship. More accurately, the bishops' behavior is outrageous and unacceptable.

Indeed, it is impossible to imagine how a Catholic bishop could successfully argue that he should be permitted to retain his American citizenship.

This is a dangerous predicament. Andrew M. Greeley is a Roman Catholic priest, best-selling novelist and sociologist at the University of Chicago's National Opinion Research Center. He recently assessed the Vatican's hierarchy appointments in America for the Religion News Service as reported in the *National Catholic Reporter*: "With unrelenting consistency in recent years, the Vatican has appointed to the American hierarchy men who are mean-spirited careerists—inept, incompetent, insensitive bureaucrats who are utterly indifferent to their clergy and laity. In all its 200-year history, the American hierarchy has never been in worse shape. This same policy has been implemented all over the Catholic world in the name of restoring to the church the loyalty of the clergy and people."[194a]

Americans can learn an important lesson from Argentina, a lesson described for the world on March 4, 1995 by a retired Argentinian naval captain, Adolfo Scilingo. During the 1976-1983 "dirty war," which was an uprising against the country's right-wing government and the Catholic Church, an estimated 4,000 dissidents were killed and 10,000 disappeared. Capt. Scilingo reported to an investigating tribunal that between 1,500 and 2,000 dissidents were thrown alive, one at a time, from airplanes at high altitudes into the ocean during 1976 and 1977 on orders from the military high command. He described in chilling testimony how he and another officer helped detainees—many weak from torture—to board the planes. Scilingo revealed that Catholic chaplains comforted military commanders after they flung political dissidents into the ocean from airplanes and that Catholic Church officials provided moral justification for the torture and murder of dissidents during the conflict.[194b]

Hebe de Bonafini, director of the Mothers of the Plaza de Mayo, a human rights group, said the church has much to repent of: "The Church has a great responsibility in everything that happened, because the Church knew that the military chaplains were paid salaries by investigating judges to participate and act in the jails extracting confessions from the prisoners." Church officials have repeatedly denied any involvement in the "dirty war." However, in April 1995, five bishops issued a statement of regret for their roles in the war.[194b]

The same Vatican officials who chose these Argentinian bishops have selected nearly all the bishops serving in the U.S. today—using the very same criteria. Father Greeley's description of the men thus appointed is most revealing. Security-survival of the institution of the Papacy is the most prized ethical value of the men in power (as has been the case for a least a millennium) and all bishops are selected because they rank this ethical value above all others. The Argentine bishops were responding to the threat posed by these dissidents to the security-survival interests of the Vatican.

Throwing young people alive out of airplanes, one by one, over the ocean was justified because this served to protect the interests of the Holy See.

Frances Kissling, president of Catholics for a Free Choice, has followed Cardinal John O'Connor's career for more than two decades: "This is a man who longs for the imperial papacy—a papacy where you had the power to burn people at the stake. When it comes to matters of internal church discipline, he is the toughest, and the meanest."[194c] The *New York Times* reports, "As the Archbishop of the media and cultural center of the United States, Cardinal O'Connor has extraordinary power among Catholic prelates. He travels to Rome and has lunch with the pope on Church business about once a month, and is widely acknowledged to have a great deal of say in the appointment of American bishops."[194c]

Are the bishops in the United States really different from their colleagues in Argentina? Given the descriptions of these men offered by Greeley and Kissling, we wonder. If this could happen in Argentina within the last 20 years, is it not possible in the U.S. today? Are American bishops not responding to dissidents in this cruel manner only because they have not yet acquired sufficient power? They have not ventured to criticize the behavior of their Argentinian counterparts because the Vatican has not instructed them to do so. There can be no doubt that the Argentinian bishops look to Rome for guidance. But after all is said and done, there was no outcry—no condemnation—from the Vatican when their role became public.

A more recent example comes from Rwanda which is predominantly Catholic. Human rights groups have charged that Catholic priests actively encouraged the murderers of more than 500,000

Tutsis in the 1994 warfare.[194d] According to a report issued by the London based Africa Rights seeking the rewards of an intimate relationship with the majority Hutu government, the bishops chose to remain silent.[194e]

KÜNG RECAPS WHERE THINGS STAND NOW

The Church is on an inevitable course of self-destruction as some bishops, theologians and historians predicted in 1870, at the time of the invention of papal infallibility. The Church has reached a dead end, as they predicted, and there is no way out. For 25 years, such a way has been sought. Millions of intelligent sincere Catholics have tried to identify a way out of a position that nearly everyone agrees has become indefensible. No one has succeeded. The Papacy as it exists today is coming to an end.

Küng summarizes where things stand: "There is no dodging the fact that in the Catholic world church history, exegesis, dogmatics, moral theology, and catechesis have all had to pay a high price...for this infallibility, which allowed for no genuine corrections and revisions....It brought on a continual conflict with history and the modern world which profoundly shook the credibility of the Catholic Church; a continual defensiveness towards new information and experiences, towards all scientific criticism, towards all possible enemies, real or imagined. And it created a gap between the Church and modern science....Enormous sacrifices were also indirectly demanded of the 'little people'—in the interests of authority, continuity, and doctrinal infallibility. The ban on contraception is only a particularly striking example of all the burdens placed on the individual conscience by the teaching presented as de facto infallible in catechisms, confessionals, religious instruction, and sermons. The exodus of countless intellectuals, the inner alienation of many believers, the lack of creative people and initiatives in the Church...the psychic disturbances, the loss of touch with reality, the mighty religious machine whose operations very often conceal the absence of inner life...Was all that necessary?" [195]

Küng is describing an institution in an advanced stage of self-destruction. Can this self-destruction be postponed, and if so, how, and for how long? This will be the subject of the next chapter. No doubt, the leadership of the Church will do everything possible to survive. The Church has enormous resources, energy, organization, direction and commitment. Paranoia has already set in. We can expect an ugly defense that will know no bounds until the very end. "This is God's institution and it must be saved at all costs," will be the battle cry in their holy war to insure institutional survival. Should we hasten the self-destruction and how?

POSTPONING SELF-DESTRUCTION OF THE CHURCH

12

12

I *AM convinced that the doctrine of infallibility is in a certain sense the key to the certainty with which the faith is confessed and proclaimed, as well as to the life and conduct of the faithful. For once this essential foundation is shaken or destroyed, the most basic truths of our faith likewise begin to break down."* [196]

> Pope John Paul II
> Excerpt from a letter sent to
> the German Bishops'
> Conference
> May 15, 1980

In this statement, Pope John Paul II acknowledges the obvious. The principle of papal infallibility is now the fundamental principle of the Church. It is the glue that holds all dogma, all Church teachings, together. Without it, the whole Catholic system would disintegrate.

For this reason, the primary focus of the Church bureaucracy is on protection of the principle of infallibility. All else is secondary. If this principle is undermined, the system will self-destruct. We should assume there is nothing these guardians of "God's institution" will not do to protect this principle.

In the last Chapter, I discussed the canonization of Pius X by Pius XII in 1954. During his canonization hearing, it was accepted that Pius X was a despot but the prevailing attitude was: "Since the faith of the Church was threatened, all such means seemed justified." It should be no surprise that the Church bureaucracy position regarding protection of the threatened principle of infallibility is the same. Obviously, all means are justified. However, is it reasonable to aid the Vatican in its quest for institutional survival at all costs? After all, the NSSM 200 researchers determined that our national and global security is gravely threatened by the desperate policies of the Vatican. Yet we are aiding the Vatican in postponing its own self-destruction. This chapter is an inquiry into some of the ways we are contributing to this postponement.

PROCLAIMING THE POPE TO BE THE WORLD'S MORAL LEADER

The Vatican's public attack on contraception has centered on the morality of contraception. Webster's dictionary defines morality as a doctrine or system of ideas concerned with conduct, or a system of principles or rules of proper conduct. For centuries the Church has relentlessly claimed that she is the *only* authority with the right to define this system of rules establishing what is right and what is wrong. This claim goes unchallenged. By default, the pope gets to make all of the rules. He decides what is moral and what is immoral. With amazing frequency, American Presidents and statesmen publicly proclaim, in effect, that the pope is moral leader of the world. By doing so, they enhance the pope's authority and power.

But if the pope must protect the principle of papal infallibility by all means at his disposal, why would he not define the system of rules concerning right and wrong in such a way as to protect his principle of infallibility? In fact, he has. The Papacy has a vested interest in defining the system and a long history of using all means necessary to insure the survival of the institution. In the Catholic system, morality is defined in terms of what will protect the Papacy.

Having been exposed to the living conditions of the world's poorest peoples on numerous occasions, I came to question the pope's system of morals. About 25 years ago, after much observation and thought, I concluded that in the deepest sense it was immoral. I cannot imagine accepting this institution's system of morality. Tens of millions of thoughtful Catholics around the world have reached the same conclusion and have left the Church.

But few speak out. Irish writer Conor Cruise O'Brien is one who has. Referring to the pope in 1980 he writes: "A good man giving bad advice is more dangerous than a nasty man giving bad advice. A good man, whom you believe to be infallible, and who gives you bad advice, can hurt you a lot, and, through you, others." [197] The British novelist and biographer A. N. Wilson, a High Anglican, reviles the pope for his distaste for the intellect: "His hatred of the intellect would appear to know no bounds. Not since the persecution of the modernists in the time of Pius X has the Western Church known such a virulent Inquisition. Any professor of theology who ventures to question the Pope's views has been ruthlessly deprived of his license to teach. Hans Kung, arguably the most distinguished theologian in the world, is only one of hundreds of academics whom the pope has muzzled....the Pope did not interest himself in the truth. If he were an illiterate peasant, this would be a pardonable vice. In an extremely intelligent former university professor, it is sinister."

Wilson continues, "Since he is manifestly intelligent, we must conclude that he knows what he is doing....But as he flies about the world, blessing the sick, kissing babies, and addressing the crowds in their own language, it must give him a very odd feeling to think that so many people accept his outrageous views and claims." [198]

John Paul II does not "interest himself in the truth." Overpopulation is the gravest threat ever faced by our species, but the pope ignores the truth. We acknowledge that this sinister man is the moral leader of the world. We permit him to make the rules in spite of his outrageous views and claims.

Our willingness to publicly accept the pope's views and claims of what is right and what is wrong is serving to postpone the inevitable self-destruction of the Papacy. Our leaders should end this unreasonable practice and let self-destruction take its course.

THE VATICAN'S "HUMAN RIGHTS' AGENDA

The Vatican similarly claims the exclusive right to define human rights. It is obvious that its definition of human rights also has been formulated to meet its institutional needs. For example, 400,000 women die each year as a result of their fertility: Half of them— 200,000—die early, in their teens or 20s, in the course of *wanted* pregnancies or childbirth. Half of them die later in their child-bearing years as a result of *unwanted* pregnancies, after they've achieved their desired family size. It is reasonable that all women should have the human right to avoid premature death posed by their own fertility by any suitable means they choose, including modern methods of contraception and safe and legal abortion. But this very basic human right does not appear on the Vatican's list.

Webster defines fraud to be an act of trickery or deceit, especially when involving misrepresentation; an act of deluding; an intentional misrepresentation, concealment, or nondisclosure for the purpose of inducing another in reliance upon it to part with some valuable thing. The Vatican is clearly committing fraud when it intentionally deceives Catholics and non-Catholics alike by describing their list of human rights, when they full well know the list was formulated in such a way as to protect the institution from self-destruction—by protecting the principle of infallibility. It is obvious to the Vatican leadership that these 200,000 women each year are paying with their lives solely to postpone the self-destruction of the Papacy.

I find this behavior shocking, indeed one of the most offensive attributes of this institution. We have the technology and resources to prevent nearly all of these deaths with little difficulty. But not only does the Vatican exclude this basic human right from its list, it has successfully thwarted all efforts to end these needless deaths by providing contraception and abortion to these women.

All American activities that might lead people to believe that Vatican concerns about human rights are genuine should be suspended—with good reason. The Vatican's incessant cries for "human rights for all" deceives billions of people into thinking that the Vatican is sincere in this concern. The resulting positive image of the Church buys time for the Church by slowing the loss of credibility, postponing self-destruction.

We should not be a party to this obvious deception. We should not, in any way, encourage people to think that the Vatican is the guardian of human rights. The credit fraudulently earned by the Church as a result of our own failure to vigorously challenge the deception will simply postpone the Vatican's self-destruction.

PRIESTS AND NUNS IN A CATCH-22 SITUATION

Frequently I'm attacked for criticizing priests and nuns who are manifestly "good people." The difficulty is that priests and nuns are caught in a wrenching Catch-22 situation. Just my describing this Catch-22 prompts angry responses. Yet the way in which we, as individuals and as a country, deal with their misfortune will determine, in large measure, how long Vatican self-destruction will be postponed.

The Catch-22 goes like this: Priests and nuns do "good works" and earn public credits. "Good works" include a wide range of activities (i.e., working for very low wages providing social services under difficult circumstances, etc.). These public credits are transferable to the hierarchy. The hierarchy can cash them in when needed to advance the Church's agenda. This system has been around for hundreds of years and it is used extensively. This system is frequently referred to by Catholic writers.

For example, the Church can define its system of human rights and leave out a few obvious ones. The Church then announces its system on the world stage and brings along a stack of these public credits and cashes them in to purchase silence from potential critics. Otherwise, they would be laughed off the stage by reasonable people for showing up with a glaringly incomplete list. If they did not have all this credit to cash in, the institution would cease to be credible. Sometimes, the Vatican does not have the credits or it is not willing to cash them in for a particular purpose, and it does lose credibility. Tens of millions of people have left the Church because its credits for good works did not weigh favorably against its discredits for bad or sinister activities undertaken in its attempt to survive.

One of the major problems faced by the Church in the United States is that it has far fewer priests and nuns than it once did to commit to earning these public credits—just at a time when its needs for such credits are exploding. This contributes to the declining credibility of the Church in America.

Priests and nuns who identify themselves as liberal and are pro-family planning and pro-abortion are caught in the Catch-22. The harder they work and the greater their good works, the more sinister behavior (like undermining family planning programs around the world) the pope and bishops can exercise without being called to account by the faithful and non-Catholics alike. Thus, the more good the liberal priests and nuns do, the more harm they do indirectly by providing cover for the sinister activities of their hierarchy. The only way the good efforts of liberal priests and nuns can have a net positive effect for humanity is for them to leave the Church and continue their efforts outside of it. We know that there are more than 20,000 ex-priests in the U.S. today. Many of them left the priesthood because they came to this same conclusion on their own. Liberal priests and nuns serve to postpone the inevitable self-destruction.

Do liberal priests and nuns aid the conservative hierarchy and postpone self-destruction of the institution in other significant ways? Yes, they do. They are vital working parts of the "mighty religious machine." They contribute to keeping the machine intact and aid the power structure in standing firm. Even though they are pro-family planning and pro-abortion, they are vital to the conservative hierarchy and their holy war against U.S. security interests as defined by NSSM 200.

The liberal priests have no power within the Church. They make no Church policy and there is no reason to hope they ever will. All hierarchy members are obedient conservatives and tend to become more conservative and more obedient with time. The grip of the ultraconservative John Paul II and his highly conservative cardinals grows ever tighter on the reins of the Church. There is little chance this grip will be lost. These conservatives will most surely elect another ultraconservative when John Paul leaves the scene. They must. If they do not, the Papacy will self-destruct quickly.

Liberal priests and nuns who believe that they can "change the Church from within" simply do not understand Papal power and the untenable position in which the pope finds himself as he oversees his self-destructing institution. Liberalization spells death for the Papacy. The only constructive action remaining for a liberal priest or nun is to leave the Church and encourage others to join them, thus allowing the inevitable self-destruction to conclude as quickly as possible. Otherwise, they should understand why they are viewed as a threat to U.S. and global security as defined in NSSM 200. By leaving the Church, they can best serve humanity, a conclusion reached by one-third of those ordained since *Humanae Vitae* was promulgated in 1968.

LIBERAL CATHOLICS—PROTECTORS OF THE CONSERVATIVE PAPACY

Often I'm told that I should not speak out against the Church because "I might offend Catholic liberals and if there is hope for change within the Church, it rests with the liberals." Since conservatives are in absolute control regarding the direction of the Church, no one's interests, except the conservatives', is served by pointing to liberals in the Church and saying "but they are on our side." They have no influence on Catholic policy making—and they will have none in the foreseeable future.

As used here, the term liberal Catholic is defined as an American Catholic who does not agree with the papal position on abortion and contraception. According to a well designed study published by Catholic Sociologist Father Andrew Greeley in the Jesuit magazine *America,* liberal Catholics account for 93 percent of all American Catholics! [199] It is stunning and tragic how little influence this overwhelming majority has on the American bishops.

As long as liberal Catholics remain in the Church, they serve the interests of the conservatives by deflecting and confusing forthright criticism of the Papacy—criticism that could further erode institutional credibility and papal authority. The liberals also serve the conservative cause in another important way. A letter sent by the six American Cardinals and the president of the National Conference of Catholic Bishops to President Clinton in June 1994, regarding the International Conference on Population and Development begins, "We speak, Mr. President...for Catholics throughout the United States..." [200] The implication is that the bishops speak for 59 million Catholics in America, giving the bishops enormous political power. Each American represents one small increment of political power. The bishops have acquired these small increments of power from each American Catholic and these small increments add up to an impressive bloc of power. They just took these increments and American Catholics have not objected. It is extremely important that American Catholics take steps to end this arrangement. As the credibility of the Papacy continues to sink, which is inevitable, American Catholics cannot predict the ways in which the pope will call upon their bishops as he desperately attempts to insure survival of the Papacy. Liberal Catholics can best serve the needs of their countrymen and the rest of humanity by bolting from the Church and encouraging others to do the same. Since *Humanae Vitae,* millions already have. (We will come back to this in Chapter 13.)

We must remember what is at stake, as illuminated by NSSM 200, and act accordingly. In no way should we assume responsibility for the painful predicament Catholics find themselves in today.

It was set in motion in 1870. Above all else, we have a high moral responsibility to protect our nation's security-survival from all threats, domestic and foreign. Nurturing liberal Catholics to participate in the population growth control movement by avoiding identification of the real opposition to population growth control undermines any hope of success. Until we identify the opposition to our movement, and educate Americans as to why and what the Catholic hierarchy is doing to thwart population growth control, we have little chance of success in dealing with the population problem. We must identify the enemy's weaknesses and exploit those weaknesses if we are to solve this problem. Some liberal Catholics will choose to leave the population movement or not to join; others will remain or join. But in any case, we cannot compromise our movement by refusing to identify our opposition, and failing to formulate our strategy so as to take advantage of its weaknesses, just so we will not offend liberal Catholics.

NON-RESPONSE OF PROTESTANT CHURCHES

Decades ago, Protestant churches had no reservations about reporting Vatican activities in the United States that they viewed as threatening to the U.S. Constitution and security. Much of this appeared in denominational publications. Such reporting is now virtually nonexistent. In discussion of the Pastoral Plan in Chapter 9, ecumenism was presented as a tool of the bishops to block potential criticism from Protestant leadership for their extensive political involvement and for their stated goals of setting government policy on abortion. However, Hasler's study suggests there is more to this: "They see danger threatening the principle of authority and, consequently, the foundations of their own inner security as well....Protestants may find a study like mine distinctly uncomfortable....we have frequently seen the churches supporting each other's authoritarian system."[201] The silence of the Protestant leadership regarding the principle of separation of church and state, and the enormous amount of political activity now conducted by the bishops, is indeed perplexing.

Is it possible that the Protestant leadership is convinced that its fortunes are closely tied to those of the Catholic Church in America? Is there a fear that if the pope's authority is destroyed, their authority also will be diminished? Is there a quiet consensus that if the credibility of the Catholic Church is destroyed, the credibility of Protestant denominations will be undermined? These questions need to be answered. Tens of millions of Protestants are depending on their leadership to protect the security of their families and to be honest about the serious threat to their national security posed by the Catholic Church as it successfully saps the political will to deal with the population problem. In any case, whatever the reason, this long silence of the Protestant leadership is helping to postpone the self-destruction of the Papacy.

LEADERSHIP OF THE POPULATION MOVEMENT

"Someone can give you information but not all the information, and although they have not 'lied' to you, they have made something appear to be something it is not."

Anonymous

With few exceptions, such as Lawrence Lader[202] and Reimert Ravenholt,[203] this quotation is applicable to most leaders of the population movement since its inception. Americans naturally look to such individuals to offer an honest and complete assessment of the population problem—not simply what they feel comfortable in sharing. The American public *knows* that *if* the Vatican were successfully preventing population growth control, our best spokesmen would tell us so, wouldn't they? For at least two decades, Americans have been deceived by those who should be bringing the message most cogently, but are unfortunately ignoring the most crucial elements of the problem. The primary issues related to the population problem have never been adequately described.

The single most important issue is lack of political will to deal with the problem particularly in America. Why did it happen, and how? What will it take to reestablish the strong commitment we had to confront the problem in 1975? These are of greatest concern. All other issues are secondary and will remain peripheral until these are addressed and American political will reestablished. The secondary issues are fine for intellectual discussions but often become serious distractions from dealing with the immediate and difficult primary issues.

It is intellectually dishonest to "make something appear to be something it is not" and "to give information but not all the information." The population leadership has been guilty of this behavior from the beginning. Continued emphasis on the secondary issues is not only a serious distraction. More importantly, by respecting the Papacy's wishes for silence, and focusing the world's attention on the secondary issues, the population movement's leaders tend to become part of the problem, rather than the spearhead of its solution.

They have, in significant ways, helped postpone the self-destruction of the Papacy. Had they honestly portrayed the impediments to population growth control, the credibility of the Catholic Church surely would have been in much steeper decline than it is in 1996.

The 1994 International Conference on Population and Development (ICPD) in Cairo was a turning point in the Vatican's stealth campaign to undermine population activities around the world. Never before had the Vatican been forced to reveal so publicly its tactics of obstruction. For the first five days of the meeting the press focused world attention on the Vatican's stand, almost alone, in thwarting all progress.

Many delegates to those sessions believe that the Holy See may have done itself irreparable harm in pushing its agenda so unrelentingly and so single-mindedly. A new image of the Vatican was crystallized in the minds of millions of deeply concerned people around the world. This new perception was best expressed when Maher Mahran, Egypt's minister of population and the host of the conference asked: "Does the Vatican rule the world? The world is not here to be dictated to. And let me tell you the delegates here represent more than five billion people in the world, and not only 190 at the Vatican."[203a] Nearly all of us present in Cairo shared Dr. Mahran's frustration. The press broadcast his comment widely. Headlines read: "Vatican isolated; Vatican Obstructs Conference." (203b) For the first time, the world recognized and accepted the reality that the Vatican is a great obstacle to population growth control. Its stealthy obstructive behavior of past decades would now be made much more difficult to maintain.

However, the Vatican did achieve numerous successes at this meeting. The most important was the retention of the Mexico City language stipulating that abortion should in no way be promoted as a method of family planning. At the Holy See's insistence, there were significant alterations in the language used in the text of the Cairo Plan of Action.[203b] Passages on abortion rights originally included in the conference draft statement were, in the end, for the most part deleted from the final document. As a result, abortion-related language was severely watered down.[203c]

What was the accomplishment of the ICPD in Cairo? Seven months later, in April 1995, 45 family planning leaders from the United States and nine Latin American nations met for three days in Mexico to assess the outcome of the ICPD Plan of Action. Since nearly 150 countries enthusiastically endorsed the plan, nearly everyone pronounced the meeting a resounding success. But was it? As each of the representatives of the nine Latin American countries stood and reported that little or no action had been taken by their governments because of the Vatican's position against family planning, it became evident that Rome had really won in Cairo.[203d] In 1996, the Republican controlled United States Congress, elected as a result of the bishops 1975 Pastoral Plan, deeply cut funding for our family planning programs abroad.

Vatican pre-conference maneuvering helped to avert another high-profile battle over abortion at the United Nations World Summit on Social Development held in March 1995 in Copenhagen, Denmark[203c] and again at the Women's Conference in Beijing in September 1995. Nothing useful came from these two conferences. The Vatican was better prepared than in Cairo and was in remarkable control. These two conferences produced no significant advances toward population stabilization.

If Americans had been told that the Vatican gravely threatened U.S. and global security in 1975, when that was definitively shown in NSSM 200, the Catholic bishops would not have been able to manipulate American policy in the innumerable ways they have. Had Americans been rightfully told that the Papacy is their enemy and why, control of population growth would surely be much further advanced today—and the Vatican would be much closer to self-destruction.

DEFECTION
OF THE FAITHFUL

13

13

There is conclusive evidence that most American Catholics are ignoring many Church teachings, in particular those related to sex. Many Catholics have assessed information on their own and determined that the Vatican positions on population growth control and immigration are untenable, and have distanced themselves from the Church. They have determined that their personal and national security are threatened by the unprecedented population growth just as many other Americans have. But none has had available to them the extensive information possessed by Father Arthur McCormack, when he wrote a lengthy article for the November 6, 1982 issue of the Catholic newspaper, *The Tablet* (London).

FATHER McCORMACK'S EXPOSÉ

Father Arthur McCormack was the Vatican consultant to the UN on population for 23 years until 1979 when he was replaced by Bishop James McHugh of New Jersey. He was probably the most knowledgeable man on the subject of population in the Catholic Church. McCormack's attack on the Vatican is the sharpest made to date on this topic. Given the forcefulness of his words, one must suspect that the Vatican and McCormack had access to a copy of NSSM 200. In his article for *The Tablet*, Father McCormack

(1) States that population growth is a serious security threat: "...the population explosion...poses a more immediate threat to human lives and to human life than the possibility of nuclear war, and nuclear explosion."

(2) Charges that the leadership of the Roman Catholic Church is blatantly intellectually dishonest:

"But Norman Borlaug [agricultural scientist and Nobel Laureate] does not fool himself, he does not blind himself to facts or pretend that theories, however plausible and well thought out, will cope with immediate pressing and complex situations. The facts behind the scientists' alarm are genuine facts, not myths. These should be so well known as to be boring to repeat, but it still seems to me that they are either not absorbed, especially...in the Church, or are deliberately overlooked or ignored."

(3) Condemns the Church for its flagrant irresponsibility in not sounding the alarm on the population explosion while protesting the possession of nuclear arms: "We hear increasingly in the Church, bishops, priests and others protesting, sometimes stridently, against even the possession of nuclear arms or the threat to use them. How many official voices are raised in the Catholic Church to warn about the other explosion—population? Even in the slums of the Third World, where there have been plenty of warnings against "immoral" methods of birth control, there has been no suggestion of a population problem of the magnitude I have indicated, or of realistic efforts to deal with it."

(4) Demands that the Church boldly state that death rates be allowed to rise if it cannot put its influence behind lowering birth rates: "The Vatican has to take one side or the other. It must put its influence behind lowering the birth rates or, if it feels this is doctrinally not feasible, boldly state that death rates must regrettably be allowed to rise rather than break what it claims is the law of God."

(5) Concludes that if the Church does not act more responsibly in dealing with overpopulation, it must be prepared to pay heavily: "Otherwise, if the chaos responsibly foreseen by extremely reputable men materializes, the Church will bear a heavy burden of responsibility."

Fourteen years have passed since McCormack warned the Vatican. Indeed, the Vatican does bear a heavy burden of responsibility, more so than any other institution or group. As the Church's leader, the pope bears the greatest responsibility for the anarchy and premature death we see everywhere. One billion people have been added to the world's population since McCormack's warning to John Paul II and we are all less secure as a result.

LAY CATHOLIC AND VATICAN SECURITY INTERESTS IN CONFLICT

American Catholics recognize that the Vatican position globally is indefensible. They also recognize that it is not in their best interests as Catholic individuals and families. In the U.S., Catholic laymen exhibit the same family planning behavior as non-Catholics, a fact we will discuss later in this chapter. Obviously, the Vatican fiercely disagrees with American lay Catholic thinking on family planning and abortion. As I noted earlier, Andrew Greeley's study found that only seven percent of U.S. Catholics support the Vatican position on abortion. [204]

There is a good reason for this. The security-survival interests of Catholic laymen are pitted against the security-survival interests of the Papacy. For many reasons—including economic, medical, and social reasons—family planning, abortion services, good sex education, population education, and the advancement of women's rights, enhance the security of laymen and their families and increase their odds of survival. But, as discussed at length earlier, the exact opposite is true for the institution of the Papacy.

OPEN BORDERS: ANOTHER CONFLICT OF INTERESTS

Likewise, Vatican demands for open borders of the U.S. are rejected by a large majority of U.S. Catholic laymen.[205] American Catholic laymen are as opposed to unrestricted immigration into the United States as non-Catholic Americans. However, a recent study by Roy Beck of the positions of religious denominations in the U.S. toward immigration highlighted this fact: "No religious group wields more power on behalf of high immigration to the U.S. than the Catholic Church. Thanks to the 1880-1914 and 1970-present Great Waves of immigration consisting primarily of Catholics, the Church towers over all other American religious groups. Its 59 million members give it immense financial, institutional and political clout, even though polls suggest the majority of its members probably don't agree with its pro-immigration stances."[206] Because of its extensive manipulation of U.S. immigration policy, the Catholic Church is mostly responsibile for the chaotic flow of illegal immigrants across our borders today.

A November 8, 1992, *National Catholic Register* article reveals why the Vatican is taking these stances. In it, Father Richard J. Ryscavage, executive director of the Migration and Refugee Services of the U.S. Catholic Conference noted that immigration is the "growing edge of Catholicism in the United States...We are in the middle of a huge wave of immigration...and most of them are Catholics...It's the key to our future and the key to why the Church is going to be very healthy in the 21st century."

Another recent study by David Simcox [207] reveals Catholic leadership positions which most Americans will find shocking:

- The U.S. does not have an inherent right to limit migration.
- Every human has a right to migrate to the U.S. and take up residence there—to seek better living conditions.
- The Catholic Church rejects the concept of national sovereignty.
- All immigrants and their offspring have a right to keep their native tongue.
- Immigration restrictions are immoral.
- The Catholic Church rejects the U.S. government distinction between political and economic refugees.

These are all official papal positions.

The study's author, David Simcox, also offers the following comment: "Archbishop Roger Mahony of Los Angeles, who presides over the United States' largest concentration of illegal aliens, put it in these terms: 'If the question is between the right of a nation to control its borders and the right of a person to emigrate in order to seek safe haven from hunger or violence (or both), we believe that the first right must give way to the second'(1987)."

For obvious reasons, American lay Catholics oppose the Vatican's view on unrestricted immigration into the U.S. While the security-survival of the Papacy is greatly enhanced by this migration, as described by Ryscavage, the security-survival of the Catholic layman and his/her family are obviously undermined for economic, educational, medical, social and other reasons. Thus, as with family planning and abortion, the security-survival interests of the Catholic layman is pitted against the security-survival interests of the Papacy.

CATHOLIC AND AMERICAN—A CONTRADICTION

It is not possible to owe allegiance to two different political entities that have conflicting security-survival interests. One entity must prevail. Most American Catholics recognize that there are many contradictions when one attempts to be both Catholic and American. The Vatican has recognized this problem for 200 years. In his book, *The Unholy Ghost: Anti-Catholicism in the American Experience* (1992), Bishop Mark J. Hurley, consultor to the Congregation for Education for the Vatican, states, "...Vatican curial prelates were skeptical that a true believer in the American proposition could be a true believer in Catholicism."

The Vatican has relied heavily on a principle it created called the primacy of conscience, on the loyalty to God over loyalty to the state [208] to demand and get allegiance. Since the pope is God's representative on earth and his spokesman, this principle translates to loyalty to the pope over loyalty to the state. Most American Catholics do not share this interpretation. President John F. Kennedy publicly denounced the Vatican's interpretation repeatedly, seriously weakening the Vatican's position in the U.S. (More about this later.)

Most American Catholics do not owe their allegiance to the Vatican as the pope would like to claim. It has been evident for decades that the Vatican does not control the Catholic voting population. It can create, finance and control political machines that do have successes but it does not control voting populations as it once did in cities with large Catholic immigrant populations. [209]

According to Bishop Hurley, "The record shows that American Catholics were held suspect both in the halls of government and in the...Vatican." [210] "While progress of Catholics in the United States is unmatched in history, yet there remains the underlying suspicion that a Catholic cannot be a true believer in the American scheme of things." [211] "For two centuries Catholics have striven to alleviate the apprehension and doubt of their fellow citizens....While these efforts have in the main been successful, yet a surprisingly significant part of mainstream American society continues to entertain doubts." [212] Catholics are sensitive to this reality.

However, according to Hurley, the Catholic hierarchy and the Vatican have not accepted what he refers to as "the secularist interpretation of the First Amendment," the theory that it meant absolute separation not merely of the state from the establishment of religion but of religion itself from public life."[213] The Vatican has its own theory about what our First Amendment means and to the extent possible, uses its own theory to determine its behavior.

For example, Hurley recalls, "During the [Kennedy] primary campaign in Oregon on May 20, 1960, the Vatican newspaper *L'Osservatore Romano* declared in Rome that the Catholic hierarchy had the right and duty to intervene in politics and to expect dutiful discipline from Catholics. The hierarchy alone, it said, has the right to judge whether the higher principles of religious and moral order are involved in political issues." [214] Though the Vatican had to do this story in order to maintain control, it did not endear it to American non-Catholics. Most American Catholics reject the Vatican concept of our first amendment and are well aware of non-Catholic objections to it.

More recently, the Vatican claimed (or repeated) the right to protect itself against harmful laws—even when democratically legislated. The central difficulty here, of course, is that what the Vatican views "harmful" to itself and its authority is just what lay Catholic men and women, as well as non-Catholics, consider beneficial to themselves and their families. In a letter sent to all American bishops by the Sacred Congregation for the Doctrine of the Faith, the most powerful Vatican office, Cardinal Ratzinger reminded them that "The Church has the responsibility to protect herself from the application of harmful laws." This letter was keep secret from 55 million American Catholics until a brief notice written by Peter Steinfels for *The New York Times* appeared July 10, 1992. The actual text remained hidden from the public until it was leaked to the press on July 15, 1992.[215]

This had to be a great embarrassment to American Catholics. From Cardinal Ratzinger: we resent the concept of American democracy. No doubt the pope had given his blessing. His message—if we don't like your democratically legislated laws, we will just ignore them and follow our own dictates. Nothing like a little anarchy for "God's" benefit, perpetrated by the Vatican against the American people.

Obviously, if an institution has the "responsibility," it also claims the "right." The Vatican exercised its "right" to protect herself from the application of harmful laws, in the autocratic way it defines "harmful," when it blocked U.S. adoption of the Rockefeller Commission recommendations and implementation of the NSSM 200 policies approved by President Ford. "To protect herself," the Church moved quickly and efficiently to kill the two most important initiatives to control population growth in American history.

In its March 1995 issue, *Church & State* reports that the Vatican claims a unique role in world politics: "The Roman Catholic Church has the right to intervene in world politics through the United Nations by virtue of its centuries of existence and its possession of the truth, a Vatican official told a Catholic newspaper recently. In an interview with the *National Catholic Register*, Archbishop Renato Raffaele Martino, the Vatican's permanent observer at the UN, defended the church's participation in last year's international population conference in Cairo. Some delegates had criticized the church for delaying the conference by refusing to approve policies related to abortion and birth control...'Our diplomacy is the oldest in the world,' Martino said...Agreeing with the [*National Catholic Reporter*] that the church speaks 'with one voice,' Martino added, '[T]he one voice is a message of salvation, found in the scriptures and lived in the tradition of the church over the centuries. It is an objective truth that remains changeless.'...Pope John Paul II echoed Martino's views during his annual New Year's address January 9..."[215a]

The *National Catholic Register* reported in its October 15, 1995 issue: "The U.S. bishops are recognized as one of the most powerful lobbyist groups on Capitol Hill."[215b] Many long-time observers are convinced that the bishops have no equal in this regard. But if "the Church speaks with one voice," as Archbishop Martino and the pope claim, then obviously the U.S. bishops are lobbying on behalf of the pope, not American Catholics. These clerics are necessarily protecting Vatican interests, but not those of American Catholics. Why?

The June 30, 1995 issue of the *National Catholic Reporter* reads: "Approximately 40 U.S. bishops have endorsed a 12-page document that challenges peers to take a less subservient, more proactive stance in relationship to the Vatican." The implication is that at present the bishops are subservient to the Vatican. The report continues: "Noting that Vatican II laid the foundation for 'significant changes in our working relationship with the whole church and with the Holy Father,' the document questioned whether collegiality is a reality or an illusion: 'When formulating documents in the past, we did not submit them to Rome until we had fully discussed them...and voted. Now they are frequently submitted beforehand by the committee chairperson, and upon receiving the results there is no dialogue. The response from Rome is treated as a directive...There is a widespread feeling that Roman documents of varying authority have for some years been systematically reinterpreting the Vatican II documents to present the minority positions at the council as the true meaning of the council.'"

"According to the document, the College of Cardinals has emerged as a 'supracollegial body' that 'weakens the role of the bishops' conferences.' But open discussion of such matters is often impeded because many bishops cling to 'strict and undifferentiated application of all Roman norms and the notion of the church as a multinational corporation with headquarters in Rome and branch offices (dioceses) around the world.'"[215c]

No one can pretend that U.S. bishops who are lobbying the Congress represent the interests of U.S. Catholics. With their 12-page statement, these 40 bishops make it clear that it is corporate interests in Rome that are protected by Church lobbying efforts in the Congress. These are often at odds with the interests of individual American Catholics, as demonstrated on innumerable occasions by their private decisions on abortion and family planning and attitude toward illegal immigration. For example, a study by the Alan Guttmacher Institute estimated that abortion rates among American Catholic women are 29 percent higher than among Protestants and that 31 percent of women who get abortions are Catholic.[215d]   Thus, in 1995 alone, when 1.52 million abortions were performed, Catholic women demonstrated on nearly half a million occasions they believed that their interests were best served by obtaining a safe, legal abortion.

In his article, "A Traitorous Shepherd," in the June 22, 1995 issue of *The Wanderer*, A.J. Matt, Jr. labels as disloyal any bishop who would represent American Catholics at the expense of the Vatican, citing the Dogmatic Constitution on the Church: "Together with their head, the Supreme Pontiff, and never apart from him, they have supreme and full authority over the universal Church; but this power cannot be exercised without the agreement of the Roman Pontiff."[215e] This arrangement is written into the Church Constitution. According to Matt, bishops who do not conform are traitors.

China offers a concrete example. In the March 26, 1995 *National Catholic Register*, the article, "In China, Catholics must choose Pope or Party," reveals that Catholic bishops in China who stay loyal to the pope must pay a price. There are two kinds of Catholicism in China: the state run Catholic Patriotic Association, which requires Catholics to swear allegiance to China and its people, and other Catholics who maintain their allegiance to Rome and represent the underground Church. The Chinese Government takes this matter very seriously. For example, Roman Catholic Archbishop, Dominic Tang, once the underground bishop of Canton, spent 22 years in prison "because he refused to renounce his allegiance to the Vatican.[215f] The Chinese government considered Tang just as traitorous as Matt labels any bishop who exercises his power without papal consent. In the United States, we do not require Catholic bishops to swear allegiance to our country—despite the fact that our security-survival interests are indisputably in direct conflict with those of the Vatican. Yet the U.S. bishops have emerged as the most powerful lobbying group on Capitol Hill.

Thomas C. Fox, editor of the *National Catholic Reporter*, in a *New York Times* article, "Rome's Lengthening Shadow: U.S. bishops squelched by Vatican," writes: "Pope John Paul II's pontificate, long characterized by the strict enforcement of church law, especially on sexual matters, is moving beyond authoritarianism. In dealing with his bishops, the Pope has abandoned the collegial guidelines set down by the second Vatican council in the 1960's; he treats them not as conferees but as his personal delegates. The bishops shudder at criticizing Rome lest their action be viewed as a sign of disloyalty....For Western Catholics, versed in pluralism and democracy, the way in which Rome is treating their bishops has one redeeming feature: it forces the bishops to share with their people the sense of powerlessness they have felt throughout this pontificate."[215g] Sadly, even if the U.S. bishops wanted to represent the interests of American Catholics in their lobbying efforts on Capitol Hill, they are powerless to do so.

In his book, *The Unholy Ghost*, Bishop Hurley admitted: "That non-Catholics had good reason to question their Catholic fellow citizens about their allegiance in the early days of the Republic can scarcely be disputed."[216] [given the behavior of the Church in Europe]. But since the early days, popes and the hierarchy have committed one hostile act after the other, keeping these suspicions in full bloom. The Church is rabidly anti-democratic and anti-American. After 200 years, nothing has changed.

There is a continuous flow of evidence. Only a few examples can be presented here. At the October 1, 1989 annual Red Mass in Washington, which is dedicated to members of the legal profession, the archbishop of Philadelphia, Anthony J. Bevilaqua, told his audience, "The time has come to restore the vital relationship between religion and law, church and society." *The Washington Times* reported that Bevilaqua blasted separation of church and state during his remarks, charging that conflicts between church and state during the past 30 years have excluded religion from public life. Stated Bevilaqua, "This opposition, this impregnable wall...cannot endure much longer." In attendance were Supreme Court Chief Justice William H. Rehnquist and associate justices Antonin Scalia, Anthony M. Kennedy and William J. Brennan, Cabinet members Louis W. Sullivan and Manuel Lujan, several congressmen and numerous judges and lawyers. Bevilaqua misses the obvious point that if the wall was impregnable, the mass when he spoke would not have taken place. [217]

In a November 1991 speech to a national religious group, Cardinal Joseph Bernardin of Chicago stated that in some circumstances it is necessary for religious groups to take direct action, rather than rely on persuasion. "While dialogue and persuasion must be religion's first impulse in the public sector," the cardinal said, "we cannot automatically exclude the possibility that, at certain moments, religious groups may have to move into the power mode in order to preserve certain basic moral values in a society....The escalating power of the communications media, for example, is a growing cause of concern because of its ever-increasing ability to mold the public ethos in the contemporary world, far more perhaps than either the political or legal realms."

Bernardin expressed concerns about the media's ability to set the terms of debate on political issues such as abortion. He was admitting that the Catholic Church must control the terms of the debate if it is to win on the abortion issue and other issues important to the papal agenda for America. The cardinal observed, "we may see a growing number of troubling situations relative to the media which only a well-organized...group of religious leaders can confront. Control of language is an immensely powerful force in any society."[218] In other words, the cardinal and his Church are now ready to suspend the U.S. Constitution in order to protect papal security interests. Freedom of speech is now clearly a threat.

In July 1993, the National Catholic Register interviewed Msgr. George Kelley, who heads the right-wing Fellowship of Catholic Scholars; "'When I became a priest [circa 1940], we had a great Church,' he says, adding that 'our system was so good I could have played golf five times a week and nobody would have missed me.' It was a time he recalls, when churches were filled and parishes operated schools which charged little or no tuition thanks to the contributions of religious order teachers. That American Church, he says, 'was the eighth wonder of the world' of Catholicism. But it has largely been lost, he says, because 'a lot of [U.S. Catholics] have become more like the culture. A lot of our people have been trained to be Americans and not to be Catholics.'"[219]

Msgr. Kelley's phraseology suggests that, in his mind, to be American (and part of the American culture), and to be Catholic, are mutually exclusive. He is also offering further evidence, with his own observations, that the Church is self-destructing as a result of exposure to American culture. Apparently, training in Catholic schools is necessary in order to become a Catholic but even then this training is often not sufficient. He also makes clear that to have a healthy Catholic Church in America, the Church must keep its followers separated from American culture (I'll touch on this further, in another context in the next Chapter).

These are but *three* examples of the realization by the Church that it cannot successfully coexist with the American Way. There have been hundreds of others in recent years. American Catholics, of course, witness these examples and, as a result, many have distanced themselves from the Church, preferring to be Americans instead.

Certainly not all Catholics wish to distance themselves from the Church. The Spring 1994 issue of *Conscience*, published by Catholics for a Free Choice, offers a superb but frightening overview of a long list of right-wing Catholic organizations which owe their allegiance to the pope. This array of organizations provide an estimated total of perhaps 200,000 activists, less than one percent of the U.S. Catholic population.[220] Their purpose: implement Vatican policy in America. This formidable collection of organizations gives new meaning to the old saying, "they are among us but they are not of us." No doubt, most are products of Catholic schools.

TODAY'S ANTI-CATHOLICS?—THE INTELLECTUALS

In *The Unholy Ghost*, referring to the Twentieth Century, Hurley states, "The most intractable indictment against Catholics was not only that...by Nativists...but more importantly and significantly by well-balanced, intelligent, tolerant, and reasonable Americans..."[221] Hurley also understands where these concerns that Americans have originate: "The repressions, quiet censorship, removal from office, and other actions gave non-Catholics, in particular, grounds for concern as to where the Church stood on basic liberties....Thanks in large measure to the Roman curial actions over the years, two centuries to be exact, those who viewed the American Catholics with distrust were not fighting straw men. There were legitimate doubts and both legitimate and illegitimate reactions. Thoughtful men and women asked fair questions..."[222] Referring to school related political campaigns in California, Hurley goes on to say, "...the campaigns not only in 1958...have revealed anti-Catholicism not primarily among the fringe groups, the marginal population, the dispossessed, but rather within the highest levels of government, of professional and business leaders, the universities, and the media."[223]

Andrew Greeley has studied the sources of anti-Catholicism in America. His findings: "It does not represent a substantial segment of the American population. It is rather limited to a small group of intellectuals and bureaucrats....But anti-Catholic and anti-religious elites do happen to have certain key positions in the national media, the universities and the federal bureaucracy."[224] In a 1978 syndicated column Greeley insists that Nativism—favoring the interests of longtime inhabitants over those of immigrants—is found "among the [American] cultural and intellectual elites."[225] Also, Louis Harris has studied this topic. His polling data give evidence that the more sophisticated were more likely to harbor anti-Catholic attitudes than the poor and less educated.[226]

President Kennedy understood and apparently agreed with the concerns of "well-balanced, intelligent, tolerant, and reasonable Americans" regarding Catholic hierarchy interference in American politics. In 1959, Kennedy offered his position on the principle of separation of Church and State: "Whatever one's religion in his private life might be, for the office holder nothing takes precedence over his oath to uphold the Constitution and all its parts—including the First Amendment and the strict separation of Church and State."[227]

On another occasion, Kennedy made an even stronger statement: "But if the time should ever come—and I do not concede any conflict to be remotely possible—when my office would require me to either violate my conscience or violate the national interest, then I would resign the office, and I hope any other conscientious public servant would do likewise."[228] Kennedy's position on the absolute separation of Church and State prompted Irish columnist for the *London Times*, Conor Cruise O'Brien, to write: "An American Catholic is a Protestant who goes to Mass. The name of John F. Kennedy comes to mind."[229] Indeed, O'Brien's description is applicable to a great many American Catholics.

During his presidential campaign, *Look Magazine* reported Kennedy as saying that "for the office-holder, nothing takes precedence over his oath to uphold the Constitution." This statement brought a sharp response from the Catholic Church on the primacy of conscience mentioned earlier, on the loyalty to God over loyalty to the state. It charged that JFK was espousing a totalitarianism with unqualified allegiance to the state, a charge which is absurd.[230] Obviously, Kennedy's position was very threatening to the influence of the Church in American political affairs.

As Americans, we would like to think that Kennedy's position on the strict separation of Church and State did not cause the Vatican much anguish. However, says Bishop Hurley, "The implication has been all along that Kennedy's stance on Church-State relations was somehow acceptable to the Catholic Church....it was not."[231] The abortion issue has given rise to the question once again: Can a Catholic politician be a full American and fully Catholic? According to Hurley: "Kennedy only muddied the waters..."[232] I think not. Kennedy's position was clearly anti-Catholic from the Vatican's perspective. But Kennedy recognized what is reasonable to "well-balanced, intelligent, tolerant and reasonable Americans—Catholic and non-Catholic.

Bishop Hurley identifies Pulitzer Prize-winning historian Arthur M. Schlesinger, Jr., close advisor to President Kennedy, and author of the 1991 best-seller, *The Disuniting of America*, as a leader of the intellectual community critical of the Catholic Bishops for their anti-abortion activities. Schlesinger berated the American Bishops for appearing to verify the fears held by many Americans that the Roman Catholic Church would try to overrule the American democratic process: "They seem to be doing their best to prove the case that Catholic politicians will not be free to act for what a majority regards as the general good."[233]

According to Hurley; "The liberal establishment led by Schlesinger presented themselves as champions of the First Amendment, specifically of the absolute separation of church and state...suggesting none too subtly that Catholics cannot be trusted, if truly convinced in their faith, fully as Americans; and claiming that Catholics do not really believe in the democratic process."[234]

Schlesinger is quoted as saying; "For years the bigots have said the Church would not hesitate to impose its will upon the general populace or to tell Catholic politicians how to act....Then Al Smith and John Kennedy said—and showed—that Catholics in politics are as free as any other American citizens to base their judgments on the national interests and the democratic process, and most Americans have come to believe them." Hurley notes that Schlesinger went on to say that New York's Cardinal O'Connor and Bishop Vaughan were changing the image of Catholics as true citizens, free to be true politicians in the American tradition. He quotes Schlesinger: "I thank heaven that Bishop Vaughan and Cardinal O'Connor were not holding forth in 1960. If they had spoken then as they speak now, John F. Kennedy would not have been elected President."[235]

In 1990, another thoughtful observer stepped forward simply to say the obvious. David R. Boldt, senior editor of the Philadelphia Inquirer, published an article titled, "The Bishops Return to a Darker Era in U.S. politics." Referring to the bishops' failure to respect the American principle of separation of church and state, Boldt said, "The Roman Catholic Church, it needs to be remembered, is quite literally an Un-American institution...not democratic...[and] sharply at odds with those that inform the laws of American secular society. And its principal policies are established by the Vatican in Rome." Boldt goes on to describe the bishops as "desperate men," an observation with which it is difficult to reasonably disagree. He concludes, "They [the bishops] intend to show that, as the organized bigots used to say, Catholic officials take orders from Rome."[236]

There is a continuous flow of examples of Catholic American intellectuals who live by the position taken by President Kennedy on separation of church and state. In Kansas, Judge Patrick Kelley sentenced some of the hundreds of Operation Rescue activists arrested in anti-abortion protests in Wichita in 1991. *The New York Times* characterized him as "a lifelong Catholic" but "a JFK Catholic," quoting a lawyer who said that "Pat is a Catholic. But like John F. Kennedy who was a president first and a Catholic second, Pat is a judge first and a Catholic second."[237]

An article by Mary Meehan appearing in the February 13, 1994 issue of the *National Catholic Register* titled "Problems of Conscience" describes a very different outcome for a Catholic public servant with a problem of conscience: "Last year Judge Joseph Moylan resigned from a juvenile court in Omaha, Neb., because a parental consent law required him to authorize abortions for minors if he found them mature enough to give informed consent. 'I simply cannot enter an order authorizing one human life to put to death another totally innocent human life,' Judge Moylan wrote in his resignation letter. He added that, since he had taken an oath to uphold the laws of Nebraska and cannot comply with this law, I am resigning my position...'" All patriotic Americans—Catholic and non-Cathoics—know that Joseph Moylan did the right thing.

Most American Catholics accept the pledge of loyalty to country necessary to being considered an American. In 1914, President Woodrow Wilson addressed an audience of recently naturalized citizens in Philadelphia: "You cannot become thorough Americans if you think of yourselves in groups. America does not consist of groups. A man who thinks of himself as belonging to a particular national group in America has not yet become an American."[238] (In the next Chapter we will examine why the Catholic Church has struggled so violently against this concept.) In 1916, Theodore Roosevelt commented: "We can have no 'fifty-fifty' allegiance in this country. Either a man is an American and nothing else, or he is not an American at all."[239]

Franklin D. Roosevelt said in 1943, "The principle on which this country was founded and by which it has always been governed, is that Americanism is a matter of mind and heart; Americanism is not, and never was, a matter of race and ancestry. A good American is one who is loyal to this country and to our creed of liberty and democracy."[240]

Most American Catholics are aware of these concepts of what it is to be an American, accept them, and live by them. Nothing contributes more to their unwillingness to conform to the demands of their bishops. They are also aware that there has been staunch opposition to Catholic schools from reasonable intellectuals for a long time. Earlier in this century, Dr. James Conant, president of Harvard University, stated: "The greater [the] proportion of our youth who fail to attend public schools and who receive their education elsewhere, the greater the threat to our democratic unity."[241] In 1875, Ulysses S. Grant campaigned on a plank that Catholic parochial schools would someday lead to another civil war.[242] Given the death of NSSM 200 and how its death came about, Grant's prediction may yet prove to be correct.

The Vatican agenda that killed NSSM 200 is alive and more aggressive than ever. A June 30, 1994 Associated Press article[243a] reported that Congressman Vic Fazio of California said that religious-right activists used stealth tactics to take over state Republican parties and impose an extreme agenda. Now that Catholics for a Free Choice has published its study of the activities of 28 right-wing Catholic organizations and exploded the myth that the religious right is a fundamentalist and evangelical Protestant movement,[243b-e] the takeover of Republican parties to which Fazio refers is correctly identified as a Vatican takeover. Our long history of tolerance is now suffering a heavy toll.

The death of NSSM 200, the takeover of political parties and numerous other examples of interference in American political life all show that the concerns expressed by President Grant and Dr. Conant regarding Catholic schools were reasonable, as the leadership of the 28 organizations reported on by CFFC were mostly Catholic school educated.

Archbishop John Ireland of St. Paul, Minnesota once said, "Americans are fair to the Catholic Church....Prejudices exist where Catholics give cause for them and seldom elsewhere."[244] Most American Catholics surely agree or more would be aligned with that tiny group created to counter anti-Catholicism, The Catholic League for Religious and Civil Rights. The vast majority of Catholics want to be and are Americans first and Catholics second—JFK Catholics. The Church representatives shout "bigot" but they are just trying to control the dissemination of information. The survival of their institution is at stake.

DISTORTION OF THE CHURCH'S IMAGE

In 1990, the Times Mirror Company, owner of a number of large U.S. newspapers, conducted a national poll, "The People, Press and Politics." This poll asked interviewees questions that would permit the measure of "favorability." Eleven political institutions were compared. The Catholic Church ranked number one with an 89 percent favorability rating, handily beating the Supreme Court, Congress and the U.S. military. Evangelical Christians were given a 53 percent rating. Among famous world leaders, including living U.S. Presidents, the pope ranked number one with a favorability rating of 88 percent. Only Vaclav Havel came within 10 points of the pope.[245]

This is either an amazing phenomenon or an impressive accomplishment by the bishops, or both. The Catholic Church in America is in serious decline. As noted earlier, half of all American priests now quit the priesthood before age 60. The average age of nuns in the U.S. is 65 years and only 3 percent are below age 40. Nearly one-third of the Catholic schools and one-fourth of the Catholic hospitals have closed in the past 30 years. Contributions by members have fallen by half in the same period, with Catholics having the lowest contribution rate of any of the major churches. Were it not for the billions of dollars received by the Church in federal, state and local tax funds, the income from corporate gifts made as a result of Catholic influence within public and private corporations, and as a result of influence within major private foundations, the Church could not possibly survive in its current form.

As noted, millions of Catholics have left the Church and become Protestants. The September 1995 New York Times/CBS News Poll revealed that 28 percent of those who had been raised as Catholics no longer considered themselves Catholic. In other words, 17 million individuals whom the bishops claim as Catholics have left the Church. In November 1979, about half of all Americans surveyed regarded the pope as a universal moral leader. By 1995, according to this survey, the proportion had fallen to 31 percent, a 40 percent drop.[245a] A 1994 Los Angeles Times survey found that 43 percent of priests and 51 percent of nuns say that things in the Church are not so good.[246] According to a study conducted by the Alan Guttmacher Institute and reported in USA Today on January 29, 1993, Catholics account for 31 percent of all abortions in the U.S. but are only 22 percent of the U.S. population. A September 1995 *Washington Post*/ABC News Poll queried: Is the Roman Catholic Church in touch with the views of Catholics in America today, or out of touch? Nearly 60 percent of both Catholics and nonCatholics responded, "out of touch." To the question, "Do you think someone who is using birth control methods other than the rhythm method can still be a good Catholic,?" Ninety-three percent of Catholics said yes. To the question, "Do you think someone who gets divorced and marries someone else without Church approval can still be a good Catholic,?" 85 percent said yes. To the question, "Do you think a woman who has an abortion for reasons other than her life being in danger can still be a good Catholic?," 69 percent said yes.[247a] The Catholic Church in the U.S. can only be described as an institution in serious decline.

How can the Church and the pope have such high favorability ratings under these circumstances? This is an important question for all Americans and the American political process. The answers will tell how the Rockefeller Commission recommendations and the NSSM 200 recommendations, and every major initiative taken thus far to control U.S. and world population growth have been killed by the Church without Americans being aware of it. We will return to this question in the next chapter.

The bishops have been permitted to make the rules on how they are reported on. This has been accomplished by using many different tools and devices and only a few will be discussed here. A 1991 study conducted by the Center for Media and Public Affairs and published by the Knights of Columbus and the Catholic League for Religious and Civil Rights, a study conducted by Catholics for use by Catholic activists, found that in spite of the fact that the Catholic Church is in precipitous decline and that half of its priest and nuns said that things in the Church are not so good, "the 'Church hierarchy' is cited more than 50 times as often as 'identified Church dissidents'!"[247] Given the state of the Church one would expect the opposite to be true. The dissenters obviously have something to talk about, but press reporting on dissension and dissenters has been successfully discouraged by the Church leadership. Given the enormous potential for dissenting opinion, the bishops' accomplishment in suppressing media coverage of this opinion is truly impressive. A reasonable question is: what other information is the Church successfully suppressing?

As mentioned in Chapter 11, the news outlets that placed the Church in a negative light were virtually all snuffed out or muzzled earlier in this century by the Knights of Columbus; this institution continues to take great pride in its early successes.[248] Its efforts in recent years and the efforts of other Catholic institutions, such as the Catholic League for Religious and Civil Rights, to suppress information that places the Church in a bad light have been mostly successful (the issue of child molestation being the only significant exception but even on this issue they do what they can.)

Any time a report appears in the press placing the Church in a bad light, almost without exception there is an immediate demand for an apology and retraction made to the reporter, editor and publisher by these Catholic thought police. Written responses and demands for publication are immediately forthcoming. These responses are usually published and it is amazing how many apologies are made and published. There are scores of examples each year and they can be found in the publications of these thought police. They eagerly share their successes with their members. But when a negative report appears in one newspaper or magazine it rarely appears in another, regardless of its newsworthiness—Carl Bernstein's *TIME* magazine article is a good example.

Economic retribution as a tool to suppress criticism was used more commonly in the last century and earlier in this century than today because it is now largely unnecessary. The long history of its use and the success enjoyed with it makes the mere threat of its use highly effective.

Perhaps far more important than the outright intimidation practiced by many of the right-wing Catholic organizations is the self-censorship practiced by reporters, editors and publishers. All know there is a line that has been drawn by the bishops that they are not to cross—and they rarely do. They are aware of the rules formulated by the bishops regarding how Church matters are to be reported—and nearly always follow them. They know they will be punished if they do not conform.

Indeed, the bishops have had far greater success in intimidating non-Catholics than in retaining their own faithful. This is not limited to the press. With 26 years in the population field, I can say from experience that the fear of retaliation by the Catholic Church has paralyzed the population movement. I have also found that the fear felt by many American politicians aware of the undemocratic activities of the Church has resulted in their silence on this issue.

The Roman Catholic Church is a political entity headquartered in Rome and controlled in Rome. Its teachings and policies are set in Rome. All of its employees work for and represent the interests of the headquarters in Rome. It has awesome political power in the U.S. and the world over. It has inviolable territory, diplomatic representation to governments around the world and its minions sit on international bodies of a purely secular nature. It has political interests, including security-survival interests which are in direct conflict with those of the United States Government and its people. But the image of the Catholic Church presented by the American press does not reflect these realities. We are led to believe that this institution is primarily religious in nature. On the contrary; numerous observers over the years, including scholar Paul Blanchard, have correctly described the Catholic Church as a political institution cloaked in religion.[249] Little has changed. The Church and its Vatican are firstly a political institution, now desperately trying to survive.

Much distortion is possible because relevant information that would limit distortion is not collected in the first place, since the Church has succeeded in blocking its collection. For example, for the bishops to claim "we speak for 59 million Americans" alone gives the Church an enormous amount of political power to manipulate government policy. It is not possible to challenge their present count of 59 million, though the actual number of Catholics who consider themselves adherents of the Catholic faith and who are willing to give the bishops permission to speak for them in the political arena is undoubtedly but a fraction of 59 million. But when politicians hear the number 59 million, they listen intently. The result—a lot of political power.

These are but a few of the reasons Americans have such a distorted view of the Church. However, American priests, nuns and laymen have a much less distorted view; it is amply documented that they are leaving the Church in droves. The test of the image is in the polling. The image of a healthy, robust and expanding American Catholic Church is clearly wrong. American Catholics are not conforming to the extent that our perceptions tell us. We are affording the Church far more deference than it deserves.

TOO MUCH EVIDENCE TO IGNORE

American Catholics, like the rest of us, cannot ignore the steady barrage of evidence that their church is in an untenable position and that the pope and the Church, as Father McCormack phrased it, "bear a heavy burden of responsibility" for much of the misery, suffering and premature death we see around the world.

There are numerous examples: The cover story of the February 1994 issue of the *Atlantic Monthly* titled "The Coming Anarchy" by Robert Kaplan links anarchy around the world, including the U.S., to overpopulation.[250] In a follow-up column in the *New York Times*, Anthony Lewis writes that overpopulation-induced environmental destruction will be "the national security issue of the early 21st century."[251] A Los Angeles Times News Service article titled, "Massive Famine Predicted Worldwide," reports on a symposium of international agricultural experts who predict eight times the shortage of food worldwide, as now seen in Africa, by the year 2000.[252]

A recent Reuters dispatch is headed, "U.N. report lists developing countries in danger of collapse," naming eight.[253] (Rwanda was the first to go.) The *New York Times* News Service reports: Pontifical Academy of Sciences recommends that couples have only two children to curb world population growth.[254] A *USA Today* article begins, "The Catholic Church, long outspoken in its opposition to abortion, is engaging in a massive and unprecedented lobbying effort to stop passage of an abortion rights bill in Congress....which would prohibit states from restricting abortion."[255] (The bishops won—the bill is now dead.) A *Los Angeles Times* News Service article is titled, "Roman Catholic bishops declare their intent to fight any legislation that provides coverage for abortions" (including the Clinton health care plan, or any alternative covering abortion).[256] A *New York Times* News Service article reports on a newly released Episcopal Church document that terms the Catholic attitude toward women "so insulting, so retrograde" that women should abandon Catholicism "for the sake of their own humanity."[257]

The *New York Times* reports that taxpayers save $4.40 for every public dollar spent to provide family planning (based on costs of baby's first two years). A *Wall Street Journal* article reports on a University of California finding that every $1 spent on family planning services saves the state $11.20 later.[259] The results of a *Washington Post-ABC News* poll in 1993 shows that the overwhelming majority of Americans favor the availability of abortion, and the percentages increased over 1992. A *Reader's Digest* article titled, "A Continent's Slow Suicide," reports, "Now the African continent is sliding back to a precolonial stage."[260] The nightly TV news stories on Haiti, Somalia, Rwanda and Bosnia reveal that these conflicts are all related to overpopulation.

These hideous stories seem endless. Of course they have the same effects on Catholics as they do on non-Catholics. "The truth shall make you free" and this steady diet of information countering the Vatican's position has emancipated Catholics from dogmas which have contributed to papal control. We have a distorted view of what American Catholics think. For decades, the Bishops have been telling us what Catholics think and most Catholics and non-Catholics alike have failed to question this arrangement. How did this arrangement come about and how is it maintained?

More importantly–how has the Vatican managed to subvert all serious efforts to deal with the over population problem without the American public's awareness of these covert operations? This is the subject of Chapters 14 and 15.

VATICAN REJECTION OF FREEDOM OF THE PRESS 14

14

" This pressure [of the Catholic Church on American journalism] is one of the most important forces in American life, and the only one about which secrecy is generally maintained, no newspaper being brave enough to discuss it, although all fear it and believe that the problem should be dragged into the open and made publicly known. (260a)"

George Seldes
1890 - 1995
Journalist and Dean of
Investigative Reporters

George Seldes was the leading observer and critic of American journalism in this century. Of his 21 books,[260b] seven deal with freedom of the press.[260c] The pressure of the Catholic Church on American journalism has been catastrophic for population growth control efforts such as the Rockefeller Commission and the NSSM 200 initiative. The secrecy imposed by the Catholic Church accounts for the near total lack of awareness of the grave threat overpopulation poses to virtually every treasured aspect of life in America. How and why journalism in this country has come to such a deplorable state will be the subject of this chapter.

As we have said, the Catholic hierarchy's hatred of freedom of the press has long been known. According to Bernhard Hasler, in his encyclical *Mirari vos*, Pope Gregory XVI (1831-1846) "condemned the ideas of liberalism. He viewed freedom of conscience as a 'false and absurd concept,' indeed a mad delusion. Freedom of the press, to his mind, could never be sufficiently abhorred and anathematized."[260d] In 1850, Pope Pius IX (1846-1878) branded freedom of the press and freedom of association as intrinsically evil.[260e] The Catholic hierarchy has never accepted the concept of freedom of the press.

By 1870, the principles of the French Revolution (1848), which included freedom of the press, had brought the Catholic Church to its knees. Newspapers everywhere were conveying the truth about Catholicism. Indeed, unrestricted journalism of the time was a major cause for the drive to adopt the principle of infallibility (see Chapter 11). According to Hasler, the Infallibilist Party "wanted to employ the infallible pope to contain the forces of unbridled journalism."[260f] On May 25, 1870, the newspaper *Unita Cattolica*, which supported adoption of the principle of infallibility, wrote, "The infallible pope must counteract and cure the prevailing abuses of unbridled freedom of the press, thanks to which journalists daily spread lies and calumny. Every day the pope can teach, condemn, and define dogma and Catholics will never be permitted to question his decisions."[260g]

With the adoption of the principle of infallibility by Pius IX and freedom of the press branded intrinsically evil by him, the Church immediately set out to "bridle" the press. In the United States, the Knights of Columbus was created in 1882 to organize the Catholic laity into a tightly controlled and responsive machine. By 1914 the Knights of Columbus had evolved into a national organization capable of intimidating anyone who criticized the Church in any way. During the period from August 1914 to January 17, 1917, the Knights succeeded, according to their own report, in shutting down 60 of the 62 or 63 newspapers in the United States that published news critical of the Catholic Church. And they bragged about it.[260h]

In 1946, Pius XII told a group of American editors that freedom of the press "does not allow a man to print what is wrong, what is known to be false, or what is calculated to undermine and destroy the moral and religious fiber of individuals and the peace and harmony of nations."[260i] The pope, of course, considers himself the supreme judge of what is wrong, false, moral, religious, peaceful and harmonious encompassing all aspects of our existence. Given the pontiff's statement, reporters, editors and publishers have only those rights given to them by the pope. Thus, any reporter, editor or publisher who defies the pope becomes fair game. These were the ground rules established by the Knights of Columbus in their crusade early in this century to destroy all American newspapers that did not conform to the dictates of the Vatican.

PAUL BLANSHARD ASSESSES VATICAN INFLUENCE

In 1949, Paul Blanshard reported on his extensive study of Catholic censorship and boycott in a book, *American Freedom and Catholic Power*. He found that, "The censorship system of the Roman Catholic Church in the United States is neither a spasmodic nor an intermittent phenomenon. It is a highly organized system of cultural and moral controls that applies not only to books, plays, magazines and motion pictures, but to persons and places....[The Church] holds the power of economic life and death over many authors, publishers and producers who must rely upon American Catholics for patronage and support."[270j]

For his analysis, Blanshard depends heavily on the writings of Catholics in good standing, including Canon law. He observes: "Catholics are taught that the Roman Catholic Church is the supreme guardian and purveyor of truth, that the Pope has infallible judgment in moral matters, and that 'union of minds requires not only a perfect accord in the one Faith, but complete submission and obedience of will to the Church and to the Roman Pontiff, as to God Himself.' The words are those of Leo XIII in his *Chief Duties of Christian Citizens*....[260k] 'The Church is not afraid of the truth,' says Father John C. Heenan in his *Priest and Penitent*, but She is very much afraid that a clever presentation of falsehood will deceive even the elect.' The Church teaches that literature is 'immoral' if it is opposed to Catholic standards, and that 'no one has a right to publish such literature any more than one has a right to poison wells or sell tainted food.'"[260l]

Blanshard quotes the most authoritative Catholic work on doctrine, Father Henry Davis's four-volume *Moral and Pastoral Theology* which instructs Catholic bishops to enforce a boycott against all of the following classes of books, as described in the priest's own words:

"1. Books by any writers which defend heresy or schism, or attempt in any way to undermine the very foundations of religion;

2. All books...which affect to prove that true divorce is permissible in the case of adultery;

3. Books which attack or hold up to ridicule any Catholic dogma, such as the creation of man, original sin, the infallibility of the Pope;

4. Books which professedly treat of, narrate, or teach matters that are lewd or obscene, such as the defense of methods of birth control."[260m]

Does the Catholic leadership have the right to suppress the press? Blanshard quotes Father Francis J. Connell, Associate Professor of Moral Theology at the Catholic University of America, who was extraordinarily frank when writing in the *American Ecclesiastical Review* for January 1946: "We believe that the rulers of a Catholic country have the right to restrict the activities of those who would lead their people away from their allegiance to the Catholic Church...they possess the right to prevent propaganda against the Church. This is merely a logical conclusion from the basic Catholic tenet that the Son of God established one religion and commanded all men to accept it under pain of eternal damnation."[260n]

Pope Pius XI was equally forthright. In an Allocution dated December 20, 1926, he stated, "Catholics may not support, favor, or read papers which are edited by men whose writings are in notable opposition to Catholic doctrine in faith and morals..."[260o]

Blanshard describes a February 11, 1928 article by a Jesuit priest, Charles J. Mullaly, that appeared in the Jesuit magazine, *AMERICA*. The article is a point-by-point description of Catholic techniques in boycotting an American newspaper and a censorship program for priests and laymen. Blanshard writes: "Father Mullaly tells with perfect candor how a priest and four or five Catholic laymen, with the help of an impressive letterhead bearing the names of prominent citizens, can terrorize any editor with the specter of a great wave of Catholic indignation."[260p] This same technique is still in use in the 1990s and numerous examples in the period 1994-1996 will be cited in the next chapter.

Mullaly offers an example of a boycott that can be used as a model in the techniques of suppression. The offending Washington, D.C., newspaper had published a series of letters-to-the-editor about a suspicious death of a young girl at a Catholic home administered by the Sisters of the Good Shepherd. "Instead of writing an indignant defense of the Sisters of the Good Shepherd," says Father

Mullaly, "and thus stimulating a controversy that would have been financially profitable to the offending paper, this Catholic Society followed a more practical method of action. Its strategy was aimed at the business office and not at the editorial department...Members of the society interviewed merchants who advertised in the paper and suggested they demand an immediate change of editorial policy, if they hoped to keep Catholic trade. No intimation of boycott was given, but these businessmen understood perfectly well that the paper was supported by their advertising, and they hastened to show sympathy for their insulted Catholic patrons.

"Priests in Washington were told to make a statement in their pulpits 'somewhat as follows': 'There is a newspaper in this city that is attacking the Sisters of the Good Shepherd. I will not mention its name. This paper is opening its columns to bigots who are insulting the purity of our Catholic Sisterhoods. I do not know what kind of Catholic each of you may be, but as for me, I will fight insults to the Holy Mother Church. I do not know what you will do; I will fling any offending newspaper from my house and will never buy it again.' Father Mullaly claimed that 'the effect was magical,' and that the offending newspaper lost forty percent of its circulation in two weeks.'...Father Mullaly, in a triumphant mood, told how the Washington Truth Society was able to function successfully as censor of the Washington press in this manner without any large membership meetings. Its actual work was done by 'one active priest in charge, two zealous laymen and a Catholic lawyer or two, ready to give legal advice free of charge. The letterhead was formidable with prominent men, but this heavy artillery was brought to bear only when urgently needed. In any city of the United States one zealous pastor with two or three active laymen, together with a legal advisor, could form a Truth Society that would batter to pieces bigotry when found in the pages of any local newspaper.'

"Father Mullaly concluded this revealing document with a platform of action for punishing critical American newspapers:

1. Do not attack a magazine or newspaper through its editorial departments but act through its business office.

2. When a magazine or newspaper is attacking your religion, write to the business manager and inform him that you will not buy the offending periodical again, and mean it...

3. Call the attention of the merchants with whom you deal to the insults and tell them that as long as they advertise in any offending paper, you will not buy their goods, and mean it...

4. Tell your news-dealer that as long as you see the magazine or newspaper on his stand as an open insult to you, you will not buy from him, and mean it."[260q]

These Catholic Truth Societies had the fervent assistance of the Knights of Columbus and the Catholic War Veterans.[260r] Blanshard offers lengthy descriptions of censorship organizations created to suppress information in books, magazines, and film and provides numerous examples of each type of censorship, but the reader is urged to refer directly to his book.[260s]

Blanshard concludes, "The machinery that the Church uses in the United States to enforce its boycott of unfriendly literature is quite elaborate....Non-Catholic publishers who print criticism of Catholic policy are threatened with boycotts and flooded with very unpleasant letters of protest. As a result of this type of pressure scarcely any publishers in the United States will even consider any manuscript that might expose them...to Catholic boycott.[260t]

"Every city editor in the United States," Blanshard goes on to say, "knows of the unofficial Catholic censorship of American news, but almost all publishers avoid discussion of the phenomenon because of the fear of Catholic reprisals. The Hierarchy itself has avoided public discussion of its boycott techniques in recent years, and has resorted more and more to quiet pressure[260u]....As a result of this policy of siege and boycott, very few publishers in the United States are courageous enough or wealthy enough to deal frankly with Catholic social policy or stories of priestly crime[260v]....Frequently the Church succeeds in intimidating the most powerful newspapers by this policy of organized protest and boycott, and, in many cases, the facts suppressed have great social significance."[260w] Unquestionably, the most important story suppressed by the Catholic Church thus far has been that by 1970, overpopulation had emerged as the greatest single threat to the security-survival of the United States and indeed all nations. But before we return to the issue of population, let's turn to an insider in American journalism, George Seldes, for more proof.

GEORGE SELDES — AMERICA'S PREMIER PRESS CRITIC

On July 2, 1995, George Seldes, author, award-winning journalist and media watchdog, died at age 104. He began his career as a reporter for the *Pittsburgh Leader* in 1909 and later went to Europe to cover World War I. From 1918 to 1928, he worked for the *Chicago Tribune*, heading bureaus in Berlin and Rome, and also reporting from Mexico. He covered the Spanish Civil War for the *New York Post* in 1936-37. He was a mainstream reporter for nearly 30 years. From 1940 to 1950, he edited the nation's first periodical of media criticism called *In Fact*—which won him a George Polk Award in 1982.[260x]

In an article, "George Seldes Leaves a Legacy of Courage," the media watchdog publication, *EXTRA!*, writes, "As a press critic, George Seldes picked up where Upton Sinclair left off. From the 1930s onward, Seldes led the way for new generations of journalists eager to search for truth wherever it might lead....I.F. Stone aptly called Seldes 'the dean and granddaddy of us investigative reporters.'"[260y] He was an American journalism insider.

While Blanshard's intensive study of the press focused on what the Catholic hierarchy said and did regarding freedom of the press, Seldes observed and reported on the actual outcomes of the hierarchy's influence over American newspapers. Very few Americans outside the journalism field appreciate the intensive influence exercised by the hierarchy over the American press at least since the adoption of the principle of papal infallibility in 1870. This influence has greatly hampered the truthful and complete reporting on all matters of concern to the Vatican—*including all matters related to population growth control*. Seldes reported on numerous examples of this influence. I will present here only one example—the Spanish Civil War—carefully documented by Seldes to show that the Catholic hierarchy's wielding of enormous influence in the press, observed for the past 25 years in population matters, is certainly not unprecedented.

But before doing so, it will be interesting to note some of Seldes's findings during several decades of intensive research. These excerpts are from his book, *Lords of the Press*:

"It was then twenty-seven years since I had started in journalism, by which time I had learned the first lesson, namely, that one must never write on controversial subjects, the first of which was religion, and that one must never report even the truth in any case in which the Catholic hierarchy might be offended."[260z]

Seldes quotes Heywood Broun, "And still more precarious is the position of the New York newspaper man who ventures any criticism of the Catholic Church. There is not a single New York editor who does not live in mortal terror of the power of this group."[260aa]

Seldes continues: "Probably the bravest thing the *News* has done has been its editorial defiance of the pressure of the Catholic Church...."[260bb] "To criticize the Catholic Church is to invite a boycott, the withdrawal of advertising, loss in circulation and in revenue."[260cc] "...almost every newspaper in the world is scared to death when any religious sect is mentioned critically."[260dd]

"Ten years ago [1929] the Catholic Church was on the defensive. Today it is on the aggressive, and there is ten times the fear of it there was a decade ago. Father Curran, of the International Catholic Truth Society, changed the policy of one newspaper because he controlled $20,000 of business (*New Republic*, December 30, 1936) and had the effrontery to boast of this outrageous attack on the freedom of the press. But it is general Catholic pressure, not $20,000, which frightens if it does not wholly corrupt many other newspapers."[260ee]

Regarding the War in Spain:

"But a new element entered into the war: the Catholic Church. It sided with the rebels. The rebels had sworn to restore the Church to power. That was one reason for the Vatican's sympathy....The American press got its first facts fairly straight. Its errors were unintentional. But from the beginning of August 1936, the Catholic hierarchy in America...began a crusade against the newspapers which truthfully reported events in Spain."[260ff]

"It is now well known that reactionary Catholics (as distinguished from liberal Catholics who are either for the Loyalist government or neutral) have used their tremendous pressure, plus threats of boycott, and the withdrawal of advertising money, to change the opinion of American newspapers regarding the war in Spain."[260gg]

"How effective the boycott against the Stern paper [*Record* publisher, Stern] was I do not know. But every newspaperman knows that the most powerful pressure group in America today is the Roman Catholic Church. I do not know whether it succeeded in curtailing the *Record* circulation or inflicting a financial blow through the withdrawal of advertising by Catholic business men. But on August 10, 1936, Publisher Stern wrote a humble letter to Cardinal Doughterty...[who] accepted the apology....I believe that every newspaperman in America who really values freedom of the press, no matter what his religious beliefs may be, will deplore this episode, and especially the *Record's* genuflections.

"And now we behold the publisher of a chain of four newspapers, four of the very tiny minority of liberal, free, independent newspapers left in America, bowing before the pressure of the Church when in fact his editorials on Spain had been true, honest, favorable to the anti-Fascist movement in Spain and applauded by all fair, liberal and intelligent men.

"Caught between the advertising pressure of big business on the one hand, and the political pressure of a religious organization on the other, the *New York Post*, *Philadelphia Record*, *Camden Courier* and *Camden Post* have had to make the usual compromises.

"I know of no better illustration of the fact that there is no completely free press in America."[260hh]

ON "CATHOLIC ISSUES" THERE IS NO FREE PRESS

From the "dean and granddaddy of investigative reporters," when it comes to issues important to the hierarchy of the Catholic Church, "...there is no free press in America." Overpopulation and its solutions—contraception, abortion, sterilization, population education, sex education, advancement of women's rights, public debate of the environment and the greenhouse effect—all threaten the authority of the pope and the survival of the institution of the Papacy. On these issues, there is no free press in America.

Of all of Seldes's conclusions, one of the most important is that secrecy is generally maintained regarding the fact that the pressure of the Catholic hierarchy on the American press is one of the most important forces in America. This pressure makes things happen or not happen depending on the needs of the hierarchy irrespective of the needs of the American people, our country and our democracy. This secrecy made possible the killing of the Rockefeller Commission and NSSM 200 initiatives and all other serious efforts to control population growth by the Catholic hierarchy.

THE SPANISH "CIVIL WAR" LESSON FOR
POPULATION GROWTH CONTROL

Over the past 25 years, American political will to deal with the overpopulation problem has been destroyed. NSSM 200 lived and died. As President Nixon's Special Message to Congress correctly predicted, these outcomes are certain to have an enormous impact on the lives of everyone on the planet. The story of the creation and demise of NSSM 200, and of how the government was thwarted in its effort to resolve the overpopulation problem, received no mention in the news media or any other information source. Few Americans are aware of what is perhaps the most important story of the 20th Century. How could it have been suppressed and for what reason?

Seldes's extensive study of the Spanish Civil War and the related control of the American press by the Catholic hierarchy is exceedingly instructive for all who are concerned about population growth control. Population growth control is by no means the first instance of absolutely pivotal Catholic hierarchy intervention in American press coverage of an important issue. The hierarchy has a history of manipulating the press to insure that Papal interests are served even at the expense of American interests.

In the 1970s and 1980s, George Seldes told us how and why in seven articles that appeared in *The Churchman* magazine, an Episcopal journal, founded in 1804, and the oldest religious publication in America. It has always been committed to the truth. (I am honored to be a contributing editor.)

After decades of intense study, in an August 1978 article, Seldes concludes: "The *New York Times* is still in fear of reprisals from the Roman Church in America, as it was during the entire Spanish War when under managing editor Edward L. James and the notorious 'Fascist phalanx in the bull-pen.' James's four, incidentally Roman Catholic, editor assistants, bowed to the 'power house on Madison Avenue,' Cardinal Spellman's residence, and a certain Father Thorning, and published scores of falsifications from Spain."[260ii] Seldes provides strong evidence to support this conclusion. For example, he cites *The New Republic* magazine: "*The New Republic*, to its credit, in 'Who Lied About Spain?' when the war was over [1939] listed the [*New York*] *Times* man with Franco as the number one falsifier." In a November 1981 article, Seldes concluded that all of

America's 1,750 daily papers were similarly terrified by "the Catholic Church propaganda campaign."[260jj] This "terror" that Seldes describes is still pervasive and has led to the disappearance of a free press in America in matters of concern to the Vatican, such as the recognition of overpopulation as a national security threat.

But let us begin the story at the beginning and allow Mr. Seldes to lay out the evidence for us item by item.

In 1931, Spain became the Republic of Spain, a liberal democracy that separated church and state, ended State monetary support for the church and adopted the principles of Freedom of Conscience, Freedom of Religion, and Freedom of the Press. The Vatican feared for the Church's very survival in Spain. There had been four insurrections since 1835, and it was the Spanish people, the poor workers and poor peasants, who burned the churches because they blamed the hierarchy for having persistently backed the upper class.[260ii] The latest uprising against the Catholic Church took place throughout the country in July, 1936.[260kk] One historian described it as "the work of masses of common people, a spontaneous uprising."[260kk] The Vatican feared that the liberal democracy with its freedoms would spell the end of the Church in Spain.

The Spanish War of 1936-39 is often called a civil war. But this was a lie from the beginning. It was not a civil war but an invasion by Hitler, Mussolini and Salazar fascists or what Seldes refers to as the Fascist Internationale in league with the Vatican. Mussolini landed 200,000 infantrymen from his Black Arrow division in Franco-held seaports and Hitler sent Goering's Condor Legion to bomb civilians,[260ll] involving an estimated 50,000 German aviators.[260jj] All this had been envisioned in Rome in 1934. Seldes writes, "Mussolini and two representatives of the plan . . . met there and even promised help in overthrowing the Republic and establishing a fascist type of government. They also met with Hitler that same year — and the confessions of the Nazis at the Nuremberg Trials confirm the plot."[260kk] There was to be an uprising of treasonous Republic officers led by Franco, the invasion by the Italian and German forces and the promulgation of the lie that this was an uprising against a communist take-over of the Republic and a "Christian crusade against atheistic communism."[260mm] The creation of this great lie would be primarily the responsibility of the Vatican.

"Cardinal Pacelli, then papal secretary, began this campaign of falsification in America when he came to Hyde Park [New York] to enlist the aid of President Franklin Roosevelt in this undertaking. Pacelli, who three years later was to become Pope Pius XII, was successful. Roman Catholic layman James Farley, a boss of the Democratic party, Cardinal Spellman, and Joseph P. Kennedy, FDR's ambassador to London, promoted Pacelli's position. Each warned Roosevelt he would lose the Catholic vote unless he embargoed arms to Spain and joined Chamberlain's so-called Neutrality Pact.

The making of the "Christian crusade against communism" myth began immediately following Pacelli's visit to America. *"The New York Times*, October 1, 1936, was informed from Rome that Pacelli had 'left for the United States of America to enlist the support of President Roosevelt and the U.S. Government for the anti-communist campaign the Pope has been waging for some time. The Holy See regards the spread of communist doctrine as the gravest and most threatening danger hanging over the world.' When the cardinal arrived in New York *The New York Times* headline read: 'Pacelli Reported Seeking Aid in U.S. in Anti-Red Drive . . .'[260mm] A myth was born.

In Spain the day before, Seldes later discovered, "The [Spanish hierarchy's] pastoral letter 'Los dos Cindados' of September 13, 1936 had converted a treasonable officer's rebellion into the 'Crusade Against Godless Communism.'"[260nn]

"Immediately following this meeting, Hitler's newspapers reported FDR had made important concessions to the Cardinal and that Pacelli 'is declared to have delivered the Catholic vote in the United States to Roosevelt.' Although this appeared at first to be a typical Nazi piece of propaganda, it seems to have been substantiated by important visits to Hyde Park in 1936 by Farley and Cardinal Spellman. In every Catholic country in Europe, Cardinals, priests and diocesan publications had openly declared themselves to be against Franco, *but not one in America did so* [emphasis added]."[260mm]

The Neutrality Act was instrumental in the demise of Republican Spain. President Roosevelt prevented guns, food and medicine from being shipped to the Republic.[260ll] Everyone understood this. "Roosevelt was re-elected in 1936, and again in 1940. The Non-Intervention Pact, originated by pro-fascists in the British Foreign

Office, remained in effect; the world press either falsified the news of the arrival of German and Italian troops, or confused enough people to prevent effective protest."[260mm]

"When in 1938, a last effort was made to lift the embargo on arms, *The Nation* said: 'The Catholics got busy and reached the President, who was fishing in southern waters. Big Church dignitaries came to Washington and talked cold politics. . .' *The Nation* report, written by Max Lerner, columnist for *The New York Post*, continues: 'only a band of heroes could have withstood the combined effort of Catholic votes, State Department leaning and authority, administrative pressure, and mental sluggishness, and the Senate Committee [considering this legislation] was not heroic . . . the biggest factor in the mind of the President was the Catholic vote. . . . It is a cold political fact that Mr. Roosevelt, who has braved concentrated wealth, has not braved the risk of losing the Catholic vote.' The repeal move in Congress failed, and the last hope for the Spanish Republic disappeared."[260mm] This blockade was responsible for the Republic's defeat.[260jj]

It was not only President Roosevelt who felt the intense Catholic pressure. When Spain's Congress opened in 1938, "a resolution was introduced in the American Congress to send greetings. Only 60 members had the courage to sign; 440 were either on the fascist side or too cowardly to declare their convictions. The 60 who signed were attacked in the Roman pulpit, the Roman Catholic press, and by the Cardinals as 'anti-American' and as 'Reds'. Cardinal Spellman and his colleagues, whose offices were referred to among newspapermen (but never by newspapers) as 'the power house', sent orders to the lobbyists to get retractions from the 60 under threat of defeat in the next elections. Many recanted." A few half-recanted, saying their greetings did not mean endorsement. Among them: Harry Byrd of Virginia and Claude Pepper of Florida. Three Senators affirmed their endorsement of the Spanish Republic. Among them: Senator Hubert Humphrey.[260mm]

Seldes goes on, "The Vatican lobby continued its work in Washington for many years after the Republic's demise, seeking quick recognition of the fascist regime, loans, admission to the United Nations."[260mm]

SPANISH BISHOPS ADMIT DECADES OF DECEPTION

The accuracy of this report on the role of the Vatican in the fascist takeover of Spain is irrefutable. Why? Because Spain's Bishops themselves openly admitted the role of the Church. Seldes writes, "The myth of a Christian crusade against Communism in Spain persisted for decades, despite honest revisionist historians. It was not until 1971 that the myth was finally destroyed by none other than the Roman Catholic hierarchy of Spain. *This important correction of history was slurred in the world press and is probably not known to more than one person in a million today* (emphasis added).

"In Madrid, September 15, 1971, Primate Cardinal Enrique Taracon presided at a Congress of the entire Roman Catholic Hierarchy, with 94 bishops and 151 priests present. . . . Although a two-thirds' vote was necessary to pass resolutions, and this one did not pass, it is significant that it received a large majority of the vote. . . . The majority confessed it had sinned in supporting the wrong side (the fascist side) in Spain and asked to be forgiven. 'We humbly recognize,' said the resolution, 'and ask pardon for it, that we failed at the proper time to be ministers of reconciliation in the midst of our people divided by a war between brothers.'"[260mm] "In 1971 — and again in 1972, 1983 and succeeding years — a majority of Spain's 94 bishops and 151 priests attending voted 60% or more for the Church's apology but never officially passed it."[260ii] By taking this action, Cardinal Taracon probably prevented widespread killing of priests and nuns upon Franco's death in 1975.

The news of these votes was almost completely suppressed in the world press. Only three minor reports on this story appeared in the United States.[260ii]

"FDR admitted his error in 1939 — but it could not be published in his lifetime. He said to his Ambassador to Madrid, Claude Bowers, who had told the truth about the great world campaign of falsehood against Spain and had urged American help: 'We have made a mistake, you have been right all along. . . .' He wrote this confession by FDR in 1954. Secretary of State Sumner Welles in his book *Time for Decision*, 1944, wrote: 'of all our blind isolationist policies the most disastrous was our attitude on the Spanish Civil War.' President Harry Truman wrote in his *Memoirs*: 'I believe it was a mistake for me to support the Neutrality Action in the first place.'"

AMERICAN HIERARCHY AND THE VATICAN MAINTAIN DECEPTION

On the other hand, "The spokesman for the American Catholic Hierarchy, who so powerfully influenced American foreign policy — Farley, Kennedy, Cardinals Hayes, Spellman and Dougherty" and the archbishops and priests and Catholic laymen who so intensely lobbied in Congress, did not join their Spanish brothers and never admitted error.[260mm] Their vital roles and that of the Vatican are unquestionable in the crushing of this liberal democracy.

The Spanish War of 1936-1939 was unspeakably brutal. All told, an estimated 500,000 to 1,000,000 of Spain's population of 25,000,000 were killed.[260nn] By 1939, an estimated 100,000 prisoners of war had been murdered by the fascists.[260jj] ". . . the official organ of the Roman Church in France, *La Croix*, was the first to report that Franco killed *every* Loyalist Republican prisoner — a tremendously important news story. That, incidentally, was also suppressed in almost the entire U.S. press."[260nn]

These Spaniards were murdered for only one reason — they believed in liberal democracy, just as we Americans do here in this country.

Seldes documents the leading role of the Vatican in the destruction of the Spanish Republic. The murder of 100,000 liberal democrat prisoners by Franco was undoubtedly made easier by Pope Pius XI. Referring to the uprising against the Roman Church throughout Spain in July, 1936, Pius XI attacked the "ruinization, destruction, villainies, barbarities by the savage forces whom it is impossible to dignify with the words human beings."[260kk] Dehumanization always makes mass murder seem less reprehensible.

"Pius XII declared publicly year after year his support for Franco. He sent Franco the Supreme Equestrian Order of the Militia of Our Lord Jesus Christ. Immediately after the war ended in 1939, Pius XII not only sent his congratulations to the fascist victor, but stated his 'Christian heroism' had 'pleased God'. On July 11, 1939 Pius XII reviewed 3,000 Spanish Legionaries in Rome and called them the defenders of the faith and the culture of their country."[260kk]

"Pius XII [also] blessed the Italian fascist army and air force on its return from Spain . . . in 1939.[260mm]

"All the American Cardinals endorsed the Franco-fascist cause except Cardinal Mundelein of Chicago. . . . Franco had awarded his decorations, usually the 'Sacred Heart of Jesus', to all the American Cardinals except Mundelein. . . . Incidentally, two well known [Catholic] laymen, Ambassador to Spain Ogden H. Hammond and Ambassador William Cameron Forbes, are also listed among the recipients of Franco's bloodstained medals."[260kk]

In the publication *Historia del Franquismo,* which began in 1976 to revise 40 years of Spanish history following Franco's death, "Issue No. 1, page 6 states: 'The rebellion of the generals was first called a Crusade for God, for Spain and for Franco' by the Church. When Franco won he received the following telegram: 'We lift our hearts to the Lord sincerely thankful that your excellency has brought a Catholic victory to Spain. . . . We send your excellency and to all the noble people of Spain our apostolic benediction. [signed] Pope Pius XII'"[260nn]

"To the Spanish press Pius XII issued the following statement for April 18, 1937: 'The nation selected by God . . . the people of Spain came to the defenses of the faith and of Christian civilization . . . God in his compassion will lead Spain on the safe road of your traditional and Catholic greatness.'"[260nn]

"Primate of Spain, Cardinal Goma . . . called the war 'a crusade for religion, for country, and for civilization' in a pastoral letter."[260nn]

Seldes offers a mountain of evidence to support his conclusions that "it was the Roman Catholic Church which was fascism's main supporter," and "It was the hierarchy which originated and propagandized the 'holy crusade against Godless Communism'. The hierarchy was as responsible as guns and planes in destroying the Republic. It monopolized schools. It propagated Fascism for 39 years."[260nn]

Why would the Vatican propagate Fascism? "The first fascist newspaper, *Arriba España,* was published August 1, 1936. One of its directors was a priest representing the Church . . . on September 16 *Arriba España* said editorially that 'Catholicism will find Fascism its best collaborator'."[260nn]

And what were the Church's rewards? "Franco repaid the Roman Catholic Church by abolishing divorce, making religious marriages obligatory and restoring taxes for the benefit of the Church — all previously banned by the Republic."[260nn]

Most important, Franco turned the schools over to the Catholic Church. Seldes offers ". . . two short abstracts from nationally used catechisms taught to two generations of children, in the hope of producing a brain-washed people which would never rebel."[2600] "In the second year of the war the Archbishop of Grenada gave his imprimatur to the catechism of the Jesuit priest Angel Maria de Arcos. This catechism was so unbelievable, so obscurantist, incredible, outrageous, that when John Langdon-Davies wrote about it in a London liberal magazine he was attacked by numerous Catholic editors, accused of making the whole thing up. He sued for libel, established the veracity of the catechism, and won his case. *Here is what the children in many eastern cities, including Granada, were taught*:

Q. Is every Liberal government hostile to the Church?

A. Evidently, since whoever is not with Christ is against Him.

Q. Then there is no grade of Liberalism that can be good?

A. None: because Liberalism is mortal sin and anti-Christian.

Q. What of Communism, Socialism, Modern Democracy, Anarchism, and the like sects?

A. They are contrary to Catholic faith, to justice, and to virtue, and as such condemned by the Church.

(In reply to another question:)

A. The Liberal system is the weapon with which the accursed Jewish race makes war on our Lord Jesus Christ, and his Church, and on the Christian people.

In 1944 the new classic catechism, known as the *Nuevo Repaldi*, and used nationally, was published and introduced into every secondary school in Spain. It consists of 112 pages, and was fully described by the U.S. press attaché in Madrid during the Spanish War, Emmet John Hughes, in his *Report from Spain*. Of the ten pages which concern themselves with the essential doctrines of Catholic faith and morals, here are a few samples:

Q. What does freedom of the press mean?

A. The right to print and publish without previous censorship all kinds of opinions, however absurd and corrupting they may be.

Q. Must the government suppress this freedom by means of censorship?

A. Obviously, yes.

Q. Why?

A. Because it must prevent the deception, calumny and corruption of its subjects, which harm the general good.

Q. Does one sin gravely who subscribes to a liberal newspaper?

A. Yes . . . Because he contributes his money to evil, places his faith in jeopardy, and gives a bad example.

Q. What rules can be given to know liberal papers?

A. The following:

1. If they call themselves liberal.

2. If they defend freedom of conscience, freedom of worship, freedom of the press, or any of the other liberal errors.

3. If they attack the Roman Pontiff, the clergy, or the religious orders.

4. If they belong to liberal parties.

5. If they comment on news or judge personalities with a liberal criterion.

6. If they unreservedly praise the good moral and intellectual qualities of liberal personalities and parties.

7. If, in reporting events concerned with the battle waged by Our Lord Jesus Christ and His Holy Church against their enemies today, they remain neutral.

Q. What is the rule to avoid error in these cases?

A. Do not read any newspaper without the previous consultation and approval of your confessor."[260oo]

These two catechisms make it clear just how strongly the Catholic Church feels about freedom of the press, as well as with what disdain and contempt it views this vital democratic principle.

OTHERS RECOGNIZE PRESS MANIPULATION

The death of NSSM 200 and the disintegration of American political determination to overcome the overpopulation problem occurred with the knowledge of only a handful of Americans over the past two decades. Has the rabidly anti-free press posture of the Catholic Church resulted in suppression of the American press in reporting on these vital topics? Could the Church, with its bishops and laymen, have had such an effect on the American press? Let us examine Seldes's findings regarding the Spanish War of 1936-39.

Of course, Seldes was by no means alone in his assessment of the Catholic leadership's corruption of the press (particularly *The New York Times*). *The Churchman* published numerous articles on this topic,[260ll] as did the *New Republic*. In their June 28, 1939, issue, "Who Lied About Spain?", *The New York Times* and its reporter, William P. Carney, headed the list.[260kk] Numerous books were also devoted to this topic (see Herbert L. Matthews, *A World in Revolution*, and Guy Talese, *History of the Times*).[260ll] Few Americans today are aware of this page of American history, or of this corruption of the principle of freedom of the press by the Catholic hierarchy, or of its implications for population growth control.

It should also be made clear that not all Catholic reporters were part of the Vatican propaganda machine. Writes Seldes, "In all justice, it must be stated that a score of noted Catholic war correspondents and noted Catholic newspapers — in Europe — reported the war honestly, detailing all the atrocities committed by the Fascist-Nazi forces. . ."[260ll] (The most famous reporter on the Loyalist (Republican) side was a Catholic named Ernest Hemingway. Other notables were Fernsworth of *The Times* and Taylor of the *Chicago Tribune*, both Catholics.)[260mm]

Seldes continues, "On May 12, 1949, one New York newspaper carried this item, *otherwise suppressed throughout the country* [emphasis added]: 'Patman Ousts Priest Lobbying for Spain'. Representative Wright Patman (D.-Texas) called a doorkeeper and had ejected from the speaker's lobby of the House the Rev. Dr. Joseph F. Thorning, editor, college professor, and *the best known propagandist* [emphasis added] for Franco's fascist regime in Spain. Throughout the war, Thorning not only praised the fascist coalition but denounced the correspondents who were reporting from the Republican side.

Seldes concluded, "Although *The New York Times* always surrendered to Father Thorning, he continued to attack it."[260mm]

We have witnessed in America since the mid-1970s the application of this same technique for control of the press on the issue of overpopulation. Although the entire press consistently genuflect to the Catholic hierarchy, they are under continuous attack for being too 'liberal' and 'anti-Catholic'. The charge of 'liberal press' is always used to attack the anti-Vatican position on every issue. This technique is used hundreds of times each day to control the American press.

In January 1977, *Historia* revealed for the first time in Spain what Seldes, Matthews, Hemingway, Fernsworth and others attempted to report in this country, that "Nazism and Fascism were accepted and became Franco's policy from the first days of the war. These facts the American press also largely suppressed, preferring to call

Hitler's and Mussolini's collaborator Franco a nationalist," asserts Seldes.[260nn]

Seldes was quite critical of the world press generally. He writes, "The world press it might be said — although no general statement is wholly true — failed its readers during the Spanish war. The democratic Republic was labeled "Red" and "Communist" at a time when there were fewer "Reds" and Communists in Spain than there are today."[260ll]

THE NEW YORK TIMES WAS THE WORST

However, he singled out *The New York Times* in his study, concluding that the newspaper was the worst offender and because of its reputation for reliability in reporting, was particularly influential in this case in a most negative sense. He was highly critical of the *Times* for its refusal to admit to its wrongdoings. He writes:

"The Army and the rulers joined the majority of the Spanish people in repudiating Franco-Fascism with the dictator's death. This left only the Fourth Estate, and notably the outstanding newspaper in the world, the most powerful and important maker of public opinion, *The New York Times*, to complete the repudiation by confessing the falsehoods and pro-fascism of the past.

"Its great opportunity came on August 1, 1977, when it published a two-column obituary of its Spanish War correspondent, Herbert L. Matthews. Instead of confessing that it had falsified history during the war by publishing slanted news and outright 100% pure lies from the Franco side, and harassed and intimidated Matthews, who risked his life and told the truth, this dirty-trick obituary added to the sad record of American journalism's failure.

"This failure of *The New York Times* to correct its false history of the fascist officers' conspiracy and rebellion —wrongly called the 'Spanish Civil War' (there were almost no Spaniards in the Franco armies: there were Germans, Italians, and the Terico and Foreign Legion of Muslims) — was so flagrant that for the second time in *Times* history, if not in all journalism's history, one of the senior editors of the *Times* was forced to criticize the *Times*. John B. Oakes wrote a 'Letter to the Editor' and it was printed!

"Matthews was one of the victims. . . . Edward L. James, then unfortunately managing editor, published falsehoods alongside Matthews' factual reports. . . . Unable to get the truth published in the *Times*, he wrote it in his book, *A World in Revolution*. Here are a few quotations:

"'McCaw had ordered the copy readers to substitute the word "Insurgents" when I sent "Italians".' (p. 26).

"'I saw two of Henday's Associated Press stories [French border] front-paged, both equally false.' (p. 35).

"'I especially took strong exceptions to the fact that in the effort to be "impartial" the *Times* had throughout alternately featured mine, Carney's and AP Henday's copy from the Franco side, regardless of news value, accuracy, and honesty.' (p. 39).

"Elsewhere in his book Matthews wrote that 'Carney was a Roman Catholic . . . in Carney's case it blinded him to any other aspect of the rebellion.' And again, 'All four of the editors who worked in the bull pen throughout the war were Roman Catholics: Robert McCaw, the assistant managing editor in charge; Neil Mac-Neil, the second man; Clarence Howell, a convert, was almost fanatically religious; and Harvey Getzloe.' These four were known in the *Times* as 'The Catholic Bull-Pen.'

"Guy Talese in his history of the *Times* refers to them as 'the Fascist phalanx in the bull-pen.'

"It might be worth noting that the *N.Y. Times* also used the services of the *Times* of London, whose correspondent in Spain, Lawrence Fernsworth, happened to be an American and a Roman Catholic. Fernsworth also wrote for the American Catholic press as well as the *N.Y. Times*. When Fernsworth once protested Editor James' mismanagement of the Spanish War news, James cabled 'Resignation accepted.' Fernsworth had not resigned; James threw him out."[2601]

The editor of *The Churchman* inserted the following note into Seldes's article:

"[Lawrence Fernsworth's . . . articles in *The Churchman* . . . titled 'A Catholic Reporter in Spain,' gave an inside story of the pressures upon an American reporter working in Spain during those war years, 1936-39. 'A political church,' he wrote, 'was not interested in honest surveys . . .' An accompanying editorial in *The Churchman* for March 1, 1940, stated: 'All too rarely does the public have the opportunity of being taken behind the scenes of dramatic events of such significance. All through the Spanish war liberal-minded Americans who attempted to counteract the falsehoods of the Roman Catholic hierarchy in reference to that conflict were bitterly attacked, as *The Churchman* was on many occasions, by Catholic leaders. When we, along with others, insisted that there were thousands of Italian troops fighting in Spain and that great numbers of German army technicians were in that country aiding Franco, we were frankly and bluntly called liars by Roman Catholic leaders. Yet, as the public now knows, we were merely recording the facts.']"[2601]

Seldes continues:

". . . *The N.Y. Times* under James, by publishing one column of falsehoods alongside one column of Matthews' eyewitness facts, served the cause of Franco and his allies, Hitler and Mussolini..."[2601]

This very same technique is being used in America today by a press manipulated by the Vatican to misinform Americans, minimizing the threat of overpopulation and, in particular, the threat of the greenhouse effect. The Vatican demand is that both sides of the issues be given equal press. An article of falsehoods is published alongside an article of facts. For example, the United Nation's task force on the greenhouse effect includes 2500 scientists. There are perhaps a half dozen people with credentials who dismiss this theory. The Vatican has successfully insisted that both groups be given equal press or, better yet, none at all. On illegal immigration, the costs to America vastly outweigh the benefits. The Vatican has succeeded in leveling the playing field using this technique of press manipulation. As a result, Americans remain unorganized on the immigration issue. The outcome: press generated confusion prevents effective protests.

Seldes continues,

"If there is any value in history, if history teaches us something and helps world civilization, the Spanish record should be set straight. The *Times* failed to do so in August 1977. Yet in 1971 Matthews concluded:

'I say that not only I, but the truth suffered. No student can today go back to the files of *The New York Times* from July 1936 and get a competent, balanced, complete journalistic picture of the Spanish Civil War. The *Times* failed its readers and posterity.'[2601]

"The war correspondents, not only Matthews and Hemingway, but the hundred or more without exception, tried to tell the world from Madrid that this was a rehearsal by Hitler and Mussolini for a world war. We said so in 1936 and every year until 1939. We warned FDR and France and England that the Nazi-Fascists, masquerading as anti-Communists, were trying out guns, tanks, and airplanes. There was destruction of whole cities, air-bombing (Guernica), destruction of whole civilian populations (Barcelona block bombing). We tried to tell the world to prepare for the Hitler-Mussolini-Japanese Anti-Komintern Pakt attack — World War II as it is now called — and by preparing, perhaps prevent it. We failed largely because of pressure by the Roman Catholic Church of the United States on the American press — by Father Thorning, Cardinal Spellman and others. And, being the most powerful opinion-making paper in America the *Times* must share a major part of the blame. Three estates — rulers, army, church — have at least confessed their sin. But not the infallible *Times.*"[2601l]

To this day *The New York Times* has not published the truth about its falsehoods and pro-fascism of the Spanish war years. We must assume that the *Times* does not want known the influence of the Catholic hierarchy at the *Times* during that era. We must also assume that the *Times* has not acted because the Catholic influence prevails in its editorial offices today.

The overthrow of democracy in Spain by the Vatican with the Spanish War of 1936-39 was viewed as a matter of great concern to the Vatican. Their success required substantial control of the press in Spain and in the United States. Halting of population growth control is far more important to the Vatican than Spain ever was and control of the press is critical. The Vatican is succeeding in thwarting population growth control because it is largely controlling the press on this issue.

Seldes singled out the *New York Times* for particular scrutiny but his studies showed that all 1,750 American newspapers with few exceptions were victimized by the Catholic leadership and that "The Catholic Church propaganda campaign [was] conducted largely by the Knights of Columbus."[7] As late as 1978, he concluded that "the *New York Times* is still in fear of reprisals from the Roman Church."

In the case of population growth control (family planning, abortion, immigration) no Catholic reporters, editors or publishers, or their counterparts in the electronic media have distinguished themselves, nor have any non-Catholics. The reason? For anyone to emerge from the pack has been made more difficult by the Vatican than it was even during the Spanish War days. Though it seems that a description of the opposition to population growth control and how the opposition operates would be newsworthy, reporters have not distinguished themselves by making this known. Despite its enormous importance, this information never appears in the press.

No doubt the influence of the Knights of Columbus with its membership of 1.5 million means that the American press is not free to report on matters that threaten the security-survival of the Papacy. But as if this were not sufficient, in recent years a new organization has been created to serve as the point of attack on the American freedom of the press — the Catholic League for Religion and Civil Rights. The next chapter is devoted to a survey of the League's chilling effect on this freedom in the 1990s.

THE CATHOLIC LEAGUE AND SUPPRESSION OF FREEDOM OF THE PRESS TODAY

15

15

The Catholic League was founded in 1973 by Jesuit priest Virgil Blum. William Donohue assumed leadership in July 1993.[260pp1] Since then, the membership has grown from 27,000 to 200,000.[260pp2] According to Donohue, the League has "won the support of all of the U.S. Cardinals and many of the Bishops as well...We are here to defend the Church from the scurrilous assaults that have been mounted against it, and we definitely need the support of the hierarchy if we are to get the job done."[260pp3] Thus it can be considered an arm of the Church. It supplements or replaces priest-controlled organizations of the past described by Blanshard and Seldes. The League apparently has a single mission: suppression of all mainstream criticism of the Roman Catholic Church.

According to Donohue, it is fortunate that, "the Catholic Church is there to provide a heady antidote to today's mindless ideas of freedom."[260pp4] He is a strong advocate of the Church's positions on restriction of the freedoms guaranteed by the American Constitution and condemned by popes for nearly two centuries, especially those regarding the press and speech. He informs us that: "the Catholic League is there to defend the Church against its adversaries."[260pp4]

There are many recognizable principles governing the behavior of the League. One is revealed in a vicious 1994 attack against the New London newspaper, *The Day,* for an editorial critical of the Catholic Church: "What is truly 'beyond understanding' is not the Catholic Church's position, it is the fact that a secular newspaper has the audacity to stick it's nose in where it doesn't belong. It is nobody's business what the Catholic Church does."[260pp5]

A second basic premise is the League's commitment to canon 1369 of the Code of Canon Law: "A person is to be punished with a just penalty, who, at a public event or assembly, or in a published writing, or by otherwise using the means of social communication, utters blasphemy, or gravely harms public morals, or rails at or excites hatred of or contempt for religion or the Church."[260pp6] Canon law is the law of the Catholic Church. All criticism of the pope or the Church is in violation of this law in one way or another. This chapter will make clear that the League follows this canon to the letter and demands that all others conform—or pay the price for their violation.

Another principle is aggressive action. Says Donohue, "I defy anyone to name a single organization that has more rabid members than the Catholic League. Our members are generous, loyal and extremely active. When we ask them to sign petitions, write to offending parties and the like, they respond with a vigor that is unparalleled...We aim to win. Obviously, we don't win them all, but our record of victories is impressive."[260pp7] To justify this stance, he identifies with Patrick Buchanan's resistance to the "Culture War" against the Catholic Church: "We didn't start this culture war against the Catholic Church, we simply want to stop it."[260pp8]

Donohue also justifies the League's aggressive behavior by claiming that it is culturally unacceptable for nonCatholics to criticize the Catholic Church. "Perhaps the most cogent remark of the day," he asserts, "came from the former Mayor of New York, Ed Koch, who politely remarked that his mother always advised him not to speak ill of other religions. It is a lesson that apparently few have learned....Non-Catholics would do well to follow the advice of Ed Koch's mom and just give it a rest. Their crankiness is wearing thin."[260pp9] This cultural norm is widely accepted in America, to the enormous benefit of the Vatican. What role, one wonders, did the Catholic Church play in its adoption? Certainly, in the case of population growth control, its consequence has been catastrophic.

The Catholic League strongly discourages criticism of the Church, especially attacks by the press. Says Donohue, "It does no good complaining about Catholic bashing if all we do is wait until the other side strikes."[260pp10] Prevention of such publications is of the essence. Yet Donohue is convinced that this is not censorship:

"The press and the radio talk shows asked me if the Catholic League was engaging in censorship by responding the way we did. As always, I informed them that only the government has the power to censor anything."[260pp11] This is patently untrue.

Another tenet enunciated by Donohue: "I think it is a gross mistake to give elevation to fringe groups. Our basic rule of thumb is this: the more mainstream the source of anti-Catholicism, the more likely it is that the Catholic League will respond....The mainstream media, after all, have the credibility and influence that the fringe lacks, and they are therefore much more likely to do real damage."[260pp12] "When major universities, TV networks and government officials engage in Catholic-baiting, it is a far more dangerous situation than the venom that emanates from certifiably fringe organizations."[260pp13] "When an establishment newspaper such as the *Sun-Sentinel* [Fort Lauderdale] offends, it cannot be ignored."[260pp14]

Donohue goes on to explain the *Sun-Sentinel* example. On February 9, 1995, it ran an ad, paid for by a Seventh Day Adventist group, which claimed that the Catholic Church is seeking to create a New World Order to take command of the world and that the Pope and the Catholic Church were in a league with Satan. "Accordingly, the Catholic League contacted the radio and television stations in the area, the opposition newspaper, and the nation's major media outlets registering its outrage and its demands. We demanded nothing less than 'an apology to Catholics and a pledge that no such ads will ever be accepted again.' We added that 'If this is not forthcoming, the Catholic League will launch a public ad campaign on its own, one that will directly target the *Sun-Sentinel*.'" "What exactly did we have in mind? We were prepared to take out ads in the opposition newspaper, registering our charge of anti-Catholic bigotry. We were prepared to pay for radio spots making our charge. We were prepared to buy billboard space along the majority arteries surrounding the Fort Lauderdale community. Why not? After all,...we are in a position to make such threats....This is the way it works: if the source of bigotry wants to deal with lousy publicity, it can elect to do so. Or it can come to its senses and knock it off. In the event the anti-Catholic bigots want to bite the bullet and stay the course, we'll do everything we can within the law to make sure that they pay a very high price for doing so."[260pp15] It goes without saying that anyone critical of the Vatican, or the hierarchy, or the Roman Catholic Church is, by definition, an anti-Catholic bigot—including Catholics themselves.

One final element makes clear the objective of the Catholic League—protection of the papacy against all criticism. Writes Donohue, "It is the conviction of the Catholic League that an attack on the Church is an attack on Catholics."[260pp16] He offers no rationale to support this theory. Obviously, millions of liberal American Catholics would disagree outright, for it is they who have been attacking the Church.

Donohue continues, "Throughout American history, the job of combating anti-Catholicism fell to the clergy, and especially to the Archbishops. But times have changed....The type of anti-Catholicism that exists in American society today is fundamentally different from the genre that marked this country's history from the outset. From colonial times to the election of John F. Kennedy as President of the United States, anti-Catholicism was vented against both individual Catholics and against the Catholic Church itself. But over the past 30 years, it has become evident that most of the Catholic-bashing centers on the institution of the Church..."[260pp17] The hierarchy cannot be effective against criticism of the institution because they are the institution. Thus, the hierarchy has had to call on the laity to protect the institution in this way. In 1971, the League's founder pointed out, "If a group is to be politically effective, issues rather than institutions must be at stake."[260pp18] In other words, the laity, if left to their own devices, will not defend the institution but they will defend their interests as individuals. Hence, the League has adopted this principle and has convinced its members that "an attack on the Church is an attack on Catholics." In this way, the institution is successfully using individual lay Catholics to shield it from all criticism.

THE CHURCH AND ITS IMAGE

The Catholic Church in America has good reason to be intensely concerned about its image and any criticism. Donohue cites a 1995 study, "Taking America's Pulse," undertaken by the National Conference (formerly known as the National Conference of Christians and Jews). Despite the almost complete suppression of all criticism of the Catholic Church in America, a majority of non-Catholic Americans (55%) believe that Catholics "want to impose their own ideas of morality on the larger society." The survey also found that 38% of non-Catholics believe that Catholics are "narrow-minded because they are too much controlled by their Church."[260pp19] Obviously, there is a highly receptive audience in this country for any justified criticisms of the Catholic Church. If the floodgates ever opened, it is unlikely that the Church would be able to close them again. Only too well understood by the hierarchy, and the Catholic League, this perhaps explains their unmitigated intolerance for criticism.

METHODS OF THE LEAGUE

Donohue has cited many of the methods used by the League, including some we have already mentioned. "We specialize in public embarrassment of public figures who have earned our wrath and that is why we are able to win so many battles: no person or organization wants to be publicly embarrassed, and that is why we specialize in doing exactly that..."[260pp20] Elsewhere he writes, "The threat of a lawsuit is the only language that some people understand. The specter of public humiliation is another weapon that must be used. Petitions and boycotts are helpful. The use of the bully pulpit—via the airwaves—is a most effective strategy. Press conferences can be used to enlighten or, alternatively, to embarrass."[260pp21] "Ads taken out in prominent national newspapers are quite effective."[260pp22]

The Catholic League's Op-Ed page advertisement which appeared in the April 10, 1995 issue of *The New York Times* attacking Disney for its release of the excellent film, "Priest," is a good example. This attack will be described more fully later. But on the Op-Ed page the following advertisement appears: "We're leading a nationwide charge against Disney, making use of every legal means available—from boycotts to stockholder revolts—all designed to send a clear and unmistakable message to Michael Eisner, chairman of Disney."[260pp23] This is only one of many staged or threatened stockholder revolts led by the League.

But probably the most effective means of suppressing criticism of the Catholic Church through the press is a constant "in your face" attack of local newspapers. In a 1995 report on the Massachusetts Chapter of the Catholic League, it is noted that the president and the executive director had been on the attack, "appearing in the media more than 600 times" in the previous five years.[260pp24] In a single state, 600 times in five years! It is no wonder that newspapers in Massachusetts are very reluctant to print any criticism of the Catholic Church, no matter how justified, given this constant barrage of punishment.

Intimidation of the media leadership and of our government by the League is achieved through the wide distribution of frequent news releases, its monthly newsletter and an annual report. In an article on the publication of its 1994 report, Donohue writes, "The purpose of the report is to educate the public and influence decision-makers in government, education and the media....The report is being distributed to all members of Congress, the White House...and to prominent members of the media and education."[260pp25] From an article regarding the 1995 annual report: "It has been sent to every Bishop and congressman in the nation, as well as to influential persons in the media and other sectors of society."[260pp26] In a February 1995 letter to the membership, Donohue announced that the 1994 report will be distributed to the press, noting "there will be little excuse left for media ignorance of Catholic-bashing."[260pp27] Individual attacks are often announced through widely distributed press releases which are bound to capture the attention of members of the press.

SUCCESS OF THE LEAGUE

The Catholic League has been remarkably successful in achieving its goals. Donohue rightfully gloats: "One of the major reasons why people are giving [donations] is the success the Catholic League has had."[260pp28] As noted earlier, membership grew from 27,000 to 200,000 in the first two years after Donohue took control. He continues, "We have had a string of victories and we have also had an unprecedented degree of media coverage. We don't win every fight but our overall record is quite good. Our presence on radio and TV, combined with coverage in newspapers and magazines—both religious and secular—is excellent."[260pp29] "We've been featured on the television program 'Entertainment Tonight' and received front page coverage from national newspapers including the *Wall Street Journal* and *The New York Times*."[260pp30] The number of apologies and promises it extracts from the nation's newspapers, TV networks and stations and programs, radio stations, activist organizations, commercial establishments, educational institutions and governments is most impressive.

The suppression of all criticism of the Catholic Church and its hierarchy is the goal of the Catholic League. The visit of the pope to the U.S. in October 1995 was a major media event. Given all the gravely serious problems faced by the Church and the enormous amount of dissent by American Catholics, as well as the growing hostility from non-Catholics as a result of the Church's interference in American policy making, one would expect wide coverage of these realities in the media during his visit. Instead, it was treated as a triumphant return.

The Catholic League believes that it played a major role in this great public relations success—and with good reason. In August 1994, it launched a campaign to intimidate the press in an astounding advance warning to media professionals preparing for the pope's visit to New York in late October. A letter signed by Donohue announced a press conference to be held just prior to the pope's visit that will present "10's of thousands of petitions from active Catholics" that have been collected over the past year.[260pp31] The petition speaks for itself—see the following page. What else but intimidation of the press is the intent of this campaign?

The November 1995 issue of the League's journal, *Catalyst*, is headlined, "Media Treat Pope Fairly; Protesters Fail to Score." Donohue writes, "By all accounts, the visit of Pope John Paul II to the United States was a smashing success. Media treatment of the papal visit was, with few exceptions, very fair. Protesters were few in number and without impact. From beginning to end, this papal visit proved to be the most triumphant of them all."[260pp32] A month later he writes, "The relatively few cheap shots that were taken at the Pope by the media in October is testimony to a change in the culture."[260pp33] And of course the desired "change in the culture" is the elimination of criticism of the pope and his hierarchy. The Catholic League is succeeding on a grand scale far beyond what all but a handful of Americans realize.

INTIMIDATION PREVENTS CRITICISM

It is clear from Donohue's own words that prevention of any criticism is the goal of the League and that intimidation is its means of achieving this end. In a fund-raising letter mailed in December

PETITION IN DEFENSE OF POPE JOHN PAUL II

We the undersigned call on the media to act responsibly when Pope John Paul II comes to New York this October.

It is not acting responsibly to give a high profile to the voices of dissident and alienated Catholics. It is not acting responsibly to focus almost exclusively on those issues of Catholic teaching that are in tension with the values of the culture; worse, it is wrong to lecture the Church on getting into line. It is not acting responsibly to neglect coverage of the good work that Catholics and the Catholic Church have done in servicing the least among us. It is not acting responsibly to continue to deride and disparage Catholic teachings in news reports, Op-Eds and cartoons. And it is not acting responsibly to deny that anti-Catholic sentiment is a force in our society.

In short, if respect for diversity is truly a value that those in the media embrace, then respect for the diversity that Catholicism offers should be readily apparent.

Signature: _____

Address: _____

_____

Date: _____

Please return in the postage-paid envelope provided.
Check here if you have included a contribution to help support our efforts. ❑
Don't send an acknowledgement of this contribution. ❑

of 1995, Donohue appeals for funds to hire more staff: "We could have done more....We could have tackled other issues, thereby adding to the number of people who will think twice before crossing Catholics again."[260pp34] From the League's 1995 Annual Report: "It is hoped that by ...[attacking critics], potential offenders will think twice before launching their assaults on Roman Catholicism."[260pp35] This statement also makes it clear that it is the protection of the institution that is the goal, not protection of individual Catholics.

It appears that the most aggressive and extensive attack in League history was one directed at Disney for its release of the movie, "Priest." In an editorial, Donohue forthrightly says that the purpose of the intensive attack on Disney is the prevention of the production of such critical movies in the future: "Our sights were set on what might be coming down the road, not on what had already happened."[260pp36]

The advice given by Ed Koch's mother—do not speak ill of other religions—has been a national ethic for nearly all of this century. This ethic, inherent in our culture, has served to suppress nearly all criticism of the Catholic Church. As a result, until its political activities were unveiled with the implementation of the bishops' Pastoral Plan for Pro-life Activities in 1975, the Church had been relatively immune from mainstream criticism. Because this ethic has served the Catholic Church so well, the Church may very well have played a major role in its inculcation into our culture. With its political activity becoming increasingly evident, critics are more than ever convinced of the need for public criticism of the Catholic Church.

However, this ethic does not protect the Church from dissent within its confines which has been growing since Vatican Council II in the 1960s, and most remarkably in recent years. The American media, to avoid flying in the face of American culture by ignoring this dearly held belief, have occasionally provided a forum for this protest. The dissenters have been a significant source of criticism. The Catholic League has not overlooked this problem—indeed, it takes it very seriously. All criticism is targeted from whatever source, including members of the Church.

For example, on January 22, 1995, CBS's "60 Minutes" broadcast a segment by Mike Wallace on the Catholic dissident group Call to Action. The Catholic hierarchy did agree to appear but dictated terms that were unacceptable to CBS. Then, according to Donohue, the Catholic League sent two letters to executive producer Barry Lando and issued the following press release on January 25: "The entire Call to Action segment was, from beginning to end, an exercise in intellectual dishonesty and journalistic malpractice. The decision to give high profile to the Catholic Church's radical fringe was pure politics, and nothing short of outrageous....Allowing extremists an uncontested opportunity to rail against the Catholic Church distorts the sentiments of most Catholics and provides succor for bigots. There is a difference between reporting dissent, and promoting it....'60 Minutes' made clear its preference, extending to the disaffected a platform that they have never earned within the Catholic community....This is propaganda at work, not journalism."[260pp37] This press release, of course, was received across America as a powerful warning to others to steer clear of Catholic dissidents. The Catholic League then launched a national postcard mailing campaign directed at Lando personally: "...we are angered over the way you continue to present the Catholic Church....We are tired of having our Church viewed from the perspective of the disaffected."[260pp38]

In another example, the League attacked the October 5, 1995 edition of "NBC Nightly News" with Tom Brokaw for providing a platform for Catholics for a Free Choice and Dignity. The League's press release included the following: "The media do a great disservice to Catholics and non-Catholics alike when Catholics for a Free Choice and Dignity are presented as though they were genuine voices in the Catholic community. The effect of such misrepresentation is to promote dissent rather than to record it. As such, it is irresponsible for the media to allow itself to become willing accomplices to public deception."[260pp39]

The continuous intimidation is bound to have its desired effect. The April 22, 1996 issue of the *New Republic* magazine criticizes the League's annual report as indicative of the League's "paranoia."[260pp40] The *New Republic* completely misses the point. One need only look at the language used in the League's attacks. It is not defense. It is intimidating language. The report is an offensive weapon used to silence critics of the Catholic Church.

SPECIFIC EXAMPLES OF THE LEAGUE'S INTIMIDATION

The Catholic League focuses it attention on five types of institutions: media, activist organizations, commercial establishments, educational institutions and governments.[260pp41] Donohue attributes the League's success, in part, to its ability to stay focused.[260pp42] The League's 1994 and 1995 annual reports alone offer 350 examples of League attacks. The numerous stunning examples from which to choose make selection for presentation difficult. These were all reported during the period from July 1994 to June 1996.

The Media

NEWSDAY—On June 1st and June 3, 1994, the Long Island daily, *Newsday*, published Bob Marlette cartoons which, according to the Catholic League, "raised pope bashing to a new level."[260pp43] An apology from *Newsday* published in the form of a "Memo to Readers" failed to satisfy the Catholic League and a petition was distributed to Long Island pastors. On July 15, Donohue met with *Newsday* publisher Anthony Marro to discuss the paper's coverage of Catholics. At the meeting, he presented 76 petitions signed by Long Island pastors expressing their concern for the way Catholics have been portrayed by the newspaper.[260pp44] This was not enough. On August 25, 1994, Donohue met with the editorial board of *Newsday* on the newspaper's coverage of Catholics. Donohue complained that the absence of practicing Catholics on the editorial board resulted in an insensitivity toward Catholics.[260pp45]

PHILADELPHIA INQUIRER—An article in the September 1994 issue of the League's journal is headlined, "Cardinal Bevilacqua Scores *Philadelphia Inquirer* for Church Coverage, Declines Interview". The *Inquirer* had requested an interview for a major story on the Archdiocese. The Cardinal refused: "I have declined your request for an interview due to your unfair and unbalanced coverage of the Archdiocese in the last year....This view is based on a review of Inquirer articles from May 1993 to May 1994. This review included 23 articles written about the Catholic Church. Of these 23 articles, eighteen were considered to be unfair and unbalanced. The unfairness and imbalance occurred in five areas including the selection of negative topics, a disregard for positive news, the use of unqualified experts, the use of negative language and a consistent omission of factual information...It is particularly frustrating to continue to read negative characterizations of the Roman Catholic Church with no regard for our role as the largest provider of social services in Southeastern Pennsylvania and our role as the most visible religious organization in the poorest areas of our city."[260pp46] The Cardinal makes clear that he feels he should be permitted to dictate what is written about his church to the letter, revealing an arrogance that could never coexist with a free press. Furthermore, that he would bring up the provision of social services by the Church, fully knowing that these services the Church provides are almost entirely funded by local, state and federal tax monies, is deceptive.

ASSOCIATED PRESS—On March 10, 1995, the Associated Press (AP), in a story on a court ruling upholding a law barring doctors from engaging in assisted suicide, disclosed that the federal appeals court judge was a Catholic. (The judge's ruling was in line with his pope's teaching on this matter.) Donohue took great offense to the AP's identification of this judge as a Catholic and sent a letter to AP executives asking for a copy of the AP policy on the matter. The League also sent a related press release to other news outlets to inform them of this offense. Darrell Christian, AP's Managing Editor wrote an apology. "The League is satisfied with AP's quick response," writes Donohue in the League's Journal, "and expects that it will not have to call attention to such errors in the future." Donohue's message to the American press was loud and clear. It is not permissible for the press to identify public servants as Catholics when they uphold Catholic teachings in their public decision-making. If so, the League will come after them.[260pp47]

DISNEY—The May 1995 issue of *Catalyst* reports in an article, "Catholic League calls for a Boycott of Disney:" "The movie 'Priest,' produced by the BBC and released by Miramax, a subsidiary of the Walt Disney Company, provoked the Catholic League to lead a storm of protest against the film and Disney. The movie is arguably the most anti-Catholic movie ever made."[260pp48] This attack on Disney represents the single greatest assault in the League's history. In an editorial, Donohue writes: "In addition to joining a boycott of everything that has the Disney label on it, we are asking everyone to sell their Disney stock. It would also send a message if everyone mailed Disney chairman Michael Eisner some old Disney toys or videos. If every Catholic League member sent even one box to Mr. Eisner, it would make an indelible impression on him."[260pp49]

The petition against Disney reads, "We, the undersigned, have a message to Disney: you bit off more than you can chew when you offended Catholics with the release of 'Priest.'...We hope that everyone at Disney thinks twice before offending Catholics again. Sadly, appeals to your goodwill mean nothing anymore. That is why we are hitting you in the pocketbook....The Catholic League has already tarnished your image and we have pledged to blacken it a little more."[260pp50]

The League placed an Op-Ed page advertisement in the April 10, 1995 issue of *The New York Times* titled "What's Happening to Disney?" It includes the statement: "So what is the Catholic League doing about this? We are leading a nationwide charge against Disney, making use of every legal means available—from boycotts to stockholder revolts—all designed to send a clear and unmistakable message to Michael Eisner, chairman of Disney."[260pp51]

But the attack did not end there. On May 2, 1995, a Catholic League member, a stockholder, asked shareholders to ratify at the November meeting of the Walt Disney Company a resolution that calls for the establishment of a religious advisory committee to insure that Disney does not produce another movie like this one.[260pp52] On April 29, the League picketed Disney's largest retail outlet in New England. A press release read: "The Catholic League intends to make the American public aware of Disney's contemptuous disregard of the sensibilities of 59 million Catholic Americans. It is Disney that is ultimately responsible for this travesty and it is Disney that will remain the focus of our protests."[260pp53]

In the July-August 1995 issue of *Catalyst*, an article, "Disney Protests Continue," reports that the League had asked the four U.S. Senators who owned Disney stock to sell it: "Mrs. Dole announced on June 2 that she was selling more than $15,000 worth of Disney stock." It reports that the League picketed the Dedham Community Theater in Dedham, Massachusetts, over the decision of the theater owner to show the anti-Catholic movie "Priest." The article also reports that numerous dioceses had sold their Disney stock and that "after nine weeks in theaters, the Hollywood Reporter's Boxoffice ranked 'Priest' 34th out of the top 35 movies nationwide."[260pp54] The January-February 1996 issue reported that upwards of 100,000 petitions were sent to Disney: "...because the movie was a flop at the box office, we do not expect to be greeted with *Priest II* anytime soon."[260pp55]

The League's campaign was not just directed to Disney but to the entire film industry and to the media in general. The message: if you place the Catholic Church in a negative light, you are going to pay.

Jane Pauley—In the June 13, 1995 airing of NBC's "Dateline ," Jane Pauley interviewed Scott O'Grady, the U.S. pilot who was rescued in Bosnia. Pauley commented "A devout Roman Catholic, O'Grady made his confirmation at age thirteen, *and unlike many of his peers never left the Church.*" The Catholic League was angered by this comment and Donohue wrote to Bob Wright, CEO of NBC, demanding that Pauley be fired immediately for this terrible offense. For maximum effect, Donohue released a statement explaining his actions to the press to insure that all got the message.[260pp56]

Bill Press—On July 16, 1995, KFI Radio [Los Angeles] talk show host Bill Press, a Roman Catholic, was critical of the pope and the Catholic Church. According to the September 1995 issue of the League's *Catalyst*, "The Catholic League issued the following statement to the press on this matter: 'The issue here is not simply the vile comments of Bill Press. The issue is the willingness of a respected radio station to keep him on payroll....The Catholic League does not want equal time to respond to Press, rather it wants him fired.'"[260pp57] By distributing this press release, the League was sending a message to everyone in the press—if you are critical of the pope or the Catholic Church, we are coming after you and your employer.

Liz Langley and the **Orlando Weekly**—Liz Langley wrote a light article about communion wafers in the August 10-16, 1995 edition. The League took great offense and issued a statement to the press that included the following: "The Langley piece is one of the most anti-Catholic articles to have appeared in some time....Accordingly, I will now mobilize a public relations offensive against the newspaper, using every tactic this side of the law to discredit the paper."[260pp58] Donohue's press release may have been meant to intimidate other reporters. Nearly a year after the incident, I talked with Editor Jeff Truesdell. Nothing ever came of the League's threats. Of course, no one ever reported this to the thousands of reporters who read the press release from Donohue.

FOX-TV—In September 1995, Mother Teresa was used to make a comedic point in a promotional spot for the Fox-TV program, The Preston Episodes. The Catholic League complained to the Los Angeles Office of Fox and "an apology was extended and a pledge not to run the offensive spot again was made."[260pp59]

BRAVO Network-"Windows"—A program which aired on September 24, 1995 on the cable network Bravo, featured a dance routine involving a priest dealing with temptation from a nun. "The Catholic League registered its outrage to Bravo, the 'Windows' producer Thomas Grimm, and Texaco Performing Arts Showcase, which sponsored the program."[260pp60] In December the League reported that Texaco had apologized for sponsoring this segment. Texaco also stated to Dr. Donohue that henceforth there would be a "screening procedure for the Texaco Performing Arts Showcase."[260pp61]

New Britain Herald— Connecticut's *New Britain Herald* published a syndicated cartoon which shows the three Magi going to visit the Baby Jesus. One of the shepherds says, "Wait...aren't we just encouraging these teen-age pregnancies?" League members complained to the newspaper that this was anti-Catholic bigotry. The newspaper issued an apology on its editorial page.[260pp62]

Ann Landers—In an interview with Christopher Buckly in the December 4, 1995 edition of the *New Yorker*, columnist Ann Landers criticized Pope John Paul II. "After first making a favorable comment about the Pope, Landers remarked, 'Of course, he's a Polack. They're very antiwomen.' ...Landers later apologized for the crack about the Pope...The Catholic League sent its own comments to the *New Yorker* and further disseminated its views via a news release and radio interviews....(T)he *Milwaukee Journal Sentinel* has decided to drop Landers' column beginning in 1996."[260pp63]

ABC's "The Naked Truth"—The League strongly attacked the January 10 edition of the ABC show "The Naked Truth." The League's letter to ABC included this threat: "We will contact the sponsors of the program and will alert our members to take action against them. Knowing our members, they won't hesitate to do so." This report, which appears in the March 1996 issue of *Catalyst*, listed the names, addresses and phone numbers of the eight sponsors of that show.[260pp64]

"Dave, Shelly & Chainsaw"-San Diego radio program—The April 1996 edition of *Catalyst* reports on an attempt by the League's

San Diego Chapter to have the "Lash Wednesday" segment of the Dave, Shelly & Chainsaw program discontinued. The local chapter charged that the "humor" was "unacceptable" and the segment must be discontinued. But it failed. At that point the national office of the Catholic League got involved and placed an ad in the *San Diego Union-Tribune* "calling attention to this outrage." This prompted media requests for interviews with the chapter president who appeared live on KGTV, the ABC affiliate. The tenor of this interview was "so controversial" that the station was pressured to invite him back a second time. "This time the television reporters were much more respectful." The League asked its members nationwide to contact the radio station General Manager and the President of PAR Broadcasting Company to demand that this segment be discontinued, providing his address, phone and fax numbers.[260pp65]

PBS' FRONTLINE—On February 6, 1996, PBS aired a program called, "Murder on 'Abortion Row'". The two hour special was a serious look at the life of John Salvi, the person who killed two women and wounded five others working at an abortion clinic in 1994. Salvi is a devout Catholic and had planned to become a Catholic priest. The Catholic League was given an opportunity to preview the program. It immediately released a statement to the press attacking the documentary which began, "The FRONTLINE program, "Murder on 'Abortion Row,'" is nothing more than a front for Planned Parenthood and an irresponsible propaganda piece against Catholicism."[260pp66]

NEWSDAY—On March 12, 1996, the Long Island newspaper, *Newsday*, ran a headline which read, "Ex-Alter Boy on Trial." The League protested. Donohue called the paper's editor: "The content and tone of his remarks assured Donohue that this would not happen again."[260pp67] *Newsday* subsequently published a League letter-to-the-editor which was very critical of the newspaper.

HBO—On May 6, 1996, Home Box Office aired "Priestly Sins: Sex and the Catholic Church." The one hour special focused on the issue of sexual abuse in the priesthood. The League issued a lengthy news release which sharply attacked HBO: "The film is classic propaganda...HBO is not the first to float the idea that a 'code of secrecy' keeps the Church from revealing the truth about clergy sexual abuse: that honor extends to the Nazis and others. The Catholic League will call on all Catholics to boycott HBO..."[260pp68]

Sony—The June 1996 issue of *Catalyst* reported on the Sony movie, "The Last Supper": "The movie, while not offensive to Catholics, nonetheless offended Catholics with its promotional material. The League...wrote a letter of protest to Sony Picture Releasing President, Jeffrey Blake. The response from Sony was decisive: 'We have taken the unusual step of modifying our marketing campaign'....The League is satisfied with this modification."[260pp69]

AP—On March 31, 1996, the Associated Press ran a story about a suburban Chicago man suspected of assassinating a Philadelphia policeman a quarter-century ago. The story, which was distributed to newspapers all over the country, mentioned that the accused was "23, a Catholic school-educated telephone repairman, when the shooting occurred." The League sent a letter of protest to the president of AP and urged all of its members to do the same, providing his name and address to them.[260pp70]

QVC Shopping Network—Continental Cablevision in New England had conducted a survey of 32,000 subscribers and found that viewers preferred to drop the Eternal Word Television Network (EWTN), the Catholic cable network, in favor of the QVC Shopping Network. The New England Chapter of the Catholic League sharply opposed this change and Continental was muscled into continuing programming of EWTM.[260pp71]

Commercial establishments

Barneys New York—On December 9, 1994, the League successfully pressured Barneys of New York, an upscale clothing store, into removing an "offensive" nativity scene from its storefront window on Madison Avenue and 61st Street. Donohue informed Barneys that it had about four hours to contact the League, otherwise the media would be contacted. "It didn't take long before Simon Doonan, a senior vice president, called Donohue and extended an apology. However, Doonan flatly declined to do anything about the exhibit. Donohue then released a statement to the media that included the following comments: "Barneys New York and Christie's have cooperated in promoting an insulting anti-Christian exhibit....Plainly put, this means that Barneys will respect the right of artists to show disrespect for the rights of Catholics. The Catholic League will disseminate this news to as wide an audience as possible. We do not accept Mr. Doonan's apology: apologies unaccompanied by corrective action do not assuage."[260pp72]

Catalyst went on to report: "Within hours of releasing this statement, the television cameras were in Dr. Donohue's office. Just about every radio and television station in New York commented on the Barney exhibit....Barneys pulled the display from the window...giving the work back to the artist....In response to all of this, Barneys took out full page ads in *The New York Times, New York Post* and *New York Daily News*, apologizing for what had happened. The ads, together with the boycotts that were instituted, wound up costing Barneys hundreds of thousands of dollars in lost sales."[260pp72] Now that's success!

Hard Rock Casino and Hotel—The December 1995 issue of *Catalyst* reports: "When the Hard Rock Casino and Hotel opened last March in Las Vegas, it featured a restored carved gothic altar in one of its cocktail bars....The offensive use of the altar has been a source of criticism by many area Catholics." The local bishop complained to the owner, Peter Morton, who said it would be removed. After seven months of inaction, the Catholic League got involved. The League outlined its strategy to the press: "...the time has now come to put public pressure on Mr. Morton. The Catholic League will contact the media in Las Vegas about this incident, and will alert the national media to it as well. We will also take out ads in the local newspapers, as well as the diocesan newspaper, requesting Catholics not to patronize the Hard Rock Casino and Hotel and to organize demonstrations in front of the establishment. We will also contact local Catholic organizations to organize phone trees and deliver their message straight to Mr. Morton. If more pressure is needed, we will bring it to bear, including a national boycott of all Hard Rock Cafes."[260pp73]

The Catholic League followed through on its promise by taking out three ads in area newspapers.[260pp74] Hard Rock quickly responded saying it would remove the altar on November 30. The report ended, "The Catholic League will announce its next move once it finds out what happens on November 30.[260pp75]

An article in its January/February 1996 issue: "Victory is Always Sweet: Hard Rock Hotel Pulls Altar" reads: "After responding to pressure brought by the Catholic League, the Hard Rock Hotel...withdrew an offensive altar from its bar...By giving the incident publicity, both nationally as well as locally, the Catholic League was able to secure the support of many influential Catholics, some of whom put pressure on Hard Rock....It cost Hard Rock approximately a quarter million dollars to remove the altar... we won."[260pp76]

Education

William Paterson College—On July 5, 1994, Professor Vernon McClean, an instructor in the African-American and Caribbean studies department at William Paterson College at Wayne, New Jersey, opened the first session of his summer class, "Racism and Sexism in a Changing America," by saying the pope is a racist. The League was contacted and it sent representatives to the college. "No one in any office would speak with us. They took great umbrage at our inquiry and were totally uncooperative. We received the same treatment from three different offices—we were either dismissed or treated as though we had no right to be questioning the incident. Following this lack of cooperation and response from the college, we issued a press release demanding an apology from the college and disciplinary action against Professor McLean. The New Jersey papers gave the issue thorough coverage and the New York radio and television media also took note."[260pp77]

After the college completed its investigation, it made a public statement that "the College is satisfied that the matter has been resolved fully and completely." The League, however was not satisfied. "Accordingly, the Catholic League called upon state officials to conduct a formal hearing on the campus of William Paterson College; Governor Christie Whitman, senior higher education officials and area legislators were contacted....But thus far she (Governor Whitman) has been mute....The Catholic League will not be satisfied until justice has been done. Our goal is not to simply chastise one college professor....We're taking the long view on this one and it would behoove people like President Speert (Paterson College president) to do likewise."[260pp77]

University of Michigan—The University of Michigan student newspaper, *The Michigan Daily*, ran a cartoon that mocked Newt Gingrich's promotion of Boys Town and also related to the pedophilia problem in the Catholic priesthood. Donohue wrote a threatening letter to Dr. James Duderstadt, President of the University of Michigan: "Enclosed is a copy of a cartoon that was run in *The Michigan Daily*....Please be advised that as president of the nation's largest Catholic civil rights organization, I am prepared to do what is necessary to rid your campus of the bigotry it presently entertains."[260pp78]

The very next issue of *Catalyst* reads: "We are happy to report that an apology from the cartoonist and a conciliatory letter from Dr. Duderstadt have brought this issue to a close."[260pp79]

Activist Organizations

The Population Institute—In a May 1995 fund-raising letter, Werner Fornos, president of The Population Institute, wrote the following: "The Vatican continues to undermine the advancements we've made in Cairo on issues of pregnancy prevention. The anti-contraceptive gestapo has vowed to double the number of its delegation (to the U.N.'s Fourth World Conference on Women in Beijing) to 28 and to turn once more to weaken the cause of reproductive rights." The July-August, 1995 issue of *Catalyst* describes the League's response in an article, "Nazi Slur of Vatican Implicates Congressmen."[260pp80]

In a news release, the Catholic League issued the following remarks: "The Population Institute proves once again that some of the anti-natalist forces are unquestionably anti-Catholic. Not content, or able, to debate the issues on their merits, these activists seek to defame the Holy See and thereby discredit its influence. Members of The Population Institute who share its politics, but not its bigotry, should make a clear and decisive break with the organization....Accordingly, the Catholic League calls upon the following advisors to The Population Institute to resign immediately: Sen. Paul Simon, Sen. Daniel K. Inouye, Sen. Barbara Boxer, Rep. Jim Leach, Rep. Robert Torricelli and Rep. Sam Gejdenson. Not to resign would be to give tacit support to anti-Catholicism...The Catholic League [also] wrote to each Congressman involved in this scandal."[260pp80]

The September 1995 issue of *Catalyst* reports: "Senator Daniel K. Inouye complied with the League's request and resigned from the Population Institute. Senator Barbara Boxer of California put The Population Institute on notice, warning that any future examples of 'inappropriate' and 'offensive' fundraising letters would lead her 'to reconsider' her position with the organization. Congressman Robert Torricelli of New Jersey...warned The Population Institute to be more careful in how it phrases its letters."[260pp81]

Anti-Defamation League—On December 1, 1995, the ADL notified the publisher, Hippocrene Books that it was granting a prestigious literary award to Richard Lukas for his book, *Did the Children Cry? Hitler's War Against Jewish and Polish Children*. Lukas was to receive the literary award, plus a prize of $1,000 on January 23, 1996 at the ADL's headquarters in New York. On January 10, the ADL's Mark Edelman, wrote to the publisher stating that a mistake had been made; that subsequent review led to a decision to reverse the initial judgment. The May 1996 issue of *Catalyst* reports, "When the Catholic League learned of what had happened, it was incensed." Donohue wrote a letter to Edelman: "For the record, I would like to know exactly why the book was selected for an award in the first place. Surely there are records of this evaluation. And I would also like to know why those reasons were found unpersuasive—and by whom—at a later date."

The report continues: "The Catholic League...did not receive a response from the ADL until the matter was favorably resolved on March 18. But the good news did not come until considerable pressure had been brought to bear. Before the ADL reversed its decision not to give the award, the attorney for author Lukas had already warned the ADL that it would be sued. When the ADL made its announcement to reinstate the award to Lukas, it noted that it still had several problems with the book. The ADL said that 'we believe the book underestimates the extent of Polish anti-Semitism before and after World War II. We believe also that, while there were heroic efforts of some Poles during this time, the book appears to vastly overestimate the number of Poles who were engaged in such courageous actions. Finally, the ADL believes the book presents a sanitized picture of Polish involvement with Jews during the War and overlooks authoritative points of view of many historians, including Polish historians.' Though justice prevailed in the end, this marks a sad chapter in the ADL's history....We hope that the ADL has learned an important lesson and that such 'mistakes' will be avoided in the future."[260pp82]

Government

The Clinton Administration—The October 1994 *Catalyst* head-line reads "League Assails Clinton Administration for Bigotry." This article reports: "In an unprecedented move, the Catholic League assailed the administration of a standing president for anti-Catholic bigotry. From the time President Clinton took office, it has become increasingly evident that his administration is insensitive at best, and downright hostile at worst, to Catholic interests. But the final straw occurred during the third weekend in August. Faith Mitchell, a spokeswoman for the State Department, charged that the Vatican's disagreement over the Cairo conference on population and development 'has to do with the fact that the conference is really calling for girls' education and improving the status of women.' That statement was so outrageous that one of our members...wrote a strong letter registering her concerns to President Clinton...and [this letter] was published as a Catholic League open letter to the President in the August 29th edition of *The New York Times*."[260pp83]

This open letter, published as a half-page advertisement sponsored by the Catholic League, ran in all editions of *The New York Times* on August 29, 1994. It viciously attacks Faith Mitchell and requests President Clinton to retract and apologize for her statement.[260pp84]

In an article published in this issue, Donohue writes: "The anti-Catholic bigots in the Clinton administration got so exercised during the Cairo conference that Leon Panetta [who is Catholic], the White House Chief of Staff, acknowledged that there was a problem with Catholic-bashing and vowed to discipline anyone who continued to chide the Vatican."[260pp85] Apparently, any criticism of the Vatican, no matter how just, is off limits.

Dr. Joycelyn Elders—In an editorial in the January-February issue of *Catalyst*, "We've Only Just Begun," Donohue writes, "We have rolled into 1995 with a string of victories. Dr. Elders is gone...Dr. Joycelyn Elders is one for the books. The very first news release I issued when I took over as president of the Catholic League in July 1993 was in opposition to the nomination of Dr. Elders as Surgeon General...Through the month of August, we pressed hard to stop her nomination: we held a press conference at the National Press Club and wrote to all the members of the Senate Judiciary

Committee, but we ultimately fell short of our objective. What we did not do, however, was give up. We continued to criticize Dr. Elders whenever she made an irresponsible statement..."[260pp86]

An article in the same issue, "Elder's Exit Applauded," reads: "The Catholic League is delighted to see that one of the most outspoken ant-Catholic bigots in the Clinton administration has been axed. Joycelyn Elders was nominated to the office of Surgeon General by President Clinton in 1993 and confirmed later by the Senate. The Catholic League opposed her nomination and confirmation from the beginning. Her anti-Catholic statements...should have alone disqualified her from a position of national influence and authority...The Catholic League continued to speak out against her during her tenure as Surgeon General."[260pp87]

This is but a very small sample of the attacks by the League over this two year period. It is unfortunate that space limits the number. These examples are presented almost entirely in the League's own words. As one surveys its material, it becomes evident that *all* criticism of the Church or anything that places the Church in a negative light is deemed anti-Catholic, despicable and impermissible. The Church is simply above all criticism. The Catholic League obviously rejects America because it rejects what America stands for, including the freedoms of speech, expression and the press. This stand taken by the Catholic League is consistent with nearly two centuries of Catholic teaching on these matters and we should expect nothing different.

Intimidation, such as has been described in this chapter, by Catholic institutions over the past hundred years, has resulted in a populace woefully ignorant of the threat to American democracy and security posed by the Church. This intimidation has made it possible for the Church to go unchallenged.

How can Americans publicly discuss the obvious conflict between American national security-survival interests and Papal security-survival interests in this environment that the Catholic League now so effectively fosters? Obviously, it is not possible. Not only were the recommendations of the Rockefeller Commission and the NSSM 200 report never implemented, they were never publicly debated. Few Americans are even aware of NSSM 200 or this conflict in security interests. Intimidation by Catholic institutions has completely suppressed appropriate investigation of this conflict. Indeed, this intimidation has shut off the flow of the kinds of facts that resulted in these recommendations—facts of which all Americans should be fully aware. Without this vital information and discussion in a public forum, there can be no democratic solution to this conflict between the interests of the nation and of the Catholic Church—a dilemma well understood by the hierarchy.

THINGS ARE SELDOM WHAT THEY SEEM

16

16

// So, as the pope visits the Rocky Mountains this week, his teachings and policies on birth control can no longer be seen merely as the business of Catholics....[they] could now instead lead to the death of us all."[261]

Georgie Anne Geyer
August 10, 1993

Most Americans have a very positive image of the pope and the Roman Catholic Church as can been seen from the study discussed in the preceding chapter. But as syndicated columnist Georgie Ann Geyer points out, this man has already taken steps that may very well cause your premature death and the premature deaths of loved ones. His behavior shows that he has no regard for your life or mine—for our souls, perhaps, but not for our lives, and especially not for our children's lives.

Geyer correctly observes that the pope is a threat to everyone on the planet. He is our enemy. Yet we have this very positive image of Pope John Paul II (the most admired world leader with a favorability rating of 88 percent)[262] and an equally positive image of his institution (the most admired political institution in the U.S. with a favorability rating of 89 percent). How can this be? How can our images be so far removed from reality? The fact is, there is a broad array of images retained by Americans that have been distorted by the Vatican to advance its own interests.

Since I began my study of the Roman Catholic Church, as it relates to population growth control, some 26 years ago, I have been amazed at the intensity of Vatican activity in the U.S. On numerous occasions, I have observed some activity (usually but not always a political activity) that did not seem reasonable. I would be offered explanations which, upon reflection, would not hold water. When I've explored these things, I would often find the Church deeply involved, seeking some gain or other.

In the U.S., the Catholic Church is a $200 billion operation,[263] composed of millions of highly organized workers with an intense sense of mission, a long history of political manipulation, and a superb track record of getting their way. Before I began my study, I had a very different idea of what church and religion meant, having been raised as a Methodist. I was completely unprepared for what I found. Many of the tears in America's social fabric are the result of Vatican attempts to advance its power, control, influence, wealth or security—at the expense of Americans and American institutions. Rarely was there evidence of Vatican involvement in these activities on the surface, but upon probing, the role of the Vatican became evident. Usually it also became evident that considerable effort had been made to mask the fact that the Vatican was a significant actor. But before presenting specific instances of such activities, a question should be considered.

HOW FAR WILL THE VATICAN GO?

How far is the Vatican willing to go to insure its survival? Some readers may be offended, but this is a valid question. In America, we have the freedom of inquiry and we should exercise it or we are sure to lose it. This is one of the most important unknowns Americans now face. If the Vatican will secretly kill the Rockefeller Commission and NSSM 200 initiatives which definitively showed that overpopulation threatens the security-survival of every American, what will it not do? Will it manipulate the initiation of U.S. warfare with other countries to divert attention from the overpopulation problem? Will it prompt a civil war in the U.S., fulfilling the prediction of President Grant, in order to undermine America's capacity to confront the overpopulation problem? Will it promote disintegration of the American social fabric to save the Papacy?

Thus far, the Vatican has had so much success at shutting down all serious efforts to control population growth that draconian actions have not yet been necessary. But what if the NSSM 200 recommendations had been implemented? Most likely, the Vatican would have done whatever it felt necessary to successfully intervene; perhaps, merely conspiring to force the resignation of a president would have been sufficient. Had they not intervened, self-destruction of the Vatican already might have been complete by now.

THE PASTORAL PLAN'S BROAD CONSEQUENCES

Few Americans appreciate how much the bishops' Pastoral Plan for Pro-Life Activities has changed America. Every community has been changed by it. Every person in America is living his/her life differently from what he/she would have had this plan not been implemented. Many of our elected representatives at all levels of government would have been different. Many positive changes in our lives, that probably would have occurred had the Rockefeller Commission and NSSM 200 recommendations been implemented, did not occur.

For example, almost surely there would be less crime, the welfare burden would be reduced and the drug problem would be smaller if the recommendations had been implemented. Why? Because family planning education would be much more widespread and integrated naturally into our pattern of family values; contraception would be encouraged; and safe, legal abortion would be much more readily available to all women. Unplanned births, about 50 percent of all U.S. births since 1975, would have been reduced dramatically. The number of poverty stricken adolescents, and men and women in their early twenties, would be much less than it is today.

Also, many negative changes in our lives have resulted from the initiatives undertaken by the bishops as a part of their Plan. The costs to us all have been enormous. Throughout the remainder of this chapter, examples of these changes will be offered. My first two books on this topic contain many more.[264]

As Byrnes concluded in his study, the National Conference of Catholic Bishops (NCCB) and United States Catholic Conference (USCC) have been consumed by the abortion issue and this Plan since they were created 27 years ago.[265] They have committed an enormous amount of energy, organization, direction and resources to the abortion and other population-related issues. This commitment has brought serious consequences throughout our society.

One of the more profound accomplishments of this Plan is the takeover of the Republican Party by the Vatican. In a July 28, 1994 *Los Angeles Times* wire service story, Jack Nelson describes the maneuvers of the Religious Right so that this takeover is all but an accomplished fact. According to Nelson, "GOP moderates have remained passive on the sidelines, unwilling to fight..."

On September 11, 1995, author, journalist and broadcaster, Bill Moyers, was given the American Jewish Committee Religious Liberty Award. In his acceptance remarks, "Echoes of the Crusades: The Radical Religious Right's Holy War on American Freedom," Moyers gives his assessment of the influence of the Religious Right: "They control the Republican Party, the House of Representatives and the Senate..."[265a]

But who are the Religious Right? The Spring 1994 issue of *Conscience*, the journal of Catholics For a Free Choice, exploded the myth that the Religious Right is a Protestant movement. It was designed, created and controlled by Catholics in response to the Pastoral Plan. These Catholics recruited opportunistic Protestants to give the appearance that Protestants were the instigators. The leadership is Catholic but the followers are often Protestant. The development of the Religious Right is described in some detail in the two books noted above, published 12 and 10 years ago, respectively. Also discussed is the Vatican takeover of the Republican Party already well underway at the time of their publication.

Even when the Pastoral Plan was first approved by the bishops, the *National Catholic Reporter* recognized that the plan would lead to a Vatican controlled political party in the United States and the newspaper went on record with this prediction.[266] Rather than creating its own political party, the Vatican chose to seize control of the Republican Party.

THE CHRISTIAN COALITION TAKEOVER OF THE REPUBLICAN PARTY

A survey by *Campaigns & Elections* magazine reported [in 1994] that the Christian Right exercised complete domination of Republican parties in 13 states and considerable control in 18 others.[266a] These facts shocked moderate Republicans and Democrats alike. It was no longer possible for the Coalition to keep its stealth campaign hidden.

At the Christian Coalition's 1995 "Road to Victory" Conference, Pat Robertson revealed his dream when the Coalition was founded in 1991. Writes Joseph L. Conn for *Church & State*: "His wish list was far from modest: a conservative majority in both houses of Congress, 30 state governorships in conservative hands and a conservative in the White House, all by 1996, and working control of one of the major political parties by 1994. During his September 8 speech, Robertson gleefully recalled those goals and boasted that his movement is not only on track, it's ahead of schedule on some points...."[266b]

A *Church & State* editorial on the Conference reported: "Pat Robertson triumphantly recounted the great distance the Christian Coalition has traveled in a short amount of time: 'I said we would have a significant voice—actually I said something else, but Ralph [Reed] said I can't say that because we got press—I said we would have a significant voice in one of the political parties by 1994 and looks like we made that one.' Robertson reminded the audience of the findings of the poll conducted by *Campaigns & Elections*, which had shocked so many. What did Coalition Executive Director Reed want Robertson to keep under wraps? Five years ago the TV preacher said, 'we want...as soon as possible to see a working majority of the Republican Party in the hands of pro-family Christians by 1996.'"[266c]

"Throughout the...conference, organizational leaders, activists and political hangers-on made it clear that the Christian Coalition is not just another interest group in American public life. It is a highly partisan religio-political army wielding a disproportionate influence in U.S. politics."[266b]

Rob Boston writing for *Church & State* after attending the September 8-9, 1995 "Road to Victory" Conference in Washington, D.C.: "...once again Reed and Robertson are being less than honest. Christian Coalition activists, in fact, have formed a partisan machine that aims to seize control of the Republican Party and place Coalition allies in public office." Deception is openly touted: "At breakout sessions, conference participants were schooled in the art of concealing their ties to the Christian Coalition, in a continuing pattern of 'stealth politics.'" Boston reports, "Speaker Cathe Halford, training director for the Texas Christian Coalition, declared:

'You all know we're in a war, we're in a spiritual war, a war for our culture, however you want to say it....Don't get intimidated that this is a big political machine you're part of. Just try to focus on those people as your neighbors.'"[266d]

Boston described one session, "Building a Neighborhood Organization": "In fact, the session had little to do with neighborhood activism; it was devoted to explaining how to get at least one Christian Coalition operative in every county precinct and how to compile information on voters, with an eye toward turning out those who are likely to support Christian Coalition candidates on election day."[266d] This is the heart of the Coalition strategy.

The results thus far: According to a report prepared by Americans United and the Interfaith Alliance Foundation, 198 members of the U.S. Congress vote with the Christian Coalition at least 86 percent of the time. At a press conference, Lynn criticized the "tangled—and growing—links between the Christian Coalition and the Republican Party...the Christian Coalition now calls the shots for a major political party."[266b]

Arthur Jones of the *National Catholic Reporter*, concludes: "Robertson and Reed have emerged as a cunningly dynamic duo that understands the weaknesses of the soft underbelly of the U.S. democratic system..."[266e] The weakness, of course, is that a determined minority can identify voters in great numbers who will vote its way if they get to the polls, then by insuring that all vote, it can sway the majority of elections. However, given the enormous Catholic commitment to the Christian Coalition one must wonder who actually discovered this soft underbelly.

The implications of this takeover for American politics at the national, state and local levels are enormous, affecting us all. Thousands of politicians at all levels whose positions have opposed the Vatican have been victims of the plan, significantly changing the American political landscape. No politician has benefited more than Senator Jesse Helms of North Carolina. This fact is documented elsewhere.[267-270]

As noted earlier, the ultimate objective of the Vatican's political machine is passage of the Human Life Amendment (HLA). As Jack Nelson pointed out, "the 1992 GOP platform called for a 'human life amendment' to the Constitution, outlawing abortion in all circumstances." It should be noted that the HLA need not be enforced to meet the needs of the Vatican. The Vatican requires only that the civil law not conflict with canon law. Then papal authority and civil authority are not pitted against one another. It is only legal abortion that threatens Papal authority.

We all have the illusion, carefully crafted by Papal propaganda, that "lives of the unborn" and "morality" are the issues. This is simply not so. It is survival of the Catholic institution and Papal power that is the issue, not the "lives of the unborn" or anything else. All countries in Latin America (all are Catholic) have higher abortion rates than the U.S. Nothing is said by the Church there. If abortion were the real issue, the Church would be speaking out even louder in Latin America than in the U.S. Only in the U.S., where it is legal, is it an important issue for the Church. Of course, few American Protestants are aware of this fact.

PROTEST DISAPPEARS FROM PROTESTANTS

Another major accomplishment of the Pastoral Plan has been its effect on Protestantism in America. The Plan has taken the protest out of the Protestant movement. Until the Pastoral Plan, Protestant denominations had no reservations about protesting or criticizing the Catholic Church. The plan specifically targeted the Protestant Churches to silence them. The bishops succeeded.

For example, the Southern Baptist Convention (SBC) has 14.7 million members and is one of the most powerful Protestant denominations. In the early 1980s, a rift began to develop between fundamentalist and moderate Baptists which did not concern theology as much as it did an authoritarian style of ministry.[271] The Catholic Church has an extremely authoritarian style of ministry. Nothing is left by the Papacy for lay interpretation. At the Baptist Convention's June 1988 meeting in San Antonio, a heated debate took place over an idea profoundly basic to all of Baptist heritage: the freedom of believers to experience God without priests, institutions or creeds acting as intermediaries." "The priesthood of the believer" is a Protestant doctrine that lay people have direct access to God and need no priestly intermediary to interpret Scripture. This is exactly the opposite of Roman Catholic belief. Baptist Convention delegates voted to invest more authority in pastors. Enraged moderates marched to the Alamo and tore up the resolution in protest. The moderates argued it would make the denomination more Catholic than Baptist.[272]

In journalist Bill Moyers's public affairs television series, "God and Politics Part II,"[273] aired on December 16, 1987, the relationship between the Baptist rift and the Pastoral Plan for Pro-Life activities became evident. It is obvious that the victory of the Baptist fundamentalists benefits the Papacy. Any split like that of the Baptists weakens the potential of a Protestant response to challenges to American democracy by the Vatican. However, in this schism, the Vatican benefits in another important way. As the so-called "conservatives" gain the upper hand in the SBC, the Baptists then enter the Catholic column on the abortion issue. The Pastoral Plan calls for the recruitment of as many non-Catholics as possible so as to mask the fact that this plan is a Catholic initiative. The bishops can now speak for 14.7 million Baptists on this issue and will wield the additional political power derived from this arrangement.

During Moyers's interview of Paul Pressler, Texas State Appellate Court Judge from Houston who engineered the split in the SBC, the Catholic connection to the Baptist rift became clear. During the interview, Moyers brought to light that Judge Pressler is on the board of directors of the Council on National Policy, along with fanatical Religious Right Catholics—Richard Viguerie, Phyllis Schlafly and Joseph Coors.

The Council on National Policy is one of the many Religious Right organizations created in response to the 1975 Pastoral Plan. By 1979, the Bishops had identified their man to engineer the Baptist rift—no doubt with a lot of the bishops' help—Judge Pressler. According to Dr. Daniel Vestal, pastor of the First Baptist Church in Midland, Texas, "I listened to a tape that Judge Pressler produced, in which he basically recounted the political plan and strategy [for conservative takeover of the SBC] that he set forth back in 1979." As Bill Moyers pressed the Judge on his relationship with the Council on National Policy—which promotes the adoption of Papal policy—the judge broke off the interview and refused to answer further questions. The Judge had been exposed—as had been the real actors behind the Baptist rift.

THE POPE'S ECUMENICAL MOVEMENT

The "ecumenical movement" is the pope's most important stratagem to silence Protestant criticism of Vatican interference in American government policy making. How does it work?

The extensive fragmentation of the Christian Church has resulted in a heavy burden of guilt for Protestants. The reason? This fragmentation is patently un-Christian. It flies in the face of the religion's fundamental principles, a constant reminder that Christ's followers reject His teachings. Protestants generally believe that unification of all Christians must be achieved if they are to live as true Christians. Guilt motivates them to strive for unity. As one New Orleans Protestant commented, "If we're going to call ourselves Christians, we have to live like it."

Criticism of one branch of Christianity by another results in disunity. Protestants have been very sensitive to this fact for much of this century. As a result, the ecumenical movement has served to silence any criticism of the Catholic Church by Protestant denominations. The outcome—complete institutional protection for the Catholic Church—compliments of well-meaning Protestants.

This reality has not been lost on the Vatican. When the Bishops Pastoral Plan for Pro-Life Activities was promulgated, Rome preempted the ecumenical initiative and began making major investments to promote ecumenism. In the last few years, Vatican interests in ecumenism have escalated sharply. "Evangelicals and Catholics Together," issued in March 1994 as an unofficial document, called on these two groups to recognize each other as Christians and to work together on common issues, such as abortion and pornography.

Adelle M. Banks reports for the Religion News Service: "The declaration was signed by such prominent evangelical leaders as Prison Fellowship founder Charles Colson and Campus Crusade for Christ founder Bill Bright. Catholic signers included Fr. Richard Neuhaus, director of the Institute on Religion and Public Life in New York, theologian Michael Novak, a winner of the Templeton Prize for Progress in Religion, Cardinal John O'Connor of New York, Archbishop Francis Stafford of Denver, and Jesuit Fr. Avery Dulles of Fordham University."

"Introducing the document last March, Neuhaus contended that not since the 16th century have Protestants and Catholics 'joined in a declaration so clear in respect to their common faith and common responsibility.' While calling the document unofficial, Neuhaus said he had 'been in contact with appropriate parties at the Holy See and they have given their strongest encouragement for the project.'"[273a]

However, many key evangelicals, including the Rev. John Ank-erberg, R.C. Sproul and the Rev. D. James Kennedy, balked, declaring that the document ought never have been written.[273a] Evangelical signers were some of the least influential in the movement while their Catholic counterparts represented the very top of the American hierarchy. This was a major initiative of the Vatican to promote the illusion that ecumenism is advancing in America. But it was only partially successful.

"THAT ALL THEY MAY BE ONE"

On May 30, 1995, the pope issued his 12th encyclical, Ut Unum Sint, "That All They May Be One," which is dedicated to the promotion of ecumenism. The message: The pope is eager to bring separated Christians back together. The encyclical was warmly received in the United States by the National Council of Churches, the nation's largest ecumenical organization. Its General Secretary, Rev. Joan B. Campbell responded: "The encyclical itself is a testament to the very spirit of Christian unity which we seek."[273b] This is precisely the response the Vatican sought. The encyclical offered the hope that unity was possible, encouraging Protestants to make every effort for its achievement—including suppressing all criticism of the Catholic Church from Protestant ranks.

Encyclicals are major declarations for Catholic clergy and the faithful. However, this one is distinctly different. It is specifically addressed to all Christians[273b] for reasons that will become apparent.

The National Catholic Register's Jean-Marie Guenois summarizes the encyclical. She quotes the pope: "Could not the real but imperfect communion existing between us persuade Church leaders and their theologians to engage with me in a patient and fraternal dialogue on this subject, a dialogue in which, leaving useless controversies behind, we could listen to one another, keeping before us only the will of Christ for His Church and allowing ourselves to be deeply moved by His plea 'that they may all be one...so that the world may believe that You have sent Me?'"

Guenois continues: "Ut Unum Sint consists of three chapters, the first on the Roman Catholic Church's commitment to ecumenism, the second on the fruits of dialogue and the third on the way to the future." The third chapter "focuses on the importance of

Christian unity for the work of evangelization." His message: We should not be wasting our energy attacking each other. We should concentrate our efforts on evangelization. Guenois continues: "While eager to preserve the Magisterium, he does express a sense of urgency about bringing Christians back together. He states bluntly in the encyclical that division among Christians 'impedes the very work of Christist.'...The very fact of calling oneself a Christian means desiring to be one with others of the same name, the Pope writes: 'To believe in Christ means to desire unity.'"[273c]

The pope goes much further. In the encyclical's point #40, the pope writes: "Relations between Christians are not aimed merely at mutual knowledge, common prayer, and dialogue. They presuppose and from now on call for every possible form of practical cooperation at all levels: pastoral, cultural, and social...Moreover, ecumenical cooperation is a true school of ecumenism, a dynamic road to unity. Unity of action leads to the full unity of faith...In the eyes of the world, cooperation among Christians becomes a form of common witness and a means of evangelization which benefits all involved."[273d]

Recalling that the pope prepared this encyclical for *all* Christians, his intent can only be described as "thinly veiled." He calls not only for Protestants to be silent about Vatican political manipulations in America so they can be the good Christians that God wants them to be, but also to cooperate with the Catholic Church in accomplishing its political agenda.

No Protestant leader protested the encyclical, though its intentions must have been clear to many. It received no negative press in the United States whatsoever. The pope's strategy is working. (It should be noted that in this encyclical, just as in *Evangelium Vitae*, the pope glorifies martyrdom. The message: the most wonderful thing one can do with one's life is to give it up in the defense of the Holy Mother Church: "This communion is already perfect in what we consider the highest point of the life of grace, 'martyria' unto death, the truest communion possible with Christ..." Why all the emphasis on martyrdom?)[273d]

An example of changed attitudes appears on the front page of the August 6, 1995 edition of the *National Catholic Register* in an article: "Catholic-Baptist ties show signs of new life: Southern Baptists and Catholics show signs of rapprochement." At the 1995 Southern Baptist Convention, Father Frank Ruff, a Catholic priest who attended his first Southern Baptist Convention in 1967, was asked to speak. It was a ground-breaking occasion. As a field representative for the National Conference of Catholic Bishops' Secretariat for Ecumenism and Interreligious Affairs, his request to address the previous year's convention had been politely turned down.[273e]

Ecumenism compromises Protestant Americans. The resulting silence has effectively shut down public debate of Vatican interference in American public policy making, gravely jeopardizing the security of all Americans as described in detail in the NSSM 200 report. The Vatican has skillfully advanced the case that an attack on the pope and the Catholic Church is an attack on all Christianity. America is certain to be in deep trouble if Protestant denominations accept this proposition. This would mean that they give the papal interpretation of the defense of Christianity a higher priority than the defense of the United States and its democracy. The outcome would be catastrophic for us all.

All of the major Protestant denominations have been affected by the Pastoral Plan and its ecumenical movement in significant ways. The Catholic Church has identified individuals who are anti-abortion, or simply opportunistic, in all of the denominations and has aided these individuals to rise to power within their denominations. The Church has helped create the illusion that the vocal anti-abortion minorities in the various denominations are the spokesmen for the denominations. More important, all criticism of the Catholic Church has been silenced, a vital outcome for the Vatican. The Protestant press which held the Vatican imposition of the Papal agenda in check in this country for 175 years has been neutralized. This arrangement has permitted the Vatican to influence American policy-making to a greater degree than would have been possible otherwise. All of our lives have been significantly affected.

EROSION OF CONFIDENCE IN OUR POLITICAL SYSTEM

The Pastoral Plan has had far-reaching effects on American political institutions, including the executive, legislative and judicial branches, which were specifically identified as targets in the plan. Organized as a result of the plan, there are thousands of

Catholics working in national, state and local governments who are responsive to the leadership of the Vatican, some out of religious belief, others simply out of opportunism. Doubtless a majority of the Catholics in our governments are "Kennedy Catholics." However, many are not and serve in the government to advance the interests of the Church. These Catholics have played havoc with American policy-making and the implementation of policy, especially in population growth control related matters. There are also opportunistic non-Catholics in our governments who serve the Vatican for personal gain or are zealots opposed to abortion and contribute to the Vatican effort.

Our government institutions are intended to protect or advance the interests of Americans. However, we have this highly organized group of Papal loyalists who do everything possible within the institutions that employ them to protect and advance Papal interests, at the expense of American interests. We have patriotic Americans pulling one way in their respective institutions in order to complete the assigned missions of their institutions. Then we have the papists pulling the other way. Some examples from Bernstein's *TIME* magazine article will be presented later.

This constant struggle erodes public confidence and trust in these institutions because most people are unaware of the conflict taking place between papists and patriotic Americans. For 19 years I have personally witnessed this conflict, particularly within institutions that are concerned with family planning, abortion and population growth control, including the U.S. Agency for International Development (AID), the old Department of Health, Education and Welfare (DHEW), the Department of Health and Human Services (HHS) and the Centers for Disease Control (CDC). Indeed, the patriots themselves are often not aware that they are involved in a conflict with the Catholic Church, which is represented by one or more of their coworkers. This constant tug-of-war is destroying the effectiveness of these institutions. Very few people recognize this serious problem—total gridlock on some issues is caused by it.

Some of the most competent people in America take positions in our government, elected and appointed officials and civil servants alike, only to leave prematurely out of disgust because they find themselves caught up in this tug-of-war, either knowingly or unknowingly, and are unable to efficiently perform the duties they were elected, appointed, or hired to do. Nothing has contributed more to the loss of the best and brightest from public service than the bishops' agenda. Others do not seek public service because of cynicism developed as a result of their own observations of this tug-of-war.

The bishops have had no reservations about corrupting these institutions to advance Papal security interests. The intervention described in the Pastoral Plan is massive and far reaching, and efficiency has suffered significantly, affecting us all. From the bishops' perspective, this is a small price to pay to save the Papacy from extinction.

One of the best examples is the presidency. When President Clinton was elected, it was clear from routinely reading an array of conservative Catholic periodicals during the course of the following year that conservative Catholics were in a state of shock. They simply could not believe this had happened.

Almost immediately, a multitude of stories began to appear in these periodicals which were obviously intended to undermine Clinton's credibility. It soon became evident that conservative Catholics were going to do everything possible to insure that there would be no second term for President Clinton. No concern was shown for potentially lasting damage to the institution of the American presidency itself. Within days of Clinton's election, open warfare was launched against the American presidency.

As soon as President Clinton took office, he was hounded by charges that were intended to embarrass him and to serve to weaken his ability to govern effectively. None of these charges, even if they were true, would result in his removal from office. However, they did serve to weaken Clinton's credibility and capability to govern. The charges served to destroy faith in President Clinton and promote cynicism toward him.

Rush Limbaugh appeared out of nowhere. There is a never before witnessed steady attack from every direction—from the floor of the House, the floor of the Senate, from radio and television talk shows, and newspaper and magazine reporters and columnists. It is an ugly, bitter, brutal, vicious attack such as Americans have seldom if ever seen a sitting president endure before. The conservative Catholic press and conservative Catholic journalists led the charge and have been the most aggressive of all.

Not surprising, Clinton's disapproval ratings have risen steadily and approximated 50 percent in mid-1994, the highest ever for a sitting president. This assault has been so intense and destructive, it is threatening to undermine the institution of the presidency itself. Cynicism toward our government has grown. Trust in our government has fallen.

Inevitably the President's ability to govern has diminished. If he does not govern well, he will be defeated in the next election. The zealots who want Clinton out of office seem to have no concern about destruction of the institution of the presidency itself. Who are these zealots? Nearly all identify with the Religious Right. Exceptions are ambitious men like Robert Dole who hungers to be the next president. The Religious Right is the design of conservative Catholics who were activated by the Pastoral Plan to advance Papal security-survival interests.

The tug-of-war taking place in our governmental institutions remains mostly unseen by the public. When a battle is perceived, such as the highly visible "Whitewater Affair," the underlying motivation is seldom understood. For example, on the August 8, 1994 "CBS Evening News," Dan Rather, in a segment on Whitewater referred to "the anti-Clinton activists" and the "Get Clinton Movement." However, no mention was made of the underlying motivation or engine of this movement. He makes no connection with the Religious Right or the Bishops' Pastoral Plan. Though Rather made no attempt to explain what is really driving the anti-Clinton campaign, we are often misled in similar circumstances.

These tugs-of-war are occurring also in our private institutions and international organizations—especially those related to population growth control—with many of the same negative consequences, undermining organizational commitment and effectiveness.

DISINFORMATION CREATES WRONG PERCEPTIONS

We are all exposed to a flow of information pointing toward the gravely threatening problem of overpopulation. But for over two decades now, surprisingly little concern for the gravity of the problem has been exhibited except by a small group of people in the field, and more recently by a growing number of environmentalists. Since the early 1970s, observers in the field have recognized that there is also a steady flow of disinformation. But they have had little reason to think that this flow is organized in any fashion, or organized and motivated by any particular institution. There are a number of individuals who have excelled in what could be called "disinformation enrichment." Three in particular come to mind: Herman Kahn, Julian Simon and Ben Wattenberg. None of them had gained distinction in the field before suddenly finding themselves at the center of the world stage disputing the work of thousands of scientists who had collectively concluded that the world is in deep trouble because of its unprecedented and uncontrolled population growth.

Herman Kahn was the first of the three. I remember watching in the 1970s with amazement as he would offer one unsound argument after the other, outrightly ignoring all of the best data available. All along I wondered how it is possible that this man would be given this incredible world platform from which to speak. How could he be taken seriously by the media, when he was scoffed at by the world scientific community? He was almost completely alone. It just did not make sense.

Next, along came the publication of an article by Julian Simon titled "Resources, Population, Environment" in *Science* in 1980.[274] This article dismissed the idea that the world has a population problem. That this article could appear in the most prestigious scientific journal in America was astounding. This article had nothing to do with science and was based on fiction as much as fact; it was a dishonest attempt to undermine the argument that the world has a population problem. The article was met with disbelief in the scientific community.

Then, along came Simon with his book, *The Ultimate Resource*, in 1981.[275] Simon attempts to make the case that it is not possible to have overpopulation; that people are the ultimate resource, and the more the better. Simon is an economist. In this book, Simon intermingles fact with fantasy throughout and misrepresents his material as fact. It was one misrepresentation of reality after the other. Simon was ridiculed by the scientific community. I could not believe that Princeton University Press had published this book. How could Simon have possibly placed this book with this publisher? This was a very serious setback for the population growth control movement. Princeton University had put its prestige behind this intellectually dishonest treatment of the issue of population growth.

At this point it became clear to me that there had to be corruption involved in the publication of the *Science* article and of the book as well. To corrupt these institutions takes a lot of influence. Who has the motivation to corrupt in this way? The institution with the most to gain by publication of these fantasies is the Vatican. Is it capable of such corruption? Certainly, if the stakes are high enough, the history of the institution suggests that they will stop at nothing.

With the publication of his article in *Science* and his book, Simon found himself at the center of the world stage. His articles and his message began to appear everywhere in newspapers and magazines. For example, in June 1981, he published a lengthy article in the *Atlantic Monthly* magazine, with the theme that nature is boundless.[276] Then in August, 1981, he published another lengthy article in the *Atlantic Monthly* attempting to make the case: the more people the better.[277a] He became a sought after public speaker and appeared often on television and radio.

No one had ever done so much to undermine public confidence in the argument advanced by the world's scientists that humanity faces a serious overpopulation problem. Years of scientific education went down the tubes. Of course, we would all like to believe that overpopulation is not a serious problem. Simon's position, the Vatican's position, caught on like wildfire. Simon's work and its apparent widespread acceptance by "scientists" caused great confusion which persists today.

Not enough people realized that Simon's support came almost entirely from the religious right. Simon wrote his book while at the University of Illinois at Champaign-Urbana. While he was there, support of his work on his book came from the Heritage Foundation, a Vatican-leaning organization created in line with the bishops' Pastoral Plan.

Simon was a visiting fellow at The Heritage Foundation when he headed a 21-member panel of "scientists" commissioned by Heritage to re-examine the 1980 Global 2000 report, which President Carter had ordered the State Department and Council on Environmental Quality to prepare, exploring probable changes in the world's population, natural resources and environment through the end of the century. The report, issued after a year-long study, expressed deep concern about continued rapid global population growth and its contribution to the depletion of natural resources and destruction of the environment.

Simon released the Heritage panel's findings at the 1982 annual meeting of the American Association for the Advancement of Science, chalking up another remarkable Vatican accomplishment. In 1984, Simon teamed up with Herman Kahn to place a book with the scientific publisher, Basil Blackwell.[277b] This 585-page book was devoted to refuting the Global 2000 report.

In March 1985, I received a telling letter from Roger Conner, Executive Director of the American Federation for Immigration Reform. It read:

"Maybe the Heritage Foundation has finally gotten rid of Julian Simon after all. He has now started his own group, written up in the enclosed column.

"Patrick Burns, our director of research and publications, has called the new group's telephone number and discovered that it is housed in an exclusive girls' finishing school financed by *Opus Dei*—an extremely right wing Catholic organization.

"I doubt that we've heard the last of Julian."

To learn of Simon's close ties to the Catholic Church did not surprise me. Let's examine some of his own words. In a September 15, 1986 letter widely distributed to journalists, Simon introduces his new organization, the Committee on Population and Economy: "Next time you work on a story concerning population, please call Committee on Population and Economy to get our point of view." In his "prospectus" he states, "The general purpose of the Committee on Population and Economy is to celebrate human life and its increase. We, plus the appended list of persons who have affiliated with us in some capacity—intend to promote belief in the value and sanctity of human life. And we hope to increase understanding that an additional human being tends to benefit rather than harm others economically."

His "partial list of general goals" includes: "Educate the public to the good news that the physical limits of our environment are receding rather than advancing....Publicize such scientific findings as those which indicate that in the long run, on average an additional human being increases the standard of living of other people rather than detracts from it, and that there is no connection between population growth or size or density and the propensity of countries toward war and violence. These findings contradict assertions without supporting evidence by the U.S. State Department and the CIA, assertions apparently made simply because they seem reasonable." Perhaps Simon is referring to NSSM 200 here.

Simon lists "Some specific tactical objectives: Disseminate writings....Provide an organizational address that the media can turn to when they seek a "contrasting" viewpoint to the Population Crisis Committee, Population Institute...and so on. As with other issues, when a population news issue arises, newspaper reporters automatically turn to organizations who make that issue their business. In the absence of an organization that speaks in favor of human life and against a doomsday view of our future, the journalist is likely simply to resort to no one....Offer an alternate source of information to the Population Resource Center which now 'briefs' government officials in a supposedly neutral fashion about population issues....Comment...on bills now before the Congress that would mandate U.S. and world "population stabilization" and that would create staffs and programs to achieve that end....'Infiltrate' church, environmental, and other groups that currently make pronouncements in favor of population control in order to provide another viewpoint."

Apparently, Simon is referring to infiltration of Protestant churches, as such discussion is forbidden in the Catholic Church. He goes on to say, "The organization will use all available education means to promote its beliefs..."

Simon lists specific planned activities: "Issue a series of articles, written for popular reading at the level of magazine articles or newspaper op-ed pieces, dealing with various aspects of our subject....This series will be sent to our list of newspaper and television journalists who cover population and the environment, many of whom we believe to be interested and who may diffuse our message." We must assume that he is referring to the Catholic journalists Pope John II referred to in addressing the International Catholic Press Union and the International Catholic Association for Radio and Television in his message, "Mass Media Need Catholic Presence," referred to earlier.

He continues, "The environmentalist and population-control organizations have developed into an effective tool the letter-to-the-editor, wherever news stories appear. We wish to create a grassroots organization with this as one of its central tasks, both in communities and on college campuses. The present state of public belief was largely created by a deluge of communications of all sorts over two decades. It will be easier for us than it was for them..."

This statement is most telling. For some who have closely followed letters-to-the-editor and op-ed columns in several different newspapers for the last decade or two, it has been evident that an organized campaign advancing the Papal position on population and abortion has been underway for a long time. Simon refers to that highly successful campaign here. Unfortunately, most readers are occasional readers and have not recognized this fact.

Simon continues, "Yet a large volume of material will be necessary to establish the legitimacy of our message...as well as to hammer home our message to the public at large. A speakers' bureau may also be part of such a grass-roots organization....We will also maintain a list of high-level scholarly speakers whom we can recommend to the media when they seek interviews on television and radio for the press."

The language used by Simon identifies his employer. His repeated use of the term, "value and sanctity of human life," is rather suggestive. However, more conclusive evidence is evident in his list of persons he says "have indicated their desire to be associated with the project." This list includes Judie Brown of the American Life League, as well as representatives of the American Enterprise Institute, The Rockford Institute, The Cato Institute, and The Heritage Foundation—all of which are identified with the Religious Right and emerged in response to the Pastoral Plan—and Georgetown University.

The highly sophisticated and prolific propaganda machine created by the bishops, which includes Simon's organization, has been effective in creating illusions which serve to counter the realities we all see with our own eyes. These realities would, in the absence of Vatican inspired propaganda, be used to make decisions to support a more effective response to the overpopulation threat to American and world security. Today, the pope is winning this war because the massive propaganda efforts on his behalf have confused the American people. Such propaganda has killed the American political will to confront the population problem. But, given the stakes for the Vatican, we should not be surprised.

With propaganda machinery in place, the Vatican set out to create many wrong perceptions, serving to undermine the scientific consensus that world overpopulation is a grave problem for the U.S.

These wrong perceptions and illusions, of course, serve as obstacles to a constructive response. Why? The constructive responses almost always include controls on population growth and immigration, threatening Vatican survival.

WRONG PERCEPTIONS — GREENHOUSE EFFECT LEADS THE LIST

Perhaps the most threatening consequence of overpopulation to the Vatican is the greenhouse effect. This consequence is terribly hard to ignore. People cannot help but take notice: wild swings in the weather, large intense storms, rising temperatures and droughts.

In June 1988, one of the nation's leading climatologists, Dr. James Hansen, director of NASA's Goddard Institute for Space Studies, declared himself "99 percent certain that the greenhouse effect is upon us." At a U.S. Senate hearing, he stated, "The greenhouse effect has been detected and is changing our climate."[278] During 1988, the United States sweltered in a heat wave and drought. News analysts warned, as *Newsweek* put it, "This year's weather was merely the foretaste of a warming trend that will, by the next century, cause unprecedented disruption in the environment, not just of the United States but of the world....This decade has seen the four hottest years of the last century and the first five months of 1988 are the warmest on record."[279]

The greenhouse effect is caused by an increase in the level of atmospheric carbon dioxide and other gases, including methane, nitrous oxides, and low-altitude ozone[280]—all a result of human activity. The more humans, the more activity, naturally. This signals the inexorable links among population growth, energy consumption, and global warming. These increased levels act as a blanket which prevents heat received from the sun from being radiated back into space.

The atmospheric carbon dioxide level has risen 27 percent since the early 1800s, and 20 percent since 1960. The level is expected to double by the third quarter of the next century. If the buildup of other greenhouse gases such as methane is considered, the same effects could occur in 50 years or less.[281]

"Most greenhouse effect forecasts call for rising sea levels, less rainfall in the interiors of continents, and hotter summers," journalist Monte Basgall reported in July 1988. "The most unsettling scenarios include an increase in severe storms, and heat and drought conditions extreme enough to force population migrations."[282]

Other science writers made equally dire forecasts: "Conditions in Southern California will resemble Death Valley."[283] "The central United States will become a desert, if predictions hold true....Three of the big models predict extreme drought to the point there will be no ability to have agricultural production in Oklahoma, Texas and Nebraska."[284] These are important food growing regions and their loss, along with other areas certain to be affected, will mean serious food shortages in the United States. It is unlikely that we will be able to feed even our current population. North Carolina State University's James Woodman believes that a climate that includes higher temperatures, elevated levels of ozone, and extreme variations in precipitation could only be bad for agriculture.

If the Earth's population, industrialization, and emissions continue to grow at present rates, a six-degree increase in temperature is expected by mid-century—a temperature level last occurring two million years ago.[285] "The potential for economic, political and social destruction is extraordinary," said biologist George Woodwell.[286] "Who could have imagined man himself rendering the earth uninhabitable?"[287]

As Newsweek's Jerry Adler and Mary Hager observed, "Trusting to luck is a risky strategy with the fate of the world at stake....The web of life is unraveling around us....The continuing thread of these environmental threats is the element of irreversibility."[288]

Norman D. Newell and Leslie Marcus have studied the positive relationship between population growth and the greenhouse effect for the period 1958-83 and found that the steady increase of carbon dioxide in the atmosphere has closely paralleled the growth of world human population, with an amazing correlation of 0.9985. The authors suggest that this relationship is so precise that carbon dioxide measurements should probably replace inaccurate census taking.[289]

According to Stephen H. Schneider, a climatologist for the National Center for Atmospheric Research in Boulder, Colorado, what he and his colleagues fear the most is rapid change. Without action, they say, the change will happen so swiftly that all forms of life will be seriously disrupted.[290]

The greenhouse effect clearly has the potential of being lethal to our life-support systems. All of this new information on the greenhouse effect cited above appeared in the American press in 1987 and 1988. A reasonable person would expect that the American people and our government would have reacted to this alarming new information. What has happened instead?

On May 6, 1989, White House Chief of Staff John H. Sununu, a devout Catholic, rejected a proposal by William Reilly, who was at that time administrator of the Environment Protection Agency (EPA), and others who wanted U.S. representatives to call for an international convention on the greenhouse effect. Reilly and the others believed it would be a strong symbolic move for President Bush to urge a convention of nations to develop a framework for agreement on ways to combat the greenhouse effect. This move was killed by the White House.[291]

On May 8, 1989, the Bush administration admitted that its Office of Management and Budget had changed conclusions about global warming data in the Congressional testimony of Dr. Hansen, over his protests. The budget office edited his text to soften the conclusions and make the prospects of change appear more uncertain.[292]

When the information cited above began appearing in 1987 and 1988, immediately we began seeing counterpoint articles to confuse the public, as well as comments from scientists not directly involved with this issue. These counterpoint articles (and numerous letters-to-the-editor) were written by people who had little or no expertise in this field. Credentials were rarely mentioned. However, there was no controversy among the most competent people in the field.

The Vatican's vast disinformation effort gave the impression to the public that there was much controversy among the scientists themselves with respect to the need to begin addressing this problem, including international communications in meetings like the one proposed by EPA Administrator, Reilly. There has been no further action on the proposed meeting, which is most certainly opposed by the pope, as it would mean the release of additional convincing evidence that we face a grave threat from overpopulation. The bottom line: nothing at all has happened.

We don't hear much about the greenhouse effect anymore. The pope's disinformation campaign is working. The public perception of the greenhouse effect is one of confusion, which has resulted in paralysis, the goal of this disinformation effort.

Columnist, Molly Ivins describes our predicament: "Bill McKibben, author of *Hope, Human and Wild*, wrote in *The Los Angeles Times* that the most curious part of this phenomenon is not that it's taking place—global warming is right where it's supposed to be, according to all the predictions by all the scientists who have studied it—but that no one is paying attention. Denial of global warming is being aided and abetted by those whom McKibben calls 'confusionists'—ideologues and industry flacks who keep trying to discredit the scientists by using inaccurate and misunderstood statistics. Rush Limbaugh, for some bizarre reason, has taken it upon himself to crusade against the idea of global warming as some kind of left-wing plot."[292a]

Perhaps the single most remarkable example of succumbing to the opposition is the Clinton Presidency. Vice-President Al Gore's performance has been astounding, but highly instructive a lesson in the struggle for power. Mark Hertsgaard writes in *The New York Times*: "To read Vice President Al Gore's 1992 book *Earth in the Balance*, one would think that from the moment he took the oath of office he would have focused on nothing but grave threats of global warming, overpopulation and runaway consumption. Instead, the Clinton administration has compiled an environmental record of retreats, defeats and half measures."

"'Even after highly publicized warnings from virtually the entire scientific community...we are doing virtually nothing to address the principal causes of this catastrophe in the making.'"

"Those words were written by Sen. Al Gore in 1991, when George Bush was in the White House. But they are no less true today. The Clinton Administration's plan against global warming relies mainly on voluntary measures that Gore himself concedes fall short of what is needed."

"Indeed, the administration has failed across the board to live up to the grand vision outlined in 'Earth in the Balance' of making 'the rescue of the environment the central organizing principle for civilization.'...[T]he Republican Congress [is] on the brink of rolling back 25 years of environmental measures."[292b]

For over 50 years, David Brower, one of the founders of the environmental movement, has been active in the struggle. Currently a Sierra Club board member, his assessment of the President is that: "Clinton has done more to harm the environment and weaken environmental regulations in three years than Presidents

Reagan and Bush did in 12 years." He characterizes President Clinton as the "Great Capitulator."[292c]

One thing is certain. Everyone expected the Clinton-Gore team to be a great positive force for the environment and that by the end of their first term, significant steps would have been taken to deal with the "greenhouse effect." Not only has nothing been accomplished, but both men have fallen silent on this vital issue.

The power of the Presidency alone has not been sufficient to overcome the strength of the opposition. But where does such power lie? Certainly not with those usually credited. Only the Holy See exerts such control in our nation's capital. The Vatican dominated Republican Congress and numerous bureaucrats throughout the government, both Catholics and opportunistic non-Catholics, have succeeded in aborting the Clinton/Gore environmental effort. The Clinton-Gore team has been no match for the Vatican team on the greenhouse effect issue, despite the convincing evidence that rapidly continues to accumulate.

GREENHOUSE EFFECT EVIDENCE CONTINUES TO MOUNT

Much of the mounting evidence that the greenhouse effect is a reality and already significantly affecting the environment is not communicated to the public. Nothing transpiring in the world today has greater implications for all our lives than the greenhouse effect. In a few decades, it will play a dominant role in what we do every day. The print news media have done a little better in bringing this problem, now only in its infancy, to our attention than their electronic counterparts where the topic is rarely mentioned. Though woefully inadequate, given the magnitude of the greenhouse effect threat to our personal security, the following evidence has appeared in the press during the past 18 months:

William K. Stevens writing for *The New York Times*: "Earth has entered a period of climatic change that is likely to cause widespread economic, social and environmental dislocation over the next century if emissions of heat trapping gases are not reduced...according to...a new assessment of the climate problem by the Intergovernmental Panel on Climate Change...a United Nations Group. The new features of the assessment—the first in five years by the panel—is that the experts are now more confident than before: That global climatic change is indeed in progress. And that at least some of the warming is due to human action...A continuing rise in sea level...most of the beaches on the U.S. East Coast would be gone in 25 years...An increase in extremes of temperature, dryness and precipitation in some regions....There is a 90 percent to 95 percent chance that climate change caused by the emission of greenhouse gases like carbon dioxide is responsible....The panel forecasts an increase in droughts like the current one in the Northeastern United States, heat waves like the one in Chicago this summer, and more fires and floods....A 'striking' retreat of mountain glaciers around the world, accompanied in the Northern Hemisphere by a shrinking snow cover in winter....Deserts are expected to expand, and the heartlands of continents to become drier. There would be more rain throughout the world....Forest trees could not migrate northward fast enough to keep up with shifting climatic zones, and some forests would disappear, the panel says."[292d]

In another *The New York Times* article, Stevens observed that 1995 was the warmest year globally since records first were kept in 1856 according to the British Meteorological Office. "The average temperature was 0.07 degrees Fahrenheit higher than the previous record set in 1990....The British figures reveal the years 1991 through 1995 to be warmer than any similar five-year period, including the two half decades of the 1980s, the warmest decade in the record to date....The NASA Goddard Institute for Space Studies in New York shows the average 1995 temperature slightly ahead of 1990 as the warmest year since 1866....Dr. James Hansen, director of the Goddard Institute predicted at least a couple more new global records will be set before 2000....The UN panel predicted ...the average global temperature will rise by a further 1.8 to 6.3 degrees, with a best estimate of 3.6 degrees, by the year 2100."[292e]

George Moffett reported that the 10 warmest years on record have occurred since 1980, the two warmest, since 1990. (*Christian Science Monitor*)[292f]

Kathy Sawyer of the *Washington Post* remarked: "After years of alarms, an international panel of scientists and government experts agreed in writing that human activities are affecting the global climate....The following language was adopted by consensus: 'The balance of evidence suggests that there is a discernible human influence on global climate.'" The delegates at a meeting in Madrid of Working Group I of the Intergovernmental Panel on Climate Change (IPCC) represented 75 nations.[292g]

Robert Lee Hotz reported (the *Los Angeles Times*): "Spring is arriving earlier every year throughout the Northern Hemisphere—possibly due to global warming—with the result that the growing season in many countries today is a week longer than 20 years ago, scientists announced...in the journal *Nature.*" [292h]

Phil Mintz for Newsday: "Ocean waves that towered 100 feet—the highest ever observed in the North Atlantic—formed during two East Coast winter storms in recent years, leaving scientists wondering if storms are becoming more intense because of global warming." Previously storm records had led them to believe that 100-foot waves should be no higher than 72 feet.[292i]

Carol Kaesuk Yoon warned in *The New York Times* that: "Plant species living high in the Alps are climbing farther up their summits to escape the heat of a warming climate, but they risk going extinct when they run out of mountain, a study has found. Surveying 26 summits, Austrian researchers reported species migrating skyward at a rate of about 3 feet a decade in this century, with some moving as fast as 12 feet a decade." If temperatures increase as predicted, all of these species will run out of mountain and become extinct.[292j]

Washington Post Columnist Jessica Mathews advised that the National Climatic Data Center has combined five indicators that greenhouse models predict will change in a warming world into a single index of climate change. "The measures include elevated temperatures, drought in the summer months and the proportion of rainfall that comes in torrential downpours....The results show that since 1980 U.S. weather has become more extreme, with an index 40 percent higher than natural fluctuation should produce. Every one of the five measures showed this trend. The study concludes that the likelihood is 90 percent to 95 percent that 'the climate is responding to increases in greenhouse gases.'"[292k]

From the Cox News Service: "Heavy downpours and howling blizzards are occurring more often than they did in the past, and some of the nation's leading climate experts say the trend is yet another sign that the Earth's climate is changing. Researchers at the National Climatic Data Center reported that 'extreme precipitation' events—the heavy downpours and snowfalls that are most likely to cause flooding, erosion and crop damage—are on the rise, not only in the United States but elsewhere in the world. 'Overall, there isn't any trend in total precipitation; we're just getting more extreme events,' said Thomas Karl, senior scientist at the Center." (2921)

This is not an exhaustive list of the American press coverage over this 18-month period. But we can say with certainty that it was sparse. "Earthweek: A Diary of the Planet," a newspaper column written by Steve Newman for Chronicle Features, offers specific and convincing evidence that, when taken collectively, change is probably underway. Some newspapers carry this column on a weekly basis. From this, we can derive a list, albeit hardly comprehensive, of world events serving as evidence that the effects of global warming are already being felt, events, largely ignored by the press, and listed below by week's ending:

The past year produced the warmest weather on record in 220 years across Austria; 1994 was almost four degrees warmer than the last record-warm year of 1775. January 6, 1995[292m]

Vast numbers of warm-water sea creatures are migrating farther north each year along the California coast in response to rising ocean temperatures. This Stanford University study begun in the early 1930s, shows that the average shoreline temperature has risen by 1.35 degrees since then. The average summer water temperature has gone up four degrees.

Even while flood waters steadily receded in rivers across northern Europe, a worsening drought in Spain wilted crops and caused water reserves to fall to dangerous levels. The drought has spread relentlessly over the Iberian Peninsula since the early 1990s and shepherds could not remember a worse drought this century. February 10, 1995[192n]

The British Antarctic Survey reported that a giant iceberg broke off from the Antarctic Peninsula. While less than 100 feet thick, the massive chunk of ice covers 1,100 square miles of ocean. The British team concluded that the breaking off of the iceberg is due to the gradual warming in the region of 4.5 degrees Fahrenheit since the 1940s.

Tibet was battered by its worst snowstorm in half a century. The northern grasslands, with 12-foot snowdrifts, were hardest hit. March 3, 1995[292o]

A surge of subtropical moisture unleashed another round of record flooding in California's Wine Country. Flooding in the Napa Valley was expected to crest at 10 feet above the record flooding of 1986. March 10, 1995[292p]

Argentine scientists warned that Antarctica's ancient ice shelf has begun to break up in warming seas. "The first thing I did was cry," lamented Dr. Rodolfo del Valle, who discovered a 40-mile long crack in the northernmost part of the Larsen Ice Shelf that runs 600 miles up the Antarctic Peninsula. United States scientists predicted in the 1970s that the melting of Antarctica's ice shelf would be one of the first clear signals of accelerating global warming.

The eastern Mediterranean Sea has suddenly warmed up far below the surface due to a new current in the Aegean Sea. The seabed has become about one degree Fahrenheit warmer in the last few years which could result in regional climate changes.

Vietnam's central highlands province of Darla is in the grip of its worst drought in several decades with most reservoirs completely dried up. March 31, 1995[292q]

A state of emergency has been declared in four northern states of Mexico, where a severe drought has withered crops and killed hundreds of thousands of cattle.

Unseasonable frost and snow across the northern half of Spain destroyed a large section of the wine crop and damaged fruits and vegetables. April 28, 1995[292r]

Searing heat and cloudless skies over Bangladesh in recent weeks have sent temperatures rising to deadly levels and helped cause the flow of the Ganges River to shrink to a trickle. May 5, 1995[292s]

Several waves of severe thunderstorms rumbling across the American Midwest and Deep South unleashed some of the worst flooding in centuries and triggered deadly tornadoes in several states.

Asia's only permanently ice-capped tropical mountain is rapidly losing its mantle of glacier ice, another sign of global warming. Ice once covered almost eight square miles of the top of the mountain in Indonesia, but now spans only one square mile at its peak. May 12, 1995[292t]

Relentless storms which have pounded the United States took a more northerly course, allowing record flooding to recede in Louisiana. Now seemingly endless waves of rain have turned the fields in the fertile Great Plains to mud, preventing cultivation.

The heat wave and drought in the eastern half of the Indian subcontinent was broken by a monsoonal storm which devastated crops and property. May 19, 1995[292u]

The southwest monsoon shows no sign of ending the unrelenting spell of high heat in parts of India and Pakistan. This year's monthlong record heat has dried up the wetlands of the Himalayan foothills, threatening endangered species.

Freakish late-season snow and rain continued to pound western parts of Canada and the United States where swollen rivers and streams swamped large tracts of farmland. Extremely rare June rains threaten a wine crop in California. June 16, 1995[292v]

Scientists studying weather patterns over the Amazon are puzzled by the discovery of sudden and violent downward-blowing winds that are destroying parts of the rain forest, causing planes to crash and threatening human life. A single episode of these sinking winds demolished a 10-square-mile jungle area in only 20 minutes. June 30, 1995[292w]

Bangladesh called in the Army to help rescue millions of people marooned by the latest floods that have swept northern parts of the country.

China continued to battle the massive flooding that has swamped 10 provinces and displaced millions of people since late May. July 14, 1995[292x]

Monsoon floods that have swept across almost half of Bangladesh since early July have killed scores of people, thousands of cattle and damaged approximately 1000 bridges and culverts.

The death toll from a brutal five-day heat wave in the American Midwest was expected to surpass 800. Temperatures soared to an all-time record of 106 degrees in Chicago, causing the greatest death toll from one event in that city since the Great Fire of 1871.

In the journal, *Nature,* scientists reported an acceleration in the melting of the Arctic ice cap, possibly signifying a long-term global warming.

Also in the journal, *Nature,* a team of European scientists wrote that Siberia is now warmer than it has been for the past 1,000 years. July 21, 1995[292y]

Tass news agency reported that the global warming has stimulated the migration of venomous snakes into the Russian Arctic. July 28, 1995[292z]

Called the floods of the century, the Chinese Army evacuated almost 1 million people in Liaoning Province where floodwaters covered 1.3 million acres. August 4, 1995[292aa]

Extreme heat and blazing summer sun sparked a new round of wildfires in the western United States, northern Mexico and parts of North Africa. In northern Baja California the mercury soared to 125 degrees. August 11, 1995[292bb]

Barely six months after experiencing some of the worst flooding in Europe this century, Holland now faces a severe shortage of water that threatens farmers with ruin.

Argentine military and civilian authorities launched a massive relief effort to bring food and supplies to southern parts of the country cut off by three weeks of severe snowstorms.

Across southern Chile, the coldest Antarctic chill in 40 years killed 250,000 sheep, cattle and horses. August 18, 1995[292cc]

The prolonged dry spell throughout northern Europe worsened with high heat and clear skies, is now taking a severe toll on the region's agriculture. Ireland's potato harvest is cooking in the earth under the hottest and driest summer on record that threatens to decimate the crop.

Savage winter conditions that lashed southern Argentina for a second week killed an estimated 1.5 million sheep and halted transportation in Patagonia.

Eastern Australia broke the record for the longest dry spell since records began 137 years ago with a total of 37 days without rain. August 25, 1995[292dd]

The luxury British liner QE2 was hit by a 95-foot tidal wave generated by the remnants of Hurricane Luis as the ship crossed the North Atlantic.

The spate of severe flash flooding around the Northern Hemisphere during the past few years may be a result of global warming, according to the U.S. Climate Analysis Center. Its findings show that the added warmth can cause clouds that burst suddenly into downpours. September 22, 1995[292ee]

A sudden and unseasonably severe snowstorm sweeping southeastern Mongolia killed nomadic herdsman and sent their 10,000 unattended head of cattle fleeing into neighboring China.

Metropolitan Denver may not recover from a freak late summer snowstorm for at least two years. Some foresters estimated that four out of every five trees in the city were destroyed or damaged when heavy and wet snow fell on the still foliated branches. September 29, 1995[292ff]

A chunk of ice measuring 82 square miles has broken loose from Antarctica due to warming waters. November 3, 1995[292gg]

Blinding blizzards moved through southern Scandinavia bringing much of the region to a standstill. "I have been a weatherman for 20 years and have never seen such a long-lasting and forceful snowstorm," said Swedish forecaster Lars-Erik Larsson.

Britain is sending $23 million in aid to southern Africa to combat a worsening drought across the region. Maize harvests have plunged 91 percent. November 24, 1995[292hh]

An international gathering of scientists and government experts in Madrid formally agreed that global warming is already occurring. The opinion of the United Nations Intergovernmental Panel on Climate Change (IPCC) is that recent temperature rises cannot be explained by natural climatic variations, leaving human influence as the only possible cause. December 1, 1995[292ii]

Scientists at the British Meteorological Office announced that the world's average temperature was 1.8 degrees Fahrenheit above normal during 1995. As predicted by computer models, some regions of the world were significantly hotter than average in 1995, like parts of Siberia where it was 5.4 degrees above normal. January 12, 1996[292jj]

British scientists reported that Antarctica's ice shelves are melting away as temperatures over the frozen continent rise by about 0.12 degrees Fahrenheit per year. At least five of the thick ice shelves that make up Antarctica have retreated dramatically over the past 50 years, during which temperatures have risen by 4.2 degrees, according to the British Antarctic Survey. January 26, 1996[292kk]

After months of fierce blizzards and temperatures as low as minus 40 degrees in western China, the army moved more than 50,000 nomads and millions of head of livestock to safer ground. Bitterly cold arctic weather also descended on much of central Canada and the midwestern United States, breaking many temperature records. February 2, 1996[292ll]

The worst blizzards of this century continue to plague much of China's Qinghai Province, threatening more than 100,000 people with starvation. March 1, 1996[292mm]

Two more waves of heavy snow in the northeastern United States put the season's snowfall totals over record levels. The 13th winter snowstorm exceeded New York City's previous record set in 1946-47.

This has been the Ukraine's harshest winter in decades. March 8, 1996[292nn]

The World Meteorological Agency announced that analysis of global weather data from 1995 reveals it to be the hottest year in recorded history. The agency's 11-page "Statement on the Status of the Global Climate 1995" also reported that there were more Atlantic hurricanes than in any year since 1933. Atmospheric concentrations of carbon dioxide and methane "greenhouse gases" are blamed for the continued increase in the average worldwide temperature.

Kenya announced it will build walls around part of two tiny islands to protect them from imminent swamping caused by the rising sea level. It is believed that the changing climate is responsible for the discernible rise in ocean levels during recent years. May 3, 1996[292oo]

Bitterly cold snowstorms, artificially-induced by cloud-seeding to put out huge fires raging across the steppes of Mongolia killed at least 5,000 head of cattle.

The worst snowstorm to strike China's northwestern Xinjiang region in half a century killed 469 swans. May 17, 1996[292pp]

A second year of severe drought in China's wheat belt has parched 17.5 million acres of crops and caused the lower reaches of the Yellow River in Shandong Province to dry up five times since January.

Unrelenting high winds after a nearly snowless winter in southern Alaska fanned huge wildfires that blackened tens of thousands of acres of forest. June 7, 1996[292qq]

Researchers in Canada announced that the permafrost, which covers a vast area of the nation's far north, is retreating. A six year study by the Geological Survey of Canada, found that the permanently frozen ground in the Mackenzie Basin has retreated by 63 to 125 miles over the past 100 years. This retreat is attributed to global warming. June 14, 1996[292rr]

The United Kingdom Climate Change Impacts Review Board announced that the country will undergo major changes during the next 50 years, with northern England and Scotland becoming wetter still and the south warmer and drier. The board warned that such changes would have a significant impact on wildlife, agriculture and ranching. The climate zones are predicted to shift 125 miles northward. July 5, 1996[292ss]

Unprecedented winter storms raging across South Africa were responsible for a blanket of heavy snow, with drifts as high as 8 feet, across the normally temperate nation. July 12, 1996[292tt]

This barrage of specific examples of what are probably the results of the greenhouse effects does get one's attention—but only if you are aware of them. Earthweek is always buried deep in the second or third section of the newspaper, with little visibility. Who cares whether we are only 90 or 95 percent certain that the greenhouse effect is causing these unprecedented events? If it should develop as predicted, the results will be catastrophic. Billions of people will die prematurely in the coming century, including millions of Americans. The ramifications of this catastrophe may well end our form of government as well. Individual security would largely disappear. With the stakes so high, why is the press largely ignoring this mountain of evidence—which literally grows weekly?

Articles appearing in the press often contain counter claims, with the result that the reader becomes skeptical of the validity of the greenhouse effect research findings. For example, the first Stevens article cited devotes nearly one-fourth of the text to opposing views and dwells on the controversy among "the scientists": "Climate forecasting is a difficult and often controversial science. One major subject of dissension is the computer models....Skeptics continue to assert, however that models fail to simulate the present climate realistically....But given the natural variability of Earth's climate and the wide fluctuations in temperature known to have occurred in the distant past, climate experts until now have been almost unanimous in saying they could not prove that emission of greenhouse gases related to human activity was playing a part in the warming....The human contribution to global warming could range from highly significant to trivial. The panel scientists say it is not yet possible to measure how much of the warming has been caused by human activity and how much is a result of natural causes."[292d]

In his second article, Stevens diminishes the importance of the findings thus far, referring to the position of the NASA Goddard Institute for Space Studies director, Dr. James Hansen: "Hansen has been one of only a few scientists to maintain steadfastly that a century-long global warming trend is being caused mostly by human influence....Other experts would go no further than the recent findings of a U.N. panel of scientists: the observed warming is 'unlikely to be entirely natural in origin' and that the weight of evidence 'suggests a discernible human influence on climate.' Previously, few scientists apart from Hansen had been willing to go even that far, contending that the relatively small warming so far could easily be a result of natural climate variability." (292e) Obviously, just by reading his own words here, it is apparent that Stevens is underscoring his case that there is much disagreement and confusion among "the scientists."

In his cited *Los Angeles Times* article, Robert Lee Hotz does much to raise doubts in the minds of readers, devoting about one-fourth of it to promoting uncertainty: "In a key but controversial report last year, a U.N. panel concluded for the first time that greenhouse gases such as carbon dioxide are probably responsible for changing the global climate...Despite the growing scientific evidence, the controversy over global warming and climate change shows no signs of abating. At the Geneva meeting earlier this week, more than 100 European and American scientists issued a joint statement condemning any major steps to reduce global warming....There is, they argue, still no scientific consensus on climate change."[292h] Who were these 100 people in Geneva? No mention is made that the United Nations panel consists of 2500 carefully selected scientists. How were these 100 people chosen? Who sponsored this meeting in Geneva? Was it arranged by the Vatican? We can be absolutely certain that Rome will make every possible effort to insure that there is never a "scientific consensus on climate change" no matter how catastrophic the greenhouse effect becomes.

Other publications simply reject the greenhouse theory. A Scripps Howard News Service article published this spring, "Global warming in dispute: Scientist raps theory of greenhouse gases," offers no reporter's name. The article begins, "The scientific squabble over global warming heated up again Wednesday with a Harvard astrophysicist's report that weather records provide 'no evidence' of a coming climatic catastrophe." (292uu) The article then blatantly misstates the data in which only scientists in the field would be familiar enough to recognize deception.

George Seldes recognized the use of these very same techniques to deceive Americans about the Spanish War of 1936-1939. And he thoroughly documented the Vatican's role in their use. There is little doubt that we are witnessing a repetition of a successful strategy as the Vatican goes about protecting its security-survival interests at any costs.

In his articles, Stevens fails to mention the enormous potential costs in lives, health, personal security and literally everything else of value to us. Why await a 100 percent certainty? A probability of 95 or 90 percent is far more than needed to act responsibly. When we suspect that a dam might break, even if there is only a 10 percent chance, we evacuate all the communities below the dam as quickly as possible. Why aren't we responding as responsibly by addressing the greenhouse effect threat? We all know that population growth control must be at the top of the list of the many solutions to the greenhouse effect problem. So does the Vatican. General acknowledgment of the problem will drive population growth control onto the public agenda as nothing has before. The threatened Vatican would prefer to prevent this realization and has a vested interest in maintaining as much confusion and skepticism as possible regarding the greenhouse effect.

If we continue on our current course, it is likely that the greenhouse effect will ultimately bring about a full-blown confrontation between Americans and the Church hierarchy. No one will be able to ignore the full fury of the consequences of the greenhouse effect. As the droughts and floods increase, as our beaches which draw 100 million Americans each year disappear, as our forests begin to die on a massive scale, and our deserts relentlessly expand, as the sea floods our coastal communities, as powerful hurricanes, huge winter storms and sweltering heat waves strike with increasing frequency, the greenhouse effect is certain to get our attention. Americans will begin to demand solutions, as well as explanations for the decades of grossly irresponsible inaction. The Vatican is going to surface as the culprit.

THE BOGUS "DEMOGRAPHIC TRANSITION" THEORY

Perhaps the single most important myth used by the Vatican to undermine concern about world population growth has been the demographic transition theory. The Vatican has promoted this myth through numerous institutions and individuals for decades. By 1975 it had largely fallen into disfavor because it was rather obvious that it was not working. However, it continues to be promoted, mostly by politicians, journalists, and foundation and population organization staffers, many of whom are Catholic. The theory is simple: the increase in well-being derived from economic development leads to a decrease in fertility.

In her book, *Population Politics: The Choices That Shape Our Future*, Virginia D. Abernethy systematically destroys the credibility of this theory. When researchers closely examined the basis for this theory in the early 1970s, they discovered that the early proponents had made assumptions about the industrialized countries that were historically dead wrong. Actually, the fertility transition to small families had occurred in the midst of desperate poverty and very high infant mortality in Europe.[293] In a *Wall Street Journal* article, "Experience Teaches Population Control Can Precede Development, and Spur It," published just before the Cairo Population Conference in September 1994, Tim Carrington cites compelling evidence that this theory is bogus. He writes that the view "Development is the best contraceptive" was widely held 20 years earlier. However, much has changed: "...there is broad agreement that the old maxim can be fully retired. Its weakness lies in the implicit suggestion that efforts to reduce fertility work only after a nation has lifted itself out of poverty. Reality suggests otherwise."[293a]

Discovery that this theory was not valid has not diminished the use of it to support the Vatican position on population growth control.

The Vatican has also promoted the illusion that U.S. foreign aid is good. For the Vatican, U.S. foreign aid *is* good. It puts tens of millions of dollars into Vatican coffers through grants to the various Catholic relief organizations. But more important, this redistribution of wealth is good for the Vatican because it discourages developing countries from facing up to their overpopulation problems and gives them a false sense of security. Abernethy makes a compelling case that in the intermediate and long run, our foreign aid is certain to result in catastrophic consequences.

Abernethy reports, "The scale of the global effort to help the third world (and the deception it fosters) can hardly be overstated. Harper's Index (March, 1989) reports that forty countries rely on foreign aid for at least a quarter of their national budgets....[when all aid is considered, of which AID money is just a small part] the United States dispersed $92 billion to developing countries in 1988 (Harper's Index, December 1989)[294a]...Experts think that, by the year

2000, 64 out of 117 third-world countries will have become dependent on donated food, and the majority of these 64 countries will be unable to support as many as half of their projected numbers."[294b]

Egypt, for example, will be dependent on imports for 80 percent of its food in the year 2000.[295] What will become of it? Where will the food imports come from when the greenhouse effect begins to take its toll on U.S. food production in a couple of decades as currently projected? The United States provides the bulk of the world's food exports.

Food is not the only problem. Abernethy summarizes, "Three billion people will lack adequate fuel wood or other energy sources. Water demand, spurred by population growth, will exceed rainfall in most of Africa, the Middle East, North Asia, and parts of Mexico, Chile, and Argentina. And, warns environmentalist Cynthia Green, 'The growing volume of untreated human wastes and toxic substances could render as much as one-fourth of the world's water supply unsafe for human consumption.'"[296]

U.S. foreign aid has made it possible for the Vatican to postpone its extinction by delaying serious population growth control efforts. But, what have been the costs to the developing countries? Developing countries have been given the implicit message that they cannot help themselves, eroding self-confidence. Says Abernethy, "Dependence on others is not a happy adult condition: Failure can be blamed on someone else; energy that could go into work or planning is dissipated in resentment when things go wrong, or in resentment simply at being dependent. Poor countries that count on foreign aid risk losing their resolve to become self-reliant. When dependence undermines self-confidence and stymies both foresight and planning, how can the future get better?"[297]

China, on the other hand, kept a firm grip on reality. It adopted self-reliance as a core tenet of national policy. In China, the one-child family is now widely, if not universally, accepted as a patriotic duty. Americans have long understood the importance of self-reliance. How much did the Vatican influence the decision-making of our law-makers in the formulation and implementation of our foreign aid policy?

Another myth promoted by the Vatican is that poverty is a distribution problem. It claims that rich countries will always have enough to share if they choose to. It adamantly rejects the idea that there is a problem of absolutely limited resources. Many developing countries buy this myth. Abernethy notes the danger of accepting it, "The results are sadly counterproductive: Poor countries are encouraged to live beyond their means in the belief that they will be bailed out, and third-world couples go on thinking that large families are affordable."[298] The results obviously meet the pope's needs.

Welfare programs in the U.S. were and continue to be strongly supported by the Vatican. As is the case of foreign aid, the Church derives billions of dollars in income from domestic welfare programs. According to the *National Catholic Reporter*, Catholic Charities USA, the nation's largest private network of local social service organizations, relies heavily on the government for its financial support: "In 1993, the latest year for which figures are available, 65 percent of Catholic Charities' income was provided by state, local and federal governments."[298a] In its March 14, 1996 issue, *The Wanderer*, a conservative national Catholic weekly, reports: "The American Church is a principal subcontractor for the government in housing, welfare, child care, health care, and education, and gets billions of dollars for its services, for which it receives very generous administrative overhead fees that keep chanceries running and provide salaries and benefits for thousands of Church bureaucrats. Thus, maintaining the welfare state—under the guise of 'compassion for the poor'—takes priority over the traditional Catholic social principles espoused by Buchanan."[298b]

But, more importantly, these programs have significantly increased fertility, especially among new immigrant arrivals[299] (most of whom are Catholic). However, these programs have had a devastating effect on the American family and social fabric. The predictions of critics of these programs at the time they were made the law of the land are now reality. The Catholic Church has taken credit for the enactment of this legislation for decades.

For years the Vatican has complained that there would be no population problem in Central and South America if the wealthy there simply redistributed their wealth. This cynical act makes the Church look like the good guys to the masses and musters support from the masses for the Church. It allows the masses to blame their problems on the wealthy. It permits the poor to avoid blame for their own conditions which are a result of simply having more children than they can afford. The Vatican wins—the poor lose.

Abernethy makes another important point: "Urging redistribution on policymakers in poor countries is almost certainly inappropriate. Hard thinking and difficult decisions seem in order because, where there is overpopulation, those who are destitute will consume, before they die, the future potential productivity of any part of the environment to which they have access. Witness the Sahel, Ethiopia, the Sudan, Haiti...Nepal, and Bangladesh."[300] The land will be denuded and the topsoil stripped away.

The Vatican is also responsible for the myth that immigration is a win-win situation when in fact the exact opposite is true. Abernethy summarizes why: "Perceived opportunities to emigrate may be just as corrosive as large-scale aid. Emigration appeals to many of the most energetic people of a society—exactly those people who would be most likely to promote constructive reform at home. One quick way to stop dissent is to expel the trouble-maker....Driving out the tree-shaker does make for soothing politics. At the same time, emigration creates a safety valve for excess population. The understanding that some people will remove themselves lifts the pressure that would otherwise encourage everyone to confront the limited nature of resources....These aspects of emigration...narrow considerably the options for helping third-world countries to help themselves."[301] Thus the developing country loses.

The American bishops lead the cry against the national identification card exactly because they know that illegal immigration control will not be possible without it. It is true that this card will infringe upon the privacy rights of citizens. (Those of us who served in the military will find this card nothing new because we were required to carry such a card throughout our service.) However, without limiting immigration through enforcement of our immigration laws, notes Abernethy: "Citizens go on losing jobs, most people's real income falls, energy security becomes a bitter joke, the environment suffers, the carrying capacity is exceeded, and Americans lose cherished values along with their privacy rights."[302] America loses.

The Vatican has created the illusion that it is not a major actor in U.S. policy making. Few Americans are aware of the intensive involvement of the Vatican in U.S. immigration policy development, most recently in the 1990 Immigration Reform Act. Abernethy acknowledges that public complacency over the Act can be traced in part to the inaccurate portrayal of future U.S. population by the U.S. Census Bureau. The Bureau's 1989 projections were criticized almost as soon as they appeared. Demographers Dennis Ahlburg and James Vaupel determined that legal and illegal immigration were being grossly underestimated.[303] However, using more accurate data for legal and illegal immigration, it was later discovered that the projected population for the U.S. in the year 2080 was 300 million off! Had this deliberate miscalculation not occurred at the Census Bureau, there is no way that the 1990 Act which further liberalized immigration law would have passed.

Abernethy does not identify the driving force behind the corruption at the Census Bureau. However, she does identify a driving force for the 1990 Act, The Heritage Foundation "whose champions are," as she says, "Julian Simon and Ben Wattenberg." As noted earlier in this chapter, The Heritage Foundation is a creation of the bishops' Pastoral Plan and is headed by a conservative Catholic, Edwin J. Feulner, Jr.

One of the great successes of the bishops' disinformation campaign has been the misleading of America in the identification of the forces encouraging an open borders arrangement for the U.S. If you ask individuals on the street who these driving forces are, they might mention a few but they never mention the Vatican. In that the Vatican is surely the most significant force, this is quite an achievement.

Perhaps its greatest success has been creation of the illusion in the U.S. that all is well within the Church, and between the Church and American democracy. This illusion is largely owed to the success that the Church has achieved in suppressing virtually all criticism of the Church in the press. A corps of Catholic organizations is committed to this activity. The pit bulls of this corps are found at the Catholic League for Religious and Civil Rights, as described in the previous chapter.

The Vatican has no use for the civil rights of American patriots—freedom of thought, of expression, of the press. Patriots have a moral responsibility to speak out when their country is threatened. This sort of intimidation over the last hundred years has resulted in a populace woefully ignorant of the threat to American democracy and security posed by the Church. This illusion has made it possible for the Church to go unchallenged.

The Vatican has also created the illusion that it does not involve itself in international organization policy making. Of course this is not so. In a recent interview, Professor Milton P. Siegel detailed how the Vatican seized control of World Health Organization (WHO) population policy making from the very beginning.[304] Siegel was Assistant Director General of WHO for its first 24 years and is considered among the world's foremost authorities on the development of WHO policy. During the third World Health Assembly (1950), the Vatican threatened to kill WHO and start their own organization if the director general, Dr. Brock Chisholm, did not stand up before the Assembly and specifically state that WHO would not get involved with family planning. He did. WHO did not get involved at all for more than a decade.

Siegel put his finger on the Vatican's motivation. Without the separation of population dynamics from WHO public health policy, the Vatican subsequently would have found it much more difficult to manipulate governments on family planning and abortion. National leaders would have been able to refer to the international consensus, as demonstrated by WHO policy. WHO, they could have insisted, has determined that family planning and abortion—like clean water, good nutrition, and immunizations—are necessary to protect public health. This was deeply threatening to the Vatican. This astounding example is reported on in greater detail in an article based on this interview found in Appendix 3, on page 559.

In its 45-year history, WHO has had a deplorable record in family planning. Its commitment has been minuscule, and even today, family planning accounts for only a tiny fraction of its budget. The Vatican continues to have considerable influence at WHO. For example, it recently succeeded in having appointed as director of the Human Reproduction Program a professor from a Catholic University in Rome, Dr. Giuseppe Benagiano, the son of Pope John Paul II's dentist. Benagiano promptly set out to kill any further clinical studies of the most important development in fertility control since the birth control pill was developed in 1960—the quinacrine pellet method of nonsurgical female sterilization.[305] This permanent method has already been used by more than 100,000 women in 15 developing countries. There have been no deaths or life-threatening injuries and it can be delivered in developing countries for under $1 US, in primitive settings by paramedical personnel. Given the current Vatican influence within WHO, it would be much better for humanity if the organization removed itself from fertility control altogether. Its behavior is similar in its relations with all other international organizations that bear on population growth control. The Vatican has succeeded with its illusion.

The Vatican's disinformation campaign has worked hard to create illusions of abundance and prosperity, that wealth is renewable and that nature is inexhaustible. The right-wing Catholic literature is full of these distortions of reality but the Vatican is also responsible for the appearance of these kinds of messages throughout media. These cornucopian fantasies are nurtured and promoted to protect the Vatican position on population growth control and thus its security-survival. The Vatican has discouraged the concept of national self-reliance, including public debate of this concept, because it recognizes that achievement of such self-reliance would be impossible without population growth control.

At the same time, the Vatican, through its disinformation efforts, has fiercely attacked the concept of carrying capacity, apparently because it makes so much common sense. But this concept immediately implies the requirement of population growth control. It has also created the illusion that Earth has an infinite capacity to absorb ever growing quantities of wastes and pollution. We get mixed signals as a result and none of us is as concerned as we would be if the Vatican were not so successful in implanting disinformation.

The steady stream of "human interest news" regarding new arrivals and regarding the plight of would-be immigrants and refugees is intensely promoted by the bishops to advance the Vatican's security interests.

The greatest accomplishment of this sophisticated and well-financed disinformation program has been its success in making immigration and population policy almost taboo subjects for public debate. Given the overwhelming importance of these subjects for the security-survival of all Americans, this success is most disheartening. If the Vatican can succeed in this country with these issues in this manner, what else may be in store?

DISUNITING OF AMERICA

In his 1993 national bestseller, *The Disuniting of America*,[306] Arthur M. Schlesinger, Jr. never mentions the Catholic Church though he does refer to religious groups. In her book, *Population Politics*, Abernethy does not mention the Catholic Church in her treatment of the subject of the disuniting of America either.[307] In fact, neither identifies who might be behind this phenomenon. They both indicate that the effort is sophisticated, is widespread, has a lot of resources, and is hell-bent to succeed. But for some reason, they do not identify who the culprits might be.

Who stands to gain from the disuniting of America? Who is threatened by a united, organized, committed America? Who stands to gain from social disorganization in America? Who has the sophistication, resources, organization and motivation to set about disuniting America?

Certainly the Vatican is a sophisticated political institution and recognizes that America's bonds of national cohesion are fragile and that factionalism can tear our country apart. Obviously, the Vatican would be gravely threatened by an influential, united, organized America committed to population growth control. It would be hard to deny that the Catholic Church has a vested interest in ethnic identification and that it has repudiated the ideal of assimilation, an American institution.

Schlesinger recognizes a serious danger relevant to the death of NSSM 200 which I will discuss further at the end of this chapter: "And when a vocal and visible minority pledges primary allegiance to their groups, whether ethnic, sexual, religious, or...political, it presents a threat to the brittle bonds of national identity that hold this diverse and fractious society together."[308] The bishops also recognize this and have used this threat on occasions too numerous to count. They are certainly prepared to use it again and again.

"The bicentennial of American independence, the centennial of the Statue of Liberty, the restoration of Ellis Island," says Schlesinger, "all turned from tributes to the melting pot into extravaganzas of ethnic distinctiveness."[309] There was a similar outcome with the 500th anniversary celebration of the arrival of Columbus in the West Indies (not America) in 1992. I watched each of these four tributes in disbelief. It looked as if these events were staged by the Catholic

Church. Support for this suspicion can be found in a later section on presidents Reagan and Bush.

Schlesinger identifies an ethnic upsurge today that "threatens to become a counter-revolution against the original theory of America as 'one people,' a common culture, a single nation."[310] He goes on to say, "The cult of ethnicity exaggerates differences, intensifies resentments and antagonisms, drives ever deeper the awful wedges between races and nationalities. The endgame is self-pity and self-ghettoization."[311] And further, "The cult of ethnicity has reversed the movement of American history, producing a nation of minorities—or at least of minority spokesmen—less interested in joining with the majority in common endeavor than in declaring their alienation...."[312] In the end, the cult of ethnicity defines the republic not as a polity of individuals but as a congeries of distinct and inviolable cultures.[313] This set of circumstances has set the stage for the fragmentation and anarchy that we already see in our inner cities today.

The Bilingual Education Act of 1968 has not worked out as planned, except if the Catholic bishops were the real planners, an intriguing possibility. In practice, bilingual education retards rather than expedites the movement of Hispanic children into the English-speaking world and it promotes segregation more than it does integration. It nourishes self-ghettoization. Bilingualism encourages concentrations of Hispanics to stay together and not be integrated.[314]

As a result, Catholic bishops now claim to speak for the millions of Hispanics living in the U.S., a status from which the bishops derive power—political power. This appears to be the only positive outcome of this Act for anybody and the bishops continue to fiercely protect the Act which has squandered billions of tax dollars. Through this Act, the bishops have made significant progress in transforming the United States into a more segregated society.

Schlesinger also notes that when a religious group claims a right to approve or veto anything that is taught in public schools, the fateful line is crossed between cultural pluralism and ethnocentrism.[315] The Vatican successfully claimed this right and vetoed in public schools all mention of the anti-democratic and anti-American teachings of the Catholic Church and all mention of history which places the Catholic Church in a negative light. As a result, we have an American populace that is blatantly ignorant of the true nature of the Catholic Church, the threat posed by the Church to the rights we claim as Americans, as well as the lengths to which the Church has gone in the past to protect its interests.

There is scant question that an attack on the common American identity is underway and that this attack has been instigated by the Vatican to promote its own interests which are presently seriously threatened. The bishops have made progress in transforming the United States into a more segregated society. They have succeeded in their efforts to impose ethnocentric, Afrocentric, and bilingual curricula on public schools, designed to hold minority children out of American society and have remarkably advanced the fragmentation of American life.

There are several advantages the bishops derive from this arrangement. One obvious advantage depends on acceptance of the bishops' proposition that they speak for these groups. At present, this proposition is thoughtlessly accepted by the media. Fragmentation will make population policies, such as those suggested by the Rockefeller Commission and NSSM 200, far more difficult to agree on and implement, a fact the bishops surely recognize. If the bishops find that anarchy in the U.S. is necessary to protect the Papacy (a likely proposition), this fragmentation sets the stage.

According to Schlesinger, "The American creed envisages a nation composed of individuals making their own choices and accountable to themselves, not a nation based on inviolable ethnic communities"[316]—accountable to their bishops or whomever. He continues, "The Constitution turns on individual rights, not on group rights"—which can leave out the bishops if their faithful choose not to follow, as with family planning and abortion.

The American creed, which he defines as the "the civic culture—the very assimilating, unifying culture,"[317] is today under siege because we let the Catholic bishops degrade history—European, Latin American, North American, and Church—allowing them to dictate its contents. Unaware of the dangers that we would have learned from a full and truthful history of the Church, we have permitted the bishops and their representatives to run grandly amok in the halls of our government. This has resulted in Papal influence on U.S. public policy making beyond what most Americans can imagine. Due to this interference, we are increasingly threatened with a grave global population problem.

INTERNATIONAL FEMINIST MOVEMENT
HIJACKED BY VATICAN

Canadian Madeline Weld has taken a serious look at the International Feminist Movement. Her findings are most revealing: "[T]he Vatican, and various allies,...categorize as racism any arguments for limiting population growth and any reasonable objections to unlimited immigration....[F]ar too many people are intimidated into silence by this form of intellectual terrorism.

"The Vatican's campaign of intellectual terrorism is advanced enormously by some feminists....Although feminists ought, theoretically, to be opponents of the pope, because they generally believe in choice on contraception and abortion, they sometimes seem more like the pope's handmaidens. A significant segment of the International Women's Movement denies that population growth is a problem and accuses anyone who disagrees with them of racism. They portray any concern with global population growth as being in inherent opposition to advancing the rights of women. Because there have been abusive population programs in the past, they argue that any program must be inherently abusive. This segment of the International Women's Movement is in danger of hijacking the whole movement."

"Because the book, *Power, Population and the Environment Women Speak,* arose from the "women's tent" of the Earth Summit, I presume it is indicative of the direction that the intelligentsia of the international women's movement is taking. That is scary, because the book is the work of idealogues, not of analysts or scholars."

"On June 5, 1995 I attended a public meeting organized by various groups, who are participating in an international effort to discredit the first conceptually new development in contraceptives in 20 years: antifertility vaccines. The development of one of these vaccines has been funded in part by the [Canadian] International Development Research Centre (IDRC). The meeting was organized by the National Action Committee on the Status of Women...Canada's largest feminist organization and Inter Pares...which has numerous Catholic sponsors. The women at that meeting were anti-science. The comment that there was a scientific consensus that the world was overpopulated was met with a comment that it was scientists who brought us the atomic bomb. Any questions pertaining to how we will solve the problems we now have were attacked with statements laying the blame for everything bad on the west. According to some of the speakers, to be concerned with population was to be genocidal toward people of other races."

"I later found out that the IDRC had offered to sponsor the Indian scientist who has been directing the research on one of these vaccines for 20 years [Prof. G.P. Talwar] to attend the meeting. The offer was turned down. The women had advertised a demonstration against the vaccine, which was mysteriously canceled...I found out that they had been planning to do a skit, but had been told that IDRC would challenge them if they misrepresented facts....What we heard at the meeting was not an objective analysis of the pros and cons of the vaccines, but a rant against genocide, eugenics and racism. To be concerned with population, we are told, was to be racist, anti-woman and anti-poor."[317a]

Unfortunately, anti-fertility vaccines are only the latest target of these feminists. They were instrumental in the near total elimination of the intrauterine device (IUD) option for American women. Today only about one percent of American women use this excellent method, while it remains the most popular one in many countries, including Finland, Norway and Sweden where medical care standards are very high. Those feminists were the storm troopers in the opposition to Depo Provera, which, though now available, was unnecessarily withheld from American women for 20 years. The latest victim is the most promising contraceptive method developed to date for people who want no more children, the quinacrine pellet method for nonsurgical female sterilization. With 26 years of experience in contraceptive development, I can attest to the extraordinary effectiveness of these destructive feminists.

Dr. Weld continues: "These feminists are very influential, because I have never seen the population issue addressed in any women's organization or publication....Yet the women at the...public disinformation...meeting I attended are impeding a solution to the world's crisis through intimidation and by spreading confusion. What motivates them?...Unfortunately, far too many sensible women are silenced by the intellectual terrorism of the feminist hijackers. To make an analogy with the U.S. civil rights movement, the Martin Luther King types of the women's movement have been shunted aside by the Louis Farrakhan types, with their own agenda of hate."

To be sure, there are Martin Luther King types. As we noted earlier, Dr. Virginia Abernethy has identified overpopulation as the single most important women's issue. Eleanor Smeal, president of the Feminist Majority, has concluded that unchecked population growth demeans the status of women and often ruins their lives. (317b) Fran P. Hosken, Women's International Network, in her comment for the cover of this book, says that nothing is more important than control over reproduction which forms the basis of all democratic institutions and equality.

"The pope's handmaidens," as Dr. Weld refers to them, must be identified and thoroughly isolated from the international feminist movement—whatever it takes. If sincere feminists fail to succeed in a complete separation from these women, the credibility of the feminist movement will share the fate suffered by the Roman Catholic Church. It will plummet. Feminist have a vital role to play in population growth control. If we fail to achieve population stabilization in the near future, all investments made in the feminist movement, by women and men alike, will be for naught.

VATICAN SETTING U.S. POLICY TO PROTECT INTERESTS

Few Americans, even few Catholics, have any idea of the extent to which the Church has gone to impose its religious dogma on all Americans, including unwilling Catholics, through law-making, judicial decision-making and the administration of government. When you ask most people the question, "How much influence do Catholic bishops have in the governing of America?" most likely they will respond: "None." The Catholic Church has successfully created the illusion that this is out of its realm.

According to Alan D. Hertzke, author of *Representing God in Washington* and a professor at the University of Oklahoma, "There's pretty good evidence that most Church members have no knowledge of what their national Church leaders are doing....Despite its absolute theological stand on many issues, the Catholic Church has proved to be one of the most effective religious forces in practical politics."[318]

David Briggs, in a December 1990 series for the Associated Press, stated: "And the Catholic Church may become the strongest power because it is willing to form coalitions with a wide range of allies."[319] These allies sometimes include opportunistic people and institutions with little concern for the well-being of this country or our people. Governments tend to fall in behind public opinion and public opinion is led by the Church on nearly all issues important to its own security.

In an August 1990 "Member Alert," Robert Maddox, executive director of the mainstream organization, Americans United for Separation of Church and State, placed in perspective just how powerful the Catholic lobbying effort really is: "The U.S. Catholic Conference enjoys an unprecedented veto power over all social legislation." That's powerful! The Catholic Church's influence is unmatched by any other U.S. institution.

The Catholic extremist Paul Weyrich heads the Center for Catholic Policy within his Free Congress Foundation. However, he also heads up the Siena Group, a coalition of 40 Roman Catholic public policy organizations.[320] If the Catholic Church were not deeply involved in the making of U.S. public policy, why would it need so many public policy organizations? Undeniably, the most powerful of all remain the National Conference of Catholic Bishops and the United States Catholic Conference, operating out of their imposing office building near the Capitol.

The Church's lobbying effort is tens of thousands of people strong on the national, state and local levels. These people are knowledgeable about the workings of government, well financed, highly organized, and deeply committed. And they are successful. For example, in November 1995, a bill prohibiting over 1 million federal employees and their dependents from choosing health insurance that covers abortion, was enacted. That same month a measure that denies abortion services for military women stationed overseas, including women serving in Bosnia, became law.[320a] On the state level, for example, in 1989 the Church managed the introduction of 270 bills in 41 state legislatures on the abortion issue alone.[321]

The costs of policies adopted as a result of the Catholic lobby, in dollar terms alone, are horrendous. For example, the costs of implementing immigration policies (policies which are shaped almost entirely by the extensive Catholic lobbying effort) were estimated by Dr. Donald L. Huddle, Professor of Economics, Rice University, to be $45 billion in 1992 alone. He projects the immigration costs to be $668.5 billion over the next decade.[322] A significant part of this money goes into Vatican coffers as the U.S.'s leading immigration service contractor. American taxpayers are footing this bill with barely a whimper.

One of the most important questions facing Americans today is: Should representatives of the Papacy be permitted any access to U.S. policy making whatsoever, given the fact that Papal security-survival interests are diametrically opposed to the security-survival interests of all Americans?

VATICAN INFLUENCE ON THE U.S. PRESIDENCY

Many Americans are victims of the illusion, carefully crafted, that the Catholic bishops have no significant influence on American presidents. No doubt the degree of influence differs from one president to the next. But they all feel and respond to this influence.

The *National Catholic Reporter*, a major national Catholic weekly newspaper, published a most revealing report in its December 29, 1989 issue. Doug Wead, special assistant to President Bush, was interviewed and quoted as saying: "He [President Bush] has been more sensitive and more accessible to the needs of the Catholic Church than any president I know of in American history." Wead indicated he felt that Bush's relationship with the American Catholic leadership was much closer than Reagan's had been: "We want the Church to feel loved and wanted, and we want them to have input." This relationship was maintained through five U.S. cardinals: Bernard Law, Joseph Bernardin, Edmund Szoka, John O'Connor, and James Hickey.

Within a month after Bush became president, all five of the cardinals had been included in meetings in the Bush family quarters. Both Law and O'Conner spent at least one overnight at the White House as guests of the president. "This has been a Catholic year," said Wead. "This administration has appointed more Catholic cabinet officers than any other in American history."

I think many Americans would be surprised to learn of this cozy relationship. It was never mentioned in the secular press—and we were left with another illusion.

However, the relationship between the Catholic Church and President Reagan is much more revealing, as described by Carl Bernstein in the cover story of the February 24, 1992 issue of *TIME* magazine, with the title: "Holy Alliance: How Reagan and the Pope

Conspired to Assist Poland's Solidarity Movement and Hasten the Demise of Communism." The agenda of the Church is far more obvious. In Chapter 7, excerpts appear from Bernstein's article regarding the Reagan Administration's adoption of the Vatican's position on birth control and abortion in U.S. foreign aid programs.

"The Catholic Team" as Bernstein described it, wielded enormous power. Bernstein reports, "The key administration players were all devout Roman Catholics—CIA chief William Casey, Allen, Clark, Haig, Walters, and William Wilson, Reagan's first ambassador to the Vatican. They regarded the U.S.—Vatican relationship as a holy alliance: the moral force of the pope and the teachings of their church combined with...their notion of American democracy." Protestants in the Reagan Administration were apparently unaware or unconcerned about this far-reaching maneuver. Or they simply felt there was nothing they could do about it.

Bernstein quotes Protestant Robert McFarlane, who served as a deputy to both Clark and Haig and later as National Security Advisor to the President: "I knew that they were meeting with [Vatican ambassador to the U.S.] Pio Laghi, and that Laghi had been to see the President, but Clark would never tell me what the substance of the discussions was." "The Catholic Team" did not include Protestants. If this was truly an American operation with strictly American interests at stake, why weren't Protestant Americans represented too? What was being hidden?

Reagan and the pope undermined and seized control of the Polish government because the Polish government seriously threatened papal security interests in Poland when that country outlawed Solidarity in 1981. Regarding direction of their operation to overthrow the Polish government, Bernstein quotes Laghi: "But I told Vernon [Vernon Walters, American ambassador to the U.N.], 'Listen to the Holy Father. We have 2,000 years of experience at this.'"

Laghi seemed to take great pleasure from the fact that the Papacy has had 20 centuries of experience in overthrowing governments. This suggests that the Vatican would stop at nothing to defend its own interests. One must read the lengthy article in *TIME* to fully appreciate the enormity of what took place, much of it illegal.

What would prevent the Vatican from putting together a team of "devout Roman Catholics," as Bernstein called them, to protect Papal security interests at the expense of U.S. security interests—if a conflict of security interests did arise? Nothing. Because that is exactly what happened.

Simple logic suggests that "The Catholic Team" was well aware of NSSM 200. Vernon Walters was the deputy director of the CIA and Alexander Haig was President Nixon's Chief of Staff when NSSM 200 was being researched and written. The Catholic Team knew that NSSM 200 had clearly determined that overpopulation gravely threatened U.S. and global security. Yet they chose to protect Papal security interests fully knowing that they were gravely undermining U.S. security. Should this behavior not be considered treasonous? Meanwhile, patriotic Americans assumed that the Reagan Administration was concerned about all aspects of U.S. security.

Bernstein's *TIME* article shows that the pope overthrew the Polish government to protect Papal security, after putting together a secret Catholic team (which excluded non-Catholics) within our government. Why would he not be prepared to assemble another "Catholic Team" to overthrow the U.S. government to further protect Papal security interests? This is a vital question to ponder.

PATRIOTISM

Webster defines patriot, "One who loves his country and zealously supports its authority and interests." He defines patriotism, "Love of country; devotion to the welfare of one's country." Webster makes no mention of the Catholic principle: "primacy of conscience: loyalty to God over loyalty to the state" discussed in Chapter 13. One must assume that God and pope are used here almost synonymously.

The "Catholic Team" described by Bernstein are not American patriots. They showed only a warped love of country and certainly did not support its interests.

In the quote appearing at the beginning of this chapter, Georgie Anne Geyer says that the pope's teachings and policies on birth control could now lead to the death of all of our countrymen. The pope's insistence on open borders for the U.S. most certainly threatens the welfare of our country and our countrymen.[323] The honest position for a patriot is a position opposed to the pope's teachings and policies on population control.

Given the obvious conflict in security-survival interests, Catholic Bishops and priests, who must place the interests of the Papacy above all else, cannot claim they are American patriots. They represent a foreign power—now rightfully recognized as our enemy. This is also true for the Catholic laymen who made up the "Catholic Team" in the Reagan Administration. Catholic Bishops have created the illusion that they are patriotic. They have defined patriotism differently from Webster—in such a way that Papal security interests are not threatened. At the same time, they have trivialized patriotism when they find it threatening.

Abernethy sums up what the American position must be: "Every nation has the sovereign right to pursue a course leading to its own survival and territorial integrity. *E pluribus unum* means that we, citizens of the United States of America, are morally obligated to act for, and avoid acting against, the best interests of our country and fellow citizens. The many became one. That is patriotism. It means loving and defending one's motherland and its people."[324] This is the moral position.

None of the illusions that I have discussed in this chapter evolved spontaneously. Given their manifest success, it is apparent that their creation has required dedicated effort and craft. The Vatican is very good at what it does. However, with sufficient effort, these illusions can be shattered, replaced with reality, accelerating the self-destruction of the Papacy.

I'll conclude this by quoting the whole of the couplet, the first line of which heads this chapter. It's from the Gilbert and Sullivan opera *H.M.S. Pinafore*:

"Things are seldom what they seem—
skim milk masquerades as cream."

In this case, Vatican security/survival policy invaded and has been masquerading as U.S. population policy, with almost certain cataclysmic results, unless we act forcefully now.

CONCLUSIONS 17

17

H OW LONG can American liberties endure? *"Our liberties are safe until the memories and experiences of the past are blotted out and the Mayflower with its band of pilgrims forgotten; until our public school system has fallen into decay and the Nation into ignorance; until legislators have resigned their functions to ecclesiastical powers and their prerogatives to priests."*[325]

President Woodrow Wilson

President Wilson's famous response to this question is haunting as we examine the life and death of NSSM 200. Regarding abortion, family planning and other population growth control related issues, the legislators have indeed "resigned their functions to ecclesiastical powers and their prerogatives to priests." We now face not only our greatest threat ever to American liberties but to our species as well. Our legislators have permitted ecclesiastical powers and priests to kill all significant initiatives to control unprecedented population growth, including the Rockefeller Commission and NSSM 200 initiatives.

WHAT IS OUR PREDICAMENT?

This problem will not vanish in the present political climate; anarchy will become inevitable. Dealing with the conflict between U.S. security-survival interests and those of the Vatican security-survival interests is an essential first step in overcoming the world population problem. The Republican Party retained the HLA in its

1996 platform, in significant part due to the efforts of presidential candidate Patrick Buchanan and his followers, including the Christian Coalition. In a February 1996 fundraising letter, Buchanan's primary motivation is made evident: "I want to talk to you today simply and directly, from my heart, about what I believe is the most important issue facing America today. That issue is the sacredness of human life, and the moral imperative facing us to fight to protect it from the moment of conception to the moment of natural death. A principal reason I'm running for president is to turn back the pro-abortion forces and keep the Republican Party firmly in the pro-life camp. And then I want to use the Presidency as a vital and powerful force to change what Pope John Paul II has so correctly called "the culture of death" that has arisen in America since 1973.

"On November 8, 1994, we made a tremendous start—electing 5 new pro-life Senators and 44 new pro-life Representatives. Now for the first time in 40 years, both houses of Congress are controlled by the Republican Party—a party solemnly sworn, in its platform, to a 100 percent pro-life position. If we elect a pro-life president in 1996, we can finally move forward to ending abortion in the United States."[86a] The stage will be set to achieve the Vatican's goal of an HLA in the U.S. Constitution. Buchanan suggests that the Republican Party has become the papal party.

Recall Bishop James McHugh's 1987 comment to Byrnes: "within twenty-four hours" of the court's action on Roe v. Wade in 1973, the bishops knew they would need to mount a political campaign in favor of a constitutional amendment prohibiting abortion. The Vatican has already seized control of the Republican Party. More on this later.

The predictions made and implied in the Rockefeller Commission and NSSM 200 reports are now coming to pass. In recent years we have seen Africa make significant strides toward returning to a pre-colonial stage. The inevitable population crash in Africa is now much more believable as a result of the images of starvation, disease and anarchy we see on our televisions almost daily.

These images have brought greater recognition that our present behavior is akin to mass madness—promoted by the Vatican. There is much telltale evidence that the Roman Catholic Church is self-destructing as it labors to extend this insanity. Institutional credibility is plummeting just as predicted by the intellectual leadership of the Church 125 years ago.

The Vatican's success in blocking and silencing the Rockefeller Commission and NSSM 200 initiatives has been a remarkable achievement with dire probable consequences for all of us. But the Vatican itself has little hope of avoiding self-destruction. It has pinned its hope on passage of the HLA which is vital to the preservation of papal authority and maintenance of power. Ultimately, the Supreme Court would have to rule that human life begins at conception.

No doubt there is hope that the Papacy can survive a prolonged period of global anarchy. The Church has proved that it can survive anarchic conditions, has a history of promoting anarchy and has on occasion profited from anarchy. There is reason to believe that the Vatican has made its choice between more immediate self-destruction and risking survival over anarchy. It is apparent that the cost in human terms is not a factor in Vatican decision-making. Indeed, from the Vatican's perspective, promotion of worldwide anarchy is a reasonable strategy.

We have been paralyzed by a myth initiated nearly 20 years ago and successfully promoted by the bishops' Pastoral Plan for Pro-Life Activities: the myth is that the Religious Right is a Protestant movement led by Protestants. This has now been debunked by Catholics for a Free Choice.

For 25 years there have been demands from non-Catholics and liberal Catholics alike that the Vatican not be identified and attacked as the enemy of population growth control; and in turn the enemy of humanity. This claim that "liberal" Catholics should be left to deal with this problem has resulted in paralysis of the movement. Catholics for a Free Choice, the liberal Catholic organization, is a tiny voice compared to the deafening silence of tens of millions of "liberal" Catholics in this country who have not identified with an organization committed to dealing with this problem. Time has run out. Syndicated columnist Georgie Anne Geyer had it right when she said the pope's policies are no longer merely the business of Catholics, since they can now lead to the death of us all.

WHY IS THIS A PREDICAMENT?

The Vatican leadership recognizes that if there is to be effective leadership in population growth control, it must come from the U.S. For this reason, its attention, energy and resources are heavily focused on America and to a lesser extent on the UN system. The U.S. is the battleground for the Vatican. In turn, it is reasonable to say the world population problem is, first of all, an American problem because we must win this battle, long ago initiated by the Vatican, before we can get on with controlling population growth. Until we do, the movement will remain paralyzed.

In this battle, the Vatican has no qualms about destroying American institutions, including democracy itself. The liberties we hold dear have been rightly recognized as gravely threatening to the Papacy at least since the 1830s. One needs only to read the teachings of the popes themselves to prove this point. Pius IX's "Syllabus of Errors" may be the most forthright. All of these attacks on democracy remain current teachings. Recent publications of the Church, including conservative weekly newspapers, document that the most reactionary principles of the Catholic Church of the past 2 centuries are operative in America today among conservative Catholics. The admiration shown by John Paul II for Pius IX and his recent announcement of his planned assault on "modernism" is very telling. What the pope refers to as "modernism" includes the liberties of American democracy.

We have been deceived by the Vatican in its use of the terms "moral" and "morality." It was a mistake to let the Vatican define these terms. Its long-standing claim of providing "moral leadership" permitted Vatican involvement in this issue. The vested interests held by the Vatican in their definitions of these terms make them unsuitable for this role. They have defined these terms in ways that protect Papal security-survival interests. The moral position is to avoid the inevitable anarchy and population crash that will occur in the absence of population growth control foreseen by NSSM 200, using the most humanitarian means.

HOW DID WE GET INTO THIS PREDICAMENT?

From the very beginning of Vatican opposition, the bishops have demanded that we all play by their rules and abide by their terms of the debate. This has given them an enormous advantage. They successfully argued that attacks on the pope, the Vatican and the Church regarding their behavior which allowed them to undermine the efforts of the population movement, were simply not permissible. This demand for silence imposed on the population movement and the press enabled the leadership of the Church to destroy major population growth control initiatives with almost no one being aware it. The bishops insisted that great care be taken by members of the movement not to offend them and their followers. And the bishops defined what was offensive. The movement meekly followed the bishops' rules. Had Americans been informed of the truth, we would not be in our present predicament.

The Vatican fully enjoys the liberties guaranteed in our Constitution, intended for our citizens. Thus Papal security interests are advanced at the expense of American citizens. The Vatican takes full advantage of the "Church's right to practice its good old American liberties of freedom of religion and freedom of speech," as David C. Carlin mockingly phrased it in his article, "Americanizing the anti-abortion argument," published in the Jesuit magazine, *America*.[326] The Church has used these liberties extensively to achieve its political goals in America—when they conflict with our country's. But should this be permitted? The Catholic Church does not represent Americans, not even Catholic Americans. It is concerned with papal interests in America—papal security-survival interests—often in direct conflict with U.S. security-survival interests and those of American Catholics. The Church can legitimately claim only the limited rights afforded to other foreign powers and institutions.

Vital to the Vatican efforts have been American priests and nuns. Their labors have made the successes of the Vatican possible. They necessarily support the pope in his crusade to save the Papacy from self-destruction, and thus have contributed significantly to our predicament. As the Church bears a heavy burden of responsibility for the chaos responsibly foreseen, to paraphrase Father McCormack, the priesthood too bears a heavy burden of responsibility.

There is little appreciation of the power, sophistication and motivation of the opponents to population growth control, even among the leaders of the population movement. The Church is a vastly superior force to any mounted against it since NSSM 200. The current collection of wrangling organizations in the population/family planning field is a manifestly inferior force. On the other hand, a fully committed U.S. Government, with an updated NSSM 200 as its blueprint, would be a formidable foe for the Vatican.

The leaders of the population movement (with the exception of Lader,[327] Ravenholt[328] and a few others) have been essential to the Vatican-created illusion that the Church is not really thwarting population growth control and for this reason they have been most helpful to the Vatican. A disproportionate number of leaders in this movement are Roman Catholic, a fact not yet satisfactorily explained. Other leaders are non-Catholic but are opportunistic and protect the Church in part to insure that opportunities they would not otherwise have continue. Opportunities, for example, for funding from corporations or foundations which may have Catholics on their governing boards, or in key executive posts. Such individuals almost surely use contraceptives, probably do not oppose abortion, but don't want to cross up the Mother Church. They may not need to take any action at all to oppose funding of a population organization—their non-Catholic associates defer to them out of what they consider personal courtesy or "good manners."

A few unsustained criticisms of the Church did surface as a result of the 1992 U.N. Conference in Rio de Janeiro on the environment and the 1994 U.N. ICPD in Cairo, but nothing came of them. Because these leaders oppose identification of their enemy, a necessary condition before a counter strategy can be formulated, these leaders have become part of the problem, not part of the solution.

Such self-censorship by both the population leadership, some of their funders, and the media appears to play a bigger role in protecting the Church from exposure of its efforts to undermine population growth control than outright overt intimidation—but is just as effective. Had there been no self-censorship, it is highly unlikely that we would be faced with this predicament.

IF WE CONTINUE AS WE ARE NOW?

If we continue on our present course, American democracy will be increasingly in jeopardy. We all recognize that democracy is an inefficient form of government—slow-moving, lots of false starts, hard choice issues avoided as long as possible—to name just a few reasons. Slack in the system is essential. Overpopulation is taking the slack out of the system—slack—a luxury a country like China no longer has. Quicker responses to changing and newly identified threats will require a more authoritarian system—an arrangement for America that the Vatican would welcome. Restrictions on freedom of speech and freedom of the press, in particular, would meet known preferences of popes going back to the 1830s.

If we continue as we are now, anarchy will be inevitable, a conclusion reached by the NSSM 200 researchers. Though there is reason to believe the Vatican may be able to survive under the conditions found in anarchy, American democracy will not. In place of anarchy many Americans would be sorely tempted to exchange most of the freedoms they enjoy today—of mind and movement, speech and vocation—for the security that an authoritarian government would offer.

The Protestant denominations and their ecumenical movement have let us down. Their insistence that the Catholic Church not be confronted concerning its blatant undemocratic involvement in American political affairs lest the ecumenical movement be undermined, will almost surely come back to haunt them. For more than 150 years, the Protestant churches played a vital role in keeping the Catholic Church in check with respect to involvement in national political affairs. Then it dropped its guard, and opportunism appears to have played an important role in this. In any case, as the role that religion has played in our failure to confront this grave national and global security threat becomes better understood, the importance of religion in American daily life will inevitably diminish. Credibility of Protestant institutions as positive forces in America will follow that of the Catholic Church—and sink.

The leadership of the population movement must consider the ethics of continuing to withhold information on the Vatican's successful efforts to undermine all population growth control initiatives. The NSSM 200 Report is one of the most important documents on this subject ever written. I first published an article on NSSM 200 and its fate more than four years ago in *The Human Quest*[329] and distributed it widely in the population field. I distributed this and subsequent articles published in *The Social Contract*[330] and *Free Inquiry*[331] to many members of the media. Not one population movement leader has published a word on NSSM 200 or its fate. NSSM 200 definitively shows that world overpopulation is a grave threat to U.S. and global security and that the only significant institutional opposition to controlling population growth is the Vatican. To withhold this information from their adherents is simply unethical.

WHAT AMERICA MUST DO

As Professor Abernathy recently reminded us, every nation has the sovereign right to pursue a course leading to its own survival. Each American is morally obligated to act for, and avoid acting against, the best interests of our country and fellow citizens. As she said: "This is patriotism." Members of the population leadership in the U.S., as well as members of the media who have censored, even self-censored, this vitally important story, have acted in an unpatriotic manner.

However, those devout conservative Roman Catholics identified by Bernstein in *TIME* as "The Catholic Team," in the Reagan Administration, must have been aware of the key findings of NSSM 200: Casey, Allen, Clark, Haig, Walters, and Wilson. They must have been aware that the security interests of the U.S. and the Papacy were in direct conflict. Ambassador Wilson admitted to collaboration with the Vatican in undermining U.S. population policy. "The Catholic Team" protected the security interests of the Vatican at the expense of the security of all Americans. No doubt there were other devout Catholic participants. This behavior was simply treasonous. Certainly, no act in the last half of the 20th century has done more to undermine U.S. security than the destruction of the NSSM 200 initiative.

NSSM 200 recommended a policy that would have meant a one-child family for America. Given that the U.S. growth rate has actually increased since 1974, we must pursue a one-child family norm as quickly as possible. The U.S. can make no greater contribution to world-wide population growth control than to lead by example. All relevant U.S. policy should promote a goal of a one-child family everywhere. We must achieve this goal as quickly as possible. We know what to do, we have the technology, the resources, the information, and the influence to make this happen. Right now, all we lack is the political will—plus a strong persistent program of population education to persuade the public (and Congress) to accept a one-child policy.

Abernathy has correctly identified overpopulation as the most important women's issue. Weld makes a compelling case that the Vatican has hyjacked the international feminist movement, undermining its credibility. The aggressive, vocal minority of feminists opposed to family planning and abortion is using the movement to advance the papal agenda, at great expense to the interests of women everywhere. They insist that overpopulation should never be the motivation for the provision of family planning services and that the importance of family planning and abortion to the advancement of women is overrated. This conflict, which has never been acknowledged, must be addressed by mainstream feminists. Otherwise, this very small minority of women will continue to be very destructive, much to the delight of the Vatican.

I cannot emphasize too strongly that the Vatican is a political power whose security interests are in conflict with those of the United States. Recognition of the differences in characteristics between conservative and liberal Catholics in America, as described by Weaver, and the implications of these differences, is vital to understanding the population problem we face. The behavior of the Church's representatives, who are virtually always conservative Catholics, is determined in Rome. There is no question that these representatives manipulate U.S. policy whenever possible, as revealed in Bernstein's *TIME* magazine article, in order to advance Papal security. The presence of its representatives thus threatens U.S. security. Anarchy will be the outcome. Civil war will be to the Vatican's advantage and will be encouraged from Rome. Americans must decide democratically whether representation of the Vatican should continue in the U.S. and if so, under what conditions. It is unpatriotic to permit the present arrangement to continue.

Probably the Vatican is lying in wait for this attack, with plans to use it to rally its troops for its holy war against American Democracy which has been underway at least since the Pastoral Plan was implemented in 1975. Until now, clerics have been the main combatants, though lay support is significant at an estimated 200,000 strong. The clerics' hired help is also significant. If they rally sufficient numbers, then the civil war that President Grant predicted may be inevitable for the very reason that he made his prediction. But we can no longer remain paralyzed by this concern that the attack will rally the Vatican troops. We must get on with it, and attacking our enemy is now a necessity. At present we are not merely at a standstill. We are losing ground.

Since overpopulation threatens the security-survival of everyone on earth, the vested interests of the Papacy in blocking all initiatives to control population growth, merely to insure its own institutional survival, makes it unfit to participate in international policy-making. Otherwise, we must accept the proposition that humanity must be entirely subordinated to the purposes of the Church, a profoundly un-American prospect. Failure to terminate Vatican representation in all relevant international bodies as soon as possible invites global catastrophe and is unethical.

If we are going to succeed with population growth control, Vatican influence must be neutralized. The most promising approach is to undermine papal authority. There are many steps which can be taken to achieve this goal. This will involve large scale but justified public criticism of the Vatican, the likes of which have not been seen before. Our approach should be to simply disseminate honest and truthful information critical of the Vatican. As long as we have a democracy in place, dissemination of this information should be sufficient to accomplish our goal.

At the present, there is very little substantive criticism of the Vatican in the U.S. This state of affairs exists because Vatican leadership understands just how threatening the flow of this information is to its institutional well-being. The Vatican will make every effort to block this initiative since it will most certainly speed institutional self-destruction. The lengths to which the Vatican will go are predictable.

We must be on guard and quick to identify Vatican activities that are designed to promote Vatican interests over U.S. interests. A good example is its initiative, evident for three years, to undermine any chances that President Clinton may have for a two-term Presidency. The propaganda campaign by conservative Catholics to undermine Clinton is vicious and unrelenting.

The self-destruction of the Papacy has been underway since *Humanae Vitae* in 1968 (if not since Vatican Council I in 1870). All activities by Americans which serve to postpone this self-destruction must be identified and terminated. A quick, massive response to hasten the self-destruction process should be considered. We have an ethical obligation to deal with the population problem as quickly as possible. Patriotism demands that we pursue this course. Other efforts to deal with this worsening dilemma have failed. Time has run out.

There is no escape from what seems to be a most unhappy truth. Only if the truth is recognized can we do anything about it. Denying the truth destroys the possibility for effective action. Failure to decide what we should do merely decides by default. These are all commonly recognized truisms that certainly apply here. We must publicly identify the enemy of population growth control and attack the enemy with sufficient force to neutralize it.

The Preamble of our U.S. Constitution reads:

> We the people of the United States, in order to form a more perfect Union, establish justice, insure domestic tranquility, provide for the common defense, promote the general welfare, and secure the blessings of liberty to ourselves and our posterity, do ordain and establish this Constitution for the United States of America.

This single sentence summarizes what our forefathers set out to secure for their posterity. All is now threatened by the grave conflict between the Papacy and the American people described in this volume. If our legislators continue, as President Wilson said, to "resign their functions to ecclesiastical powers and their prerogatives to priests," how long can American liberties endure?

REFERENCES

1. Ehrlich PR. The Population Bomb. New York: Ballantine Books, 1968.
2. Hardin G. The Tragedy of the Commons. Science 1968;162:1243-8.
3. Beck R. Religions and the Environment: Commitment High Until U.S. Population Issues Raised. The Social Contract 1993;3:76-89.
4a. Nixon R. Special Message to the Congress on Problems of Population Growth, July 18, 1969. Public Papers of the Presidents, No. 271, p. 521, Office of the Federal Register, National Archives, Washington, DC, 1971.
4b. Commission on Population Growth and the American Future. Population and the American Future. Washington, DC: U.S. Government Printing Office, 1972. 176 pp.
4c. Nixon R. Statement About the Report of the Commission on Population Growth and the American Future, May 5, 1972. Public Papers of the Presidents, No. 142, p. 576, Office of the Federal Register, National Archives, Washington, DC, 1974.
5. National Security Council. NSSM 200: Implications of worldwide population growth for U.S. security and overseas interests. Washington, DC, December 10, 1974. (See Chapter 3, p. 70 of this volume.)
6. Ibid., p. 556.
7. Ibid., p. 445.
8. Ibid., p. 73.
9. Ibid., p. 76.
10. Ibid., p. 518.
11. Ibid., p. 73.
12. Ibid., p. 78.
13. Byrnes TA. Catholic Bishops in American Politics. Lawrenceville, New Jersey: Princeton University Press, 1991. p. 66.
14. Ibid., p. 4.
15. Schmidt AW. Personal Communication. August 28,1992.
16. Scheuer J. A disappointing outcome: United States and World Population Trends since the Rockefeller Commission. The Social Contract 1992;Summer:203-206.
17. Byrnes, op. cit., p. 143.
18. National Security Council, op. cit. (See page 492, Appendix 2, this volume)
19. Ibid. (See page 549, Appendix 2, this volume)
20. Byrnes, op. cit., p. 70.
21. Ibid., p. 73.
22. Ibid., p. 74.
23. Ibid.
24. Ravenholt RT. Pronatalist Zealotry and Population Pressure Conflicts: How Catholics Seized Control of U.S. Family Planning Programs. Center for Research on Population and Security, Research Triangle Park, NC 27709. May 1991, 27 pp.
25. Byrnes, op. cit., p. 76.
26. Beck, op. cit.

27.   Byrnes, op. cit., p. 41.
28.   Ibid., p. 48.
29.   Ibid., p. 49.
30.   Ibid.
31.   Ibid.
32.   Ibid., p. 143.
33.   Ibid., p. 144.
33a.   Blanshard P. American Freedom and Catholic Power. Boston: The Beacon Press, 1950. p.46 [Quoted from the Catholic Almanac]
33b.   Ibid. p.50. [Quoted from Leo XIII's encyclical, Chief Duties of Christian Citizens.]
33b1.   Davies M. Religious Liberty and the Secular State. Catholic Family News. August 1996. p. 1.
33b2.   Weaver MJ. Being Right: Conservative Catholics in America. Huntington: Indiana University Press, 1995.
33b3.   Heckler-Feltz C. The burden of being Catholic and right. National Catholic Reporter August 9, 1996. p. 13.
33c.   Langan J. Defending life even unto death. National Catholic Register, September 17, 1996, p.1.
33d.   Baumann P. The Pope vs. the Culture of Death. New York Times, October 8, 1995, OP-ED.
33e.   Czech Philosopher Accuses Vatican of Undermining Democracy. The Churchman's Human Quest, January-February, 1996, p.21.
33f.   Be Defenders of Life, Says Cardinal Lopez Trujillo. The Wanderer, October 12, 1995, p.7.
33g.   Bohlen C. Pope Offers 'Gospel of Life' vs. 'Culture of Death.' New York Times, March 31, 1995, p.A1.
33h.   Donovan J. 'At home,' the Pope's encyclical takes beating. National Catholic Register, April 23, 1995, p.1.
33i.   Steinfels P. U.S. Responds on Established Lines. New York Times, March 31, 1995, p.A5.
33j.   Pope's Letter: A 'Sinister' World Has Led to 'Crimes Against Life.' New York Times, March 31, 1995, p.A4.
34.   Likoudis P. Vatican letter calls on bishops to oppose homosexual rights laws. The Wanderer 1992 July 30;1.
35.   Vaillancourt JG. Papal Power: A Study of Vatican Control Over Lay Catholic Elites. Berkeley:University of California Press, 1980.
36.   Schwartz M. Persistent Prejudice: Anti-Catholicism in America. Huntington, Indiana: Our Sunday Visitor, 1984. p. 132.
37.   King HV. Cardinal O'Connor Declares That Church Teaching On Abortion Underpins All Else. The Wanderer, April 23, 1992. p. 1.
38.   Jones A. Vatican, "International Agencies Hone Family, Population Positions." National Catholic Reporter (reprinted in Conscience, May/June 1984. p. 7.
39.   Murphy FX, Erhart JF. Catholic perspectives on population issues. Pop Bulletin 1975;30(6):3-31.
40.   Hasler, AB. How the Pope Became Infallible. Garden City, New York: Doubleday, 1981.
41.   Ibid. (cover)
42.   Vaillancourt, op. cit., p. 2.
43.   Hasler, op. cit., p. 270.
44.   Byrnes, op. cit., p. 29.
45.   Ibid., p. 44.
46.   Ibid., p. 45.
47.   Ibid., p. 46.
48.   Bernstein C. The Holy Alliance. TIME, February 24, 1992.
49.   Byrnes, op. cit., p. 58.
50.   Ibid., p. 57.
51.   Ibid.
52.   Ibid., p. 59.
53.   Ibid.

54.   Blum VC. Public policy making: Why the churches strike out. America
        1971;124(9):224-8.
55.   Mumford SD. A second report on the Catholic bishops' pastoral plan for pro-life
        activities: its implications for democracy in North Carolina, viewed in a
        world context. Center for Research on Population and Security, Research
        Triangle Park, NC 27709. October 1988, 15 pp.
56.   Blum, op. cit.
57.   Ibid.
58.   Ibid.
59.   Ibid.
60.   Mumford SD. American Democracy & The Vatican: Population Growth and
        National Security. Amherst, New York: Humanist Press, 1984. 268 pp.
61.   Mumford SD. The Pope and the New Apocalypse: The Holy War Against Family
        Planning. Research Triangle Park, North Carolina: Center for Research on
        Population and Security, 1986. 82 pp.
62.   Mumford SD. The Catholic bishops' pastoral plan for pro-life activities and its
        implications for Democracy in North Carolina. Research Triangle Park,
        North Carolina: Center for Research on Population and Security, 1987.
63.   Bernstein, op. cit.
63a.   News Release from The Free Press, A Division of Macmillan, Inc. for the book
        Abortion Politics: Mutiny In the Ranks of the Right by Michele McKeegan.
        1992.
63b.   Conn JL. Behind The Mask. Church & State November 1994. p. 4.
64.   Ravenholt, op. cit.
65.   Mumford, op. cit., 1984.
66.   Mumford, op. cit., 1986.
67.   Mumford, op. cit., 1988.
68.   Paige C. The Right To Lifers: Who They Are, How They Operate, Where They Get
        Their Money. New York: Summit Books, 1983.
69.   Mumford, op. cit., 1984.
70.   Mumford, op. cit., 1986.
71.   Paige, op. cit., p. 195.
72.   Ibid., p. 112.
73.   Willis E. Abortion Rights: Overruling pro-Fascist. The Village Voice. February 4,
        1980, p. 7.
74.   Paige, op. cit., p. 112.
75.   Anonymous. Bennett, Bork Launch Catholic Campaign to Promote Church Views.
        Church & State, October 1991, p. 16.
76.   Conn JL. Unholy Matrimony. Church & State, April 1993.
77.   Bork ME. Fundraising letter addressed to "Fellow Catholic American" from the
        Catholic Campaign for America, 1994.
78.   Kaufman I. Patrick Buchanan: 'Right From The Beginning.' Our Sunday Visitor,
        August 28, 1988, p. 3.
78a.   Kosova W, Isikoff M, Brant M. The Buchanan Files. NEWSWEEK February 26, 1996.
        p. 25.
78b.   Ferrara J. Pat Buchanan vs. Liberal Establishment. Catholic Family News May
        1996. p. 11.
79.   Conn, op. cit., 1993.
80.   Ibid.
81.   Ibid.
82.   Ibid.
83.   Anonymous. The Wanderer. September 9, 1993, p. 9.
84.   Anonymous. Buchanan To Address 'Catholic Action' Summit In New Jersey.
        Church & State, June 1993, p. 13.
85.   Ibid.
86.   Paige, op. cit.
86a.   Buchanan PJ. Candidate for President fundraising letter. February 1996. p. 1.
87.   Lader L. Politics, Power & the Church. New York: Macmillan, 1987.
88.   Mumford, op. cit., 1984.

89.	Mumford, op. cit., 1986.

89.   Mumford, op. cit., 1986.
90.   Mumford, op. cit., 1988.
91.   Conn, op. cit., 1993.
92.   Paige, op. cit., p. 155, 167.
93.   Conn, op. cit., 1993.
94.   Ibid.
95.   Ibid.
96.   Ibid.
96a. Banks AM. 'Contract' poses quandary for Coalition. National Catholic Reporter May 5, 1995. p. 3.
96b. Birnbaum JH. The Gospel According to Ralph. Time May 15, 1995. p. 28.
96c. Membership 'deceptive,' group says. National Catholic Reporter January 19, 1996. p. 8.
96d. Mullen PH. Christian Coalition eyes Catholic clout. National Catholic Register October 15, 1996. p. 1.
96e. Boston R. Pat Robertson And Church-State Separation: A Track Record of Deception. Church & State April 1996, p. 9.
96f. Conn JL. Papal Blessing? Church & State November 1995. p.4.
96g. Likoudis P. Christian Coalition Casting a New Net to Catch Catholics. Wanderer September 28, 1995. p. 1.
96h. A 1996 Catholic Alliance fund raising letter signed by Maureen Roselli.
96i. Catholics and the Line Between Church and State. New York Times October 8, 1995.
97.   Hasler, op. cit., p. 25.
98.   Hasler, op. cit.
99.   Ibid., p. 27.
100. Ibid., p. 150.
101. Ibid., p. 15.
102. Ibid., p. 281.
103. Ibid., p. 36.
104. Ibid., p. 37.
105. Ibid., p. 164.
106. Ibid., p. 39.
107. Ibid., p. 43.
108. Ibid., p. 81.
109. Ibid., p. 45.
110. Ibid., p. 39.
111. Ibid., p. 52.
112. Ibid., p. 52.
113. Ibid., p. 39.
114. Ibid., p. 293.
115. Ibid., p. 5.
116. Ibid., p. 238.
117. Ibid., p. 43.
118. Ibid., p. 17.
119. Ibid., p. 109.
120. Ibid.
121. Ibid.
122. Ibid., p. 115.
123. Ibid., p. 118.
124. Ibid., p. 120.
125. Ibid., p. 125.
127. Ibid., p. 126.
128. Ibid., p. 127.
129. Ibid.
130. Ibid., p. 14.
131. Ibid., p. 277.
132. Ibid., p. 141.
133. Ibid., p. 14.
134. Ibid., p. 15.

135.   Ibid., p. 27.
136.   Ibid., p. 313.
137.   Ibid., p. 37.
138.   Ibid., p. 237.
139.   Ibid.
140.   Ibid., p. 276.
141.   Kauffman CJ. Anti-Catholicism and the Knights of Columbus. In: Riley P, Shaw R, eds. Anti-Catholicism in the Media. Huntington, Indiana: Our Sunday Visitor, 1993. p. 239.
142.   Anonymous. New York Archdiocese Gets Credit, Taxpayers Get Bill. Freethought Today, October 1993, p. 4.
142a.   Flanders L. Far-Right Militias and Anti-Abortion Violence: When Will Media See the Connection? *Extra!* July/August 1995. p. 11.
143.   Greenberger RS, Langley M. Col. North's Ideology and Zealousness Led Him to Contras' Cause. Wall Street Journal, December 31, 1986, p. 1.
144.   Grier P. Col. Oliver North: Beyond the Cartoon to a Complex Man. The Christian Science Monitor, December 26, 1986, p. 1.
145.   Hasler, op. cit., p. 277.
146.   Ibid., p. 137.
147.   Ibid., p. 46.
148.   Ibid., p. 48.
149.   Ibid.
150.   Ibid., p. 172.
151.   Ibid., p. 173.
152.   Ibid., p. 58.
153.   Ibid., p. 72.
154.   Ibid., p. 127.
155.   Ibid., p. 178.
156.   Ibid., p. 228.
157.   Ibid., p. 230.
158.   Ibid., p. 215.
159.   Ibid., p. 240.
160.   Ibid., p. 278.
161.   Ibid.
162.   Ibid., p. 116.
163.   Ibid.
164.   Ibid., p. 132.
165.   Ibid., p. 135.
166.   Ibid., p. 150.
167.   Ibid., p. 192.
168.   Ibid., p. 207.
169.   Ibid., p. 225.
170.   Ibid., p. 227.
171.   Ibid., p. 142.
172.   Ibid., p. 244.
173.   Ibid., p. 284.
174.   Filteau J. Theologian: U.S. Catholics Yet to Make Mark on Culture. The Florida Catholic, November 11, 1988. p. 1.
175.   Ibid.
176.   Hasler, op. cit., p. 284.
177.   Ibid., p. 26.
177a.   Anonymous. '92 Status Report/ Vocations. The Catholic Church Extension Society, Chicago.
177b.   Feuerherd P. New seminarians reflect papal vision. National Catholic Register October 15, 1995. p. 1.
177c.   Report documents decline in seminaries. The Wanderer February 16, 1995. p. 3.
178.   Anonymous. Los Angeles Times' Survey Released. The Wanderer, March 3, 1994, p. 3.
179.   Anonymous. A Call to Renew a Church We Love. CORPUS, Seattle.

180. Steinfels P. Catholic Orders Need 'Dramatic' Change to Survive, Study Says. New York Times, September 20, 1992.

181. O'Sullivan G. Catholicism's New Cold War: The Church Militant Lurches Rightward. The Humanist, September/October 1993, p. 27.

182. Steinfels, op. cit.

183. Anonymous. Catholic Church Depends on Parochial Schools for Clergy, Worshippers. Church & State, February 1991, p. 15.

184. Steinfels, op. cit.

185. Shaw R. A 'dirty little secret,' National Catholic Register, October 10, 1993, p. 5.

185a. In Government We Trust. Voice of Reason Summer 1995. p. 2.

186. Anonymous. Missionary Congress to be Held in Peru Feb. 3-8. National Catholic Register, p. 7.

186a. We are the Church. Nordamerikanische Wochen-Post December 16, 1995.

186b. Bohlen C. Catholic dissent against pope is increasing. News & Observer November 26, 1995. p. 11A.

187. Hasler, op. cit., p. 264.

188. Ibid., p. 284.

189. Ibid., p. 248.

190. Ibid., p. 294.

191. Ibid., p. 252.

192. Ibid., p. 277.

192a. Roberts Tom. Bishops should read this book on sex abuse. National Catholic Reporter September 8, 1995. p. 31.

192b. Bishops Issue Letter Condemning Pedophilia. The Wanderer November 2, 1995. p. 7.

192c. Donohue WA. Catholic League's 1994 Report on Anti-Catholicism. New York:Catholic League for Religious and Civil Rights 1995. p. 19.

192d. Wirpsa L. Blowing whistle on sex abuse means new career for priest. National Catholic Reporter September 15, 1996.

192e. Pedophile Priest Crisis 'Overblown.' National Catholic Reporter March 24, 1996. p. 2.

192f. Bishop Named in $280 Million Lawsuit. The Wanderer May 2, 1996. p. 3.

193. Hasler, op. cit., p. 283.

194. Ibid., p. 270.

194a. Greeley AM. Look out for the ambitious clerics in purple. National Catholic Reporter September 15, 1995. p. 4.

194b. Catholic Chaplains Condoned Argentina's 'Dirty War,' Former Officer Charges. Church & State May 1995. p. 17.

194c. Bumiller E. As Pope's Important Ally, Cardinal Shines High in Hierarchy. New York Times October 8, 1995. p. 41.

194d. People, not church, blamed for genocide. News & Observer (Raleigh) March 21, 1996. p. 14A.

194e. Rwandan Bishops Accused of Ignoring Genocide. Church & State November 1995. p. 22.

195. Hasler, op. cit., p. 195.

196. Ibid., p. 313.

197. O'Brien CC. People, Vol. 7, No. 1, November 1, 1980.

198. Wilson AN. Heroes & Villains. The Independent Magazine. April 14, 1990, p. 54.

199. Greeley AM. Who are the Catholic conservatives? America, 1991;165(7):158-62.

200. Hickey J. et al. Dear Mr. President. National Catholic Register, July 3, 1994, p. 3.

201. Hasler, op. cit., p. 309.

202. Lader, op. cit.

203. Ravenholt, op. cit.

203a. Cairo and beyond. Open File September 1995. p. 5.

203b. Renato Martino on Cairo's achievement. National Catholic Register February 5, 1995. p. 1.

203c. Barbera M. In Copenhagen, another U.N. summit. National Catholic Register February 26, 1995. p. 1.

203d. Collins DA. Personal Communication. April 11, 1995.

204.   Greeley, op. cit.
205.   Beck, op. cit.
206.   Ibid.
207.   Simcox D. The Catholic Hierarchy and Immigration: Boundless Compassion, Limited Responsibility. The Social Contract 1993;3:90-95.
208.   Hasler, op. cit., p. 81.
209.   Byrnes, op. cit., p. 27.
210.   Hurley MJ. The Unholy Ghost: Anti-Catholicism in the American Experience. Huntington, Indiana: Our Sunday Vistor, 1992. p. 12.
211.   Ibid. p. 10.
212.   Ibid. p. 12.
213.   Ibid. p. 141.
214.   Ibid. p. 143.
215.   Likoudis, op. cit.
215a.   Vatican Claims Unique Role in World Politics. Church & State March 1995. p. 22.
215b.   Mullen PH. Christian Coalition eyes Catholic clout. National Catholic Register October 15, 1995. p. 1.
215c.   40 bishops say church needs way to dialogue with Rome. National Catholic Reporter June 30, 1995. p. 3.
215d.   Henshaw SK, Host K. Family Planning Perspectives.
215e.   Matt AJ. A Traitorous Shepherd. The Wanderer June 22, 1995 p. 4.
215f.   Mullen PH. In China, Catholics must choose Pope or Party. National Catholic Register March 26, 1995. p. 1.
215g.   Fox TC. Rome's Lengthening Shadow. New York Times November 14, 1994.
216.   Hurley, op. cit., p. 269.
217.   Anonymous. Archbishop Calls For Church-State Unity At Red Mass. Church & State, November 1989.
218.   Anonymous. Chicago Cardinal Endorses 'Power Mode' For Churches, Advances Opus Dei Movement. Church & State, February 1991, p. 15.
219.   Feuerherd P. Fighting The Good Fight. National Catholic Register, July 27, 1993. p. 3.
220.   Askin S. The Catholic Right. Conscience, Spring 1994. p. 6.
221.   Hurley, op. cit., p. 44.
222.   Ibid., p. 52.
223.   Ibid., p. 180.
224.   Ibid., p. 158.
225.   Ibid., p. 285.
226.   Ibid., p. 159.
227.   Ibid., p. 143.
228.   Ibid., p. 146.
229.   Ibid.
230.   Ibid., p. 81.
231.   Ibid., p. 141.
232.   Ibid., p. 81.
233.   Ibid., p. 128.
234.   Ibid., p. 129.
235.   Ibid., p. 132.
236.   Ibid., p. 138.
237.   Ibid., p. 146.
238.   Schlesinger AM, Jr. The Disuniting of America. New York: W.W. Norton, 1992. p. 35.
239.   Ibid.
240.   Ibid., p. 37.
241.   Hurley, op. cit., p. 181.
242.   Ibid., p. 26.
243a.   Lawrence J. Democrats step up attacks against 'radical right.' (Raleigh) News and Observer, June 30, 1994, p. 1.
243b.   Kissling F, Shannon D. Who's Right? Conscience, Spring 1994, p. 2.
243c.   Askin, op. cit.
243d.   Askin S. The US Catholic Hierarchy. Conscience, Spring 1994, p. 8.
243e.   Askin S. Prominent Catholic Organizations. Conscience, Spring 1994, p. 13.

244.	Hurley, op. cit., p. 45.
245.	Robinson MJ. A Fine Study: But How Much Does It Matter? In: Riley P, Shaw R, eds. Anti-Catholicism in the Media. Huntington, Indiana: Our Sunday Visitor, 1993. p. 179.
245a.	Niebuhr G. Most Catholics Admire the Pope, but Many Don't Feel Bound by His Teachings. New York Times October 1, 1995. p. 15.
245b.	Mulligan HA. Excitement builds for papal visit to U.S. News & Observer (Raleigh) October 4, 1995. p. 8A.
246.	Anonymous. Los Angeles Times' Survey Released. The Wanderer, March 3, 1994. p. 3.
247.	Robinson, op. cit., p. 176.
247a.	Goodstein L, Morin R. Love the Messenger; Not His Message: American Catholics believe in the pope, but think the church is out of sync. Washington Post (National Weekly Edition) October 9-15, 1995. p. 37.
248.	Kauffman, op. cit.
249.	Blanshard P. American Freedom and Catholic Power. Boston:Beacon Press, 1949.
250.	Kaplan R. The Coming Anarchy. Atlantic Monthly, February 1994, p. 44.
251.	Lewis A. A Bleak Vision of What's in Store For The World. New York Times News Service, March 11, 1994.
252.	Walters, DKH. Massive Famine Predicted. (Raleigh) News & Observer. January 30, 1993, p. 1.
253.	Anonymous. U.N. Report Lists Developing Countries in Danger of Collapse. (Raleigh) News & Observer, June 2, 1994.
254.	Cowell A. Scientists Associated With Vatican Urge Limits On Population Growth. New York Times News Service, June 16, 1994.
255.	Hall M. Church Mail-In Targets Abortion: Catholics Papering Congress. USA TODAY, January 29, 1993, p. 3A.
256.	Anonymous. Abortion Opposed in Health Reform: Roman Catholic Bishops Declare Their Intent To Fight Any Legislation That Provides Coverage For Abortions. Los Angeles Times News Service, July 14, 1994.
257.	Goldman AL. In Newark, Two Clerics Battle Over Statements On Women. New York Times, January 31, 1991, A16.
258.	Lewin T. Study Shows Taxpayers Save If Public Aids In Birth Control. New York Times, February 26, 1990.
259.	Bacon KH. Bush Backs Away From Birth-Control Program As Congress Braces For a Tough Fight On Issue. The Wall Street Journal, February 2, 1990. P. A12.
260.	Anonymous. A Continent's Slow Suicide. Reader's Digest, May 1993. p. 110.
260ii.	Seldes G. Reformation in Spain, 454 Years Late. The Churchman August-September 1978. p. 6.
260jj.	Seldes G. 'LIBERAL' — A New Dirty Word. The Churchman November 1981. p. 6.
260kk.	Seldes G. Lies Not Meant For Light. The Churchman January 1979. p. 10.
260ll.	Seldes G. Falsehoods of the Spanish War. The Churchman October 1977. p. 7.
260mm.	Seldes G. "Christian" Anti-Communist Crusade. The Churchman October 1972. p. 11.
260nn.	Seldes G. The Roman Church and Franco. The Churchman December 1978. p. 10.
260oo.	Seldes G. Catholic Spain's Suppressed News. The Churchman November 1978. p. 8.
260pp1.	Donohue W. We've Only Just Begun. Catalyst January-February 1995. p. 3.
260pp2.	Christian Coalition Conference a Success. Catalyst October 1995. p. 15.
260pp3.	Donohue W. A Banner Year for the Catholic League. Catalyst July-August 1994. p. 3.
260pp4.	Christian Coalition Conference a Success. Catalyst October 1995. p. 15.
260pp5.	Women's Ordination Letter Draws Liberal Media Fire: Editorial Criticism of Papal Letter Earns Response. Catalyst July-August 1994. p. 8.
260pp6.	Sheridan A. Ignatian Society Petitions Cardinal Hickey to Remove Fr. Drinan's Faculties. The Wanderer July 18, 1996. p. 1.
260pp7.	Donohue W. Our Members Make This a Special Christmas. Catalyst December 1995. p. 3.
260pp8.	Ibid.

260pp9. Donohue W. The Vatican, Women and Non-Catholics. Catalyst July-August 1994. p. 7.

260pp10. Letter sent to the Catholic League Membership signed by League President William Donohue. June 1995.

260pp11. Donohue W. The Message From Florida Is: Bigots Beware. Catalyst April 1995. p. 3.

260pp12. Ibid.

260pp13. Donohue W. Catholic League's 1994 Report on Anti-Catholicism. New York: Catholic League for Religious and Civil Rights. p. 2.

260pp14. Donohue W. The Message From Florida Is: Bigots Beware. Catalyst April 1995. p. 3.

260pp15. Ibid.

260pp16. Donohue W. Catholic League's 1994 Report on Anti-Catholicism. New York: Catholic League for Religious and Civil Rights. p. 2.

260pp17. Ibid.

260pp18. Blum VC. Public Policy Making: Why the Churches Strike Out. America March 6, 1971. p. 224.

260pp19. Anti-Catholicism Nation's Worst Prejudice. Catalyst July-August 1995. p. 13.

260pp20. Donohue W. Our Members make This a Special Christmas. Catalyst December 1995. p. 3.

260pp21. Donohue W. A Banner Year for the Catholic League. Catalyst July-August 1994. p. 3.

260pp22. Letter sent to the Catholic League Membership signed by League President William Donohue. June 1995.

260pp23. Catholic League Op-Ed page ad which appeared in the April 10, 1995 issue of the New York Times, "What's Happening to Disney?" signed by William A. Donohue, President.

260pp24. The Catholic Action League of Massachusetts Forms. The Wanderer October 8, 1995. p. 8.

260pp25. Report On Anti-Catholicism Released. Catalyst April 1995. p. 1.

260pp26. Report On Anti-Catholicism Released. Catalyst May 1996. p. 1.

260pp27. Letter sent to the Catholic League Membership signed by League President William Donohue. February 1995.

260pp28. Donohue W. A Banner Year for the Catholic League. Catalyst July-August 1994. p. 3.

260pp29. Ibid.

260pp30. Letter sent to the Catholic League Membership signed by League President William Donohue. September 1995.

260pp31. Catholic League letter announcing a press conference signed by League President William Donohue. August 1994.

260pp32. Media Treat Pope Fairly; Protesters Fail to Score. Catalyst November 1995. p. 1.

260pp33. Donohue W. Our Members make This a Special Christmas. Catalyst December 1995. p. 3.

260pp34. Catholic League fundraising letter signed by William Donohue mailed December 1995.

260pp35. Donohue W. Catholic League's 1995 Report on Anti-Catholicism. New York: Catholic League for Religious and Civil Rights. p. 4.

260pp36. Donohue W. The Fallout Over "Priest." Catalyst June 1995. p. 3.

260pp37. "60 Minutes" Rigs Show Against Catholic Church. Catalyst March 1995. p. 1.

260pp38. Give It To "60 Minutes".... Catalyst March 1995. p. 4A.

260pp39. Media Treat Pope Fairly; Protesters Fail to Score. Catalyst November 1995. p. 1.

260pp40. We're "Paranoid." Catalyst June 1996. p. 1.

260pp41. Report On Anti-Catholicism Released. Catalyst May 1996. p. 1.

260pp42. Donohue W. Our Members make This a Special Christmas. Catalyst December 1995. p. 3.

260pp43. Newsday's Marlette Offends Twice in One Week. Catalyst July-August 1994. p. 8.

260pp44. Meeting with Newsday Editor. Catalyst September 1994. p. 2.

260pp45. Meeting with Newsday Editorial Board. Catalyst October 1994. p. 2.

260pp46. Cardinal Bevilacqua Scores Philadelphia Inquirer For Church Coverage, Declines Interview. Catalyst September 1994. p. 6.

260pp47. AP Responds to League Complaint. Catalyst May 1995. p. 1.

260pp48. Catholic League Calls for Boycott of Disney. Catalyst May 1995. p. 1.

260pp49. Donohue W. There's Anger in the Land. Catalyst May 1995. p. 3.

260pp50. Petition Against Disney. Catalyst May 1995. p. 5.

260pp51. What's Happening to Disney?, a Catholic League Op-Ed page ad which appeared in the April 10, 1995 issue of The New York Times. Catalyst May 1995. p. 12.

260pp52. Disney Targeted By Resolution. Catalyst June 1995. p. 1.

260pp53. League Pickets Disney. Catalyst June 1995. p. 14.

260pp54. Disney Protests Continue. Catalyst July-August 1995. p. 4.

260pp55. Disney Gets Present From Catholic League. Catalyst January-February 1996. p. 9.

260pp56. Jane Pauley Shows Anti-Catholic Bias. Catalyst July-August 1995. p. 15.

260pp57. KFI Radio (Los Angeles) Insults Catholics. Catalyst September 1995. p. 5.

260pp58. Orlando Newspaper Insults Catholics. Catalyst October 1995. p. 6.

260pp59. Media Wars on Catholicism: Fox Promo Withdrawn. Catalyst November 1995. p. 4.

260pp60. Media Wars on Catholicism: Bravo Makes Obscene Show. Catalyst November 1995. p. 5.

260pp61. Texaco Apologizes, Bravo Condescends. Catalyst December 1995. p. 13.

260pp62. You Can Make a Difference. Catalyst December 1995. p. 2.

260pp63. Ann (S)Landers Lashes Out at Pope and Polish People. Catalyst January-February 1996. p. 10.

260pp64. ABC Show "The Naked Truth" Ridicules Catholicism. Catalyst March 1996. p. 4.

260pp65. San Diego Radio Program Mocks Catholicism, Drawing League Response. Catalyst April 1996. p. 1.

260pp66. PBS' "FRONTLINE" Exploits Catholicism in Abortion Program. Catalyst April 1996. p. 6.

260pp67. Protest of Bias Yields Favorable Result. Catalyst May 1996. p. 13.

260pp68. HBO Offers Tabloid Look at Catholic Church. Catalyst June 1996. p. 1.

260pp69. League Protest of "The Last Supper" Pays Off. Catalyst June 1996. p. 4.

260pp70. AP Red Flags Catholic Religion. Catalyst June 1996. p. 13.

260pp71. New England Chapter Helps Save EWTN. Catalyst June 1996. p. 13.

260pp72. League Pressures N.Y. Store To Remove Offensive Creche. Catalyst January-February 1995. p. 1.

260pp73. Hard Rock Hotel in Las Vegas Offends Catholics. Catalyst December 1995. p. 4.

260pp74. Why is the Hard Rock Hotel Offending Catholics? Catalyst December 1995. p. 5.

260pp75. Hard Rock Hotel in Las Vegas Offends Catholics. Catalyst December 1995. p. 4.

260pp76. Hard Rock Hotel Pulls Altar. Catalyst January-February 1996. p. 6.

260pp77. Pope Defamed at New Jersey State College. Catalyst September 1994. p. 1.

260pp78. University of Michigan Cartoon Draws Swift League Response. Catalyst March 1995. p. 11.

260pp79. University of Michigan Cartoonist Apologizes. Catalyst April 1995. p. 2.

260pp80. Nazi Slur of Vatican Implicates Congressmen. Catalyst July-August 1995. p. 1.

260pp81. Senator Inouye Resigns From Population Institute After League Protest. Catalyst September 1995. p. 4.

260pp82. Protest Stirs ADL to Restore Prize to Author. Catalyst May 1996. p. 6.

260pp83. League Assails Clinton Administration for Bigotry. Catalyst October 1994. p. 1.

260pp84. Open Letter To The President. This half-page ad sponsored by the Catholic League ran in all editions of The New York Times on August 29, 1994. *Catalyst* October 1994. p. 8.

260pp85. Donohue W. The Holy See, Cairo and The Pundits. Catalyst October 1994. p. 11.

260pp86. Donohue W. We've Only Just Begun. Catalyst January-February 1995. p. 3.

260pp87. Elder's Exit Applauded. Catalyst January-February 1995. p. 4.

261. Geyer GA. Catholicism's Modern Galileo Affair. Dallas Morning News, August 10, 1993.

262.   Robinson, op. cit., p. 179.
263.   Lader, op. cit., p. 101.
264a.   Mumford, op. cit., 1984.
264b.   Mumford, op. cit., 1986.
265.   Byrnes, op. cit, p. 143.
265a.   Moyers B. Echoes of the Crusades. Church & State December 1995. p. 16.
266.   Byrnes, op. cit., p. 143.
266a.   Birnbaum JH. The Gospel According to Ralph. TIME May 15, 1995. p. 28.
266b.   Conn JL. Power Trip. Church & State October 1995. p. 4.
266c.   Reckless Driving on the Road to Victory. *Church & State* October 1995. p. 14.
266d.   Boston R. Stealth Strategy. Church & State October 1995. p. 8.
266e.   Jones A. Coalition wants to dominate GOP. National Catholic Reporter. September
         22, 1995. p. 5.
267.   Mumford, op. cit., 1984.
268.   Mumford, op. cit., 1986.
269.   Mumford, op. cit., 1987.
270.   Mumford, op. cit., 1988.
271.   Ackerman T. The Baptist Rift. (Raleigh) News & Observer, July 17, 1988, p. 1D.
272.   Ibid.
273.   Moyers B. God & Politics: The Battle for the Bible. Public Affairs Television.
         December 16, 1987. Transcript from Journal Graphics, Inc. New York. p. 13.
273a.   Banks AM. Pact with Catholics alarms evangelicals. _____273.
273b.   Associated Press. Pope urges unity among Christians in 12th encyclical. News &
         Observer (Raleigh) May 31, 1995.
273c.   Guenois JM. For the sake of unity, a fresh look at the papal role. National Catholic
         Register June 25, 1995. p. 1.
273d.   Rice CE. The Catholic Alliance Has a Truth In Labeling Problem. The Wanderer
         March 28, 1996.
273e.   Hays C. Catholic-Baptist ties show signs of new life. National Catholic Register
         August 6, 1996. p. 1.
274.   Simon JL. Resources, population, environment: an oversupply of false bad news.
         Science, 208(4451) June 1980, p. 1431.
275.   Simon JL. The Ultimate Resource. Princeton, New Jersey: Princeton University
         Press, 1981.
276.   Simon JL. The scarcity of raw materials: a challenge to the conventional wisdom.
         Atlantic Monthly. June 1981, p. 33.
277a.   Simon JL. World population growth: an anti-doomsday view. Atlantic Monthly,
         August 1981, p. 70.
277b.   Simon JL. The resourceful earth: a response to Global 2000. New York: Basil
         Blackwell, 1984.
278.   Begley S, Miller M, Hager M. Inside the Greenhouse: Heat Waves. Newsweek, July
         11, 1988. p. 16.
279.   Ibid.
280.   Basgall M. The Greenhouse Monster. (Raleigh) News & Observer, July 24, 1988, p.
         1D.
281.   Manuel J. Getting Warmer. Leader, August 4, 1988, p. 9.
282.   Basgall, op. cit.
283.   O'Conner, DB. The Greenhouse Effect. Leader, December 31, 1987, p. 10.
284.   Ibid.
285.   Anonymous. Rising Oceans Could Trigger Devastation. Chapel Hill Newspaper,
         June 13, 1988, p. 2.
286.   Ibid.
287.   Begley, op. cit.
288.   Adler J, Hager M. Stretched to the Limit. Newsweek, July 11, 1988, p. 23.
289.   Newell ND, Marcus L. Carbon Dioxide and People. Palaios Vol. 2, 1987. p. 101.
290.   Wilford JN. Greenhouse effect sparks dire warning. (Raleigh) News & Observer,
         July 19, 1988, p. 1.
291.   Shabecoff P. Scientist's words on global warming changed by OMB to soften
         conclusions. (Raleigh) News & Observer, May 8, 1989, p. 1A.

292.   Anonymous. White House rejects environmental move. (Raleigh) News &
          Observer, May 7, 1989, p. 20A.
292a.   Ivins M. Warning of Warming. News & Observer (Raleigh) September 13, 1995.
292b.   Hertsgaard M. Environmental Meltdown, News & Observer (Raleigh) April 11,
          1995. p. 13A.
292c.   Brower D. For Earth, it's Nader, not Clinton. News & Observer (Raleigh) July 24,
          1996. p. 13A.
292d.   Stevens WK. Panel says Earth's warming could spur wide disruptions. News &
          Observer (Raleigh) September 19, 1995. p. 1.
292e.   Stevens WK. Earth's temperature rising. News & Oberver (Raleigh) January 4,
          1996. p. 1.
292f.   Moffett G. Grain Glut Gone as Global Supply Shrinks. The Christian Science
          Monitor. April 3, 1996. p. 1.
292g.   Sawyer K. Panel says humans influence climate. News & Observer (Raleigh)
          December 3, 1995.
292h.   Hotz RL. Northern Hemisphere spring arrives earlier, scientists find. News &
          Observer (Raleigh) July 12, 1996. p. 21A.
292i.   Mintz P. Big East Coast waves ripple scientific calm. News & Observer (Raleigh)
          June 3, 1995. p. 9B.
292j.   Yoon CK. Alpine plants climb to escape warming. News & Observer (Raleigh)
292k.   Mathews J. Senator Helms' atmosphere. News & Observer (Raleigh) June 2, 1995. p. 15A.
292l.   Cox News Service. Downpours, blizzards measured more often. News & Observer
          (Raleigh) September 21, 1995. p. 8A.
292m.   Newman S. Earthweek: A Diary of the Planet. News & Observer (Raleigh)
          January 9, 1996. p. 5B.
292n.   Ibid., February 13, 1995. p. 5B.
292o.   Ibid., March 6, 1995. p. 5B.
292p.   Ibid., March 13, 1995.
292q.   Ibid., April 3, 1995. p. 5B.
292r.   Ibid., May 1, 1995. p. 5B.
292s.   Ibid., May 8, 1995. p. 5B.
292t.   Ibid., May 15, 1995. p. 5B.
292u.   Ibid., May 22, 1995. p. 5B.
292v.   Ibid., June 19, 1995. p. 5B.
292w.   Ibid., July 3, 1995. p. 5B.
292x.   Ibid., July 17, 1995.
292y.   Ibid., July 24, 1995.
292z.   Ibid., July 31, 1995. p. 5B.
292aa.   Ibid., August 7, 1995.
292bb.   Ibid., August 14, 1995. p. 5B.
292cc.   Ibid., August 21, 1995.
292dd.   Ibid., August 28, 1995. p. 8D.
292ee.   Ibid., September 25, 1995. p. 2C
292ff.   Ibid., October 2, 1995. p. 2C.
292gg.   Ibid., November 6, 1995.
292hh.   Ibid., November 27, 1995. p. 2C.
292ii.   Ibid., December 4, 1995. p. 2C.
292jj.   Ibid., January 15, 1996. p. 2C.
292kk.   Ibid., January 29, 1996. p. 2C.
292ll.   Ibid., February 5, 1996. p. 2C.
292mm.   Ibid., March 4, 1996.
292nn.   Ibid., March 11, 1996. p. 2C.
292oo.   Ibid., May 6, 1996. p. 2C.
292pp.   Ibid., May 20, 1996. p.2C.
292qq.   Ibid., June 10, 1996. p. 2C.
292rr.   Ibid., June 17, 1996. p. 2C.
292ss.   Ibid., July 8, 1996. p. 2C.
292tt.   Ibid., July 15, 1996. p. 2C.

292uu. Scripps Howard News Service. Global warming in dispute. News & Observer (Raleigh) April 11, 1996. p. 11A.
293.   Abernethy VA. Population Politics: The Choices That Shape Our Future. New York: Insight Books, 1993.
293a.   Carrington T. Experience Teaches Population Control Can Precede Development, and Spur It. The Wall Street Journal August 8, 1994.
294a.   Abernethy, op. cit., p. 118.
294b.   Ibid., p. 140.
295.   Ibid., p. 43.
296.   Ibid., p. 140.
297.   Ibid., p. 116.
298.   Ibid., p. 140.
298a.   Edwards RT. Nonprofits fight Istook amendment. National Catholic Reporter September 22, 1995. p. 4.
299.   Abernethy, op. cit., p. 203.
300.   Ibid., p. 162.
301.   Ibid., p. 141.
302.   Ibid., p. 281.
303.   Ibid., p. 260.
304.   Mumford SD. Vatican control of World Health Organization population policy. The Humanist 1993;53(2):21-5.
305.   Editorial. Death of a study: WHO, what, and why. The Lancet, April 23, 1994, p. 987.
306.   Schlesinger, op. cit.
307.   Abernethy, op. cit.
308.   Schlesinger, op. cit., p. 113.
309.   Ibid., p. 42.
310.   Ibid., p. 42.
311.   Ibid., p. 102.
312.   Ibid., p. 112.
313.   Ibid., p. 117.
314.   Ibid., p. 108.
315.   Ibid., p. 98.
316.   Ibid., p. 134.
317.   Ibid., p. 131.
317a.   Weld M. Address to the Humanist Association of Canada, Guelph, Ontario, June 23, 1995. p. 5.
318.   Briggs, D. Evangelicals' White House Clout Fades. (Raleigh) News & Observer, December 26, 1990, p. 2A.
319.   Ibid.
320.   Conn, op. cit.
320a.   Michaelman K. NARAL Membership fundraising letter. January 1996. p. 1.
321.   Wattleton F. 1992 letter to Planned Parenthood Federation of America supporters. New York.
322.   Anonymous. Immigration costs taxpayers $45 billion in 1992. Population/Environment Balance Report, December 1993, p. 1.
323.   Simcox, op. cit.
324.   Abernethy, op. cit., p. 297.
325.   Public Papers of Woodrow Wilson [Authorized Edition], Part I, Vol. 1, page 62. In:The Great Quotations compiled by George Seldes. Secaucus, New Jersey: Castle Books, 1966.
326.   Carlin DC Jr. Americanizing the anti-abortion argument. America,
327.   Lader, op. cit.
328.   Ravenholt, op. cit.
329.   Mumford SD. Papal Power: U.S. Security Population Directive Undermined by Vatican with Ecumenism a Tool. Human Quest, May-June 1992, p. 15.
330.   Mumford SD. National Security Study Memorandum 200: World Population Growth and U.S. Security. The Social Contract. Winter 1992-93, p. 2.
331.   Mumford SD. Overcoming Overpopulation: The Rise and Fall of American Political Will. Free Inquiry, Spring 1994, p. 23.

Appendix 1

The World Population Plan of Action.

Adopted by consensus of the 137 countries
represented at the
United Nations World Population Conference
at Bucharest, August 1974.

Appendix 1

WORLD POPULATION
PLAN OF ACTION

August 1976

Adopted by the
World Population
Conference
Bucharest, 1974

Agency for International Development
Washington, D.C. 20523

World Population Plan of Action

The World Population Conference.

Having due regard for human aspirations for a better quality of life and for rapid socio-economic development,

Taking into consideration the interrelationship between population situations and socio-economic development,

Decides on the following World Population Plan of Action as a policy instrument within the broader context of the internationally adopted strategies for national and international progress:

A. Background to the Plan

1. The promotion of development and improvement of quality of life require coordination of action in all major socio-economic fields including that of population, which is the inexhaustible source of creativity and a determining factor of progress. At the international level a number of strategies and programmes whose explicit aim is to affect variables in fields other than population have already been formulated. These include the Provisional Indicative World Plan for Agricultural Development of the Food and Agriculture Organization of the United Nations (FAO), the United Nations/FAO World Food Programme, the International Labour Organisation's World Employment Programme, the Action Plan for the Human Environment, the United Nations World Plan of Action for the Application of Science and Technology to Development, the Programme of Concerted Action for the Advancement of Women, and, more comprehensively, the International Development Strategy for the Second United Nations Development Decade. The Declaration on the Establishment of a New International Economic Order and the Programme of Action to achieve it, adopted by the United Nations General Assembly at its sixth special session (resolutions 3201 and 3202 (S-VI) of 1 May 1974), provide the most recent over-all framework for international co-operation. The explicit aim of the World Population Plan of Action is to help co-ordinate population trends and the trends of economic and social development. The basis for an effective solution of population problems is, above all, socio-economic transformation. A population policy may have a certain success if it constitutes an integral part of socio-economic development; its contribution to the solution of world development problems is hence only partial, as is the case with the other sectoral strategies. Consequently, the Plan of Action must be considered as an important component of the system of international strategies and as an instrument of the international community for the promotion of economic development, quality of life, human rights and fundamental freedoms.

2. The formulation of international strategies is a response to universal recognition of the existence of important problems in the world and the need for concerted national and international action to achieve their solution. Where trends of population growth, distribution and structure are out of balance with social, economic and environmental factors, they can, at certain stages of development, create additional difficulties for the achievement of sustained development. Policies whose aim is to affect population trends must not be considered substitutes for socio-economic development policies but as being integrated with those policies in order to facilitate the solution of certain problems facing both developing and developed countries and to promote a more balanced and rational development.

3. Throughout history the rate of growth of world population averaged only slightly above replacement levels. The recent increase in the growth rate began mainly as a result of the decline in mortality during the past few centuries, a decline that has accelerated significantly during recent decades. The inertia of social structures and the insufficiency of economic progress, especially when these exist in the absence of profound socio-cultural changes, partly explain why in the majority of developing countries the decline in mortality has not been accompanied by a parallel decline in fertility. Since about 1950, the world population growth rate has risen to 2 per cent a year. If sustained, this will result in a doubling of the world's population every 35 years. However, national rates of natural growth range widely, from a negative rate to well over 3 per cent a year.

4. The consideration of population problems cannot be reduced to the analysis of population trends only. It must also be borne in mind that the present situation of the developing countries originates in the unequal processes of socio-economic development which have divided peoples since the beginning of the modern era. This inequity still exists and is intensified by lack of equity in international economic relations with consequent disparity in levels of living.

5. Although acceleration in the rate of growth of the world's population is mainly the result of very large declines in the mortality of developing countries, those declines have been unevenly distributed. Thus, at present, average expectation of life at birth is 63 years in Latin America, 57 years in Asia and only a little over 46 years in Africa, compared with more than 71 years in the developed regions. Furthermore, although on average less than one in 40 children dies before reaching the age of 1 year in the developed regions, one in 15 dies before reaching that age in Latin America, one in 10 in Asia and one in 7 in Africa. In fact, in some developing regions, and particularly in African countries, average expectation of life at birth is estimated to be less than 40 years and one in 4 children dies before the age of 1 year. Consequently, many developing countries consider reduction of mortality, and particularly reduction of infant mortality, to be one of the most important and urgent goals.

6. While the right of couples to have the number of children they desire is accepted in a number of international instruments, many couples in the world are unable to exercise that right effectively. In many parts of the world, poor economic conditions, social norms, inadequate knowledge of effective methods of family regulation and the unavailability of contraceptive services result in a situation in which couples have more children than they desire or feel they can properly care for. In certain countries, on the other hand, because of economic or biological factors, problems of involuntary sterility and of subfecundity exist, with the result that many couples have fewer children than they desire. Of course, the degree of urgency attached to dealing with each of these two situations depends upon the prevailing conditions within the country in question.

7. Individual reproductive behaviour and the needs and aspirations of society should be reconciled. In many developing countries, and particularly in the large countries of Asia, the desire of couples to achieve large families is believed to result in excessive national population growth rates and Governments are explicitly attempting to reduce those rates by implementing specific policy measures. On the other hand, some countries are attempting to increase desired family size, if only slightly.

8. Throughout the world, urban populations are growing in size at a considerably faster rate than rural populations. As a result, by the end of this century, and for the first time in history, the majority of the world's population will be living in urban areas. Urbanization is an element of the process of modernization. Moreover, while in certain countries this process is efficiently managed and maximum use is made of the advantages this management presents, in others urbanization takes place in an uncontrolled manner and is accompanied by overcrowding in certain districts, an increase in slums, deterioration of the environment, urban unemployment and many other social and economic problems.

9. In most of the developing countries, although the rate of urban population growth is higher than the growth rate in rural areas, the latter is still significant. The rural population of developing countries is growing at an average rate of 1.7 per cent a year, and in some instances at a faster rate than that of the urban population in developed countries. Furthermore, many rural areas of heavy emigration, in both developed and developing countries, are being depleted of their younger populations and are being left with populations whose age distribution is unfavourable to economic development. Thus, in many countries, the revitalization of the countryside is a priority goal.

10. For some countries international migration may be, in certain circumstances, an instrument of population policy. At least two types of international migration are of considerable concern to many countries in the world: the movement of migrant workers with limited skills, and the movement of skilled workers and professionals. Movements of the former often involve large numbers and raise such questions as the fair and proper treatment in countries of immigration, the breaking up of families and other social and economic questions in countries both of emigration and immigration. The migration of skilled workers and professionals results in a "brain drain", often from less developed to more developed countries, which is at present of considerable concern to many countries and to the international community as a whole. The number of instruments on these subjects and the increased involvement of international organizations reflect international awareness of these problems.

11. A population's age structure is greatly affected by its birth rates. For example, declining fertility is the main factor underlying the declining proportion of children in a population. Thus, according to the medium projections of the United Nations, the population of less than 15 years of age in the developing countries is expected to decline from an average of more than 41 per cent of total population in 1970 to an average of about 35 per cent in 2000. However, such a decline in the proportion of children will be accompanied by an increase in their numbers at an average of 1.7 per cent a year. The demand for educational services is expected to increase considerably, in view of both the existing backlog and the continuously increasing population of children which ought to enter and remain in schools; therefore the supply of educational services must be increased. With regard to the population 15 to

29 years of age, an increase in both their proportion and number is expected in the developing countries. Consequently, unless very high
rates of economic development are attained, in
many of these countries, and particularly where
levels of unemployment and underemployment
are already high, the additional difficulties will
not be overcome at least until the end of this
century. Furthermore, in both developed and
developing countries, the greatly changing social and economic conditions faced by youth
require a better understanding of the problems
involved and the formulation and implementation of policies to resolve them.

12. Declining birth rates also result in a gradual aging of the population. Because birth rates
have already declined in developing countries,
the average proportion of the population aged
65 years and over in these countries makes up
10 per cent of the total population, whereas
it makes up only 3 per cent in developing
countries. However, aging of the population
in developing countries has recently begun, and
is expected to accelerate. Thus, although the
total population of these countries is projected
to increase by an average of 2.3 per cent a year
between 1970 and 2000, the population 65
years and over is expected to increase by 3.5
per cent a year. Not only are the numbers and
proportions of the aged increasing rapidly but
the social and economic conditions which face
them are also rapidly changing. There is an
urgent need, in those countries where such
programmes are lacking, for the development
of social security and health programmes for
the elderly.

13. Because of the relatively high proportions of children and youth in the populations of developing countries, declines in fertility levels in those countries will not be fully reflected in declines in population growth rates until some decades later. To illustrate this demographic inertia, it may be noted that, for developing countries, even if replacement levels of fertility—approximately two children per completed family—had been achieved in 1970 and maintained thereafter, their total population would still grow from a 1970 total of 2.5 billion to about 4.4 billion before it would stabilize during the second half of the twenty-first century. In these circumstances, the population of the world as a whole would grow from 3.6 billion to 5.8 billion. This example of demographic inertia, which will lead to a growing population for many decades to come, demonstrates that whatever population policies may be formulated, socio-economic development must accelerate in order to provide for a significant increase in levels of living. Efforts made by developing countries to speed up economic growth must be viewed by the entire international community as a global endeavour to improve the quality of life for all people of the world, supported by a just utilization of the world's wealth, resources and technology in the spirit of the new international economic order. It also demonstrates that countries wishing to affect their population growth must anticipate future demographic trends and take appropriate decisions and actions in their plans for economic and social development well in advance.

B. Principles and Objectives of the Plan

14. This Plan of Action is based on a number of principles which underlie its objective and are observed in its formulation. The formulation and implementation of population policies is the sovereign right of each nation. This right is to be exercised in accordance with national objectives and needs and without external interference, taking into account universal solidarity in order to improve the quality of life of the peoples of the world. The main responsibility for national population policies and programmes lies with national authorities. However, international co-operation should play an important role in accordance with the principles of the United Nations Charter. The Plan of Action is based on the following principles:

(a) The principal aim of social, economic and cultural development, of which population goals and policies are integral parts, is to improve levels of living and the quality of life of the people. Of all things in the world, people are the most precious. Man's knowledge and ability to master himself and his environment will continue to grow. Mankind's future can be made infinitely bright;

(b) True development cannot take place in the absence of national independence and liberation. Alien and colonial domination, foreign occupation, wars of aggression, racial discrimination, *apartheid* and neocolonialism in all its forms, continue to be among the greatest obstacles to the full emancipation and progress of the developing countries and all the people involved. Co-operation among nations on the basis of national sovereignty is essential for development. Development also requires recognition of the dignity of the individual, appreciation for the human person and his self-determination, as well as the elimination of discrimination in all its forms;

(c) Population and development are inter-related: population variables influence develop-ment variables and are also influenced by them; thus the formulation of a World Population Plan of Action reflects the international com-munity's awareness of the importance of popu-lation trends for socio-economic development, and the socio-economic nature of the recom-mendations contained in this Plan of Action reflects its awareness of the crucial role that development plays in affecting population trends;

(d) Population policies are constituent ele-ments of socio-economic development policies, never substitutes for them; while serving socio-economic objectives, they should be consistent with internationally and nationally recognized human rights of individual freedom, justice and the survival of national, regional and minority groups;

(e) Independently of the realization of eco-nomic and social objectives, respect for human life is basic to all human societies;

(f) All couples and individuals have the basic right to decide freely and responsibly the num-ber and spacing of their children and to have the information, education and means to do so; the responsibility of couples and individuals in the exercise of this right takes into account the needs of their living and future children, and their responsibilities towards the community;

(g) The family is the basic unit of society and should be protected by appropriate legislation and policy;

(h) Women have the right to complete inte-gration in the development process particularly by means of an equal access to education and equal participtaion in social, economic, cultural and political life. In addition, the necessary measures should be taken to facilitate this inte-gration with family responsibilities which should be fully shared by both partners;

(i) Recommendations in this Plan of Action regarding policies to deal with population problems must recognize the diversity of conditions within and among different countries;

(j) In the democratic formulation of national population goals and policies, consideration must be given, together with other economic and social factors, to the supplies and characteristics of natural resources and to the quality of the environment and particularly to all aspects of food supply including productivity of rural areas. The demand for vital resources increases not only with growing population but also with growing *per capita* consumption; attention must be directed to the just distribution of resources and to the minimization of wasteful aspects of their use throughout the world;

(k) The growing interdependence among nations makes international action increasingly important to the solution of development and population problems. International strategies will achieve their objective only if they ensure that the underprivileged of the world achieve, urgently, through structural, social and economic reforms, a significant improvement in their living conditions;

(l) This Plan of Action must be sufficiently flexible to take into account the consequences of rapid demographic changes, societal changes and changes in human behaviour, attitudes and values;

(m) The objectives of this Plan of Action should be consistent with the purposes and principles of the United Nations Charter, the Universal Declaration of Human Rights and with the objectives of the Second United Nations Development Decade; however, changes in demographic variables during the Decade are largely the result of past demographic events and changes in demographic trends sought during the Decade have social and economic repercussions up to and beyond the end of this century.

15. Guided by these principles, the primary aim of this Plan of Action is to expand and deepen the capacities of countries to deal effectively with their national and subnational population problems and to promote an appropriate international response to their needs by increasing international activity in research, the exchange of information, and the provision of assistance on request. In pursuit of this primary aim, the following general objectives are set for this Plan of Action:

(a) To advance understanding of population at global, regional, national and subnational levels, recognizing the diversity of the problems involved;

(b) To advance national and international understanding of the interrelationship of demographic and socio-economic factors in development: on the one hand, of the nature and scope of the effect of demographic factors on the attainment of goals of advancing human welfare, and, on the other hand, the impact of broader social, economic and cultural factors on demographic behaviour;

(c) To promote socio-economic measures and programmes whose aim is to affect, *inter alia*, population growth, morbidity and mortality, reproduction and family formation, population distribution and internal migration, international migration and, consequently, demographic structures;

(d) To advance national and international understanding of the complex relations among the problems of population, resources, environment and development, and to promote a unified analytical approach to the study of these inter-relationships and to relevant policies;

(e) To promote the status of women and the expansion of their roles, their full participation in the formulation and implementation of socio-economic policy, including population policies, and the creation of awareness among all women of their current and potential roles in national life;

(f) To recommend guidelines for population policies consistent with national values and goals and with internationally recognized principles;

(g) To promote the development and implementation of population policies where necessary, including improvement in the communication of the purposes and goals of those policies to the public and the promotion of popular participation in the formulation and implementation;

(h) To encourage the development and good management of appropriate education, training, statistical research, information and family health services as well as statistical services in support of the above principles and objectives.

C. Recommendations for Action

1. Population goals and policies

(a) *Population growth*

16. According to the United Nations medium population projections, little change is expected to occur in average rates of population growth either in the developed or in the developing regions by 1985. According to the United Nations low variant projections, it is estimated that, as a result of social and economic development and population policies as reported by countries in the Second United Nations Inquiry on Population and Development, population growth rates in the developing countries as a whole may decline from the present level of 2.4 per cent per annum to about 2 per cent by 1985 and may remain below 0.7 per cent per annum in the developed countires. In this case the world-wide rate of population growth would decline from 2 per cent to about 1.7 per cent.

17. Countries which consider that their present or expected rates of population growth hamper their goals of promoting human welfare are invited, if they have not yet done so, to consider adopting population policies, within the framework of socio-economic development, which are consistent with basic human rights and national goals and values.

18. Countries which aim at achieving moderate or low population growth should try to achieve it through a low level of birth and death rates. Countries wishing to increase their rate of population growth should, when mortality is high, concentrate efforts on the reduction of mortality, and where appropriate, encourage an increase in fertility and encourage immigration.

19. Recognizing that *per capita* use of world resources is much higher in the developed than in the developing countries, the developed countries are urged to adopt appropriate policies in population, consumption and investment, bearing in mind the need for fundamental improvement in international equity.

(b) *Morbidity and mortality*

20. The reduction of morbidity and mortality to the maximum feasible extent is a major goal of every human society. It should be achieved in conjunction with massive social and economic development. Where mortality and morbidity rates are very high, concentrated national and international efforts should be applied to reduce them as a matter of highest priority in the context of societal change.

21. The short-term effect of mortality reduction on population growth rates is symptomatic of the early development process and must be viewed as beneficial. Sustained reductions in fertility have generally been preceded by reductions in mortality. Although this relationship is complex, mortality reduction may be a prerequisite to a decline in fertility.

22. It is a goal of this Plan of Action to reduce mortality levels, particularly infant and maternal mortality levels, to the maximum extent possible in all regions of the world and to reduce national and subnational differentials therein. The attainment of an average expectation of life of 62 years by 1985 and 74 years by the year 2000 for the world as a whole would require by the end of the century an increase of 11 years for Latin America, 17 years for Asia and 28 years for Africa.

23. Countries with the highest mortality levels should aim by 1985 to have an expectation of life at birth of at least 50 years and an infant mortality rate of less than 120 per thousand live births.

24. It is recommended that national and international efforts to reduce general morbidity and mortality levels be accompanied by particularly vigorous efforts to achieve the following goals:

(*a*) Reduction of foetal, infant and early childhood mortality and related maternal morbidity and mortality;

(*b*) Reduction of involuntary sterility, subfecundity, defective births and illegal abortions;

(*c*) Reduction or, if possible, elimination of differential morbidity and mortality within countries, particularly with regard to differentials between regions, urban and rural areas, social and ethnic groups, and the sexes;

(*d*) Eradication, wherever possible, or control of infectious and parasitic diseases, undernutrition and malnutrition; and the provision of a sufficient supply of potable water and adequate sanitation;

(*e*) Improvement of poor health and nutritional conditions which adversely affect working-age populations and their productivity and thus undermine development efforts;

(*f*) Adoption of special measures for reducing mortality from social and environmental factors and elimination of aggression as a cause of death and poor health.

25. It is recommended that health and nutrition programmes designed to reduce morbidity and mortality be integrated within a comprehensive development strategy and supplemented by a wide range of mutually supporting social policy measures; special attention should be given to improving the management of existing health, nutrition and related social services and to the formulation of policies to widen their coverage so as to reach, in particular, rural, remote and underprivileged groups.

26. Each country has its own experience in preventing and treating diseases. Promotion of interchange of such experience will help to reduce morbidity and mortality.

(c) *Reproduction, family formation and the status of women*

27. This Plan of Action recognizes the variety of national goals with regard to fertility and does not recommend any world family-size norm.

28. This Plan of Action recognizes the necessity of ensuring that all couples are able to achieve their desired number and spacing of children and the necessity of preparing the social and economic conditions to achieve that desire.

29. Consistent with the Proclamation of the International Conference on Human Rights, the Declaration on Social Progress and Development, the relevant targets of the Second United Nations Development Decade and the other international instruments on the subject, it is recommended that all countries:

(a) Respect and ensure, regardless of their over-all demographic goals, the right of persons to determine, in a free, informed and responsible manner, the number and spacing of their children;

(b) Encourage appropriate education concerning responsible parenthood and make available to persons who so desire advice and the means of achieving it;

(c) Ensure that family planning, medical and related social services aim not only at the prevention of unwanted pregnancies but also at the elimination of involuntary sterility and subfecundity in order that all couples may be permitted to achieve their desired number of children, and that child adoption may be facilitated;

(d) Seek to ensure the continued possibility of variations in family size when a low fertility level has been established or is a policy objective;

(e) Make use, wherever needed and appropriate, of adequately trained professional and auxiliary health personnel, rural extension, home economics and social workers, and non-governmental channels, to help provide family planning services and to advise users of contraceptives;

(f) Increase their health manpower and health facilities to an effective level, redistribute functions among the different levels of professionals and auxiliaries in order to overcome the shortage of qualified personnel and establish an effective system of supervision in their health and family planning services;

(g) Ensure that information about, and education in, family planning and other matters which affect fertility are based on valid and proven scientific knowledge, and include a full account of any risk that may be involved in the use or non-use of contraceptives.

30. Governments which have family planning programmes are invited to consider integrating and co-ordinating those services with health and other services designed to raise the quality of family life, including family allowances and maternity benefits, and to consider including family planning services in their official health and social insurance systems. As concerns couples themselves, family planning policy should also be directed towards the promotion of the psycho-social harmony and mental and physical well-being of couples.

31. It is recommended that countries wishing to affect fertility levels give priority to implementing development programmes and educational and health strategies which, while contributing to economic growth and higher standards of living, have a decisive impact upon demographic trends, including fertility. International co-operation is called for to give priority to assisting such national efforts in order that these programmes and strategies be carried into effect.

32. While recognizing the diversity of social, cultural, political and economic conditions among countries and regions, it is nevertheless agreed that the following development goals generally have an effect on the socio-economic context of reproductive decisions that tends to moderate fertility levels:

(a) The reduction of infant and child mortality, particularly by means of improved nutrition, sanitation, maternal and child health care, and maternal education;

(b) The full integration of women into the development process, particularly by means of their greater participation in educational, social, economic and political opportunities, and especially by means of the removal of obstacles to their employment in the nonagricultural sector wherever possible. In this context, national laws and policies, as well as relevant international recommendations, should be reviewed in order to eliminate discrimination in, and remove obstacles to, the education, training, employment and career advancement opportunities for women;

(c) The promotion of social justice, social mobility and social development, particularly by means of a wide participation of the population in development and a more equitable distribution of income, land, social services and amenities;

(d) The promotion of wide educational opportunities for the young of both sexes, and the extension of public forms of pre-school education for the rising generation;

(e) The elimination of child labour and child abuse and the establishment of social security and old-age benefits;

(f) The establishment of an appropriate lower limit for age at marriage.

33. It is recommended that Governments consider making provision, in both their formal and non-formal educational programmes, for informing their people of the consequences of existing or alternative fertility behaviour for the well-being of the family, for educational and psychological development of children and for the general welfare of society, so that an informed and responsible attitude to marriage and reproduction will be promoted.

34. Family size may also be affected by incentive and disincentive schemes. However, if such schemes are adopted or modified it is essential that they should not violate human rights.

35. Some social welfare programmes, such as family allowances and maternity benefits, may have a positive effect on fertility and may hence be strengthened when such an effect is desired. However, such programmes should not, in principle, be curtailed if the opposite effect on fertility is desired.

36. The projections in paragraph 16 of future declines in rates of population growth, and those in paragraph 22 concerning increased expectation of life, are consistent with declines in the birth rate of the developing countries as a whole from the present level of 38 per thousand to 30 per thousand by 1985; in these projections, birth rates in the developed countries remain in the region of 15 per thousand. To achieve by 1985 these levels of fertility would require substantial national efforts, by those countries concerned, in the field of socio-economic development and population policies, supported, upon request, by adequate international assistance. Such efforts would also be required to achieve the increase in expectation of life.

37. In the light of the principles of this Plan of Action, countries which consider their birth rates detrimental to their national purposes are invited to consider setting quantitative goals and implementing policies that may lead to the attainment of such goals by 1985. Nothing herein should interfere with the sovereignty of any Government to adopt or not to adopt such quantitative goals.

38. Countries which desire to reduce their birth rates are invited to give particular consideration to the reduction of fertility at the extremes of female reproductive ages because of the salutary effects this may have on infant and maternal welfare.

39. The family is recognized as the basic unit of society. Governments should assist families as far as possible to enable them to fulfil their role in society. It is therefore recommended that:

(a) The family be protected by appropriate legislation and policy without discrimination as to other members of society:

(b) Family ties be strengthened by giving recognition to the importance of love and mutual respect within the family unit:

(c) National legislation having direct bearing on the welfare of the family and its members, including laws concerning age at marriage, inheritance, property rights, divorce, education, employment and the rights of the child, be periodically reviewed, as feasible, and adapted to the changing social and economic conditions and with regard to the cultural setting:

(d) Marriages be entered into only with the free and full consent of the intending spouses:

(e) Measures be taken to protect the social and legal rights of spouses and children in the case of dissolution or termination of marriage by death or other reason.

40. It is also recommended that:

(a) Governments should equalize the legal and social status of children born in and out of wedlock as well as children adopted;

(b) The legal responsibilities of each parent towards the care and support of all their children should be established.

41. Governments should ensure full participation of women in the educational, social, economic and political life of their countries on an equal basis with men. It is recommended that:

(a) Education for girls as well as boys should be extended and diversified to enable them to contribute more effectively in rural and urban sectors, as well as in the management of food and other household functions;

(b) Women should be actively involved both as individuals and through political and non-governmental organizations, at every stage and every level in the planning and implementation of development programmes, including population policies;

(c) The economic contribution of women in households and farming should be recognized in national economies;

(d) Governments should make a sustained effort to ensure that legislation regarding the status of women complies with the principles spelled out in the Declaration on the Elimination of Discrimination against Women and other United Nations declarations, conventions and international instruments, to reduce the gap between law and practice through effective implementation, and to inform women at all socio-economic levels of their legal rights and responsibilities.

42. Equal status of men and women in the family and in society improves the over-all quality of life. This principle of equality should be fully realized in family planning where each spouse should consider the welfare of the other members of the family.

43. Improvement of the status of women in the family and in society can contribute, where desired, to smaller family size, and the opportunity for women to plan births also improves their individual status.

(d) *Population distribution and internal migration*

44. Urbanization in most countries is characterized by a number of adverse factors: drain from rural areas through migration of individuals who cannot be absorbed by productive employment in urban areas, serious disequilibrium in the growth of urban centres, contamination of the environment, inadequate housing and services and social and psychological stress. In many developing countries, adverse consequences are due in large part to the economic structures resulting from the dependent situation of those countries in the international economic system; the correction of these shortcomings requires as a matter of priority the establishment of equitable economic relations among peoples.

45. Policies aimed at influencing population flows into urban areas should be co-ordinated with policies relating to the absorptive capacity of urban centres as well as policies aimed at eliminating the undesirable consequences of excessive migration. In so far as possible, those policies should be integrated into plans and programmes dealing with over-all social and economic development.

46. In formulating and implementing internal migration policies, Governments are urged to consider the following guidelines, without prejudice to their own socio-economic policies:

(*a*) Measures should be avoided which infringe the right of freedom of movement and residence within the borders of each State as enunciated in the Universal Declaration of Human Rights and other international instruments;

(*b*) A major approach to a more rational distribution of the population is that of planned and more equitable regional development, particularly in the advancement of regions which are less favoured or developed by comparison with the rest of the country;

(*c*) In planning development, and particularly in planning the location of industry and business and the distribution of social services and amenities, Governments should take into account not only short-term economic returns or alternative patterns but also the social and environmental costs and benefits involved as well as equity and social justice in the distribution of the benefits of development among all groups and regions;

(*d*) Population distribution patterns should not be restricted to a choice between metropolitan and rural life: efforts should be made to establish and strengthen networks of small and medium-size cities to relieve the pressure on the large towns, while still offering an alternative to rural living;

(*e*) Intensive programmes of economic and social improvement should be carried out in the rural areas through balanced agricultural development which will provide increased income to the agricultural population, permit an effective expansion of social services and include measures to protect the environment and conserve and increase agricultural resources;

(*f*) Programmes should be promoted to make accessible to scattered populations the basic social services and the support necessary for increased productivity, for example by consolidating them in rural centres.

47. Internal migration policies should include the provision of information to the rural population concerning economic and social conditions in the urban areas, including information on the availability of employment opportunities.

48. In rural areas and areas accessible to rural populations, new employment opportunities, including industries and public works programmes, should be created, systems of land tenure should be improved and social services and amenities provided. It is not sufficient to consider how to bring the people to existing economic and social activities; it is also important to bring those activities to the people.

49. Considerable experience is now being gained by some countries which have implemented programmes for relieving urban pressures, revitalizing the countryside, inhabiting sparsely populated areas and settling newly reclaimed agricultural land. Countries having such experience are invited to share it with other countries. It is recommended that international organizations make available upon request coordinated technical and financial assistance to facilitate the settlement of people.

50. The problems of urban environment are a consequence not only of the concentration of inhabitants but also of their way of life, which can produce harmful effects, such as wasteful and excessive consumption and activities which produce pollution. In order to avoid such effects in those countries experiencing this problem, a development pattern favouring balanced and rational consumption is recommended.

(e) *International migration*

51. It is recommended that Governments and international organizations generally facilitate voluntary international movement. However, such movements should not be based on racial considerations which are to the detriment of indigenous populations. The significance of international migration varies widely among countries, depending upon their area, population size and growth rate, social and economic structure and environmental conditions.

52. Governments which consider international migration to be important to their countries, either in the short or the long run, are urged to conduct, when appropriate, bilateral or multilateral consultations, taking into account the principles of the Charter of the United Nations, the Universal Declaration of Human Rights, the relevant resolutions of the United Nations system and other international instruments, with a view to harmonizing those of their policies which affect these movements. It is recommended that international organizations make available upon request co-ordinated technical and financial assistance to facilitate the settlement of people in countries of immigration.

53. Problems of refugees and displaced persons arising from forced migration, including their right of return to homes and properties, should also be settled in accordance with the relevant Principles of the Charter of the United Nations, the Universal Declaration of Human Rights and other international instruments.

54. Countries that are concerned with the outflow of migrant workers and wish to encourage and assist those remaining workers or returning workers should make particular efforts to create favourable employment opportunities at the national level. More developed countries should co-operate, bilaterally or through regional organizations and the international community, with less developed countries, to achieve these goals through the increased availability of capital, technical assistance, export markets and more favourable terms of trade and choice of production technology.

55. Countries receiving migrant workers should provide proper treatment and adequate social welfare services for them and their families, and should ensure their physical safety and security, in conformity with the provisions of the relevant conventions and recommendations of the International Labour Organisation and other international instruments.

56. Specifically, in the treatment of migrant workers, Governments should work to prevent discrimination in the labour market and in society through lower salaries or other unequal conditions, to preserve their human rights, to combat prejudice against them and to eliminate obstacles to the reunion of their families. Governments should enable permanent immigrants to preserve their cultural heritage *inter alia* through the use of their mother tongue. Laws to limit illegal immigration should relate not only to the illegal migrants themselves but also to those inducing or facilitating their illegal action and should be promulgated in conformity with international law and basic human rights. Governments should bear in mind humanitarian considerations in the treatment of aliens who remain in a country illegally.

57. Since the outflow of qualified personnel from developing to developed countries seriously hampers the development of the former, there is an urgent need to formulate national and international policies to avoid the "brain drain" and to obviate its adverse effects, including the possibility of devising programmes for large-scale communication of appropriate technological knowledge mainly from developed countries to the extent that it can be properly adjusted and appropriately absorbed.

58. Developing countries suffering from heavy emigration of skilled workers and professionals should undertake extensive educational programmes, manpower planning, and investment in scientific and technical programmes. They should also undertake other programmes and measures to better match skills with employment opportunities and to increase the motivation of such personnel to contribute to the progress of their own country. Measures should be taken to encourage the return of scientists and skilled personnel to specific job vacancies.

59. Foreign investors should employ and train local personnel and use local research facilities to the greatest possible extent in conformity with the policies of the host country. Subject to their consent, the location of research facilities in host countries may aid them to a certain extent in retaining the services of highly skilled and professional research workers. Such investment should, of course, in no circumstances inhibit national economic development. International co-operation is needed to improve programmes to induce skilled personnel to return to, or remain in, their own countries.

60. Where immigration has proved to be of a long-term nature, countries are invited to explore the possibilities of extending national civil rights to immigrants.

61. The flow of skilled workers, technicans and professionals from more developed to less developed countries may be considered a form of international co-operation. Countries in a position to do so should continue and increase this flow with full respect for the sovereignty and equality of recipient countries.

62. Countries affected by significant numbers of migrant workers are urged, if they have not yet done so, to conclude bilateral or multilateral agreements which would regulate migration, protect and assist migrant workers, and protect the interests of the countries concerned. The International Labour Organisation should promote concerted action in the field of protection of migrant workers, and the United Nations Commission on Human Rights should help, as appropriate, to ensure that the fundamental rights of migrants are safeguarded.

(f) *Population structure*

63. All Governments are urged, when formulating their development policies and programmes, to take fully into account the implications of changing numbers and proportions of youth, working-age groups and the aged, particularly where such changes are rapid. Countries should study their population structures to determine the most desirable balance among age groups.

64. Specifically, developing countries are urged to consider the implications which the combination of the characteristically young age structure and moderate to high fertility has on their development. The increasing number and proportion of young persons in the populations of developing countries requires appropriate development strategies, priority being accorded to their subsistence, health, education, training and incorporation in the labour force through full employment as well as their active participation in political, cultural, social and economic life.

65. Developing countries are invited to consider the possible economic, social and demographic effects of population shifts from agriculture to non-agricultural industries. In addition to fuller utilization of labour and improvements in productivity and the levels of living, promotion of non-agricultural employment should aim at such changes in the socio-economic structure of manpower and population as would affect demographically relevant behaviour of individuals. All countries are invited to consider fully giving appropriate support and assistance to the World Employment Programme and related national employment promotion schemes.

66. Similarly, the other countries are urged to consider the contrary implications of the combination of their aging structure with moderate to low or very low fertility. All countries should carry out, as part of their development programmes, comprehensive, humanitarian and just programmes of social security for the elderly.

67. In undertaking settlement and resettlement schemes and urban planning, Governments are urged to give adequate attention to questions of age and sex balance and, particularly, to the welfare of the family.

2. Socio-economic policies

68. This Plan of Action recognizes that economic and social development is a central factor in the solution of population problems. National efforts of developing countries to accelerate economic growth should be assisted by the entire international community. The implementation of the International Development Strategy for the Second United Nations Development Decade, and the Declaration and the Programme of Action on the New International Economic Order as adopted at the sixth special session of the General Assembly should lead to a reduction in the widening gap in levels of living between developed and developing countries and would be conducive to a reduction in population growth rates particularly in countries where such rates are high.

69. In planning measures to harmonize population trends and socio-economic change, human beings must be regarded not only as consumers but also as producers. The investment by nations in the health and education of their citizens contributes substantially to productivity. Consequently, plans for economic and social development and for international assistance for this purpose should emphasize the health and education sectors. Likewise, patterns of production and technology should be adapted to each country's endowment in human resources. Decisions on the introduction of technologies affording significant savings in employment of manpower should take into account the relative abundance of human resources. To this end it is recommended that efforts should be intensified to determine for each country the technologies and production methods best suited to its working population situation and to study the relationship between population factors and employment.

70. It is imperative that all countries, and within them all social sectors, should adapt themselves to more rational utilization of natural resources, without excess, so that some are not deprived of what others waste. In order to increase the production and distribution of food for the growing world population it is recommended that Governments give high priority to improving methods of food production, the investigation and development of new sources of food and more effective utilization of existing sources. International co-operation is recommended with the aim of ensuring the provision of fertilizers and energy and a timely supply of food-stuffs to all countries.

3. Promotion of knowledge and policies

71. In order to achieve the population objectives of this Plan of Action and to put its policy recommendations adequately into effect, measures need to be undertaken to promote knowledge of the relationships and problems involved, to assist in the development of population policies and to elicit the co-operation and participation of all concerned in the formulation and implementation of these policies.

(a) *Data collection and analysis*

72. Statistical data on the population collected by means of censuses, surveys or vital statistics registers are essential for the planning of investigations and the provision of a basis for the formulation, evaluation and application of population and development policies. Countries that have not yet done so are urged to tabulate and analyse their census and other data and make them available to national policy-making bodies in order to fulfil these objectives.

73. It is up to each country to take a population census in accordance with its own needs and capabilities. However, it is recommended that a population census be taken by each country between 1975 and 1985. It is also recommended that those censuses give particular attention to data relevant to development planning and the formulation of population policies. In order to be of greatest value, it is recommended that the data be tabulated and made available as quickly as possible, together with an evaluation of the quality of the information and the degree of coverage of the census.

74. All countries that have not yet done so are encouraged to establish a continuing capability for taking household sample surveys and to establish a long-term plan for regular collection of statistics on various demographic and interrelated socio-economic variables, particularly those relating to the improvement of levels of living, well-being and level of education of individuals, factors which relate closely to problems affecting population. All countries are invited to co-operate with the World Fertility Survey.

75. In line with the objectives of the World Programme for the Improvement of Vital Statistics, countries are encouraged to establish or improve their vital registration system, as a long-term objective, and to enact laws relevant to the improvement of vital registration. Until this improvement is completed, the use of alternative methods is recommended, such as sample surveys, to provide up-to-date information on vital events.

76. Developing countries should be provided with technical co-operation, equipment and financial support to develop or improve the population and related statistical programmes mentioned above. Provision for data-gathering assistance should cover fully the need for evaluating, analysing and presenting the data in a form most appropriate to the needs of users.

77. Governments that have not yet done so are urged to establish appropriate services for the collection, analysis and dissemination of demographic and related statistical information.

(b) *Research*

78. This Plan of Action gives high priority to research activities in population problems (including unemployment, starvation and poverty) and to related fields, particularly to research activities that are important for the formulation, evaluation and implementation of the population policies consistent with full respect for human rights and fundamental freedoms as recognized in international instruments of the United Nations. Although research designed to fill gaps in knowledge is very urgent and important, high priority should be given to research oriented to the specific problems of countries and regions, including methodological studies. Such research is best carried out in the countries and regions themselves and by competent persons especially acquainted with national and regional conditions. The following areas are considered to require research in order to fill existing gaps in knowledge:

(a) The social, cultural and economic determinants of population variables in different developmental and political situations, particularly at the family and micro levels;

(b) The demographic and social processes occurring within the family cycle through time and, particularly, in relation to alternative modes of development;

(c) The development of effective means for the improvement of health, and especially for the reduction of maternal, foetal, infant and early childhood mortality;

(d) The study of experiences of countries which have major programmes of internal migration with a view to developing guidelines that are helpful to policy-makers of those countries and of countries that are interested in undertaking similar programmes;

(e) Projections of demographic and related variables including the development of empirical and hypothetical models for simulating possible future trends;

(f) The formulation, implementation and evaluation of population policies including: methods for integrating population inputs and goals in development plans and programmes; means for understanding and improving the motivations of people to participate in the formulation and implementation of population programmes; study of education and communication aspects of population policy; analysis of population policies in their relationship to other socio-economic development policies, laws and institutions, including the possible influences of the economic system on the social, cultural and economic aspects of population policies; translation into action programmes of policies dealing with the socio-economic determinants of fertility, mortality, internal migration and distribution and international migration;

(g) The collection, analysis and dissemination of information concerning human rights in relation to population matters and the preparation of studies designed to clarify, systematize and more effectively implement those human rights;

(h) The review and analysis of national and international laws which bear directly or indirectly on population factors;

(i) The assessment and improvement of existing and new methods of fertility regulation
by means of research, including basic biological
and applied research; the evaluation of the impact, both in short-term and long-term effects,
of different methods of fertility regulation on
ethical and cultural values and on mental and
physical health; and the assessment and study
of policies for creating social and economic
conditions so that couples can freely decide on
the size of their families;

(j) The evaluation of the impact of different
methods of family planning on the health conditions of women and members of their families;

(k) The interrelationships among patterns of
family formation, nutrition and health, reproductive biology, and the incidence, causes and
treatment of sterility;

(l) Methods of improving the management,
delivery and utilization of all social services
associated with population, including family
welfare and, when appropriate, family planning;

(m) Methods for the development of systems
of social, demographic and related economic
statistics in which various sets of data are inter-
linked, with a view to improving insight into
the interrelationships of variables in these
fields;

(n) The interrelations of population trends
and conditions and other social and economic
variables, in particular the availability of human
resources, food and natural resources, the quality of the environment, the need for health, education, employment, welfare, housing and other
social services and amenities, promotion of
human rights, the enhancement of the status
of women, the need for social security, political
stability, discrimination and political freedom;

(o) The impact of a shift from one family size pattern to another on biological and demographic characteristics of the population;

(p) The changing structure, functions and dynamics of the family as an institution, including the changing roles of men and women, attitudes towards and opportunities for women's education and employment; the implications of current and future population trends for the status of women; biomedical research on male and female fertility, and the economic, social and demographic benefits to be derived from the integration of women in the development process;

(q) Development of social indicators, reflecting the quality of life as well as the interrelations between socio-economic and demographic phenomena, should be encouraged. Emphasis should also be given to the development of socio-economic and demographic models.

79. National research requirements and needs must be determined by Governments and national institutions. However, high priority should be given, wherever possible, to research that has wide relevance and international applicability.

80. National and regional research institutions dealing with population and related questions should be assisted and expanded as appropriate. Special efforts should be made to co-ordinate the research of those institutions by facilitating the exchange of their research findings and the exchange of information on their planned and ongoing research projects.

(c) *Management, training, education and information*

81. There is a particular need for the development of management in all fields related to population, with national and international attention and appropriate support given to programmes dealing with its promotion.

82. A dual approach to training is recommended: an international programme for training in population matters concomitant with national and regional training programmes adapted and made particularly relevant to conditions in the countries and regions of the trainees. While recognizing the complementarity of these two approaches, national and regional training should be given the higher priority.

83. Training in population dynamics and policies, whether national, regional or international, should, in so far as possible, be interdisciplinary in nature. The training of population specialists should always be accompanied by relevant career development for the trainees in their fields of specialization. Training should deal not only with population variables but also with inter-relationships of these variables with economic, social and political variables.

84. Training in the various aspects of population activities, including the management of population programmes should not be restricted to the higher levels of specialization but should also be extended to personnel at other levels, and, where needed, to medical, paramedical and traditional health personnel, and population programme administrators. Such training should impart an adequate knowledge of human rights in accordance with international standards and an awareness of the human rights aspect of population problems.

85. Training in population matters should be extended to labour, community and other social leaders, and to senior government officials, with a view to enabling them better to identify the population problems of their countries and communities and to help in the formulation of policies relating to them.

86. Owing to the role of education in the progress of individuals and society and the impact of education on demographic behaviour, all countries are urged to further develop their formal and informal educational programmes; efforts should be made to eradicate illiteracy, to promote education among the youth and abolish factors discriminating against women.

87. Educational institutions in all countries should be encouraged to expand their curricula to include a study of population dynamics and policies, including, where appropriate, family life, responsible parenthood and the relation of population dynamics to socio-economic development and to international relations. Governments are urged to co-operate in developing a world-wide system of international, regional and national institutions to meet the need for trained manpower. Assistance to the less developed countries should include, as appropriate, the improvement of the educational infrastructure such as library facilities and computer services.

88. Governments are invited to use all available means for disseminating population information.

89. Governments are invited to consider the distribution of population information to enlighten both rural and urban populations, through the assistance of governmental agencies.

90. Voluntary organizations should be encouraged, within the framework of national laws, policies and regulations, to play an important role in disseminating population information and ensuring wider participation in population programmes, and to share experiences regarding the implementation of population measures and programmes.

91. International organizations, both governmental and non-governmental, should strengthen their efforts to distribute information on population and related matters, particularly through periodic publications on the world population situation, prospects and policies, the utilization of audio-visual and other aids to communication, the publication of non-technical digests and reports, and the production and wide distribution of newsletters on population activities. Consideration should also be given to strengthening the publication of international professional journals and reviews in the field of population.

92. In order to achieve the widest possible dissemination of research results, translation activities should be encouraged at both the national and international levels. In this respect, the revision of the *Multilingual Demographic Dictionary* [1] and its publication in additional languages are strongly recommended.

93. The information and experience resulting from the World Population Conference and the World Population Year relating to the scientific study of population and the elaboration of population policies should be synthesized and disseminated by the United Nations.

(d) *Development and evaluation of population policies*

94. Where population policies or programmes have been adopted, systematic and periodic evaluations of their effectiveness should be made with a view to their improvement.

95. Population measures and programmes should be integrated into comprehensive social and economic plans and programmes and this integration should be reflected in the goals, instrumentalities and organizations for planning within the countries. In general, it is suggested that a unit dealing with population aspects be created and placed at a high level of the national administrative structure and that such a unit be staffed with qualified persons from the relevant disciplines.

---

[1] United Nations publication, Sales No. 58.XIII.4.

D. Recommendations for Implementation

Role of National Governments

96. The success of this Plan of Action will largely depend on the actions undertaken by national Governments. To take action, Governments are urged to utilize fully the support of intergovernmental and non-governmental organizations.

97. This Plan of Action recognizes the responsibility of each Government to decide on its own policies and devise its own programmes of action for dealing with the problems of population and economic and social progress. Recommendations, in so far as they relate to national Governments, are made with due regard to the need for variety and flexibility in the hope that they may be responsive to major needs in the population field as perceived and interpreted by national Governments. However, national policies should be formulated and implemented without violating, and with due promotion of, universally accepted standards of human rights.

98. An important role of Governments with regard to this Plan of Action is to determine and assess the population problems and needs of their countries in the light of their political, social, cultural, religious and economic conditions; such an undertaking should be carried out systematically and periodically so as to promote informed, rational and dynamic decision-making in matters of population and development.

99. The effect of national action or inaction in the fields of population may, in certain circumstances, extend beyond national boundaries; such international implications are particularly evident with regard to aspects of morbidity, population concentration and international migration, but may also apply to other aspects of population concern.

2. Role of international co-operation

100. International co-operation, based on the peaceful coexistence of States having different social systems, should play a supportive role in achieving the goals of the Plan of Action. This supportive role could take the form of direct assistance, technical or financial, in response to national and regional requests and be additional to economic development assistance, or the form of other activities, such as monitoring progress, undertaking comparative research in the area of population, resources and consumption, and furthering the exchange among countries of information and policy experiences in the field of population and consumption. Assistance should be provided on the basis of respect for sovereignty of the recipient country and its national policy.

101. The General Assembly of the United Nations, the Economic and Social Council, the Governing Council of the United Nations Development Programme/United Nations Fund for Population Activities and other competent legislative and policy-making bodies of the specialized agencies and the various intergovernmental organizations are urged to give careful consideration to this Plan of Action and to ensure an appropriate response to it.

102. Countries sharing similar population conditions and problems are invited to consider jointly this Plain of Action, exchange experience in relevant fields and elaborate those aspects of the Plan that are of particular relevance to them. The United Nations regional economic commissions and other regional bodies of the United Nations system should play an important role towards this end.

103. There is a special need for training in the field of population. The United Nations system, Governments and, as appropriate, non-governmental organizations are urged to give recognition to that need and priority to the measures necessary to meet it, including information, education and services for family planning.

104. Developed countries, and other countries able to assist, are urged to increase their assistance to developing countries in accordance with the goals of the Second United Nations Development Decade and, together with international organizations, make that assistance available in accordance with the national priorities of receiving countries. In this respect, it is recognized, in view of the magnitude of the problems and the consequent national requirements for funds, that considerable expansion of international assistance in the population field is required for the proper implementation of this Plan of Action.

105. It is suggested that the expanding, but still insufficient, international assistance in population and development matters requires increased co-operation; the United Nations Fund for Population Activities is urged, in co-operation with all organizations responsible for international population assistance, to produce a guide for international assistance in population matters which would be made available to recipient countries and institutions and be revised periodically.

106. International non-governmental organizations are urged to respond to the goals and policies of this Plan of Action by co-ordinating their activities with those of other non-governmental organizations, and with those of relevant bilateral and multilateral organizations, by expanding their support for national institutions and organizations dealing with population questions, and by co-operating in the promotion of widespread knowledge of the goals and policies of the Plan of Action, and, when requested, by supporting national and private institutions and organizations dealing with population questions.

3. Monitoring, review and appraisal

107. It is recommended that monitoring of population trends and policies discussed in this Plan of Action should be undertaken continuously as a specialized activity of the United Nations and reviewed biennially by the appropriate bodies of the United Nations system, beginning in 1977. Because of the shortness of the intervals, such monitoring would necessarily have to be selective with regard to its informational content and should focus mainly on new and emerging population trends and policies.

108. A comprehensive and thorough review and appraisal of progress made towards achieving the goals and recommendations of this Plan of Action should be undertaken every five years by the United Nations system. For this purpose the Secretary-General is invited to make appropriate arrangements taking account of the existing structure and resources of the United Nations system, and in co-operation with Governments. It is suggested that the first such review be made in 1979 and be repeated each five years thereafter. The findings of such systematic evaluations should be considered by the Economic and Social Council with the object of making, whenever necessary, appropriate modifications of the goals and recommendations of this Plan.

109. It is urged that both the monitoring and the review and appraisal activities of this Plan of Action be closely co-ordinated with those of the International Development Strategy for the Second United Nations Development Decade and any new international development strategy that might be formulated.

Appendix 2

NSSM 200 Study Report Text.

Parts One and Two
(main body of the report).

Appendix 2

NSSM 200:

IMPLICATIONS OF WORLDWIDE POPULATION GROWTH
FOR U.S. SECURITY AND OVERSEAS INTERESTS

December 10, 1974

CLASSIFIED BY Harry C. Blaney, III
SUBJECT TO GENERAL DECLASSIFICATION SCHEDULE OF
EXECUTIVE ORDER 11652 AUTOMATICALLY DOWN-
GRADED AT TWO YEAR INTERVALS AND DECLASSIFIED
ON DECEMBER 31, 1980.

This document can only be declassified by the White House.

Declassified/Released on ___7/3/89___
under provisions of E.O. 12356
by F. Graboske, National Security Council

TABLE OF CONTENTS

Executive Summary   (see pages 65-82)

Part One—Analytical Section
Chapter I World Demographic Trends   437-454
Chapter II Population and World Food Supplies   455-461
Chapter III Minerals and Fuel   461-471
Chapter IV Economic Development and
        Population Growth   471-478
Chapter V Implications of Population Pressures for
            National Security   479-490
Chapter VI World Population Conference   491-498

Part Two—Policy Recommendations
Section I A U.S. Global Population Strategy   499-512
Section II Action to Create Conditions for Fertility
            Decline: Population and a Development
            Assistance Strategy   512
A. General Strategy and Resource for A.I.D. Assistance   512-521
B. Functional Assistance Programs to Create
    Conditions for Fertility Decline   521-536
C.   Food for Peace Program and Population   536-538
Section III International Organizations and other
            Multilateral Population Programs   538
A.   UN Organization and Specialized Agencies   539-540
B.   Encouraging Private Organizations   540-541
Section IV   Provision and Development of Family
            Planning Services, Information and
            Technology   541
A. Research to Improve Fertility Control Technology   541-544
B. Development of Low-Cost Delivery Systems   545-552
C. Utilization of Mass Media and Satellite Communi-
    cations System for Family Planning   552-556
Section V Action to Develop Worldwide Political and   556-558
            Popular Commitment to Population Stability

PART ONE. ANALYTICAL SECTION

CHAPTER I - WORLD DEMOGRAPHIC TRENDS

INTRODUCTION

The present world population growth is unique. Rates of increase are much higher than in earlier centuries, they are more widespread, and have a greater effect on economic life, social justice, and—quite likely—on public order and political stability. The significance of population growth is enhanced because it comes at a time when the absolute size and rate of increase of the global economy, need for agricultural land, demand for and consumption of resources including water, production of wastes and pollution have also escalated to historically unique levels. Factors that only a short time ago were considered separately now have interlocking relationships, inter-dependence in a literal sense. The changes are not only quantitatively greater than in the past but qualitatively different. The growing burden is not only on resources but on administrative and social institutions as well.

Population growth is, of course, only one of the important factors in this new, highly integrated tangle of relationships. However, it differs from the others because it is a determinant of the demand sector while others relate to output and supply. (Population growth also contributes to supply through provision of manpower; in most developing countries, however, the problem is not a lack of but a surfeit of hands.) It is, therefore, most pervasive, affecting what needs to be done in regard to other factors. Whether other problems can be solved depends, in varying degrees, on the extent to which rapid population growth and other population variables can be brought under control.

HIGHLIGHTS OF CURRENT DEMOGRAPHIC TRENDS

Since 1950, world population has been undergoing unprecedented growth. This growth has four prominent features:
1. It is unique, far more rapid than ever in history.
2. It is much more rapid in less developed than in developed regions.
3. Concentration in towns and cities is increasing much more rapidly than overall population growth and is far more rapid in LDCs than in developed countries.
4. It has a tremendous built-in momentum that will inexorably double populations of most less developed countries by 2000 and will treble or quadruple their populations before leveling off—unless far greater efforts at fertility control are made than are being made.

    Therefore, if a country wants to influence its total numbers through population policy, it must act in the immediate future in order to make a substantial difference in the long run.

For most of man's history, world population grew very slowly. At the rate of growth estimated for the first 18 centuries A.D., it required more than 1,000 years for world population to double in size. With the beginnings of the industrial revolution and of modern medicine and sanitation over two hundred years ago, population growth rates began to accelerate. At the current growth rate (1.9 percent) world population will double in 37 years.
    -   By about 1830, world population reached 1 billion. The second billion was added in about 100 years by 1930. The third billion in 30 years by 1960. The fourth will be reached in 1975.
    -   Between 1750-1800 less than 4 million were being added, on the average, to the earth's population each year. Between 1850-1900, it was close to 8 million. By 1950 it had grown to 40 million. By 1975 it will be about 80 million.

In the developed countries of Europe, growth rates in the last century rarely exceeded 1.0-1.2 percent per year, almost never 1.5 percent. Death rates were much higher than in most LDCs today.

In North America where growth rates were higher, immigration made a significant contribution. In nearly every country of Europe, growth rates are now below 1 percent, in many below 0.5 percent. The natural growth rate (births minus deaths) in the United States is less than 0.6 percent. Including immigration (the world's highest) it is less than 0.7 percent.

In less developed countries growth rates average about 2.4 percent. For the People's Republic of China, with a massive, enforced birth control program, the growth rate is estimated at under 2 percent. India's is variously estimated from 2.2 percent, Brazil at 2.8 percent, Mexico at 3.4 percent, and Latin America at about 2.9 percent. African countries, with high birth as well as high death rates, average 2.6 percent; this growth rate will increase as death rates go down.

The world's population is _now_ about 3.9 billion; 1.1 billion in the developed countries (30 percent) and 2.8 billion in the less developed countries (70 percent).

In 1950, only 28 percent of the world's population or 692 million, lived in urban localities. Between 1950 and 1970, urban population expanded at a rate twice as rapid as the rate of growth of total population. In 1970, urban population increased to 36 percent of world total and numbered 1.3 billion. By 2000, according to the UN's medium variant projection, 3.2 billion (about half of the total) of world inhabitants will live in cities and towns.

In developed countries, the urban population varies from 45 to 85 percent; in LDCs, it varies from close to zero in some African states to nearly 100 percent in Hong Kong and Singapore.

In LDCs, urban population is projected to _more than triple_ in the remainder of this century, from 622 million in 1970 to 2,087 in 2000. Its proportion in total LDC population will thus increase from 25 percent in 1970 to 41 percent in 2000. This implies that by the end of this century LDCs will reach half the level of urbanization projected for DCs (82 percent) (See Appendix Table 1).

The enormous built-in _momentum_ of population growth in the less developed countries (and to a degree in the developed countries) is, if possible, even more important and ominous than current population size and rates of growth. Unlike a conventional explosion, population growth provides a continuing chain reaction. This momentum springs from (1) high fertility levels of LDC populations and (2) the very high percentage of maturing young people in populations. The typical developed country, Sweden for example, may have 25% of the population under 15 years of age. The typical developing country has 41% to 45% or its population under 15. This means that a tremendous number of future parents, compared to existing parents, are already born. Even if they have fewer children per family than their parents, the increase in population will be very great.

Three projections (not predictions), based on three different assumptions concerning fertility, will illustrate the generative effect of this building momentum.

a. Present fertility continued: If present fertility rates were to remain constant, the 1974 population 3.9 billion would increase to 7.8 billion by the hear 2000 and rise to a theoretical 103 billion by 2075.

b. U.N. "Medium Variant": If present birth rates in the developing countries, averaging about 38/1000 were further reduced to 29/1000 by 2000, the world's population in 2000 would be 6.4 billion, with over 100 million being added each year. At the time stability (non-growth) is reached in about 2100, world population would exceed 12.0 billion.

c. Replacement Fertility by 2000: If replacement levels of fertility were reached by 2000, the world's population in 2000 would be 5.9 billion and at the time of stability, about 2075, would be 8.4 billion. ("Replacement level" of fertility is not zero population growth. It is the level of fertility when couples are limiting their families to an average of about two children. For most countries, where there are high percentages of young people, even the attainment of replacement levels of fertility means that the population will continue to grow for additional 50-60 years to much higher numbers before leveling off.)

It is reasonable to assume that projection (a) is unreal since significant efforts are already being made to slow population growth and because even the most extreme pro-natalists do not argue that the earth could or should support 103 billion people. Famine, pestilence, war, or birth control will stop population growth far short of this figure.

The U.N. medium variant (projection (b)) has been described in a publication of the U.N. Population Division as "a synthesis of the results of efforts by demographers of the various countries and the

U.N. Secretariat to formulate realistic assumptions with regard to future trends, in view of information about present conditions and past experiences." Although by no means infallible, these projections provide plausible working numbers and are used by U.N. agencies (e.g., FAO, ILO) for their specialized analyses. One major shortcoming of most projections, however, is that "information about present conditions" quoted above is not quite up-to-date. Even in the United States, refined fertility and mortality rates become available only after a delay of several years.

Thus, it is possible that the rate of world population growth has actually fallen below (or for that matter increased from) that assumed under the U.N. medium variant. A number of less developed countries with rising living levels (particularly with increasing equality of income) and efficient family planning programs have experienced marked declines in fertility. Where access to family planning services has been restricted, fertility levels can be expected to show little change.

It is certain that fertility rates have already fallen significantly in Hong King, Singapore, Taiwan, Fiji, South Korea, Barbados, Chile, Costa Rica, Trinidad and Tobago, and Mauritius (See Table 1). Moderate declines have also been registered in West Malaysia, Sri Lanka, and Egypt. Steady increases in the number of acceptors at family planning facilities indicate a likelihood of some fertility reduction in Thailand, Indonesia, the Philippines, Colombia, and other countries which have family planning programs. On the other hand, there is little concrete evidence of significant fertility reduction in the populous countries of India, Bangladesh, Pakistan, etc.[1]

1   Of 82 countries for which crude birth rates are available for 1960 and 1972, 72—or 88 percent—experienced a decline in birth rates during this period. The 72 countries include 29 developed countries and 24 independent territories, including Hong Kong and Puerto Rico. The 19 sovereign LDCs include Mexico, Guatemala, El Salvador, Panama, Jamaica, Tunisia, Costa Rica, Chile, Fiji, Jauritius, Trinidad and Tobago, Singapore, Barbados, Taiwan, Egypt, Sri Lanka, Guyana, West Malaysia, and Algeria. (ISPC, US Bureau of the Census).

Table 1. Declines in Total Fertility Rates: Selected Years

Country	Year	Fertility level	Annual average fertility decline (Percent)
Hong Kong	1961	5,170	4.0
	1971	3,423	
Singapore	1960	5,078	6.4
	1970	3,088	
Taiwan	1960	5,750	3.6
	1970	4,000	
South Korea	1960	6,184	4.4
	1970	3,937	
West Malaysia	1960	5,955	1.6
	1970	5,051	
Sri Lanka	1960	5,496	2.4
	1970	4,414	
Barbados	1960	4,675	5.3
	1970	2,705	
Chile	1960	5,146	3.4
	1970	3,653	
Costa Rica	1960	7,355	3.9
	1970	4,950	
Trinadad & Tobago	1960	5,550	4.8
	1970	3,387	
Mauritius	1960	5,897	5.4
	1970	3,387	

Table 1. Declines in Total Fertility Rates: Selected Years (c			
Country	Year	Fertility level	Annual average fertility decline (Percent)
Egypt	1960	6,381	2.2
	1970	5,095	
Fiji	1960	5,503	5.4
	1970	3,841	

Source of basic data: ISPC, U.S. Bureau of the Census

Total Fertility Rate: Number of children a woman would have if she were to bear them at the prevailing rate in each five-year age group of woman's reporductive span (ages 15-19, 20-24...45-49). Rates in this table refer to number of children per 1,000 women.

Projection (c) is attainable if countries recognize the gravity of their population situation and make a serious effort to do something about it.

The differences in the size of total population projected under the three variants become substantial in a relatively short time.

By 1985, the medium variant projects some 342 million fewer people than the constant fertility variant and the replacement variant is 75 million lower than the medium variant.

By the year 2000 the difference between constant and medium fertility variants rises to 1.4 billion and between the medium and replacement variants, close to 500 million. By the year 2000, the span between the high and low series—some 1.9 billion—would amount to almost half the present world population.

Most importantly, perhaps, by 2075 the constant variant would have swamped the earth and the difference between the medium and replacement variants would amount to 3.7 billion. (Table 2.) The significance of the alternative variants is that they reflect the difference between a manageable situation and potential chaos with widespread starvation, disease, and disintegration for many countries.

Table 2. World Population Growth Under Different Assumptions Concerning Fertility: 1970-2075					
	Constant Fertility Variant		Medium Fertility Variant		Replacement Fertility Variant
	Millions	Growth*	Millions	Growth*	Millions	Growth*
1970	3,600	–	3,600	–	3,600	–
1985	5,200	2.4%	4,858	2.0%	4,783	1.8%
2000	7,800	2.8%	6,407	1.9%	5,923	1.4%
2075	103,000	3.4%	12,048	0.84%	8,357	0.46%

*Annual average growth rate since preceding date.

Furthermore, after replacement level fertility is reached, family size need not remain at an average of two children per family. Once this level is attained, it is possible that fertility will continue to decline below replacement level. This would hasten the time when a stationary population is reached and would increase the difference between the projection variants. The great momentum of population growth can be seen even more clearly in the case of a single country—for example, Mexico. Its 1970 population was 50 million. If its 1965-1970 fertility were to continue, Mexico's population in 2070 would theoretically number 2.2 billion. If its present average of 6.1 children per family could be reduced to an average of about 2 (replacement level fertility) by 1980-85, its population would continue to grow for about sixty years to 110 million. If the two-child average could be reached by 1990-95, the population would stabilize in sixty more years at about 22 percent higher—134 million. If the two-child average cannot be reached for 30 years (by 2000-05), the population at stabilization would grow by an additional 24 percent to 167 million.

Similar illustrations for other countries are given below.

Table 3. Projected Population Size Under Different Assumptions Concerning Fertility: 1970-2070

Country	Fertility assumption	Population in millions 1970	2000	2070	Ratio of 2070 to 1970 population
Venezuela	Constant fertility	11	31	420	38.2
	Replacement fertility by:				
	2000-05		22	34	3.1
	1990-95		20	27	
	1980-85		18	22	
Indonesia	Constant fertility	120	294	4,507	37.6
	Replacement fertility by:				
	2000-05		214	328	2.7
	1990-95		193	275	2.3
	1980-85		177	236	2.0
Morocco	Constant fertility	16	54	1,505	14.1
	Replacement fertility by:				
	2000-05		35	58	3.6
	1990-95		30	44	2.8
	1980-85		26	35	2.2

Source of basic data: ISPC, U.S. Bureau of the Census

As Table 3. indicates, alternative rates of fertility decline would have significant impact on the size of a country's population by 2000. They would make enormous differences in the sizes of the stabilized populations, attained some 60 to 70 years after replacement level fertility is reached. Therefore, it is of the utmost urgency that governments now recognize the facts and implications of population growth determining the ultimate population sizes that make sense for their countries and start vigorous programs at once to achieve their desired goals.

FUTURE GROWTH IN MAJOR REGIONS AND COUNTRIES
Throughout the projected period 1970 to 2000, less developed regions will grow more rapidly than developed regions. The rate of growth in LDCs will primarily depend upon the rapidity with which family planning practices are adopted.

Differences in the growth rates of DCs and LDCs will further aggravate the striking demographic imbalances between developed and less developed countries. Under the U.N. medium projection variant, by the year 2000 the population of less developed countries would double, rising from 2.5 billion in 1970 to 5.0 billion (Table 4). In contrast, the overall growth of the population of the developed world during the same period would amount to about 26 percent, increasing from 1.08 to 1.37 billion. Thus, by the year 2000 almost 80 percent of world population would reside in regions now considered less developed and over 90 percent of the annual increment to world population would occur there.

TABLE 4. TOTAL POPULATION, DISTRIBUTION, AND RATES OF GROWTH, by Major Region: 1970-2000
(UN "medium" projection variant)

Major Region and Country	Total Population					Growth	
	1970		1985	2000		1970-2000	
	Mil-lions	Per-cent	Mil-lions	Mil-lions	Per-cent	Mil-lions	Annual average rate
WORLD TOTAL	3,621	100.0	4,858	6,407	100.0	2,786	1.9%
DEVELOPED COUNTRIES	1,084	29.9	1,234	1,368	21.4	284	0.8%
Market economies	736	20.3	835	920	14.4	184	0.7%
US							
Japan							
Centrally planned economies							
USSR							
LESS DEVELOPED COUNTRIES	2,537	70.1	3,624	5,039	78.6	2,502	2.3%
Centrally planned economies*	794	21.9	1,007	1,201	18.7	407	1.4%
China							
Market economies	1,743	38.1	2,616	3,838	59.9	2,095	2.7%
East Asia	49	1.4	66	83	1.3	34	1.8%
South Asia	1,090	30.1	1,625	2,341	36.5	1,251	2.6%
Eastern South Asia	264	7.3	399	574	9.0	310	2.6%
Indonesia	120	3.3	177	250	3.9	130	2.5%
Middle South Asia	749	20.7	1,105	1,584	24.7	835	2.5%
Indian sub-continent**	691	19.1	1,016	1,449	22.6	758	2.5%
Western South Asia	77	2.1	121	183	2.9	106	2.9%

TABLE 4. TOTAL POPULATION, DISTRIBUTION, AND RATES OF GROWTH, by Major Region: 1970-2000
(UN "medium" projection variant)

Major Region and Country	Total Population					Growth	
	1970		1985	2000		1970-2000	
	Mil- lions	Per- cent	Mil- lions	Mil- lions	Per- cent	Mil- lions	Annual average rate
Africa	352	9.7	536	884	13.1	482	2.9%
Nigeria***	55	1.5	84	135	2.1	80	3.0%
Egypt	33	0.9	47	66	1.0	33	2.3%
Latin America	248	6.8	384	572	8.9	324	2.8%
Caribbean	26	0.7	36	48	0.8	22	2.2%
Central America	67	1.8	109	173	2.7	106	3.2%
Mexico	50	1.4	83	132	2.1	82	3.3%
Tropical S. America	155	4.3	239	351	5.5	196	2.8%
Brazil	95	2.6	145	212	3.3	117	2.7%
Colombia	22	0.6	35	51	0.8	29	2.9%
Oceania	4	0.1	6	9	0.1	5	2.6%

*   Centrally planned economies include PRChina, North Korea, North Vietnam and Mongolia

**   [National Archives photocopy not legible]

***   [National Archives photocopy not legible]

The paucity of reliable information on all Asian communist countries and the highly optimistic assumptions concerning China's fertility trends implicit in U.N. medium projections[1] argue for disaggregating the less developed countries into centrally planned economies and countries with market economies. Such disaggregation reflects more accurately the burden of rapidly growing populations in most LDCs.

As Table 4. shows, the population of countries with centrally planned economies, comprising about 1/3 of the 1970 LDC total, is projected to grow between 1970 and 2000 at a rate well below the LDC average of 2.3 percent. Over the entire thirty-year period, their growth rate averages 1.4 percent, in comparison with 2.7 percent for other LDCs. Between 1970 and 1985, the annual rate of growth in Asian communist LDCs is expected to average 1.6 percent and subsequently to decline to an average of 1.2 percent between 1985 and 2000. The growth rate of LDCs with market economies, on the other hand, remains practically the same, at 2.7 and 2.6 percent, respectively. Thus, barring both large-scale birth control efforts (greater than implied by the medium variant) or economic or political upheavals, the next twenty-five years offer non-communist LDCs little respite from the burdens of rapidly increasing humanity. Of course, some LDCs will be able to accommodate this increase with less difficulty than others.

Moreover, short of Draconian measures there is no possibility that any LDC can stabilize its population at less than double its present size. For many, stabilization will not be short of three times their present size.

NATO and Eastern Europe. In the west, only France and Greece have a policy of increasing population growth—which the people are successfully disregarding. (In a recent and significant change from traditional positions, however, the French Assembly overwhelmingly endorsed a law not only authorizing general availability of contraceptives but also providing that their cost be borne by the social security system.) Other western NATO members have

1   The size of the Chinese population, its age distribution and rate of growth are widely disputed, not only among western observers but apparently within China itself. Recent estimates vary from "over 700 million," a figure used consistently by PRChina's representatives to U.N. meetings, to 920 million estimated for mid-1974 by U.S. Department of Commerce, Bureau of Economic Analysis.

no policies.[1] Most provide some or substantial family planning services. All appear headed toward lower growth rates. In two NATO member countries (West Germany and Luxembourg), annual numbers of deaths already exceed births, yielding a negative natural growth rate.

Romania, Hungary, Bulgaria, and Czechoslovakia have active policies to increase their population growth rates—despite the reluctance of their people to have larger families. Within the USSR, fertility rates in RSFSR and the republics of Ukraine, Latvia, and Estonia are below replacement level. This situation has prevailed at least since 1969-1970 and, if continued, will eventually lead to negative population growth in these republics. In the United States, average fertility also fell below replacement level in the past two years (1972 and 1973). There is a striking difference, however, in the attitudes toward this demographic development in the two countries. While in the United States the possibility of a stabilized (non-growing) population is generally viewed with favor, in the USSR there is perceptible concern over the low fertility of Slavs and Balts (mostly by Slavs and Balts). The Soviet government, by all indications, is studying the feasibility of increasing their sagging birth rates. The entire matter of fertility-bolstering policies is circumscribed by the relatively high costs of increasing fertility (mainly through increased outlays for consumption goods and services) and the need to avoid the appearance of ethnic discrimination between rapidly and slowly growing nationalities.

U.N. medium projections to the year 2000 show no significant changes in the relative demographic position of the western alliance countries as against eastern Europe and the USSR. The population of the Warsaw Pact countries will remain at 65 percent of the populations of NATO member states. If Turkey is excluded, the Warsaw Pact proportion rises somewhat from 70 percent in 1970 to 73 percent by 2000. This change is not of an order of magnitude that in itself will have important implications for east-west power relations. (Future growth of manpower in NATO and Warsaw Pact nations has not been examined in this Memorandum.)

Of greater potential political and strategic significance are prospective changes in the populations of less developed regions both among themselves and in relation to developed countries.

---

1   Turkey has a policy of population control.

Africa. Assessment of future demographic trends in Africa is severely impeded by lack of reliable base data on the size, composition, fertility and mortality, and migration of much of the continent's population. With this important limitation in mind, the population of Africa is projected to increase from 352 million in 1970 to 834 million in 2000, an increase of almost 2.5 times. In most African countries, population growth rates are likely to increase appreciably before they begin to decline. Rapid population expansion may be particularly burdensome to the "least developed" among Africa's LDCs including—according to the U.N. classification—Ethiopia, Sudan, Tanzania, Uganda, Upper Volta, Mali, Malawi, Niger, Burundi, Guinea, Chad, Rwanda, Somalia, Dahomey, Lesotho, and Botswana. As a group, they numbered 104 million in 1970 and are projected to grow at an average rate of 3.0 percent a year, to some 250 million in 2000. This rate of growth is based on the assumption of significant reductions in mortality. It is questionable, however, whether economic and social conditions in the foreseeable future will permit reductions in mortality required to produce a 3 percent growth rate. Consequently, the population of the "least developed" of Africa's LDCs may fall short of the 250 million figure in 2000.

African countries endowed with rich oil and other natural resources may be in a better economic position to cope with population expansion. Nigeria falls into this category. Already the most populous country on the continent, with an estimated 55 million people in 1970 (see footnote to Table 4), Nigeria's population by the end of this century is projected to number 135 million. This suggests a growing political and strategic role for Nigeria, at least in Africa south of the Sahara.

In North Africa, Egypt's population of 33 million in 1970 is projected to double by 2000. The large and increasing size of Egypt's population is, and will remain for many years, an important consideration in the formulation of many foreign and domestic policies not only of Egypt but also of neighboring countries.

Latin America. Rapid population growth is projected for tropical South American which includes Brazil, Colombia, Peru, Venezuela, Ecuador and Bolivia. Brazil, with a current population of over 100 million, clearly dominates the continent demographically; by the end of this century, its population is projected to reach the 1974 U.S. level of about 212 million people. Rapid economic growth prospects—if they are not diminished by demographic over-growth—portend a growing power status for Brazil in Latin America and on the world scene over the next 25 years.

The Caribbean which includes a number of countries with promising family planning programs (Jamaica, Trinidad and Tobago, Cuba, Barbados and also Puerto Rico) is projected to grow at 2.2 percent a year between 1970 and 2000, a rate below the Latin American average of 2.8 percent.

Perhaps the most significant population trend from the view-point of the United States is the prospect that Mexico's population will increase from 50 million in 1970 to over 130 million by the year 2000. Even under most optimistic conditions, in which the country's average fertility falls to replacement level by 2000, Mexico's population is likely to exceed 100 million by the end of this century.

South Asia. Somewhat slower rates are expected for Eastern and Middle South Asia whose combined population of 1.03 billion in 1970 is projected to more than double by 2000 to 2.20 billion. In the face of continued rapid population growth (2.5 percent), the prospects for the populous Indian subregion, which already faces staggering economic problems, are particularly bleak. South and Southeast Asia's population will substantially increase relative to mainland China; it appears doubtful, however, that this will do much to enhance their relative power position and political influence in Asia. On the contrary, preoccupation with the growing internal economic and social problems resulting from huge population increases may progressively reduce the ability of the region, especially India, to play an effective regional and world power role.

Western South Asia, demographically dominated by Turkey and seven oil-rich states (including Saudi Arabia, Iraq, and Kuwait) is projected to be one of the fastest growing LDC regions, with an annual average growth rate of 2.9 percent between 1970 and 2000. Part of this growth will be due to immigration, as for example, into Kuwait.

The relatively low growth rate of 1.8 percent projected for East Asian LDCs with market economics reflects highly successful family planning programs in Taiwan, South Korea, and Hong Kong.

The People's Republic of China (PRC). The People's Republic of China has by far the world's largest population and, potentially, severe problems of population pressure, given its low standard of living and quite intensive utilization of available farm land resources. Its last census in 1953 recorded a population of 583 million, and PRC officials have cited a figure as high as 830 million for 1970. The Commerce Department's Bureau of Economic Analysis projects a slightly higher population, reaching 920 million by 1974. The present population growth rate is about two percent.

Conclusion

Rapid population growth in less developed countries has been mounting in a social milieu of poverty, unemployment and underemployment, low educational attainment, widespread malnutrition, and increasing costs of food production. These countries have accumulated a formidable "backlog" of unfinished tasks. They include economic assimilation of some 40 percent of their people who are pressing at, but largely remain outside the periphery of the developing economy; the amelioration of generally low levels of living; and in addition, accommodation of annually larger increments to the population. The accomplishment of these tasks could be intolerably slow if the average annual growth rate in the remainder of this century does not slow down to well below the 2.7 percent projected, under the medium variant, for LDCs with market economics. How rapid population growth impedes social and economic progress is discussed in subsequent chapters.

Appendix Table 1

Projected Growth of Urban Population Selected Years 1965-2000(U.N. Medium Variant)

Year	World Population			DC Population			LDC Population		
	Total (millions)	Urban (millions)	Percent urban	Total (millions)	Urban (millions)	Percent urban	Total (millions)	Urban (millions)	Percent urban
1965	3,289	1,158	35.2	1,037	651	62.8	2,252	507	22.5
1970	3,621	1,315	36.3	1,084	693	63.9	2,537	622	24.5
1980	4,401	1,791	40.7	1,183	830	70.2	3,2'3	961	29.9
1990	5,346	2,419	45.3	1,282	977	76.2	4,064	1,443	35.5
2000	6,407	3,205	50.0	1,368	1,118	81.8	5,039	2,087	41.4

Note: The 'urban' population has been estimated in accordance with diverse national definitions of that term.

Rates of Growth of Urban and Rural Populations, 1970-2000 (U.N. Medium Variant)

	World Population			DC Population			LDC Population		
	Total	Urban	Rural	Total	Urban	Rural	Total	Urban	Rural
1970-2000 Total growth (percent)	76.9	143.7	38.8	26.2	61.3	-36.1	98.6	235.5	54.2
Annual average growth (percent)	1.9	3.0	1.1	0.8	1.6	-1.5	2.3	4.1	1.5

CHAPTER II. POPULATION AND WORLD FOOD SUPPLIES

Rapid population growth and lagging food production in developing countries, together with the sharp deterioration in the global food situation in 1972 and 1973, have raised serious concerns about the ability of the world to feed itself adequately over the next quarter century and beyond.

As a result of population growth, and to some extent also of increasing affluence, world food demand has been growing at unprecedented rates. In 1900, the annual increase in world demand for cereals was about 4 million tons. By 1950, it had risen to about 12 million tons per year. By 1970, the annual increase in demand was 30 million tons (on a base of over 1,200 million tons). This is roughly equivalent to the annual wheat crop of Canada, Australia, and Argentina combined. This annual increase in food demand is made up of a 2% annual increase in population and a 0.5% increased demand per capita. Part of the rising per capita demand reflects improvement in diets of some of the peoples of the developing countries. In the less developed countries about 400 pounds of grain is available per person per year and is mostly eaten as cereal. The average North American, however, uses nearly a ton of grain a year, only 200 pounds directly and the rest in the form of meat, milk, and eggs for which several pounds of cereal are required to produce one pound of the animal product (e.g., five pounds of grain to produce one pound of beef).

During the past two decades, LDCs have been able to keep food production ahead of population, notwithstanding the unprecedentedly high rates of population growth. The basic figures are summarized in the following table: [calculated from data in USDA, The World Agricultural Situation, March 1974]:

INDICES OF WORLD POPULATION AND FOOD PRODUCTION
(excluding Peoples Republic of China)
1954=100

	WORLD			DEVELOPED COUNTRIES			LESS DEVELOPED COUNTRIES		
		Food production			Food production			Food production	
	Popu-lation	Total	Per Capita	Popu-lation	Total	Per Capita	Popu-lation	Total	Per Capita
1954	100	100	100	100	100	100	100	100	100
1973	144	170	119	124	170	138	159	171	107
Compound Annual Increase (%)									
	1.9	2.8	0.9	1.1	2.8	1.7	2.5	2.9	0.4

It will be noted that the relative gain in LDC total food production was just as great as for advanced countries, but was far less on a per capita basis because of the sharp difference in population growth rates. Moreover, within the LDC group were 24 countries (including Indonesia, Nigeria, the Philippines, Zaire, Algeria, Guyana, Iraq, and Chile) in which the rate of increase of population growth exceeded the rate of increase in food production; and a much more populous group (including India, Pakistan, and Bangladesh) in which the rate of increase in production barely exceeded population growth but did not keep up with the increase in domestic demand. [World Food Conference, Preliminary Assessment, 8 May 1974; U.N. Document E/CONF. 65/PREP/6, p. 33.]

General requirements have been projected for the years 1985 and 2000, based on the UN Medium Variant population estimates and allowing for a very small improvement in diets in the LDCs.

A recent projection made by the Department of Agriculture indicates a potential productive capacity more than adequate to meet world cereal requirements (the staple food of the world) of a population of 6.4 billion in the year 2000 (medium fertility variant) at roughly current relative prices.

This overall picture offers little cause for complacency when broken down by geographic regions. To support only a very modest improvement in current cereal consumption levels (from 177 kilograms per capita in 1970 to 200-206 kilograms in 2000) the projections show an alarming increase in LDC dependency on imports. Such imports are projected to rise from 21.4 million tons in 1970 to 102-122 million tons by the end of the century. Cereal imports would increase to 13-15 percent of total developing country consumption as against 8 percent in 1970. As a group, the advanced countries cannot only meet their own needs but will also generate a substantial surplus. For the LDCs, analyses of food production capacity foresee the physical possibility of meeting their needs, provided that (a) weather conditions are normal, (b) yields per unit of area continue to improve at the rates of the last decade, bringing the average by 1985 close to present yields in the advanced countries, and (c) a substantially larger annual transfer of grains can be arranged from the surplus countries (mainly North America), either through commercial sales or through continuous and growing food aid. The estimates of production capacity do not rely on major new technical breakthroughs in food production methods, but they do require the availability and application of greatly increased quantities of fertilizers, pesticides, irrigation water, and other inputs to modernized agriculture, together with continued technological advances at past rates and the institutional and administrative reforms (including vastly expanded research and extension services) essential to the successful application of these inputs. They also assume normal weather conditions. Substantial political will is required in the LDCs to give the necessary priority to food production.

There is great uncertainty whether the conditions for achieving food balance in the LDCs can in fact be realized. Climatic changes are poorly understood, but a persistent atmospheric cooling trend since 1940 has been established. One respectable body of scientific opinion believes that this portends a period of much wider annual frosts, and possibly a long-term lowering of rainfall in the monsoon areas of Asia and Africa. Nitrogen fertilizer will be in world short supply into the late 1970s, at least; because of higher energy prices, it may also be more costly in real terms than in the 1960s. Capital investments for irrigation and infrastructure and the organizational requirements for securing continuous improvements in agricultural yields may well be beyond the financial and administrative capacity of many LDCs. For some of the areas under heaviest population pressure, there is little or no prospect for foreign exchange earnings to cover constantly increasing imports of food.

While it is always unwise to project the recent past into the long-term future, the experience of 1972-73 is very sobering. The coincidence of adverse weather in many regions in 1972 brought per capita production in the LDCs back to the level of the early 1960s. At the same time, world food reserves (mainly American) were almost exhausted, and they were not rebuilt during the high production year of 1973. A repetition under these conditions of 1972 weather patterns would result in large-scale famine of a kind not experienced for several decades—a kind the world thought had been permanently banished.

Even if massive famine can be averted, the most optimistic forecasts of food production potential in the more populous LDCs show little improvement in the presently inadequate levels and quality of nutrition. As long as annual population growth continues at 2 to 3 percent or more, LDCs must make expanded food production the top development priority, even though it may absorb a large fraction of available capital and foreign exchange.

Moderation of population growth rates in the LDCs could make some difference to food requirements by 1985, a substantial difference by 2000, and a vast difference in the early part of the next century. From the viewpoint of U.S. interests, such reductions in LDC food needs would be clearly advantageous. They would not reduce American commercial markets for food since the reduction in LDC food requirements that would result from slowing population growth would affect only requests for concessional or grant food assistance, not commercial sales. They would improve the prospects for maintaining adequate world food reserves against climatic emergencies. They would reduce the likelihood of periodic famines in region after region, accompanied by food riots and chronic social and political instability. They would improve the possibilities for long-term development and integration into a peaceful world order.

Even taking the most optimistic view of the theoretical possibilities of producing enough foods in the developed countries to meet the requirements of the developing countries, the problem of increased costs to the LDCs is already extremely serious and in its future may be insurmountable. At <u>current</u> prices the anticipated import requirements of 102-122 million tons by 2000 would raise the cost of developing countries' imports of cereals to $16-20[1] billion by that year compared with $2.5 billion in 1970. Large as they may seem even these estimates of import requirements could be on the low side if the developing countries are unable to achieve the Department of Agriculture's assumed increase in the rate of growth of production.

The FAO in its recent "Preliminary Assessment of the World Food Situation Present and Future" has reached a similar conclusion:

What is certain is the enormity of the food import bill which might face the developing countries . . . In addition [to cereals] the developing countries . . . would be importing substantial amounts of other foodstuffs. clearly the financing of international food trade on this scale would raise very grave problems.

At least three-quarters of the projected increase in cereal imports of developing countries would fall in the poorer countries of South Asia and North and Central Africa. The situation in Latin America which is projected to shift from a modest surplus to a modest deficit area is quite different. Most of this deficit will be in Mexico and Central America, with relatively high income and easily exploitable transportation links to the U.S.

The problem in Latin America, therefore, appears relatively more manageable.

It seems highly unlikely, however, that the poorer countries of Asia and Africa will be able to finance nearly like the level of import requirements projected by the USDA. Few of them have dynamic export-oriented industrial sectors like Taiwan or South Korea or rich raw material resources that will generate export earnings fast enough to keep pace with food import needs. Accordingly, those countries where large-scale hunger and malnutrition are already present face the bleak prospect of little, if any, improvement in the food intake in the years ahead barring a major foreign financial food aid program, more rapid expansion of domestic food production, reduced population growth or some combination of all three. Worse yet, a series of crop disasters could transform some of them into classic Malthusian cases with famines involving millions of people.

1   At $160.00 per ton.

While foreign assistance probably will continue to be forthcoming to meet short-term emergency situations like the threat of mass starvation, it is more questionable whether aid donor countries will be prepared to provide the sort of massive food aid called for by the import projections on a long-term continuing basis.

Reduced population growth rates clearly could bring significant relief over the longer term. Some analysts maintain that for the post-1985 period a rapid decline in fertility will be crucial to adequate diets worldwide. If, as noted before, fertility in the developing countries could be made to decline to the replacement level by the year 2000, the world's population in that year would be 5.9 billion or 500 million below the level that would be attained if the UN medium projection were followed. Nearly all of the decline would be in the LDCs. With such a reduction the projected import gap of 102-122 million tons per year could be eliminated while still permitting a modest improvement in per capita consumption. While such a rapid reduction in fertility rates in the next 30 years is an optimistic target, it is thought by some experts that it could be obtained by intensified efforts if its necessity were understood by world and national leaders. Even more modest reductions could have significant implications by 2000 and even more over time.

Intensive programs to increase food production in developing countries beyond the levels assumed in the U.S.D.A. projections probably offer the best prospect for some reasonably early relief, although this poses major technical and organizational difficulties and will involve substantial costs. It must be realized, however, that this will be difficult in all countries and probably impossible in some—or many. Even with the introduction of new inputs and techniques it has not been possible to increase agricultural output by as much as 3 percent per annum in many of the poorer developing countries. Population growth in a number of these countries exceeds that rate.

Such a program of increased food production would require the widespread use of improved seed varieties, increased applications of chemical fertilizers and pesticides over vast areas and better farm management along with bringing new land under cultivation. It has been estimated, for example, that with better varieties, pest control, and the application of fertilizer on the Japanese scale, Indian rice yields could theoretically at least, be raised two and one-half times current levels. Here again very substantial foreign assistance for imported materials may be required for at least the early years before the program begins to take hold.

The problem is clear. The solutions, or at least the directions we must travel to reach them are also generally agreed. What will be required is a genuine commitment to a set of policies that will lead the international community, both developed and developing countries, to the achievement of the objectives spelled out above.

CHAPTER III - MINERALS AND FUEL

Population growth per se is not likely to impose serious constraints on the global physical availability of fuel and non-fuel minerals to the end of the century and beyond.

This favorable outlook on reserves does not rule out shortage situations for specific minerals at particular times and places. Careful planning with continued scientific and technological progress (including the development of substitutes) should keep the problems of physical availability within manageable proportions.

The major factor influencing the demand for non-agricultural raw materials is the level of industrial activity, regional and global. For example, the U.S., with 6% of the world's population, consumes about a third of its resources. The demand for raw materials, unlike food, is not a direct function of population growth. The current scarcities and high prices for most such materials result mainly from the boom conditions in all industrialized regions in the years 1972-73.

The important potential linkage between rapid population growth and minerals availability is indirect rather than direct. It flows from the negative effects of excessive population growth in economic development and social progress, and therefore on internal stability, in overcrowded under-developed countries. The United States has become increasingly dependent on mineral imports from developing countries in recent decades, and this trend is likely to continue. The location of known reserves of higher-grade ores of most minerals favors increasing dependence of all industrialized regions on imports from less developed countries. The real problems of mineral supplies lie, not in basic physical sufficiency, but in the politico-economic issues of access, terms for exploration and exploitation, and division of the benefits among producers, consumers, and host country governments.

In the extreme cases where population pressures lead to endemic famine, food riots, and breakdown of social order, those conditions are scarcely conducive to systematic exploration for mineral deposits or the long-term investments required for their exploitation. Short of famine, unless some minimum of popular aspirations for material improvement can be satisfied, and unless the terms of access and exploitation persuade governments and peoples that this aspect of the international economic order has "something in it for them," concessions to foreign companies are likely to be expropriated or subjected to arbitrary intervention. Whether through government action, labor conflicts, sabotage, or civil disturbance, the smooth flow of needed materials will be jeopardized. Although population pressure is obviously not the only factor involved, these types of frustrations are much less likely under conditions of slow or zero population growth.

Reserves.

Projections made by the Department of Interior through the year 2000 for those fuel and non-fuel minerals on which the U.S. depends heavily for imports[1] support these conclusions on physical resources (see Annex). Proven reserves of many of these minerals appear to be more than adequate to meet the estimated accumulated world demand at 1972 relative prices at least to the end of the century. While petroleum (including natural gas), copper, zinc, and tin are probable exceptions, the extension of economically exploitable reserves as a result of higher prices, as well as substitution and secondary recovery for metals, should avoid long-term supply restrictions. In many cases, the price increases that have taken place since 1972 should be more than sufficient to bring about the necessary extension of reserves.

These conclusions are consistent with a much more extensive study made in 1972 for the Commission on Population Growth and the American Future.[2]

As regards fossil fuels, that study foresees adequate world reserves for at least the next quarter to half century even without

1   Aluminum, copper, iron ore, lead, nickel, tin, uranium, zinc, and petroleum (including natural gas).
2   Population, Resources and the Environment edited by Ronald Ridker, Vol. III of the Commission Research Report.

major technological breakthroughs. U.S. reserves of coal and oil shale are adequate well into the next century, although their full exploitation may be limited by environmental and water supply factors. Estimates of the U.S. Geological Survey suggest recoverable oil and gas reserves (assuming sufficiently high prices) to meet domestic demand for another two or three decades, but there is also respectable expert opinion supporting much lower estimates; present oil production is below the peak of 1970 and meets only 70 percent of current demands.[1] Nevertheless, the U.S. is in a relatively strong position on fossil fuels compared with the rest of the industrialized world, provided that it takes the time and makes the heavy investments needed to develop domestic alternatives to foreign sources.

In the case of the 19 non-fuel minerals studied by the Commission it was concluded there were sufficient proven reserves of nine to meet cumulative world needs at current relative prices through the year 2020.[2] For the ten others[3] world proven reserves were considered inadequate. However, it was judged that moderate price increases, recycling and substitution could bridge the estimated gap between supply and requirements.

The above projections probably understate the estimates of global resources. "Proved Reserves," that is known supplies that will be available at present or slightly higher relative costs 10 to 25 years from now, rarely exceed 25 years' cumulative requirements, because industry generally is reluctant to undertake costly exploration to meet demands which may or may not materialize in the more distant future. Experience has shown that additional reserves are discovered as required, at least in the case of non-fuel minerals, and "proved reserves" have generally remained constant in relation to consumption.

The adequacy of reserves does not of course assure that supplies will be forthcoming in a steady stream as required. Intermediate problems may develop as a result of business miscalculations regarding the timing of expansion to meet requirements. With the

1   For a recent review of varying estimates on oil and gas reserves, see "Oil and Gas Resources," Science, 12 July 84, pp. 127-130 (Vol. 185).
2   Chromium, iron, nickel, vanadium, magnesium, phosphorous, pottassium, cobalt, and nitrogen.
3   Manganese, molybdenum, tungsten, aluminum, copper, lead, zinc, tin, titanium, and sulphur.

considerable lead time required for expanding capacity, this can result in periods of serious shortage for certain materials and rising prices as in the recent past. Similarly, from time to time there will be periods of overcapacity and falling prices. Necessary technical adjustments required for the shift to substitutes or increased recycling also may be delayed by the required lead time or by lack of information.

An early warning system designed to flag impending surpluses and shortages, could be very helpful in anticipating these problems. Such a mechanism might take the form of groups of experts working with the UN Division of Resources. Alternatively, intergovernmental commodity study groups might be set up for the purpose of monitoring those commodities identified as potential problem areas.

Adequate global availability of fuel and non-fuel minerals is not of much benefit to countries who cannot afford to pay for them. Oil supplies currently are adequate to cover world needs, but the quadrupling of prices in the past year has created grave financial and payment problems for developed and developing countries alike. If similar action to raise prices were undertaken by supplies of other important minerals, an already bad situation would be intensified. Success in such efforts is questionable, however; there is no case in which the quantities involved are remotely comparable to the cases of energy; and the scope for successful price-gouging or cartel tactics is much smaller.

Although the U.S. is relatively well off in this regard, it nonetheless depends heavily on mineral imports from a number of sources which are not completely safe or stable. It may therefore be necessary, especially in the light of our recent oil experience, to keep this dependence within bounds, in some cases by developing additional domestic resources and more generally by acquiring stockpiles for economic as well as national defense emergencies. There are also possible dangers of unreasonable prices promoted by producer cartels and broader policy questions of U.S. support for commodity agreements involving both producers and consumers. Such matters, however, are in the domain of commodity policy rather than population policy.

At least through the end of this century, changes in population growth trends will make little difference to total levels of requirements for fuel and other minerals. Those requirements are related much more closely to levels of income and industrial output, leaving the demand for minerals substantially unaffected. In the longer run, a lower ultimate world population (say 8 to 9 billion rather than 12 to 16 billion) would require a lower annual input of depletable resources directly affected by population size as well as a much lower volume of food, forest products, textiles, and other renewable resources.

Whatever may be done to guard against interruptions of supply and to develop domestic alternatives, the U.S. economy will require large and increasing amounts of minerals from abroad, especially from less developed countries.[1] That fact gives the U.S. enhanced interest in the political, economic, and social stability of the supplying countries. Wherever a lessening of population pressures through reduced birth rates can increase the prospects for such stability, population policy becomes relevant to resource supplies and to the economic interests of the United States.

ANNEX

OUTLOOK FOR RAW MATERIALS

I. Factors Affecting Raw Material Demand and Supply

Some of the key factors that must be considered in evaluating the future raw materials situation are the stage of a country's economic development and the responsiveness of the market to changes in the relative prices of the raw materials.

Economic theory indicates that the pattern of consumption of raw materials varies with the level of economic activity. Examination of the intensity-of-use of raw materials (incremental quantity of raw material needed to support an additional unit of GNP) show that after a particular level of GNP is reached, the intensity of use of raw materials starts to decline. Possible explanations for this decline are:

1. In industrialized countries, the services component of GNP expands relative to the non-services components as economic growth occurs.

---

1   See National Commission on Materials Policy, Towards a National Materials Policy: Basic Data and Issues, April 1972.

2. Technological progress, on the whole, tends to lower the intensity-of-use through greater efficiency in the use of raw materials and development of alloys.

3. Economic growth continues to be characterized by substitution of one material by another and substitution of synthetics for natural materials.[1]

Most developed countries have reached this point of declining intensity-of-use.[2] For other countries that have not reached this stage of economic development, their population usually goes through a stage of rapid growth prior to industrialization. This is due to the relative ease in the application of improved health care policies and the resulting decline in their death rates, while birth rates remain high. Then the country's economy does begin to industrialize and grow more rapidly, the initial rapid rise in industrial production results in an increasing intensity-of-use of raw materials, until industrial production reached the level where the intensity-of-use begins to decline.

As was discussed above, changes in the relative prices of raw materials change the amount of economically recoverable reserves. Thus, the relative price level, smoothness of the adjustment process, and availability of capital for needed investment can also be expected to significantly influence raw materials' market conditions. In addition, technological improvement in mining and metallurgy permits lower grade ores to be exploited without corresponding increases in costs.

The following table presents the 1972 net imports and the ratio of imports to total demand for nine commodities. The net imports of these nine commodities represented 99 percent of the total trade deficit in minerals.

---

1 <u>Materials Requirements Abroad in the Year 2000</u>, research project prepared for National Commission on Materials Policy by the Wharton School, University of Pennsylvania; pp. 9-10
2 United Nations Symposium on Population; Resources, and Environment, Stockholm, 9/26-10/5/73, E/Conf. 6-/CEP/3, p. 35.

Commodity	1972 Net Imports ($Millions)*	Ratio of Imports to Total Demand
Aluminum	48.38	.286
Copper	206.4	.160
Iron	424.5	.049
Lead	102.9	.239
Nickel	477.1	.704
Tin	220.2	.943
Titanium	256.5	.469
Zinc	294.8	.517
Petroleum (including natural gas)	5,494.5	.246

The primary sources of these US imports during the period 1969-1972 were:

Commodity	Source & %
Aluminum	–Canada 76%
Copper	–Canada 31%, Peru 27%, Chile 22%
Iron	–Canada 50%, Venezuela 31%
Lead	–Canada 29%, Peru 21%, Australia 21%
Nickel	–Canada 82%, Norway 8%
Tin	–Malaysia 64%, Thailand 27%
Titanium	–Japan 73%, USSR 19%
Zinc (Ore)	–Canada 60%, Mexico 24%
Zinc (Metal)	–Canada 48%, Australia 10%
Pertroleum (crude)	–Canada 42%
Petroleum (crude)	–Venezuela 17%

II. World Reserves

The following table shows estimates of the world reserve position for these commodities. As mentioned earlier, the quantity of

* The values are based on U.S. 1972 prices for materials in primary form, and in some cases do not represent commercial value of the crude material. Source: Bureau of Mines.

economically recoverable reserves increases with higher prices.
The following tables, based on Bureau of Mines information, provide estimates of reserves at various prices. (All prices are in
constant 1972 dollars.)

Aluminum (Bauxite)

Price (per pound primary aluminum)

	Price A	Price B	Price C	Price D
	.23	.29	.33	.36

Reserves (billion short tons, aluminum content)

World	3.58	3.76	4.15	5.21
U.S.	.01	.02	.04	.09

Copper

Price (per pound refined copper)

	.51	.60	.75

Reserves (million short tons)

World	370	418	507
U.S.	83	93	115

Gold

Price (per troy ounce)

	58.60	90	100	150

Reserves (million troy ounce)

World	1,000	1,221	1,588	1,850
U.S.	82	120	200	240

Iron

Price (per short ton of primary iron contained in ore)

	17.80	20.80	23.80

Reserves (billion short tons iron content)

World	96.7	129.0	206.0
U.S.	2.0	2.7	18.0

Lead

Price (per pound primary lead metal)

	.15	.18	.20

Reserves (million short tons, lead content)

	.15	.18	.20
World	96.0	129.0	144.0
U.S.	36.0	51.0	56.0

Nickel

Price (per pound of primary metal)

	1.53	1.75	2.00	2.25

Reserves (millions short tons)

	1.53	1.75	2.00	2.25
World	46.2	60.5	78.0	99.5
U.S.	.2	.2	.5	.5

Tin

Price (per pound primary tin metal)

	1.77	2.00	2.50	3.00

Reserves (thousands of long tons – tin content)

	1.77	2.00	2.50	3.00
World	4,180	5,500	7,530	9,290
U.S.	5	9	100	200

Titanium

Price (per pound titanium in pigment)

	.45	.55	.60

Reserves (thousands short tons titanium content)

	.45	.55	.60
World	158,000	222,000	327,000
U.S.	32,400	45,000	60,000

Zinc

Price (per pound, prime western zinc delivered)

	.18	.25	.30

Reserves (million short tons, zinc content)

	.18	.25	.30
World	131	193	260
U.S.	30	40	50

Petroleum

Data necessary to quantify reserve-price relationships are not available. For planning purposes, however, the Bureau of Mines used the rough assumption that a 100% increase in price would increase reserves by 10%. The average 1972 U.S. price was $3.39/bbl. with proven world reserves of 666.9 billion bbls. and U.S. reserves of 36.3 billion barrels. Using the Bureau of Mines assumption, therefore, a doubling in world price (a U.S. price of $6.78/bbl.) would imply world reserves of 733.5 billion bbls. and U.S. reserves of 39.9 billion barrels.

Natural Gas

Price (wellhead price per thousand cubic feet)			
.186	.34	.44	.55
Reserves (trillion cubic feet)			
World			
1,156	6,130	10,240	15,599
U.S.			
266	580	900	2,349

It should be noted that these statistics represent a shift in 1972 relative prices and assume constant 1972 technology. The development of new technology or a more dramatic shift in relative prices can have a significant impact on the supply of economically recoverable reserves. Aluminum is a case in point. It is the most abundant metallic element in the earth's crust and the supply of this resource is almost entirely determined by the price. Current demand and technology limit economically recoverable reserves to bauxite sources. Alternate sources of aluminum exist (e.g., alunite) and if improved technology is developed making these alternate sources commercially viable, supply constraints will not likely be encountered.

The above estimated reserve figures, while representing approximate orders of magnitude, are adequate to meet projected accumulated world demand (also very rough orders of magnitude) through the year 2000. In some cases, modest price increases above the 1972 level may be required to attract the necessary capital investment.

CHAPTER IV - ECONOMIC DEVELOPMENT AND POPULATION GROWTH

Rapid population growth adversely affects every aspect of economic and social progress in developing countries. It absorbs large amounts of resources needed for more productive investment in development. It requires greater expenditures for health, education and other social services, particularly in urban areas. It increases the dependency load per worker so that a high fraction of the output of the productive age group is needed to support dependents. It reduces family savings and domestic investment. It increases existing severe pressures on limited agricultural land in countries where the world's "poverty problem" is concentrated. It creates a need for use of large amounts of scarce foreign exchange for food imports (or the loss of food surpluses for export). Finally, it intensifies the already severe unemployment and underemployment problems of many developing countries where not enough productive jobs are created to absorb the annual increments to the labor force.

Even in countries with good resource/population ratios, rapid population growth causes problems for several reasons: First, large capital investments generally are required to exploit unused resources. Second, some countries already have high and growing unemployment and lack the means to train new entrants to their labor force. Third, there are long delays between starting effective family planning programs and reducing fertility, and even longer delays between reductions in fertility and population stabilization. Hence there is substantial danger of vastly overshooting population targets if population growth is not moderated in the near future.

During the past decade, the developing countries have raised their GNP at a rate of 5 percent per annum as against 4.8 percent in developed countries. But at the same time the LDCs experienced an average annual population growth rate of 2.5 percent. Thus their per capita income growth rate was only 2.5 percent and in some of the more highly populated areas the increase in per capita incomes was less than 2 percent. This stands in stark contrast to 3.6 percent in the rich countries. Moreover, the low rate means that there is very little change in those countries whose per capita incomes are

$200 or less per annum. The problem has been further exacerbated in recent months by the dramatic increases in oil and fertilizer prices. The World Bank has estimated that the incomes of the 800 million inhabitants of the countries hardest hit by the oil crisis will grow at less than 1% per capita per year of the remainder of the 1970s. Taking account of inequalities in income distribution, there will be well over 500 million people, with average incomes of less than $100 per capita, who will experience either no growth or negative growth in that period.

Moderation of population growth offers benefits in terms of resources saved for investment and/or higher per capita consumption. If resource requirements to support fewer children are reduced and the funds now allocated for construction of schools, houses, hospitals and other essential facilities are invested in productive activities, the impact on the growth of GNP and per capita income may be significant. In addition, economic and social progress resulting from population control will further contribute to the decline in fertility rates. The relationship is reciprocal, and can take the form of either a vicious or a virtuous circle.

This raises the question of how much more efficient expenditures for population control might be than in raising production through direct investments in additional irrigation and power projects and factories. While most economists today do not agree with the assumptions that went into early overly optimistic estimates of returns to population expenditures, there is general agreement that up to the point when cost per acceptor rises rapidly, family planning expenditures are generally considered the best investment a country can make in its own future.

II. Impact of Population Growth on Economic Development[1]

In most, if not all, developing countries high fertility rates impose substantial economic costs and restrain economic growth. The main adverse macroeconomic effects may be analyzed in three general categories: (1) the saving effect, (2) "child quality" versus "child quantity", and (3) "capital deepening" versus "capital widening." These three categories are not mutually exclusive, but they

---

1   There is no subhead or subsection "I" in the NSSM 200 response document provided by the National Archives. This is probably just a numbering error in the orignial typescript, rather than indicative of missing text. —Ed.

highlight different familial and social perspectives. In addition, there are often longer-run adverse effects on agricultural output and the balance of payments.

(1) The saving effect. A high fertility economy has perforce a larger "burden of dependency" than a low fertility economy, because a larger proportion of the population consists of children too young to work. There are more non-working people to feed, house and rear, and there is a smaller surplus above minimum consumption available for savings and investment. It follows that a lower fertility rate can free resources from consumption; if saved and invested, these resources could contribute to economic growth. (There is much controversy on this; empirical studies of the savings effect have produced varying results.)

(2) Child quality versus quantity. Parents make investment decisions, in a sense, about their children. Healthier and better-educated children tend to be economically more productive, both as children and later as adults. In addition to the more-or-less conscious trade-offs parents can make about more education and better health per child, there are certain biologic adverse effects suffered by high birth order children such as higher mortality and limited brain growth due to higher incidence of malnutrition. It must be emphasized, however, that discussion of trade-offs between child quality and child quantity will probably remain academic with regard to countries where child mortality remains high. When parents cannot expect most children to survive to old age, they probably will continue to "over-compensate", using high fertility as a form of hedge to insure that they will have some living offspring able to support the parents in the distant future.

(3) Capital deepening versus widening. From the family's viewpoint high fertility is likely to reduce welfare per child; for the economy one may view high fertility as too rapid a growth in labor force relative to capital stock. Society's capital stock includes facilities such as schools and other educational inputs in addition to capital investments that raise workers' outputs in agriculture and manufacturing. For any given rate of capital accumulation, a lower population growth rate can help increase the amount of capital and education per worker, helping thereby to increase output and income per capita. The problem of migration to cities and the derived demand for urban infrastructure can also be analyzed as problems

of capital widening, which draw resources away from growth-generating investments.

In a number of the more populous countries a fourth aspect of rapid growth in numbers has emerged in recent years which has profound long-run consequences. Agricultural output was able to keep pace or exceed population growth over the many decades of population rise prior to the middle of this century, primarily through steady expansion of acreage under cultivation. More recently, only marginal unused land has been available in India, Thailand, Java, Bangladesh, and other areas. As a result (a) land holdings have declined in size, and (b) land shortage has led to deforestation and overgrazing, with consequent soil erosion and severe water pollution and increased urban migration. Areas that once earned foreign exchange through the export of food surpluses are now in deficit or face early transition to dependence on food imports. Although the scope for raising agricultural productivity is very great in many of these areas, the available technologies for doing so require much higher capital costs per acre and much larger foreign exchange outlays for "modern" inputs (chemical fertilizer, pesticides, petroleum fuels, etc.) than was the case with the traditional technologies. Thus the population growth problem can be seen as an important long-run, or structural, contributor to current LDC balance of payments problems and to deterioration of their basic ecological infrastructure.

Finally, high fertility appears to exacerbate the maldistribution of income which is a fundamental economic and social problem in much of the developing world. Higher income families tend to have fewer children, spend more on the health and education of these children, have more wealth to pass on to these children in contrast to the several disadvantages that face the children of the poor. The latter tend to be more numerous, receiving less of an investment per child in their "human capital", leaving the children with economic, educational and social constraints similar to those which restrict the opportunities of the parents. In short, high fertility contributes to the intergenerational continuity of maldistributions of income and related social and political problems.

III. The Effect of Development on Population Growth

The determinants of population growth are not well understood, especially for low income societies. Historical data show that declining fertility in Europe and North America has been associated with declining mortality and increasing urbanization, and generally with "modernization." Fertility declined substantially in the West without the benefit of sophisticated contraceptives. This movement from high fertility and high mortality to low fertility and low mortality is known as the "demographic transition". In many low income countries mortality has declined markedly since World War II (in large part from reduction in epidemic illness and famine), but fertility has remained high. Apart from a few pockets of low fertility in East Asia and the Caribbean, a significant demographic transition has not occurred in the third world. (The Chinese, however, make remarkable claims about their success in reducing birth rates, and qualified observers are persuaded that they have had unusual success even though specific demographic information is lacking.)

There is considerable, incontestable evidence in many developing countries that a larger (though not fully known) number of couples would like to have fewer children than possible generally there—and that there is a large unsatisfied demand by these couples for family planning services. It is also now widely believed that something more that family planning services will be needed to motivate other couples to want smaller families and all couples to want replacement levels essential to the progress and growth of their countries.

There is also evidence, although it is not conclusive, that certain aspects of economic development and modernization are more directly related to lowered birth rates than others, and that selective developmental policies may bring about a demographic transition at substantially lower per capita income levels than in Europe, North America, and Japan.[1] Such selective policies would focus on improved health care and nutrition directed toward reduced infant and child mortality; universal schooling and adult literacy, especially for women; increasing the legal age of marriage; greater opportunities for female employment in the money economy; improved old-age social security arrangements; and agricultural modernization focussed on small farmers. It is important that this focus

---

1   See James E. Kocher, Rural Development, Income Distribution, and Fertility Decline (Population Council, New York, 1973), and William Rich, Smaller Families through Social and Economic Progress (Overseas Development Council, Wash., 1973).

be made in development programs because, given today's high population densities, high birth rates, and low income levels in much of Asia, Africa, and Latin America, if the demographic transition has to await overall development and modernization, the vicious circle of poverty, people, and unemployment may never be broken.

The causes of high birth rates in low income societies are generally explained in terms of three factors:

a. <u>Inadequacy of information and means</u>. Actual family size in many societies is higher than desired family size owing to ignorance of acceptable birth control methods or unavailability of birth control devices and services. The importance of this factor is evidenced by many sociological investigations on "desired family size" versus actual size, and by the substantial rates of acceptance for contraceptives when systematic family planning services are introduced. This factor has been a basic assumption in the family planning programs of official bilateral and multilateral programs in many countries over the past decade. Whatever the actual weight of this factor, which clearly varies from country to country and which shifts with changes in economic and social conditions, there remains without question a significant demand for family planning services.

b. <u>Inadequacy of motivation for reduced numbers of children</u>. Especially in the rural areas of underdeveloped countries, which account for the major share of today's population growth, parents often want large numbers of children (especially boys) (i) to ensure that some will survive against the odds of high child mortality, (ii) to provide support for the parents in their old age, and (iii) to provide low cost farm labor. While these elements are present among rural populace, continued urbanization may reduce the need for sons in the longer term. The absence of educational and employment opportunities for young women intensifies these same motivations by encouraging early marriage and early and frequent maternity. This factor suggests the crucial importance of selective development policies as a means of accelerating the reduction of fertility.

c. The "time lag". Family preferences and social institutions that favor high fertility change slowly. Even though mortality and economic conditions have improved significantly since World War II in LDCs, family expectations, social norms, and parental practice are slow to respond to these altered conditions. This factor leads to the need for large scale programs of information, education, and persuasion directed at lower fertility.

The three elements are undoubtedly intermixed in varying proportions in all underdeveloped countries with high birth rates. In most LDCs, many couples would reduce their completed family size if appropriate birth control methods were more easily available. The extent of this reduction, however, may still leave their completed family size at higher than mere replacement levels—i.e., at levels implying continued but less rapid population growth. Many other couples would not reduce their desired family size merely if better contraceptives were available, either because they see large families as economically beneficial, or because of cultural factors, or because they misread their own economic interests.

Therefore, family planning supply (contraceptive technology and delivery systems) and demand (the motivation for reduced fertility) would not be viewed as mutually exclusive alternatives; they are complementary and may be mutually reinforcing. The selected point of focus mentioned earlier—old age security programs, maternal and child health programs, increased female education, increasing the legal age of marriage, financial incentives to "acceptors", personnel,—are important, yet better information is required as to which measures are most cost-effective and feasible in a given situation and how their cost-effectiveness compares to supply programs.

One additional interesting area is receiving increasing attention: the distribution of the benefits of development. Experience in several countries suggests that the extent to which the poor, with the highest fertility rates, reduce their fertility will depend on the extent to which they participate in development. In this view the average level of economic development and the average amount of modernization are less important determinants of population growth than is the specific structure of development. This line of investigation suggests that social development activities need to be more precisely targeted than in the past to reach the lowest income people, to counteract their desire for high fertility as a means of alleviating certain adverse conditions.

IV. Employment and Social Problems

Employment, aside from its role in production of goods and services, is an important source of income and of status or recognition to workers and their families. The inability of large segments of the economically active population in developing countries to find jobs offering a minimum acceptable standard of living is reflected in a widening of income disparities and a deepening sense of economic, political and social frustration.

The most economically significant employment problems in LDCs contributed to by excessive population growth are low worker productivity in production of traditional goods and services produced, the changing aspirations of the work force, the existing distribution of income, wealth and power, and the natural resource endowment of a country.

The political and social problems of urban overcrowding are directly related to population growth. In addition to the still-high fertility in urban areas of many LDC's, population pressures on the land, which increases migration to the cities, adds to the pressures on urban job markets and political stability, and strains, the capacity to provide schools, health facilities, and water supplies.

It should be recognized that lower fertility will relieve only a portion of these strains and that its most beneficial effects will be felt only over a period of decades. Most of the potential migrants from countryside to city over the coming 15 to 20 years have already been born. Lower birth rates do provide some immediate relief to health and sanitation and welfare services, and medium-term relief to pressures on educational systems. The largest effects on employment, migration, and living standards, however, will be felt only after 25 or 30 years. The time lags inherent in all aspects of population dynamics only reinforce the urgency of adopting effective policies in the years immediately ahead if the formidable problems of the present decade are not to become utterly unmanageable in the 1990s and beyond the year 2000.

CHAPTER V—IMPLICATIONS OF POPULATION PRESSURES FOR NATIONAL SECURITY

It seems well understood that the impact of population factors on the subjects already considered—development, food requirements, resources, environment—adversely affects the welfare and progress of countries in which we have a friendly interest and thus indirectly adversely affects broad U.S. interests as well.

The effects of population factors on the political stability of these countries and their implications for internal and international order or disorder, destructive social unrest, violence and disruptive foreign activities are less well understood and need more analysis. Nevertheless, some strategists and experts believe that these effects may ultimately be the most important of those arising from population factors, most harmful to the countries where they occur and seriously affecting U.S. interests. Other experts within the U.S. Government disagree with this conclusion.

A recent study* of forty-five local conflicts involving Third World countries examined the ways in which population factors affect the initiation and course of a conflict in different situations. The study reached two major conclusions:

1. ". . . population factors are indeed critical in, and often determinants of, violent conflict in developing areas. Segmental (religious, social, racial) differences, migration, rapid population growth, differential levels of knowledge and skills, rural/urban differences, population pressure and the spacial location of population in relation to resources—in this rough order of importance—all appear to be important contributions to conflict and violence...

2. Clearly, conflicts which are regarded in primarily political terms often have demographic roots: Recognition of these relationships appears crucial to any understanding or prevention of such hostilities."

It does not appear that the population factors act alone or, often, directly to cause the disruptive effects. They act through intervening elements—variables. They also add to other causative factors turning what might have been only a difficult situation into one with disruptive results.

* Choucri, Nazli, Professor of Political Science, M.I.T. — "Population Dynamics and Local Conflict; A Cross-National Study of Population and War, A Summary," June 1974.

This action is seldom simple. Professor Philip Hauser of the University of Chicago has suggested the concept of "population complosion" to describe the situation in many developing countries when (a) more and more people are born into or move into and are compressed in the same living space under (b) conditions and irritations of different races, colors, religions, languages, or cultural backgrounds, often with differential rates of population growth among these groups, and (c) with the frustrations of failure to achieve their aspirations for better standards of living for themselves or their children. To these may be added pressures for and actual international migration. These population factors appear to have a multiplying effect on other factors involved in situations of incipient violence. Population density, the "overpopulation" most often thought of in this connection, is much less important.

These population factors contribute to socio-economic variables including breakdowns in social structures, underemployment and unemployment, poverty, deprived people in city slums, lowered opportunities for education for the masses, few job opportunities for those who do obtain education, interracial, religious, and regional rivalries, and sharply increased financial, planning, and administrative burdens on governmental systems at all levels.

These adverse conditions appear to contribute frequently to harmful developments of a political nature: Juvenile delinquency, thievery and other crimes, organized brigandry, kidnapping and terrorism, food riots, other outbreaks of violence; guerilla warfare, communal violence, separatist movements, revolutionary movements and counter-revolutionary coups. All of these bear upon the weakening or collapse of local, state, or national government functions.

Beyond national boundaries, population factors appear to have had operative roles in some past politically disturbing legal or illegal mass migrations, border incidents, and wars. If current increased population pressures continue they may have greater potential for future disruption in foreign relations.

Perhaps most important, in the last decade population factors have impacted more severely than before on availabilities of agricultural land and resources, industrialization, pollution and the environment. All this is occurring at a time when international communications have created rising expectations which are being frustrated by slow development and inequalities of distribution.

Since population factors work with other factors and act through intervening linkages, research as to their effects of a political nature is difficult and "proof" even more so. This does not mean, however, that the causality does not exist. It means only that U.S. policy decisions must take into account the less precise and programmatic character of our knowledge of these linkages.

Although general hypotheses are hard to draw, some seem reasonably sustainable:

1. Population growth and inadequate resources. Where population size is greater than available resources, or is expanding more rapidly than the available resources, there is a tendency toward internal disorders and violence and, sometimes, disruptive international policies or violence. The higher the rate of growth, the more salient a factor population increase appears to be. A sense of increasing crowding, real or perceived, seems to generate such tendencies, especially if it seems to thwart obtaining desired personal or national goals.

2. Populations with a high proportion of growth. The young people, who are in much higher proportions in many LDCs, are likely to be more volatile, unstable, prone to extremes, alienation and violence than an older population. These young people can more readily be persuaded to attack the legal institutions of the government or real property of the "establishment," "imperialists," multinational corporations, or other—often foreign—influences blamed for their troubles.

3. Population factors with social cleavages. When adverse population factors of growth, movement, density, excess, or pressure coincide with racial, religious, color, linguistic, cultural, or other social cleavages, there will develop the most potentially explosive situations for internal disorder, perhaps with external effects. When such factors exist together with the reality or sense of relative deprivation among different groups within the same country or in relation to other countries or peoples, the probability of violence increases significantly.

4. Population movements and international migrations. Population movements within countries appear to have a large role in disorders. Migrations into neighboring countries (especially those richer or more sparsely settled), whether legal or illegal, can provoke negative political reactions or force.

There may be increased propensities for violence arising simply from technological developments making it easier—e.g., international proliferation and more ready accessibility to sub-national groups of nuclear and other lethal weaponry. These possibilities make the disruptive population factors discussed above even more dangerous.

Some Effects of Current Population Pressures

In the 1960s and 1970s, there have been a series of episodes in which population factors have apparently had a role—directly or indirectly—affecting countries in which we have an interest.

El Salvador-Honduras War. An example was the 1969 war between El Salvador and Honduras. Dubbed the "Soccer War", it was sparked by a riot during a soccer match, its underlying cause was tension resulting from the large scale migration of Salvadorans from their rapidly growing, densely populated country to relatively uninhabited areas of Honduras. The Hondurans resented the presence of migrants and in 1969 began to enforce an already extant land tenancy law to expel them. El Salvador was angered by the treatment given its citizens. Flaring tempers on both sides over this issue created a situation which ultimately led to a military clash.

Nigeria. The Nigerian civil war seriously retarded the progress of Africa's most populous nations and caused political repercussions and pressures in the United States. It was fundamentally a matter of tribal relationships. Irritations among the tribes caused in part by rapidly increasing numbers of people, in a situation of inadequate opportunity for most of them, magnified the tribal issues and may have helped precipitate the war. The migration of the Ibos from Eastern Nigeria, looking for employment, led to competition with local peoples of other tribes and contributed to tribal rioting. This unstable situation was intensified by the fact that in the 1963 population census returns were falsified to inflate the Western region's population and hence its representation in the Federal Government. The Ibos of the Eastern region, with the oil resources of the country, felt their resources would be unjustly drawn on and attempted to establish their independence.

Pakistan-India-Bangladesh 1970-71. This religious and nationalistic conflict contains several points where a population factor at a crucial time may have had a causal effect in turning events away from peaceful solutions to violence. The Central Government in West Pakistan resorted to military suppression of the East Wing after the election in which the Awami League had an overwhelming victory in East Pakistan. This election had followed two sets of circumstances. The first was a growing discontent in East Pakistan at the slow rate of economic and social progress being made and the Bengali feeling that West Pakistan was dealing unequally and unfairly with East Pakistan in the distribution of national revenues. The first population factor was the 75 million Bengalis whom the 45 million West Pakistanis sought to continue to dominate. Some observers believe that as a recent population factor the rapid rate of population growth in East Pakistan seriously diminished the per capita improvement from the revenues made available and contributed significantly to the discontent. A special aspect of the population explosion in East Pakistan (second population factor) was the fact that the dense occupation of all good agricultural land forced hundreds of thousands of people to move into the obviously unsafe lowlands along the southern coast. They became victims of the hurricane in 1970. An estimated 300,000 died. The Government was unable to deal with a disaster affecting so many people. The leaders and people of East Pakistan reacted vigorously to this failure of the Government to bring help.

It seems quite likely that these situations in which population factors played an important role led to the overwhelming victory of the Awami League that led the Government to resort to force in East Pakistan with the massacres and rapes that followed. Other experts believe the effects of the latter two factors were of marginal influence in the Awami League's victory.

It further seems possible that much of the violence was stimulated or magnified by population pressures. Two groups of Moslems had been competing for jobs and land in East Bengal since the 1947 partition. "Biharis" are a small minority of non-Bengali Moslems who chose to resettle in East Pakistan at that time. Their integration into Bengali society was undoubtedly inhibited by the deteriorating living conditions of the majority Bengalis. With the Pakistan army crackdown in March, 1971, the Biharis cooperated with the authorities, and reportedly were able thereby to improve their economic conditions at the expense of the persecuted Bengalis. When the tables were turned after independence, it was the Biharis who were persecuted and whose property and jobs were seized. It seems likely that both these outbursts of violence were induced or enlarged by the population "complosion" factor.

The violence in East Pakistan against the Bengalis and particularly the Hindu minority who bore the brunt of Army repression led to the next population factor, the mass migration during one year of nine or ten million refugees into West Bengal in India. This placed a tremendous burden on the already weak Indian economy. As one Indian leader in the India Family Planning Program said, "The influx of nine million people wiped out the savings of some nine million births which had been averted over a period of eight years of the family planning program."

There were other factors in India's invasion of East Bengal, but it is possible that the necessity of returning these nine or ten million refugees to east Bengal—getting them out of India—may have played a part in the Indian decision to invade. Certainly, in a broader sense, the threat posed by this serious, spreading instability on India's eastern frontier—an instability in which population factors were a major underlying cause—a key reason for the Indian decision.

The political arrangements in the Subcontinent have changed, but all of the underlying population factors which influenced the dramatic acts of violence that took place in 1970-71 still exist, in worsening dimensions, to influence future events.

Additional illustrations. Population factors also appear to have had indirect causal relations, in varying degrees, on the killings in Indonesia in 1965-6, the communal slaughter in Rwanda in 1961-2 and 1963-4 and in Burundi in 1972, the coup in Uganda in 1972, and the insurrection in Sri Lanka in 1971.

Some Potential Effects of Future Population Pressures

Between the end of World War II and 1975 the world's population will have increased about one and a half billion—nearly one billion of that from 1960 to the present. The rate of growth is increasing and between two and a half and three and a half billion will be added by the year 2000, depending partly on the effectiveness of population growth control programs. This increase of the next 25 years will, of course, pyramid on the great number added with such rapidity in the last 25. The population factors which contributed to the political pressures and instabilities of the last decades will be multiplied.

PRC - The demographic factors of the PRC are referred to on page 79 above. The Government of the PRC has made a major effort to feed its growing population.

Cultivated farm land, at 107 million hectares, has not increased significantly over the past 25 years, although farm output has substantially kept pace with population growth through improved yields secured by land improvement, irrigation extension, intensified cropping, and rapid expansion in the supply of fertilizers.

In 1973 the PRC adopted new, forceful population control measures. In the urban areas Peking claimed its birth control measures had secured a two-child family and a one percent annual population growth, and it proposes to extend this development throughout the rural areas by 1980.

The political implications of China's future population growth are obviously important but are not dealt with here.

Israel and the Arab States. If a peace settlement can be reached, the central issue will be how to make it last. Egypt with about 37 million today is growing at 2.8% per year. It will approximate 48 million by 1985, 75 million by 1995, and more than 85 million by 2000. It is doubtful that Egypt's economic progress can greatly exceed its population growth. With Israel starting at today's population of 3.3 million, the disparity between its population and those of the Arab States will rapidly increase. Inside Israel, unless Jewish immigration continues, the gap between the size of the Arab and Jewish populations will diminish. Together with the traditional animosities—which will remain the prime determinants of Arab-Israeli conflict—these population factors make the potential for peace and for U.S. interests in the area ominous.

India-Bangladesh. The Subcontinent will be for years the major focus of world concern over population growth. India's population is now approximately 580 million, adding a million by each full moon. Embassy New Delhi (New Delhi 2115, June 17, 1974) reports:

"There seems no way of turning off the faucet this side of 1 billion Indians, which means India must continue to court economic and social disaster. It is not clear how the shaky and slow-growing Indian economy can bear the enormous expenditures on health, housing, employment, and education, which must be made if the society is even to maintain its current low levels."

Death rates have recently increased in parts of India and episodes like the recent smallpox epidemic have led Embassy New Delhi to add:

"A future failure of the India food crop could cause widespread death and suffering which could not be overcome by the GOI or foreign assistance. The rise in the death rate in several rural areas suggests that Malthusian pressures are already being felt."

And further:

"Increasing political disturbances should be expected in the future, fed by the pressures of rising population in urban areas, food shortages, and growing scarcities in household commodities. The GOI has not been very successful in alleviating unemployment in the cities. The recent disturbances in Gujarat and Bihar seem to be only the beginning of chronic and serious political disorders occurring throughout India."

There will probably be a weakening, possibly a breakdown, of the control of the central government over some of the states and local areas. The democratic system will be taxed and may be in danger of giving way to a form of dictatorship, benevolent or otherwise. The existence of India as a democratic buttress in Asia will be threatened.

Bangladesh, with appalling population density, rapid population growth, and extensive poverty will suffer even more. Its population has increased 40% since the census 13 years ago and is growing at least 3% per year. The present 75 million, or so, unless slowed by famine, disease, or massive birth control, will double in 23 years and exceed 170 million by 2000.

Requirements for food and other basic necessities of life are growing at a faster rate than existing resources and administrative systems are providing them. In the rural areas, the size of the average farm is being reduced and there is increasing landlessness. More and more people are migrating to urban areas. The government admits a 30% rate of unemployment and underemployment.

Already, Embassy Dacca reports (Dacca 3424, June 19, 1974) there are important economic-population causes for the landlessness that is rapidly increasing and contributing to violent crimes of murder and armed robbery that terrorize the ordinary citizen.

"Some of the vast army of unemployed and landless, and those strapped by the escalating cost of basic commodities, have doubtless turned to crime."

Three paragraphs of Embassy Dacca's report sharply outline the effect on U.S. political interests we may anticipate from population factors in Bangladesh and other countries that, if present trends are not changed, will be in conditions similar to Bangladesh in only a few years.

"Of concern to the U.S. are several probable outcomes as the basic political, economic and social situation worsens over the coming decades. Already afflicted with a crisis mentality by which they look to wealthy foreign countries to shore up their faltering economy, the BDG will continue to escalate its demands on the U.S. both bilaterally and internationally to enlarge its assistance, both of commodities and financing. Bangladesh is now a fairly solid supporter of third world positions, advocating better distribution of the world's wealth and extensive trade concessions to poor nations. As its problems grow and its ability to gain assistance fails to keep pace, Bangladesh's positions on international issues likely will become radicalized, inevitably in opposition to U.S. interests on major issues as it seeks to align itself with others to force adequate aid.

"U.S. interests in Bangladesh center on the development of an economically and politically stable country which will not threaten the stability of its neighbors in the Subcontinent nor invite the intrusion of outside powers. Surrounded on three sides by India and sharing a short border with Burma, Bangladesh, if it descends into chaos, will threaten the stability of these nations as well. Already Bengalis are illegally migrating into the frontier provinces of Assam and Tripura, politically sensitive areas of India, and into adjacent Burma. Should expanded out-migration and socio-political collapse in Bangladesh threaten its own stability, India may be forced to consider intervention, although it is difficult to see in what way the Indians could cope with the situation.

"Bangladesh is a case study of the effects of few resources and burgeoning population not only on national and regional stability but also on the future world order. In a sense, if we and other richer elements of the world community do not meet the test of formulating a policy to help Bangladesh awaken from its economic and demographic nightmare, we will not be prepared in future decades to deal with the consequences of similar problems in other countries which have far more political and economic consequences to U.S. interests."

Africa—Sahel Countries. The current tragedy of the Sahel countries, to which U.S. aid in past years has been minimal, has suddenly cost us an immense effort in food supplies at a time when we are already hard pressed to supply other countries, and domestic food prices are causing strong political repercussions in the U.S. The costs to us and other donor countries for aid to help restore the devastated land will run into hundreds of millions. Yet little attention is given to the fact that even before the adverse effect of the continued drought, it was population growth and added migration of herdsmen to the edge of the desert that led to cutting the trees and cropping the grass, inviting the desert to sweep forward. Control of population growth and migration must be a part of any program for improvement of lasting value.

Panama. The troublesome problem of jurisdiction over the Canal Zone is primarily due to Panamanian feelings of national pride and a desire to achieve sovereignty over its entire territory. One Panamanian agreement in pursuing its treaty goals is that U.S. control over the Canal Zone prevents the natural expansion of Panama City, an expansion needed as a result of demographic pressures. In 1908, at the time of the construction of the Canal, the population of the Zone was about 40,000. Today it is close to the same figure, 45,000. On the other hand, Panama City, which had some 20,000 people in 1908, has received growing migration from rural areas and now has over 500,000. A new treaty which would give Panama jurisdiction over land now in the Zone would help alleviate the problems caused by this growth of Panama City.

Mexico and the U.S. Closest to home, the combined population growth of Mexico and the U.S. Southwest presages major difficulties for the future. Mexico's population is growing at some 3.5% per year and will double in 20 years with concomitant increases in demands for food, housing, education, and employment. By 1995, the present 57 million will have increased to some 115 million and, unless their recently established family planning program has great success, by 2000 will exceed 130 million. More important, the numbers of young people entering the job market each year will expand even more quickly. These growing numbers will increase the pressure of illegal emigration to the U.S., and make the issue an even more serious source of friction in our political relations with Mexico.

On our side, the Bureau of the Census estimates that as more and more Americans move to the Southwestern States the present 40,000,000 population may approximate 61,000,000 by 1995. The domestic use of Colorado River water may again have increased the salinity level in Mexico and reopened that political issue.

Amembassy Mexico City (Mexico 4953, June 14, 1974) summarized the influences of population factors on U.S. interests as follows:

"An indefinite continuation of Mexico's high population growth rate would increasingly act as a brake on economic (and social) improvement. The consequences would be noted in various ways. Mexico could well take more radical positions in the international scene. Illegal migration to the U.S. would increase. In a country where unemployment and under-employment is already high, the entry of increasing numbers into the work force would only intensify the pressure to seek employment in the U.S. by whatever means. Yet another consequence would be increased demand for food imports from the U.S., especially if the rate of growth of agricultural production continues to lag behind the population growth rate. Finally, one cannot dismiss the spectre of future domestic instability as a long term consequence, should the economy, now strong, falter."

UNCTAD, the Special UNGA, and the UN. The developing countries, after several years of unorganized maneuvering and erratic attacks have now formed tight groupings in the Special Committee for Latin American Coordination, the Organization of African States, and the Seventy-Seven. As illustrated in the Declaration of Santiago and the recent Special General Assembly, these groupings at times appear to reflect a common desire to launch economic attacks against the United States and, to a lesser degree, the European developed countries. A factor which is common to all of them, which retards their development, burdens their foreign exchange, subjects them to world prices for food, fertilizer, and necessities of life and pushes them into disadvantageous trade relations is their excessively rapid population growth. Until they are able to overcome this problem, it is likely that their manifestations of antagonism toward the United States in international bodies will increase.

Global Factors

In industrial nations, population growth increases demand for industrial output. This over time tends to deplete national raw materials resources and calls increasingly on sources of marginal profitability and foreign supplies. To obtain raw materials, industrial nations seek to locate and develop external sources of supply. The potential for collisions of interest among the developing countries is obvious and has already begun. It is visible and vexing in claims for territorial waters and national sovereignty over mineral resources. It may become intense in rivalries over exploring and exploiting the resources of the ocean floor.

In developing countries, the burden of population factors, added to others, will weaken unstable governments, often only marginally effective in good times, and open the way for extremist regimes. Countries suffering under such burdens will be more susceptible to radicalization. Their vulnerability also might invite foreign intervention by stronger nations bent on acquiring political and economic advantage. The tensions within the Have-not nations are likely to intensify, and the conflicts between them and the Haves may escalate.

Past experience gives little assistance to predicting the course of these developments because the speed of today's population growth, migrations, and urbanization far exceeds anything the world has seen before. Moreover, the consequences of such population factors can no longer be evaded by moving to new hunting or grazing lands, by conquering new territory, by discovering or colonizing new continents, or by emigration in large numbers.

The world has ample warning that we all must make more rapid efforts at social and economic development to avoid or mitigate these gloomy prospects. We should be warned also that we all must move as rapidly as possible toward stabilizing national and world population growth.

CHAPTER VI - WORLD POPULATION CONFERENCE

From the standpoint of policy and program, the focal point of the World Population Conference (WPC) at Bucharest, Romania, in August 1974, was the World Population Plan of Action (WPPA). The U.S. had contributed many substantive points to the draft Plan. We had particularly emphasized the incorporation of population factors in national planning of developing countries' population programs for assuring the availability of means of family planning to persons of reproductive age, voluntary but specific goals for the reduction of population growth and time frames for action.

As the WPPA reached the WPC it was organized as a demographic document. It also related population factors to family welfare, social and economic development, and fertility reduction. Population policies and programs were recognized as an essential element, but only one element of economic and social development programs. The sovereignty of nations in determining their own population policies and programs was repeatedly recognized. The general impression after five regional consultative meetings on the Plan was that it had general support.

There was general consternation, therefore, when at the beginning of the conference the Plan was subjected to a slashing, five-pronged attack led by Algeria, with the backing of several African countries; Argentina, supported by Uruguay, Brazil, Peru and, more limitedly, some other Latin American countries; the Eastern European group (less Romania); the PRC and the Holy See. Although the attacks were not identical, they embraced three central elements relevant to U.S. policy and action in this field:

1.Repeated references to the importance (or as some said, the pre-condition) of economic and social development for the reduction of high fertility. Led by Algeria and Argentina, many emphasized the "new international economic order" as central to economic and social development.

2.Efforts to reduce the references to population programs, minimize their importance and delete all references to quantitative or time goals.

3.Additional references to national sovereignty in setting population policies and programs.

The Plan of Action

Despite the initial attack and continuing efforts to change the conceptual basis of the world Population Plan of Action, the Conference adopted by acclamation (only the Holy See stating a general reservation) a complete World Population Plan of Action. It is less urgent in tone than the draft submitted by the U.N. Secretariat but in several ways more complete and with greater potential than that draft. The final action followed a vigorous debate with hotly contested positions and forty-seven votes. Nevertheless, there was general satisfaction among the participants at the success of their efforts.

a. Principles and Aims

The Plan of Action lays down several important principles, some for the first time in a U.N. document.

1. Among the first-time statements is the assertion that the sovereign right of each nation to set its own population policies is "to be exercised ... taking into account universal solidarity in order to improve the quality of life of the peoples of the world." (Para 13) This new provision opens the way toward increasing responsibility by nations toward other nations in establishing their national population policies.

2. The conceptual relationship between population and development is stated in Para 13(c):

Population and development are interrelated: population variables influence development variables and are also influenced by them; the formulation of a World Population Plan of Action reflects the international community's awareness of the importance of population trends for socio-economic development, and the socio-economic nature of the recommendations contained in this Plan of Action reflects its awareness of the crucial role that development plays in affecting population trends.

3. A basic right of couples and individuals is recognized by Para 13(f), for the first time in a single declarative sentence:

All couples and individuals have the basic human right to decide freely and responsibly the number and spacing of their children and to have the information, education and means to do so;

4. Also for the first time, a U.N. document links the responsibility of child-bearers to the community [Para 13(f) continued]:

The responsibility of couples and individuals in the exercise of this right takes into account the needs of their living and future children, and their responsibilities towards the community.

It is now possible to build on this newly-stated principle as the right of couples first recognized in the Tehran Human Rights Declaration of 1968 has been built on.

5. A flat declaration of the right of women is included in Para 13(h):

Women have the right to complete integration in the development process particularly by means of an equal participation in educational, social, economic, cultural and political life. In addition, the necessary measures should be taken to facilitate this integration with family responsibilities which should be fully shared by both partners.

6. The need for international action is accepted in Para 13(k):

The growing interdependence of countries makes the adoption of measures at the international level increasingly important for the solution of problems of development and population problems.

7. The "primary aim" of the Plan of Action is asserted to be "to expand and deepen the capacities of countries to deal effectively with their national and subnational population problems and to promote an appropriate international response to their needs by increasing international activity in research, the exchange of information, and the provision of assistance on request."

b. Recommendations

The Plan of Action includes recommendations for: population goals and policies; population growth; mortality and morbidity; reproduction; family formation and the status of women; population distribution and internal migration; international migration; population structure; socio-economic policies; data collection and analysis; research; development and evolution of population policies; the role of national governments and of international cooperation; and monitoring, review and appraisal.

A score of these recommendations are the most important:

1. Governments should integrate population measures and programs into comprehensive social and economic plans and programs and their integration should be reflected in the goals, instrumentalities and organizations for planning within the countries. A unit dealing with population aspects should be created and placed at a high level of the national administrative structure. (Para 94)

2. Countries which consider their population growth hampers attainment of their goals should consider adopting population policies—through a low level of birth and death rates. (Para 17, 18)

3. Highest priority should be given to reduction in mortality and morbidity and increase of life expectancy and programs for this purpose should reach rural areas and underprivileged groups. (Para 20-25)

4. Countries are urged to encourage appropriate education concerning responsible parenthood and make available to persons who so desire advice and means of achieving it. [Para 29(b)]

5. Family planning and related services should aim at prevention of unwanted pregnancies and also at elimination of involuntary sterility or subfecundity to enable couples to achieve their desired number of children. [Para 29 (c)]

6. Adequately trained auxiliary personnel, social workers and non-government channels should be used to help provide family planning services. [Para 29(e)]

7. Governments with family planning programs should consider coordinating them with health and other services designed to raise the quality of life.

8. Countries wishing to affect fertility levels should give priority to development programs and health and education strategies which have a decisive effect upon demographic trends, including fertility. [Para 31] International cooperation should give priority to assisting such national efforts. Such programs may include reduction in infant and child mortality, increased education, particularly for females, improvement in the status of women, land reform and support in old age. [Para 32]

9. Countries which consider their birth rates detrimental to their national purposes are invited to set quantitative goals and implement policies to achieve them by 1985. [Para 37]

10. Developed countries are urged to develop appropriate policies in population, consumption and investment, bearing in mind the need for fundamental improvement in international equity.

11. Because the family is the basic unit of society, governments should assist families as far as possible through legislation and services. [Para 39]

12. Governments should ensure full participation of women in the educational, economic, social and political life of their countries

on an equal basis with men. [Para 40] (A new provision, added at Bucharest.)

13. A series of recommendations are made to stabilize migration within countries, particularly policies to reduce the undesirable consequences of excessively rapid urbanization and to develop opportunities in rural areas and small towns, recognizing the right of individuals to move freely within their national boundaries. [Para 44-50]

14. Agreements should be concluded to regulate the international migration of workers and to assure non-discriminatory treatment and social services for these workers and their families; also other measures to decrease the brain drain from developing countries. [Para 51-62]

15. To assure needed information concerning population trends, population censuses should be taken at regular intervals and information concerning births and deaths be made available at least annually. [Para 72-77]

16. Research should be intensified to develop knowledge concerning the social, economic and political interrelationships with population trends; effective means of reducing infant and childhood mortality; methods for integrating population goals into national plans, means of improving the motivation of people, analysis of population policies in relation to socio-economic development, laws and institution; methods of fertility regulation to meet the varied requirement of individuals and communities, including methods requiring no medical supervision; the interrelations of health, nutrition and reproductive biology; and utilization of social services, including family planning services. [Para 78-80]

17. Training of management on population dynamics and administration, on an interdisciplinary basis, should be provided for medical, paramedical, traditional health personnel, program administrators, senior government officials, labor, community and social leaders. Education and information programs should be undertaken to bring population information to all areas of countries. [Paras 81-92]

18. An important role of governments is to determine and assess the population problems and needs of their countries in the light of their political, social, cultural, religious and economic conditions; such an undertaking should be carried out systematically and periodically so as to provide informed, rational and dynamic

decision-making in matters of population and development. [Para 97]

20. The Plan of Action should be closely coordinated with the International Development Strategy for the Second United Nations Development Decade, reviewed in depth at five year intervals, and modified as appropriate. [Paras 106-108]

The Plan of Action hedges in presenting specific statements of quantitative goals or a time frame for the reduction of fertility. These concepts are included, however, in the combination of Paras 16 and 36, together with goals [Para 37] and the review [Para 106]. Para 16 states that, according to the U.N low variant projections, it is estimated that as a result of social and economic development and population policies as reported by countries in the Second United Nations Inquiry on Population and Development, population growth rates in the developing countries as a whole may decline from the present level of 2.4% per annum to about 2% by 1985; and below 0.7% per annum in the developed countries. In this case the worldwide rate of population growth would decline from 2% to about 1.7%. Para 36 says that these projections and those for mortality decline are consistent with declines in the birth rate of the developing countries as a whole from the present level of 38 per thousand to 30 per thousand by 1985. Para 36 goes on to say that "To achieve by 1985 these levels of fertility would require substantial national efforts, by those countries concerned, in the field of socio-economic development and population policies, supported, upon request, by adequate international assistance." Para 37 then follows with the statement that countries which consider their birth rates detrimental to their national purposes are invited to consider setting quantitative goals and implementing policies that may lead to the attainment of such goals by 1985. Para 106 recommends a comprehensive review and appraisal of population trends and policies discussed in the Plan of Action should be undertaken every five years and modified, wherever needed, by ECOSOC.

Usefulness of the Plan of Action

The World Population Plan of Action, despite its wordiness and often hesitant tone, contains all the necessary provisions for effective population growth control programs at national and international levels. It lacks only plain statements of quantitative goals with time frames for their accomplishment. These will have to be added by individual national action and development as rapidly as possible in further U.N. documents. The basis for suitable goals exists in paragraphs 16, 36, 37, and 106, referred to above. The U.N. low variant projection used in these paragraphs is close to the goals proposed by the United States and other ECAFE nations:

–   For developed countries –
    replacement levels of fertility by 1985;
    stationary populations as soon as practicable.
–   For developing countries –
    replacement levels in two or three decades.
–   For the world –
    a 1.7% population growth rate by 1985 with 2% average for the developing countries and 0.7% average for developed countries;
    replacement level of fertility for all countries by 2000.

The dangerous situation evidenced by the current food situation and projections for the future make it essential to press for the realization of these goals. The beliefs, ideologies and misconceptions displayed by many nations at Bucharest indicate more forcefully than ever the need for extensive education of the leaders of many governments, especially in Africa and some in Latin America. Approaches leaders of individual countries must be designed in the light of their current beliefs and to meet their special concerns. These might include:

1. Projections of population growth individualized for countries and with analyses of relations of population factors to social and economic development of each country.

2. Familiarization programs at U.N. Headquarters in New York for ministers of governments, senior policy level officials and comparably influential leaders from private life.

3. Greatly increased training programs for senior officials in the elements of demographic economics.

4. Assistance in integrating population factors in national plans, particularly as they relate to health services, education, agricultural resources and development, employment, equitable distribution of income and social stability.

5. Assistance in relating population policies and family planning programs to major sectors of development: health, nutrition,

agriculture, education, social services, organized labor, women's activities, community development.

6. Initiatives to implement the Percy amendment regarding improvement in the status of women.

7. Emphasis in assistance and development programs on development of rural areas.

All these activities and others particularly productive are consistent with the Plan of Action and may be based upon it.

Beyond these activities, essentially directed at national interests, a broader educational concept is needed to convey an acute understanding of the interrelation of national interests and world population growth.

PART TWO.
POLICY RECOMMENDATIONS

I. Introduction - A U.S. Global Population Strategy

There is no simple single approach to the population problem which will provide a "technological fix". As the previous analysis makes clear the problem of population growth has social, economic and technological aspects all of which must be understood and dealt with for a world population policy to succeed. With this in mind, the following broad recommended strategy provides a framework for the development of specific individual programs which must be tailored to the needs and particularities of each country and of different sectors of the population within a country. Essentially all its recommendations made below are supported by the World Population Plan of action drafted at the World Population Conference.

A. Basic Global Strategy

The following basic elements are necessary parts of a comprehensive approach to the population problem which must include both bilateral and multilateral components to achieve success. Thus, USG population assistance programs will need to be coordinated with those of the major multilateral institutions, voluntary organizations, and other bilateral donors.

The common strategy for dealing with rapid population growth should encourage constructive actions to lower fertility since population growth over the years will seriously negate reasonable prospects for the sound social and economic development of the peoples involved.

While the time horizon in this NSSM is the year 2000 we must recognize that in most countries, especially the LDCs, population stability cannot be achieved until the next century. There are too many powerful socio-economic factors operating on family size decisions and too much momentum built into the dynamics of population growth to permit a quick and dramatic reversal of current trends. There is also even less cause for optimism on the rapidity of socio-economic progress that would generate rapid fertility reduction in the poor LDCs than on the feasibility of extending family planning services to those in their populations who may wish to take advantage of them. Thus, at this point we cannot know with certainty when world population can feasibly be stabilized, nor can we state with assurance the limits of the world's ecological "carrying capability". But we can be certain of the desirable direction of change and can state as a plausible objective the target of achieving replacement fertility rates by the year 2000.

Over the past few years, U.S. government-funded population programs have played a major role in arousing interest in family planning in many countries, and in launching and accelerating the growth of national family planning programs. In most countries, there has been an initial rapid growth in contraceptive "acceptors" up to perhaps 10% of fertile couples in a few LDCs. The acceleration of previous trends of fertility decline is attributable, at least in part, to family planning programs.

However, there is growing appreciation that the problem is more long term and complex than first appeared and that a short term burst of activity or moral fervor will not solve it. The danger in this realization is that the U.S. might abandon its commitment to assisting in the world's population problem, rather than facing up to it for the long-run difficult problem that it is.

From year to year we are learning more about what kind of fertility reduction is feasible in differing LDC situations. Given the laws of compound growth, even comparatively small reductions in fertility over the next decade will make a significant difference in total numbers by the year 2000, and a far more significant one by the year 2050.

The proposed strategy calls for a coordinated approach to respond to the important U.S. foreign policy interest in the influence of population growth on the world's political, economic and ecological systems. What is unusual about population is that this foreign policy interest must have a time horizon far beyond that of most other objectives. While there are strong short-run reasons for population programs, because of such factors as food supply, pressures on social service budgets, urban migration and social and political instability, the major impact of the benefits - or avoidance of catastrophe - that could be accomplished by a strengthened U.S. commitment in the population area will be felt less by those of us in the U.S. and other countries today than by our children and grandchildren.

B. Key Country priorities in U.S. and Multilateral Population Assistance

One issue in any global population strategy is the degree of emphasis in allocation of program resources among countries. The options available range from heavy concentration on a few vital large countries to a geographically diverse program essentially involving all countries willing to accept such assistance. All agencies believe the following policy provides the proper overall balance.

In order to assist the development of major countries and to maximize progress toward population stability, primary emphasis would be placed on the largest and fastest growing developing countries where the imbalance between growing numbers and development potential most seriously risks instability, unrest, and international tensions. These countries are: India, Bangladesh, Pakistan, Nigeria, Mexico, Indonesia, Brazil, The Philippines, Thailand, Egypt, Turkey, Ethiopia, and Colombia. Out of a total 73.3 million worldwide average increase in population from 1970-75 these countries contributed 34.3 million or 47%. This group of priority countries includes some with virtually no government interest in family planning and others with active government family planning programs which require and would welcome enlarged technical and financial assistance. These countries should be given the highest priority within AID's population program in terms of resource allocations and/or leadership efforts to encourage action by other donors and organizations.

However, other countries would not be ignored. AID would provide population assistance and/or undertake leadership efforts with respect to other, lower priority countries to the extent that the availability of funds and staff permits, taking into account of such factors as : long run U.S. political interests; impact of rapid population growth on its development potential; the country's relative contribution to world population growth; its financial capacity to cope with the problem; potential impact on domestic unrest and international frictions (which can apply to small as well as large countries); its significance as a test or demonstration case; and opportunities for expenditures that appear particularly cost-effective (e.g. it has been suggested that there may be particularly cost-effective opportunities for supporting family planning to reduce the lag between mortality and fertility declines in countries where death rates are still declining rapidly); national commitment to an effective program.

For both the high priority countries and the lower priority ones to which funds and staff permit aid, the form and content of our assistance or leadership efforts would vary from country to country, depending on each nation's particular interests, needs, and receptivity to various forms of assistance. For example, if these countries are receptive to U.S. assistance through bilateral or central AID funding, we should provide such assistance at levels commensurate with the recipient's capability to finance needed actions with its own funds, the contributions of other donors and organizations, and the effectiveness with which funds can be used.

In countries where U.S. assistance is limited either by the nature of political or diplomatic relations with those countries or by lack of strong government desire. In population reduction programs, external technical and financial assistance (if desired by the countries) would have to come from other donors and/or from private and international organizations, many of which receive contributions from AID. The USG would, however, maintain an interest (e.g. through Embassies) in such countries' population problems and programs (if any) to reduce population growth rates. Moreover, particularly in the case of high priority countries, we should be alert to opportunities for expanding our assistance efforts and for demonstrating to their leaders the consequences of rapid population growth and the benefits of actions to reduce fertility.

In countries to which other forms of U.S. assistance are provided but not population assistance, AID will monitor progress toward achievement of development objectives, taking into account the extent to which these are hindered by rapid population growth, and will look for opportunities to encourage initiation of or improvement in population policies and programs.

In addition, the U.S. strategy should support in these LDC countries general activities (e.g. bio-medical research or fertility control methods) capable of achieving major breakthroughs in key problems which hinder reductions in population growth.

C. Instruments and Modalities for Population Assistance

Bilateral population assistance is the largest and most invisible "instrument" for carrying out U.S. policy in this area. Other instruments include: support for and coordination with population programs of multilateral organizations and voluntary agencies; encouragement of multilateral country consortia and consultative groups to emphasize family planning in reviews of overall recipient progress and aid requests; and formal and informal presentation of views at international gatherings, such as food and population conferences. Specific country strategies must be worked out for each of the highest priority countries, and for the lower priority ones. These strategies will take account of such factors as: national attitudes and sensitivities on family planning; which "instruments" will be most acceptable, opportunities for effective use of assistance; and need of external capital or operating assistance.

For example, in Mexico our strategy would focus on working primarily through private agencies and multilateral organizations to encourage more government attention to the need for control of population growth; in Bangladesh we might provide large-scale technical and financial assistance, depending on the soundness of specific program requests; in Indonesia we would respond to assistance requests but would seek to have Indonesia meet as much of program costs from its own resources (i.e. surplus oil earnings) as possible. In general we would not provide large-scale bilateral assistance in the more developed LDCs, such as Brazil or Mexico. Although these countries are in the top priority list our approach must take account of the fact that their problems relate often to government policies and decisions and not to larger scale need for concessional assistance.

Within the overall array of U.S. foreign assistance programs, preferential treatment in allocation of funds and manpower should be given to cost-effective programs to reduce population growth;

including both family planning activities and supportive activities in other sectors.

While some have argued for use of explicit "leverage" to "force" better population programs on LDC governments, there are several practical constraints on our efforts to achieve program improvements. Attempts to use "leverage" for far less sensitive issues have generally caused political frictions and often backfired. Successful family planning requires strong local dedication and commitment that cannot over the long run be enforced from the outside. There is also the danger that some LDC leaders will see developed country pressures for family planning as a form of economic or racial imperialism; this could well create a serious backlash.

Short of "leverage", there are many opportunities, bilaterally and multilaterally, for U.S. representations to discuss and urge the need for stronger family planning programs. There is also some established precedent for taking account of family planning performance in appraisal of assistance requirements by AID and consultative groups. Since population growth is a major determinant of increases in food demand, allocation of scarce PL 480 resources should take account of what steps a country is taking in population control as well as food production. In these sensitive relationships, however, it is important in style as well as substance to avoid the appearance of coercion.

D. <u>Provision and Development of Family Planning Services, Information and Technology</u>

Past experience suggests that easily available family planning services are a vital and effective element in reducing fertility rates in the LDCs.

Two main advances are required for providing safe and effective fertility control techniques in the developing countries:

1. <u>Expansion and further development of efficient low-cost systems to assure the full availability of existing family planning services, materials and information to the 85% of LDC populations not now effectively reached.</u> In developing countries willing to create special delivery systems for family planning services this may be the most effective method. In others the most efficient and acceptable method is to combine family planning with health or nutrition in multi-purpose delivery systems.

2. Improving the effectiveness of present means of fertility control, and developing new technologies which are simple, low cost, effective, safe, long-lasting and acceptable to potential users. This involves both basic developmental research and operations research to judge the utility of new or modified approaches under LDC conditions.

Both of these goals should be given very high priority with necessary additional funding consistent with current or adjusted divisions of labor among other donors and organizations involved in these areas of population assistance.

E. Creating Conditions Conducive to Fertility Decline

It is clear that the availability of contraceptive services and information is not a complete answer to the population problem. In view of the importance of socio-economic factors in determining desired family size, overall assistance strategy should increasingly concentrate on selective policies which will contribute to population decline as well as other goals. This strategy reflects the complementarity between population control and other U.S. development objectives, particularly those relating to AID's Congressional mandate to focus on problems of the "poor majority" in LDC's.

We know that certain kinds of development policies—e.g., those which provide the poor with a major share in development benefits—both promote fertility reductions and accomplish other major development objectives. There are other policies which appear to also promote fertility reduction but which may conflict with non-population objectives (e.g., consider the effect of bringing a large number of women into the labor force in countries and occupations where unemployment is already high and rising).

However, AID knows only approximately the relative priorities among the factors that affect fertility and is even further away from knowing what specific cost-effective steps governments can take to affect these factors.

Nevertheless, with what limited information we have, the urgency of moving forward toward lower fertility rates, even without complete knowledge of the socio-economic forces involved, suggests a three-pronged strategy:

1. High priority to large-scale implementation of programs affecting the determinants of fertility in those cases where there is probable cost-effectiveness, taking account of potential impact on population growth rates; other development benefits to be gained; ethical considerations; feasibility in light of LDC bureaucratic and political concerns and problems; and timeframe for accomplishing objectives.

2. High priority to experimentation and pilot projects in areas where there is evidence of a close relationship to fertility reduction but where there are serious questions about cost-effectiveness relating either to other development impact (e.g., the female employment example cited above) or to program design (e.g., what cost-effective steps can be taken to promote female employment or literacy).

3. High priority to comparative research and evaluation on the relative impact on desired family size of the socio-economic determinants of fertility in general and on what policy scope exists for affecting these determinants.

In all three cases emphasis should be given to moving action as much as possible to LDC institutions and individuals rather than to involving U.S. researchers on a large scale.

Activities in all three categories would receive very high priority in allocation of AID funds. The largest amounts required should be in the first category and would generally not come from population funds. However, since such activities (e.g., in rural development and basic education) coincide with other AID sectoral priorities, sound project requests from LDC's will be placed close to the top in AID's funding priorities (assuming that they do not conflict with other major development and other foreign policy objectives).

The following areas appear to contain significant promise in effecting fertility declines, and are discussed in subsequent sections.

- providing minimal levels of education especially for women;
- reducing infant and child mortality;
- expanding opportunities for wage employment especially for women;
- developing alternatives to "social security" support provided by children to aging parents;

- pursuing development strategies that skew income growth toward the poor, especially rural development focussing on rural poverty;
- concentrating on the education and indoctrination of the rising generation of children regarding the desirability of smaller family size.

The World Population Plan of Action includes a provision (paragraph 31) that countries trying for effective fertility levels should give priority to development programs and health and education strategies which have a decisive effect upon demographic trends, including fertility. It calls for international information to give priority to assisting such national efforts. Programs suggested (paragraph 32) are essentially the same as those listed above.

Food is another of special concern in any population strategy. Adequate food stocks need to be created to provide for periods of severe shortages and LDC food production efforts must be reenforced to meet increased demand resulting from population and income growth. U.S. agricultural production goals should take account of the normal import requirements of LDC's (as well as developed countries) and of likely occasional crop failures in major parts of the LDC world. Without improved food security, there will be pressure leading to possible conflict and the desire for large families for "insurance" purposes, thus undermining other development and population control efforts.

F. Development of World-Wide Political and Popular Commitment to Population Stabilization and Its Associated Improvement of Individual Quality of Life.

A fundamental element in any overall strategy to deal with the population problem is obtaining the support and commitment of key leaders in the developing countries. This is only possible if they can clearly see the negative impact of unrestricted population growth in their countries and the benefits of reducing birth rates - and if they believe it is possible to cope with the population problem through instruments of public policy. Since most high officials are in office for relatively short periods, they have to see early benefits or the value of longer term statesmanship. In each specific case, individual leaders will have to approach their population problems within the context of their country's values, resources, and existing priorities.

Therefore, it is vital that leaders of major LDCs themselves take the lead in advancing family planning and population stabilization, not only within the U.N. and other international organizations but also through bilateral contacts with leaders of other LDCs. Reducing population growth in LDCs should not be advocated exclusively by the developed countries. The U.S. should encourage such a role as opportunities appear in its high level contact with LDC leaders.

The most recent forum for such an effort was the August 1974 U.N. World Population Conference. It was an ideal context to focus concerted world attention on the problem. The debate views and highlights of the World Population Plan of action are reviewed in Chapter VI.

The U.S. strengthened its credibility as an advocate of lower population growth rates by explaining that, while it did not have a single written action population policy, it did have legislation, Executive Branch policies and court decisions that amounted to a national policy and that our national fertility level was already below replacement and seemed likely to attain a stable population by 2000.

The U.S. also proposed to join with other developed countries in an international collaborative effort of research in human reproduction and fertility control covering bio-medical and socio-economic factors.

The U.S. further offered to collaborate with other interested donor countries and organizations (e.g., WHO, UNFPA, World Bank, UNICEF) to encourage further action by LDC governments and other institutions to provide low-cost, basic preventive health services, including maternal and child health and family planning services, reaching out into the remote rural areas.

The U.S. delegation also said the U.S. would request from the Congress increased U.S. bilateral assistance to population-family planning programs, and additional amounts for essential functional activities and our contribution to the UNFPA if countries showed an interest in such assistance.

Each of these commitments is important and should be pursued by the U.S. Government.

It is vital that the effort to develop and strengthen a commitment on the part of the LDC leaders not be seen by them as an industrialized country policy to keep their strength down or to reserve resources for use by the "rich" countries. Development of such a perception could create a serious backlash adverse to the cause of population stability. Thus the U.S. and other "rich" countries should take care that policies they advocate for the LDC's would be acceptable within their own countries. (This may require public debate and affirmation of our intended policies.) The "political" leadership role in developing countries should, of course, be taken whenever possible by their own leaders.

The U.S. can help to minimize charges of an imperialist motivation behind its support of population activities by repeatedly asserting that such support derives from a concern with:

(a) the right of the individual couple to determine freely and responsibly their number and spacing of children and to have information, education, and means to do so; and

(b) the fundamental social and economic development of poor countries in which rapid population growth is both a contributing cause and a consequence of widespread poverty.

Furthermore, the U.S. should also take steps to convey the message that the control of world population growth is in the mutual interest of the developed and developing countries alike.

Family planning programs should be supported by multilateral organizations wherever they can provide the most efficient and acceptable means. Where U.S. bilateral assistance is necessary or preferred, it should be provided in collaboration with host country institutions—as is the case now. Credit should go to local leaders for the success of projects. The success and acceptability of family planning assistance will depend in large measure on the degree to which it contributes to the ability of the host government to serve and obtain the support of its people.

In many countries today, decision-makers are wary of instituting population programs, not because they are unconcerned about rapid population growth, but because they lack confidence that such programs will succeed. By actively working to demonstrate to such leaders that national population and family planning programs have achieved progress in a wide variety of poor countries, the U.S. could help persuade the leaders of many countries that the investment of funds in national family planning programs is likely to yield high returns even in the short and medium term. Several examples of success exist already, although regrettably they tend to come from LDCs that are untypically well off in terms of income growth and/or social services or are islands or city states.

We should also appeal to potential leaders among the younger generations in developing countries, focusing on the implications of continued rapid population growth for their countries in the next 10-20 years, when they may assume national leadership roles.

Beyond seeking to reach and influence national leaders, improved world-wide support for population-related efforts should be sought through increased emphasis on mass media and other population education and motivation programs by the U.N., USIA, and USAID. We should give higher priorities in our information programs world-wide for this area and consider expansion of collaborative arrangements with multilateral institutions in population education programs.

Another challenge will be in obtaining the further understanding and support of the U.S. public and Congress for the necessary added funds for such an effort, given the competing demands for resources. If an effective program is to be mounted by the U.S., we will need to contribute significant new amounts of funds. Thus there is need to reinforce the positive attitudes of those in Congress who presently support U.S. activity in the population field and to enlist their support in persuading others. Public debate is needed now.

Personal approaches by the President, the Secretary of State, other members of the Cabinet, and their principal deputies would be helpful in this effort. Congress and the public must be clearly informed that the Executive Branch is seriously worried about the problem and that it deserves their further attention. Congressional representatives at the World Population Conference can help.

An Alternative View

The above basic strategy assumes that the current forms of assistance programs in both population and economic and social development areas will be able to solve the problem. There is however, another view, which is shared by a growing number of experts. It believes that the outlook is much harsher and far less tractable than commonly perceived. This holds that the severity of the population problem in this century which is already claiming the lives of more than 10 million people yearly, is such as to make likely continued widespread food shortage and other demographic catastrophes, and, in the words of C.P. Snow, we shall be watching people starve on television.

The conclusion of this view is that mandatory programs may be needed and that we should be considering these possibilities now.

This school of thought believes the following types of questions need to be addressed:

Should the U.S. make an all out commitment to major limitation of world population with all the financial and international as well as domestic political costs that would entail?

Should the U.S. set even higher agricultural production goals which would enable it to provide additional major food resources to other countries? Should they be nationally or internationally controlled?

On what basis should such food resources then be provided? Would food be considered an instrument of national power? Will we be forced to make choices as to whom we can reasonably assist, and if so, should population efforts be a criterion for such assistance?

Is the U.S. prepared to accept food rationing to help people who can't/won't control their population growth?

Should the U.S. seek to change its own food consumption patterns toward more efficient uses of protein?

Are mandatory population control measures appropriate for the U.S. and/or for others?

Should the U.S. initiate a major research effort to address the growing problems of fresh water supply, ecological damage, and adverse climate?

While definitive answers to those questions are not possible in this study given its time limitations and its implications for domestic policy, nevertheless they are needed if one accepts the drastic and persistent character of the population growth problem. Should the choice be made that the recommendations and the options given below are not adequate to meet this problem, consideration should be given to a further study and additional action in this field as outlined above.

Conclusion

The overall strategy above provides a general approach through which the difficulties and dangers of population growth and related problems can be approached in a balanced and comprehensive basis. No single effort will do the job. Only a concerted and major effort in a number of carefully selected directions can provide the hope of success in reducing population growth and its unwanted dangers to world economic will-being and political stability. There are no "quick-fixes" in this field.

Below are specific program recommendations which are designed to implement this strategy. Some will require few new resources; many call for major efforts and significant new resources. We cannot simply buy population growth moderation for nearly 4 billion people "on the cheap".

II. Action to Create Conditions for Fertility Decline: Population and a Development Assistance Strategy

A. General Strategy and Resource Allocations for AID Assistance

Discussion:

1. Past Program Actions

Since inception of the program in 1965, AID has obligated nearly $625 million for population activities. These funds have been used primarily to (1) draw attention to the population problem, (2) encourage multilateral and other donor support for the worldwide population effort, and (3) help create and maintain the means for attacking the problem, including the development of LDC capabilities to do so.

In pursuing these objectives, AID's population resources were focussed on areas of need where action was feasible and likely to be effective. AID has provided assistance to population programs in some 70 LDCs, on a bilateral basis and/or indirectly through private organizations and other channels. AID currently provides bilateral assistance to 36 of these countries. State and AID played an important role in establishing the United Nations Fund for Population Activities (UNFPA) to spearhead multilateral effort in population as a complement to the bilateral actions of AID and other donor countries. Since the Fund's establishment, AID has been the largest single contributor. Moreover, with assistance from AID a number of private family planning organizations (e.g., Pathfinder Fund, International Planned Parenthood Foundation, Population Council) have significantly expanded their worldwide population programs. Such organizations are still the main supporters of family planning action in many developing countries.

AID actions have been a major catalyst in stimulating the flow of funds into LDC population programs - from almost nothing ten years ago, the amounts being spent from all sources in 1974 for programs in the developing countries of Africa, Latin America, and Asia (excluding China) will total between $400 and $500 million. About half of this will be contributed by the developed countries bilaterally or through multilateral agencies, and the balance will come from the budgets of the developing countries themselves. AID's contribution is about one-quarter of the total - AID obligated $112.4 million for population programs in FY 1974 and plans for FY 1975 program of $137.5 million.

While world resources for population activities will continue to grow, they are unlikely to expand as rapidly as needed. (One rough estimate is that five times the current amount, or about $2.5 billion in constant dollars, will be required annually by 1985 to provide the 2.5 billion people in the developing world, excluding China, with full-scale family planning programs). In view of these limited resources AID's efforts (in both fiscal and manpower terms) and through its leadership the efforts of others, must be focussed to the extent possible on high priority needs in countries where the population problem is the most acute. Accordingly, AID last year began a process of developing geographic and functional program priorities for use in allocating funds and staff, and in arranging and adjusting divisions of labor with other donors and organizations active in the worldwide population effort. Although this study has not yet been completed, a general outline of a U.S. population assistance strategy can be developed from the results of the priorities studied to date. The geographic and functional parameters of the strategy are discussed under 2. and 3. below. The implications for population resource allocations are presented under 4.

2. Geographic Priorities in U.S. Population Assistance

The U.S. strategy should be to encourage and support, through bilateral, multilateral and other channels, constructive actions to lower fertility rates in selected developing countries. Within this overall strategy and in view of funding and manpower limitations, the U.S. should emphasize assistance to those countries where the population problem is the most serious.

There are three major factors to consider in judging the seriousness of the problem:

The first is the country's contribution to the world's population problem, which is determined by the size of its population, its population growth rate, and its progress in the "demographic transition" from high birth and high death rates to low ones.

The second is the extent to which population growth impinges on the country's economic development and its financial capacity to cope with its population problem.

The third factor is the extent to which an imbalance between growing numbers of people and a country's capability to handle the problem could lead to serious instability, international tensions, or conflicts. Although many countries may experience adverse consequences from such imbalances, the troublemaking regional or international conditions might not be as serious in some places as they are in others.

Based on the first two criteria, AID has developed a preliminary rank ordering of nearly 100 developing countries which, after review and refinement, will be used as a guide in AID's own funding and manpower resource allocations and in encouraging action through AID leadership efforts on the part of other population assistance instrumentalities. Applying these three criteria to this rank ordering, there are 13 countries where we currently judge the problem and risks to be the most serious. They are: Bangladesh, India, Pakistan, Indonesia, Philippines, Thailand, Egypt, Turkey, Ethiopia, Nigeria, Brazil, Mexico, and Colombia. Out of a total 67 million worldwide increase in population in 1972 these countries contributed about 45%. These countries range from those with virtually no government interest in family planning to those with active government family planning programs which require and would welcome enlarged technical and financial assistance.

These countries should be given the highest priority within AID's population program in terms of resource allocations and/or leadership efforts to encourage action by other donors and organizations. The form and content of our assistance or leadership efforts would vary from country-to-country (as discussed in 3. below), depending on each country's needs, its receptivity to various forms of assistance, its capability to finance needed actions, the effectiveness with which funds can be used, and current or adjusted divisions of labor among the other donors and organizations providing population assistance to the country. AID's population actions would also need to be consistent with the overall U.S. development policy toward each country.

While the countries cited above would be given highest priority, other countries would not be ignored. AID would provide population assistance and/or undertake leadership efforts with respect to other countries to the extent that the availability of funds and staff permits, taking account of such factors as: a country's placement in AID's priority listing of LDCs; its potential impact on domestic unrest and international frictions (which can apply to small as well as large countries); its significance as a test or demonstration case; and opportunities for expenditures that appear particularly cost-effective (e.g. its has been suggested that there may be particularly cost-effective opportunities for supporting family planning to reduce the lag between mortality and fertility declines in countries where death rates are still declining rapidly).

3. Mode and Content of U.S. Population Assistance

In moving from geographic emphases to strategies for the mode and functional content of population assistance to both the higher and lower priority countries which are to be assisted, various factors need to be considered: (1) the extent of a country's understanding of its population problem and interest in responding to it; (2) the specific actions needed to cope with the problem; (3) the country's need for external financial assistance to deal with the problem; and (4) its receptivity to various forms of assistance.

Some of the countries in the high priority group cited above (e.g. Bangladesh, Pakistan, Indonesia, Philippines, Thailand) and some lower priority countries have recognized that rapid population growth is a problem, are taking actions of their own to deal with it, and are receptive to assistance from the U.S. (through bilateral or central AID funding) and other donors, as well as to multilateral support for their efforts. In these cases AID should continue to provide such assistance based on each country's functional needs, the effectiveness with which funds can be used in these areas, and current or adjusted divisions of labor among other donors and organizations providing assistance to the country. Furthermore, our assistance strategies for these countries should consider their capabilities to finance needed population actions. Countries which have relatively large surpluses of export earning and foreign exchange reserves are unlikely to require large-scale external financial assistance and should be encouraged to finance their own commodity imports as well as local costs. In such cases our strategy should be to concentrate on needed technical assistance and on attempting to play a catalytic role in encouraging better programs and additional host country financing for dealing with the population problem.

In other high and lower priority countries U.S. assistance is limited either by the nature of political or diplomatic relations with those countries (e.g. India, Egypt), or by the lack of strong government interest in population reduction programs (e.g. Nigeria, Ethiopia, Mexico, Brazil). In such cases, external technical and financial assistance, if desired by the countries, would have to come from other donors and/or from private and international organizations (many of which receive contributions from AID). The USG would, however, maintain an interest (e.g. through Embassies) in such countries' population problems and programs (if any) to reduce population growth rates. Moreover, particularly in the case of high priority countries to which U.S. population assistance is now limited for one reason or another, we should be alert to opportunities for expanding our assistance efforts and for demonstrating to their leaders the consequences of rapid population growth and the benefits of actions to reduce fertility.

In countries to which other forms of U.S. assistance are provided but not population assistance, AID will monitor progress toward achievement of development objectives, taking into account the extent to which these are hindered by rapid population growth, and will look for opportunities to encourage initiation of or improvement in population policies and programs.

In addition, the U.S. strategy should support general activities capable of achieving major breakthroughs in key problems which hinder attainment of fertility control objectives. For example, the development of more effective, simpler contraceptive methods through bio-medical research will benefit all countries which face the problem of rapid population growth; improvements in methods for measuring demographic changes will assist a number of LDCs in determining current population growth rates and evaluating the impact over time of population/family planning activities.

4. Resource Allocations for U.S. Population Assistance

AID funds obligated for population/family planning assistance rose steadily since inception of the program ($10 million in the FY 1965-67 period) to nearly $125 million in FY 1972. In FY 1973, however, funds available for population remained at the $125 million level; in FY 1974 they actually declined slightly, to $112.5 million because of a ceiling on population obligations inserted in the legislation by the House Appropriations Committee. With this plateau in AID population obligations, worldwide resources have not been adequate to meet all identified, sensible funding needs, and we therefore see opportunities for significant expansion of the program.

Some major actions in the area of creating conditions for fertility decline, as described in Section IIB, can be funded from AID resources available for the sectors in question (e.g., education, agriculture). Other actions come under the purview of population ("Title X") funds. In this latter category, increases in projected budget requests to the Congress on the order of $35-50 million annually through FY 1980—above the $137.5 million requested by FY 1975—appear appropriate at this time. Such increases must be accompanied by expanding contributions to the worldwide population effort from other donors and organizations and from the LDCs themselves, if significant progress is to be made. The USG should take advantage of appropriate opportunities to stimulate such contributions from others.

Title X Funding for Population

Year		Amount ($ million)
FY 1972	– Actual Obligations	123.3
FY 1973	– Actual Obligations	125.6
FY 1974	– Actual Obligations	112.4
FY 1975	– Request to Congress	137.5
FY 1976	– Projection	170
FY 1977	– Projection	210
FY 1978	– Projection	250
FY 1979	– Projection	300
FY 1980	– Projection	350

These Title X funding projections for FY 1976-80 are general magnitudes based on preliminary estimates of expansion or initiation of population programs in developing countries and growing requirements for outside assistance as discussed in greater detail in other sections of this paper. These estimates contemplated very substantial increases in self-help and assistance from other donor countries.

Our objective should be to assure that developing countries make family planning information, educational and means available to all their peoples by 1980. Our efforts should include:

Increased A.I.D. bilateral and centrally-funded programs, consistent with the geographic priorities cited above.

Expanded contributions to multilateral and private organizations that can work effectively in the population area.

Further research on the relative impact of various socio-economic factors on desired family size, and experimental efforts to test the feasibility of larger-scale efforts to affect some of these factors.

Additional bio-medical research to improve the existing means of fertility control and to develop new ones which are safe, effective, inexpensive, and attractive to both men and women.

Innovative approaches to providing family planning services, such as the utilization of commercial channels for distribution of contraceptives, and the development of low-cost systems for delivering effective health and family planning services to the 85% of LDC populations not now reached by such services.

Expanded efforts to increase the awareness of LDC leaders and publics regarding the consequences of rapid population growth and to stimulate further LDC commitment to actions to reduce fertility.

We believe expansions in the range of 35-50 million annually over the next five years are realistic, in light of potential LDC needs and prospects for increased contributions from other population assistance instrumentalities, as well as constraints on the speed with which AID (and other donors) population funds can be expanded and effectively utilized. These include negative or ambivalent host government attitudes toward population reduction programs; the need for complementary financial and manpower inputs by recipient governments, which must come at the expense of other programs they consider to be high priority; and the need to assure that new projects involve sensible, effective actions that are likely to reduce fertility. We must avoid inadequately planned or implemented programs that lead to extremely high costs per acceptor. In effect, we are closer to "absorptive capacity" in terms of year-to-year increases in population programs than we are, for example, in annual expansions in food, fertilizer or generalized resource transfers.

It would be premature to make detailed funding recommendations by countries and functional categories in light of our inability to predict what changes—such as in host country attitudes to U.S. population assistance and in fertility control technologies—may occur which would significantly alter funding needs in particular geographic or functional areas. For example, AID is currently precluded from providing bilateral assistance to India and Egypt, two significant countries in the highest priority group, due to the nature of U.S. political and diplomatic relations with these countries. However, if these relationships were to change and bilateral aid could be provided, we would want to consider providing appropriate population assistance to these countries. In other cases, changing U.S.-LDC relationships might preclude further aid to some countries. Factors such as these could both change the mix and affect overall magnitudes of funds needed for population assistance. Therefore, proposed program mixes and funding levels by geographic and functional categories should continue to be examined on an annual basis during the regular USG program and budget review processes which lead to the presentation of funding requests to the Congress.

Recognizing that changing opportunities for action could substantially affect AID's resource requirements for population assistance, we anticipate that, if funds are provided by the Congress at the levels projected, we would be able to cover necessary actions related to the highest priority countries and also those related to lower priority countries, moving reasonably far down the list. At this point, however, AID believes it would not be desirable to make priority judgments on which activities would not be funded if Congress did not provide the levels projected. If cuts were made in these levels we would have to make judgments based on such factors as the priority rankings of countries, then-existing LDC needs, and divisions of labor with other actors in the population assistance area.

If AID's population assistance program is to expand at the general magnitudes cited above, additional direct hire staff will likely be needed. While the expansion in program action would be primarily through grants and contracts with LDC or U.S. institutions, or through contributions to international organizations, increases in direct hire staff would be necessary to review project proposals, monitor their implementation through such instrumentalities, and evaluate their progress against pre-established goals. Specific direct hire manpower requirements should continue to be considered during the annual program and budget reviews, along with details of program mix and funding levels by country and functional category, in order to correlate staffing needs with projected program actions for a particular year.

Recommendations

1. The U.S. strategy should be to encourage and support, through bilateral, multilateral and other channels, constructive action to lower fertility rates in selected developing countries. The U.S. should apply each of the relevant provisions of its World Population Plan of Action and use it to influence and support actions by developing countries.

2. Within this overall strategy, the U.S. should give highest priority, in terms of resource allocation (along with donors) to efforts to encourage assistance from others to those countries cited above where the population problem is most serious, and provide assistance to other countries as funds and staff permit.

3. AID's further development of population program priorities, both geographic and functional, should be consistent with the general strategy discussed above, with the other recommendations of this paper and with the World Population Plan of Action. The strategies should be coordinated with the population activities of other donors countries and agencies using the WPPA as leverage to obtain suitable action.

4. AID's budget requests over the next five years should include a major expansion of bilateral population and family planning programs (as appropriate for each country or region), of functional activities as necessary, and of contributions through multilateral channels, consistent with the general funding magnitudes discussed above. The proposed budgets should emphasize the country and functional priorities outlined in the recommendations of this study and as detailed in AID's geographic and functional strategy papers.

II. B. Functional Assistance Programs to Create Conditions for Fertility Decline

Introduction

Discussion

It is clear that the availability of contraceptive services and information, important as that is, is not the only element required to address the population problems of the LDCs. Substantial evidence shows that many families in LDCs (especially the poor) consciously prefer to have numerous children for a variety of economic and social reasons. For example, small children can make economic contributions on family farms, children can be important sources of support for old parents where no alternative form of social security exists, and children may be a source of status for women who have few alternatives in male-dominated societies.

The desire for large families diminishes as income rises. Developed countries and the more developed areas in LDCs have lower fertility than less developed areas. Similarly, family planning programs produce more acceptors and have a greater impact on fertility in developed areas than they do in less developed areas. Thus, investments in development are important in lowering fertility rates. We know that the major socio-economic determinants of fertility are strongly interrelated. A change in any one of them is likely to produce a change in the others as well. Clearly development per se is a powerful determinant of fertility. However, since it is unlikely that most LDCs will develop sufficiently during the next 25-30 years, it is crucial to identify those sectors that most directly and powerfully affect fertility.

In this context, population should be viewed as a variable which interacts, to differing degrees, with a wide range of development programs, and the U.S. strategy should continue to stress the importance of taking population into account in "non-family planning" activities. This is particularly important with the increasing focus in the U.S. development program on food and nutrition, health and population, and education and human resources; assistance programs have less chance of success as long as the numbers to be fed, educated, and employed are increasing rapidly.

Thus, to assist in achieving LDC fertility reduction, not only should family planning be high up on the priority list for U.S. foreign assistance, but high priority in allocation of funds should be given to programs in other sectors that contribute in a cost-effective manner in reduction in population growth.

There is a growing, but still quite small, body of research to determine the socio-economic aspects of development that most directly and powerfully affect fertility. Although the limited analysis to date cannot be considered definitive, there is general agreement that the five following factors (in addition to increases in per capita income) tend to be strongly associated with fertility declines: education, especially the education of women; reductions in infant mortality; wage employment opportunities for women; social security and other substitutes for the economic value of children; and relative equality in income distribution and rural development. There are a number of other factors identified from research, historical analysis, and experimentation that also affect fertility, including delaying the average age of marriage, and direct payments (financial incentive) to family planning acceptors.

There are, however, a number of questions which must be addressed before one can move from identification of factors associated with fertility decline to large-scale programs that will induce fertility decline in a cost-effective manner. For example, in the case of female education, we need to consider such questions as: did the female education cause fertility to decline or did the development process in some situations cause parents both to see less economic need for large families and to indulge in the "luxury" of educating their daughters? If more female education does in fact cause fertility declines, will poor high-fertility parents see much advantage in sending their daughters to school? If so, how much does it cost to educate a girl to the point where her fertility will be reduced (which occurs at about the fourth-grade level)? What specific programs in female education are most cost-effective (e.g., primary school, non-formal literacy training, or vocational or pre-vocational training)? What, in rough quantitative terms, are the non-population benefits of an additional dollar spent on female education in a given situation in comparison to other non-population investment alternatives? What are the population benefits of a dollar spent on female education in comparison with other population-related investments, such as in contraceptive supplies or in maternal and child health care systems? And finally, what is the total population plus non-population benefit of investment in a given specific program in female education in comparison with the total population plus non-population benefits of alternate feasible investment opportunities?

As a recent research proposal from Harvard's Department of Population Studies puts this problem: "Recent studies have identified more specific factors underlying fertility declines, especially, the spread of educational attainment and the broadening of non-traditional roles for women. In situations of rapid population growth, however, these run counter to powerful market forces. Even when efforts are made to provide educational opportunities for most of the school age population, low levels of development and restricted employment opportunities for academically educated youth lead to high dropout rates and non-attendance..."

Fortunately, the situation is by no means as ambiguous for all of the likely factors affecting fertility. For example, laws that raise the minimum marriage age, where politically feasible and at least partially enforceable, can over time have a modest effect on fertility at negligible cost. Similarly, there have been some controversial, but remarkably successful, experiments in India in which financial incentives, along with other motivational devices, were used to get large numbers of men to accept vasectomies. In addition, there appear to be some major activities, such as programs aimed to improve the productive capacity of the rural poor, which can be well justified even without reference to population benefits, but which appear to have major population benefits as well.

The strategy suggested by the above considerations is that the volume and type of programs aimed at the "determinants of fertility" should be directly related to our estimate of the total benefits (including non-population benefits) of a dollar invested in a given proposed program and to our confidence in the reliability of that estimate. There is room for honest disagreement among researchers and policy-makers about the benefits, or feasibility, of a given program. Hopefully, over time, with more research, experimentation and evaluation, areas of disagreement and ambiguity will be clarified, and donors and recipients will have better information both on what policies and programs tend to work under what circumstances and how to go about analyzing a given country situation to find the best feasible steps that should be taken.

Recommendations:

1. AID should implement the strategy set out in the World Population Plan of Action, especially paragraphs 31 and 32 and Section I ("Introduction - a U.S. Global Population Strategy") above, which calls for high priority in funding to three categories of programs in areas affecting fertility (family-size) decisions:

a. Operational programs where there is proven cost-effectiveness, generally where there are also significant benefits for non-population objectives;

b. Experimental programs where research indicates close relationships to fertility reduction but cost-effectiveness has not yet been demonstrated in terms of specific steps to be taken (i.e., program design); and

c. Research and evaluation on the relative impact on desired family size of the socio-economic determinants of fertility, and on what policy scope exists for affecting these determinants.

2. Research, experimentation and evaluation of ongoing programs should focus on answering the questions (such as those raised above, relating to female education) that determine what steps can and should be taken in other sectors that will in a cost-effective manner speed up the rate of fertility decline. In addition to the five areas discussed in Section II. B 1-5 below, the research should also cover the full range of factors affecting fertility, such as laws and norms respecting age of marriage, and financial incentives. Work of this sort should be undertaken in individual key countries to determine the motivational factors required there to develop a preference for small family size. High priority must be given to testing feasibility and replicability on a wide scale.

3. AID should encourage other donors in LDC governments to carry out parallel strategies of research, experimentation, and (cost-effective well-evaluated) large-scale operations programs on factors affecting fertility. Work in this area should be coordinated, and results shared.

4. AID should help develop capacity in a few existing U.S. and LDC institutions to serve as major centers for research and policy development in the areas of fertility-affecting social or economic measures, direct incentives, household behavior research, and evaluation techniques for motivational approaches. The centers should provide technical assistance, serve as a forum for discussion, and generally provide the "critical mass" of effort and visibility which has been lacking in this area to date. Emphasis should be given to maximum involvement of LDC institutions and individuals.

The following sections discuss research experimental and operational programs to be undertaken in the five promising areas mentioned above.

1. Providing Minimal Levels of Education, Especially for Women

Discussion

There is fairly convincing evidence that female education especially of 4th grade and above correlates strongly with reduced desired family size, although it is unclear the extent to which the female education causes reductions in desired family size or whether it is a faster pace of development which leads both to increased demand for female education and to reduction in desired family size. There is also a relatively widely held theory—though not statistically validated—that improved levels of literacy contribute to reduction in desired family size both through greater knowledge of family planning information and increasing motivational factors related to reductions in family size. Unfortunately, AID's experience with mass literacy programs over the past 15 years has yielded the sobering conclusion that such programs generally failed (i.e. were not cost-effective) unless the population sees practical benefits to themselves from learning how to read—e.g., a requirement for literacy to acquire easier access to information about new agricultural technologies or to jobs that require literacy.

Now, however, AID has recently revised its education strategy, in line with the mandate of its legislation, to place emphasis on the spread of education to poor people, particularly in rural areas, and relatively less on higher levels of education. This approach is focused on use of formal and "non-formal" education (i.e., organized education outside the schoolroom setting) to assist in meeting the human resource requirements of the development process, including such things as rural literacy programs aimed at agriculture, family planning, or other development goals.

Recommendations

1. Integrated basic education (including applied literacy) and family planning programs should be developed whenever they appear to be effective, of high priority, and acceptable to the individual country. AID should continue its emphasis on basic education, for women as well as men.

2. A major effort should be made in LDCs seeking to reduce birth rates to assure at least an elementary school education for virtually all children, girls as well as boys, as soon as the country can afford it (which would be quite soon for all but the poorest countries). Simplified, practical education programs should be developed. These programs should, where feasible, include specific curricula to motivate the next generation toward a two-child family average to assure that level of fertility in two or three decades. AID should encourage and respond to requests for assis-

tance in extending basic education and in introducing family planning into curricula. Expenditures for such emphasis on increased practical education should come from general AID funds, not population funds.

II. B
2. Reducing Infant and Child Mortality

Discussion:

High infant and child mortality rates, evident in many developing countries, lead parents to be concerned about the number of their children who are likely to survive. Parents may overcompensate for possible child losses by having additional children. Research to date clearly indicates not only that high fertility and high birth rates are closely correlated but that in most circumstances low net population growth rates can only be achieved when child mortality is low as well. Policies and programs which significantly reduce infant and child mortality below present levels will lead couples to have fewer children. However, we must recognize that there is a lag of at least several years before parents (and cultures and subcultures) become confident that their children are more likely to survive and to adjust their fertility behavior accordingly.

Considerable reduction in infant and child mortality is possible through improvement in nutrition, inoculations against diseases, and other public health measures if means can be devised for extending such services to neglected LDC populations on a low-cost basis. It often makes sense to combine such activities with family planning services in integrated delivery systems in order to maximize the use of scarce LDC financial and health manpower resources (See Section IV). In addition, providing selected health care for both mothers and their children can enhance the acceptability of family planning by showing concern for the whole condition of the mother and her children and not just for the single factor of fertility.

The two major cost-effective problems in maternal-child health care are that clinical health care delivery systems have not in the past accounted for much of the reduction in infant mortality and that, as in the U.S., local medical communities tend to favor relatively expensive quality health care, even at the cost of leaving large numbers of people (in the LDC's generally over two-thirds of the people) virtually uncovered by modern health services.

Although we do not have all the answers on how to develop inexpensive, integrated delivery systems, we need to proceed with operational programs to respond to ODC requests if they are likely to be cost-effective based on experience to date, and to experiment on a large scale with innovative ways of tackling the outstanding problems. Evaluation mechanisms for measuring the impact of various courses of action are an essential part of this effort in order to provide feedback for current and future projects and to improve the state of the art in this field.

Currently, efforts to develop low-cost health and family planning services for neglected populations in the LDC's are impeded because of the lack of international commitment and resources to the health side. For example:

A. The World Bank could supply low-interest credits to LDCs for the development of low-cost health-related services to neglected populations but has not yet made a policy decision to do so. The Bank has a population and health program and the program's leaders have been quite sympathetic with the above objective. The Bank's staff has prepared a policy paper on this subject for the Board but prospects for it are not good. Currently, the paper will be discussed by the Bank Board at its November 1974 meeting. Apparently there is some reticence within the Bank's Board and in parts of the staff about making a strong initiative in this area. In part, the Bank argues that there are not proven models of effective, low-cost health systems in which the Bank can invest. The Bank also argues that other sectors such as agriculture, should receive higher priority in the competition for scarce resources. In addition, arguments are made in some quarters of the Bank that the Bank ought to restrict itself to "hard loan projects" and not get into the "soft" area.

A current reading from the Bank's staff suggests that unless there is some change in the thinking of the Bank Board, the Bank's policy will be simply to keep trying to help in the population and health areas but not to take any large initiative in the low-cost delivery system area.

The Bank stance is regrettable because the Bank could play a very useful role in this area helping to fund low-cost physical structures and other elements of low-cost health systems, including rural health clinics where needed. It could also help in providing low-cost loans for training, and in seeking and testing new approaches to reaching those who do not now have access to health and family planning services. This would not be at all inconsistent with our and the Bank's frankly admitting that we do not have all the "answer" or cost-effective models for low-cost health delivery systems. Rather they, we and other donors could work together on experimentally oriented, operational programs to develop models for the wide variety of situations faced by LDCs.

Involvement of the Bank in this area would open up new possibilities for collaboration. Grant funds, whether from the U.S. or UNFPA, could be used to handle the parts of the action that require short lead times such as immediate provision of supplies, certain kinds of training and rapid deployment of technical assistance. Simultaneously, for parts of the action that require longer lead times, such as building clinics, World Bank loans could be employed. The Bank's lending processes could be synchronized to bring such building activity to a readiness condition at the time the training programs have moved along far enough to permit manning of the facilities. The emphasis should be on meeting low-cost rather than high-cost infrastructure requirements.

Obviously, in addition to building, we assume the Bank could fund other local-cost elements of expansion of health systems such as longer-term training programs.

AID is currently trying to work out improved consultation procedures with the Bank staff in the hope of achieving better collaborative efforts within the Bank's current commitment of resources in the population and health areas. With a greater commitment of Bank resources and improved consultation with AID and UNFPA, a much greater dent could be made on the overall problem.

B. The World Health Organization (WHO) and its counterpart for Latin America, the Pan American Health Organization (PAHO), currently provide technical assistance in the development and implementation of health projects which are in turn financed by international funding mechanisms such as UNDP and the International Financial Institutions. However, funds available for health actions through these organizations are limited at present. Higher priority by the international funding agencies to health actions could expand the opportunities for useful collaborations among donor institutions and countries to develop low-cost integrated health and family planning delivery systems for LDC populations that do not now have access to such services.

Recommendations:

The U.S. should encourage heightened international interest in and commitment of resources to developing delivery mechanisms for providing integrated health and family planning services to neglected populations at costs which host countries can support within a reasonable period of time. Efforts would include:

1. Encouraging the World Bank and other international funding mechanisms, through the U.S. representatives on the boards of these organizations, to take a broader initiative in the development of inexpensive service delivery mechanisms in countries wishing to expand such systems.

2. Indicating U.S. willingness (as the U.S. did at the World Population Conference) to join with other donors and organizations to encourage and support further action by LDC governments and other institutions in the low-cost delivery systems area.

A. As offered at Bucharest, the U.S. should join donor countries, WHO, UNFPA, UNICEF and the World Bank to create a consortium to offer assistance to the more needy developing countries to establish their own low-cost preventive and curative public health systems reaching into all areas of their countries and capable of national support within a reasonable period. Such systems would include family planning services as an ordinary part of their overall services.

B. The WHO should be asked to take the leadership in such an arrangement and is ready to do so. Apparently at least half of the potential donor countries and the EEC's technical assistance program are favorably inclined. So is the UNFPA and UNICEF. The U.S., through its representation on the World Bank Board, should encourage a broader World Bank initiative in this field, particularly to assist in the development of inexpensive, basic health service infrastructures in countries wishing to undertake the development of such systems.

3. Expanding Wage Employment Opportunities, Especially for Women

Discussion

Employment is the key to access to income, which opens the way to improved health, education, nutrition, and reduced family size. Reliable job opportunities enable parents to limit their family size and invest in the welfare of the children they have.

The status and utilization of women in LDC societies is particularly important in reducing family size. For women, employment outside the home offers an alternative to early marriage and childbearing, and an incentive to have fewer children after marriage. The woman who must stay home to take care of her children must forego the income she could earn outside the home. Research indicates that female wage employment outside the home is related to fertility reduction. Programs to increase the women's labor force participation must, however, take account of the overall demand for labor; this would be a particular problem in occupations where there is already widespread unemployment among males. But other occupations where women have a comparative advantage can be encouraged.

Improving the legal and social status of women gives women a greater voice in decision-making about their lives, including family size, and can provide alternative opportunities to childbearing, thereby reducing the benefits of having children.

The U.S. Delegation to the Bucharest Conference emphasized the importance of improving the general status of women and of developing employment opportunities for women outside the home and off the farm. It was joined by all countries in adopting a strong statement on this vital issue. See Chapter VI for a fuller discussion of the conference.

Recommendations:

1. AID should communicate with and seek opportunities to assist national economic development programs to increase the role of women in the development process.

2. AID should review its education/training programs (such as U.S. participant training, in-country and third-country training) to see that such activities provide equal access to women.

3. AID should enlarge pre-vocational and vocational training to involve women more directly in learning skills which can enhance their income and status in the community (e.g. paramedical skills related to provision of family planning services).

4. AID should encourage the development and placement of LDC women as decision-makers in development programs, particularly those programs designed to increase the role of women as producers of goods and services, and otherwise to improve women's welfare (e.g. national credit and finance programs, and national health and family planning programs).

5. AID should encourage, where possible, women's active participation in the labor movement in order to promote equal pay for equal work, equal benefits, and equal employment opportunities.

6. AID should continue to review its programs and projects for their impact on LDC women, and adjust them as necessary to foster greater participation of women - particularly those in the lowest classes - in the development process.

4. <u>Developing Alternatives to the Social Security Role Provided By Children to Aging Parents</u>

<u>Discussion</u>:

In most LDCs the almost total absence of government or other institutional forms of social security for old people forces dependence on children for old age survival. The need for such support appears to be one of the important motivations for having numerous children. Several proposals have been made, and a few pilot experiments are being conducted, to test the impact of financial incentives designed to provide old age support (or, more tangentially, to increase the earning power of fewer children by financing education costs parents would otherwise bear). Proposals have been made for son-insurance (provided to the parents if they have no more than three children), and for deferred payments of retirement benefits (again tied to specified limits on family size), where the payment of the incentive is delayed. The intent is not only to tie the incentive to actual fertility, but to impose the financial cost on the government or private sector entity only after the benefits of the avoided births have accrued to the economy and the financing entity. Schemes of varying administrative complexity have been developed to take account of management problems in LDCs. The economic and equity core of these long-term incentive proposals is simple: the government offers to return to the contracting couple a portion of the economic dividend they generate by avoiding births, as a direct trade-off for the personal financial benefits they forego by having fewer children.

Further research and experimentation in this area needs to take into account the impact of growing urbanization in LDCs on traditional rural values and outlooks such as the desire for children as old-age insurance.

Recommendation:

AID should take a positive stance with respect to exploration of social security type incentives as described above. AID should encourage governments to consider such measures, and should provide financial and technical assistance where appropriate. The recommendation made earlier to establish an "intermediary" institutional capacity which could provide LDC governments with substantial assistance in this area, among several areas on the "demand" side of the problem, would add considerably to AID's ability to carry out this recommendation.

5. Pursuing Development Strategies that Skew Income Growth Toward the Poor, Especially Rural Development Focussing on Rural Poverty

Income distribution and rural development: The higher a family's income, the fewer children it will probably have, except at the very top of the income scale. Similarly, the more evenly distributed the income in a society, the lower the overall fertility rate seems to be since better income distribution means that the poor, who have the highest fertility, have higher income. Thus a development strategy which emphasizes the rural poor, who are the largest and poorest group in most LDCs would be providing income increases to those with the highest fertility levels. No LDC is likely to achieve population stability unless the rural poor participate in income increases and fertility declines.

Agriculture and rural development is already, along with population, the U.S. Government's highest priority in provision of assistance to LDCs. For FY 1975, about 60% of the $1.13 billion AID requested in the five functional areas of the foreign assistance legislation is in agriculture and rural development. The $255 million increase in the FY 1975 level authorized in the two year FY 1974 authorization bill is virtually all for agriculture and rural development.

AID's primary goal in agriculture and rural development is concentration in food output and increases in the rural quality of life; the major strategy element is concentration on increasing the output of small farmers, through assistance in provision of improved technologies, agricultural inputs, institutional supports, etc.

This strategy addresses three U.S. interests: First, it increases agricultural output in the LDCs, and speeds up the average pace of their development, which, as has been noted, leads to increased acceptance of family planning. Second, the emphasis on small farmers and other elements of the rural poor spreads the benefits of development as broadly as is feasible among lower income groups. As noted above spreading the benefits of development to the poor, who tend to have the highest fertility rates, is an important step in getting them to reduce their family size. In addition, the concentration on small farmer production (vs., for example, highly mechanized, large-scale agriculture) can increase on and off farm rural job opportunities and decrease the flow to the cities. While fertility levels in rural areas are higher than in the cities, continued rapid migration into the cities at levels greater than the cities' job markets or services can sustain adds an important destabilizing element to development efforts and goals of many countries. Indeed, urban areas in some LDCs are already the scene of urban unrest and high crime rates.

Recommendation

AID should continue its efforts to focus not just on agriculture and rural development but specifically on small farmers and on labor-intensive means of stimulating agricultural output and on other aspects of improving the quality of life of the rural poor, so that agriculture and rural development assistance, in addition to its importance for increased food production and other purposes, can have maximum impact on reducing population growth.

6. <u>Concentration on Education and Indoctrination of The Rising Generation of Children Regarding the Desirability of Smaller Family Size</u>

Discussion:

Present efforts at reducing birth rates in LDCs, including AID and UNFPA assistance, are directed largely at adults now in their reproductive years. Only nominal attention is given to population education or sex education in schools and in most countries none is given in the very early grades which are the only attainment of 2/3-3/4 of the children. It should be obvious, however, that efforts at birth control directed toward adults will with even maximum success result in acceptance of contraception for the reduction of births only to the level of the desired family size—which knowledge, attitude and practice studies in many countries indicate is an average of four or more children.

The great necessity is to convince the masses of the population that it is to their individual and national interest to have, on the average, only three and then only two children. There is little likelihood that this result can be accomplished very widely against the background of the cultural heritage of today's adults, even the young adults, among the masses in most LDCs. Without diminishing in any way the effort to reach these adults, the obvious increased focus of attention should be to change the attitudes of the next generation, those who are now in elementary school or younger. If this could be done, it would indeed be possible to attain a level of fertility approaching replacement in 20 years and actually reaching it in 30.

Because a large percentage of children from high-fertility, low-income groups do not attend school, it will be necessary to develop means to reach them for this and other educational purposes through informal educational programs. As the discussion earlier of the determinants of family size (fertility) pointed out, it is also important to make significant progress in other areas, such as better health care and improvements in income distribution, before desired family size can be expected to fall sharply. If it makes economic sense for poor parents to have large families twenty years from now, there is no evidence as to whether population education or indoctrination will have sufficient impact alone to dissuade them.

Recommendation

1. That U.S. agencies stress the importance of education of the next generation of parents, starting in elementary schools, toward a two-child family ideal.

2. That AID stimulate specific efforts to develop means of educating children of elementary school age to the ideal of the two-child family and that UNESCO be asked to take the lead through formal and informal education.

General Recommendation for UN Agencies

As to each of the above six categories State and AID should make specific efforts to have the relevant UN agency, WHO, ILO, FAO, UNESCO, UNICEF, and the UNFPA take its proper role of leadership in the UN family with increased program effort, citing the World Population Plan of Action.

II. C. Food for Peace Program and Population

Discussion:

One of the most fundamental aspects of the impact of population growth on the political and economic well-being of the globe is its relationship to food. Here the problem of the interrelationship of population, national resources, environment, productivity and political and economic stability come together when shortages of this basic human need occur.

USDA projections indicate that the quantity of grain imports needed by the LDCs in the 1980s will grow significantly, both in overall and per capita terms. In addition, these countries will face year-to-year fluctuations in production due to the influence of weather and other factors.

This is not to say that the LDCs need face starvation in the next two decades, for the same projections indicate an even greater increase in production of grains in the developed nations. It should be pointed out, however, that these projections assume that such major problems as the vast increase in the need for fresh water, the ecological effects of the vast increase in the application of fertilizer, pesticides, and irrigation, and the apparent adverse trend in the global climate, are solved. At present, there are no solutions to these problems in sight.

The major challenge will be to increase food production in the LDCs themselves and to liberalize the system in which grain is transferred commercially from producer to consumer countries. We also see food aid as an important way of meeting part of the chronic shortfall and emergency needs caused by year-to-year variation at least through the end of this decade. Many outside experts predict just such difficulties even if major efforts are undertaken to expand world agricultural output, especially in the LDCs themselves but also in the U.S. and in other major feed grain producers. In the longer run, LDCs must both decrease population growth and increase agricultural production significantly. At some point the "excess capacity" of the food exporting countries will run out. Some countries have already moved from a net food exporter to a net importer of food.

There are major interagency studies now progressing in the food area and this report cannot go deeply into this field. It can only point to serious problems as they relate to population and suggest minimum requirements and goals in the food area. In particular, we believe that population growth may have very serious negative consequences on food production in the LDCs including over-expectations of the capacity of the land to produce, downgrading the ecological economics of marginal areas, and overharvesting the seas. All of these conditions may affect the viability of the world's economy and thereby its prospects for peace and security.

Recommendations:

Since NSC/CIEP studies are already underway we refer the reader to them. However the following, we believe, are minimum requirements for any strategy which wishes to avoid instability and conflict brought on by population growth and food scarcity:

(1) High priority for U.S. bilateral and multilateral LDC Agricultural Assistance; including efforts by the LDCs to improve food production and distribution with necessary institutional adjustments and economic policies to stimulate efficient production. This

must include a significant increase in financial and technical aid to promote more efficient production and distribution in the LDCs.

(2) Development of national food stocks* (including those needed for emergency relief) within an internationally agreed framework sufficient to provide an adequate level of world food security;

(3) Expansion of production of the input elements of food production (i.e., fertilizer, availability of water and high yield seed stocks) and increased incentives for expanded agricultural productivity. In this context a reduction in the real cost of energy (especially fuel) either through expansion in availability through new sources or decline in the relative price of oil or both would be of great importance;

(4) Significant expansion of U.S. and other producer country food crops within the context of a liberalized and efficient world trade system that will assure food availability to the LDCs in case of severe shortage. New international trade arrangements for agricultural products, open enough to permit maximum production by efficient producers and flexible enough to dampen wide price fluctuations in years when weather conditions result in either significant shortfalls or surpluses. We believe this objective can be achieved by trade liberalization and an internationally coordinated food reserve program without resorting to price-oriented agreements, which have undesirable effects on both production and distribution;

(5) The maintenance of an adequate food aid program with a clearer focus on its use as a means to make up real food deficits, pending the development of their own food resources, in countries unable to feed themselves rather than as primarily an economic development or foreign policy instrument; and

(6) A strengthened research effort, including long term, to develop new seed and farming technologies, primarily to increase yields but also to permit more extensive cultivation techniques, particularly in LDCs.

III. Internation Organizations and other Multilateral Population Programs

---

* The Department of Agriculture favors U.S. commercial interests holding any national stocks in an international network of stockpiles.

A. UN Organization and Specialized Agencies

Discussion

In the mid-sixties the UN member countries slowly began to agree on a greater involvement of the United Nations in population matters. In 1967 the Secretary-General created a Trust Fund to finance work in the population field. In 1969 the Fund was renamed the United Nations Fund for Population Activities (UNFPA) and placed under the overall supervision of the United Nations Development Program. During this period, also, the mandates of the Specialized Agencies were modified to permit greater involvement by these agencies in population activities.

UNFPA's role was clarified by an ECOSOC resolution in 1973: (a) to build up the knowledge and capacity to respond to the needs in the population and family planning fields; (b) to promote awareness in both developed and developing countries of the social, economic, and environmental implications of population problems; (c) to extend assistance to developing countries; and (d) to promote population programs and to coordinate projects supported by the UNFPA.

Most of the projects financed by UNFPA are implemented with the assistance of organizations of the Untied Nations system, including the regional Economic Commission, United Nations Children's Fund (UNICEF), International Labour Organization (ILO), Food and Agriculture Organization (FAO), United Nations Educational Scientific and Cultural Organization (UNESCO), the World Health Organization (WHO). Collaborative arrangements have been made with the International Development Association (IDA), an affiliate of the World Bank, and with the World Food Programme.

Increasingly the UNFPA is moving toward comprehensive country programs negotiated directly with governments. This permits the governments to select the implementing (executing) agency which may be a member of the UN system or a non-government organization or company. With the development of the country program approach it is planned to level off UNFPA funding to the specialized agencies.

UNFPA has received $122 million in voluntary contributions from 65 governments, of which $42 million was raised in 1973. The

Work Plan of UNFPA for 1974-77 sets a $280 million goal for
fund-raising, as follows:
 –   1974 – $54 million
     1975 – $64 million
     1976 – $76 million
     1977 – $86 million

Through 1971 the U.S. had contributed approximately half of
all the funds contributed to UNFPA. In 1972 we reduced our
matching contribution to 48 percent of other donations, and for 1973
we further reduced our contribution to 45%. In 1973 requests for
UNFPA assistance had begun to exceed available resources. This
trend has accelerated and demand for UNFPA resources is now
strongly outrunning supply. Documented need for UNFPA assistance during the years 1974-77 is $350 million, but because the
UNFPA could anticipate that only $280 million will be available it
has been necessary to phase the balance to at least 1978.

Recommendations

The U.S. should continue its support of multilateral efforts in
the population field by:

a) increasing, subject to congressional appropriation action, the
absolute contribution to the UNFPA in light of 1) mounting demands for UNFPA Assistance, 2) improving UNFPA capacity to
administer projects, 3) the extent to which UNFPA funding aims at
U.S. objectives and will substitute for U.S. funding, 4) the prospect
that without increased U.S. contributions the UNFPA will be unable
to raise sufficient funds for its budget in 1975 and beyond;

b) initiating or participating in an effort to increase the resources from other donors made available to international agencies
that can work effectively in the population area as both to increase
overall population efforts and, in the UNFPA, to further reduce the
U.S. percentage share of total contributions; and

c) supporting the coordinating role which UNFPA plays
among donor and recipient countries, and among UN and other
organizations in the population field, including the World Bank.

B. Encouraging Private Organizations

Discussion:

The cooperation of private organizations and groups on a national, regional and world-wide level is essential to the success of a comprehensive population strategy. These groups provide important intellectual contributions and policy support, as well as the delivery of family planning and health services and information. In some countries, the private and voluntary organizations are the only means of providing family planning services and materials.

Recommendations:

AID should continue to provide support to those private U.S. and international organizations whose work contributes to reducing rapid population growth, and to develop with them, where appropriate, geographic and functional divisions of labor in population assistance.

IV. Provision and Development of Family Planning Services, Information and Technology

In addition to creating the climate for fertility decline, as described in a previous section, it is essential to provide safe and effective techniques for controlling fertility.

There are two main elements in this task: (a) improving the effectiveness of the existing means of fertility control and developing new ones; and (b) developing low-cost systems for the delivery of family planning technologies, information and related services to the 85% of LDC populations not now reached.

Legislation and policies affecting what the U.S. Government does relative to abortion in the above areas is discussed at the end of this section.

A. Research to Improve Fertility Control Technology
Discussion

The effort to reduce population growth requires a variety of birth control methods which are safe, effective, inexpensive and attractive to both men and women. The developing countries in particular need methods which do not require physicians and which are suitable for use in primitive, remote rural areas or urban slums by people with relatively low motivation. Experiences in family planning have clearly demonstrated the crucial impact of improved technology on fertility control.

None of the currently available methods of fertility control is completely effective and free of adverse reactions and objectionable characteristics. The ideal of a contraceptive, perfect in all these respects, may never be realized. A great deal of effort and money will be necessary to improve fertility control methods. The research to achieve this aim can be divided into two categories:

1. Short-term approaches: These include applied and developmental work which is required to perfect further and evaluate the safety and role of methods demonstrated to be effective in family planning programs in the developing countries.

Other work is directed toward new methods based on well established knowledge about the physiology of reproduction. Although short term pay-offs are possible, successful development of some methods may take 5 years and up to $15 million for a single method.

2. Long-term approaches: The limited state of fundamental knowledge of many reproductive processes requires that a strong research effort of a more basic nature be maintained to elucidate these processes and provide leads for contraceptive development research. For example, new knowledge of male reproductive processes is needed before research to develop a male "pill" can come to fruition. Costs and duration of the required research are high and difficult to quantify.

With expenditures of about $30 million annually, a broad program of basic and applied bio-medical research on human reproduction and contraceptive development is carried out by the Center for Population Research of the National Institute of Child Health and Human Development. The Agency for International Development annually funds about $5 million of principally applied research on new means of fertility control suitable for use in developing countries.

Smaller sums are spent by other agencies of the U.S. Government. Coordination of the federal research effort is facilitated by the activities of the Interagency Committee on Population Research. This committee prepares an annual listing and analyses of all government supported population research programs. The listing is published in the Inventory of Federal Population Research.

A variety of studies have been undertaken by non-governmental experts including the U.S. Commission on Population Growth and the American Future. Most of these studies indicate that the United States effort in population research is insufficient. Opinions differ on how much more can be spent wisely and effectively but an additional $25-50 million annually for bio-medical research constitutes a conservative estimate.

Recommendations:

A stepwise increase over the next 3 years to a total of about $100 million annually for fertility and contraceptive research is recommended. This is an increase of $60 million over the current $40 million expended annually by the major Federal Agencies for bio-medical research. Of this increase $40 million would be spent on short-term, goal directed research. The current expenditure of $20 million in long-term approaches consisting largely of basic bio-medical research would be doubled. This increased effort would require significantly increased staffing of the federal agencies which support this work. Areas recommended for further research are:

1. Short-term approaches: These approaches include improvement and field testing of existing technology and development of new technology. It is expected that some of these approaches would be ready for use within five years. Specific short term approaches worthy of increased effort are as follows:

a. Oral contraceptives have become popular and widely used; yet the optimal steroid hormone combinations and doses for LDC populations need further definition. Field studies in several settings are required.

Approx. Increased Cost: $3 million annually.

b. Intra-uterine devices of differing size, shape, and bioactivity should be developed and tested to determine the optimum levels of effectiveness, safety, and acceptability.

Approx. Increased Cost: $3 million annually.

c. Improved methods for ovulation prediction will be important to those couples who wish to practice rhythm with more assurance of effectiveness than they now have.

Approx. Increased Cost: $3 million annually.

d. Sterilization of men and women has received wide-spread acceptance in several areas when a simple, quick, and safe procedure is readily available. Female sterilization has been improved

by technical advances with laparoscopes, culdoscopes, and greatly simplifies abdominal surgical techniques. Further improvements by the use of tubal clips, trans-cervical approaches, and simpler techniques can be developed. For men several current techniques hold promise but require more refinement and evaluation.
Approx. Increased Cost $6 million annually.

e. Injectable contraceptives for women which are effective for three months or more and are administered by para-professionals undoubtedly will be a significant improvement. Currently available methods of this type are limited by their side effects and potential hazards. There are reasons to believe that these problems can be overcome with additional research.
Approx. Increased Cost: $5 million annually.

f. Leuteolytic and anti-progesterone approaches to fertility control including use of prostaglandins are theoretically attractive but considerable work remains to be done.
Approx. Increased Cost: $7 million annually.

g. Non-Clinical Methods. Additional research on non-clinical methods including foams, creams, and condoms is needed. These methods can be used without medical supervision.
Approx. Increased Cost; $5 million annually.

h. Field studies. Clinical trials of new methods in use settings are essential to test their worth in developing countries and to select the best of several possible methods in a given setting.
Approx. Increased Cost: $8 million annually.

2. Long-term approaches: Increased research toward better understanding of human reproductive physiology will lead to better methods of fertility control for use in five to fifteen years. A great deal has yet to be learned about basic aspects of male and female fertility and how regulation can be effected. For example, an effective and safe male contraceptive is needed, in particular an injection which will be effective for specified periods of time. Fundamental research must be done but there are reasons to believe that the development of an injectable male contraceptive is feasible. Another method which should be developed is an injection which will assure a woman of regular periods. The drug would be given by para-professionals once a month or as needed to regularize the menstrual cycle. Recent scientific advances indicate that this method can be developed.
Approx. Increased Cost: $20 million annually.

B. Development of Low-cost Delivery Systems

Discussion

Exclusive of China, only 10-15% of LDC populations are currently effectively reached by family planning activities. If efforts to reduce rapid population growth are to be successful it is essential that the neglected 85-90% of LDC populations have access to convenient, reliable family planning services. Moreover, these people—largely in rural but also in urban areas—not only tend to have the highest fertility, they simultaneously suffer the poorest health, the worst nutritional levels, and the highest infant mortality rates.

Family planning services in LDCs are currently provided by the following means:

1. Government-run clinics or centers which offer family planning services alone;

2. Government-run clinics or centers which offer family planning as part of a broader based health service;

3. Government-run programs that emphasize door to door contact by family planning workers who deliver contraceptives to those desiring them and/or make referrals to clinics;

4. Clinics or centers run by private organizations (e.g., family planning associations);

5. Commercial channels which in many countries sell condoms, oral contraceptives, and sometimes spermicidal foam over the counter;

6. Private physicians.

Two of these means in particular hold promise for allowing significant expansion of services to the neglected poor:

1. Integrated Delivery Systems. This approach involves the provision of family planning in conjunction with health and/or nutrition services, primarily through government-run programs. There are simple logistical reasons which argue for providing these services on an integrated basis. Very few of the LDCs have the resources, both in financial and manpower terms, to enable them to deploy individual types of services to the neglected 85% of their populations. By combining a variety of services in one delivery mechanism they can attain maximum impact with the scarce resources available.

In addition, the provision of family planning in the context of broader health services can help make family planning more acceptable to LDC leaders and individuals who, for a variety of reasons (some ideological, some simply humanitarian) object to family planning. Family planning in the health context shows a concern for the well-being of the family as a whole and not just for a couple's reproductive function.

Finally, providing integrated family planning and health services on a broad basis would help the U.S. contend with the ideological charge that the U.S. is more interested in curbing the numbers of LDC people than it is in their future and well-being. While it can be argued, and argued effectively, that limitation of numbers may well be one of the most critical factors in enhancing development potential and improving the chances for well-being, we should recognize that those who argue along ideological lines have made a great deal of the fact that the U.S. contribution to development programs and health programs has steadily shrunk, whereas funding for population programs has steadily increased. While many explanations may be brought forward to explain these trends, the fact is that they have been an ideological liability to the U.S. in its crucial developing relationships with the LDCs. A.I.D. currently spends about $35 million annually in bilateral programs on the provision of family planning services through integrated delivery systems. Any action to expand such systems must aim at the deployment of truly low-cost services. Health-related services which involve costly physical structures, high skill requirements, and expensive supply methods will not produce the desired deployment in any reasonable time. The basic test of low-cost methods will be whether the LDC governments concerned can assume responsibility for the financial, administrative, manpower and other elements of these service extensions. Utilizing existing indigenous structures and personnel (including traditional medical practitioners who in some countries have shown a strong interest in family planning) and service methods that involve simply-trained personnel, can help keep costs within LDC resource capabilities.

2. Commercial Channels. In an increasing number of LDCs, contraceptives (such as condoms, foam and the Pill) are being made available without prescription requirements through commercial

channels such as drugstores.* The commercial approach offers a practical, low-cost means of providing family planning services, since it utilizes an existing distribution system and does not involve financing the further expansion of public clinical delivery facilities. Both A.I.D. and private organizations like the IPPF are currently testing commercial distribution schemes in various LDCs to obtain further information on the feasibility, costs, and degree of family planning acceptance achieved through this approach. A.I.D. is currently spending about $2 million annually in this area.

In order to stimulate LDC provision of adequate family planning services, whether alone or in conjunction with health services, A.I.D. has subsidized contraceptive purchases for a number of years. In FY 1973 requests from A.I.D. bilateral and grantee programs for contraceptive supplies—in particular for oral contraceptives and condoms—increased markedly, and have continued to accelerate in FY 1974. Additional rapid expansion in demand is expected over the next several years as the accumulated population/family planning efforts of the past decade gain momentum.

While it is useful to subsidize provision of contraceptives in the short term in order to expand and stimulate LDC family planning programs, in the long term it will not be possible to fully fund demands for commodities, as well as other necessary family planning actions, within A.I.D. and other donor budgets. These costs must ultimately be borne by LDC governments and/or individual consumers. Therefore, A.I.D. will increasingly focus on developing contraceptive production and procurement capacities by the LDCs themselves. A.I.D. must, however, be prepared to continue supplying large quantities of contraceptives over the next several years to avoid a detrimental hiatus in program supply lines while efforts are made to expand LDC production and procurement actions. A.I.D. should also encourage other donors and multilateral organizations to assume a greater share of the effort, in regard both to the short-term actions to subsidize contraceptive supplies and the longer-term actions to develop LDC capacities for commodity production and procurement.

---

* For obvious reasons, the initiative to distribute prescription drugs through commercial channels should be taken by local government and not by the US Government.

Recommendations:

1. A.I.D. should aim its population assistance program to help achieve adequate coverage of couples having the highest fertility who do not now have access to family planning services.

2. The service delivery approaches which seem to hold greatest promise of reaching these people should be vigorously pursued. For example:

a. The U.S. should indicate its willingness to join with other donors and organizations to encourage further action by LDC governments and other institutions to provide low-cost family planning and health services to groups in their populations who are not now reached by such services. In accordance with Title X of the AID Legislation and current policy, A.I.D. should be prepared to provide substantial assistance in this area in response to sound requests.

b. The services provided must take account of the capacities of the LDC governments or institutions to absorb full responsibility, over reasonable timeframes, for financing and managing the level of services involved.

c. A.I.D. and other donor assistance efforts should utilize to the extent possible indigenous structures and personnel in delivering services, and should aim at the rapid development of local (community) action and sustaining capabilities.

d. A.I.D. should continue to support experimentation with commercial distribution of contraceptives and application of useful findings in order to further explore the feasibility and replicability of this approach. Efforts in this area by other donors and organizations should be encouraged. Approx. U.S. Cost: $5-10 million annually.

3. In conjunction with other donors and organizations, A.I.D. should actively encourage the development of LDC capabilities for production and procurement of needed family planning contraceptives.

Special Footnote: While the agencies participating in this study have no specific recommendations to propose on abortion the following issues are believed important and should be considered in the context of a global population strategy.

Abortion

1. Worldwide Abortion Practices

Certain facts about abortion need to be appreciated:

No country has reduced its population growth without resorting to abortion.

Thirty million pregnancies are estimated to be terminated annually by abortion throughout the world. The figure is a guess. More precise data indicate about 7 percent of the world's population live in countries where abortion is prohibited without exception and 12 percent in countries where abortion is permitted only to save the life of the pregnant woman. About 15 percent live under statutes authorizing abortion on broader medical grounds, that is, to avert a threat to the woman's health, rather than to her life, and sometimes on eugenic and/or juridical grounds (rape, etc.) as well. Countries where social factors may be taken into consideration to justify termination of pregnancy account for 22 percent of the world's population and those allowing for elective abortion for at least some categories of women, for 36 percent. No information is available for the remaining 8 percent; it would appear, however, that most of these people live in areas with restrictive abortion laws.

The abortion statutes of many countries are not strictly enforced and some abortions on medical grounds are probably tolerated in most places. It is well known that in some countries with very restrictive laws, abortions can be obtained from physicians openly and without interference from the authorities. Conversely, legal authorization of elective abortion does not guarantee that abortion on request is actually available to all women who may want their pregnancies terminated. Lack of medical personnel and facilities or conservative attitudes among physicians and hospital administrators may effectively curtail access to abortion, especially for economically or socially deprived women.

2. U.S. Legislation and Policies Relative to Abortion

Although the Supreme Court of the United States invalidated the abortion laws of most states in January 1973, the subject still remains politically sensitive. U.S. Government actions relative to abortion are restricted as indicated by the following Federal legislation and the resultant policy decisions of the concerned departments and agencies.

    a.　A.I.D. Program

The predominant part of A.I.D.'s population assistance program has concentrated on contraceptive or foresight methods. A.I.D. recognized, however, that under developing country conditions foresight methods not only are frequently unavailable but often fail because of ignorance, lack of preparation, misuse and non-use. Because of these latter conditions, increasing numbers of women in the developing world have been resorting to abortion, usually under unsafe and often lethal conditions. Indeed, abortion, legal and illegal, now has become the most widespread fertility control method in use in the world today. Since, in the developing world, the increasingly widespread practice of abortion is conducted often under unsafe conditions, A.I.D. sought through research to reduce the health risks and other complexities which arise from the illegal and unsafe forms of abortion. One result has been the development of the Menstrual Regulation Kit, a simple, inexpensive, safe and effective means of fertility control which is easy to use under LDC conditions.

    Section 114 of the Foreign Assistance Act of 1961 (P.L. 93-189), as amended in 1974, adds for the first time restrictions on the use of A.I.D. funds relative to abortion. The provision states that "None of the funds made available to carry out this part (Part I of the Act) shall be used to pay for the performance of abortions as a method of family planning or to motivate or coerce any person to practice abortions."

    In order to comply with Section 114, A.I.D. has determined that foreign assistance funds will not be used to:

    (i) procure or distribute equipment provided for the purpose of inducing abortions as a method of family planning.

    (ii) directly support abortion activities in LDCs. However, A.I.D. may provide population program support to LDCs and institutions as long as A.I.D. funds are wholly attributable to the permissible aspects of such programs.

    (iii) information, education, training, or communication programs that promote abortion as a method of family planning. However, A.I.D. will continue to finance training of LDC doctors in the latest techniques used in obstetrics-gynecology practice, and will not disqualify such training programs if they include pregnancy termination within the overall curriculum. Such training is provided only at the election of the participants.

(iiii) pay women in the LDCs to have abortions as a method of family planning or to pay persons to perform abortions or to solicit persons to undergo abortions.

A.I.D. funds may continue to be used for research relative to abortion since the Congress specifically chose not to include research among the prohibited activities.

A major effect of the amendment and policy determination is that A.I.D. will not be involved in further development or promotion of the Menstrual Regulation Kit. However, other donors or organizations may become interested in promoting with their own funds dissemination of this promising fertility control method.

b. DHEW Programs

Section 1008 of the Family Planning Services and Population Research Act of 1970 (P.L. 91-572) states that "None of the funds appropriated under this title shall be used in programs where abortion is a method of family planning." DHEW has adhered strictly to the intent of Congress and does not support abortion research. Studies of the causes and consequences of abortion are permitted, however.

The Public Health Service Act Extension of 1973 (P.L. 93-45) contains the Church Amendment which establishes the right of health providers (both individuals and institutions) to refuse to perform an abortion if it conflicts with moral or religious principles.

c. Proposed Legislation on Abortion Research

There are numerous proposed Congressional amendments and bills which are more restrictive on abortion research than any of the pieces of legislation cited above.

It would be unwise to restrict abortion research for the following reasons:

1. The persistent and ubiquitous nature of abortion.

2. Widespread lack of safe abortion technique.

3. Restriction of research on abortifacient drugs and devices would:

a . Possibly eliminate further development of the IUD.

b. Prevent development of drugs which might have other beneficial uses. An example is methotrexate (R) which is now used to cure a hitherto fatal tumor of the uterus—choriocarcinoma. This drug was first used as an abortifacient.

C. Utilization of Mass Media and Satellite Communications Systems for Family Planning

1. Utilization of Mass Media for Dissemination of Family Planning Services and Information

The potential of education and its various media is primarily a function of (a) target populations where socio-economic conditions would permit reasonable people to change their behavior with the receipt of information about family planning and (b) the adequate development of the substantive motivating context of the message. While dramatic limitations in the availability of any family planning related message are most severe in rural areas of developing countries, even more serious gaps exist in the understanding of the implicit incentives in the system for large families and the potential of the informational message to alter those conditions.

Nevertheless, progress in the technology for mass media communications has led to the suggestion that the priority need might lie in the utilization of this technology, particularly with large and illiterate rural populations. While there are on-going efforts they have not yet reached their full potential. Nor have the principal U.S. agencies concerned yet integrated or given sufficient priority to family planning information and population programs generally.

Yet A.I.D.'s work suggests that radio, posters, printed material, and various types of personal contacts by health/family planning workers tend to be more cost-effective than television except in those areas (generally urban) where a TV system is already in place which reaches more than just the middle and upper classes. There is great scope for use of mass media, particularly in the initial stages of making people aware of the benefits of family planning and of services available; in this way mass media can effectively complement necessary interpersonal communications.

In almost every country of the world there are channels of communication (media) available, such, as print media, radio, posters, and personal contacts, which already reach the vast majority of the population. For example, studies in India - with only 30% literacy, show that most of the population is aware of the government's family planning program. If response is low it is not because of lack of media to transmit information.

A.I.D. believes that the best bet in media strategy is to encourage intensive use of media already available, or available at relatively low cost. For example, radio is a medium which in some countries already reaches a sizeable percentage of the rural population; a recent A.I.D. financed study by Stanford indicates that radio is as effective as television, costs one-fifth as much, and offers more opportunities for programming for local needs and for local feedback.

Recommendations

USAID and USIA should encourage other population donors and organizations to develop comprehensive information and educational programs dealing with population and family planning consistent with the geographic and functional population emphasis discussed in other sections. Such programs should make use of the results of AID's extensive experience in this field and should include consideration of social, cultural and economic factors in population control as well as strictly technical and educational ones.

2. Use of U.S. broadcast satellites for dissemination of family planning and health information to key LDC countries

Discussion:

One key factor in the effective use of existing contraceptive techniques has been the problem of education. In particular, this problem is most severe in rural areas of the developing countries. There is need to develop a cost-effective communications system designed for rural areas which, together with local direct governmental efforts, can provide comprehensive health information and in particular, family planning guidance. One new supporting technology which has been under development is the broadcast satellite. NASA and Fairchild have now developed an ATS (Applied Technology Satellite), now in orbit, which has the capability of beaming educational television programs to isolated areas via small inexpensive community receivers.

NASA's sixth Applications Technology Satellite was launched into geosynchronous orbit over the Galapagos Islands on May 30, 1974. It will be utilized for a year in that position to deliver health and educational services to millions of Americans in remote regions of the Rocky Mountain States, Alaska and Appalachia. During this period it will be made available for a short time to Brazil in order to demonstrate how such a broadcast satellite may be used to provide signals to 500 schools in their existing educational television network 1400 miles northeast of Rio de Janeiro in Rio Grande do Norte.

In mid-1975, ATS-6 will be moved to a point over the Indian Ocean to begin beaming educational television to India. India is now developing its broadcast program materials. Signals picked up from one of two Indian ground transmitters will be rebroadcast to individual stations in 2500 villages and to ground relay installations serving networks comprising 3000 more. This operation over India will last one year, after which time India hopes to have its own broadcast satellite in preparation.

Eventually it will be possible to broadcast directly to individual TV sets in remote rural areas. Such a "direct broadcast satellite," which is still under development, could one day go directly into individual TV receivers. At present, broadcast satellite signals go to ground receiving stations and are relayed to individual television sets on a local or regional basis. The latter can be used in towns, villages and schools.

The hope is that these new technologies will provide a substantial input in family planning programs, where the primary constraint lies in informational services. The fact, however, is that information and education does not appear to be the primary constraint in the development of effective family planning programs. AID itself has learned from costly intensive inputs that a supply oriented approach to family planning is not and cannot be fully effective until the demand side - incentives and motivations - are both understood and accounted for.

Leaving this vast problem aside, AID has much relevant experience in the numerous problems encountered in the use of modern communications media for mass rural education. First, there is widespread LDC sensitivity to satellite broadcast, expressed most vigorously in the Outer Space Committee of the UN. Many countries don't want broadcasts of neighboring countries over their own territory and fear unwanted propaganda and subversion by hostile broadcasters. NASA experience suggests that the U.S. must tread very softly when discussing assistance in program content. International restrictions may be placed on the types of proposed broadcasts and it remains technically difficult to restrict broadcast area coverage to national boundaries. To the extent programs are developed jointly and are appreciated and wanted by receiving countries, some relaxation in their position might occur.

Agreement is nearly universal among practitioners of educational technology that the technology is years ahead of software or content development. Thus cost per person reached tend to be very high. In addition, given the current technology, audiences are limited to those who are willing to walk to the village TV set and listen to public service messages and studies show declining audiences over time with large audiences primarily for popular entertainment. In addition, keeping village receivers in repair is a difficult problem. The high cost of program development remains a serious constraint, particularly since there is so little experience in validifying program content for wide general audiences.

With these factors it is clear that one needs to proceed slowly in utilization of this technology for the LDCs in the population field.

Recommendations:

1. The work of existing networks on population, education, ITV, and broadcast satellites should be brought together to better consolidate relative priorities for research, experimentation and programming in family planning. Wider distribution of the broad AID experience in these areas would probably be justified. This is particularly true since specific studies have already been done on the experimental ATS-6 programs in the U.S., Brazil, and India and each clearly documents the very experimental character and high costs of the effort. Thus at this point it is clearly inconsistent with U.S. or LDC population goals to allocate large additional sums for a technology which is experimental.

2. Limited donor and recipient family planning funds available for education/motivation must be allocated on a cost-effectiveness basis. Satellite TV may have opportunities for cost-effectiveness primarily where the decision has already been taken—on other than family planning grounds—to undertake very large-scale rural TV

systems. Where applicable in such countries satellite technology should be used when cost-effective. Research should give special attention to costs and efficiency relative to alternative media.

3. Where the need for education is established and an effective format has been developed, we recommend more effective exploitation of existing and conventional media: radio, printed material, posters, etc., as discussed under part I above.

V. Action to Develop World-Wide Political and Popular Commitment to Population Stability

Discussion:

A far larger, high-level effort is needed to develop a greater commitment of leaders of both developed and developing countries to undertake efforts, commensurate with the need, to bring population growth under control.

In the United States, we do not yet have a domestic population policy despite widespread recognition that we should—supported by the recommendations of the remarkable Report of the Commission on Population Growth and the American Future.

Although world population growth is widely recognized within the Government as a current danger of the highest magnitude calling for urgent measures, it does not rank high on the agendas of conversations with leaders of other nations.

Nevertheless, the United States Government and private organizations give more attention to the subject than any donor countries except, perhaps, Sweden, Norway and Denmark. France makes no meaningful contribution either financially or verbally. The USSR no longer opposes efforts of U.S. agencies but gives no support.

In the LDCs, although 31 countries, including China, have national population growth control programs and 16 more include family planning in their national health services—at least in some degree—the commitment by the leadership in some of these countries is neither high nor wide. These programs will have only modest success until there is much stronger and wider acceptance of their real importance by leadership groups. Such acceptance and support will be essential to assure that the population information, education and service programs have vital moral backing, administrative capacity, technical skills and government financing.

Recommendations:

1. Executive Branch

a. The President and the Secretary of State should make a point of discussing our national concern about world population growth in meetings with national leaders where it would be relevant.

b. The Executive Branch should give special attention to briefing the Congress on population matters to stimulate support and leadership which the Congress has exercised in the past. A program for this purpose should be developed by S/PM with H and AID.

2. World Population Conference

a. In addition to the specific recommendations for action listed in the preceding sections, U.S. agencies should use the prestige of the World Population Plan of Action to advance all of the relevant action recommendations made by it in order to generate more effective programs for population growth limitation. AID should coordinate closely with the UNFPA in trying to expand resources for population assistance programs, especially from non-OECD, non-traditional donors.

The U.S. should continue to play a leading role in ECOSOC and General Assembly discussions and review of the WPPA.

3. Department of State

a. The State Department should urge the establishment at U.N. headquarters of a high level seminar for LDC cabinet and high level officials and non-governmental leaders of comparable responsibility for indoctrination in population matters. They should have the opportunity in this seminar to meet the senior officials of U.N. agencies and leading population experts from a variety of countries.

b. The State Department should also encourage organization of a UNFPA policy staff to consult with leaders in population programs of developing countries and other experts in population matters to evaluate programs and consider actions needed to improve them.

c. A senior officer, preferably with ambassadorial experience, should be assigned in each regional bureau dealing with LDCs or in State's Population Office to give full-time attention to the development of commitment by LDC leaders to population growth reduction.

d. A senior officer should be assigned to the Bureau of International Organization Affairs to follow and press action by the Specialized Agencies of the U.N. in population matters in developing countries.

e. Part of the present temporary staffing of S/PM for the purposes of the World Population Year and the World Population Conference should be continued on a permanent basis to take advantage of momentum gained by the Year and Conference.

Alternate View on 3.c.

c. The Department should expand its efforts to help Ambassadorial and other high-ranking U.S.G. personnel understand the consequences of rapid population growth and the remedial measures possible.

d. The Department would also give increased attention to developing a commitment to population growth reduction on the part of LDC leaders.

e. Adequate manpower should be provided in S/PM and other parts of the Department as appropriate to implement these expanded efforts.

4. A.I.D. should expand its programs to increase the understanding of LDC leaders regarding the consequences of rapid population growth and their commitment to undertaking remedial actions. This should include necessary actions for collecting and analyzing adequate and reliable demographic data to be used in promoting awareness of the problem and in formulating appropriate policies and programs.

5. USIA. As a major part of U.S. information policy, the improving but still limited programs of USIA to convey information on population matters should be strengthened to a level commensurate with the importance of the subject.

Appendix 3

The World Health Organization
and The Vatican.

Vatican Control of World Health
Organization Population Policy:
An Interview with Milton P. Siegel
Assistant Director General,
World Health Organization, 1946-1970.

Appendix 3

The Vatican and World Population Policy

An Interview with Milton P. Siegel

by Stephen D. Mumford

There is a growing consensus among international public-health leaders that the gains made by their earliest practitioners are about to be lost as a result of overpopulation. The hideous scourge of premature death in Africa that we have been witnessing on our television screens for the last decade is spreading throughout the continent along with civil war.

Somalia is presently the focus of our attention, but there are many other African countries which are all but certain to slip into chaos. CIA director Robert Gates has predicted that, within the next year, there will be 30 million people starving in Africa alone.

A December 20, 1992, article from the National Geographic News Service identifies the fundamental problem in Africa: "Along with war and drought, the third horseman of the African apocalypse has been overpopulation. There are simply more people trying to live on the land than the land can support." The article goes on to observe: "There doesn't seem to be any long-term solution short of transporting millions of Somalis out of there and leaving enough living space for the people and cattle that remain." But no country will accept these millions of Somalis and the tens of millions of other Africans who face the same prospect.

The result will be an explosion in premature deaths, just as some of the delegates who shaped United Nations health policy in the late 1940s had predicted. These leaders in public health recognized that the choice was not *whether* population growth would be controlled but *how*. Would birth control be implemented along with "death control," or would population-growth control be left to implacable na-

> *Editor's Note: One of the bleakest facts of this century has been the unchecked growth in world population, with its resulting strain on the planet's life-support systems and misery for countless millions of human beings. This represents an ethical failure of catastrophic proportions on the part of the peoples of the democratic West who, while providing the medical and agricultural advances which make it feasible for all people to live longer, healthier lives, have at the same time allowed their governments to be manipulated by the Vatican and other religious interests to block effective dissemination of the knowledge and use of population-growth-control measures. As documented in what follows, the source of this calamity is to be found in the early days of the United Nations Organization, when the Western democracies that controlled the agenda of such UNO agencies as the fledgling World Health Organization caved in to political pressure from the Vatican out of fear of its influence on their Catholic voters. In today's more secular Western democracies, the power of the Vatican to control the votes of its adherents is much diminished. However, we can see that on questions such as population-growth control, this decrease in Vatican political power is offset in the United States by the increased power of fundamentalist Protestantism and on the international scene by rising fundamentalist Islam.*

ture through starvation and starvation-related diseases? They argued that this was the real choice they were making as they shaped World Health Organization policy. These leaders understood that, in the not-too-distant future, overpopulation would be a major—and *preventable*—cause of death.

But these people of vision lost that debate in the 1940s, and now premature death on an appalling scale is just getting underway in Africa. It is reasonable to predict that more than half of the Africans alive today will die prematurely, and that a substantial majority of African children born in this decade will die either in this decade or the next.

Because of his position and the length of his tenure, Milton P. Siegel is considered among the world's foremost authorities on the development of World Health Organization policy. In this videotaped interview (available from the Center for Research on Population and Security, P.O. Box 13067, Research Triangle Park, NC 27709, for $19), he reveals the influence of the Vatican in shaping WHO policy, particularly in blocking adoption of the concept that overpopulation is a grave public-health threat—a concept which, in WHO's early years, enjoyed a broad consensus among member countries.

Without this separation of population dynamics from WHO public-health policy, the Vatican would have found it much more difficult to subsequently manipulate governments on such issues as family planning and abortion. National leaders would have been able to refer to the international consensus, as demonstrated by WHO policy. WHO, they could have insisted, has determined that family planning and abortion—like clean water, good nutrition, and immunizations—are necessary to protect public health.

Professor Siegel has now decided to speak out on the subject. As he was involved in the World Health Organization at an early stage, his personal experience provides ample evidence that the Vatican influenced WHO policy development from the outset, during the early period of the Interim Commission in 1946. In its 44-year history, this international health body has had a deplorable record in family planning. Its commitment has been miniscule, and even today family planning accounts for only a tiny fraction of its budget.

Professor Siegel joined the World Health Organization in 1946, when it was still in its formative stages—under the umbrella of the United Nations, created just the year before. Because of Siegel's earlier work in North America and the Middle East, he was asked, in effect, to be one of WHO's "founding fathers." So he came on board on the senior staff of the Interim Commission. Dr. Brock Chisholm of Canada was the executive director of the commission. The Interim Commission set up the permanent organization with headquarters in Geneva, Switzerland, and Dr. Chisholm was chosen to be WHO's first director general.

MUMFORD: In your role as assistant director general of WHO, you were in a position to know all of the essential facts that went into all WHO policy-making decisions, weren't you?

SIEGEL: I feel it might be useful for me to point out my participation in, first, the creation of the World Health Organization, and my role as assistant director general for 24 years, which is when I reached retirement age. I attended every meeting of the World Health Assembly and every session of the executive board. The board met twice a year. The Health Assembly met annually, and I was present, exercising my functions at these meetings. I didn't miss a single one.

MUMFORD: How did Dr. Chisholm regard family planning in those early days as a potential concern for WHO?

SIEGEL: He considered it absolutely essential. . . . Brock Chisholm was a realist, and he firmly believed that overpopulation was a threat—a security threat, if you will— to all the nations of the world. And that steps must be taken, and it should be considered part of health function to do something about population-growth control.

MUMFORD: Did you and Brock Chisholm ever discuss the opposition to family planning?

SIEGEL: Yes, we had to. It was an issue even before I joined the Interim Commission. I joined the commission a year after it was created.

MUMFORD: When did you first start witnessing this opposition to WHO involvement with family planning?

SIEGEL: Well, my first exposure to it—the initial stages of opposition to family planning by the Catholic church—started as soon as I joined WHO and word reached me that this was a real problem. I was visited by one of the representatives of the Vatican in Geneva, who wanted to know who I was and where I came from and what I believed in. And I politely invited him out of my office, because I did not consider that I was under any obligation to reveal anything that I knew to someone outside the organization—whether it was someone from the Vatican or any other organized group. So they couldn't get any information out of me.

But as a result, I had the beginnings of conversations with my colleagues, particularly with Dr. Chisholm.

MUMFORD: What was the basis of opposition within WHO to the discussion of population and population problems?

SIEGEL: Well, the position simply was that population-growth control, family planning, or whatever you want to call it, was not a health problem and therefore should not even be debated. That was the position of Ireland, Italy, Lebanon, and later on Belgium. The issue of population growth came up at every meeting WHO held.

You couldn't separate population problems from health in the minds of most of the delegates. But these few countries—particularly those which were dominated by the Vatican—didn't want to see that discussed in a health organization. Because as soon as you introduce anything under the subject of health—whether it's peace, security, or family planning—it's pretty hard to argue against improving the health of people. These countries knew that, and they tried to defend themselves by saying, "These are political considerations and shouldn't be discussed in a health arena."

MUMFORD: Wasn't the question of religion, as such, ever raised in the discussion?

SIEGEL: Well, it was raised indirectly. Religion always was raised indirectly one way or another. But sometimes they would simply call it politics.

I think one can provide many illustrative examples of the way in which politics has interfered with the progress of health. And the influence of religion never did show itself until the Vatican began to use its influence through the church organizational structure, which, incidentally, probably is one of the best organizational structures the world's ever seen.

So, one way or another, sometimes surreptitiously, the Catholic church used its influence to defeat, if you will, any movement toward family planning or birth control.

MUMFORD: I've read—and we've discussed—that in the second World Health Assembly the representative from Ceylon commented that the security and peace of the world is threatened by population growth, and that the need for birth control must be considered internationally. What reaction was there to this?

SIEGEL: Well, it's interesting to note the fact that the second World Health Assembly was not held in Geneva, it was in Rome.

The environment which we were subjected to in Rome for the second World Health Assembly made it particularly difficult for anyone to make the kind of statement made by that man, the representative of the country that was then called Ceylon. . . . But he still had the courage to get up and make that statement about the importance of peace and security and health, and the role that health can play with regard to population control or family planning or what I choose to call management of population growth.

MUMFORD: Yes, I recall how action was stymied in the second World Health Assembly. What happened at the third assembly?

SIEGEL: When we reached the third World Health Assembly, which was back again in Geneva . . . for the first time to my recollection a strong effort was made in the steering committee to add the subject of population and family planning to the agenda to be discussed at the third World Health Assembly.

Well, the delegation of Ceylon was on the steering committee that drafted the agenda to go to the Health Assembly for approval, and the delegates did their utmost to argue that population for them was an exceedingly serious problem, because they were a small island with a relatively large population, considering the size of the island. And they felt that population just had to be considered by the World Health Organization, and for that reason they were making very strong efforts to get the steering committee to allow the subjects of family planning and population to be added to the suggested agenda.

When that hit the assembly for its approval of the agenda, it was the delegate from Ireland—Dr. Hourihane—who made a rather strong, forceful statement (in the style which was the one style he could handle extremely well), saying there were two major religions, and his country was one of them—that is, the major part of its population was one of the religions—which absolutely refused to permit its delegation to participate in any meeting where the problem of family planning was being discussed.

When the vote came on the subject of whether to put population and family planning on the agenda, the vote was 30 against, one in favor, and there were somewhere between four and six abstentions.

MUMFORD: So Ireland simply intimidated just about everyone. While the Catholic opposition was developing earlier, how did Dr. Chisholm react? Was he concerned?

SIEGEL: Oh, he was very concerned because he was beginning to feel pressure from the member states of WHO that were predominantly Catholic in all respects—politically and in the development of their programs. And they were putting pressure on Brock Chisholm as director general of WHO to do as little as possible about family planning. Then later on, as time went by, when they weren't very successful in influencing the development of the program, they became extremely difficult and put considerable pressure on the director general to do *nothing* about family planning. It took them about three years before they could get the kind of resolutions or consensus in our annual meetings of the Health Assembly to prevent the director from proposing programs that included such things as family planning.

> *Dr. Chisholm was being pressured by certain member states of WHO to do nothing about family planning.*

MUMFORD: It took them three years? You're talking about the Catholic church's representatives?

SIEGEL: Well, they had to work through government representatives because they couldn't speak officially; they didn't have the prerogative of being recognized to speak at a meeting of the World Health Assembly or any of its subsidiary bodies unless they were invited. So they operated through the countries where they knew they had influence. I think it's a well-known fact who those countries are. Two outstanding ones are Ireland and Italy.

Then later on, the Belgians became very much involved, and it was the Belgian and Irish delegates—the chief delegates—who went to Brock Chisholm and demanded that he make a clear statement to the assembly that he would not propose any family-planning programs in any of the annual programs and budget of the organization. They threatened that, if he didn't do that at the then-ongoing Health Assembly, which was, I think, the third (1950), they would withdraw from the organization and take steps to destroy the organization. They went so far as to use these words threatening him—that, if he didn't do what they wanted him to do, they would first withdraw and then create a new organization altogether and destroy the World Health Organization.

Among the people Chisholm talked to was myself. Who else he talked to, I don't know, but I think I was the only one of his top policy-makers with whom he discussed this. I told him that he should not allow himself to be virtually blackmailed into taking the action they wanted him to take. "Let them go ahead and withdraw and see what happens," I advised.

Well, he did not want to do that because his term as director general only had a couple more years to run, and he didn't want to leave that problem in the hands of his successor. He knew that he was not going to remain for a second term as director general, having already served two years as executive director of the Interim Commission.

> *The Belgian and Irish Delegations threatened to withdraw from WHO and take steps to destroy the organization.*

So he made a statement to the Health Assembly in full complete session that he would not, as long as he was director general, do anything to include family planning in the programming of the organization. And that put a stop to anything that had been going on previously.

Now the only thing that was going on previously was a program in India which took place almost from the outset of the organization—because the then-minister of health of India was a woman, not a doctor, who was formerly secretary to Mahatma Gandhi, and she was a converted Catholic dead set against any kind of family-planning programs in India. The Vatican would accept the idea of the use of the rhythm method but no contraceptives.

We provided an expert, whose name was Abraham Stone, to go to India to try to set up a program for the rhythm method, together with the minister of health—whose name, incidentally, was Rajkumari Amrit Kaur. She was a princess; that's what *rajkumari* means. I knew her well, and she was a charming person and certainly a great supporter of WHO; but her being a converted Catholic made her more Catholic than the pope, and she refused to support any kind of family-planning program.

When the rhythm method failed miserably—it produced absolutely no results—then there was nothing else that was acceptable to her. It was only after she retired as minister of health that India began to do something about family planning.

MUMFORD: How very sad. At last, Chisholm felt he had to knuckle under.

SIEGEL: After what had happened at the third World Health Assembly, the fourth—which was in 1951 in Geneva—didn't even touch the subject. It was almost taken for granted that it would simply be a repetition of what had happened at the third Assembly—and therefore let's not waste time at the fourth.

And so we get to the fifth World Health Assembly, in 1952. I have equated the fifth assembly in my own mind with the death knell of WHO's involvement in population—primarlily because of the pressure put on the director general by, particularly, the governments of Ireland and Belgium.

MUMFORD: So I gather Dr. Chisholm's capitulation at the third World Health Assembly wasn't quite the end of it, was it?

SIEGEL: The representative of Ceylon at the fifth World Health Assembly was Dr. Wickremsinghe, and, in referring to the population problem he said: "We must therefore always regard the population problem as a vital one, and see how, without violating any religious beliefs or moral standards, we could solve this problem in a scientific and careful manner." This then led to a proposal by one of the outstanding members of the delegations that came to WHO meetings—Dr. Karl Evang from Norway. The Scandinavian countries, as most people know, have almost always been in favor of doing something about family planning. This has particularly been true of Norway, Sweden, and Denmark.

Dr. Karl Evang was an outstanding public-health person in the world and spoke absolutely perfect English. He proposed, after hearing what the representative from Ceylon had to say, that it was time to establish an expert committee to examine the problem and report on the health aspects of the population problem.

His proposal met with the support of representatives of a number countries; I won't take time to list them all, but, of course, one of them was Sweden and another Ceylon. The group of countries under the influence of the Vatican proposed another resolution: that, from a purely medical stand-point, population problems do not require any particular action on the part of WHO at the present time.

In the meantime, the delegate from India, whom I knew quite well (incidentally, he was a gynecologist and obstetrician from Madras, India), proposed a resolution that an expert committee should be set up with the aim of acquiring knowledge with regard to the spacing of children and birth-control problems as well as the other health aspects of population.

MUMFORD: So, two countries proposed expert committees?

SIEGEL: After heated debate, discussion was closed, and it was time to put the resolutions to a vote.

One of the members said he didn't understand what was taking place, because, as he understood it, discussion of the subject had already been declared closed and he didn't see why it should be reopened. The chair of the committee, being mindful of what the problem was growing into, suggested that, in the interest of harmony and conciliation, the best procedure would be to withdraw *all* the resolutions. And that was accepted by consensus.

MUMFORD: What was the implication?

SIEGEL: Well, the implication of that was that nothing happened; the discussion was closed and there was no resolution. Therefore, the director general having already made his statement that he would not include family planning in any program as long as he was director general—but he only had another year to two to go—the result was that the organization did absolutely nothing about fam-

ily planning for a period of somewhere between seven and nine years.

That gave me an awful lot of problems; every time I'd go to New York, I'd be jumped on at the United Nations because of WHO's failure to take what the United Nations considered to be the kind of action that WHO was the appropriate organization to deal with.

The failure of WHO to be able to do anything during this period to which I referred—seven to nine years—was clearly the result of the very effective job done by the Vatican and its representatives, not only at WHO but at meetings of the United Nations and other organizations.

The United Nations itself, first by its division of social affairs, tried to do something about the population problem and was very disappointed that WHO had been placed in a position where it was virtually stopped and prevented from doing anything. That probably had a great deal of influence in the United Nations on the establishment of the United Nations Fund for Population Activities, which it set up because WHO had miserably failed to do what the United Nations had hoped it would do.

MUMFORD: Do you think the Vatican exerts pressure on WHO even today?

SIEGEL: I believe that the Catholic church still has considerable influence on WHO's policies and program development.

Stephen D. Mumford is the director of the Center for Research on Population and Security. Much of the history covered by Professor Siegel in this interview about the intrusion of the Catholic church into the development of WHO population policy is also covered in The United Nations and the Population Question *by Richard Symonds and Michael Carder, a Population Council book, published by McGraw-Hill in 1973.*

INDEX

A

A World in Revolution, 273
Abernethy, Virginia D.
 on demographic transition theory, 341-45
 on the disuniting of America, 348
 on overpopulation and women's issues, 353
 on patriotism, 358
Abortion
 banned by **Humanae Vitae**, 124
 clinics, bombings of, 196-97
 Commission on Population and the
  American Future recommendation on, 49
 Evangelium Vitae on, 117-20
 Latin America rates of, 311
 legalization of,
  papal authority threatened by, 123-26
  Vatican's concern about, 110-11
 Vatican Declaration on Abortion, 111
  Christians duties defined in, 112
Adler, Jerry, on the greenhouse effect, 326
Administrative records
 Commission on Population and the American Future recommendations on, 55
Adoption, Commission on Population and the American Future
  recommendation on, 48
Africa
 cereal imports and, 459
 demographic trends in, 451
  potential effects of, 488
 unseasonable weather in, 336
Africa Rights, on Rwanda murders, 211
Agency for International Development (AID)
 crippling of family planning program, 101-2
 declining confidence in, 317
 strategy/resources for, 512-21
Ahlburg, Dennis, on immigration estimations, 345
AID (Agency for International Development)
 crippling of family planning program, 101-2
 declining confidence in, 317
 strategy/resources for, 512-21
AIDS programs, NSDM 314 on, 89-90
Alan Guttmacher Institute, on abortion rates of American Catholic women, 236
Alaska, unseasonable weather in, 337
Algeria, food supplies and, 456
Aliens, illegal, Commission on Population and the American Future
  recommendation on, 51
Allen, Richard V.
 Catholic Campaign for America and, 173
 Reagan's "Catholic Team" and, 132, 356
Amazon, unseasonable weather in, 334
America. See United States
American Association for the Advancement of Science, Julian Simon and, 322
American Cause, 175
American Center for Law and Justice, Keith Fournier, 178
American Enterprise Institute, Julian Simon and, 324
American Federation for Immigration Reform, 322
American Freedom and Catholic Power, 255
American Jewish Committee Religious Liberty Award, 308
American Life League, Julian Simon and, 324
American Life Lobby, 166
Americans United for Separation of Church and State
 on Christian Coalition control of Congress, 310
 on size of Christian Coalition, 179
 on Vatican influence on U.S. policy, 354
Ankerberg, John (Rev.), rejects **Evangelicals and Catholics Together**
  agreement, 314
Ann Landers, Catholic League attack on, 293
Antarctica, ice shelf breaking up, 333, 336
Anti-Defamation League, Catholic League attack on, 299
Anti-family planning crusade, origin of, 126-27
Anti-fertility vaccines, feminists attack on, 351-52
Arab states, demographic trends in, potential effects of, 485
Arctic, ice cap melting, 334
Argentina
 "dirty war" of, Catholic Church and, 209
 unseasonable weather in, 335
Asia
 cereal imports and, 459
 demographic trends in, 452
Associated Press, Catholic League attack on, 290, 295
Astarita, Joseph J., Catholic Campaign for America and, 174
At Home the Pope's Encyclical Takes a Beating, 121
Australia, unseasonable weather in, 335
Authority

papal,
 despotic, 206-7
 papal power and, 123
 threatened by population growth control, 123-26
 versus state, 111-22

B

Bangladesh
 demographic trends in, potential effects of, 486-88
 food supplies and, 456
 population,
  assistance to, 501, 514, 515
  pressure effects in, 483-84
 results of overpopulation of, 344
 unseasonable weather in, 333, 334
Banks, Adelle M.
 on Christian Coalition, 178
 on **Evangelicals and Catholics Together** issued document, 313
Barneys New York, Catholic League attack on, 295-96
Basgall, Monte, on the greenhouse effect, 325-26
Baumann, Paul, **The Pope vs. the Culture of Death**, 121
Beck, Roy, on U.S. immigration, 231
Behavior, research, Commission on Population and the American Future
  recommendations on, 55
Being Right: Conservative Catholics in America, 115
Belohradsky, Vaclav, reaction to **Evangelium Vitae**, 117
Benagiano, Giuseppe, appointed director of Human Reproduction Program, 346
Bendyna, Mary, on Catholics in Christian Coalition, 179, 180
Bennett, William
 Catholic Campaign for America and, 172
 Road to Victory speaker, 179-80
Bernardin, Joseph L. (Cardinal)
 on direct action versus persuasion, 238
 George Bush and, 355
 meeting with Jimmy Carter, 1976 election, 100-101
Bernstein, Carl, 247
 The U.S. and the Vatican on Birth Control, 133
 on Reagan's "Catholic Team", 132, 356-57
 on the Vatican alliance with Ronald Reagan, 355-57
Bevilaqua, Anthony J.
 on church-state relationship, 238
 Philadelphia Inquirer and, 289-90
Bilingual Education Act of, 1968, 349
Birth control
 banned by **Humanae Vitae**, 124
 Papal Commission on Population and Birth Control and, 124
Birth rates. See Fertility, rates
Bishops. See Catholic bishops
Blake, Jeffrey, Catholic League letter to, 295
Blanshard, Paul, on Catholic censorship, 255-58
Blum, Virgil
 Catholic League and, 279
 guidelines offered by, 161-62
 Public Policy Making: Why the Churches Strike Out, 155
Boldt, David R., on bishops view of church and state, 242
Bolivia, demographic trends in, 451
Bork, Mary Ellen, Catholic Campaign for America and, 173
Borlaug, Norman, 230
Bosco, John (Saint), refers to pope as "God on earth", 198
Boston, Rob, on honesty of Christian Coalition, 309-10
Botswana, demographic trends in, 451
Boutwell, Jeffrey H., **Environmental Change and Violent Conflict**, 107-8
Bowers, Claude, apologized to by FDR, 266
Boxer, Barbara
 Catholic League calls to resign from The Population Institute, 298
 warns The Population Institute, 298
Boycotts
 Charles J. Mullaly on, 256-58
 Henry Davis on, 255-56
Bravo Network, Catholic League attack on, 293
Brazil
 demographic trends in, 451-52
 population, assistance to, 501, 514
Brennan, William J., Red Mass in Washington attendee, 238
Briggs, David, on Vatican influence on U.S. policy, 353-54
Bright, Bill, signer of **Evangelicals and Catholics Together** agreement, 313
Brimelow, Peter, U.S. population projections, 107
British Antarctic Survey, on icebergs and warming temperatures, 332
British Meteorological Office, on world's warming temperature, 336
Brokaw, Tom, criticized by Catholic League, 288
Broun, Heywood, on freedom of the press, 260
Brower, David, on the Clinton administration's environmental record, 328-29
Brown, Judie, Julian Simon and, 324

Buchanan, Patrick
  Catholic Campaign for America and, 173
  comment on Richard M. Nixon's re-election, 96
  on Franco, 173
  HLA in Republican Party platform and, 176, 362
  Road to Victory speaker, 180
  Winning the Cultural War speech, 175
Buckly, Christopher, Ann Landers interview and, 293
Burch, Thomas
  Papal Commission on Population and Birth Control assignment, 125
  on threat to Papal authority, 124
Bureau of Alcohol, Tobacco, and Firearms, abortion clinic attacks and, 196-97
Burns, Patrick, 322
Burundi, demographic trends in, 451
Bush, George (President)
  anti-abortion judges appointed by, 165
  Catholic bishops relationship with, 355
  rejects holding a greenhouse effect convention, 327
  Vatican control of policy under, 163-64
Byrd, Harry, greetings to Spain's Congress and, 265
Byrnes, Timothy A.
  on 1976 presidential election, 99-102
  Catholic Bishops in American Politics, 95
  on Catholic Bishops political strength, 96
  notes shift in Catholic bishops political emphasis, 131-32

C

Cairo Plan of Action, 225
Califano, Joseph, appointed Secretary of Health, Education and Welfare, 101
Call to Action, 287-88
Callahan, Patrick Henry, founder of Commission on Religious Prejudices, 196
Campbell, Joan B., on **Ut Unum Sint, That All They May Be One**, 314
Canada, unseasonable weather in, 334
Carey, Hugh, **Challenge to Catholic Americans**, 174
Carrington, Tom, on demographic transition theory, 341
Carter, Jimmy
  concern about Catholic voters, 99
  meeting with National Catholic Conference of Bishops, 100-101
Casey, Robert, **Road to Victory** speaker, 179
Casey, William, Reagan's "Catholic Team" and, 132, 356
Catechism, 269
Catholic Alliance, with Christian Coalition, 180-83
Catholic Association for Radio and Television (Unda), 157
Catholic bishops
  changing views of American, 208
  Christian Coalition,
    alliance with, 180-83
    created by, 177
  dilemma of American, 237
  as lobbyists, 235
  national identification program and, 344
  patriotism and, 358
  political,
    emphasis shift from local/state to federal government, 131-32
    strength of, 96
  recent appointments of, 209-10
  response to Roe v. Wade, 137
  Rwanda and, 211
  Spanish, deception of admitted, 266
  weakened by College of Cardinals, 236
Catholic Bishops in American Politics, 95
Catholic Campaign for America (CCA), 172-73
Catholic censorship, 255-58
Catholic Charities USA, government funds relied on by, 343
Catholic Church of America
  distorted image of, 245-48
  see also Roman Catholic Church
Catholic Eucharistic Congress, Gerald Ford wins support at, 102
Catholic Hospital Association, **Pastoral Plan for Pro-Life Activities** and, 158-59
Catholic Lawyers Association
  called on to attack Roe v. Wade decision, 161
  Pastoral Plan for Pro-Life Activities and, 158
Catholic League, 279-302
  attack on,
    60 Minutes, 287-88
    The Naked Truth, 293
    The Population Institute, 298-99
    Ann Landers, 293
    Anti-Defamation League, 299
    Associated Press, 290, 295
    Barneys New York, 295
    Bill Press, 292
    Bravo Network, 293

Clinton administration, 300
    Dave, Shelly & Chainsaw, 293-94
    Disney, 287, 290-92
    Dr. Joycelyn Elders, 300-301
    Fox-TV, 293
    Hard Rock Casino and Hotel, 296-97
    HBO, 294-95
    Jane Pauley, 292
    Liz Langley, 292
    NBC Nightly News, 288
    New Britain Herald, 293
    Newsday, 289, 294
    Orlando Weekly, 292
    PBS' Frontline, 294
    Philadelphia Inquirer, 289-90
    QC Shopping Network, 295
    Sony, 295
    University of Michigan, 297-98
    William Paterson College, 297
  on censorship, 280-82
  founding of, 279
  image of the Catholic Church and, 282-83
  methods used by, 283-84
    examples of, 289-302
  purpose of, 279
  success of, 284-85
Catholic League calls for a Boycott of Disney, 290
Catholic League for Religious and Civil Rights, 244
  study on Catholic church image, 246, 247
Catholic orders, dropping membership of, 204
Catholic Patriotic Association, 237
Catholic Physicians Guilds, **Pastoral Plan for Pro-Life Activities** and, 158
Catholic Press Association, **Pastoral Plan for Pro-Life Activities** and, 156-58
Catholic Principles of Politics, 114
Catholic schools, declining number of, 204
"Catholic Team," Ronald Reagan's, 356-57
Catholic Truth Societies, censorship and, 258
Catholic voters
  Richard M. Nixon's need for, 95-96
  seen as swing vote in 1976 election, 99
Catholic War Veterans, censorship and, 258
Catholics
  citizenship contradicts religious affiliation, 233-39
  conservative versus liberal, 115-16
  liberal, 220-22
  Vatican in conflict with, 231
  within Christian Coalition, 179-80
  see also Roman Catholic Church
Catholics for a Free Choice and Dignity, 210, 288
  on creation of the Religious Right, 308
  on Catholic right-wing organizations, 239, 244
The Cato Institute, Julian Simon and, 324
CCA (Catholic Campaign for America, 172-73
CDC (Centers for Disease Control), declining confidence in, 317
Censorship, 255-58
  Catholic Truth Societies and, 258
  Charles J. Mullaly on, 256-58
  William Donohue on, 280-82
Census, mid-decade, Commission on Population and the American Future recommendations, 54
Census Bureau
  projections by,
    immigration, 345
    U.S. population, 107
Center for Catholic Policy, 354
Center for Media and Public Affairs, on Catholic church image, 246
Centers for Disease Control (CDC), declining confidence in, 317
Central America, cereal imports and, 459
Chad, demographic trends in, 451
Challenge to Catholic Americans, 174
Chief Duties of Christian Citizens, 112, 255
Child care, Commission on Population and the American Future recommendation on, 48
Children
  born out of wedlock, Commission on Population and the American Future recommendation, 48
  inadequate motivation for reducing, 476
  quality versus quantity, 473
Chile, unseasonable weather in, 335
China
  demographic trends in, 452-53
    potential effects of, 485
  one-child policy, 342
  unseasonable weather in, 334, 336, 337
Chisholm, Brock, Vatican threat to, 346
Christian, Darrell, apology to Catholic League by, 290
Christian Coalition, 178-80

Catholic alliance with, 180-83
creation of, 177
HLA in Republican Party platform and, 176, 362
Pat Robertson and, 176-78, 309
Republican Party takeover by, 308-11
size of, 179
Christopher, Warren
Stanford address, 4-5
opposition to, 5
The Church and the Future, 206
The Churchman's Human Quest, Czech Philosopher Accuses Vatican
of Undermining Democracy, 117
Civil strife, renewable resource scarcity and, 108
Clark, William, Reagan's "Catholic Team" and, 132, 356
Clarkson, Fred, on anti-abortion militants/militias, 197
Clinton, Bill (President)
Catholic League criticism of administration of, 300
election of, conservative Catholics response to, 318-19
on the greenhouse effect, 328
Coal, U.S. reserves of, 463
College of Cardinals, relationship with Bishops, 236
Colombia
demographic trends in, 451
population, assistance to, 501, 514
Colson, Charles, signer of Evangelicals and Catholics Together
agreement, 313
Commercial establishments, examples of Catholic League intimidation of, 295-97
Commission on Population and Birth, 19, 207
Commission on Population Growth and the American Future, 462
compilation of recommendations of, 47-57
creation of, 20
areas of inquiry, 36-38
called for, 36
Richard M. Nixon's remarks, 45-46
establishment of called for, 16
findings,
renounced by Richard M. Nixon, 21, 95-96
submitted, 21
Commission on Religious Prejudices, critical press and, 196
Committee on Population and Economy, 322
purpose of, 322-23
Committee for the Survival of a Free Congress, 166
Community creation, National Commission on Urban Growth
recommendations on, 34
Conant, James, on parochial schools, 244
Conception, papal infallibility and, 207-8
Conflict, renewable resource scarcity and, 108
Congregation for the Doctrine of the Faith, 120
Conn, Joseph L.
on Catholic aid to Pat Robertson, 178
Christian Coalition and, 177
on political views of Pope John Paul and Pat Robertson, 180
Connell, Francis J. (Father), on suppressing the press, 256
Conner, Roger, on Julian Simon, 322
Constitution, John F. Kennedy on upholding, 241
Contraception, Commission on Population and the American Future
recommendation on, 48
Cooke, Terence (Cardinal), Richard M. Nixon's letter to, 95-96
Coors, Joseph, Paul Pressler and, 312
Council on National Policy, Paul Pressler on board of, 312
Council of Social Advisers, Commission on Population and the American
Future on, 57
Cox News Service, on the greenhouse effect, 331-32
Culture of Life, Culture of Death, 120
Czech Philosopher Accuses Vatican of Undermining Democracy, 117
Czechoslovakia, population growth, policy to increase, 450

D

Dahomey, demographic trends in, 451
Dave, Shelly & Chainsaw, Catholic League attack on, 293-94
Davies, Michael, Religious Liberty and the Secular State, 114
Davis, Henry, on book boycotts, 255-56
de Arcos, Angel Maria, catechism, 269
de Bonafini, Hebe, on Catholic Church and Argentina's "dirty war", 209-10
Decree on the Bishops' Pastoral Office in the Church, 110
Defending life even unto death, 117, 120-21
Democracy
confidence eroded in, 316-19
rejected by Pius IX, 112-13, 191
as threat to Papacy, 171-72
Vatican's rejection of, 111-22
not a means to an end, 119
"weak underbelly" of, 310
Demographic transition theory, 340-47
Demographic trends, 65-66, 437-54
current, 437-45
future, 446-54

Department of Agriculture, on world cereal requirements, 456
Department of Community Development, Commission on Population and the
American Future recommendation on, 56
Department of Health, Education, and Welfare (DHEW), declining
confidence in, 317
Department of Health and Human Services (HHS)
Commission on Population and the American Future recommendation on, 56
declining confidence in, 317
Depo Provera, feminist prevented distribution of, 352
Developing countries, population growth in, 30-31
DHEW (Department of Health, Education and Welfare), declining confidence
in, 317
Did the Children Cry? Hitler's War Against Jewish and Polish Children, 299
Diocesan Plan, proposed, 161-62
Disinformation, wrong perceptions created by, 319-25
Disney, Catholic League attack on, 287, 290-92
The Disuniting of America, 241, 348
Dole, Robert, 319
Donohue, William
assumes Catholic League leadership, 279
on criticism of the Catholic Church, 280-82
Donovan, Jeffrey, At Home the Pope's Encyclical Takes a Beating, 121
Dooling, John F. (Judge), Hyde Amendment and, 167-68
Doonan, Simon, Catholic League attempted intimidation of, 295
Dornan, Robert K., Catholic Campaign for America and, 173
Duderstadt, James, Catholic League letter to, 297-98
Dulles, Avery (Jesuit Fr.)
signer of Evangelicals and Catholics Together agreement, 313
on stifled Catholic intellectual development, 202-3
Dupanloup, Felix, on Pius IX, 193

E

Eagle Forum, 166
Earth in the Balance, 328
Earthweek: A Diary of the Planet, 332
Echoes of the Crusades: The Radical Religious Right's Holy War on
American Freedom, 308
Economic growth and development, NSSM 200 on, 67-70, 471-78
Ecuador, demographic trends in, 451
Ecumenical
activity, need for, 159-60
movement, Protestants silenced by, 312-13
Edelman, Mark, withdraws award to Richard Lukas, 299
Education, examples of Catholic League intimidation of, 297-98
Egypt
demographic trends in, 451
potential effects of, 485
food imports dependency of, 342
population, assistance to, 501, 514
Ehrlich, Paul, The Population Bomb, 19
El Salvador-Honduras war, population pressures role in, 482
Elders, Joycelyn, Catholic League attack on, 300-301
Elder's Exit Applauded, 301
Ellis, John Tracy, on stifled Catholic intellectual development, 203
Elwell, Marlene
Catholic Campaign for America and, 174
Christian Coalition and, 177
Emigration, effects of, 344
Employment, population growth and, 478
Environmental Change and Violent Conflict, 107-8
Equal Rights Amendment (ERA)
Commission on Population and the American Future recommendation on, 48
enactment called for, 21
Equal rights for women, Commission on Population and the American Future
recommendation, 48
ERA (Equal Rights Amendment)
Commission on Population and the American Future recommendation on, 48
enactment called for, 21
Estonia, population growth rate in, 450
Eternal Word Television Network, Catholic League and, 295
Ethiopia
demographic trends in, 451
population, assistance to, 501, 514
results of overpopulation, 344
Ethnic conflicts, renewable resource scarcity and, 108
Europe, unseasonable weather in, 335
Evangelicals and Catholics Together, 313
Evangelium Vitae, 117-20
Italian response to, 121
United States response to, 121
ex cathedra. See Papal infallibility
Experience Teaches Population Control Can Precede Development and
Spur It, 341

F

Falwell, Jerry, recruited by Paul Weyrich, 177
Family planning

Father Arthur McCormack's position on, 127
services,
Commission on Population and the American Future recommendation on, 50-51
provision/development of, 504-5
utilization of mass media for, 552-56
World Health Organization and, 246-47
Farley, James, lobbies for Catholic Church, 243
Fascism, supported by Catholic Church, 267-69
Fazio, Vic, on religious-right stealth tactics, 244
FCF (Free Congress Foundation), 161
Fellowship of Catholic Scholars, 239
Feminist Majority, on women's status and overpopulation, 353
Fernsworth, Lawrence, Spanish "Civil War" and, 273
Fertility, control,
Commission on Population and the American Future recommendation on, 50
technique improvements, 541-44
health care services and, Commission on Population and the American Future recommendation on, 50
rates,
actions to promote decline in, 512-58
create conditions for decline of, 505-7, 521-36
declining, **442-43**
economic impact of, 472-74
projections based on, 440-46
Fertilizer, world supply of, 457
Fideles, Christi, on capturing America for Catholics, 175
Finland, intrauterine devices and, 352
First amendment, Vatican rejection of, 233-34
Food for Peace Program, 536-38
Food supplies, adequacy of, 66-67, 455-61
Forbes, William Cameron, **Sacred Heart of Jesus** decoration and, 268
Ford, Gerald (President)
on Catholic voters concerns, 99
endorses NSSM, 200, 15
National Conference of Catholic Bishops and, 102
NSDM 314 and, 15-16, 22-23
response to NSSM, 200, 22-23
succeeded to presidency, 98
Foreign aid, Vatican benefits from, 341
Foreign Assistance Act, anti-abort amendment added to, 101
Fornos, Werner, Catholic League attack on, 298
Fournier, Keith
American Center for Law and Justice and, 178
Catholic Campaign for America and, 174
Fox, Thomas C., **Rome's Lengthening Shadow: U.S. bishops squelched by Vatican**, 237
Fox-TV, Catholic League attack on, 293
Franco, Francisco
Patrick Buchanan on, 173
receives congratulations from Pius XII, 268
supported by,
American Cardinals, 267-68
Hitler and Mussolini, 263
The New York Times, 272-76
Vatican, 268-69
Free Congress Foundation (FCF), 161, 166, 354
Paul Weyrich and, 177
Free Speech Advocates, Christian Coalition and, 177
Freedom of association, condemned by Pope Pius IX, 191, 192, 254
Freedom of conscience
condemned by Pope Gregory XVI, 253-54
Pius IX condemns, 191
Freedom of press, 195
"Catholic issues" and, 261
Francis J. Connell on, 256
George Seldes on, 253, 259-61
Gregory XVI on, 253-54
Pius IX on, 191, 192, 254
Pius XII on, 254
Vatican rejection of, 253-76
Freedom of speech, Pius IX condemns, 191, 192
French Revolution, papacy and, 190
Frontline, Catholic League attack on, 294
Fuels, adequacy of, 67, 461-71

G

Gejdenson, Sam, Catholic League calls to resign from **The Population Institute**, 298
General Assembly of the Presbyterian Church, stance on population control, 19-20
George Seldes Leaves a Legacy of Courage, 259
Getzloe, Harvey, 273
Geyer, Georgie Ann, on Pope John Paul II, **305**
Giblin, Gerry, on origin of the Catholic Alliance, 181
Gilligan, John J., appointed AID Administrator, 101

Gingrich, Newt, **The Michigan Daily** mocks, 297
Global warming. See Greenhouse effect
God and Politics Part II, 312
GOP
Christian Coalition takeover of, 308-11
Vatican takeover of, 308
Gore, Al (Vice President), change of position on greenhouse effect, 328
Government
authority of, papal authority pitted against, 111-22
Commission on Population and the American Future recommendation on,
data distribution, 54
organizational changes, 56
examples of Catholic League intimidation of, 300-302
population growth, dealing with, 38-40
Gracida, Rene (Bishop), Catholic Campaign for America and, 174
Grant, Ulysses S., on parochial schools, 244
Greeley, Andrew M. (Father)
on anti-Catholicism, 240
on liberal Catholics, 221
on Vatican appointments, 209, 210
Green, Cynthia, on untreated human waste, 342
Greenhouse effect
evidence of, 325-27, 329-40
Vatican disinformation effort about, 327-29
Gregorovius, Ferdinand, on Pius IX, 192
Gregory XVI (Pope)
condemned liberalism, 253-54
papal infallibility claimed by, 189-90
Guenois, Jean-Marie, on **Ut Unum Sint, That All They May Be One**, 314-15
Guinea, demographic trends in, 451
Guyana, food supplies and, 456

H

Haig, Alexander, Reagan's "Catholic Team" and, 132
Haiti, results of overpopulation of, 344
Halford, Cathe, 309
Hammond, Ogden H., **Sacred Heart of Jesus** decoration and, 268
Hanretty, Patrick M., Catholic Campaign for America and, 174
Hansen, James
on the greenhouse effect, 325, 329-30, 338-39
conclusions changed by Bush administration over his protest, 327
Hard Rock Casino and Hotel, Catholic League attacked by, 296-97
Hardin, Garrett, **The Tragedy of the Commons**, 19
Harper's Index, on foreign aid, 341-42
Harris, Louis, 240
Hasler, Bernhard
anti-family planning crusade and, 126
on binding nature of doctrine of infallibility, 194
describes Pius IX, 192
on freedom of the press, 253-54
How the Pope Became Infallible, 125
papal infallibility,
church credibility and, 200
consequences of, 201
elasticity of, 189
importance of, 194-95
seen as self-destructive, 199
on silence of Protestant churches, 222
Hauser, Philip, on "population complosion", 480
HBO, Catholic League attack on, 294
Health care, Commission on Population and the American Future recommendation on, 50
Heckler-Feltz, Cheryl, on conservative Catholics, 115-16
Heenan, John C. (Father), **Priest and Penitent**, 255
Helms, Jesse, 310
anti-abortion amendment, Foreign Assistance Act and, 101
The Heritage Foundation, 166
1990 Immigration Reform Act and, 345
Julian Simon and, 321-22, 324
Hertzke, Alan D., on Vatican influence on U.S. policy, 353
Hesburgh, Theodore (Father), offered AID Administrator position, 101
HHS (Department of Health and Human Services), declining confidence in, 317
Hickey, James (Cardinal), George Bush and, 355
Historia del Franquismo, on Pius XII's message congratulation Franco on victory, 268
Hitler, Franco supported by, 263
HLA (Human Life Amendment), 164, 310-11
importance of, 171
ratification drive intensification, 172-76
retained in Republican Party platform, 176
Holland, unseasonable weather in, 335
Holy Alliance: How Reagan and the Pope Conspired to Assist Poland's Solidarity Movement and Hasten the Demise of Communism, 355-56
Holz, Robert Lee, on the greenhouse effect, 331

Homer-Dixon, Thomas F., **Environmental Change and Violent Conflict**, 107-8
Hosken, Fran P., on control of reproduction, 353
How the Pope Became Infallible, 125
Howell, Clarence, 273
Huddle, Donald L., on Vatican influence on U.S. policy, 354-55
Hughes, Emmet John, on **Nuevo Repaldi** catechism, 269-70
Human Life Amendment (HLA), 164, 310-11
   importance of, 171
   ratification drive intensification, 172-76
   retained in Republican Party platform, 176, 361-62
Human Reproduction Program, Giuseppe Benagiano appointed director of, 346
Human rights, Vatican's agenda of, 217-18
Humanae Vitae, 208
   abortion/birth control banned by, 124
      harm caused by, 203-4
   rejected by majority, 208
Humphrey, Hubert, greetings to Spain's Congress and, 265
Hungary, population growth, policy to increase, 450
Hurley, Mark J. (Bishop)
   on conflict between being a Catholic and an American, 233, 237, 240
   identifies M. Schlesinger as anti-Catholic, 241-42
   on John F. Kennedy's church-state stance, 241
Hyde Amendment, 167-68

I

Icard, Henri, on papal infallibility, 199, 200
Il Manifesto, on the **Evangelium Vitae**, 121
Illegal aliens, Commission on Population and the American Future recommendation on, 51
Immaculate Conception, Pius IX and, 190
Immigration
   Commission on Population and the American Future recommendation on, 51
   effects of, 344
   1990 Immigration Reform Act, 344
   Vatican's stance on, 231-32
In China Catholics must choose Pope or Party, 237
India
   demographic trends in, potential effects of, 485-86
   food supplies and, 456
   population,
      assistance to, 501, 514
      pressure effects in, 483-84
   unseasonable weather in, 333-34
Indonesia
   food supplies and, 456
   population, assistance to, 501, 514
Infallibilists, 198
Infallibility. See Papal infallibility
Infallible? An Inquiry, 208
Inouye, Daniel K.
   The Population Institute, 298
Intellect, papal distaste for, 217
Intellectuals, as anti-Catholics, 240-44
Interfaith Alliance Foundation, on Christian Coalition control of Congress, 310
Intergovernmental Panel on Climate Change (IPCC), on the greenhouse effect, 330-31, 536
International Catholic Office for Film and Cinema (OCIC), 157
International Catholic Press Union (UCIP), 157
International Catholic Truth Society, 260
International Conference on Population and Development, 221, 224
International migration, Commission on Population and the American Future recommendation on, 54
International Planned Parenthood Federation, funding to canceled, 133
International strife, renewable resource scarcity and, 108
Intimidation
   Catholic League methods of, 283-84
      examples of, 289-302
   criticism prevented by, 285, 287-88
Intrauterine device (IUD), attacked by feminists, 352
IPCC (Intergovernmental Panel on Climate Change), on the greenhouse effect, 330-31, 336
Iraq
   demographic trends in, 452
   food supplies and, 456
Ireland, John (Archbishop), on prejudice, 244
Ireland, unseasonable weather in, 335
Israel, demographic trends in, potential effects of, 485
IUD (Intrauterine device), attacked by feminists, 352
Ivins, Molly, on the greenhouse effect, 328

J

James, Edward L., on reporting on Spanish "Civil War", 272-73
Jesuits, lead papal infallibility movement, 199
John Paul I (Pope), throne/crown dispensed with, 194
John Paul II (Pope)

on church self-protection, 235
in conflict with American bishops, 208
on contraception and threat to the papacy, 188-89
New York's Central Park Mass and, 181
Papal Commission on Population and Birth Control and, 124
on papal infallibility, **215**
Petition in Defense of Pope John Paul II, 286
throne/crown dispensed with, 194
Ut Unum Sint, That All They May Be One issued, 314-15
view of Protestants, Jews and secularists, 122
see also Wojtyla, Karol (Archbishop of Cracow)
John XXII (Pope), papal infallibility condemned by, 189
John XXIII (Pope), papal infallibility doctrine and, 207
Joint Committee on Population, Commission on Population and the American Future recommendation on, 57
Jones, Arthur, on Pat Robertson and Ralph Reed, 310

K

Kahn, Herman, 322
   disinformation and, 320
Kelley, George (Msgr.), on Catholics becoming Americans, 239
Kelley, Patrick, criticism of, 243
Kennedy, Anthony M., Red Mass in Washington attendee, 238
Kennedy, James (Rev.), rejects **Evangelicals and Catholics Together** agreement, 314
Kennedy, John F. (President)
   denounced supremacy of church over state, 233
   on separation of church and state, 240-41
Kennedy, Joseph P., lobbies for Catholic Church, 243
Kenya, unseasonable weather in, 337
Keyes, Alan, **Road to Victory** speaker, 180
Kissinger, Henry
   NSSM 200,
      cover memo, 61-62
      directions for undertaking, 22
Kissling, Frances, on Cardinal John O'Connor, 210
Knights of Columbus
   censorship and, 258
   freedom of the press and, 254
   purpose of, 196
   study on Catholic church image, 246
Kraus, Franz Xaver
   on Pius IX, 192
   on self-destruction due to papal infallibility, 199
Küng, Hans
   on Church's teaching on contraception, 203
   deprived of teaching, 217
   on function of infallibility, 193-94
   Infallible? An Inquiry, 208
   papal infallibility,
      discussed by, 211-12
      effect of doctrine of, 194
      function of doctrine of, 193-94
   Pius IX described by, 191-92
Kuwait, demographic trends in, 452

L

Lader, Lawrence, 223
Laghi, Pio (Cardinal)
   American foreign aid and, 133
   Ronald Reagan and, 356
Lando, Barry, Catholic League criticism of, 287-88
Langan, Janine, **Defending life even unto death**, 117, 120-21
Langley, Liz, Catholic League attack on, 292
Larsson, Lars-Erik, on unusual Scandinavian weather, 336
Latin America
   abortion in, 311
   cereal imports and, 459
   demographic trends in, 451-52
   Protestant church growth in, 204-5
Latvia, population growth rate in, 450
Law, Bernard (Cardinal), George Bush and, 355
Law
   church self-protection and, 234
   Vatican's right to protect self from, 122-23
Lawmakers, intimidation of, 165-66
Leach, Jim, Catholic League calls to resign from **The Population Institute**, 298
Leo XIII (Pope), **Chief Duties of Christian Citizens**, 112, 255
Lerner, Max, on Vatican pressure on Franklin D. Roosevelt, 265
Lesotho, demographic trends in, 451
Levin, Sander, 164
   Office of Population dismemberment and, 101
Liberal Catholics, 220-22
Liberalism
   condemned by Pope Gregory XVI, 253-54
   Pius IX condemns, 191, 192
Life Amendment Political Action Committee, 166

Likoudis, Paul, on origins of Catholic Alliance, 181
Limbaugh, Rush, 318
  on the greenhouse effect, 328
Lords of the Press, 259
Los dos Cindados, 264
Loyalty, to God over state, 233
Lujan, Manuel, Red Mass in Washington attendee, 238
Lukas, Richard
  Anti-Defamation League award and, 299
Lynch, Frank, Catholic Campaign for America and, 174
Lynn, Barry, on size of Christian Coalition, 179

M

MacNeil, Neil, 273
Maddox, Robert, on Vatican influence on U.S. policy, 354
Mahony, Roger (Archbishop), on immigration versus national sovereignty, 232
Mahran, Maher, on Vatican population stance, 224
Malawi, demographic trends in, 451
Mali, demographic trends in, 451
Marcus, Leslie, on the greenhouse effect, 326
Marlette, Bob, Catholic League intimidation and, 289
Marro, Anthony, Catholic League intimidation and, 289
Martino, Renato Rafaele, on church self-protection, 235
Martino, Rocco L., Catholic Campaign for America and, 174
Martyrdom
  described, 121
  Ut Unum Sint, That All They May Be One and, 315
Mary's Assumption, myth of, 205-6
Mass Media, utilization of, 552-56
Mass Media Needs Catholic Presence, 157
Massive Famine Predicted Worldwide, 249
Mathews, Jessica, on the greenhouse effect, 331
Matt, A.J. Jr., on bishops loyalty, 236
Matthews, Herbert L.
  A World in Revolution, 271
  New York Times and, 272-73
McCarthy, Joseph, Patrick Buchanan on, 173
McCaw, Robert, 273
McCormick, Arthur (Father)
  exposé of Vatican by, 229-30
  position on Vatican's family planning policy, 127
McFarlane, Robert, on Reagan's "Catholic Team", 356
McHugh, James (Bishop)
  response to Roe v. Wade, 137, 362
  on Roe v. Wade, 176
  Vatican consultant to the UN, 229
McKibben, Bill, on the greenhouse effect, 328
McLean, Vernon, Catholic League attack on, 297
Media, examples of Catholic League intimidation of, 289-95
Media Treat Pope Fairly; Protesters Fail to Score, 285
Mediterranean Sea, warming of, 333
Meehan, Mary, on Judge Joseph Moylan's resignation, 243
Mexico
  cereal imports and, 459
  demographic trends in, potential effects of, 488-89
  drought in, 333
  population, assistance to, 514
Michelis, Friedrich, describes Pius IX, 200
The Michigan Daily, Catholic League attack on, 297-98
Migration, Commission on Population and the American Future
  recommendation on, 52, 54
Migration and Refugee Services, 232
Minerals
  adequacy of, 67, 461-71
  reserves of, 462-65
  world, 468-71
Minorities, Commission on Population and the American Future
  recommendation on, 52
Minors, contraception and, Commission on Population and the
  American Future recommendation on, 49
Mintz, Phil, on the greenhouse effect, 331
Mirari vos, 189-90
  freedom of the press and, 253-54
Mitchell, Faith, Catholic League and, 300
Moffett, George, on the greenhouse effect, 330
Monaghan, Thomas
  Catholic Campaign for America and, 174
  Marlene Elwell and, 177
Monaghan, Thomas Patrick, counsel to Pat Robertson's American
  Center for Law and Justice, 177
Mongolia, unseasonable weather in, 335, 337
Moral Majority, 166
  Jerry Falwell recruited to lead, 177
Moral and Pastoral Theology, on book boycotts, 255-56
Mothers of the Plaza de Mayo, 209
Moyers, Bill

on SBC rift, 312
  on Vatican control of GOP, 308
Moylan, Joseph, resignation of, 243
Mullaly, Charles J., on censorship and boycotts, 256-58
Murder on Abortion Row, 294
Mussolini, Franco supported by, 263

N

National Action Committee on the Status of Women, 351
National Catholic Alliance Voter Mobilization Campaign, 182
National Commission on Urban Growth, community creation recommended by, 34
National Committee for a Human Life Amendment, 166
National Conference of Catholic Bishops
  created, 98
  energy committed to abortion/population related issues by, 307
  establishment of, 110
  Gerald Ford, and, 102
  letter to Bill Clinton, 221
  meeting with Jimmy Carter, 100-101
National Conservative Political Action Committee, 166
National Council of Churches, welcomes **Ut Unum Sint, That All They May Be One**, 314
National Empowerment Television (NET), 178
National identification card program, 344
National Institute of Population Science, 56
National Right to Life Committee, 166
National security, population pressures and, 479-90
National Security Council, NSSM 200 responsibilities assigned to, 23
National Security Decision Memorandum 314 (NSDM 314), 15-16
  text of, 89-92
National Security Study Memorandum 200. See NSSM 200
National sovereignty, Vatican's rejection of, 232
Nazi Slur of Vatican Implicates Congressman, 298
NBC Nightly News, criticized by Catholic League, 288
Nelson, Jack, on Vatican takeover of Republican Party, 308
Nepal, results of overpopulation of, 344
NET (National Empowerment Television), 178
Neuhaus, Richard J. (Fr.)
  Catholic Campaign for America and, 174
  signer of **Evangelicals and Catholics Together** agreement, 313
Neutrality Act, demise of republican Spain and, 264
New Britain Herald, Catholic League attack on, 293
New Republic, on Catholic League, 288
New Right Movement, 166
New York City Archdiocese, funded by taxes, 196
Newman, Steve, on the greenhouse effect, 332
Newsday
  Catholic League,
    attack on, 294
    intimidation of, 289
Niger, demographic trends in, 451
Nigeria
  demographic trends in, 451
  food supplies and, 456
  population,
    assistance to, 501, 514
    pressure effects in, 482
Nitrogen fertilizer, world supply of, 457
Nixon, Richard M.
  Commission on Population Growth and the American Future, remarks at establishment of, 45-46
  letter to Cardinal Terence Cooke, 95-96
  need for Catholic vote in re-election, 95-96
  Population and the American Future, findings renounces by, 21, 95-96
  Problems on Population Growth speech, 16-17
  resigns from presidency, 98
  Special Message on Problems of Population Growth, 20
    text of, 29-41
Non-Intervention Pact, 264
North, Oliver, religious affiliation hidden by press, 197
North America, seen as missionary region, 204
Norway, intrauterine devices and, 352
Novak, Michael, signer of **Evangelicals and Catholics Together** agreement, 313
NSDM 314
  issued by Gerald Ford, 15-16, 22-23, 95
    National Security Council responsibilities concerning, 23
NSSM 200
  emphasis of, 17
  endorsed by Gerald Ford, 15
  executive summary, 63-86
    adequacy of world food supplies, 66-67
    dealing with population growth, 71-72
    economic development and population growth, 67-70
    key points in full report, 83-86
    minerals and fuel, 67
    policy follow-up and coordination, 79-80
    policy recommendations, 72-79

political effects of population factors, 70-71
population growth by major region, 82
world demographic trends, 65-66
Henry Kissinger,
cover memo by, 61-62
directions for undertaking, 22
National Security Council responsibilities concerning, 23
opposition to, 98-103
recommendations, 24
study initiated, 97
text of,
actions for decline in fertility rates, 512-58
demographic trends, 437-54
economic development/population growth and, 471-78
executive summary, 65-82
food supplies and, 455-61
minerals/fuel and, 461-71
policy recommendations, 499-558
population pressures on national security, 479-90
U.S. global population strategy, 512-21
World Population Conference, 491-98
Vatican only opposition to, 109, 131
Nuevo Repaldi, 269
Nuns
catch-22 of, 218-20
increasing average age of, 204
Nuremberg trials, fascists support of Franco confirmed at, 263

O

O'Brien, Conor Cruise
American Catholic defined by, 241
on papal infallibility, 216-17
OCIC (International Catholic Office for Film and Cinema), 157
O'Connor, John J. (Cardinal)
Catholic Campaign for America and, 173
disposition/power of, 210
George Bush and, 355
M. Schlesinger on, 242
signer of **Evangelicals and Catholics Together** agreement, 313
on threat to Papal authority, 124
Office of Population Affairs Government, Commission on Population and the American Future recommendation, 56
Office of Population Growth and Distribution, Commission on Population and the American Future commendation, 56
Oil
reserves of, 470-71
U.S., 463
Old Catholic Church, creation of, 199
Orlando Weekly, Catholic League attack on, 292

P

Paige, Connie, **The Right to Life: Who They Are, How They Operate, How They Get Their Money**, 166
Pakistan
food supplies and, 456
population,
assistance to, 501, 515
pressure effects in, 483-84
Panama, demographic trends in, potential effects of, 488
Panel of the United Nations Association, 31
Paneta, Leon, promises to discipline staffers who chide the Vatican, 300
Papacy
anti-family planning crusade and, 126-27
authority of,
papal power and, 123
pitted against governmental authority, 111-22
dangers faced in 19th century, 190-91
democracy as threat to, 171-72
importance of infallibility to, 194-95
infallibility of. See Papal infallibility
proclaimed as world's moral leader, 216-17
threatened by population growth control, 123-26
Papal Commission on Population and Birth Control, on birth control, 124
Papal infallibility
Cardinal Joseph Ratzinger on, 120
collides with conception, 207-8
consequences of, 200-205
declaration of, 125-26
dissenters predictions about, 199-200
freedom of the press and, 254
as fundamental principle of the Church, 215
Hans Küng on, 193-94, 211-12
history of, 189-90
importance of, 193-94
to the pope, 194-95
new papal image created by, 198-99
population problem and, 187

as response to 19th century challenges, 190-91
seen as self-destructive, 199
as threat to papacy, 188-89
Papal law, imposition of, 172
Papal Power: A Study of Vatican Control Over Lay Catholic Elites, 123
Papal primacy, 189
consequences of, 200-205
Papal security, National Conference of Catholic Bishops and, 98
Papal States, loss of, 190
Pastoral Constitution on the Church in the Modern World, 110
Pastoral Plan for Pro-Life Activities, 137-38, 287
analysis of, 156-59
consequences of, 307-8
creation of 'new right' and, 166-67
district pro-life group objectives, 152
ecumenical activity and, 159-60
public information effort and, 160
implementation of, 151-52
intimating lawmakers and, 165-66
John F. Dooling (Judge) and, 167-68
judicial activity and, 160-61
proposed diocesan plan, 161-62
Religious Right created in response to, 308
"sanitized" plan excerpts, 150-51
sanitized version, 163-65
Southern Baptist Convention rift and, 312
text of, 139-49
Patriotism, 357-58
definitions of, 357
Paul VI (Pope)
Commission on Population and Birth and, 19, 207
rejects majority position, 19, 207-8
in conflict with American bishops, 208
Humanae Vitae and, 124, 208
papal infallibility and, 126
tiara laid aside by, 194
Pauley, Jane, Catholic League attack on, 292
The People, Press and Politics, 245
People's Republic of China (PRC)
demographic trends in, 452-53
potential effects of, 485
one child policy, 342
unseasonable weather in, 334, 336, 337
Pepper, Claude, greetings to Spain's Congress and, 265
Persistent Prejudice: Anti-Catholicism in America, 124
Petition in Defense of Pope John Paul II, 286
Petroleum
reserves of, 470-71
U.S., 463
Philadelphia Inquirer, Catholic League intimidation of, 289-90
Philippines
food supplies and, 456
population, assistance to, 501, 514, 515
Pius IX (Pope)
capital punishments ordered by, 190
condemns,
freedom of association, 191, 192, 254
freedom of conscience, 191
freedom of press, 191, 192, 254
description of, 191-93
legacy of, 193
on papal infallibility as dogma, 190
Quata Cura, modern errors listed in, 112-13, 191
referred to as "God on earth", 198
Pius X (Pope)
canonized, 207, 215
separation of church and state condemned by, 114
Pius XI (Pope), on censorship, 256
Pius XII (Pope)
awards Franco **Supreme Equestrian Order of the Militia of Our Lord Jesus Christ**, 267
canonized Pius X, 207, 215
congratulates Franco on Spanish "Civil War" victory, 268
on freedom of the press, 254
proclamation on Mary's assumed into heaven, 205
Planned Parenthood, on anti-abortion militants/militias, 197
Pokorsky, Jerry (Father), **Road to Victory** speaker, 180
Policy on Global Population Issues memo, 7-13
Policy recommendations
follow-up/coordination of, 79-80
NSSM, 200, 72-79
Political will, Vatican's role in destroying, 109
Politics, population growth affects on, 70-71
Pontifical Council for the Family, 120
Poor, Commission on Population and the American Future recommendation on, 52
The Pope vs. the Culture of Death, 117, 121

Pope John XXIII, **Commission on Population and Birth** established by, 19
Population
Commission on Population and the American Future recommendations on,
   distribution, 52, 55
   education, 47
   intercensal estimates, 55
   stabilization, 51
   statistics, 53
   survey, 54
   trends, 437-54
     current, 437-46
     future, 446-54
   urban expansion, 52, 439
The Population Institute, Catholic League attack on, 298
Population and the American Future
published, 20
recommendations of, 20-21
see also Rockefeller Commission Report
Population assistance
instruments/modalities for, 503-4
key country priorities in, 501-3
The Population Bomb, 19
Population Education Act, enactment called for, 21
Population goals, NSDM 314 on, 91-92
Population growth
by major region, 82
control,
   Father Arthur McCormack's position on, 127
   papacy threatened by, 13-16
   Presbyterian Church stance on, 19-20
   Spanish "Civil War" as lesson for, 262-65
develop actions to stabilize, 556-58
developing countries, 30-31
economic impact of, 472-74
effects of,
   development on, 474-78
   potential, 484-89
goals/requirements for dealing with, 71-72
inadequate resources and, 481
international migrations and, 481
national security and, 479-90
need for international cooperation, 31-32
NSSM 200 on, 471-78
political,
   effects of, 70-71
   instability and, 481
social cleavages and, 481
stabilization plan development for, 507-11
in the United States, 32-36
world, 29
   demographic trends, 65-66
Population Growth Control: The Next Move is America's, 17
Population movement, leadership of, 223-25
Population Politics: The Choices That Shape Our Future, 341, 348
Population programs
NSDM 314,
   on developing, 91
   on funding of, 90
Poverty, as a distribution problem, 342-43
Power, Population and the Environment Women Speak, 351
PRC. *See* People's Republic of China (PRC)
Preliminary Assessment of the World Food Situation Present and Future, 459
Presbyterian Church, stance on population control, 19-20
Press, Bill, Catholic League attack on, 292
Press
freedom of, 195
   Pius IX condemns, 191, 192
   see also Freedom of press
manipulation of, 270-72
powerless, 195-98
Pressler, Paul, on connection with Catholic organizations, 312
Priest Lobbying for Spain, 271
Priest and Penitent, 255
Priesthood, drop in numbers entering, 204
Priestly Sins: Sex and the Catholic Church, 294
Priests, catch-22 of, 218-20
Private agencies, Commission on Population and the American Future recommendation on, 57
Problems on Population Growth and the American Future, 16-17
Pro-life groups, objectives of, 152
Protestant churches
growth of in Latin America, 204-5
silence of, 222-23
Protestants

fragmentation guilt feelings and, 313
protest disappears from, 311-12
Public Policy Making: Why the Churches Strike Out, 155
Publishers, Catholic boycotts and, 258

Q

Quata Cura, modern errors listed in, 112-13, 191
Quinacrine pellet, opposition to, 352
QVC Shopping Network, Catholic League attack on, 295

R

Racism and Sexism in Changing America, 297
Rather, Dan, on the **Whitewater Affair**, 319
Rathjens, George W., **Environmental Change and Violent Conflict**, 107-8
Ratzinger, Joseph (Cardinal)
on church self-protection, 234
on papal infallibility, 120
on Vatican self-protection, 122-23
Rausch, James (Bishop), relationship with Andrew Young, 100
Ravenholt, R.T., 223
   Pronatalist Zealotry and Population Pressure Conflicts: How Catholics Seized Control of U.S. Family Planning Programs, 100
   removed from AID position, 101
Raw materials
demand/supply of, factors affecting, 465-66
world reserves of, 467-71
Reagan, Ronald (President)
anti-abortion judges appointed by, 165
Catholic bishops relationship with, 355-56
"Catholic Team" of, 132, 356-57
foreign aid policy, changed to appease Vatican, 133
Vatican control of policy under, 163-64
Red Mass in Washington, 238
Reed, Ralph, 309
on Christian Coalition and Catholics, 180-81
Rehnquist, William H., Red Mass in Washington attendee, 238
Reilly, William, greenhouse effect warning by rejected, 327
Religious Liberty and the Secular State, 114
Religious Right, 166
creation of, 96, 308
Religious Roundtable, 166
Renewable resources, civil/international strife and, 108
Representing God in Washington, 353
Republican Party
Christian Coalition takeover over of, 308-11
Vatican takeover of, 308, 362
Research
NSDM 314 on, 90
social/behavioral, Commission on Population and the American Future recommendations on, 55
Resources, Population, Environment, 320
Resources, renewable, civil/international strife and, 108
Rice, Charles
on pope gaining power to approve "natural law", 180
on solving current societal problems, 175
Right to Life Party, 166
Right to Life Political Action Committee, 166
Road to Victory Conference, 179
Robertson, Pat
call for "religious liberty" amendment, 180
Catholic Campaign for America and, 174
Christian Coalition and, 176-78
on dream/progress of the Christian Coalition, 309
on Protestants and Catholics drawing together, 181
recruited by Paul Weyrich, 177
Rockefeller, John D. 3rd
chaired **Commission on Population Growth and the American Future**, 20
on opposition to Rockefeller Commission Report, 97
Panel of the United Nations Association and, 31
Rockefeller Commission Report
on opposition to,
   James Scheuer, 97
   John D. Rockefeller, 96-97
Papacy survival and, 131
see also **Population and the American Future**
The Rockford Institute, Julian Simon and, 324
Roe v. Wade, 132
Bishop James McHugh on, 176, 362
Catholic bishops response to, 137
Catholic Lawyers Association and, 161
judicial activity since, 160-61
Pastoral Plan for Pro-Life Activities,
   district pro-life group objectives, 152
   implementation of, 151-52
   in response to, 137-38
   "sanitized" plan excerpts, 150-51

text of, 139-49
Roman Catholic Church
    alliance with Christian Coalition, 180-83
    distorted image of, 245-48
    image of, 282-83
    losing touch with reality, 205-6
    opposition to NSSM, 200, 98-103
    see also Catholic
Romania, population growth, policy to increase, 450
Rome's Lengthening Shadow: U.S. bishops squelched by Vatican, 237
Roosevelt, Franklin D. (President)
    admits mistake over Spanish "Civil War", 266
    on being an American, 243
    lobbied by Cardinal Pacelli, 264
Roosevelt, Theodore (President), on being an American, 243
Roselli, Maureen
    Catholic Alliance headed by, 181
    membership drive letter, 181-82
    on size of Christian Coalition, 179
Ruff, Frank (Father), speaks at Southern Baptist Convention, 315-16
Rural areas, Commission on Population and the American Future
    recommendation on, 53
Rwanda
    demographic trends in, 451
    murders encouraged by priests in, 210-11
Ryan, John A. (Msgr.), Catholic Principles of Politics, 114
Ryscavage, Richard J. (Father), on immigration, 232

S

Sacred Congregation for the Doctrine of the Faith
    on church self-protection, 234
    on Vatican protecting itself, 122-23
Sacred Heart of Jesus decoration, awarded to American Cardinals, 268
Sahel countries
    demographic trends in, potential effects of, 488
    results of overpopulation of, 344
Satellite communications, utilization of mass media for, 552-56
Saudi Arabia, demographic trends in, 452
Sawyer, Kathy, on the greenhouse effect, 330-31
SBC (Southern Baptist Convention)
    Father Frank Ruff speaks at, 315-16
    rift between fundamentalists and moderates, 311-12
        Bill Moyers on, 312
        Pastoral Plan for Pro-Life Activities and, 312
Scalia , Anthony, Red Mass in Washington attendee, 238
Scandinavia, unseasonable weather in, 336
Scheuer, James, on criticism of Rockefeller Commission Report, 97
Schlafly, Phyllis
    Catholic Campaign for America and, 173
    Paul Pressler and, 312
Schlesinger, Arthur M.
    on disuniting America, 348-50
    identified as anti-Catholic, 241-43
Schmieder, Steven, Catholic Campaign for America and, 174
Schneider, Stephen H., on the greenhouse effect, 326
Schwartz, Michael, Persistent Prejudice: Anti-Catholicism in America, 124
Science, as enemy of the Vatican, 202
Scientific American, Environmental Change and Violent Conflict, 107-8
Scilingo, Adolfo, on Argentina's "dirty war" and the Catholic Church and, 209
Scowcroft, Brent
    National Security Decision Memorandum 314 (NSDM 314), text, 89-92
    NSSM 200 and, 22
Seldes, George, on freedom of the press, 253, 259-61
Seminaries, drop in numbers entering, 204
Separation of church and state
    Anthony J. Bevilaqua on, 238
    condemned by Pope Pius X, 114
    Evangelium Vitae and, 117-20
    on John F. Kennedy, 240
    John F. Kennedy on, 240-41
    Papacy opposed to, 112
    Quata Cura and, 112-13
    Rocco L. Martino on, 174
Settle, Stephen, on imposition of papal law, 172
Sex education, Commission on Population and the American Future
    recommendation on, 47
Shakespeare, Frank, Catholic Campaign for America and, 173
Shaw, Russel, Catholic Campaign for America and, 173-74
Siberia, warming of, 334
Siegel, Milton, The Vatican and World Population Policy, 515-17
Siena Group, 354
Sietel, Milton P., on Vatican control of World Health Organization, 346
Silva, John, Murder on Abortion Row and, 294
Simcox, David, on immigration, 232
Simon, Julian
    1990 Immigration Reform Act and, 345
    disinformation disseminated by, 320-24

Simon, Paul, Catholic League calls to resign from The Population Institute, 298
Simons, Franceos, infallibility challenged by, 208
Sixty 60 Minutes, Catholic League attack on, 287-88
Smeal, Eleanor, on women's status and overpopulation, 353
Smith, Chris, 181
Social behavior, research on, Commission on Population and the American
    Future recommendations on, 55
Social problems, population growth and, 478
Society of Catholic Social Scientists, 175
Somalia, demographic trends in, 451
Sony, Catholic League attack on, 295
South Africa, unseasonable weather in, 338
South America, demographic trends in, 451
Southern Baptist Convention (SBC)
    Father Frank Ruff speaks at, 315-16
    rift between fundamentalists and moderates, 311-12
        Bill Moyers on, 312
        Pastoral Plan for Pro-Life Activities and, 312
Spain
    bishops, of deception by admitted to, 266
    Neutrality Act and, 264
    Nuevo Repaldi catechism of, 269-70
    unseasonable weather in, 333
Spanish Civil War
    American Cardinals support of Franco during, 267-68
    casualties/murders during, 267
    Catholic support of rebels during, 260
    Spanish Bishops apologize for deception about, 266
    Vatican interests and, 127
Special groups, Commission on Population and the American Future
    recommendation on, 53
Special Message on Problems of Population Growth, 20
    text of, 29-41
Sproul, R.C., rejects Evangelicals and Catholics Together agreement, 314
Stafford, Francis, signer of Evangelicals and Catholics Together
    agreement, 173
Stanford University, rising shoreline temperature study, 332
State population agencies, Commission on Population and the American
    Future recommendation on, 57
Statistics
    Commission on Population and the American Future,
        administrative records, 54
        population/vital, 53
Steinfels, Peter, response to Evangelium Vitae, 122
Sterilization, voluntary, Commission on Population and the American Future
    recommendation on, 49
Stevens, William K., on the greenhouse effect, 329-30, 338-39
Sudan
    demographic trends in, 451
    results of overpopulation of, 344
Sullivan, John H., 164
    aided in selecting Jimmy Carter's political appointees, 101
Sullivan, Louis W., Red Mass in Washington attendee, 238
Sununu, John H., rejects William Reilly proposal on greenhouse effect, 327
Sweden, intrauterine devices and, 352
Szoka, Edmund (Cardinal), George Bush and, 355

T

Taking America's Pulse, 282
Talese, Guy, on the Fascist phalanx, 273
Tang, Dominic, loyalty of, 237
Tanzania, demographic trends in, 451
Taracon, Enrique (Primate Cardinal), on Spanish Bishops deception, 266
Tass new agency, on venomous snake migration, 334
Teenagers, services for, Commission on Population and the American
    Future recommendation on, 51
Text of
    world Population Plan of Action, 399-402
    recommendations for action, 403-32
Thailand, population, assistance to, 501, 514, 515
That All They May Be One, issued, 314
Thorning, Joseph F. (Father), propagandist Franco supporter, 271
Tibet, blizzard in, 332
Time for Decision, 266
Torricelli, Robert
    Catholic League calls to resign from The Population Institute, 298
    warns The Population Institute, 298-99
The Tragedy of the Commons, 19
Training
    Commission on Population and the American Future recommendation on,
        health care providers,50
        professional, 55
Truesdell, Jeff, 292
Trujillo, Alfonso Lopez (Cardinal), on Church is at war with democracy, 120
Truman, Harry (President), calls Neutrality Action a mistake, 266
Turkey
    demographic trends in, 452

population, assistance to, 501, 514
Tyrell, George, **The Church and the Future**, 206

U

UCIP (International Catholic Press Union), 157
Uganda, demographic trends in, 451
Ukraine
 population growth rate in, 450
 unseasonable weather in, 337
The Ultimate Resource, 320-21
UN World Population Conference, World Population Plan of Action
 adopted by, **22**
Unda (Catholic Association for Radio and Television), 157
The Unholy Ghost: Anti-Catholicism in the American Experience,
 233, 237, 240
United Kingdom Climate Change Impacts Review Board, on changing
 weather, 338
United Nations, world population and, called to assume leadership on, 31
United Nations Fund for Population Activities, funding to canceled, 133
United Nations World Population Conference, Vatican only opposition
 to, 131
United Nations World Summit on Social Development, 225
United States
 demographic trends in, potential effects of, 488-89
 disuniting of, 348-51
 fertility rate in, 450
 global population strategy, 499-512
 minerals/fuel, 461
  primary sources of, **467**
  reserves, 462-65
 policy versus Vatican interests, 353-55
 population,
  assistance mode/content of, 515-17
  assistance priorities, 514-15
  assistance resource allocations, 517-20
  projections, 32-36, 107
 unseasonable weather in, 333-35
 Vatican security issue versus, 127
The U.S. and the Vatican on Birth Control, 133
U.S. Catholic Conference, Migration and Refugee Services and, 232
United States Catholic Conference (USCC), established, 110
U.S. Climate Analysis Center, on global warming, 335
U.S. Geological Survey, on U.S. oil/coal reserves, 463
University of Michigan, Catholic League attack on, 297-98
Upper Volta, demographic trends in, 451
Urban, expansion, Commission on Population and the American
 Future recommendation on, 52
USCC. *See* United States Catholic Conference (USCC)
Ut Unum Sint, issued, 314

V

Vaillancourt, Jean-Guy
 on need for papal infallibility, 191
 **Papal Power: A Study of Vatican Control Over Lay Catholic
 Elites**, 123
Vatican
 abortion and, concern over legalizing, 110-11
 alliance with Ronald Reagan, 355-57
 anti-family planning crusade and, 126-27
 in conflict with lay Catholics, 231
 Council II, 110-11
 demands open borders of U.S., 231
 democracy,
  rejected by, 111-22
  as threat to, 171-72
 demographic transition theory promoted by, 340-41
 endorses **Evangelicals and Catholics Together** agreement, 313
 Franco rewards to, 268-69
 free press rejected by, 253-76
 "human rights" agenda of, 217-18
 influence on U.S. presidency, 355-57
 insuring survival of, 306-7
 International Feminist Movement and, 351-53
 opposition to NSSM, 200, 98-103
 opposition to NSSM 200,
  only institution to do so, 109, 131
  reasons for, 110-33
 policy control under Ronald Reagan and George Bush, 163-64
 on poverty as a distribution problem, 342-43
 press manipulation by, 270-72
 proclaiming pope as world's moral leader, 216-17
 rejection of national sovereignty, 232
 Republican Party takeover by, 308, 362
 right to protect self from harmful laws, 122-23
 science as enemy of, 202
 Spanish Republic destruction lead by, 267
 U.S. policy and interests of, 353-55

Vatican Council I
 papal infallibility declared by, 125-26, 189-90
 papal primacy declared by, 189
Vatican Council II, growth of internal criticism since, 287
Vatican Declaration on Abortion, 111
 Christian's duties described in, 112
Vaupel, James, on immigration estimations, 345
Venezuela, demographic trends in, 451
Vestel, Daniel, on Paul Pressler, 312
Victory is Always Sweet: Hard Rock Hotel Pulls Alter, 296
Viguerie, Richard, Paul Pressler and, 312
Vital statistics, Commission on Population and the American Future
 recommendation on, 53
Voluntary sterilization, Commission on Population and the American Future
 recommendation on, 49
von Baltha, Hand Urs, on papal infallibility, 199
von Dollinger, Ignaz, on despotic papal authority, 207

W

Wallace, Mike, Catholic League criticism of, 287-88
Walters, Vernon, Reagan's "Catholic Team" and, 132, 356
War
 NSSM 200 prediction of, 108-9
 renewable resource scarcity and, 108
Wattenberg, Ben, 1990 Immigration Reform Act and, 345
Wead, Doug, on Vatican influence on U.S. presidency, 355
Weaver, Mary Jo, **Being Right: Conservative Catholics in America**, 115
Weld, Madeline
 on the International Feminist Movement, 351-52
 on the "pope's handmaidens", 353
Welfare programs, Vatican support of U.S., 343
Welles, Sumner, on Spanish "Civil War", 266
Weyrich, Paul
 Christian Coalition and, 177
 Free Congress Foundation and, 161
 Vatican influence on U.S. policy and, 354
What's Happening to Disney?, 291
Whitewater Affair, 319
Whitman, Christie, Catholic League attack on William Preston College and, 297
Who Lied About Spain, 262, 270
WHO (World Health Organization)
 control of, 346
 family planning and, 246-47
William Paterson College, Catholic League attack on, 297
Wilson, A.N., on papal distaste for the intellect, 217
Wilson, William A.
 Catholic Campaign for America and, 173
 on foreign aid and the Vatican, 133
 Reagan's "Catholic Team" and, 356
Wilson, Woodrow (President)
 on being an American, 243
 on endurance of America, **361**
Winning the Cultural War, 175
Wojtyla, Karol (Archbishop of Cracow)
 major author of **Humanae Vitae** and, 124
 Papal Commission on Population and Birth Control and, 124
 see also John Paul II (Pope)
Women, equal rights for, Commission on Population and the American Future
 recommendation on, 48
Women's International Network, 353
Woodman, James, on the greenhouse effect, 326
Woodwell, George, on the greenhouse effect, 326
World
 adequacy of food supplies for, 66-67
 demographic trends, 65-66, 437-54
 population goals, NSDM 314 on, 92-93
The World Agricultural Situation, 455
World Conference on Population, 133
World Health Organization (WHO)
 control of, 346
 family planning and, 346-47
World Population Conference
 NSSM 200 on, 491-98
 World Population Plan of Action,
  adopted by, **22**
  text of, 391-432
 Vatican opposition to, 131
A World in Revolution, 271
Wykes, Tom, Catholic Campaign for America and, 174

Y

Yoon, Carol Kaesuk, on the greenhouse effect, 331
Young, Andrew, meeting with Bishop James Rausch, 100

Z

Zablocki, Clement, opposition to AID family planning, 101
Zaire, food supplies and, 456

DR. STEPHEN D. MUMFORD is president of the Center for Research on Population and Security. For more than 20 years his principal research interest has been the relationship between world population growth and national and global security. While on military duty in Asia, he first recognized the linkage between political instability and population pressures. A graduate of the University of Kentucky College of Agriculture, Mumford was commissioned in the Army Medical Service Corps, leaving active duty with the rank of Captain. He received his master's degree in public health and doctorate in population studies from the University of Texas. In the course of his work he has traveled widely in Third World countries. For more than two decades he has been a lead scientist in the evaluation of sterilization methods, including the quinacrine pellet nonsurgical method of female sterilization, collaborating with scientists in more than 20 countries. He is a member of the Board of Directors of The Churchman Associates. In addition to publishing two books on biomedical and social aspects of family planning, as well as scientific articles in more than a score of journals, his three earlier major works in his primary field of specialization are these: *Population Growth Control: The Next Move is America's* (New York: Philosophical Library, 1977), *American Democracy and the Vatican: Population Growth and National Security* (Amherst, New York: Humanist Press, 1984) and *The Pope and the New Apocalypse: The Holy War Against Family Planning* (Research Triangle Park, North Carolina: Center for Research on Population and Security, 1986).

World overpopulation has long been recognized by our government as a grave threat to U.S. and global security — even exceeding the danger posed by nuclear war. However, all efforts to address this new threat have been blocked — for the same astonishing reason.

In 1968, public awareness of the population problem and the political commitment to confront it were just beginning to peak. In 1969, President Richard M. Nixon responded. In a rare Special Message to Congress, he announced the creation of the Commission on Population Growth and the American Future. Its task: to make a series of recommendations that could be used to formulate a comprehensive population policy for this country. After two years of intensive study, the Commission made more than 70 recommendations, constituting the foundation of an excellent policy. Nothing ever came of this report. Not one recommendation was ever adopted. To this day the U.S. does not have a population policy.

Then, in 1974, the first World Population Conference was held in Bucharest. By consensus, the 137 countries present adopted the World Population Plan of Action. Had it been implemented, the world would be very different today. But it was not.

In April 1974, in National Security Study Memorandum 200 (NSSM 200), President Nixon directed that an investigation be undertaken by all government departments and agencies with significant intelligence gathering capabilities to determine if world overpopulation did threaten the security of the United States. This included The National Security Council, the CIA, the Defense, Agriculture and State Departments, and the Agency for International Development. Their report concluded, "World population growth is widely recognized within the Government as a current danger of the highest magnitude calling for urgent measures....There is a major risk of severe damage [from